Transforming Special Education Through Artificial Intelligence

Annette G. Walters
Independent Researcher, USA

IGI Global
Publishing Tomorrow's Research Today

Published in the United States of America by
IGI Global Scientific Publishing
701 East Chocolate Avenue
Hershey, PA, 17033, USA
Tel: 717-533-8845
Fax: 717-533-8661
E-mail: cust@igi-global.com
Website: https://www.igi-global.com

Library of Congress Cataloging-in-Publication Data

Names: Walters, Annette, 1973- editor.
Title: Transforming special education through artificial intelligence / edited by: Annette G. Walters.
Description: Hershey, PA : Information Science Reference, [2025] | Includes bibliographical references and index. | Summary: "The primary objective of this book is to enhance the comprehension of Artificial Intelligence (AI) in the context of Special Education (SE). This publication will offer a thorough examination of the advantages and disadvantages linked to AI in specialized instruction, along with its potential implications in terms of legality, ethics, and instruction"-- Provided by publisher.
Identifiers: LCCN 2024039282 (print) | LCCN 2024039283 (ebook) | ISBN 9798369355381 (hc) | ISBN 9798369355398 (sc) | ISBN 9798369355404 (ebook)
Subjects: LCSH: Artificial intelligence--Educational applications. | Special education--Technological innovations. | Students with disabilities--Education.
Classification: LCC LB1028.43 .T77 2024 (print) | LCC LB1028.43 (ebook) | DDC 370.285/63--dc23/eng/20241011
LC record available at https://lccn.loc.gov/2024039282
LC ebook record available at https://lccn.loc.gov/2024039283

Vice President of Editorial: Melissa Wagner
Managing Editor of Acquisitions: Mikaela Felty
Managing Editor of Book Development: Jocelynn Hessler
Production Manager: Mike Brehm
Cover Design: Phillip Shickler

British Cataloguing in Publication Data
A Cataloguing in Publication record for this book is available from the British Library.

Table of Contents

Detailed Table of Contents

The current chapter critically highlights the advancement of Artificial Intelligence (AI) and how it has reshaped the field practice of special education. AI is transforming global education, particularly for students with disabilities. It enables personalised, scalable learning experiences that enhance engagement and teaching efficacy. Tools like VR simulations, Google Glass, and Lexplore assist with social interactions and reading difficulties. AI applications, such as ALEKS and Q-interactive, adjust learning difficulty based on student responses, while platforms like Carnegie Learning and DreamBox offer personalised feedback. AI's integration with evidence-based practices like Universal Design for Learning (UDL) has maximised learning outcomes. Research indicates significant AI benefits in special education and allied fields, including speech-language therapy, occupational therapy, and clinical psychology.

This chapter explores the intersection of artificial intelligence (AI) and personalized learning, highlighting the potential to revolutionize accessibility and inclusivity in special education. Drawing from psychological and pedagogical research, the chapter delves into the nuanced impact of AI-driven tools' capacity to transform instruction, enrich educational experiences, and bolster access to various disciplines. Challenges, bias, and potential exclusionary barriers emerge, necessitating a critical examination of how AI's potential transformative impact reshapes the landscape of inclusion and accessibility in the educational sphere. By identifying emerging challenges and proposing pathways for advancement, the chapter underscores the importance of ensuring that AI technologies advance rather than hinder inclusive and accessible educational practices, with an ultimate aim to establish a more accessible learning environment tailored to the diverse needs of students with disabilities.

The integration of Artificial Intelligence (AI) into the educational sector has revolutionized traditional teaching methods, presenting both opportunities and challenges. While extensive discussions have explored AI's role in general education, its specific applications and implications in Special Education (SE) remain underexplored. This chapter aims to bridge that gap by examining the potential of AI to provide personalized, data-driven support for students with disabilities. We will explore how AI can facilitate early detection of learning disabilities, enhance individualized learning plans, and improve communication between educators and stakeholders. Additionally, we will address the ethical considerations, data privacy issues, and potential biases inherent in AI systems. By offering a balanced view of the promises and pitfalls of AI in SE, this chapter seeks to equip educators, policymakers, and researchers with the knowledge necessary to harness AI responsibly and effectively.

Artificial Intelligence affects all the major players in the education sector and has become the new normal in the current and upcoming era. This chapter aims to probe specifically and introduce inclusivity in the education sector with an interdisciplinary approach of AI for students with hearing disability, visual impairment, mobility dysfunction, and intellectual challenges. Teaching and learning pedagogies from educational institutions are emphasized to understand the importance of inclusion of AI in special education. Several techniques that provide personalized hand-holding to special students are also particularized. Ethical policy has been taken into considerations for special education that trusted technical involvement through artificial intelligence. Comprehensive understanding of the potential advantages of AI and challenges are included in the chapter. Applications of artificial intelligence in the same are due to the multiplicity of difficulties encountered in special education, thus the study has been found imperative to cater different needs of each special student.

Artificial Intelligence (AI) is swiftly reshaping modern education through innovations in classroom management, personalized learning, and administrative effectiveness. This chapter investigates AI's diverse impact on education, emphasizing its role in improving accessibility and inclusivity. AI employs advanced algorithms and data analysis to customize educational content, pacing, and teaching methods to meet individual student requirements, thereby enhancing engagement and minimizing disruptions. Automated assessment tools deliver immediate feedback, enabling educators to concentrate on interactive teaching. Furthermore, AI applications in Special Education offer personalized learning experiences that enhance cognitive and social skills for students with diverse needs. Additionally, AI adoption in education is gaining traction in the Arab world to meet the demands of the Fourth Industrial Revolution and enhance learning outcomes.

This chapter addresses the topic of equitable instruction using Artificial Intelligence for Executive Functioning skills of students with disabilities. The chapter will have the following content: Types of EF needs: This will outline varied EF needs with classroom examples on how the needs are reflected. Overview of AI tools for EF: AI has the potential to act as a digital assistant in creating to-do lists, prioritize, and set reminders like a personal assistant. This section will cover popular AI tools such as ChatGPT, Grammarly, PowerPoint Speaker Coach, Motion, LightKey, etc., with specific examples of use. Approaching EF needs from an equitable perspective using AI: This section will outline the AI tools that can help with EF, with specific application examples and uses. Cultural and linguistic diversity considerations will be included. Case study examples: This will include brief case studies of SWD with EF deficits in planning, prioritizing, organizing, problem solving, time management, etc.

This chapter will primarily examine the utilization of AI in special education, focusing on the perspectives of educators and parents. It will also explore the level of awareness and impact of AI in special education in India. More over, this research will assess the various tools currently employed in special education and the potential for incorporating AI in different areas of this field in the future. The satisfaction level of students and the scope of AI implementation will also be analyzed. The study will further investigate the difficulties, obstacles, and concerns surrounding the use of AI in special education within India. By separately considering the opinions and viewpoints of instructors and parents of children with special needs, this study addresses both classroom and non-classroom implementations of AI in special education. Moreover, it ensures that individual challenges specific to each domain are taken into consideration.

The preparation of special education practitioners is a field that is ever-evolving. To that end, this paper aims to demonstrate the utility and increased opportunity of embedding artificial intelligence (AI) tools within the preparation programs of special educators, particularly as it is contextualize within the community college space. Additionally, this paper attempts to establish an abbreviated research base for AI within education-centered literature, particularly as this piece illustrates the impact of community college and specific coursework that is used to provide learning opportunities for students studying the fundamentals of special education. Last, this document illustrates how AI may be used as an engaging component to special education coursework to improve the ways in which special education teacher-educators, i.e., research-practitioners who train and provide academic and professional development for special educators, design and develop coursework within settings of teaching and learning.

The integration of artificial intelligence (AI) technology into special education teacher preparation programs represents a transformative approach to addressing the complex needs of diverse learners. By leveraging AI, teachers can enhance pedagogical competencies, foster inclusive classroom environments, and optimize instructional practices tailored to individual student needs. Furthermore, using AI in special education promotes innovation, efficiency, and effectiveness. This chapter presents initial findings from preservice special education teachers regarding their experiences learning to use AI technologies in the context of supporting students with disabilities through 1) effective lesson plan development, 2) implementation of evidence-based practices, and 3) identifying ways that AI can support their individual challenges.

Artificial intelligence (AI) has the potential to radically change a wide range of disciplines, including special education. Given the chronic issues with recruitment and retention of personnel involved in services for people with disabilities, automating professional development and training represents a promising application of AI. However, powerful technologies such as AI often produce adverse or unintended consequences. This chapter discusses the ethical implications of a line of research involving the integration of AI into immersive virtual reality (VR)— 'smart' VR—designed to teach practitioners a research-based behavior intervention for children with intellectual and developmental disabilities. Specific sections describe the impetus and potential advantages of smart VR, delineate the development and evaluation of the training, and identify concerns related to the use of similar applications in special education.

Preface

In the ever-evolving landscape of education, the intersection of Artificial Intelligence (AI) and Special Education (SE) presents both an exhilarating frontier and a complex challenge. As editors of this reference book, we are motivated by a shared commitment to explore and illuminate this intersection, aiming to equip educators, policymakers, and stakeholders with the knowledge and insights needed to harness AI's potential for students with disabilities.

The promise of AI lies in its ability to personalize learning experiences, offer real-time data insights, and enhance collaboration among educators, parents, and students. For students with disabilities, these capabilities could mean the difference between struggling to keep pace and flourishing in a supportive environment tailored to their unique needs. However, the integration of AI into Special Education is not without its ethical dilemmas and concerns. Issues surrounding data privacy, algorithmic bias, and the potential diminishing of human connection in educational settings must be addressed with careful consideration and transparency.

This book serves as a comprehensive exploration of the dual nature of AI in SE: its transformative potential and the critical challenges it poses. Each chapter provides a thorough examination of various facets of AI, including its applications, benefits, and ethical implications. Through case studies and real-life examples, we aim to showcase successful implementations that highlight the positive impact of AI on learning outcomes while also discussing the obstacles that may arise.

Our goal is to foster a deeper understanding of how AI can be effectively utilized to support students with disabilities, ensuring they receive the individualized attention and resources necessary for their success. By encouraging informed discussions about AI's role in SE, we aspire to empower educators to make thoughtful decisions about technology integration in their classrooms.

As we embark on this journey together, we invite you to engage with the content, challenge the assumptions, and envision a future where AI is a valuable ally in Special Education—an ally that promotes equity, access, and inclusive educational practices for all students.

Chapter 1: Reshaping Special Education: Strategic Use of Artificial Intelligence

In this foundational chapter, we critically assess how Artificial Intelligence (AI) is reshaping the landscape of special education. The author highlights the innovative tools and technologies that foster personalized learning experiences for students with disabilities, including virtual reality simulations and adaptive learning platforms. By integrating AI with evidence-based practices like Universal Design for Learning (UDL), we explore how these advancements improve engagement and instructional effectiveness. This chapter also underscores the significant benefits of AI across related fields, demonstrating its potential to transform educational practices on a global scale.

Chapter 2: Enhancing Special Education Using AI: The Intersection of Personalized Learning and Inclusivity

This chapter delves into the powerful intersection of AI and personalized learning, examining how these innovations can enhance accessibility and inclusivity in special education. Drawing on psychological and pedagogical research, the author highlights the transformative impact of AI tools on educational experiences. While recognizing the challenges and potential biases associated with AI, the chapter advocates for critical reflection on how to leverage technology to create more inclusive environments for students with disabilities, ensuring that AI serves to advance equitable educational practices.

Chapter 3: Artificial Intelligence in Special Education: Enhancing Learning Outcomes for Students with Disabilities

Here, we bridge the gap in discussions surrounding AI's application in special education. This chapter provides an in-depth analysis of how AI can offer personalized, data-driven support tailored to the unique needs of students with disabilities. It explores the potential for early detection of learning disabilities and the enhancement of individualized education plans. The chapter does not shy away from addressing ethical considerations and data privacy issues, equipping readers with a nuanced understanding of AI's promises and pitfalls within special education.

Chapter 4: The Potential of Artificial Intelligence to Enhance Special Education

Focusing on inclusivity, this chapter examines AI's role in supporting students with diverse disabilities, including hearing impairments and mobility challenges. By emphasizing pedagogical strategies that integrate AI, the author highlights various techniques that provide personalized support for students. Ethical policies surrounding AI's involvement in special education are also discussed, painting a comprehensive picture of how AI can address the multifaceted challenges faced by special education practitioners.

Chapter 5: Promoting Accessibility and Personalizing Learning Experiences through AI

This chapter investigates the multifaceted impacts of AI in education, particularly regarding accessibility and personalized learning. It discusses how AI tools can customize educational content and teaching methods to enhance engagement and reduce disruptions. The author highlights the role of AI in Special Education as a means to support cognitive and social skill development while also addressing the growing demand for effective learning strategies in the face of rapid technological advancement.

Chapter 6: Creating Academically Advanced Learning Environments for Gifted Students Through Artificial Intelligence

In this exploration of AI's role in enhancing learning environments for gifted students, the chapter examines how educators can leverage AI to create cognitively stimulating experiences. By posing critical questions about AI's capacity to tailor instruction and assessments for advanced learners, the author highlights the interplay between AI and human intelligence. Ethical considerations and future research implications are also discussed, providing a roadmap for educators aiming to foster academic excellence.

Chapter 7: Artificial Intelligence in Special Education: AI Therapeutic Pedagogy for Language Disorders

Focusing on language impairments, this chapter explores how AI can address challenges faced by students with Language-Based Learning Disorders (LBLDs). It assesses the effectiveness of AI technologies in supporting articulation, fluency, and broader language skills. The author discusses both the potential benefits and limitations of AI interventions, offering insights into how AI can enhance assessment and remediation strategies for language disorders in special education.

Chapter 8: Can Artificial Intelligence Facilitate Mathematics Instruction?

This chapter delves into the potential of AI in mathematics education, examining its applications in creating adaptive learning environments and supporting students with special needs. The author reviews various AI tools that enhance engagement and facilitate personalized learning experiences, emphasizing the importance of mathematics as a foundational skill. Through this exploration, the chapter showcases how AI can transform the teaching and learning of mathematical concepts.

Chapter 9: Specializing Instruction with the Use of Artificial Intelligence

Examining the transformative power of AI in delivering specialized instruction, this chapter discusses how AI can personalize educational experiences. It highlights the ways in which AI applications can analyze student data to create individualized learning paths, ensuring that diverse educational needs are met. The author offers a vision for future AI-powered learning environments that promote inclusion and effectiveness in special education.

Chapter 10: Executive Functioning Skills and Artificial Intelligence

This chapter addresses the integration of AI to support executive functioning skills among students with disabilities. It outlines various needs associated with executive functioning and presents AI tools that can assist students in planning, prioritizing, and organizing tasks. By examining case studies and practical applications, the author emphasizes the importance of equitable instruction and the potential for AI to enhance the educational experience for students with executive functioning deficits.

Chapter 11: Role of AI in Special Education in India

Focusing on the Indian context, this chapter explores the utilization of AI in special education through the perspectives of educators and parents. The author assesses the awareness and impact of AI tools currently in use, as well as the challenges and barriers to effective implementation. By examining both classroom and non-classroom applications of AI, this chapter offers valuable insights into the unique needs of students with disabilities in India.

Chapter 12: Embracing Artificial Intelligence Tools to Enrich Special Education Teacher Preparation

This chapter investigates the role of AI tools in preparing special education practitioners, particularly within community college settings. By establishing a research base for AI in teacher preparation, the author highlights how AI can enhance coursework and provide engaging learning opportunities for future educators. This discussion underscores the necessity of integrating AI into training programs to better equip educators to meet the needs of diverse learners.

Chapter 13: Exploring AI in Special Education With A Qualitative Study: AI and Special Education Preservice Teachers

Through qualitative research, this chapter examines the experiences of preservice special education teachers as they learn to utilize AI technologies. The findings reveal how AI can enhance pedagogical skills, foster inclusive environments, and optimize instructional practices. The author emphasizes the importance of AI in supporting effective lesson planning and evidence-based practices, ultimately preparing future educators to better serve students with disabilities.

Chapter 14: Using AI to Support the Transition from Schooling to Employment for Autistic Individuals

This chapter addresses the critical transition from education to employment for individuals with autism spectrum disorder (ASD). It explores the potential of generative AI tools, like ChatGPT, to support communication, social skills training, and information access during this transition. By synthesizing existing literature, the author highlights the advantages of AI while advocating for its integration with professional guidance to ensure successful outcomes for autistic individuals entering the workforce.

Chapter 15: Implications of Artificial Intelligence for Special Education Technology

This chapter investigates the wide-ranging applications of AI in special education, focusing on how it can enhance data-driven decision-making, behavioral therapies, and adaptive learning platforms. The author discusses the role of AI-driven assistive technologies and the ethical considerations surrounding their use. By emphasizing the need for professional development and stakeholder cooperation, this chapter outlines a framework for effectively integrating AI into special education practices.

Chapter 16: Reflections on AI-Augmented Professional Development in Special Education: Promises and Pitfalls

In this chapter, the author examines the potential of AI to revolutionize professional development for special education practitioners. Highlighting both the opportunities and challenges presented by AI, the discussion includes the integration of AI into immersive virtual reality for training educators. Ethical implications and concerns about the unintended consequences of AI use in training are addressed, providing a balanced view of this innovative approach.

Chapter 17: Artificial Intelligence: Solutions in Special Education

The concluding chapter synthesizes the discussions throughout the book, emphasizing the transformative potential of AI in special education. It reexamines the challenges and ethical considerations surrounding AI implementation, advocating for responsible practices that maximize its benefits for students with disabilities. The author provides a forward-looking perspective on how AI can shape the future of special education, offering actionable solutions and recommendations for stakeholders.

Thank you for joining us in this critical conversation. Together, we can shape a more inclusive and effective educational landscape that truly transforms the learning experiences of students with disabilities.

Chapter 1
Reshaping Special Education:
Strategic Use of Artificial Intelligence

Wasim Ahmad
https://orcid.org/0000-0002-2106-7824
National Institute for the Empowerment of Persons With Intellectual Disabilities, Navi Mumbai, India

Rishu Raj
https://orcid.org/0009-0003-5440-8837
National Institute for the Empowerment of Persons With Intellectual Disabilities, Navi Mumbai, India

Ruchika Shokeen
https://orcid.org/0009-0003-3322-9389
National Institute for the Empowerment of Persons With Intellectual Disabilities, Navi Mumbai, India

ABSTRACT

The current chapter critically highlights the advancement of Artificial Intelligence (AI) and how it has reshaped the field practice of special education. AI is transforming global education, particularly for students with disabilities. It enables personalised, scalable learning experiences that enhance engagement and teaching efficacy. Tools like VR simulations, Google Glass, and Lexplore assist with social interactions and reading difficulties. AI applications, such as ALEKS and Q-interactive, adjust learning difficulty based on student responses, while platforms like Carnegie Learning and DreamBox offer personalised feedback. AI's integration with evidence-based practices like Universal Design for Learning (UDL) has maximised learning outcomes.

DOI: 10.4018/979-8-3693-5538-1.ch001

Research indicates significant AI benefits in special education and allied fields, including speech-language therapy, occupational therapy, and clinical psychology.

INTRODUCTION

Artificial Intelligence (AI) is tremendously reshaping the global education landscape in the 21 century. The strategic use of AI can help to adapt to the learning needs of students with disabilities. The effective use of use AI enables an innovative, scalable personalized learning experience that is vital for both student engagement and the effective teaching-learning process. Panjwani-Charania & Zhai (2023) identified seven types of artificial intelligence from the literature: adaptive learning, facial expression, chat robot, communication assistant, mastery learning, intelligent tutor and interactive robot.

Fitria (2021) talked about advanced technologies such as Virtual Reality (VR) simulations, Brain Power's tools, and Google Glass are innovatively employed to aid individuals with autism in enhancing social interactions. Additionally, Lexico supports students experiencing reading difficulties through real-time feedback and personalized learning solutions. Cutting-edge technologies such as Lexplore, which utilizes eye-tracking technology to identify reading difficulties, enable educators to intervene proactively. Google Expeditions and Labster offer immersive virtual field trips, lab simulations, and interactive experiences (Parmaxi & Athanasiou, 2021). ALEKS provides personalized learning experiences, allowing students to master course topics through a continuous cycle of mastery, knowledge retention, and positive feedback (Sun et al., 2021). Q-interactive adjusts question difficulty based on student responses, providing accurate assessments of their knowledge and skills. ScootPad and Edpuzzle assist educators in discovering and organizing educational materials. Carnegie Learning, endorsed by the U.S. Department of Education's What Works Clearinghouse (2010), emphasizes effective instructional strategies. DreamBox Learning delivers personalized instruction and feedback to students (Wang & Woodworth, 2011; What Works Clearinghouse, 2013).

AI refers to the remarkable capability of machines to execute cognitive tasks such as thinking, perceiving, learning, problem-solving, and decision-making. Initially envisioned as a technology that could emulate human intelligence, AI has evolved to transcend its original conception. With unprecedented advancements in data collection, processing, and computational power, intelligent systems are now deployed to undertake a myriad of tasks, enhance connectivity, and boost productivity. As AI's capabilities have dramatically expanded, so too has its utility across a growing array of fields. AI comprises a constellation of technologies that enable machines to act with heightened levels of intelligence, emulating human capabilities in sensing, comprehending, and acting. For instance, computer vision and audio processing allow machines to actively perceive the world by acquiring and processing images, sounds, and speech. Natural language processing and inference engines empower AI systems to analyze and understand the information collected (National Institute for Transforming India Aayog, 2023).

Employing deep learning to assimilate and scrutinize existing course materials, textbooks, and curricula, the technology generates bespoke learning resources, including customized textbooks, chapter summaries, and multiple-choice assessments. In a recent hackathon organized by National Institute for Transforming of India Aayog, the spotlight was on 'ReadEx,' an innovative Android application that leverages Natural Language Processing to generate real-time questions, offers content recommendations, and creates flashcards (National institute for transforming of India Aayog, 2023).

BACKGROUND

Special education has evolved significantly over the years, but many of the foundational methods from the past have shaped contemporary practices. Here are some of the old methods used in special education: segregated special education (Fitch, 2003), medical model (science direct), behavioristic approach, Individualized instruction (science direct), resource room (Al-Zoubi, & Rahman, 2012) pull out programs (Fernandez, et al., 2016) developmental approaches, task analysis (Schworm 1979; Ahmad et al., 2022; Yadav et al. 2022).

Segregated classrooms were established for students with disabilities, placing them in separate educational settings away from their peers. While these environments provided tailored resources and specialized support, they often limited social interaction with non-disabled peers and set lower expectations for the students. The Medical Model treated disabilities primarily as medical conditions requiring cure or management, emphasizing diagnosis and treatment but often focusing excessively on deficits rather than recognizing the strengths and potential of individuals (Ahmad et al., 2022; Yadav et al., 2022).

Behaviorist approaches, a method pioneered by B.F. Skinner, employed techniques like operant conditioning (rewards and punishments) to shape behaviours. This method effectively modifies specific behaviors and skills but was sometimes criticized for their rigidity and lack of attention to the underlying causes of behaviors. Individualized instruction & tailored teaching to meet the unique needs of each student, involving curriculum modifications, varied teaching strategies and customized assessments. This approach offered personalized learning experiences but was often time-consuming and resource-intensive (Adetunji & Zaman, 2022).

Resource rooms allowed students to divide their time between general education classrooms and specialized resource rooms. This model provided a balance of integration and specialized support but faced challenges in coordinating efforts between regular and special education teachers. Next method is Pull-out services, which involved specialists removing students from their regular classrooms for short periods to provide targeted instruction or therapy, offering focused, intensive help on specific skills but disrupting routines and potentially leading to stigma (Ahmad et al., 2022; Yadav et al., 2022).

Developmental approaches emphasized child development stages, offering instruction appropriate to each stage and providing a holistic view of child development. However, this method sometimes fails to address the unique developmental pace of children with disabilities. Another method is task analysis; the process of breaking down tasks into smaller, more manageable steps and teaching each step individually, making it easier for students to master complex tasks. While effective, this method could be very time consuming and might not generalize well to new situations (Ahmad et al., 2022; Yadav et al., 2022).

RESHAPING SPECIAL EDUCATION

Reshaping special education encompasses the evolution and enhancement of practices, policies, and methodologies aimed at educating and supporting students with disabilities. This transformative process involves updating and refining traditional methods to more effectively address the diverse needs of these students, fostering inclusion, and ensuring equitable access to educational opportunities. Advanced AI assessment tools augment the capabilities of teachers and parents, providing more precise and comprehensive evaluations of each child's unique needs and progress (Drigas, 2012).

KEY ASPECTS OF RESHAPING SPECIAL EDUCATION

Inclusion and Mainstreaming: This approach integrates students with disabilities into inclusive settings alongside their non-disabled peers, thereby enhancing social interaction, reducing stigma, and fostering diversity and mutual understanding among all students (Fitch, 2003).

Individualized Education Programs (IEPs): IEPs are comprehensive, personalized education plans that delineate specific goals, accommodations, and support services for each student. These plans ensure that education is meticulously tailored to the unique needs and abilities of each student, fostering an environment where they can thrive and achieve their full potential (Kurth et al., 2022).

Universal Design for Learning (UDL): UDL creates flexible curricula designed to accommodate a diverse array of learning styles and abilities from the outset. This approach makes education accessible to all students, minimizing the need for specialized accommodations by integrating inclusive practices into the core of educational planning (Cardona et al., 2023).

Assistive Technology: This entails utilizing an array of tools and devices, such as communication aids, specialized software, and adaptive equipment, to support and enhance the learning experiences of students with disabilities. By fostering greater independence and improving learning capabilities, these technologies play a crucial role in inclusive education. The World Health Organization projects that the number of individuals with cognitive, sensory, or mobility impairments requiring assistive technology will surge to 3.5 billion by 2050 (Barua et al., 2022).

Collaborative Learning Environment: In this team-oriented approach, general and special education teachers unite to plan, instruct, and assess students. By combining their expertise, they provide more comprehensive support, ensuring a richer and more inclusive educational experience for all students (Jameel & Arsalan, 2024).

Response to Intervention: It entails early identification and targeted support for students with learning and behavioral needs through tiered levels of intervention. This proactive approach aims to prevent academic challenges and minimize the necessity for specialized education services by providing timely and structured support (Hunt et al., 2021).

Social-Emotional Learning: Incorporating it into the curriculum assists students with disabilities in cultivating essential social and emotional skills, thereby bolstering their overall well-being and academic achievement. Additionally, social robots are utilized to engage with humans in ways that are both social and emotional, enhancing interactive learning experiences (Sharma et al., 2023).

Family and Community Involvement: Involving families and communities in the educational process fosters a supportive network that amplifies the effectiveness of educational interventions and nurtures students' learning and development (Eden et al., 2024).

Professional Development for Educators: Sustaining ongoing training and resources ensures that educators are consistently abreast of current best practices and the latest advancements in special education research, thereby equipping them with the requisite knowledge to effectively cater to the diverse needs of every student (Donath et al., 2023).

Simultaneously, the objective of Artificial Intelligence in Education is to refine educational methodologies through advancements in AI technology. This vision is in harmony with the UNESCO Beijing Consensus, advocating for the effective integration of AI into education. The growing focus on AI within the educational sphere underscores its potential to fundamentally transform the roles of educators, administrators, and academic institutions alike (Garg, & Sharma, 2020).

DEVELOPING IEP THORUGH AI

AI is revolutionizing the development of IEPs for individuals with disabilities in several transformative ways. These transformative ways according to McGrath (2023) are following:

Personalized Learning: AI customizes learning experiences by analyzing student strengths, weaknesses, and learning styles. It adjusts task difficulty and content presentation accordingly to optimize learning outcomes (Jian, 2023).

Real-time Progress Monitoring: AI enables continuous monitoring and provides instant feedback, allowing educators to make timely adjustments in the process of conducting IEPs based on students' current needs and styles. This capability harnesses sensor-based data to track students' learning progressions, facilitating real-time content adjustments and personalized instruction (Lamb, Choi, & Owens, 2023).

Augmented Accessibility: AI technologies such as speech-to-text and real-time translation bolster inclusivity by facilitating active participation in educational settings.

Data-Driven Decision Making: AI leverages extensive datasets to discern intricate patterns, guiding refined educational strategies and targeted interventions.

Tailored Assessments: AI designs individualized evaluations to meticulously gauge academic progress and pinpoint areas necessitating additional support.

Virtual Mentors and Facilitators: AI-powered virtual assistants and tutors extend educational assistance beyond conventional classrooms, augmenting learning experiences.

Prognostic Analytics: Through data analysis, AI anticipates forthcoming challenges, prompting preemptive measures and early detection of potential obstacles.

Concurrent Collaboration Platforms: AI optimizes communication and resource accessibility among educators, therapists, guardians, and learners, fostering synergistic educational frameworks.

The Various AI Based Applications Contributing in Developing IEP for Students with Special Needs are:

1. IEP Writer- The IEP Composer is a comprehensive tool designed to aid educators in the formulation and management of IEPs. It features templates, progress tracking capabilities, and robust reporting functionalities, ensuring adherence to educational standards and regulatory requirements.

2. Goalbook Toolkit- facilitates educators in setting and monitoring personalized objectives for students. It offers a repository of goals aligned with educational standards, accompanied by benchmarks and an array of strategies and resources to support the diverse learning needs of students (Webb et al., 2023).
3. n2y Unique Learning System- 2y's Unique Learning Framework provides a suite of specialized tools tailored for use in special education contexts. It encompasses differentiated instructional materials, assessment tools, and mechanisms for monitoring student progress, all meticulously tailored to meet individualized student requirements (Huron & Ohio, 2024; n2y, 2021).
4. Frontline Special Ed & Interventions- Frontline Education offers an extensive suite designed for the management of special education programs. This suite includes functionalities for developing IEPs, monitoring student progress, and ensuring compliance with regulatory standards.
5. ClassDojo- ClassDojo serves as a versatile classroom management tool adaptable for use within the framework of IEPs. It enables educators to monitor both behavioral and academic progress, facilitate communication with parents, and provide updates on student performance (Konrad, 2022).
6. Learning Ally- Learning Ally provides a comprehensive collection of audiobooks and supplementary resources specifically designed to support students with learning disabilities. These resources can be seamlessly integrated into IEPs, offering accessible learning materials tailored to the individual needs of students (International Dyslexia Association, n.d; learning Ally, n.d).
7. Remind- a communication platform facilitating seamless interaction among educators, students, and parents. It serves to keep all stakeholders abreast of a student's academic progress and any updates to their IEP (Nisbet et al., 2017).
8. Special Needs for Special Kids- This platform offers a diverse array of resources and tools tailored explicitly for special education contexts. It encompasses customizable lesson plans, engaging activities, and comprehensive assessments designed to cater to the unique requirements of individual students.

AI BRINGING OF UNIVERSAL DESIGN OF LEARNING

AI applications can significantly enhance the implementation of UDL by supporting its three core principles (Gupta & Ahmad, 2022):

Multiple Means of Representation: AI tools offer content in multiple modalities, encompassing text, audio, and video formats, thereby accommodating varied learning preferences

Multiple Means of Engagement: AI functionalities foster student involvement through interactive and adaptable activities, tailoring learning experiences to individual needs and preferences.

Multiple Means of Action and Expression: AI tools empower students to showcase their understanding using diverse methods such as written responses, oral presentations, and visual representations, aligning with the principle of supporting multiple pathways for demonstration.

AI-Driven Applications That Supports UDL Principles

1. **Kurzweil 3000**: An AI-powered literacy support tool offering text-to-speech, language translation, and study skills support, providing content in multiple formats (Kurzweil, 2019).
2. **CAST's UDL Tools**: Tools and resources like UDL Studio, providing customisable templates and interactive activities to engage diverse learners.
3. **Read & Write by Text-help**: An AI-based literacy tool with features such as text-to-speech, speech-to-text, and word prediction, making content accessible to all students (Mosito et al., 2017).
4. **Microsoft Learning Tools**: Integrated into apps like OneNote, Word, and Outlook, these tools offer immersive reader, dictation, and text-to-speech, supporting varied learning preferences (Namachivayam, 2021; Abdullah et al., 2021).
5. **Classkick**: An interactive platform that enables teachers to provide real-time feedback and support, using AI to identify and address individual student needs (Chua et al., 2021).
6. **Quizlet**: Uses AI to create adaptive learning experiences with customisable flashcards and quizzes, supporting multiple learning styles (Setiawan & Wiedarti, 2020; Hough, 2018)
7. **Pear Deck**: Integrates with Google Slides and Microsoft PowerPoint to create interactive presentations, using AI to analyse student responses and engagement. (Juanis et al., 2023; Tholfsen, 2020).
8. **Edpuzzle**: Allows creation of interactive video lessons with embedded questions and assessments, ensuring accessible and engaging content Alvarez and Mischel (2024) have also talked about advantage of Edpuzzle.
9. **Kami**: A digital classroom app with text-to-speech, annotation, and collaboration features, providing multiple means of engagement and expression (Newsroom, 2019).
10. **Coby by Don Johnston**: An AI-driven writing tool offering word prediction, speech recognition, and text-to-speech, aiding students with writing difficulties.

AI FOR ASSISTIVE TECHNOLOGY

AI applications are increasingly providing powerful assistive technologies for individuals with intellectual disabilities, enhancing their ability to learn, communicate, and engage with their environment (lannone, & Giansanti, 2023; de Freitas et al., 2022n.d).

Weitzman (2023) in article "Empowering individuals with disabilities through AI technology" have mentioned several assistive technologies. It can be categorized using some notable AI-driven applications as given:

1. Speech Generating Devices (SGDs):
    - **Proloquo2Go:** Uses AI to predict words and phrases, providing a voice for individuals with speech difficulties.
    - **Predictable:** AI-driven app that predicts and vocalises sentences typed by the user, adapting to their communication patterns over time.
2. Learning and Cognitive Support:
    - **CogniFit:** AI-based platform offering personalised brain games and activities to improve cognitive abilities.
    - **Elevate:** Creates personalised training programs to enhance cognitive skills such as focus, memory, and problem-solving.
3. Educational Tools:
    - **Learning Ally:** Provides audiobooks and educational resources tailored to students with learning disabilities, using AI to match content to learner needs.
    - **ModMath:** Digital platform that helps students with dysgraphia and dyslexia solve math problems without handwriting issues.
    - Text-to-speech technology, supportive e-text, and electronic books (Mosito et al., 2017).
4. Communication Aids:
    - **Tobii Dynavox:** Eye-tracking technology that uses AI to interpret eye movements for communication and computer access ((Duffy et al., 2018)
    - **Voiceitt:** AI-driven speech recognition app that understands non-standard speech patterns, aiding communication for individuals with speech impairments.
5. Daily Living and Independence:
    - **Amazon Alexa and Google Assistant:** Smart assistants that use AI to help manage daily tasks and control smart home devices with voice commands.

- **Seeing AI:** Microsoft app that describes the world around visually impaired users using AI, aiding in daily navigation.

6. Behavioural and Emotional Support:
   - **ReThink:** AI-based app designed to reduce cyberbullying by detecting offensive language and promoting positive behavior.
   - **Autism Therapy with Robots:** AI-driven robots like NAO and Milo engage children with autism in interactive social and emotional learning activities.
7. Reading and Writing Aids:
   - **Kurzweil 3000:** Uses AI for text-to-speech, language translation, and study aids, making reading and writing accessible for individuals with learning disabilities. (Kurzweil Education, 2019).
   - **Ghotit Real Writer and Reader:** AI app that provides accurate spelling and grammar corrections, text-to-speech, and word prediction for dyslexia and dysgraphia.
8. Social Skills Development:
   - **Emotiplay:** Uses AI to help individuals with autism understand and interpret emotions through interactive games.
   - **Mentegram:** AI-powered mental health platform that provides personalised feedback and support for developing social and emotional skills.
9. Visual Impairments:
   - **Be My Eyes:** Connects visually impaired users with sighted volunteers via video call for assistance with everyday tasks.
   - **OrCam MyEye:** Wearable device using AI to read text, recognize faces, and identify products, providing audio feedback to the user (Granquist et al., 2021).
10. Hearing Impairments:
    - **AVA:** Provides real-time transcription of spoken conversations, aiding group discussions for hearing-impaired individuals.
    - **RogerVoice:** Transcribes phone calls in real-time, allowing users to read conversations.
11. Mobility Impairments:
    - **Liftware:** AI-enabled utensils that stabilise hand tremors, helping individuals with Parkinson's or essential tremor eat independently.
    - **WHILL Autonomous Drive System:** AI-powered electric wheelchairs that navigate autonomously, providing greater mobility.
12. Mental Health and Emotional Support:
    - **Woebot:** AI-powered chatbot offering cognitive behavioral therapy (CBT) and emotional support.

- **Replika:** AI chatbot that provides companionship and mental health support, learning from user interactions for personalised responses.

13. Speech and Language Disorders:
    - **Proloquo2Go:** AAC app using AI to predict and suggest words and phrases for individuals with speech difficulties.
    - **Predictable:** Text-to-speech app using AI to predict user intent for efficient communication.
14. Learning Disabilities:
    - **Kurzweil 3000:** Literacy support tool offering text-to-speech, language translation, and study aids for learning disabilities. (Kurzweil Education, 2019).
    - **Ghotit Real Writer and Reader:** Provides advanced spelling and grammar corrections, text-to-speech, and word prediction for dyslexia and dysgraphia (Prenner, 2015).
    - **ModMath:** Digital platform for solving math problems, aiding students with dysgraphia and dyslexia.

AI has revolutionized assistive technology for Persons with Disabilities, enhancing accessibility, independence, and quality of life across various disability types.

AI FOR COLLABORATIVE TEACHING MODEL

AI is profoundly reshaping collaborative pedagogical paradigms through its augmentation of communication, streamlining of administrative duties, and facilitation of bespoke learning encounters. E-learning, elucidated in the aforementioned discourse stands as a pivotal tool in the educational arsenal (Tan, Lee, & Lee, 2022). The Collaborative Learning framework espouses myriad advantages over competitive or individualistic methodologies drawing from the insights of Johnson (1989) and Pantiz (1999), have delineated more than fifty merits of Collaborative Learning, stratified into four principal categories (Laal & Ghodsi, 2012):

Social Advantages: CL nurtures a social support infrastructure among learners, fosters diverse perspectives among students and faculty, promotes a constructive milieu for modeling and exercising cooperation, and cultivates cohesive learning communities.

Psychological Benefits: It bolsters learners' self-regard, diminishes anxiety levels, and fosters favorable dispositions towards educators.

Academic Gains: CL cultivates critical thinking competencies, engages learners actively in the educational process, enhances classroom performance and academic outcomes, exemplifies effective conflict resolution and problem-solving strategies, enables tailored instruction even in expansive lecture settings, and motivates learners within academic environments.

Alternative Assessment Techniques: Alternative assessment techniques integrate collaborative teaching practices with diverse assessment methodologies. These categories underscore the comprehensive advantages of adopting collaborative learning strategies in educational settings (Laal et al., 2014).

AI's impact on collaborative teaching is multifaceted, as highlighted in the discourse on personalized education:

Personalized Learning: Tailoring each student's learning experience to meet their individual needs involves adjusting learning pace, materials, sequence, technologies, instructional methods, and support.

Adaptive Learning Systems: Platforms like DreamBox and Knewton utilize AI to adapt learning content based on students' performance, facilitating collaborative efforts in crafting personalized lesson plans (Wang, & Woodworth, 2011; Fitria, 2021).

Additionally, research explores innovative educational technologies such as Head-Mounted Displays (HMDs) for immersive learning scenarios. Studies by Johnston, Miller, Shing, Ravindran, and Rahmadiva demonstrate applications using HMDs, virtual environments like CAVE systems, and interactive tools such as Leap Motion, enhancing engagement and learning efficacy (Mahini, 2024).

Intelligent Tutoring Systems exemplify cutting-edge educational tools such as Carnegie Learning, which deliver instantaneous feedback and personalized instruction. These systems empower educators to tailor collaborative endeavors according to individual student requirements (Fitria, 2021).

Enhanced Communication and Collaboration:

In the realm of virtual collaborative platforms, AI-integrated tools like Google Classroom and Microsoft Teams revolutionize teacher-student-parent communication. Automated reminders, assignment tracking, and real-time feedback amplify the power of collaboration, enriching support systems, establishing achievable goals, and facilitating early interventions.

Automating Administrative Tasks (Munawar, 2023):

AI-driven scheduling solutions streamline class timetables, meetings, and collaborative planning sessions, optimizing resource allocation and time management (Fitria, 2021; Tahiru, 2021).

Professional Development:

Personalized Professional Development (PD) initiatives harness AI's analytical prowess to identify educators' strengths and areas for growth. Tailored PD programs foster collaborative learning among teachers, promoting continuous improvement (Cardona et al., 2023).

Virtual Coaches and Mentors:

AI-powered virtual coaching platforms like AI Coach by Better Lesson offer personalized guidance and feedback to educators. These tools nurture collaborative growth and skill enhancement among teachers (Fitria, 2021).

Student Support and Intervention:

Early Warning Systems powered by AI detect at-risk students through data analysis, enabling collaborative efforts for timely interventions and support strategies.

Behavioral Analytics:

AI tools monitor and analyze student behavior, empowering educators to adopt collaborative approaches in classroom management and student well-being support (Sharma et al., 2023).

Content Creation and Sharing:

AI-generated content tools like Content Technologies Inc. facilitate customized educational materials. Teachers collaborate on modifying and adapting content to cater to diverse student needs (Khosravi et al., n.d).

Resource Repositories:

AI-powered platforms such as OER Commons harness machine learning to recommend pertinent open educational resources (OER), tailored to teachers' collaborative inputs and preferences (Khosravi et al., 2023).

Enhanced Student Engagement:

Innovative approaches like gamification and interactive learning leverage AI to create adaptive games and engaging lessons. These tools empower educators to collaboratively integrate immersive educational experiences into their curricula, enhancing student engagement and skill optimization (Smiderle et al., 2020).

AI-Powered Assistants:

Virtual assistants like Alexa for Education facilitate collaborative classroom activities by providing real-time support to students and teachers alike. These assistants enhance interactive learning environments and foster collaborative problem-solving (Darvishi et al., 2024).

Data-Driven Decision Making:

Learning Analytics: AI platforms such as BrightBytes offer robust data analytics capabilities, enabling teachers to collaboratively analyze student performance comprehensively. These insights inform data-driven decisions aimed at enhancing learning outcomes (Toyokawa et al., 2023).

Predictive Analytics: AI's predictive analytics capabilities forecast future academic trends and student needs, empowering educators to collaboratively devise proactive instructional strategies. Platforms like TeachFX provide AI-powered instructional feedback that promotes meaningful student discourse.

ROLE OF ARTIFICIAL INTELLIGENCE IN EARLY INTERVENTION

Artificial Intelligence (AI) plays a pivotal role in enabling early interventions in education through its capabilities to identify at-risk students, personalize learning experiences, and provide timely and targeted assistance. Georgopoulos et al. (2003) introduced a differential diagnosis tool utilizing fuzzy cognitive maps, a symbolic representation in soft computing, to distinguish Specific Language Impairment from conditions like dyslexia and autism. Successful testing on clinical cases underscored its efficacy in medical diagnostics.

Students with speech disorders benefit from advanced tools like the computer-based Speech Therapy system, enhanced with a fuzzy expert system based on forward chaining. This improvement led to the development of LOGOMON, designed to recommend optimal therapeutic interventions tailored to individual students (Sharma et al., 2023).

Key AI-Enabled Early Intervention Methods Include:

1. Predictive Analytics: AI harnesses historical data to detect patterns indicative of potential academic or behavioral issues. Platforms such as BrightBytes and Panorama Education utilize machine learning algorithms for predictive analytics, aiding educators in identifying students at risk of academic underachievement or dropout (Munro et al., 2019; Klimova et al., 2023).
2. Early Warning Systems: AI-driven systems monitor student indicators like attendance, grades, and engagement levels, alerting educators to intervene promptly and provide necessary support (Baneres et al., 2020).
3. Behavioral Analytics: Tools like ClassDojo employ AI to track and analyze real-time student behavior, offering immediate feedback and facilitating positive behavioral interventions. AI-Augmented Learning and Applied Behavior Analytics (AI-ABA) platforms enhance personalized treatment and learning plans for individuals with Autism and other neurodevelopmental conditions, promoting self-regulation through reinforcement-based virtual reality and mobile platforms (Ghafghazi et al., 2021).
4. Communication Platforms: AI enhances platforms like Google Classroom and Microsoft Teams, facilitating real-time communication and collaboration among educators, students, and parents, ensuring timely interventions and informed contributions. The School Automation System (MIS/ERP) integrates web-based applications, providing a unified interface for Parents, Students, Teachers, and School Administration (National Informatics Centre, n.d).
5. Parent and Teacher Portals: AI-driven portals offer immediate updates on student performance and intervention outcomes, fostering effective collaboration between parents and educators to support student progress. E-learning, which typically reduces study time by 40-60% compared to traditional settings, allows students to learn at their own pace through interactive videos, simulations, and applications, accessible via communication tools such as Microsoft Teams. The efficacy of these methods lies not only in their selection but in their ability to support emotional well-being, particularly crucial during remote learning periods (Marin & Popovici, 2022).
6. Learning Analytics: Platforms like Classcraft utilize AI to analyze student engagement and performance data, aiding educators in identifying students requiring additional support and informing early intervention strategies through data-driven decision-making. Toyokawa et al. (2023) utilized the LEAF learning system to analyze students' handwriting data from interactions in a Japanese

elementary school's resource room, visualizing learning behaviors and difficulties to support learners with special needs effectively.

7. Customizable Reports: AI tools generate detailed reports on student progress, pinpointing areas of concern and suggesting interventions tailored to individual student needs, thereby enabling educators to optimize instructional strategies (Marin & Popovici, 2022).
8. AI-Powered Communication Platforms: Tools like ClassTag and Remind leverage AI to streamline communication between teachers, parents, and students, automating updates, reminders, and personalized messages to enhance home-school partnerships (Marin & Popovici, 2022).
9. Language Translation: AI-powered services such as Google Translate bridge language barriers, ensuring non-English-speaking families receive critical information in their native languages (Garg & Sharma, 2020).
10. Real-Time Progress Reports: AI generates and delivers real-time progress reports to parents, offering insights into their child's academic performance, attendance, and behavior.
11. Homework and Assignment Tracking: AI assists parents in monitoring their child's homework and assignments, with platforms like Google Classroom providing visibility into assignments, deadlines, and submission statuses.
12. Interactive Learning Activities: AI recommends personalized learning activities for parents to engage in with their children at home, promoting parental involvement in education. Microsoft's Equadex, tailored for children with learning disabilities and autism, provides a mobile-navigated environment for enhanced communication and understanding through visual presentations (Wang'ang'a, 2024).
13. AI Assistive Devices: Technologies like Microsoft Translator aid learners with hearing impairments by translating spoken language into visible captions through headsets, supporting comprehension across 60 languages (Roach, 2018). Advanced hearing aids, employing deep learning and AI, enhance auditory experiences with features like sound scene analysis, real-time language translation, and sound protection (Garg & Sharma, 2020).
14. **Community Portals:** AI-driven platforms have pioneered community portals tailored for seamless resource sharing, event organization, and collaborative project management. Platforms such as Nextdoor, originally designed for local neighborhoods, can be adeptly adapted to foster collaboration and engagement within school communities.
15. **Parental Workshops and Training:** AI designs and recommends workshops and training sessions for parents based on their needs and interests. Platforms like Coursera and edX offer courses on supporting children's learning at home. Parent training programs have proven useful for the prevention and treatment

of behavior problems (Michelson et al., 2013; Pidano & Allen, 2015; Forgatch & Gewirtz, 2018; Zisser-Nathenson et al., 2018). Different parent training programs have already been implemented using BITs, proving to be effective in reducing disruptive behavior, improving the sense of parental self-efficacy, and developing parental skills (Bausback & Bunge, 2021; Cefai et al., 2010; Corralejo & Rodriguez, 2018; Morawska et al., 2014; Sourander et al. 2016). However, till now no parental training a been given by AI chatbot (Entenberg et al., 2021). Technology enhances parental workshop and training (McCall et al., 2023; Entenberg et al., 2021).

16. **Resource Recommendations:** AI further empowers parents by curating and recommending educational resources, articles, and videos that facilitate their support of their child's learning and developmental milestones. Tools like Pocket adeptly aggregate and suggest pertinent content, catering to diverse parental needs. In the realm of educational technology, several computer-based tools have emerged to aid children with dyslexia, such as the Phonological Awareness Educational Software, enhancing phonological awareness among readers. Additionally, specialized interventions like the LIFEisGAME for children with autism facilitate comprehension of facial expressions, while the Smart Tutoring Model facilitates enhanced learning experiences for children with various learning disabilities (Garg & Sharma, 2020).

ROLE OF ARTIFICIAL INTELLIGENCE IN ASSESSMENT

The integration of A.I in education represents a profound revolution in the industry, fundamentally altering its aims and methodologies. AI applications have enabled personalized learning experiences tailored to individual student aptitudes and needs. AI algorithms now include sophisticated assessment tools capable of analyzing cognitive, physical, and emotional abilities sourced from diverse data inputs. These tools empower occupational therapists and special education professionals to craft highly personalized intervention plans. Furthermore, AI-driven assistive technologies such as robotic devices and smartphone systems have significantly enhanced the autonomy and quality of life for individuals with disabilities. These technologies provide tailored support across daily activities, mobility, and communication needs.

Recent research highlighted in “Artificial Intelligence and Sensor Technologies: The Future of Education for Students with and without Intellectual and Developmental Disabilities” underscores the transformative potential of cost-effective, precise sensor technologies, generative AI, and neurotechnologies. These innovations offer unprecedented real-time insights into students' learning progress and cognitive states. In essence, AI's integration in education marks a pivotal shift towards adaptive and inclusive learning environments, promising to revolutionize educational practices and support frameworks for diverse student populations (Medenica et al., 2023).

1) The Cognitive Assessment and Rehabilitation Environment (CAREN) system, developed by Aulisio, Han, and Glueck, (2020) is an AI-based assessment tool that uses virtual reality, motion capture, and AI algorithms to evaluate cognitive functions like attention, memory, and executive functions in individuals with cognitive impairments. By analyzing user interactions within the virtual reality environment, AI algorithms capture data on cognitive performance, offering valuable insights into an individual's abilities. This aids in accurate assessment and personalized intervention planning (Medenica et al., 2023; Aulisio et al., 2020).
2) The Kinect-based Movement Assessment System uses AI algorithms and Kinect's depth-sensing technology to assess motor skills and movement patterns in individuals with motor impairments. The AI analyzes body movements to detect and quantify impairments accurately, providing objective measurements of motor performance. This enables therapists to evaluate progress, adapt treatment plans, and customize interventions to individual needs (Medenica et al., 2023; Gal et al., 2015).
3) The Computerized Dynamic Assessment System focuses on evaluating cognitive abilities and learning potential in individuals with learning disabilities or developmental disorders. Computerized Dynamic Assessment System utilizes adaptive algorithms to tailor the assessment tasks based on the individual's responses, allowing for personalized and targeted evaluations of cognitive strengths and weaknesses (Medenica et al., 2023).
4) The Language Assessment Remediation and Screening Procedure is an AI-powered tool used to assess language skills and identify impairments, especially in individuals with developmental language disorders. Its AI algorithms analyze linguistic data, such as syntax and morphology, to evaluate language abilities and pinpoint areas needing intervention and support. (Medenica et al., 2023; Nayak et al., 2005).
5) Assessing reading comprehension tests will not only allow timely feedback to students but also can provide feedback to education researchers, parents and teachers. In this study two systems are described. The first is based on latent semantic analysis, which needs a reasonable level of handwriting recognition performance. The second developed an Artificial Neural Network (ANN) which is based on features collected from the handwriting image. Both systems were trained and evaluated using a test-bed of essays written in response to prompts in statewide reading comprehension tests and scored by humans. Even though

there were observed errors in word recognition during the evaluation of this platform scoring performance still remains a promising tool (Srihari et al., 2008).

6) Kohli et al., (2010) introduced a systematic approach for the identification of dyslexia at an early stage by using ANN . This approach is amongst the first attempts which have been made for addressing the dyslexia identification problems with the use of ANN.
7) Jain et al. (2009) proposed a model called Perceptron based Learning Disability Detector. It is an artificial neural network model for identifying difficulties in reading (dyslexia), in writing (dysgraphia) and in mathematics (dyscalculia) using curriculum based test conducted by special educators.
8) Pavlopoulos et al. (2008) developed a neural network approach enhanced by Genetic Programming for self-assessment in e-learning environments. This method evaluates user responses to both single and multiple questions across various learning domains: grammar, reading, writing, letter recognition, alphabetical order, and spelling. The Genetic Programming Neural Network (GPNN) methodology proves effective for students struggling in these areas, particularly benefiting those with physical or sensory impairments. The platform successfully assessed user responses, suggesting potential for developing an intelligent e-tutor through generalised assessment processes (Drigas & Ioannidou, 2012).

By harnessing AI technologies, these tools provide objective and personalized assessments of cognitive abilities, language skills, driving performance, and social-emotional well-being. The integration of AI algorithms enables precise evaluations, tailored interventions, and data-driven decision-making, enhancing the overall assessment process and promoting better outcomes for individuals with various disabilities and impairments.

ROLE OF ARTIFICIAL IN PERSONALISED LEARNING

AI algorithms in education are adept at analyzing students' learning patterns and abilities, thereby offering personalized recommendations and adaptive learning experiences that cater specifically to individual needs. For instance, Squirrel AI Learning stands out as a prime example of such a platform. It employs adaptive learning algorithms designed to customize educational content and instructional approaches according to each student's unique learning pace, preferences, and areas of knowledge gaps. This continuous assessment and curriculum adjustment process are aimed at maximizing learning outcomes and supporting students in achieving their academic objectives with greater efficiency.

ROLE OF ROBOT IN RESHAPING SPECIAL EDUCATION

Robots designed for children with special needs, such as the IRIS educational robot, play a transformative role that extends beyond traditional education. These robots are instrumental in fostering not only educational growth but also enhancing social, personal, and recreational skills within school and community settings, particularly notable in Pennsylvania.

These robotic companions are equipped to assist with essential daily activities like dressing, eating, and mobility. Utilizing advanced AI algorithms, they can tailor their assistance to the specific needs and preferences of each individual, providing highly personalized and adaptive support. Numerous studies have underscored the efficacy of robots in engaging children with autism during interventions. They excel in capturing attention and motivating children, thereby facilitating effective teaching of targeted skills.

In summary, these robotic technologies represent a significant advancement in supporting holistic development among children with special needs, leveraging AI to offer tailored assistance and fostering comprehensive skill development across various domains (Lee et al., 2012; Lee & Obinata, 2013; Wainer et al., 2010).

Jamsa et al. (2014) delved into the realm of AI algorithms applied in proactive fall detection systems, employing sophisticated sensor technologies like accelerometers and gyroscopes. These systems leverage machine learning algorithms to discern patterns of movement indicative of falls amidst regular daily activities.

Zammarchi and Conversano (2021) underscored the pervasive use of eye-tracking technology in exploring social interaction levels among individuals with autism. Lorenzo et al. (2020) posited virtual reality as particularly well-suited for the diverse learning styles of individuals with autism, highlighting its potential in educational settings. Barua et al. (2022) emphasized the facilitative role of AI tools in supporting social interactions among individuals with autism.

Studies in the literature extensively document the efficacy of robots in imparting crucial skills to individuals with autism. These skills encompass initiating and sustaining interactions, establishing eye contact, mastering turn-taking, recognizing emotions, fostering joint attention, and facilitating imitation (Pennisi et al., 2016; Saleh et al., 2021).

In the paper "GenAI, Robots, and Inclusive Special Education: Autism Spectrum Disorder in the Age of Generative AI," it is argued that individuals with autism often exhibit a preference for interacting with robots over humans a phenomenon widely studied in robotics research. For example, Tapus et al. (2012) observed that participants with autism initiated more interactions with the Robot Nao than with humans, displaying prolonged periods of eye contact with the robot. According to feedback from a parent at our institution, her child with autism expresses a preference for conversing with robots rather than teachers due to the predictability and perceived control in these interactions. The paper emphasizes that robots effectively engage and motivate individuals with autism during interventions, capturing their attention and significantly enhancing learning outcomes (Sağdıç et al., 2024).

ARTIFICIAL INTELLIGENCE CREATING ADAPTIVE LEARNING

Adaptive learning utilizes AI algorithms to dynamically tailor interventions or learning experiences based on an individual's responses and progress. In educational and rehabilitation contexts, these systems continuously monitor performance, adjust task difficulty, and deliver instant feedback (Malach, & Javorcik, 2019). This personalised approach fosters individual skill development, encourages mastery learning, and boosts engagement and motivation (Medenica et al., 2023). It also helps in learning spelling for dyslexic students (Kast et al., 2011).

1) Al-driven virtual reality platforms have also been utilised to facilitate personalised interventions and adaptive learning. Researchers (Ke & Im, 2013) explored the use of VR environments combined with Al algorithms to create immersive and interactive therapeutic experiences.
2) These platforms adapt the virtual reality scenarios and activities based on the individual's performance, providing personalised challenges and feedback. AI algorithms analyse the user's interactions within the virtual reality environment, enabling therapists to assess progress, tailor interventions, and create realistic simulations for skill development and functional training.
3) Collaborative virtual environments employ AI algorithms to generate interactive virtual agents engaging in social interactions with users. These environments utilize natural language processing and emotional intelligence algorithms to interpret and respond to user input, nurturing meaningful social interactions and fostering social skill development. Pelachaud et al. (n.d) introduced the Virtual Interactive Social Agent system, designed specifically to facilitate communication and interaction within virtual environments (Medenica et al., 2023).
4) Baschera and Gross (2010) developed an adaptive spelling training system targeting students grappling with spelling difficulties. This platform incorporates an inference algorithm adept at handling unstructured input containing multiple errors defined by distinct error patterns. Using Poisson regression with a linear link function, the algorithm evaluates challenges associated with specific error patterns to tailor remedial strategies.

5) Melis et al. (2001) pioneered ActiveMath, a web-based intelligent tutoring system specializing in mathematics education. ActiveMath operates as an Intelligent Tutoring System, enabling students to learn autonomously within their preferred environment. It employs diverse AI techniques for adaptive course generation, student modeling, feedback provision, interactive exercises, and semantic web-compatible knowledge representation. ActiveMath empowers students to initiate their learning journey, assess their grasp of concepts, and set learning goals, adjusting course content and recommendations accordingly. An integrated eye-tracking mechanism monitors student attention and reading patterns, enhancing learning engagement and efficacy.
6) Anthony et al. (2008) developed an Intelligent Tutoring System tailored for algebra equation-solving, a challenging subject for many students. This platform, known as Cognitive Tutors, accepts natural handwriting input and presents interactive problem-solving scenarios. In Cognitive Tutor Algebra, students engage in modeling, graphing functions, and solving equations, receiving real-time feedback and guidance. The Freehand Formula Entry System, trained on extensive student data, supports diverse mathematical topics and learner profiles, particularly benefiting students with special educational needs like those with Down syndrome (Drigas & Ioannidou, 2023).
7) Sebe et al. (2006) developed an emotion recognition tool that integrates visual and audio cues for human-computer interaction. In addition to identifying the six universal emotions (happy, surprise, angry, disgust, fear, and sad), this application can detect other affective states such as interest, boredom, confusion, and frustration. It is applicable to all children but particularly effective for those with speech difficulties and in training children with autism, who often struggle with understanding emotions. The approach analyses 11 affective states across 38 subjects using Bayesian Networks for bimodal fusion. The model incorporates a variable indicating whether the user is speaking. Facial features such as eyebrows, eyelids, and mouth movements are tracked to quantify specific facial expressions. Testing on 38 graduate and undergraduate students from diverse fields demonstrated significantly improved emotion recognition accuracy when integrating both visual and audio information. (Drigas & Ioannidou, 2023; Sebe et al., n.d)
8) Advanced technologies such as virtual reality, augmented reality, AI, robotics, and eye-tracking are increasingly integrated into educational settings. Eye-tracking technology, highlighted by Zammarchi and Conversano (2021), is commonly used to study social interactions in individuals with autism. Lorenzo et al. (2020) suggest that Virtual Reality is well-suited to the learning styles of individuals with autism. Barua et al. (2022) indicate that AI tools facilitate social

interaction among individuals with autism. These advancements are expected to significantly support individuals with autism across various domains.

To effectively harness new streams of real-time process data, it is crucial to develop frameworks and tools like generative artificial intelligence. These tools will illustrate methods for large-scale research and application, aiming to establish a fully adaptive, student-centered classroom environment. By integrating neurocognitive, psychophysiological, and other process data alongside existing machine learning and big data frameworks, educators and researchers in special education can gain deeper insights into how learning tasks, assessments, and student interactions contribute to cognitive functions (e.g., reasoning and thinking), affective aspects (e.g., motivation and engagement), and behavioral outcomes (e.g., practices and strategies) within classroom settings (Drigas & Ioannidou, 2012).

AI AMELIORATING SPECIFIC CONDITIONS

AI-supported applications are transforming the support provided to children with autism, improving their communication skills (Sağdıç et al., 2023), social skills (Riedl et al., 2009), and IEP (Rakap, 2023). They also facilitate the recording of behavioral issues and stereotypical movements (Amiri et al., 2017), as well as conducting skill analyses (Srinivasan & Parthasarathi, 2013). For example, Sağdıç et al. (2023) developed an AI-based educational application featuring cartoon characters that use applied behavior analysis to teach individuals with autism how to respond to questions and follow instructions. This innovative approach enables autism individuals to acquire target behaviors through interactive tablet-based cartoons, reducing reliance on traditional teacher-led methods (Sağdıç et al., 2024).

A Netherlands-based start-up has developed an AI-powered smartphone app called GnoSys, offering a groundbreaking and affordable solution for translating sign language into text and speech in real time. Utilising neural networks and computer vision, GnoSys recognises sign language from video and translates it into speech through smart algorithms. This app enables teachers in inclusive settings to better understand and meet the needs of their hearing-impaired students. This paper will focus on teaching Hearing Impaired students in special schools using GnoSys, Live Transcribe, Sound Amplifier, iCommunicator, and Virtual Reality. Moreover, a "poor man's eye-tracker" is designed which is able to trace child's attention and reading time in detail (Israni, 2019).

Not only GnoSys but also VoiceOver and TalkBack integrated by iPhone and Android respectively. Siri, Apple's virtual assistant, orchestrates seamless interactions, akin to Cortana by Microsoft and Google Assistant. Aira and Be My Eyes converge in their mission, connecting sighted volunteers with visually impaired users to navigate complex tasks such as airport gate finding.

Seeing AI stands out as a versatile app on iOS, adept at interpreting and narrating documents captured by the smartphone camera, including banknotes and product barcodes (Fitria, 2021). For those with speech impediments like Parkinson's, Voiceitt harnesses AI to decipher challenging speech patterns, fostering clearer communication. In the domain of navigation, tools like Google Maps, Moovit, Wheelmap, Soundscape, and Evelity empower individuals with disabilities to traverse urban landscapes confidently (New York City). Embracing inclusivity means ensuring everyone, irrespective of their abilities, can access essential services. For instance, Braille AI Tutor revolutionizes Braille education with AI-driven speech recognition and interactive learning, pivotal for integrating blind individuals into the workforce and broader society. Seeing AI on iOS excels at document interpretation, image recognition, and even emotion detection from facial expressions, while Lookout on Android offers a swift Quick Scan Mode for rapid text assessment. Google's Project Guideline pioneers an AI-enabled system enabling blind individuals to independently navigate paths painted on the ground using their smartphone, headphones, and a guiding harness. Accessible document validation tools like Microsoft Accessibility Checker and Adobe Accessibility Checker uphold equal access to information for students and professionals with disabilities, reinforcing their capacity to thrive in educational and professional realms.

BENEFITS FOR INDIVIDUALS WITH AUTISM USING AI

There have been several benefits of AI for making the lives of people with disabilities comfortable. The use of AI is also being used for screening, identification, assessment, diagnosis and certification (Bertacchini et al., 2023; Bozkurt, 2020; Bozkurt, 2023d; Bozkurt & Sharma, 2023; Molenaar et al., 2022):

- **Early Diagnosis**: AI provides objective early assessments of risk, enabling timely access to educational services.
- **Personalised Learning**: AI tailors educational materials to individual learning styles.
- **Multi-Sensory Engagement**: Technologies enhance learning by engaging multiple senses, boosting motivation and retention.
- **Interactive Environments**: AI-powered simulations create engaging and realistic learning scenarios.
- **Rapid Content Delivery and Feedback**: AI efficiently generates and evaluates educational content, providing quick feedback.

- **Increased Efficiency**: AI assists teachers in preparing materials and reports, saving time.
- **Predictable Teaching**: AI creates stable, anxiety-reducing learning environments.
- **High Motivation**: Individuals with Autism often prefer technology-based learning.
- **24/7 Accessibility**: AI enables continuous, anytime-anywhere education.
- **Assistant Teacher**: AI aids in skill analysis, individualized planning, and performance measurement, reducing teacher workload.
- **Alternative Communication**: AI enhances communication for non-verbal individuals with AUTISM.
- **Behavioral Tracking**: AI monitors and analyzes behaviors, offering real-time feedback to prevent outbursts.
- **Social Skills Training**: AI simulations provide safe environments for practicing social interactions.
- **Game-Based Learning**: AI gamifies educational content, making learning more enjoyable and engaging.

WAY FORWARD

To effectively harness the potential of AI, organizations should form interdisciplinary teams, fostering collaboration with industry experts and academic research institutions. Initiating pilot projects and involving stakeholders from the outset is essential for assessing feasibility and securing commitment. It is imperative to maintain transparent communication regarding the benefits and risks of AI, delineating clear roles and responsibilities to streamline operations. Continuous training and support are vital to cultivate a culture of innovation, while robust feedback mechanisms and regular review cycles are necessary to monitor progress and inform adjustments. Investing in advanced data analytics enhances the evaluation process, enabling organizations to measure outcomes effectively. Sharing best practices across the industry encourages continual improvement and learning.

Promoting a culture of experimentation and strengthening external partnerships can significantly bolster resources and expertise, ensuring a seamless integration of AI technologies with minimal disruption. This strategic approach not only accelerates AI adoption but also maximizes its potential to drive transformative outcomes (Khairi & Yhya Alhafidh, 2024).

CONCLUSION

When the opportunities presented by AI as an assistive technology are properly utilized and well-integrated into the education of students with special needs, the results are satisfying. Reshaping special education through the sophisticated strategies of Artificial Intelligence unveils a transformative horizon, one teeming with promise for enriching the personalized learning journeys of students with disabilities. AI's marvels lie in its ability to craft bespoke educational pathways, deliver instantaneous and nuanced feedback, and provide adaptive resources finely tuned to the unique needs of each learner. This technological alchemy empowers educators to meticulously monitor student progress, discern areas of challenge, and tailor interventions with precision and empathy.

Yet, amidst this digital renaissance, we must tread with vigilance. Ethical considerations concerning data privacy, the inclusive design of AI systems, and the indispensable role of human oversight are paramount. The confluence of AI and special education harbors the potential to cultivate greater autonomy, engagement, and academic triumphs for students with disabilities. Nevertheless, such integration must be navigated with a blend of innovation and circumspection, ensuring that the essence of inclusive and thoughtful education remains at its core.

REFERENCES

N2Y. 2021, October 21). *N2Y wins Special Education Solution of the Year designation in 6th annual EdTech Breakthrough Awards program*. PR Newswire. https://www.prnewswire.com/news-releases/n2y-wins-special-education-solution-of-the-year-designation-in-6th-annual-edtech-breakthrough-awards-program-302166212.html

n2y. (2004). Unique Learning System [Educational software]. Retrieved from https://www.n2y.com/unique-learning-system/ on 1 June 2024.

Ahmad, W., Parween, S., & Nazli. (2022). Concept of Normalization, Mainstreaming, Integration, and Inclusive Education: Implications in Educational Program. In Ahmad, W., Chavan, B.S., & Gupta, R.K. (Eds.), Comprehensive Textbook on Disability (pp. 8-12). New Delhi: Jaypee Brothers Medical Publishers.

Al-Obaydi, L. H., Pikhart, M., & Klimova, B. (2023). ChatGPT and the general concepts of Education: Can Artificial Intelligence-driven Chatbots Support the process of Language Learning? [IJET]. *International Journal of Emerging Technologies in Learning*, 18(21), 39–50. DOI: 10.3991/ijet.v18i21.42593

Al-Zoubi, S. M., & Rahman, M. S. B. A. (2012). The Effect of Resource Room on improving Reading and Arithmetic Skills for Learners with Learning Disabilities. The. *International Journal of Scientific Research in Education*, 5(4), 269–277. Retrieved June 1, 2024, from http://www.ijsre.com

Ally, L. (1948). About us. Retrieved from https://www.learningally.org/About-Us on 1 June 2024.

Ally, L. (2011). Learning Ally. https://learningally.org retrieved on 1 June 2024.

Almodaires, A. A., Almutairi, F. M., & Almsaud, T. E. A. (2021). Pre-Service Teachers' Perceptions of the Effectiveness of Microsoft. *International Education Studies*, 14(9), 108–121. DOI: 10.5539/ies.v14n9p108

Alvarez-Alvarez, C., & Mischel, L. (2024). Edpuzzle for E-learning: A Study of Perceived Advantages and Limitations. *International Journal of Education and Development Using Information and Communication Technology*, 20(1), 134–145.

Amazon. (2014). Amazon Alexa. Retrieved from https://www.amazon.com/alexa on 1 June 2024.

Amiri, A. M., Peltier, N., Goldberg, C., Sun, Y., Nathan, A., Hiremath, S. V., & Mankodiya, K. (2017). WearSense: Detecting autism stereotypic behaviors through smartwatches. *Healthcare (Basel)*, 5(11), 2–9. DOI: 10.3390/healthcare5010011

Anthony, L., Yang, J., & Koedinger, K. R. (2008). Toward Next-Generation Intelligent tutors: Adding natural Handwriting Input. *IEEE MultiMedia*, 15(3), 64–68. DOI: 10.1109/MMUL.2008.73

AssistiveWare. (2009). *Proloquo2Go*. AssistiveWare. https://www.assistiveware.com/products/proloquo2go

Aulisio, M. C., Han, D. Y., & Glueck, A. C. (2020). Virtual reality gaming as a neurorehabilitation tool for brain injuries in adults: A systematic review. *Brain Injury : [BI]*, 34(10), 1322–1330. DOI: 10.1080/02699052.2020.1802779

Bañeres, D., Rodríguez, M. E., Guerrero-Roldán, A. E., & Karadeniz, A. (2020). An Early Warning System to Detect at-risk Students in online Higher Education. *Applied Sciences (Basel, Switzerland)*, 10(13), 1–28. DOI: 10.3390/app10134427

Barua, P. D., Vicnesh, J., Gururajan, R., Oh, S. L., Palmer, E., Azizan, M. M., & Acharya, U. R. (2022). Artificial intelligence enabled personalized assistive tools to enhance education of children with neurodevelopmental disorders: A review. *International Journal of Environmental Research and Public Health*, 19(3), 1–26. DOI: 10.3390/ijerph19031192

Baschera, G.-M., & Gross, M. (2010). Poisson-based inference for perturbation models in adaptive spelling training. *International Journal of Artificial Intelligence in Education*, 20, 333–360. DOI: 10.3233/JAI-2010-011

Bausback, K. B., & Bunge, E. L. (2021). Meta-analysis of parent training programs utilizing behavior intervention technologies. *Social Sciences (Basel, Switzerland)*, 10(10), 367. DOI: 10.3390/socsci10100367

Bertacchini, F., Demarco, F., Scuro, C., Pantano, P., & Bilotta, E. (2023). A social robot connected with ChatGPT to improve cognitive functioning in autism subjects. *Frontiers in Psychology*, 14, 1232177. DOI: 10.3389/fpsyg.2023.1232177

Betsy, & Eubanck, G. (2012). *About ModMath*. Retrieved June 1, 2024, from https://www.modmath.com

Bozkurt, A. (2020). Educational technology research patterns in the realm of the digital knowledge age. *Journal of Interactive Media in Education*, 2020(1), 1–17. DOI: 10.5334/jime.570

Bozkurt, A. (2023d). ChatGPT, generative artificial intelligence, and algorithmic paradigm shift. *CRES Journal Critical Reviews in Educational Sciences*, 4(1), 63–72. DOI: 10.59320/alanyazin.1283282

Bozkurt, A., & Sharma, R. C. (2023). Generative AI and prompt engineering: The art of whispering to let the genie out of the algorithmic world. *Asian Journal of Distance Education*, 18(2), i–vii. DOI: 10.5281/zenodo.8174941

Breznitz, S., & Nachshon, I. (1999). Development of CogniFit. Retrieved from https://www.cognifit.com on 1 June 2024.

Cardona, M. A., Rodríguez, R. J., & Ishmael, K. (2023). Artificial Intelligence and the Future of Teaching and Learning. Office of Educational Technology, U.S. Department of Education, 1-67. Retrieved from https://tech.ed.gov

Carnegie Learning, Inc. (n.d.). *Carnegie Learning*. Retrieved from https://www.carnegielearning.com on 27 June 2024.

CAST. (2011). *UDL guidelines* [Web tool]. Retrieved from https://udlguidelines.cast.org on 1 June 2024.

Cefai, J., Smith, D., & Pushak, R. E. (2010). Parenting wisely: Parent training via CD-ROM with an Australian sample. *Child & Family Behavior Therapy*, 32(1), 17–33. DOI: 10.1080/07317100903539709

Chermesh, O. (2009). *Ghotit Real Writer and Reader*. Retrieved from https://www.ghotit.com on 20 June 2024.

Chua, N. A., Soon, G. Y., Mansor, N. R. B. M., Rashid, R. A., Ahmad, M., Musa, A., Rahman, N. A. A., Noh, C. H. C., Ibrahim, M. Y., & Dollah@Abdullah, A. B. (2021). 'CLASSKICK' an interactive online app to support students' learning: A case study on Mandarin as a foreign learning. *Journal of Physics: Conference Series,* 1874(1), 012084. IOP Publishing. https://doi.org/DOI: 10.1088/1742-6596/1874/1/012084

Corralejo, S. M., & Rodríguez, D. M. M. (2018). Technology in parenting programs: A systematic review of existing interventions. *Journal of Child and Family Studies*, 27(9), 1–15. DOI: 10.1007/s10826-018-1117-1

Darvishi, A., Khosravi, H., Sadiq, S., Gašević, D., & Siemens, G. (2024). Impact of AI assistance on student agency. *Computers & Education*, 210, 104967. DOI: 10.1016/j.compedu.2023.104967

de Freitas, M. P., Piai, V. A., Farias, R. H., Fernandes, A. M. R., de Moraes, R. A. G., & Leithardt, V. R. Q. (2022). Artificial Intelligence of Things Applied to Assistive Technology: A Systematic Literature Review. *Sensors (Basel)*, 22(21), 8531. DOI: 10.3390/s22218531

Don Johnston Incorporated. (2006). *Coby*. Don Johnston Incorporated.

Donath, J. L., Lüke, T., Graf, E., Tran, U. S., & Götz, T. (2023). Does professional development effectively support the implementation of inclusive education? A meta-analysis. *Educational Psychology Review*, 35(30), 30. Advance online publication. DOI: 10.1007/s10648-023-09752-2

Drigas, A., & Ioannidou, R.-E. (2012). Artificial intelligence in special education: A decade review. *International Journal of Engineering Education*, 28(1), 135–146.

Duchemin, T., & Doevendans, P. (2014). AVA. Retrieved from https://www.ava.me/blog on 20 June 2024.

Duffy, E. I., Garry, J., Talbot, L., Pasternak, D., Flinn, A., Minardi, C., Dookram, M., Grant, K., Fitzgerald, D., Rubano, J., Vosswinkel, J., & Jawa, R. S. (2018). A pilot study assessing the spiritual, emotional, physical/environmental, and physiological needs of mechanically ventilated surgical intensive care unit patients via eye tracking devices, head nodding, and communication boards. *Trauma Surgery & Acute Care Open*, 3(1), e000180. DOI: 10.1136/tsaco-2018-000180

Ebo, B. A. (2018). Constructivism or Behaviorism: What is the Best Method to Teach Special Needs Students? *Journal of Healthcare, Science and the Humanities*, 8(2), 45–56.

Eden, C. A., Nneamaka, O. N., & Adeniyi, I. S.Chima Abimbola EdenOnyebuchi Nneamaka ChisomIdowu Sulaimon Adeniyi. (2024). Parent and community involvement in education: Strengthening partnerships for social improvement. *International Journal of Applied Research in Social Sciences*, 6(3), 372–382. DOI: 10.51594/ijarss.v6i3.894

Edpuzzle, Inc. (n.d). Edpuzzle. Retrieved [27th June 2024], from https://edpuzzle.com on 20 June 2024.

Emotiplay. (n.d). Emotiplay. Retrieved from https://www.emotiplay.com/blog/ on 1 June 2024.

Entenberg, G. A., Areas, M., Roussos, A. J., Maglio, A. L., Thrall, J., Escoredo, M., & Bunge, E. L. (2021). Using an artificial intelligence-based chatbot to provide parent training: Results from a feasibility study. *Social Sciences (Basel, Switzerland)*, 10(11), 426. DOI: 10.3390/socsci10110426

Er, M., Andres, E., Budenbender, J., Frischauf, A., Goguadze, G., Libbrecht, P., Pollet, M., & Ullrich, C. (2001). ActiveMath: A generic and adaptive web-based learning environment. *Artificial Intelligence in Education, 12.*

Er, M., & Siekmann, J. (2004). ActiveMath: An intelligent tutoring system for mathematics. In Rutkowski, L., Siekmann, J., Tadeusiewicz, R., & Zadeh, L. A. *(Eds.),Seventh International Conference on Artificial Intelligence and Soft Computing (ICAISC)* (pp. 91–101). Springer-Verlag. https://doi.org/DOI: 10.1007/978-3-540-24844-6_12

Eynon-Lynch, R., & Eynon-Lynch, M. (2015). *Pear Deck.* Pear Deck, Inc.

Fernandez, N., & Hynes, J. W. (2016). The Efficacy of Pullout Programs in Elementary Schools: Making it work. *The Journal of Multidisciplinary Graduate Research*, 2 (3),32-47. Retrieved from https://www.shsu.edu/academics/education/journal-of-multidisciplinary-graduate-research/documents/2016/Article%203%20-%202016%20-%20Fernandez%20and%20Hynes.pdf on 1 June 2024.

Fitch, F. (2003). Inclusion, exclusion, and ideology: Special education students' changing sense of self. *The Urban Review*, 35(3), 233–252. DOI: 10.1023/A:1025733719935

Fitria, T. N. (2021, December). Artificial Intelligence in Education: Using AI tools for Teaching and Learning Process [Conference paper]. *ResearchGate*. https://www.researchgate.net/publication/357447234

Forgatch, M. S., & Gewirtz, A. H. (2018). The evolution of the Oregon Model of Parent Management Training: An Intervention for Antisocial Behavior in Children and Adolescents. In Weisz, J. R., & Kazdin, A. E. (Eds.), *Evidence-based psychotherapies for children and adolescents* (pp. 85–102). The Guilford Press.

Fridenson-Hayo, S., Berggren, S., Lassalle, A., Tal, S., Pigat, D., Meir-Goren, N., O'Reilly, H., Ben-Zur, S., Bölte, S., Baron-Cohen, S., & Golan, O. (2017). 'Emotiplay': A serious game for learning about emotions in children with autism: Results of a cross-cultural evaluation. *European Child & Adolescent Psychiatry*, 26(8), 979–992. DOI: 10.1007/s00787-017-0968-0

Frontline Education. (1998). Special Ed & Interventions [Educational software]. Retrieved from https://www.frontlineeducation.com/products/special-education-interventions/ on 1 June 2024.

Gal, N., Andrei, D., Nemeş, D. I., Nădăşan, E., & Stoicu-Tivadar, V. (2015). A Kinect based intelligent e-rehabilitation system in physical therapy. *Studies in Health Technology and Informatics*, 210, 489–493.

Gander, T., & Shaw, B. (2024). AI in education 2023: Understanding the impact on effective pedagogy, inclusive learning and equitable outcomes. *He Rourou*, 1(1), 15. DOI: 10.54474/herourou.v1i1.9137

Garg, S., & Sharma, S. (2020). Impact of Artificial Intelligence in Special Need Education to Promote Inclusive Pedagogy. *International Journal of Information and Education Technology (IJIET)*, 10(7), 514–519. DOI: 10.18178/ijiet.2020.10.7.1418

Georgopoulos, V. C., Malandraki, G. A., & Stylios, C. D. (2003). A fuzzy cognitive map approach to differential diagnosis of specific language impairment. *Artificial Intelligence in Medicine*, 29(3), 261–278. DOI: 10.1016/S0933-3657(02)00076-3

Ghafghazi, S., Carnett, A., Neely, L., Das, A., & Rad, P. (2021). AI-augmented Behavior Analysis for Children with Developmental Disabilities: Building towards Precision Treatment. Child and Adolescent Policy and Research Institute (CAPRI); *Secure AI Laboratory for Autonomy* (AILA). 1-6.

Google. (2016). Google Assistant. Retrieved from https://assistant.google.com on 1 June 2024.

Granquist, C., Sun, S. Y., Montezuma, S. R., Tran, T. M., Gage, R., & Legge, G. E. (2021). Evaluation and Comparison of Artificial Intelligence Vision Aids: Orcam MyEye 1 and Seeing AI. *Journal of Visual Impairment & Blindness*, 115(4), 277–285. DOI: 10.1177/0145482X211027492

Gupta, R. K., & Ahmad, W. (2022). Universal Design for Learning. In Ahmad, W., Chavan, B. S., & Gupta, R. K. (Eds.), *Comprehensive Textbook on Disability* (pp. 558–563). Jaypee Brothers Medical Publishers.

Herrero, S., & Sabrià, Q. (2013). *Edpuzzle*. Edpuzzle, Inc.

Hough, L. (2018, May 22). Tool in school: Quizlet. ED. Magazine, Harvard Graduate School of Education. https://www.gse.harvard.edu/news/ed/18/05/tool-school-quizlet

Hunt, X., Saran, A., White, H., & Kuper, H. (2021). PROTOCOL: Effectiveness of Interventions for Improving Educational Outcomes for People With Disabilities in Low- and Middle-income Countries: A Systematic Review. *Campbell Systematic Reviews*, 17(4), e1197. DOI: 10.1002/cl2.1197

Huron & Ohio., (2024, June 6). n2y wins "Special Education Solution of the Year" designation in 6th annual EdTech Breakthrough Awards program: Prestigious international awards program recognizes outstanding educational technology products and companies [Press release]. PR Newswire.

Iannone, A., & Giansanti, D. (2023). Breaking Barriers-The Intersection of AI and Assistive Technology in Autism Care: A Narrative Review. *Journal of Personalized Medicine*, 14(1), 41. DOI: 10.3390/jpm14010041

International Dyslexia Association. (n.d). IDA and Learning Ally to get struggling readers much-needed help. https://dyslexiaida.org/ida-and-learning-ally-to-get-struggling-readers-much-needed-help/

Israni, B. (2019). *Combining artificial intelligence with special education.*

Jain, K., Manghirmalani, P., Dongardive, J., & Abraham, S. (2009). Computational diagnosis of learning disability. *International Journal of Recent Trends in Engineering*, 2(3), 64–69.

Jameel, T., & Arsalan, H. (2024). *Adapting education for the AI era: Strategies for generative AI integration.* https://doi.org/DOI: 10.13140/RG.2.2.10251.50723

Jämsä, T., Kangas, M., Vikman, I., Nyberg, L., & Korpelainen, R. (2014). Fall detection in older people: From laboratory to real-life. *Proceedings of the Estonian Academy of Sciences*, 63(3), 341–345. DOI: 10.3176/proc.2014.3.08

Jeannel, O. (2012). Roger Voice. Retrieved from https://rogervoice.com/solutions/the-rogervoice-app/ on 1 June 2024.

Jian, M. (2023). Personalized learning through AI. *Advances in Engineering Innovation*, 5(1), 16–19. Advance online publication. DOI: 10.54254/2977-3903/5/2023039

Johnson, D., & Johnson, R. T. (2015). Cooperation and competition. In *International encyclopedia of the social & behavioral sciences: Second edition* (pp. 856–861). https://doi.org/DOI: 10.1016/B978-0-08-097086-8.24051-8

Johnson, D. W., & Johnson, R. (1989). *Cooperation and competition: Theory and research.* Interaction Book Company.

Juanis, A. A., Anak Mundu, J., & Tati, J. S. (2023). Student's engagement with interactive online learning by Pear Deck. *Jurnal Pengajian Umum / Journal of General Studies, 1.* https://myjms.mohe.gov.my/index.php/jpu/article/view/22743

Kast, M., Baschera, G.-M., Gross, M., Jäncke, L., & Meyer, M. (2011). Computer-based Learning of Spelling Skills in Children with and without Dyslexia. *Annals of Dyslexia*, 61(2), 177–200. DOI: 10.1007/s11881-011-0052-2

Ke, F., & Im, T. (2013). Virtual-reality-based social interaction training for children with high-functioning autism. *The Journal of Educational Research*, 106(6), 441–461. DOI: 10.1080/00220671.2013.832999

Khairi, F., & Yhya Alhafidh, F. (2024). *Navigating the five stages of AI adoption in higher education: A simplified guide.* https://doi.org/DOI: 10.13140/RG.2.2.15679.52641

Khosravi, H., Denny, P., Moore, S., & Stamper, J. (2023). Learnersourcing in the age of AI: Student, educator, and machine partnerships for content creation. *Computers and Education: Artificial Intelligence*, 5, 100151. DOI: 10.1016/j.caeai.2023.100151

Kim, Y. D., Hong, J. W., Kang, W. S., Baek, S. S., Lee, H. S., & An, J. (2010). Design of robot-assisted observation system for therapy and education of children with autism. In Ge, S. S., Li, H., Cabibihan, J. J., & Tan, Y. K. (Eds.), *Social robotics* (Vol. 6414, pp. 218–227). Springer., DOI: 10.1007/978-3-642-17248-9_23

Kinteract. (n.d). Kinteract. Retrieved June 27, 2024, from https://www.kinteract.co.uk/ on 1 June 2024.

Klimova, B., Pikhart, M., & Kacetl, J. (2023). Ethical issues of the use of AI-driven mobile apps for education. *Frontiers in Public Health*, 10, 1118116. DOI: 10.3389/fpubh.2022.1118116

Kohli, M., & Prasad, T. (2010). Identifying dyslexic students by using artificial neural networks. *Lecture Notes in Engineering and Computer Science*, 2183, 118.

Konrad, A. (2022, July 21). ClassDojo won Over Classrooms. Now it's on a $125 million mission to bring kids to the metaverse. *Forbes*.

Kopf, B., & Kopf, D. (2011). Remind [Mobile app]. Remind. https://www.remind.comNisbet, Kelsey and Opp, Allison. (2017). Effects of the Remind App on Parent-Teacher Communication at a Mixed-Income Middle School. Retrieved from Sophia, the St. Catherine University repository website: (https://sophia.stkate.edu/maed/227) on 1 June 2024.

Kurth, J. A., Turner, E. L., Gerasimova, D., Hicks, T. A., Zagona, A., Lansey, K., Mansouri, M. C., Lyon, K. J., Jameson, M., Loyless, R., & Pace, J. R. (2022). An investigation of IEP quality associated with Special Education Placement for Students with Complex Support Needs. *Research and Practice for Persons with Severe Disabilities : the Journal of TASH*, 47(4), 244–260. DOI: 10.1177/15407969221134923

Kurzweil Education. (1996). Kurzweil 3000 [Computer software]. Retrieved from https://www.kurzweiledu.com, on 1 June 2024.

Laal, M., & Ghodsi, S. M. (2012). Benefits of collaborative learning. *Procedia: Social and Behavioral Sciences*, 31, 486–490. DOI: 10.1016/j.sbspro.2011.12.091

Laal, M., Khattami-Kermanshahi, Z., & Laal, M. (2014). Teaching and education: Collaborative style. *Procedia: Social and Behavioral Sciences*, 116, 4057–4061. DOI: 10.1016/j.sbspro.2014.01.890

Labs, E. (2014). Elevate - Brain Training [Mobile application software]. App Store. https://www.elevateapp.com

Labs, W. (2017). Woebot. Retrieved from https://woebothealth.com on 2 June 2024.

Lamb, R., Choi, I., & Owens, T. (2023). Artificial intelligence and sensor technologies: The future of special education for students with intellectual and developmental disabilities. *Global Journal of Intellectual & Developmental Disabilities*, 11(3), 555814. Advance online publication. DOI: 10.19080/GJIDD.2023.11.555814

Learning Ally. (n.d). Learning Ally: Audiobooks for students with dyslexia & learning disabilities. https://learningally.org/

Lee, J., & Obinata, G. (2013, March). Developing therapeutic robot for children with autism: A study on exploring colour feedback. In *Human-Robot Interaction (HRI), 8th Association for Computing Machinery/Institute of Electrical and Electronics Engineers (ACM/IEEE)* (pp. 10–15). IEEE. https://doi.org/DOI: 10.1109/HRI.2013.6483557

Lee, J., Takehashi, H., Nagai, C., & Obinata, G. (2012). Design of a therapeutic robot for interacting with autistic children through interpersonal touch. In *IEEE RO-MAN: The 21st IEEE International Symposium on Robot and Human Interactive Communication* (pp. 712–717). IEEE. https://doi.org/DOI: 10.1109/ROMAN.2012.6343835

Libbrecht, P., & Melis, E. (2006). Methods to access and retrieve mathematical content in ActiveMath. In A. Iglesias & N. Takayama (Eds.), *Mathematical software - ICMS 2006* (Vol. 4151, pp. 331–342). Springer. https://doi.org/DOI: 10.1007/11832225_33

Lift lab. (2012). Liftware. Retrieved from https://www.liftware.com, on 1 June 2024.

Lorenzo, G., Lorenzo-Lledó, A., Lledó Carreres, A., & Pérez-Vázquez, E. (2020). Approach from a bibliometric perspective of the educational application of virtual reality in people with autism spectrum disorder. *Education in the Knowledge Society*, 21(4), 1–14. DOI: 10.14201/eks.19522

Luka.inc (2017). Replika. Retrieved from https://replika.ai on 1 June 2024.

Mahini, S. (2024). Virtual reality as a tool for children with autism spectrum disorder. *Digital Technologies Research and Applications*, 3(1), 16–23. DOI: 10.54963/dtra.v3i1.211

Malach, J., & Javorcik, T. (n.d.). Conditions and bases of incorporation of artificial intelligence into Czech school environment. *European Conference on Learning and Instruction (EClAlR)*. https://doi.org/DOI: 10.34190/EClAlR.19.077

Marin, I., & Popovici, D. (2022). Teachers-students-parents digital portal need analysis designed for abroad studies. In *Proceedings of the 14th International Conference on Education and New Learning Technologies (EDULEARN)* (pp. 3373–3382). https://doi.org/DOI: 10.21125/edulearn.2022.0826

Massoumeh, Z., & Jamshidi, L. (2012). An investigation of medical model and special education methods. *Procedia: Social and Behavioral Sciences*, 46, 5802–5804. DOI: 10.1016/j.sbspro.2012.06.518

McCall, M. P., Anton, M. T., Highlander, A., Loiselle, R., Forehand, R., Khavjou, O., & Jones, D. J. (2023). Technology-enhanced behavioral parent training: The relationship between technology use and efficiency of service delivery. *Behavior Modification*, 47(5), 1094–14. DOI: 10.1177/01454455231165937

McGrath, D. (2023, July 12). Using AI to write IEPs: A tool to help educators reduce workload. *Edutopia*. https://www.edutopia.org/article/using-ai-write-ieps-help-educators-reduce-workload/

McGraw-Hill. (n.d). ALEKS. Retrieved, from https://www.aleks.com on 27 June 2024.

Medenica, V., Ivanović, L., Ristic, I., & Čolić, G. (2023). *Artificial intelligence in occupational therapy and special education and rehabilitation*. https://doi.org/DOI: 10.7251/ZSAN2302033M

Mentegram. (n.d). Mentegram. Retrieved from https://mentegram.com.au/how-it-works/ on 1 June 2024.

Michelson, D., Davenport, C., Dretzke, J., Barlow, J., & Day, C. (2013). Do Evidence-based Interventions work when Tested in the "real world?" A Systematic Review and Meta-analysis of Parent Management Training for the Treatment of Child Disruptive Behavior. *Clinical Child and Family Psychology Review*, 16(1), 18–34. DOI: 10.1007/s10567-013-0128-0

Microsoft. (1975). Accessibility Tools for Learning. Retrieved June 28, 2024, from https://www.microsoft.com/en-in/education/learning-tools/accessibility-tools

Microsoft. (2017). Seeing AI. Retrieved from https://www.microsoft.com/seeing-ai on 1 June 2024.

Mohammad, S., Adetunji, M. S., & Zaman, T. U. (2022). Special education: Learning theories and educational models. In Javan, B. S., Ahmad, W., & Gupta, R. K. (Eds.), *Comprehensive Textbook on Disability* (pp. 13–22). Jaypee Brothers Medical Publishers.

Molenaar, I., de Mooij, S., Azevedo, R., Bannert, M., Järvelä, S., & Gašević, D. (2022). Measuring self-regulated learning and the role of AI: Five years of research using multichannel data. *Computers in Human Behavior*, 139, 1–9. DOI: 10.1016/j.chb.2022.107540

Morawska, A., Tometzki, H., & Sanders, M. R. (2014). An Evaluation of the Efficacy of a Triple P-Positive Parenting Program podcast series. *Journal of Developmental and Behavioral Pediatrics*, 35(2), 128–137. DOI: 10.1097/DBP.0000000000000020

Mosito, C. P., Warnick, A. M., & Esambe, E. E. (2017). Enhancing Reading Abilities of Learners with Intellectual Impairments through Computer Technology. *African Journal of Disability*, 6, 206. DOI: 10.4102/ajod.v6i0.206

Munro, E. (2019). *Predictive analytics in child protection* (CHESS Working Paper No. 2019-03). Durham University. https://www.dur.ac.uk/resources/chess/CHESSWorkingPaper2019-03.pdf

Namachivayam, A. (2021). An Appraisal of Microsoft Teams and Its Features. 462-478.

National Informatics Centre. (n.d.). KVS Shala Darpan. Retrieved on june 1, 2024, from https://information.nic.in/kvs-shala-darpan

National Institute for Transforming India Aayog. (2023). National Strategy for Artificial Intelligence. Government of India. Retrieved from https://www.niti.gov.in/sites/default/files/2023-03/National-Strategy-for-Artificial-Intelligence.pdf) on 27th June 2024.

Nayak, J., Bhat, P. S., Acharya, R. U. V., & Aithal, U. V. (2005). Classification and analysis of speech abnormalities. *ITBM-RBM*, 26(5–6), 319–327. DOI: 10.1016/j.rbmret.2005.05.002

Newsroom (2019, July 21). How Education Software Company Kami entered America's Classrooms. University of Auckland Centre for Innovation and Entrepreneurship. https://www.example.com/kami-article retrieved on 20 June 2024.

Panitz, T. (1999). Benefits of cooperative learning in relation to student motivation. In Theall, M. (Ed.), *Motivation from within: Approaches for encouraging faculty and students to excel* (pp. 59–68). Josey-Bass Publishing.

Panjwani-Charani, S., & Zhai, X. (2023). AI for Students with Learning Disabilities: A Systematic Review. In *X. Zhai & J. Krajcik (2023), Uses of Artificial Intelligence in STEM Education* (pp. 1–28). Oxford University Press.

Parmaxi, A., Athanasiou, A., & A Demetriou, A. (2021). Introducing a Student-led Application of Google Expeditions: An exploratory study. *Educational Media International*, 58(3), 1–23. DOI: 10.1080/09523987.2021.1908497

Pavlopoulos, J., Vrettaros, J., Vouros, G., & Drigas, A. S. (2008). The development of a self-assessment system for the learners' answers with the use of GPNN. In Lytras, M. D., Carroll, J. M., Damiani, E., & Tennyson, R. D. (Eds.), *Emerging technologies and information systems for the knowledge society: WSKS 2008* (Vol. 5288, pp. 332–340). Springer., DOI: 10.1007/978-3-540-87781-3_37

Pennisi, P., Tonacci, A., Tartarisco, G., Billeci, L., Ruta, L., Gangemi, S., & Pioggia, G. (2016). Autism and Social Robotics: A Systematic Review. *Autism Research: official journal of the International Society for Autism Research,* 9(2), 165–83. https://doi.org/DOI: 10.1002/aur.1527

Pidano, A. E., & Allen, A. R. (2015). The Incredible Years series: A Review of the Independent Research base. *Journal of Child and Family Studies*, 24(7), 1898–1916. DOI: 10.1007/s10826-014-9991-7

Pilling, K. (2015). Special Needs for Special Kids [Mobile app]. Special Needs for Special Kids. https://www.specialneedsforspecialkids.org

Prenner. (2015, August 5). *Ghotit Real Writer.* Dyslexia Help at the University of Michigan. https://dyslexiahelp.umich.edu/home/ghotit-real-writer

Puglisi, A., Caprì, T., Pignolo, L., Gismondo, S., Chilà, P., Minutoli, R., Marino, F., Failla, C., Arnao, A. A., Tartarisco, G., Cerasa, A., & Pioggia, G. (2022). Social Humanoid Robots for Children with Autism Spectrum Disorders: A Review of Modalities, Indications, and Pitfalls. *Children (Basel, Switzerland)*, 9(7), 953. DOI: 10.3390/children9070953

Rakap, S. (2024). Chatting with GPT: Enhancing Individualized Education Program Goal Development for Novice Special Education Teachers. *Journal of Special Education Technology*, 39(3), 339–348. DOI: 10.1177/01626434231211295

Riedl, M., Arriaga, R., Boujarwah, F., Hong, H., Isbell, J., & Heflin, J. (2009). Graphical social scenarios: Toward intervention and authoring for adolescents with high functioning autism. In 2009 AAAI Fall Symposium Series. AAAI. https://cdn.aaai.org/ocs/945/945-4144-1-PB.pdf

Roach, J. (2018). AI technology helps students who are deaf learn. *Microsoft.* https://blogs.microsoft.com/ai/ai-powered-captioning/

Robokind. (n.d). Milo Robot. Retrieved from https://www.robokind.com/advanced-social-robots on 1 June 2024.

Rowland, A., Do, P., & Aylward, J. (2014). Classkick. https://www.classkick.com

Sağdıç, A., Canpolat Çığ, N., Çelenk, U., Takı, Z., Çetin, İ., Feyzullahoğlu, P., Altuğ Ateş, M., & Doğan, O. (2023). Teaching following instructions and responding skills to children with autism with an AI-supported mobile application. In *ICERI2023 Proceedings* (pp. 7658-7664). IATED. https://doi.org/DOI: 10.21125/iceri.2023.1920

Sağdıç, A., Elumar-Efe, E., & Sani-Bozkurt, S. (2024). GenAI, robots, and inclusive special education: Autism spectrum disorder in the age of generative AI. In Sharma, R., & Bozkurt, A. (Eds.), *Transforming education with generative AI: Prompt engineering and synthetic content creation* (pp. 309–326). IGI Global., DOI: 10.4018/979-8-3693-1351-0.ch015

Saleh, M. A., Hashim, H., Mohamed, N. N., & Almisreb, A. A. (2020). Robots and autistic children: A review. *Periodicals of Engineering and Natural Sciences*, 8(3), 1247–1262. DOI: 10.21533/pen.v8i3.790

Santos, L., Annunziata, S., Geminiani, A., Ivani, A., Giubergia, A., Garofalo, D., Caglio, A., Brazzoli, E., Lipari, R., Carrozza, M. C., Ambrosini, E., Olivieri, I., & Pedrocchi, A. (2023). Applications of robotics for autism spectrum disorder: A scoping review. *Review Journal of Autism and Developmental Disorders*. Advance online publication. DOI: 10.1007/s40489-023-00402-5

Schipor, O., Pentiuc, S., & Schipor, M.-D. (2010). Improving computer-based speech therapy using a fuzzy expert system. *Computer Information*, 29(1), 303–318.

Schworm, R. (1979). Task Analysis in Special Education: Definition and Clarification. *Journal of Special Education Technology*, 2(3), 37–44. DOI: 10.1177/016264347900200305

ScootPad Corporation. (n.d). ScootPad. Retrieved from https://www.scootpad.com 27th June 2024.

Sebe, N., Cohen, I., Gevers, T., & Huang, T. S. (2006). Emotion recognition based on joint visual and audio cues. In *Proceedings of the 18th International Conference on Pattern Recognition (ICPR'06)* (pp. 1136–1139). IEEE. https://doi.org/DOI: 10.1109/ICPR.2006.489

Setiawan, M. R., & Wiedarti, P. (2020). The effectiveness of Quizlet application towards students' motivation in learning vocabulary. *Studies in English Language and Education*, 7(1), 83–95. DOI: 10.24815/siele.v7i1.15359

Shamim, M., Ademola, A. H., & Uz, Z. T. (2022). Special education: Learning theories and educational models. In B. S. Chavan, W. Ahmad, R. K. Gupta, M. Shamim, A. H. Ademola, & Z. T. Uz (Eds.), *Comprehensive textbook on disability*. Jaypee Brothers Medical Publishers (P) Ltd. https://doi.org/DOI: 10.5005/jp/books/18613_5

Sharma, S., Tomar, V., Yadav, N., & Aggarwal, M. (2023). Impact of AI-based special education on educators and students. In *Advances in educational technologies and instructional design book series* (pp. 47–66). IGI Global., DOI: 10.4018/979-8-3693-0378-8.ch003

Shashua, A., & Aviram, Z. (2010). OrCam MyEye. Retrieved from https://www.orcam.com, 1 June 2023.

Smiderle, R., Rigo, S. J., Marques, L. B., Peçanha de Miranda Coelho, J. A., & Jaques, P. A. (2020). The impact of gamification on students' learning, engagement, and behavior based on their personality traits. *Smart Learning Environments*, 7(1), 3. DOI: 10.1186/s40561-019-0098-x

SoftBank Robotics. (n.d). NAO Robot. Retrieved from https://emea.softbankrobotics.com/industries/higher-education on 1 june 2024.

Sourander, A., McGrath, P. J., Ristkari, T., Cunningham, C., Huttunen, J., Lingley-Pottie, P., Hinkka-Yli-Salomäki, S., Kinnunen, M., Vuorio, J., Sinokki, A., Fossum, S., & Unruh, A. (2016). Internet-Assisted Parent Training Intervention for Disruptive Behavior in 4-Year-Old Children: A Randomized Clinical Trial. *JAMA Psychiatry*, 73(4), 378–387. DOI: 10.1001/jamapsychiatry.2015.3411

Srihari, S., Collins, J., Srihari, R., Srinivasan, H., Shetty, S., & Brutt-Griffler, J. (2008). Automated Scoring of Handwritten essays in Reading Comprehension tests. *Artificial Intelligence*, 172(3), 300–324. DOI: 10.1016/j.artint.2007.06.005

Srinivasan, B., & Parthasarathi, R. (2013). An intelligent task analysis approach for special education based on MIRA. *Journal of Applied Logic*, 11(1), 137–145. DOI: 10.1016/j.jal.2012.12.001

Sun, S., Else-Quest, N., Hodges, L., French, A., & Dowling, R. (2021). The effects of ALEKS on mathematics learning in K-12 and higher education: A meta-analysis. *Investigations in Mathematics Learning*, 13(3), 1–15. DOI: 10.1080/19477503.2021.1926194

Sutherland, A. (2005). Quizlet. https://www.quizlet.com

Tahiru, F. (2021). AI in education: A systematic literature review. *Journal of Cases on Information Technology*, 23(1), 1–20. DOI: 10.4018/JCIT.2021010101

Tan, S. C., Lee, A. V. Y., & Lee, M. (2022). A systematic review of artificial intelligence techniques for collaborative learning over the past two decades. *Computers and Education: Artificial Intelligence*, 3, 100097. DOI: 10.1016/j.caeai.2022.100097

Tapus, A., Peca, A., Aly, A., Pop, C., & Jisa, L.. (2012). Children with autism social engagement in interaction with Nao, an imitative robot: A series of single case experiments. *Interaction Studies: Social Behaviour and Communication in Biological and Artificial Systems*, 13(3), 315–347. DOI: 10.1075/is.13.3.01tap

Therapy Box Ltd. Predictable, [Mobile application software]. Retrieved on 1 June 2024.

Tholfsen, M. (2020, January 13). Pear Deck integrates with Microsoft Immersive Reader to make Learning more Accessible for all. Microsoft Tech Community. https://techcommunity.microsoft.com/t5/education-blog/pear-deck-integrates-with-microsoft-immersive-reader-to-make/ba-p/1101740

Toyokawa, Y., Horikoshi, I., Majumdar, R., & Ogata, H. (2023). Challenges and Opportunities of AI in Inclusive Education: A case Study of Data-enhanced Active Reading in Japan. *Smart Learning Environments*, 10(67), 1–19. DOI: 10.1186/s40561-023-00286-2

Voiceitt Ltd. (2012). Voiceitt. Retrieved from https://www.voiceitt.com on 2 June 2024.

Wainer, J., Ferrari, E., Dautenhahn, K., & Robins, B. (2010). The effectiveness of using a robotics class to foster collaboration among groups of children with autism in an exploratory study. *Personal and Ubiquitous Computing*, 14(5), 445–455. DOI: 10.1007/s00779-009-0266-z

Wang, H. (2013). Instruction in American academic libraries. In Wang, H., & Latham, B. (Eds.), *Academic libraries in the US and China* (pp. 3–49). Chandos Publishing., DOI: 10.1016/B978-1-84334-691-3.50001-9

Wang, H., & Woodworth, K. (2011). *Evaluation of Rocketship Education's use of DreamBox Learning's online mathematics program.* Center for Education Policy, SRI International. https://www.sri.com/publication/evaluation-rocketship-educations-use-dreambox-learnings-online-mathematics-program/

Wang'ang'a, A. W. (2024). Consequences of Artificial Intelligence on Teaching and Learning in Higher Education in Kenya. *Literature Review East African Journal of Education Studies*, 7(1), 202–215. DOI: 10.37284/eajes.7.1.1718

Wang'ang'a, A. W. (2024). Consequences of Artificial Intelligence on Teaching and Learning in Higher Education in Kenya. *Literature Review East African Journal of Education Studies*, 7(1), 202–215. DOI: 10.37284/eajes.7.1.1718

Webb, J. J., Cook, M. A., Grant, A. A., & Ross, S. M. (2023). *A study of educator attitudes and beliefs and Goalbook Toolkit usage* (Doctoral dissertation). Johns Hopkins University. Available from Johns Hopkins University Repository. https://jscholarship.library.jhu.edu/server/api/core/bitstreams/a052eaae-7035-4200-b8a1-e9260ffa92b0/content

Weitzman, T. (2023, June 16). Empowering individuals with disabilities through AI technology. *Forbes Business Council*. https://www.forbes.com/sites/forbesbusinesscouncil/2023/06/16/empowering-individuals-with-disabilities-through-ai-technology/

What Works Clearinghouse. (2010, August 31). *Carnegie Learning curricula and Cognitive Tutor software*. U.S. Department of Education, Institute of Education Sciences. https://ies.ed.gov/ncee/wwc/InterventionReport/Index/408

What Works Clearinghouse. (2013). Elementary School Mathematics December 2013: DreamBox Learning. U.S. Department of Education, Institute of Education Sciences. https://ies.ed.gov/ncee/wwc/Docs/InterventionReports/wwc_dreambox_123013.pdf

Whill. (n.d). Whill Autonomous Drive System. Retrieved from https://www.whill.us on 2 June 2024.

Wiberg, H. H. (2012). Be My Eyes. Retrieved from https://www.bemyeyes.com on 2 June 2024.

Yadav, S. K., Dutt, P. R. C., & Ahmad, W. (2022). Historical Perspective of Special Education in India and Abroad. In Chavan, B. S., Ahmad, W., & Gupta, R. K. (Eds.), *Comprehensive Textbook on Disability* (pp. 23–29). Jaypee Brothers Medical Publishers.

Yoo, J. D. (2011). Goalbook Toolkit. https://goalbookapp.com/ retrieved on 2 June 2024

Zammarchi, G., & Conversano, C. (2021). Application of eye tracking technology in medicine: A bibliometric analysis. *Vision (Basel)*, 5(4), 56. DOI: 10.3390/vision5040056

Zisser-Nathenson, A. R., Herschell, A. D., & Eyberg, S. M. (2018). Parent-child interaction therapy and the treatment of disruptive behavior disorders. In Weisz, J. R., & Kazdin, A. E. (Eds.), *Evidence-Based Psychotherapies for Children and Adolescents* (pp. 103–121). The Guilford Press.

Chapter 2
Enhancing Special Education Using AI:
The Intersection of Personalized Learning and Inclusivity

Lynn Scott
https://orcid.org/0009-0008-5198-5811
Indiana State University, USA

Tahnee Wilder
https://orcid.org/0000-0003-3007-1590
University of Central Florida, USA

Tiffanie Zaugg
https://orcid.org/0000-0001-6992-893X
University of Central Florida, USA

Annette Romualdo
University of Minnesota, Duluth, USA

ABSTRACT

This chapter explores the intersection of artificial intelligence (AI) and personalized learning, highlighting the potential to revolutionize accessibility and inclusivity in special education. Drawing from psychological and pedagogical research, the chapter delves into the nuanced impact of AI-driven tools' capacity to transform instruction, enrich educational experiences, and bolster access to various disciplines. Challenges, bias, and potential exclusionary barriers emerge, necessitating a critical examination of how AI's potential transformative impact reshapes the landscape of inclusion and accessibility in the educational sphere. By identifying emerging challenges and proposing pathways for advancement, the chapter underscores the importance of

DOI: 10.4018/979-8-3693-5538-1.ch002

ensuring that AI technologies advance rather than hinder inclusive and accessible educational practices, with an ultimate aim to establish a more accessible learning environment tailored to the diverse needs of students with disabilities.

ENHANCING ACCESSIBILITY AND PERSONALIZED LEARNING FOR STUDENTS WITH DISABILITIES

Artificial intelligence (AI) stands at the forefront of educational transformation, offering unprecedented opportunities to design and customize curricular learning environments which meet the unique needs of each student, revolutionizing accessibility and personalized education.

The surge in interest in AI synchronously aligns with global movements toward greater societal equity, and acknowledgment that accessibility is a foundational element of fairness (UNESCO, 2023). Accessibility refers to the usability of products and services by all individuals, regardless of how the user encounters them (Interaction Design Foundation, 2016). The authors explore AI's nuanced impact on the promotion of increased accessibility and personalized learning for children who receive special education services. Utilizing findings from psychological and pedagogical studies (Baskara, 2023; Goswami, 2004; Harry, 2023; Hopcan et al., 2023; Tapalova & Zhiyenbayeva, 2022; Van der Vorst & Jelicic, 2019), the authors aim to foster forward thinking in this domain.

ARTIFICIAL INTELLIGENCE IN SPECIAL EDUCATION

Artificial intelligence (AI) has the potential to revolutionize the special education field, transforming how educators individualize learning and support for students with disabilities. Traditional means of providing individualized instruction can be labor intensive and makeshift in nature, particularly as students with disabilities are included in the general education classroom and special educators are tasked with modifying and adapting grade level curriculum across content areas (Agran et al., 2020). Thompson et al. (2020) found educators reported using informal, ad hoc approaches to planning support for students with disabilities in general education classrooms. Educators identified challenges, such as time constraints, lack of resources and training, and lack of systemized problem-solving processes.

Given the significant academic and social-emotional benefits of including students with disabilities in the general education classroom (Agran et al., 2020; de Boer et al., 2013), it is imperative teachers are equipped with necessary tools to facilitate this integration, including technology to support diverse learning needs. By leveraging AI tools in the classroom, educators can efficiently and dynamically customize learning environments to meet the needs of each student, thereby dramatically reducing the labor-intensive nature of special education case management. AI-powered tools can assist in almost every aspect of the K-12 classroom—revolutionizing individualized student access to reading, writing, and mathematics, in addition to the arts and even the physical education classroom (Chen, 2009; Pearson et al., 2010). AI tools can personalize pace and level of content, based on a student's present level of understanding, to increase student engagement in learning (Marino et al., 2024). According to OpenAI (2023), ChatGPT has the potential to provide immediate and dynamically tailored social stories, visual schedules, first-then boards, choice boards, task analyses, communication boards, social scripts, visual timers, individualized adaptive physical education plans, modified activities, specialized equipment ideas, flexible teaching method ideas, adaptive supplies suggestions, UDL suggestions based on content, suggestions for wraparound community supports, and sensory tool options—all customized to student need/s, as identified by the educator. Large Language AI models, such as ChatGPT, provide impromptu, personalized support for both the educator and their students (OpenAI, 2023).

Artificial Intelligence (AI), when employed as assistive technology, manifests as a transformative force enhancing accessibility and inclusivity for individuals with disabilities, yet it diverges from traditional assistive tools through its dynamic, adaptive learning capabilities and sophisticated data processing. Some of these advancements have significantly enhanced accessibility, communication, and community engagement, as described in Table 1 (OHCHR, 2022). In the realm of cognitive and learning support, Artificial intelligence technologies, such as Microsoft's Hexis-Antara© convert content into Braille, and the Google Braille AI Tutor utilizes gamification to improve literacy skills among visually impaired learners (SmartClick, 2022). Enhancements via augmentative and alternative communication (AAC) devices for children with disabilities enable effective participation in daily social and educational activities (Neamtu et al., 2019). Further, AI assists in reducing educational barriers for students with disabilities by providing tools for accessible online mathematics and enhancing document accessibility for complex layouts in STEM education (Marino et al., 2023).

Table 1. Examples of Artificial Intelligence in Special Education

Solution Example	Functionality	Enhancement to Accessibility and Inclusivity	Challenges in Implementation
AI-powered Autonomous Vehicles (e.g. Waymo, 2023)	Provides autonomous transportation solutions to enhance accessibility for individuals with physical disabilities (OHCHR, 2022)	Facilitates community engagement and independence for individuals with physical disabilities by offering reliable transportation options (OHCHR, 2022)	High cost of development and deployment, regulatory and safety concerns, and the need for infrastructure modifications
AI Communication Aids (e.g. Microsoft Seeing AI, 2023)	Facilitate communication by reducing reciprocity and learning gaps (OHCHR, 2022)	Improves social interaction and learning opportunities for individuals with communication impairments, promoting greater inclusivity (OHCHR, 2022)	High costs and need for specialized training, potential issues with real-time accuracy and privacy concerns
Augmentative and Alternative Communication Devices (e.g. Tobii Dynavox, 2023)	Enable effective participation in daily social and educational activities for children with disabilities (Neamtu et al., 2019)	Provides tools for children with disabilities to communicate effectively, enhancing their participation and inclusivity in various settings (Neamtu et al., 2019)	High costs, the need for individualized customization, and the requirement for training educators and caregivers
Accessible Online Mathematics Tools (e.g. Mod Math, 2023)	Provide accessible tools for online mathematics to reduce educational barriers (Marino et al., 2023)	Supports students with disabilities in STEM education by offering accessible mathematics tools, promoting inclusivity and equal learning opportunities (Marino et al., 2023)	Integration with existing curricula, ensuring tool accessibility across different platforms, and providing sufficient training and support

continued on following page

Table 1. Continued

Solution Example	Functionality	Enhancement to Accessibility and Inclusivity	Challenges in Implementation
Large Language Model AI (e.g. ChatGPT, 2023)	Facilitate spontaneous, adaptive creation of social stories, visual schedules, first-then boards, visual timers, choice boards, social scripts, task analysis (step-by-step) guides, communication board templates, customization, social scripts, sensory tool recommendations, provide alignment to standards, and tailor reading to level (OpenAI, 2024)	Potential to enhance understanding of grade-level curriculum; promote communication with typical peers, provide structure and routine; promote autonomy, independence, and choice; promote regulation and focus; support transitions (OpenAI, 2024)	Challenges with accuracy and reliability, as the provided information may be outdated or incorrect; content appropriateness should be verified by human-in-the-loop; potential FERPA violations with data sharing; teacher's lack of familiarity and comfort with modality
Enhanced Document Accessibility Tools (e.g. Texthelp, 2023)	Enhance document accessibility for complex layouts in STEM education (Marino et al., 2023)	Supports students with disabilities in accessing and comprehending complex STEM materials, promoting inclusivity and equal learning opportunities (Marino et al., 2023)	Ensuring compatibility with various document formats, high costs of implementation, and need for regular updates and technical support

These examples highlight how AI, used as assistive technology (AT), can not only improve practical daily functioning but also foster inclusivity in educational settings, preparing a foundation for continuous innovation in how educational services are delivered to students with disabilities (Marino et al., 2023; Marino et al., 2024). However, the rapid advancement and integration of artificial intelligence (AI) into these areas have introduced complex challenges that threaten to undermine progress (Akgun & Greenhow, 2021).

Challenges and Considerations to Implementation

AI tools designed for personalized learning must be equipped to adapt to the unique needs of students with disabilities. Customization of learning for students with disabilities can be multi-faceted and (traditionally) resource-intensive. High costs associated with individualized customization and the need for specialized training for educators and caregivers can complicate the implementation process (Marino et al., 2024; USDOE, 2023). The adaptability of AI to different learning styles and needs varies, potentially limits its efficacy for some students with disabilities (Marino et al., 2024). A systematic review conducted by Moriña et al. (2023) highlights the challenges and potential solutions in utilizing personalized learning for students with disabilities. The adoption of AI technologies in special education faces several barriers, including the potential exorbitant cost of implementation, varying levels of digital literacy among students and educators, the need for stable internet connections, privacy concerns, and the challenge of integrating new technology with existing educational materials. While the high cost of selected AI technologies constitutes a significant obstacle to widespread adoption, addressing the other challenges is equally crucial for the successful implementation of personalized learning in special education settings. Overcoming these barriers requires a comprehensive approach that includes financial support, professional development for educators, digital literacy training for students, robust infrastructure, data protection measures, and thoughtful integration strategies.

The high cost associated with implementing AI technologies in special education poses significant challenges, ranging from the initial investment in research and development to ongoing expenses related to subscriptions, training, and support. For instance, AI-powered communication aids necessitate substantial funding for research, development, and regulatory compliance (Moriña et al., 2023; Rice & Dunn, 2023). Many AI tools operate on subscription models, leading to recurring costs that can strain fluctuating educational budgets, especially as educational funding may correlate directly with academic outcomes (. Expenses associated with software licenses, premium features, and continuous updates can be prohibitive, particularly for underfunded schools and districts.

Effective AI implementation in special education can demand extensive training for educators. Resistance from educators unfamiliar with technology can further complicate the adoption process and integration of new technology into the classroom (Francom et al., 2021). Ongoing training is needed, as AI technologies evolve rapidly, necessitating regular updates to educators' knowledge and skills (Kizilcec, 2023). From a student perspective, varying levels of digital literacy among students with disabilities can hinder the effective use of AI solutions. Ensuring all users can competently navigate these technologies is crucial for their success. Continuous updates and support are necessary to maintain compatibility and address technical issues (Kuleto et al., 2021).

To overcome these challenges, educational institutions must prioritize professional development programs that focus on AI literacy and provide educators with the necessary tools and resources to effectively integrate AI into their teaching practices (ISTE, 2023). Tailored training and assistance should be offered to ensure students with disabilities can fully benefit from AI-powered learning solutions (Rice & Dunn, 2023). By addressing financial barriers and investing in comprehensive training and support, special education can harness the potential of AI technologies to create more inclusive and accessible learning environments for all students (Marino et al., 2024).

Many AI tools rely on robust internet connectivity to function effectively. Inconsistent or inadequate internet access can disrupt the use of these tools, particularly in rural or underserved areas (Moriña et al., 2023). AI technologies that involve real-time data processing, such as transcription services and image recognition, pose privacy concerns. The constant capture and analysis of data raises issues related to data security and student privacy (Huang, 2023). Schools must implement stringent data protection measures to safeguard sensitive information and comply with privacy regulations.

Integrating AI tools with existing educational materials and curricula is another significant challenge. Many AI solutions are designed to work within specific frameworks, making it difficult to align with established teaching practices and resources (Akgun & Greenhow, 2021). For example, learning management platforms such as Blackboard, Moodle, or Canvas manage course assignments, assessments, and communication through the use of application programming interfaces with set protocols owned and controlled by a specific company; often restricting integration of AI tools seamlessly. While AI powered adaptive learning platforms use real-time analysis of students' performance and learning styles to tailor educational experiences their use of complex algorithms and data analytics often conflict with the rigid, one-size-fits-all structure of conventional curricula, making it challenging for teachers to synchronize with existing lesson plans and assessment strategies. Misalignment can lead to inefficiencies and hinder the seamless incorporation of AI into the learning environment. Ensuring compatibility and coherence between AI tools and traditional educational materials requires careful planning and coordination (Ifenthaler & Schumacher, 2023). Developers need to invest significant effort to ensure compatibility and seamless operation across different environments.

While AI has the potential to revolutionize personalized learning in special education, its implementation faces multifaceted challenges. Addressing these challenges requires substantial investment, comprehensive training programs, robust technical support, and careful planning to integrate AI solutions with existing educational frameworks (Akgun & Greenhow, 2021; Moriña et al., 2023). By tackling these issues, educational institutions can harness the full potential of AI to enhance accessibility, inclusivity, and personalized learning experiences for students with disabilities.

Biases in AI Systems

Artificial intelligence systems, widely employed in diverse sectors, are increasingly tasked with making decisions that significantly impact individuals and society. However, these systems are not immune to biases, which can arise at various stages, including dataset creation, problem formulation, and data analysis (Srinivasan & Chander, 2021). Biases in AI can result from historical data encoding societal prejudices or from the design and implementation choices of developers (Ntoutsi et al., 2020). For instance, biased data can cause AI systems to perpetuate unfair treatment based on race, gender, or other demographic factors, thereby exacerbating social inequalities rather than mitigating them (Rejmaniak, 2021). Additionally, cognitive biases inherent in human decision-making can influence the design and development of AI systems, leading to biased outcomes (Soleimani et al., 2021).

Brian Christian, in his book "The Alignment Problem," explores how AI systems can inadvertently perpetuate and even exacerbate existing biases present in the data they are trained on, leading to unfair outcomes in applications such as hiring, law enforcement, and loan approvals. He emphasizes the necessity of aligning AI systems with human values and ethical principles to mitigate these biases and ensure fairer, more equitable technology deployment (Akgun & Greenhow, 2021; Christian, 2020). Biases in AI systems (Srinivasan & Chander, 2021) and the need for safety and trust (Varona & Suárez, 2022) are also significant concerns.

Addressing these biases requires a multifaceted approach, including ethical guidelines, legal frameworks, and technical solutions to detect and mitigate biases (Ntoutsi et al., 2020). One proposed strategy is the integration of human-centric AI, which incorporates human oversight and ethical considerations into AI systems to enhance fairness and transparency (Harfouche et al., 2023). Biases in AI systems are multifaceted and require comprehensive strategies involving ethical, legal, and technical measures to ensure fair and unbiased outcomes (Akgun & Greenhow, 2021; Christian, 2020; CIDDL, 2024).

SAFETY, TRANSPARENCY, AND TRUST

Concerns regarding safety, transparency, and trust in AI are increasingly critical as AI systems become more integrated into various domains, including healthcare, governance, and industry. The safety of AI systems is paramount, especially in high-stakes environments where errors can lead to significant harm. Over-trusting AI systems can lead to serious safety issues, as demonstrated by studies on human-AI collaboration that highlight the dangers of improper trust calibration (Okamura & Yamada, 2020). To address these issues, it is essential to enhance transparency in AI systems. Transparency involves providing clear and understandable explanations for AI decisions, which can help users better trust and appropriately rely on AI systems (Schmidt et al., 2020). However, transparency alone does not always lead to increased trust. In some cases, greater transparency can reveal the limitations and uncertainties of AI systems, potentially diminishing trust (Schmidt et al., 2020).

Trust in AI is dependent not only on transparency but also on the ethical and fair operation of these systems. Trustworthy AI must be robust, fair, and accountable, ensuring that AI systems do not inadvertently perpetuate biases or make unfair decisions (Liu et al., 2021). For instance, the introduction of Supplier's Declarations of Conformity (SDoC) for AI services aims to increase trust by providing detailed documentation of the AI's performance, safety, and security measures (Hind et al., 2018). These measures foster a more comprehensive understanding and confidence in AI systems, promoting their broader acceptance and utilization (Mehrotra et al., 2023).

Ensuring the safety, transparency, and trustworthiness of AI systems requires a multifaceted approach that includes proper trust calibration, transparent operations, and robust ethical standards. Such efforts are essential to mitigate risks and enhance the reliability and acceptance of AI technologies (Okamura & Yamada, 2020).

Exclusionary Impact

Total bans on AI in school districts may hinder personalized learning for individuals with disabilities, which limits access to AT and related educational tools — potentially impeding the advancement of learning initiatives (ISTE, 2023). For example, since its inception in 2009, Grammarly has been an assistive technology tool, providing invaluable support for students with disabilities by enhancing their writing through advanced grammar, punctuation, and style checking. However, recent shifts in policy have seen some school districts and colleges banning use after the company disclosed its reliance on AI technologies. The case of a college student placed on academic probation solely for utilizing Grammarly to proofread her paper highlighted this change in acceptance, underscoring the growing concerns and regulatory responses toward AI-driven tools in educational settings (Settembre, 2024). This incident reflects a broader hesitation among educational institutions to integrate AI tools that may compromise academic integrity or privacy. The potential consequences of such bans on students' learning and academic performance are a matter of serious concern (Menezes, 2024).

The relevance of a range of barriers to the implementation and use of AI has been identified. These include difficulties in collaboration between different disciplines (Dafoe et al., 2020), a lack of organizational capabilities and individual competencies (Bérubé et al., 2021), and the need for AI systems to understand human-like meaning (Mitchell, 2019). The conceptual hurdles to AI implementation and use are primarily centered around teacher responsibilities.

Personalized Learning Environments: A Transformative Approach (PLE)

Personalized Learning Environments (PLE) represent a systematic approach to education that focuses on tailoring instruction to meet each student's neurogentic profiles, e.g. strengths, preferences, needs, and goals (Chen, 2009; Pearson et al., 2010; Wong et al., 2017). This approach aims to create well-rounded educational experiences that enhance students' access to diverse disciplines and essential 21st-century work skills (Horváth, 2020; Swan, 2017). A crucial component of PLEs is the emphasis on cultivating system change, which underscores the necessity of fostering an environment that supports continuous improvement and innovation (Caro et al., 2023; Filatov et al., 2019; Ronksley-Pavia, 2024). To achieve this, states are encouraged to nurture a culture of experimentation and flexibility within their educational systems. This involves allowing schools to pilot new approaches and scale successful models, thus promoting innovative practices in teaching and learning (KnowledgeWorks, 2020; National Forum on Education Statistics, 2019). Equally important are responsive funding systems that adapt to the evolving needs of schools and students. These systems must ensure equitable resource distribution, prioritize support for high-need areas, and support innovative educational models that can drive systemic change (KnowledgeWorks, 2020; National Forum on Education Statistics, 2019). Personalized Learning Environments (PLE) offer a transformative approach to education by tailoring instruction to meet the unique needs of each student; fostering essential skills for success in the modern world. The State Policy Framework for Personalized Learning by KnowledgeWorks (2020) serves as a comprehensive guide for states aiming to revolutionize their education systems through personalized learning. The framework outlines four primary strategies essential for this transformation to tailor learning environments in support of equitable and accessible change catering to unique student needs: Empowering Student Learning, Cultivating Systems Change, Building Capacity, and Ensuring Quality (See Figure 1) (KnowledgeWorks, 2020).

Figure 1. Primary Strategies for Transformational Change

Note: This figure demonstrates the four primary strategies offered by The State Policy Framework for Personalized Learning by Knowledge Works (2020) as a transformative approach to education through personalized learning environments.

Empower Student Learning

Artificial Intelligence (AI) is set to revolutionize Personalized Learning Environments (PLEs), significantly enhancing their ability to cater to individual student needs and empower student learning through advanced, adaptive technologies. Central to this structure is the focus on empowering student learning, which involves creating equitable conditions that cater to the needs of all students, particularly those historically underserved (Aggarwal et al., 2023). This includes providing tailored interventions, ensuring access to high-quality resources, developing personalized learning pathways, and implementing balanced assessment systems that evaluate both academic and social-emotional competencies (Aggarwal et al., 2023)

According to the Office of Educational Technology report, Artificial Intelligence and the Future of Teaching and Learning: Insights and Recommendations (2023), AI-driven technologies empower student learning through several key mechanisms. Artificial intelligence enhances adaptivity within PLEs by dynamically adjusting educational content, pace, and instructional methods to match individual student performance and preferences. This personalized approach ensures that each student receives relevant and effective learning experiences tailored to their unique needs (KnowledgeWorks, 2020; Office of Educational Technology, 2023). A practical example of AI's impact on PLEs is the use of Intelligent Tutoring Systems (ITS). Similar to one-on-one tutoring, ITS provides step-by-step guidance and feedback. These systems monitor student progress, identify areas of difficulty, and offer targeted interventions, fostering a supportive and responsive learning environment. By delivering real-time, personalized feedback, ITS significantly enhances student understanding and retention of complex concepts (KnowledgeWorks, 2020; Office of Educational Technology, 2023). AI facilitates more natural and intuitive interactions within PLEs. Traditional educational technologies often rely on limited interaction methods, but AI-enabled systems support human-like interactions. For instance, students can engage in dialogue with AI tutors, receive spoken feedback, or interact with adaptive virtual agents. Resulting in a more engaging and effective learning experience, closely aligned with natural communication and learning styles (Office of Educational Technology, 2023).

Continuous support is also offered to students, beyond the school day, by AI, ensuring access to personalized learning resources and assistance when needed. Fortuitously supporting and reinforcing learning and promptly addressing gaps in understanding (KnowledgeWorks, 2020). In conclusion, PLEs are revolutionized by AI through adaptive, personalized, and engaging learning experiences. By leveraging AI technologies, more effective and inclusive learning environments can be created, catering to individual student needs and empowering them to achieve their full potential (Office of Educational Technology, 2023).

Build Capacity

Building capacity in PLEs faces several barriers, including a lack of understanding and support from leadership, insufficient infrastructure, and concerns about data privacy and algorithmic bias (Wang, 2021). Educators recognize that AI-driven tools can significantly enhance personalized learning but are also aware of the new risks they bring. Educators have expressed concerns about the fairness of AI recommendations and the potential for these systems to reinforce existing biases if not properly managed (Akgun & Greenhow, 2021; Marino et al., 2023). Moreover, the rapid advancement of AI technologies requires that educational leaders and policymakers stay informed and develop robust policies to govern their use. This includes ensuring that AI tools comply with laws such as the Family Educational Rights and Privacy Act (FERPA, 1974) and the Individuals with Disabilities Education Act (IDEA, 2005). The need for continuous improvement processes, stakeholder engagement, and evidence-based interventions to address these challenges continues (Marino et al., 2024).

A comprehensive approach to addressing barriers includes training for educators, investment in infrastructure, and the development of ethical guidelines to ensure the effective and equitable implementation of AI in education (Akgun & Greenhow, 2021; ISTE, 2023; Marino et al., 2024; Wang, 2021), notably understanding and support from leadership (Wang, 2021). Capacity building is sustained and scaled through initiatives based on a shared vision for student success that aligns with personalized learning principles. This requires collaborative leadership at all levels—state, district, and school—to ensure coherent policy implementation and a unified commitment to student achievement. In addition, educators and leaders require comprehensive support, including professional development on instructional strategies, data use, and creating inclusive learning environments to ensure effective implementation (Gillett-Swan & Grant-Smith, 2018; KnowledgeWorks, 2020).

Ensure Quality

Ensuring quality in personalized learning systems requires maintaining high standards and accountability. Gillett-Swan & Grant-Smith, (2018) offer a framework on managing impacts and maintaining quality of life while placing emphasis on high standards and accountability in personalized learning systems. Criteria for success must be defined to guide the design, implementation, and evaluation of such educational practices. Balanced assessment systems, using both formative assessments (like regular quizzes and classroom feedback) and summative assessments (such as standardized tests and final projects), offer a holistic view of student learning and inform instructional methods. Establishing metrics to measure the effectiveness of personalized learning initiatives allows for tracking progress, identifies areas for improvement, and celebrates successes. As PLEs and AI systems more readily follow principles to ensure quality and trustworthiness in model development educators trust AI-driven recommendations.

Human oversight is essential in personalized learning and AI to address biases or inaccuracies, ensuring that AI-driven recommendations are fair and effective for all students. Integrating these principles allows AI to significantly enhance personalized learning environments, making education more adaptive, inclusive, and effective.

Aligning AI technologies with educational goals and best practices supports continuous improvement and equity in student learning outcomes (KnowledgeWorks, 2020; Office of Educational Technology, 2023). Ensuring the quality of PLEs fosters a broader impact while cultivating systems change essential for sustaining advancements and creating an environment that supports continuous improvement and innovation for SWD (Pearson et al., 2010). Initiatives necessitate encouraging a culture of experimentation, providing responsive funding, and engaging stakeholders to ensure effective implementation and scalability of personalized learning.

Cultivate Systemic Reform

The need for robust change to guarantee quality and equity in personalized learning for SWD is imperative. Ensuring continuous enhancement and upholding high standards while addressing the diverse needs of marginalized student populations requires fostering a culture of innovation, aligning resources, and building capacity (Waldron & McLeskey, 2010). Achieving a large-scale vision of change necessitates leveraging cutting-edge tools and approaches within the interdisciplinary methods of learning science (Pearson et al., 2010). Researchers in learning science employ interdisciplinary methodologies to enhance innovation and creativity, aiming to improve both learning processes and educational environments (Nathan & Sawyer, 2014; Sawyer, 2014). Such efforts aim to create educational systems that provide equitable access and empower all students to succeed (Tripp & Shortlidge, 2019).

Systemic educational reform for SWD driven by inclusion calls for collaborative efforts and a shared vision (Waldron & McLeskey, 2010). Interdisciplinary methods within the learning sciences and advanced technologies can develop new pedagogical knowledge that improves student outcomes (Guerriero, 2017). Expert panels worldwide recognize the evolving nature of teaching and advocate for integrating learning sciences into educational practice (Guerriero, 2017; Kalil, 2017; McKenney, 2018). Despite 30 years of advancements, the impact of the learning sciences on education has been largely overlooked, resulting in slow integration into educational practices (Graesser, 2013; Tokuhama-Espinosa, 2019). Graesser (2013) proposed that learning science technologies were destined to penetrate educational practices to focus on cognition, emotion, and motivation. AI may be the tipping point for integrating the learning sciences into personalized learning by harnessing data-driven insights to tailor educational experiences to individual student needs, bridging the gap between theoretical research and practical application.

These processes involve leveraging data to inform decision-making (Graesser, 2013), ensuring educational strategies are grounded in evidence and tailored to address specific challenges. Engaging stakeholders, including educators, parents, and community members, in continuous feedback loops is essential to creating a collaborative and responsive educational environment (Collier et al., 2015). Applying evidence-based interventions from the learning sciences further supports the objective of fostering a culture of continuous improvement, ensuring that all initiatives are effective and impactful (Chen, 2009; Diamond, 2013; Graham & Harris, 2003; Pearson et al., 2010; Pintrich, 2000; Zimmerman, 2000). Through these comprehensive strategies, Personalized Learning Environments can significantly enhance the educational landscape, providing students with the skills and knowledge necessary for success in the modern world.

Insights from Neuroscience and Learning Sciences

Neuroscience and the learning sciences have provided valuable insights into understanding and supporting learners with special educational needs. The concept of neuroplasticity, which refers to the brain's ability to reorganize and form new neural connections in response to learning and experience (Doidge, 2007; Wong et al., 2017), has particularly revolutionized this field. This understanding challenges the notion that learning difficulties are fixed and immutable, suggesting instead that targeted interventions can help rewire the brain and improve learning outcomes. For example, research has shown that intensive, systematic instruction can lead to significant gains in reading skills for students with dyslexia, accompanied by changes in brain activity patterns (Archer & Hughes, 2011; Graham & Harris, 2003; Robson et al., 2020; Ruan et al., 2022).

Executive functions, such as attention, working memory, and cognitive flexibility, play a crucial role in learning and academic performance (Diamond, 2013; Wong et al., 2017). Students with diverse educational needs often experience challenges in these areas, which can impact their ability to acquire and apply new knowledge and skills. AI-powered adaptive learning systems can be designed to target and strengthen executive functions by providing structured, scaffolded learning experiences that gradually increase in complexity and require learners to exercise these skills (Molenaar et al., 2023; Robson et al., 2020). Moreover, neuroscience research has highlighted the importance of multi-sensory learning experiences in enhancing memory and understanding (Shams & Seitz, 2008; Wong et al., 2017). Engaging multiple senses, such as vision, hearing, and touch, can create richer, more robust neural representations of information. An important consideration for learners with sensory processing challenges or specific sensory preferences is the integration of multi-sensory elements in educational technology tools. These tools, which include visual aids, auditory cues, and tactile experiences, can greatly improve the accessibility and engagement of the learning process for these students.

The learning sciences have also contributed important insights into designing effective educational interventions for learners with disabilities. One key principle is the importance of providing explicit, systematic instruction that breaks down complex skills into smaller, more manageable components (Archer & Hughes, 2011; Wong et al., 2017). This approach is especially beneficial for students with learning disabilities, who may struggle to infer patterns and rules from implicit or unstructured learning experiences (Archer & Hughes, 2011; Ruan et al., 2022). Another insight from the learning sciences is the value of collaborative and social learning experiences in promoting engagement, motivation, and deeper understanding (Hmelo-Silver, 2004). Learners with disabilities may face social and communication challenges that can hinder their ability to participate in group learning activities. However, EdTech tools that facilitate online collaboration, such as discussion forums, wikis, and virtual classrooms, can provide alternative avenues for these students to interact with their peers and contribute to shared knowledge-building.

Finally, the learning sciences emphasize the importance of formative assessment and data-driven decision-making in optimizing learning outcomes (Black & Wiliam, 2009). By continuously monitoring student progress and adjusting instruction based on individual needs and performance, educators can ensure that each learner receives the support they need to succeed. AI-powered learning analytics tools can automate this process by collecting and analyzing real-time data on student interactions, providing insights into learning patterns, and recommending targeted interventions (Molenaar et al., 2023).

Self-regulated and Self-directed Learning

Self-regulation and self-directed learning are crucial concepts in education and the learning sciences, particularly in the context of special education (Chen, 2009). These approaches empower learners to take control of their own learning process, setting goals, monitoring progress, and adapting strategies to optimize their performance. By fostering these skills and considering the Extended Mind Theory, educators can help students with special educational needs develop the autonomy and resilience needed to overcome learning challenges and succeed academically.

The Extended Mind Theory, proposed by Clark and Chalmers (1998), suggests that the human mind is not limited to the brain but extends into the environment through the use of tools and technologies. This theory has significant implications for special education, as it suggests that students with different needs can adapt and learn to use technology as an extension of their cognitive abilities. For example, teachers use graphic organizers to help break down the writing process into manageable steps in brainstorming, organizing thoughts, and outlining. The act of physically writing on paper helps students externalize their mental processes and provide a visual representation of their ideas. The graphic organizer serves as an extension of a student's mind, allowing him to organize his thoughts more effectively and reducing the cognitive load associated with the writing process (Clark & Chalmers, 1998).

Similarly, assistive technologies as seen in Table 1, such as document accessibility tools, e.g. text-to-speech software or adaptive learning applications, can serve as cognitive extensions for students with learning difficulties. For instance, a student with dyslexia can use text-to-speech software to access and engage with written content, bypassing the challenges associated with decoding and reading fluency. The software becomes an extension of the student's mind, allowing them to comprehend and process information more effectively (Clark & Chalmers, 1998). By incorporating assistive technologies and learning tools into their educational experiences, these students can enhance their self-regulation and self-directed learning skills (Molenaar et al., 2023).

Self-regulation and self-directed learning are crucial concepts in education, particularly in the context of special education. These approaches empower learners to take control of their own learning process, setting goals, monitoring progress, and adapting strategies to optimize their performance. Self-regulation refers to the ability to manage one's thoughts, emotions, and behaviors in pursuit of a goal (Zimmerman, 2000). In the context of learning, self-regulation involves setting academic goals, planning and organizing learning activities, monitoring comprehension and progress, and adjusting strategies as needed (Pintrich, 2000).

For students with special educational needs, self-regulation can be particularly challenging. These learners may struggle with executive functions, such as attention, working memory, and impulse control, which are essential for effective self-regulation (Diamond, 2013). They may also face social, emotional, or behavioral difficulties that can impact their ability to manage their learning experiences (Molenaar et al., 2023). However, research has shown that self-regulation skills can be taught and developed through explicit instruction, modeling, and practice (Graham & Harris, 2003). For example, a student with ADHD may have difficulty maintaining attention during independent work tasks, leading to incomplete assignments and frustration (Diamond, 2013; Graham & Harris, 2003). To support this student's self-regulation skills, the teacher can implement a self-monitoring strategy. The teacher works with the student to create a checklist that breaks down the task into smaller, manageable steps. The student uses the checklist to monitor their progress, checking off each step as they complete it. The teacher also models the use of the checklist and provides verbal prompts and encouragement throughout the process. Over time, the student learns to internalize the self-monitoring strategy, improving their ability to maintain attention and complete tasks independently. Explicit instruction and practice of self-regulation skills can help students with special educational needs develop the tools necessary to manage their learning experiences more effectively (Graham & Harris, 2003).

Call to Action

The necessity for a call to action to advance special education through artificial intelligence (AI) is both urgent and compelling. The absence of innovative, personalized learning solutions significantly impacts the lives of students with disabilities, leading to missed opportunities for academic and social development (Gillett-Swan & Grant-Smith, 2018). Without the integration of AI-driven technologies, many SWD continue to face barriers that hinder their inclusion in general education classrooms and limit their potential. Immediate, concerted efforts to adopt and implement AI in special education are essential to addressing these challenges head-on. By mobilizing educators, policymakers, and stakeholders to embrace AI as a transformative tool, we can create equitable, inclusive, and adaptive learning environments for all students. The future success and well-being of students with disabilities depend on our collective commitment to fostering innovation and inclusivity in education. AI as a transformative tool aligns with Kotter's 8-step process for leading change (Kotter, 2012). By following steps encapsulating change in climate, engagement, and execution, we can create equitable, inclusive, and adaptive learning environments for all students. The future success and well-being of students with disabilities depends on our collective commitment to fostering innovation and inclusivity in education.

Climate for Change

Creating a climate conducive to change is the first step towards revolutionizing special education by integrating AI. This section emphasizes the need to generate a sense of urgency around the current special education deficiencies and AI's transformative potential to address these gaps. By building strong leadership and forming a cohesive vision for change, educators and stakeholders can set the stage for a collaborative, concerted effort to enhance personalized learning and inclusivity for SWD (Milat et al., 2013). Establishing a climate for change ensures that the educational community is prepared, motivated, and aligned towards the common goal of integrating AI to foster an inclusive learning environment.

Create Urgency. In the realm of enhancing special education through AI, creating a sense of urgency is paramount. AI integration can revolutionize personalized learning and inclusivity for SWD. Recognizing the current gaps in special education services and the potential of AI to bridge these gaps can galvanize stakeholders to act swiftly (Waldron & McLeskey, 2010). Highlighting the immediate benefits, such as improved learning outcomes and increased engagement for SWD, underscores the necessity for rapid adoption and integration of AI technologies in educational settings (Alsobeh & Woodward, 2023).

Build Leadership. Effective building level leadership is crucial to driving change in special education through AI. Educational leaders must champion the cause, demonstrating a commitment to leveraging AI for personalized learning (KnowledgeWorks, 2020; Wang, 2021). By building a coalition of educators, administrators, parents, and policymakers, leaders can foster a supportive environment for implementing AI-driven inclusive practices. Leadership must also focus on professional development, ensuring that teachers are well-equipped to use AI tools effectively to support SWD (ISTE, 2024; Marino et al., 2023; UNESCO, 2023; Wang, 2021).

Form a Vision for Change. A clear, compelling vision for integrating AI in special education can inspire and guide efforts toward inclusivity (Marino et al., 2023). Articulating how AI can facilitate personalized learning experiences that cater to the unique needs of students with disabilities promotes their inclusion in general education classrooms (Marino et al., 2024). By setting ambitious yet achievable goals, the vision can serve as a roadmap for educators and stakeholders, aligning their efforts towards a common objective of enhanced inclusivity and personalized education (KnowledgeWorks, 2020).

Engagement

Engagement is critical in enlisting the support and active participation of all stakeholders in the journey towards AI-driven improvements in special education. Creating a unified vision that resonates with educators, parents, students, and policymakers alike holds significant importance. By fostering a shared commitment to the vision of personalized learning and inclusivity, and by empowering stakeholders with the necessary tools and knowledge, we can mobilize collective action (KnowledgeWorks, 2020). Engagement ensures that the efforts to integrate AI in special education are supported by a broad coalition, enhancing the likelihood of successful and sustainable implementation.

Enlist a Unified Vision. To foster engagement, enlisting a unified vision that encompasses the perspectives and aspirations of all stakeholders, including those with disabilities, is essential (Hughes et al., 2022). Emphasize the transformative potential of AI in creating personalized learning pathways for students with disabilities, ensuring the principle of "Nothing About Us Without Us" is upheld (Charlton, 1998). Engaging teachers, parents, students, and policymakers in collaborative dialogue ensures that the vision reflects a collective commitment to inclusivity. By aligning everyone's efforts towards this shared goal, the educational community can work cohesively to implement AI-driven solutions effectively (Wang, 2021).

Empower Action. Empowering action involves equipping educators and stakeholders with the necessary tools, knowledge, and resources to implement AI in special education (Kadaruddin, 2023). Providing professional development opportunities, access to cutting-edge AI technologies, and fostering a culture of innovation encourages proactive efforts towards inclusivity. By empowering educators to experiment with AI tools and adapt their teaching strategies, schools can create dynamic, responsive learning environments that support the diverse needs of SWD (Kirongo et al., 2022).

Execution

Successful implementation and sustainability of AI initiatives in special education require a strategic approach that emphasizes generating quick wins, sustaining acceleration, and instituting lasting change. This section focuses on the practical steps necessary to embed AI-driven personalized learning and inclusive practices within the educational system. By demonstrating early successes, maintaining momentum through continuous innovation, and developing policies and infrastructure to support long-term integration, we can ensure that AI becomes an integral part of special education. Implementation and sustainability efforts guarantee the benefits of AI are not only realized in the short term but are also preserved and expanded over time to create a truly inclusive educational environment (Tanveer et al., 2020).

Generate Quick Wins. Generating quick wins is vital for demonstrating the immediate benefits of AI in special education. Identifying and implementing small-scale AI projects that yield tangible improvements in student engagement and learning outcomes can build momentum and validate the efficacy of AI tools (Neeharika & Riyazuddin, 2023). These early successes can serve as proof-of-concept, encouraging broader adoption and continued investment in AI-driven educational strategies (Hughes et al., 2022).

Sustain Acceleration. Sustaining acceleration requires maintaining the momentum generated by initial successes and continuously driving innovation (Lasrado, 2019). Regular evaluation and refinement of AI initiatives are essential to ensuring they remain effective and relevant (Badmus, 2023). Providing ongoing support and resources for educators, as well as fostering a culture of continuous improvement, helps sustain the acceleration of AI integration in special education. By consistently pushing the boundaries of what AI can achieve, schools can enhance their capacity to support SWD (Schrauben et al., 2019).

Institute Change. Instituting lasting change involves embedding AI-driven personalized learning and inclusivity practices into the fabric of the educational system (Aggarwal, 2023). Achieving this goal necessitates comprehensive policy development, robust infrastructure, and a commitment to equity (Badawy, 2023).

Ensuring that AI initiatives are scalable and adaptable to different contexts helps institutionalize these practices (Milat et al., 2013). By creating an inclusive, adaptive educational environment, schools can better serve SWD and ensure their meaningful inclusion in general education classrooms (Walker et al., 2023).

The intersection of personalized learning and inclusivity through AI presents an unprecedented opportunity to enhance special education. As educators, administrators, and policymakers, we must act with urgency and vision to integrate AI into our educational practices. Let us build strong leadership, engage all stakeholders in a unified vision, and empower action at every level. By generating quick wins, sustaining momentum, and instituting lasting change, we can create an inclusive educational landscape where every student, regardless of their abilities, can thrive. Embrace AI as a catalyst for inclusion and equity, and commit to transforming special education for the betterment of all students (Alsobeh & Woodward, 2023).

CONCLUSION

Artificial intelligence (AI) offers promising opportunities to support students with disabilities by leveraging self-regulated learning theories to enhance the educational experience of individuals with diverse needs in inclusive settings (Molenaar et al., 2023; Ruan et al., 2022). Self-regulated learning empowers students to take an active, metacognitive role in their educational journey by setting goals, monitoring progress, and adjusting strategies (Zimmerman, 2008). By remaining metacognitively, motivationally, and behaviorally active in their learning, students can benefit from interventions that teach skills and raise self-efficacy for learning (Schunk & Ertmer, 2000). Personalized learning models, which tailor instruction to individual abilities, interests, and experiences, align with this paradigm, fostering optimal engagement and achievement (Prain et al., 2013).

AI design that aligns with motivational, cognitive, and contextual factors of self-regulation can optimize human-AI synergies (Roll & Wylie, 2016; Ruan et al., 2022). Chatbots and virtual assistants, for example, can act as on-demand metacognitive coaches, modeling self-regulatory processes such as planning, monitoring, and reflection (Grawemeyer et al., 2017). However, educators and students with disabilities must participate in the design process to create AI supports that are equitable, empowering, and aligned with self-determined learning (Luckin, 2017; Moon, 2023).

As education increasingly leverages AI capabilities, researchers must critically examine how to harmonize self-regulated learning theory with AI-enabled personalized instruction (Molenaar et al., 2023). Studies by Sancenon et al. (2022) and Heng et al. (2021) document variations in experience and underscore the importance of personalized learning approaches catering to individualized needs and contexts, fostering more effective practices, and improving student outcomes. The future of education lies in harnessing AI's computational strengths while preserving human-centric values of autonomy, identity, and agency (Molenaar et al., 2023; Robson et al., 2020). Consequently, as AI and personalized learning evolve, examining the reshaping of inclusion and accessibility becomes critical (Molenaar et al., 2023; Ruan et al., 2022). Through this lens, the authors aim to identify emerging challenges and propose pathways to ensure AI technologies advance inclusive and accessible practices rather than hinder them.

References

Aggarwal, D. (2023). Exploring the scope of artificial intelligence (AI) for lifelong education through personalised & adaptive learning. *Journal of Artificial Intelligence. Machine Learning and Neural Network*, 4(01), 21–26. DOI: 10.55529/jaimlnn.41.21.26

Aggarwal, D., Sharma, D., & Saxena, A. (2023). Adoption of artificial intelligence (AI) for development of smart education as the future of a sustainable education system. *Journal of Artificial Intelligence. Machine Learning and Neural Network*, 3(06), 23–28. DOI: 10.55529/jaimlnn.36.23.28

Agran, M., Jackson, L., Kurth, J. A., Ryndak, D., Burnette, K., Jameson, M., Zagona, A., Fitzpatrick, H., & Wehmeyer, M. (2020). Why aren't students with severe disabilities being placed in general education classrooms: Examining the relations among classroom placement, learner outcomes, and other factors. *Research and Practice for Persons with Severe Disabilities : the Journal of TASH*, 45(1), 4–13. DOI: 10.1177/1540796919878134

Akgun, S., & Greenhow, C. (2021). Artificial intelligence in education: Addressing ethical challenges in K-12 settings. *AI and Ethics*, 2(3), 431–440. DOI: 10.1007/s43681-021-00096-7 PMID: 34790956

Alsobeh, A., & Woodward, B. (2023). AI as a partner in learning: A novel student-in-the-Loop framework for enhanced student engagement and outcomes in higher education. *Proceedings of the 24th Annual Conference on Information Technology Education.* DOI: 10.1145/3585059.3611405

Archer, A. L., & Hughes, C. A. (2011). Explicit Instruction: Effective and efficient teaching (what works for special-needs learners). *The Journal of Special Education*, 36(4), 186–205.

Badawy, M. (2023). Integrating artificial intelligence and big data into smart healthcare systems: A comprehensive review of current and future directions. *Artificial Intelligence Evolution. 4*(2),133-135. https://doi.org?DOI: 10.37256/aie/4220232980

Badmus, O. (2023). Application of AI technology in program management. *Journal of Engineering Research and Reports*, 25(8), 48–55. DOI: 10.9734/jerr/2023/v25i8958

Baskara, R. (2023). Personalised learning with AI: Implications for Ignatian pedagogy. [International Journal of Educational Best Practices]. *IJEBP*, 7(1), 1–16. DOI: 10.31258/ijebp.v7n1.p1-16

Bérubé, M., Giannelia, T., & Vial, G. (2021). Barriers to the Implementation of AI in Organizations: Findings from a Delphi Study. *Proceedings of the 54th Hawaii International Conference on System Sciences*. 1-10. https://doi.org/DOI: 10.24251/HICSS.2021.805

Black, P., & Wiliam, D. (2009). Developing the theory of formative assessment. *Educational Assessment, Evaluation and Accountability*, 21(1), 5–31. DOI: 10.1007/s11092-008-9068-5

Caro, M. F., Quitian, L., Giraldo, J. C., & Lengua-Cantero, C. (2023, November). A Formal Model for Personalized Learning Path using Artificial Intelligence for Instructional Planning with a Focus on 21st-Century Skills and Environmental Awareness. In *2023 IEEE Colombian Caribbean Conference (C3)* (pp. 1-6). IEEE. DOI: 10.1109/C358072.2023.10436195

Charlton, J. I. (1998). *Nothing about us without us: Disability oppression and empowerment*. University of California Press.

Chen, C.-M. (2009). Personalized E-learning system with self-regulated learning assisted mechanisms for promoting learning performance. *Expert Systems with Applications*, 36(5), 8816–8829. DOI: 10.1016/j.eswa.2008.11.026

Christian, B. (2020). *The Alignment Problem: Machine Learning and Human Values*. W.W. Norton & Company.

Clark, A., & Chalmers, D. (1998). The extended mind. *Analysis*, 58(1), 7–19. DOI: 10.1093/analys/58.1.7

Collier, M., Keefe, E., & Hirrel, L. (2015). Preparing special education teachers to collaborate with families. *School Community Journal*, 25, 117–136.

Dafoe, A., Hughes, E., Bachrach, Y., Collins, T., McKee, K., Leibo, J., Larson, K., & Graepel, T. (2020). Open Problems in Cooperative AI. *ArXiv*, abs/2012.08630.

de Boer, A., Pijl, S. J., Post, W., & Minnaert, A. (2013). Peer acceptance and friendships of students with disabilities in general education: The role of child, peer, and classroom variables. *Social Development*, 22(4), 831–844. DOI: 10.1111/j.1467-9507.2012.00670.x

Diamond, A. (2013). Executive functions. *Annual Review of Psychology*, 64(1), 135–168. DOI: 10.1146/annurev-psych-113011-143750 PMID: 23020641

Doidge, N. (2007). *The Brain That Changes Itself: Stories of Personal Triumph from the Frontiers of Brain Science*. Viking Penguin.

Family Educational Rights and Privacy Act (FERPA), 20 U.S.C. § 1232g; 34 CFR Part 99 (1974).

Filatov, V., Zolotukhin, O., Yerokhin, A., & Kudryavtseva, M. (2019, September). Personalized adaptation of learning environments. In *2019 IEEE 8th International Conference on Advanced Optoelectronics and Lasers (CAOL)* (pp. 584-587). IEEE. DOI: 10.1109/CAOL46282.2019.9019525

Francom, G. M., Lee, S. J., & Pinkney, H. (2021). Technologies, Challenges and Needs of K-12 Teachers in the Transition to Distance Learning during the COVID-19 Pandemic. *TechTrends*, 65(4), 589–601. DOI: 10.1007/s11528-021-00625-5 PMID: 34223560

Gillett-Swan, J., & Grant-Smith, D. (2018). A framework for managing the impacts of work-integrated learning on student quality of life. *International Journal of Work-Integrated Learning*, 19(2), 129–140. https://eprints.qut.edu.au/223863/

Goswami, U. (2004). Neuroscience, education and special education. *British Journal of Special Education*, 31(4), 175–183. DOI: 10.1111/j.0952-3383.2004.00352.x

Graesser, A. C. (2013). Evolution of advanced learning technologies in the 21st century. *Theory into Practice*, 52(1), 93–101. DOI: 10.1080/00405841.2013.795446

Graham, S., & Harris, K. R. (2003). *Writing Better: Teaching Writing Process and Self-Regulation to Students with Learning Problems*. Brookes Publishing.

Grawemeyer, B., Holmes, W., Mavrikis, M., Hansen, A., Loibl, K., & Gutiérrez-Santos, S. (2017). Affective versus cognitive behavior modeling for better educational outcomes. In Leonidis, A., & Bouras, C. (Eds.), *UMAP 2017: Proceedings of the 25th Conference on User Modeling, Adaptation, and Personalization* (pp. 268-279). Springer. DOI: 10.1007/978-3-319-93843-1_19

Guerriero, S. (Ed.). (2017). *Educational research and innovation pedagogical knowledge and the changing nature of the teaching profession*. OECD Publishing., DOI: 10.1787/9789264270695-

Harfouche, A., Quinio, B., & Bugiotti, F. (2023). Human-Centric AI to Mitigate AI Biases. *Journal of Global Information Management*, 31(5), 1–23. Advance online publication. DOI: 10.4018/JGIM.331755

Harry, A., & Sayudin, S. (2023). Role of AI in education. [INJURITY]. *Interdisciplinary Journal and Humanity*, 2(3), 260–268. DOI: 10.58631/injurity.v2i3.52

Heng, L. E., Voon, W. P., Jalil, N. A., Kwun, C. L., Chieh, T. C., & Subri, N. F. (2021). Personalization of learning content in learning management system. *Proceedings of the 2021 10th International Conference on Software and Computer Applications*. DOI: 10.1145/3457784.3457819

Hind, M., Mehta, S., Mojsilovic, A., Nair, R., Ramamurthy, K., Olteanu, A., & Varshney, K. R. (2018). Increasing trust in AI services through supplier's declarations of conformity. *arXiv*. https://arxiv.org/abs/1808.07261

Hmelo-Silver, C. E. (2004). Problem-based learning: What and how do students learn? *Educational Psychology Review*, 16(3), 235–266. DOI: 10.1023/B:EDPR.0000034022.16470.f3

Hopcan, S., Polat, E., Ozturk, M. E., & Ozturk, L. (2023). Artificial intelligence in special education: A systematic review. *Interactive Learning Environments*, 31(10), 7335–7353. DOI: 10.1080/10494820.2022.2067186

Horváth, I. (2020). Personalized learning opportunity in 3D VR. In 2020 11th IEEE International Conference on Cognitive Infocommunications (CogInfoCom) (pp. 425-430). Mariehamn, Finland. DOI: 10.1109/CogInfoCom50765.2020.9237895

Huang, L. (2023). *Ethics of artificial intelligence in education: Student privacy and data protection*. Science Insights Education Frontiers., DOI: 10.15254.sief.23.re202

Hughes, C., Dieker, L., Glavey, E., Hines, R., Wilkins, I., Ingraham, K., Bukaty, C., Ali, K., Shah, S., Murphy, J., & Taylor, M. (2022). RAISE: Robotics & AI to improve STEM and social skills for elementary school students. *Frontiers in Virtual Reality*, 3, 968312. Advance online publication. DOI: 10.3389/frvir.2022.968312

Ifenthaler, D., & Schumacher, C. (2023). Reciprocal issues of artificial and human intelligence in education. *Journal of Research on Technology in Education*, 55(1), 1–6. DOI: 10.1080/15391523.2022.2154511

Interaction Design Foundation. (2016, June 1). What is accessibility? Interaction Design Foundation - IxDF. https://www.interaction-design.org/literature/topics/accessibility

International Society for Technology in Education (ISTE). (2023, July). *Bringing AI to school: Tips for School Leaders*. https://cms-live-media.iste.org/Bringing_AI_to_School-2023_07.pdf?_ga=2.148286964.278272055.1709340314-1629594781.1707762420

Kadaruddin, K. (2023). *Empowering education through generative AI: Innovative instructional strategies for tomorrow's learners*. International Journal of Business, Law, and Education., DOI: 10.56442/ijble.v4i2.215

Kalil, T. (2017). Policy entrepreneurship at the White House. *Innovations: Technology, Governance, Globalization*, 11(3/4), 4–21. DOI: 10.1162/inov_a_00253

Kennett, D. W., Gardner, A., Scott, L., Patterson, M. S., Zhang, L., & Carter, R. A. (2022). Choice and voice: Emerging questions of personalised professional learning. *Practice*, 4(2), 103–109. DOI: 10.1080/25783858.2022.2086061

Kirongo, A., Bundi, D., Kitaria, D., Huka, G., & Muketha, G. (2022). *Implementation of AI-based assistive technologies for learners with physical disabilities in Kenya: a practical design thinking approach.* African Journal of Science, Technology and Social Sciences., DOI: 10.58506/ajstss.v1i1.71

Kizilcec, R. F. (2023). To Advance AI Use in Education, Focus on Understanding Educators. *International Journal of Artificial Intelligence in Education*, 34(1), 12–19. DOI: 10.1007/s40593-023-00351-4 PMID: 37359103

KnowledgeWorks. (2020). *State policy framework for personalized learning.* KnowledgeWorks. https://knowledgeworks.org/resources/state-policy-framework-personalized-learning/

Kornbluh, M. (2020). Untold student stories: Examining educational budget cuts within urban school settings. *Journal of Urban Affairs*, 42(5), 731–749. DOI: 10.1080/07352166.2019.1607748

Kotter, J. P. (2012). *Leading change*. Harvard business press.

Kuleto, V., Ilić, M., Dumangiu, M., Ranković, M., Martins, O. M., Păun, D., & Mihoreanu, L. (2021). Exploring opportunities and challenges of artificial intelligence and machine learning in higher education institutions. *Sustainability (Basel)*, 13(18), 10424. DOI: 10.3390/su131810424

Lasrado, F. (2019). *Sustaining Innovation and Future Research Implications.* Fostering Creativity and Innovation., DOI: 10.1007/978-3-319-99121-4_6

Liu, H., Wang, Y., Fan, W., Liu, X., Li, Y., Jain, S., Liu, Y., Jain, A., & Tang, J. (2021). Trustworthy AI: A Computational Perspective. *ACM Transactions on Intelligent Systems and Technology*, 14(1), 1–59. DOI: 10.1145/3546872

Luckin, R. (2017). Towards Artificial Intelligence-based Assessment Systems. *Nature Human Behaviour, 1*, 0028. https://doi.org/DOI: 10.1038/s41562-016-0028

Marino, M. T., Basham, J. D., Courtade, G., Hott, B. L., Howorth, S. K., Goldman, S. R., & Vasquez, E. (2024). Inclusive intelligence: The impact of AI on education for all learners. Center for Innovation, Design, and Digital Learning (CIDDL). https://ciddl.org/inclusive-intelligence-the-impact-of-ai-on-education-for-all-learners/

Marino, M. T., Vasquez, E., Dieker, L., Basham, J., & Blackorby, J. (2023). The future of artificial intelligence in special education technology. *Journal of Special Education Technology*, 38(3), 404–416. DOI: 10.1177/01626434231165977

McKenney, S. (2018). How can the learning sciences (better) impact policy and practice? *Journal of the Learning Sciences*, 27(1), 1–7. DOI: 10.1080/10508406.2017.1404404

Mehrotra, S., Degachi, C., Vereschak, O., Jonker, C., & Tielman, M. (2023). A systematic review on fostering appropriate trust in human-AI interaction. *ARXiv*, abs/2311.06305. https://doi.org//arXiv.2311.06305DOI: 10.48550

Menezes, D. (2024). Student fights AI cheating allegations for using Grammarly. NewsNation. https://www.newsnationnow.com/business/tech/ai/student-fights-academic-probation-ai-tool/

Microsoft. (2023). Seeing AI. Retrieved from https://www.seeingai.com/

Milat, A., King, L., Bauman, A., & Redman, S. (2013). The concept of scalability: Increasing the scale and potential adoption of health promotion interventions into policy and practice. *Health Promotion International*, 3(28), 285–298. DOI: 10.1093/heapro/dar097 PMID: 22241853

Mitchell, M. (2019). *Artificial Intelligence: A Guide for Thinking Humans*. Farrar, Straus and Giroux.

ModMath. (2023). ModMath. Retrieved from https://www.modmath.com/

Molenaar, I., de Mooij, S., Azevedo, R., Bannert, M., Järvelä, S., & Gašević, D. (2023). Measuring self-regulated learning and the role of AI: Five years of research using multimodal multichannel data. *Computers in Human Behavior*, 139, 107540. DOI: 10.1016/j.chb.2022.107540

Moon, M. (2023). Searching for inclusive artificial intelligence for social good: Participatory governance and policy recommendations for making AI more inclusive and benign for society. *Public Administration Review*, 83(6), 1496–1505. DOI: 10.1111/puar.13648

Moriña, A., Carballo, R., & Castellano-Beltran, A. (2023). A systematic review of the benefits and challenges of technologies for the learning of university students with disabilities. *Journal of Special Education Technology*, 39(1), 41–50. DOI: 10.1177/01626434231175357

Nathan, M. J., & Sawyer, R. K. (2014). Foundations of the learning sciences. In Sawyer, R. K. (Ed.), *The Cambridge Handbook of the Learning Sciences* (2nd ed., pp. 21–43). Cambridge University Press. DOI: 10.1017/CBO9781139519526.004

National Forum on Education Statistics. (2019). Forum Guide to Personalized Learning Data (NFES2019160). U.S. Department of Education. Washington, DC: National Center for Education Statistics.

Neamtu, R., Camara, A., Pereira, C., & Ferreira, R. (2019). Using artificial intelligence for augmentative alternative communication for children with disabilities. In Lamas, D., Loizides, F., Nacke, L., Petrie, H., Winckler, M., & Zaphiris, P. (Eds.), Lecture Notes in Computer Science: Vol. 11746. *Human-Computer Interaction – INTERACT 2019*. Springer., DOI: 10.1007/978-3-030-29381-9_15

Neeharika, C., & Riyazuddin, Y. (2023). Artificial Intelligence in Children with Special Need Education. *2023 International Conference on Intelligent Data Communication Technologies and Internet of Things*, 519-523. DOI: 10.1109/IDCIoT56793.2023.10053420

Ntoutsi, E., Fafalios, P., Gadiraju, U., Iosifidis, V., Nejdl, W., Vidal, M., Ruggieri, S., Turini, F., Papadopoulos, S., Krasanakis, E., Kompatsiaris, I., Kinder-Kurlanda, K., Wagner, C., Karimi, F., Fernández, M., Alani, H., Berendt, B., Kruegel, T., Heinze, C., & Staab, S. (2020). Bias in data-driven artificial intelligence systems—An introductory survey. *Wiley Interdisciplinary Reviews. Data Mining and Knowledge Discovery*, 10(3), e1356. DOI: 10.1002/widm.1356

Office of Educational Technology. (2023). *Artificial intelligence and the future of teaching and learning: Insights and recommendations*. U.S. Department of Education. https://tech.ed.gov/ai-report-2023

Office of the High Commissioner for Human Rights (OHCHR). (2022, May 9.). Humanity should get the best from AI, not the worst - UN disability. https://www.ohchr.org/

Okamura, K., & Yamada, S. (2020). Adaptive trust calibration for human-AI collaboration. *PLoS One*, 15(2), e0229132. Advance online publication. DOI: 10.1371/journal.pone.0229132 PMID: 32084201

Open, A. I. (2023). ChatGPT (June 2023 version) [Large language model]. https://www.openai.com/

Pearson, E., Gkatzidou, V., & Green, S. (2010). From a personal Learning environment to an adaptable personal learning environment: Meeting the needs and preferences of disabled learners. 2010 10th IEEE International Conference on Advanced Learning Technologies, 333–335. DOI: 10.1109/ICALT.2010.94

Pintrich, P. R. (2000). The role of goal orientation in self-regulated learning. In *Handbook of Self-Regulation* (pp. 451–502). Academic Press. DOI: 10.1016/B978-012109890-2/50043-3

Prain, V., Cox, P., Deed, C., Dorman, J., Edwards, D., Farrelly, C., Keeffe, M., Lovejoy, V., Mow, L., Sellings, P., Waldrip, B., & Yager, Z. (2013). Personalised learning. *Journal of Educational Psychology*, 38(1), 54–68. DOI: 10.1080/01443410.2013.857010

Rejmaniak, R. (2021). Bias in Artificial Intelligence Systems. *Białostockie Studia Prawnicze*, 26(3), 25–42. DOI: 10.15290/bsp.2021.26.03.02

Rice, M. F., & Dunn, S. (2023). The use of artificial intelligence with students with identified disabilities: A systematic review with critique. *Computers in the Schools*, 40(4), 370–390. Advance online publication. DOI: 10.1080/07380569.2023.2244935

Robson, D. A., Allen, M. S., & Howard, S. J. (2020). Self-regulation in childhood as a predictor of future outcomes: A meta-analytic review. *Psychological Bulletin*, 146(4), 324–354. DOI: 10.1037/bul0000227 PMID: 31904248

Roll, I., & Wylie, R. (2016). Evolution and revolution in artificial intelligence in education. *International Journal of Artificial Intelligence in Education*, 26(2), 582–608. DOI: 10.1007/s40593-016-0110-3

Ronksley-Pavia, M. (2024). Curriculum in special school contexts: A collaged framework for personalised, individual student learning. *Curriculum Journal*, 35(1), 56–72. DOI: 10.1002/curj.235

Ruan, M., Peng, X., & Zhang, Y. (2022). Modeling self-regulated learning with AI: A case study using multimodal data. In Aleven, V., Roll, I., & Koedinger, K. R. (Eds.), Lecture Notes in Computer Science: Vol. 13291. *Artificial Intelligence in Education* (pp. 90–101). Springer., DOI: 10.1007/978-3-031-06017-9_7

Samara, M., George, T., & Ali, M. (2021). AI-based adaptive intelligent systems: A comprehensive review. *iJAI, 4*(3), 319-330. https://doi.org/DOI: 10.1016/j.jai.2021.11.005

Sancenon, V., Wijaya, K., Wen, X. Y., Utama, D. A., Ashworth, M., Ng, K. H., Cheong, A., & Neo, Z. (2022). A new web-based personalized learning system improves student learning outcomes. *International Journal of Virtual and Personal Learning Environments*, 12(1), 1–21. DOI: 10.4018/IJVPLE.295306

Sawyer, R. K. (2014). The future of learning: Grounding educational innovation in the learning sciences. In Sawyer, R. K. (Ed.), *The Cambridge Handbook of the Learning Sciences* (2nd ed., pp. 726–746). Cambridge University Press. DOI: 10.1017/CBO9781139519526.043

Schiff, D. (2021). Out of the lab and into the classroom: The future of artificial intelligence in education. *AERA Open*. Advance online publication. DOI: 10.1177/23328584211037513

Schmidt, P., Biessmann, F., & Teubner, T. (2020). Transparency and trust in artificial intelligence systems. *Journal of Decision Systems*, 29(2), 260–278. DOI: 10.1080/12460125.2020.1819094

Schrauben, K., Owen-DeSchryver, J., & Cale, S. (2019). STRIVE to improve educational outcomes: Supporting students with disabilities in the general education classroom. *Educational Psychology*, 58(16), 171–185. Advance online publication. DOI: 10.5604/01.3001.0013.6372

Schunk, D., & Ertmer, P. (2000). Self-Regulation and academic learning. Handbook of Self-Regulation, 631–649. DOI: 10.1016/B978-012109890-2/50048-2

Settembre, J. (2024). College student put on academic probation for using Grammarly: "AI violation. https://nypost.com/2024/02/21/tech/student-put-on-probation-for-using-grammarly-ai-violation/

Shams, L., & Seitz, A. R. (2008). Benefits of multisensory learning. *Trends in Cognitive Sciences*, 12(11), 411–417. DOI: 10.1016/j.tics.2008.07.006 PMID: 18805039

SmartClick. (2022). Machine Learning Solutions & Artificial Intelligence https://www.smartclick.ai/

Soleimani, M., Intezari, A., Taskin, N., & Pauleen, D. (2021). Cognitive biases in developing biased artificial intelligence recruitment systems. In *Proceedings of the 54th Hawaii International Conference on System Sciences* (pp. 1-9). DOI: 10.24251/HICSS.2021.620

Srinivasan, R., & Chander, A. (2021). Biases in AI Systems. *ACM Queue; Tomorrow's Computing Today*, 19(2), 45–64. DOI: 10.1145/3466132.3466134

Swan, C. (2017). Personalized learning: Understandings and effectiveness in practice. *Journal of Initial Teacher Inquiry*, 3, 3–6. DOI: 10.26021/834

Tanveer, M., Hassan, S., & Bhaumik, A. (2020). Academic Policy Regarding Sustainability and Artificial Intelligence (AI). *Sustainability (Basel)*, 12(22), 9435. DOI: 10.3390/su12229435

Tapalova, O., & Zhiyenbayeva, N. (2022). Artificial intelligence in education: AIEd for personalised learning pathways. *Electronic Journal of e-Learning*, 20(5), 639–653. https://files.eric.ed.gov/fulltext/EJ1373006.pdf. DOI: 10.34190/ejel.20.5.2597

Texthelp. (2023). Equatio. Retrieved from https://www.texthelp.com/

Thompson, J. R., Walker, V. L., Felce, D., Jenkins, R., Kerr, M., Lowe, K., & Linehan, C. (2020). Planning supports for students with intellectual disability in general education classrooms. *Inclusion (Washington, D.C.)*, 8(1), 27–42. DOI: 10.1352/2326-6988-8.1.27

Tobii Dynavox. (2023). *Tobii Dynavox I-Series*. Retrieved from Tobii Dynavox.

Tokuhama-Espinosa, T. (2019). The learning sciences framework in educational leadership. *Frontiers in Education*, 4(136), 1–20. DOI: 10.3389/feduc.2019.00136

Tripp, B., & Shortlidge, E. (2019). A Framework to guide undergraduate education in interdisciplinary science. *CBE Life Sciences Education*, 18(2), es3. Advance online publication. DOI: 10.1187/cbe.18-11-0226 PMID: 31120394

United Nations Educational, Scientific and Cultural Organization (UNESCO). (2023). Guidance for generative AI in education and research. https://unesdoc.unesco.org/ark:/48223/pf0000386693

U.S. Department of Education. Office of Educational Technology, Artificial Intelligence and Future of Teaching and Learning: Insights and Recommendations, Washington, DC, 2023. https://tech.ed.gov

Van der Vorst, T., & Jelicic, N. (2019). *Artificial intelligence in education: Can AI bring the full potential of personalized learning to education? 30th European Conference of the International Telecommunications Society (ITS): "Towards a Connected and Automated Society", Helsinki, Finland, 16th-19th June, 2019, International Telecommunications Society*. ITS., https://hdl.handle.net/10419/205222

Varona, D., & Suárez, J. (2022). Discrimination, Bias, Fairness, and Trustworthy AI. *Applied Sciences (Basel, Switzerland)*, 12(12), 5826. Advance online publication. DOI: 10.3390/app12125826

Vembi Technologies. (2024). Hexis-Antara: Braille reader for visually impaired children. Retrieved from https://vembi.in/wp/hexis/

Waldron, N., & McLeskey, J. (2010). Establishing a Collaborative School Culture Through Comprehensive School Reform. *Journal of Educational & Psychological Consultation*, 20(1), 58–74. DOI: 10.1080/10474410903535364

Walker, V., Carpenter, M., Kittelman, A., & Rowe, D. (2023). Supports planning to improve access and participation in general education classrooms for students with disabilities. *Teaching Exceptional Children*, 55(4), 232–235. DOI: 10.1177/00400599231167479

Wang, Y. (2021). When artificial intelligence meets educational leaders' data-informed decision-making: A cautionary tale. *Studies in Educational Evaluation*, 69, 100872. DOI: 10.1016/j.stueduc.2020.100872

Waymo. (2023). Waymo Self-Driving Cars. Retrieved from Waymo

Wong, P. C. M., Vuong, L. C., & Liu, K. (2017). Personalized learning: From neurogenetics of behaviors to designing optimal language training. *Neuropsychologia*, 98, 192–200. DOI: 10.1016/j.neuropsychologia.2016.10.002 PMID: 27720749

Zimmerman, B. J. (2000). Attaining self-regulation. *Handbook of self-regulation*, 13–39. DOI: 10.1016/B978-012109890-2/50031-7

Zimmerman, B. J. (2008). Investigating self-regulation and motivation: Historical background, methodological developments, and future prospects. *American Educational Research Journal*, 45(1), 166–183. DOI: 10.3102/0002831207312909

Chapter 3
Artificial Intelligence in Special Education: Enhancing Learning Outcomes for Students With Disabilities

R. Krishna Kumari
https://orcid.org/0000-0002-1802-628X
Career Development Centre, SRM Institute of Science and Technology, India

ABSTRACT

The integration of Artificial Intelligence (AI) into the educational sector has revolutionized traditional teaching methods, presenting both opportunities and challenges. While extensive discussions have explored AI's role in general education, its specific applications and implications in Special Education (SE) remain underexplored. This chapter aims to bridge that gap by examining the potential of AI to provide personalized, data-driven support for students with disabilities. We will explore how AI can facilitate early detection of learning disabilities, enhance individualized learning plans, and improve communication between educators and stakeholders. Additionally, we will address the ethical considerations, data privacy issues, and potential biases inherent in AI systems. By offering a balanced view of the promises and pitfalls of AI in SE, this chapter seeks to equip educators, policymakers, and researchers with the knowledge necessary to harness AI responsibly and effectively.

INTRODUCTION

The educational field has been greatly impacted by the emergence of Artificial Intelligence (AI). This transformative technology has spurred a plethora of discussions, informative sessions, and diverse perspectives on the reliability and authen-

DOI: 10.4018/979-8-3693-5538-1.ch003

ticity of utilizing AI in general education. Yet, amidst this burgeoning discourse, there is a noticeable gap in information and dialogue regarding the intersection of AI and Special Education (SE). This book aims to delve deeply into this specific area, offering a comprehensive understanding that will bridge this gap. AI has the potential to offer substantial advantages for students with disabilities, provided certain parameters and criteria are met. These potential benefits are vast and multifaceted, encompassing personalized learning experiences, early detection and intervention of learning difficulties, and enhanced communication and collaboration among educators, parents, and stakeholders (Bhatti et al., 2024). However, various factors need to be taken into account when considering the implementation of AI in SE to ensure these benefits are fully realized (Kharbat et al., 2021).

A key consideration is the need for personalized and individualized support for students with disabilities. AI has the capability to analyze vast amounts of data and provide tailored learning experiences for each student, taking into account their unique needs and learning styles (Garg & Sharma, 2020). This personalized approach can significantly bridge the gap between students with disabilities and their peers, ensuring that each student receives the specific support they require to succeed academically. For example, AI-driven tools can adapt learning materials to match the pace and level of understanding of individual students, thereby enhancing their engagement and comprehension (Mehta et al., 2023). Additionally, AI can play a crucial role in the early detection and intervention of learning difficulties and disabilities. By analyzing patterns in student behavior and performance, AI systems can identify potential learning challenges at an early stage (Ali et al., 2023). This early identification allows educators to intervene promptly, providing appropriate support and resources before the issues escalate (Hopcan et al., 2023). Early intervention is critical in mitigating the long-term impacts of learning disabilities, making AI an invaluable tool in the proactive management of special education needs (Confer, 2023).

Furthermore, AI can enhance communication and collaboration between educators, parents, and other stakeholders involved in the education of students with disabilities (Kalonde et al., 2024). By providing real-time data and insights, AI facilitates more effective decision-making and coordination of efforts (Şen & Akbay, 2023). For instance, AI can generate detailed progress reports that highlight a student's achievements and areas needing improvement, enabling all parties to stay informed and aligned in their support strategies (Jadán-Guerrero et al., 2024). This enhanced communication ensures that everyone involved is equipped with the necessary information to support the student's learning and development effectively (Huera et al., 2024).

However, while the potential benefits of AI in SE are significant, it is crucial to acknowledge the ethical considerations and potential challenges associated with its use. There are valid concerns about data privacy, bias in AI algorithms, and the risk of AI diminishing human interaction and empathy in the educational setting (Rice & Dunn, 2023). Data privacy is a paramount concern, as the use of AI involves collecting and analyzing sensitive information about students. Ensuring that this data is protected and used responsibly is essential to maintaining trust and safeguarding student privacy (Zdravkova, 2022). Bias in AI algorithms is another critical issue. If not properly addressed, biases in the data used to train AI systems can lead to unfair and inaccurate outcomes (Zdravkova et al., 2022). This is particularly concerning in SE, where vulnerable populations could be adversely affected. Therefore, it is imperative that AI systems are developed and implemented with a strong emphasis on fairness, transparency, and accountability (Kumar et al., 2023).

Moreover, the potential for AI to replace human interaction and empathy in education raises significant concerns. While AI can provide valuable support and insights, it cannot replicate the nuanced understanding and emotional connection that human educators bring to their interactions with students (Mehta et al., 2023). Ensuring that AI is used to augment rather than replace human involvement is crucial in maintaining the empathetic and supportive environment that is essential for effective special education (Bhatti et al., 2024).

Overall, the intersection of AI and Special Education holds great promise for improving outcomes for students with disabilities. By leveraging the capabilities of AI in a thoughtful and responsible manner, educators can provide more personalized and effective support for these students, ultimately helping them to reach their full potential (Kharbat et al., 2021). The chapters included in this book will provide comprehensive insights into the future of education, specifically focusing on the transformative potential of AI in Special Education. Through detailed analyses, case studies, and discussions on ethical considerations, this work aims to equip educators, policymakers, and stakeholders with the knowledge and tools needed to harness AI effectively and ethically in the service of students with disabilities.

Objectives

The primary objective of this book is to enhance the comprehension of Artificial Intelligence (AI) in the context of Special Education (SE). This publication will offer a thorough examination of the advantages and disadvantages linked to AI in specialized instruction, along with its potential implications in terms of legality, ethics, and instruction. It will delve into a comprehensive analysis of the pros and cons of AI in the field of learning and teaching. By delving into the different facets of AI in special education, this work will contribute to a more profound understanding of how AI can be efficiently employed to aid and enrich the educational journeys of students with disabilities. This work will explore case studies and real-life examples of how AI has been successfully integrated into special education programs, showcasing the positive impact it can have on students' learning outcomes and overall educational experience. It will also address concerns and challenges surrounding the use of AI in special education, such as data privacy, bias, and the potential for technology to replace human interaction in the classroom.

The ultimate goal of this chapter is to provide educators, policymakers, and other stakeholders in the field of special education with a comprehensive overview of the current landscape of AI in education, as well as practical guidance on how to effectively implement and leverage AI technologies to support students with disabilities. By fostering a deeper understanding of the opportunities and challenges presented by AI in special education, this book aims to empower educators to make informed decisions about the use of technology in their classrooms and ensure that all students have access to the resources and support they need to succeed.

BACKGROUND AND LITERATURE REVIEW

Historical Context of AI in Education

The integration of Artificial Intelligence (AI) into education has a history that spans several decades, marked by continuous innovation and development. The journey of AI in education can be traced through several key phases, each characterized by significant technological advancements and evolving educational applications. Figure 1 shows the timeline of AI in education.

Figure 1. Timeline of AI in education

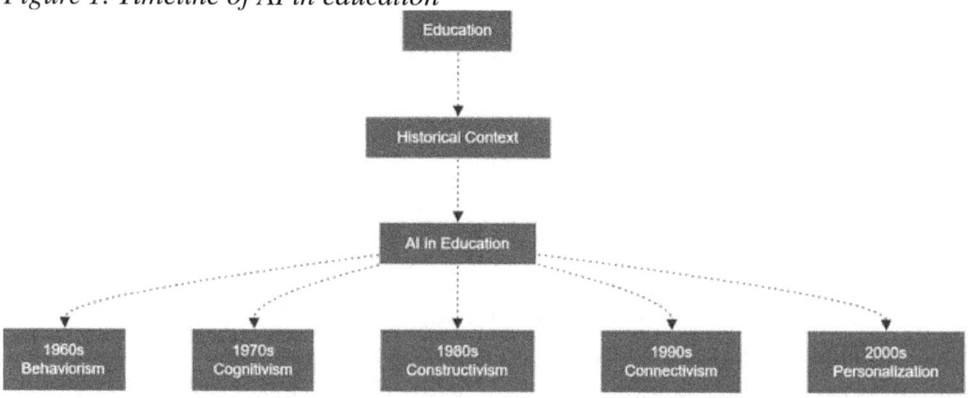

1970s-1980s: The Emergence of Intelligent Tutoring Systems (ITS)

The concept of Intelligent Tutoring Systems (ITS) emerged in the 1970s and 1980s, laying the groundwork for the use of AI in personalized learning. ITS aimed to simulate the guidance and feedback provided by human tutors, adapting to the individual needs of students. Early ITS were developed to provide personalized instruction in various subjects, particularly mathematics and computer programming. These systems used rule-based algorithms to deliver content and feedback, adjusting to the learner's responses.

One notable example from this era is the SCHOLAR system, developed by Jaime Carbonell in the early 1970s. SCHOLAR was designed to teach geography through a dialog-based approach, engaging students in interactive question-and-answer sessions. Despite the limited computational power of the time, SCHOLAR demonstrated the potential of AI to provide personalized and adaptive learning experiences.

1990s: Advancements in Computational Power and Algorithms

By the 1990s, advancements in computational power and algorithms enabled more sophisticated AI applications in education. Tools such as cognitive tutors, which offered step-by-step assistance in subjects like mathematics, became more common. These early AI systems were primarily rule-based, relying on predefined logic and heuristics to guide their interactions with students.

One significant development was the Cognitive Tutor system, developed by researchers at Carnegie Mellon University. This system used cognitive models to represent the processes students use to solve problems, allowing it to provide targeted hints and feedback based on the student's current understanding. Cognitive Tutors were implemented in classrooms and showed promising results in improving student achievement, particularly in mathematics.

2000s: The Advent of Machine Learning

The 2000s saw the advent of machine learning, a subfield of AI that allows systems to learn from data rather than relying solely on pre-programmed rules. This paradigm shift enabled the development of more adaptive and intelligent educational technologies. AI-driven platforms like Khan Academy and Coursera began to incorporate machine learning algorithms to personalize learning experiences, track student progress, and provide targeted recommendations.

Machine learning enabled these platforms to analyze vast amounts of student data, identifying patterns and making predictions about student performance. For example, Khan Academy's learning platform uses machine learning algorithms to recommend practice exercises and instructional videos tailored to each student's learning needs. This approach helps to ensure that students receive the right level of challenge and support, fostering a more personalized and effective learning experience.

2010s: The Rise of Deep Learning and Natural Language Processing (NLP)

In the past decade, AI in education has expanded rapidly with the advent of deep learning, natural language processing (NLP), and other advanced AI techniques. These technologies have given rise to sophisticated applications such as automated grading systems, intelligent virtual assistants, and AI-powered learning management systems that offer real-time feedback and support to students.

Deep learning, a subset of machine learning, involves neural networks with many layers that can learn complex patterns from large datasets. This technology has been used to develop automated grading systems that can assess student essays and provide feedback on grammar, style, and content. For example, automated essay scoring systems like E-Rater, developed by Educational Testing Service (ETS), use deep learning algorithms to evaluate written responses with a level of accuracy comparable to human graders.

Natural language processing (NLP) has also revolutionized educational applications by enabling AI systems to understand and generate human language. Intelligent virtual assistants, such as IBM's Watson Tutor, use NLP to engage students in interactive dialogues, answering questions, and providing explanations. These virtual assistants can offer personalized tutoring and support, helping students to overcome learning challenges and achieve their academic goals.

2020s: AI-powered Adaptive Learning Platforms

Today, AI continues to transform education through innovative applications and research. AI-powered adaptive learning platforms, such as DreamBox and Smart Sparrow, provide personalized learning paths based on real-time data analysis. These systems continually adjust the content and pace of instruction to match each student's progress, ensuring an optimal learning experience.

In addition to personalized learning, AI is being used to enhance administrative and support functions in education. Predictive analytics tools help educators identify at-risk students and intervene early to provide necessary support. AI-driven chatbots assist with administrative tasks, such as answering student queries and managing course enrollments, freeing up educators to focus more on teaching and mentoring.

Looking forward, the integration of AI in education is expected to continue evolving, driven by ongoing advancements in AI technologies and pedagogical research. Emerging trends include the use of AI for immersive learning experiences through augmented reality (AR) and virtual reality (VR), as well as the development of more sophisticated AI systems that can understand and respond to the emotional and social needs of students.

Thus, the historical context of AI in education reflects a journey of continuous innovation and improvement. From the early days of rule-based Intelligent Tutoring Systems to the current era of machine learning and deep learning, AI has progressively enhanced the ability to provide personalized, adaptive, and effective educational experiences. As AI technologies continue to advance, their potential to transform education and support diverse learning needs, including those in Special Education, will only grow stronger.

Current State of AI in Special Education

The application of Artificial Intelligence (AI) in Special Education (SE) is a more recent development, but it holds significant promise for transforming the educational experiences of students with disabilities. AI technologies are being used in various capacities to support SE, offering innovative solutions that enhance learning, accessibility, communication, and early intervention. Here, we delve into the current state of AI in SE, exploring its diverse applications, potential benefits, and the challenges that need to be addressed for broader adoption and scalability (see Table 1). One prominent application of AI in SE is the use of adaptive learning platforms that cater to the unique needs of students with disabilities. These platforms leverage AI algorithms to adjust the difficulty level and presentation of educational content based on the student's performance and preferences. For example, AI can modify the complexity of reading materials or offer alternative representations of mathematical problems to accommodate different learning styles.

AI is also being used to develop assistive technologies that support communication and interaction for students with disabilities. Speech-to-text and text-to-speech systems, powered by NLP, are helping students with hearing or speech impairments to communicate more effectively. Similarly, AI-driven eye-tracking and gesture-recognition technologies are enabling students with physical disabilities to interact with digital content in more accessible ways. Furthermore, AI is facilitating the early detection and diagnosis of learning disabilities. Machine learning algorithms can analyze student performance data to identify patterns indicative of specific learning challenges, such as dyslexia or ADHD. Early detection allows for timely interventions, tailored support plans, and better educational outcomes for students.

Table 1. AI in Special Education

Category	Description	Benefits	Challenges	Considerations	Example
Adaptive Learning Platforms	AI algorithms personalize learning content (difficulty, format) based on student performance and preferences.	* Addresses diverse learning styles * Provides targeted practice and support * Fosters engagement and motivation	* Limited content availability for all areas * Potential for over-reliance on AI over teacher expertise * Algorithmic bias in content selection	* Requires ongoing development and content updates * Regular human oversight and teacher input crucial	* DreamBox Learning (math) * Smart Sparrow (e-learning)
Assistive Technologies	AI-powered tools enhance communication and interaction for students with disabilities.	* Improves accessibility to educational materials * Enables independent learning and participation * Promotes self-confidence and communication skills	* Cost of technology and implementation * Need for training and support for students and educators * Potential technical difficulties	* Data privacy and security concerns * Importance of user-centered design and accessibility standards	* Google Live Transcribe (speech-to-text) * Kurzweil 3000 (text-to-speech) * Tobii Dynavox (eye-tracking) * Leap Motion (gesture recognition)
Early Detection and Diagnosis	Machine learning analyzes student data to identify patterns indicative of learning disabilities.	* Enables early intervention and support * Improves long-term educational outcomes * Provides valuable insights for educators and specialists	* Accuracy of AI models in identifying specific disabilities * Potential for misdiagnosis or over-identification * Ethical implications of data collection and use	* Requires robust data sets and diverse representation * Ongoing research and development to refine algorithms * Transparency in data collection and usage practices	* CortiQ (EEG analysis) * Ninaad (dyslexia identification)
Enhanced Communication and Collaboration	AI generates data and insights to facilitate communication among educators, parents, and stakeholders.	* Informs data-driven decision making * Promotes collaboration and shared understanding * Provides real-time progress reports for students	* Teacher workload in managing data and reports * Potential for information overload or misinterpretation * Ensuring accessibility of data visualizations	* Focus on actionable insights and clear communication * Develop user-friendly interfaces and reporting tools * Ongoing training and support for educators	*BrightBytes (data analytics) * Classcraft (classroom management)

Challenges and Considerations

Despite these advancements, the integration of AI in SE is still in its nascent stages, and there is considerable potential for further innovation and development. Current implementations are often pilot projects or limited to specific contexts, highlighting the need for broader adoption and scalability.

Data Privacy and Security: The use of AI in SE involves collecting and analyzing sensitive information about students, raising significant concerns about data privacy and security. Ensuring that student data is protected and used ethically is crucial for maintaining trust and safeguarding privacy.

Bias in AI Algorithms: AI systems can inadvertently perpetuate existing biases present in the data used to train them. This can lead to unfair and discriminatory outcomes, particularly in SE, where diverse student needs must be equitably addressed. Developing AI algorithms that are fair, transparent, and accountable is essential to avoid bias and ensure equitable treatment for all students.

Implementation and Scalability: Integrating AI into SE requires significant resources, training, and infrastructure. Ensuring that schools and educators are equipped to effectively implement and scale AI technologies is a substantial challenge. Providing professional development and support for educators is crucial to help them harness the potential of AI in their teaching practices.

Ethical Considerations: The ethical use of AI in SE involves navigating complex issues related to consent, autonomy, and the potential consequences of AI decisions on students' lives. Establishing ethical frameworks and guidelines is necessary to govern the responsible use of AI in this context.

Thus, the current state of AI in Special Education reflects a burgeoning field with significant promise for improving educational outcomes for students with disabilities. While there are challenges to address, the potential benefits of AI in providing personalized learning experiences, enhancing accessibility, facilitating early intervention, and improving communication and collaboration are substantial. By continuing to innovate and develop AI technologies with careful consideration of ethical, privacy, and implementation issues, educators and stakeholders can work towards a more inclusive and effective educational environment for all students.

THE POTENTIAL OF AI IN SPECIAL EDUCATION

Artificial Intelligence (AI) holds significant potential to transform Special Education (SE) by offering innovative solutions to longstanding challenges. Below, we explore the key areas where AI can make a substantial impact: personalized learning experiences, early detection and intervention of learning disabilities, and enhancing communication and collaboration among stakeholders.

Personalized Learning Experiences

Customization and Adaptation

• AI can analyze individual student performance data to tailor educational content to their unique needs. For example, adaptive learning platforms can adjust the complexity of reading materials or offer alternative representations of mathematical problems based on a student's progress and learning style.

• AI systems provide immediate feedback, helping students understand their mistakes and learn more effectively. This instant feedback loop can be particularly beneficial for students with disabilities, who may require more frequent and specific guidance.

Engagement and Motivation

• AI-driven tools, such as educational games and interactive simulations, can make learning more engaging and fun. These tools often include features that adapt to the student's pace and preferences, maintaining their interest and motivation.

• AI can help students set realistic learning goals and track their progress toward achieving them. Personalized dashboards can show students and their educators how they are progressing, which can be highly motivating and provide a sense of accomplishment.

Case Studies and Examples

• Programs like Carnegie Learning's Cognitive Tutor use AI to provide step-by-step assistance in subjects like mathematics, adapting in real-time to the student's responses.

• Tools like Duolingo use AI to customize lessons based on the user's performance, offering a model that could be applied to various subjects in SE.

Early Detection and Intervention of Learning Disabilities

Pattern Recognition and Diagnosis

- AI can sift through vast amounts of data to identify patterns indicative of learning disabilities such as dyslexia, ADHD, or autism spectrum disorder (ASD). By analyzing metrics such as reading speed, error rates, and response times, AI can detect potential issues that might not be immediately evident to human observers.
- Machine learning models can predict the likelihood of a student developing a learning disability based on early performance data, allowing for preemptive action.

Timely Interventions

- Once a learning disability is detected, AI can help develop tailored intervention plans that address the specific needs of the student. These plans can include recommended teaching strategies, resources, and accommodations.
- AI systems can continuously monitor the effectiveness of interventions, making adjustments as needed to ensure the student receives the most effective support.

Case Studies and Examples

- AI-driven programs like Lexplore use eye-tracking technology and machine learning to identify reading difficulties in young children, enabling early and targeted intervention.
- AI applications like Brain Power's Empower Me use wearables and AI to analyze behavioral patterns in children with autism, helping caregivers and educators tailor their approaches.

Enhancing Communication and Collaboration Among Stakeholders

Streamlining Communication

- AI platforms can facilitate real-time sharing of student performance data among teachers, parents, and specialists. This ensures that all stakeholders have up-to-date information and can collaborate effectively on the student's educational plan.
- AI can automate the generation of progress reports, Individualized Education Program (IEP) updates, and other documentation, reducing the administrative burden on educators and allowing them to focus more on direct interaction with students.

Decision-Making Support

- AI systems can provide educators and parents with actionable insights derived from data analysis, helping them make informed decisions about the student's educational needs and interventions.
- Platforms that incorporate AI can include features like shared calendars, task management, and communication channels that facilitate better coordination among all parties involved in the student's education.

Case Studies and Examples

- AI-driven systems like Frontline Education offer comprehensive tools for managing IEPs, including progress tracking, compliance checks, and communication features.
- Apps such as ClassDojo and Remind use AI to help teachers communicate more efficiently with parents, sharing updates and feedback in real-time.

AI has the potential to revolutionize Special Education by providing personalized learning experiences, facilitating early detection and intervention of learning disabilities, and enhancing communication and collaboration among stakeholders. By leveraging AI technologies thoughtfully and ethically, educators can significantly improve educational outcomes for students with disabilities, ensuring they receive the support and resources they need to thrive. This exploration underscores the need for continued innovation and investment in AI applications tailored to the unique challenges and opportunities in Special Education.

CASE STUDIES AND REAL-LIFE EXAMPLES

The integration of Artificial Intelligence (AI) in Special Education (SE) is showing promise worldwide, with various implementations demonstrating significant improvements in educational outcomes for students with disabilities. This section explores specific case studies and real-life examples, analyzing their results and distilling key lessons learned from these implementations.

Successful Implementations of AI in Special Education

1. **Lexplore: AI-driven Early Literacy Assessment**

   Overview: Lexplore employs AI and eye-tracking technology to assess reading skills in children. By analyzing eye movements, the system can identify reading difficulties, such as dyslexia, early on.

Outcomes: Schools using Lexplore report that early identification of reading challenges allows for timely and targeted interventions, leading to improved reading skills and student confidence. The data-driven approach provides objective insights, often identifying issues that traditional assessments miss.

Lessons Learned: Lexplore's success highlights the importance of early screening and the power of AI in providing objective, data-driven insights. This case study underscores the need for schools to invest in technology that can aid in early detection and intervention.

2. **Brain Power: Empower Me for Autism**

   Overview: Empower Me is a suite of AI-powered wearable devices designed to support children with autism. These devices use machine learning to analyze behavioral data and provide real-time feedback to caregivers and educators.

   Outcomes: The use of Empower Me has led to improved social interactions, communication skills, and reduced anxiety in children with autism. The ability to provide real-time data and feedback enables immediate adjustments in support strategies, enhancing the effectiveness of interventions.

   Lessons Learned: Empower Me demonstrates the potential of AI to provide personalized, real-time support. The involvement of caregivers and educators in the implementation process is crucial to ensure the technology is used effectively and benefits the students.

3. **Carnegie Learning's MATHia**

   Overview: MATHia is an AI-driven math tutoring program that provides personalized instruction based on each student's progress and learning needs. It adjusts the difficulty and type of problems in real-time to support individual learning paths.

   Outcomes: Students using MATHia show significant improvements in math proficiency compared to traditional teaching methods. The program's adaptive nature helps keep students engaged and motivated, which is especially beneficial for those with learning disabilities.

   Lessons Learned: MATHia underscores the effectiveness of AI in creating personalized learning experiences that adapt to individual student needs. Continuous monitoring and real-time adjustments are key components of its success.

Analysis of Specific Programs and Their Outcomes

1. **Knewton: Adaptive Learning Platform**

Overview: Knewton is an adaptive learning platform that uses AI to personalize educational content across various subjects. The platform adjusts learning pathways based on real-time analysis of student performance.

Outcomes: Schools using Knewton report increased student engagement and higher achievement scores. The platform's ability to identify and address individual learning gaps is particularly beneficial for students with learning disabilities.

Lessons Learned: Knewton's success highlights the necessity of integrating AI seamlessly into existing curricula and the value of real-time data in supporting personalized learning. The platform's adaptability to different subjects and contexts enhances its utility.

2. **Microsoft's Seeing AI**

   Overview: Seeing AI is an app designed to assist visually impaired individuals by using AI to describe people, text, and objects through a smartphone camera. The app provides real-time auditory feedback to users.

   Outcomes: Visually impaired students using Seeing AI report greater independence and confidence in navigating both educational and everyday environments. The app's user-friendly interface and accurate real-time descriptions enhance accessibility and participation.

   Lessons Learned: Seeing AI underscores the importance of accessibility-focused design in AI applications. This case study illustrates the significant impact such tools can have on enhancing independence and engagement for students with disabilities.

3. **Cognii Virtual Learning Assistant**

   Overview: Cognii offers an AI-powered virtual learning assistant that engages students in natural language dialogue to reinforce learning. It provides personalized tutoring and instant feedback.

   Outcomes: Schools using Cognii observe improved critical thinking and writing skills among students. The interactive nature of the virtual assistant helps students articulate their thoughts and receive immediate guidance, enhancing their learning experience.

   Lessons Learned: Cognii highlights the potential of AI to enhance higher-order thinking skills. Interactive and responsive educational tools play a significant role in engaging students and fostering deeper learning.

Lessons Learned from These Implementations

1. **Early and Continuous Engagement**
    - o **Stakeholder Involvement**: Successful implementations emphasize the need for involving educators, students, and parents from the outset. This ensures AI tools are user-friendly and meet actual needs.
    - o **Training and Support**: Providing adequate training and ongoing support for educators is crucial. Educators need to understand how to integrate AI tools effectively into their teaching practices.
2. **Customization and Flexibility**
    - o **Tailored Solutions**: AI implementations in SE need to be flexible and customizable to address the diverse needs of students with disabilities. One-size-fits-all approaches are less effective.
    - o **Real-Time Adjustments**: The ability of AI systems to make real-time adjustments based on student performance is a key factor in their success. Continuous monitoring and adaptation help maintain student engagement and improve learning outcomes.
3. **Ethical Considerations and Data Privacy**
    - o **Privacy Protections**: Ensuring robust data privacy and security measures is essential. Trust in AI tools can only be built if students' personal information is safeguarded.
    - o **Bias Mitigation**: Efforts must be made to identify and mitigate biases in AI algorithms. Diverse and representative training data are critical to developing fair and unbiased AI systems.
4. **Measurable Outcomes**
    - o **Evidence-Based Impact**: Successful implementations often have clear metrics for measuring impact, such as academic performance improvements, engagement levels, and user satisfaction. Regular assessments help refine and enhance AI tools.
5. **Sustainability and Scalability**
    - o **Resource Allocation**: Adequate resources, including funding and infrastructure, are necessary to sustain and scale AI initiatives in SE. Pilot programs should plan for long-term integration and expansion.
    - o **Scalability Plans**: Planning for scalability ensures that successful AI tools can be expanded to benefit a broader student population without losing effectiveness.

The case studies and real-life examples demonstrate the transformative potential of AI in Special Education. By providing personalized learning experiences, facilitating early detection and intervention of learning disabilities, and enhancing communication and collaboration, AI can significantly improve educational outcomes for students with disabilities. However, the successful implementation of AI requires careful consideration of stakeholder involvement, customization, ethical considerations, and scalability. These lessons learned can guide future efforts to harness AI's full potential in Special Education, ensuring that all students receive the support and resources they need to thrive.

ETHICAL CONSIDERATIONS AND CHALLENGES

The integration of Artificial Intelligence (AI) into Special Education (SE) offers substantial benefits but also raises several ethical considerations and challenges (see Figure 2). To ensure responsible and effective implementation, it is crucial to address concerns related to data privacy, bias in AI algorithms, and the potential impact on human interaction and empathy in education. This section provides a detailed exploration of these key ethical issues.

Figure 2. Flowchart of Ethical Considerations and Challenges in AI for Special Education

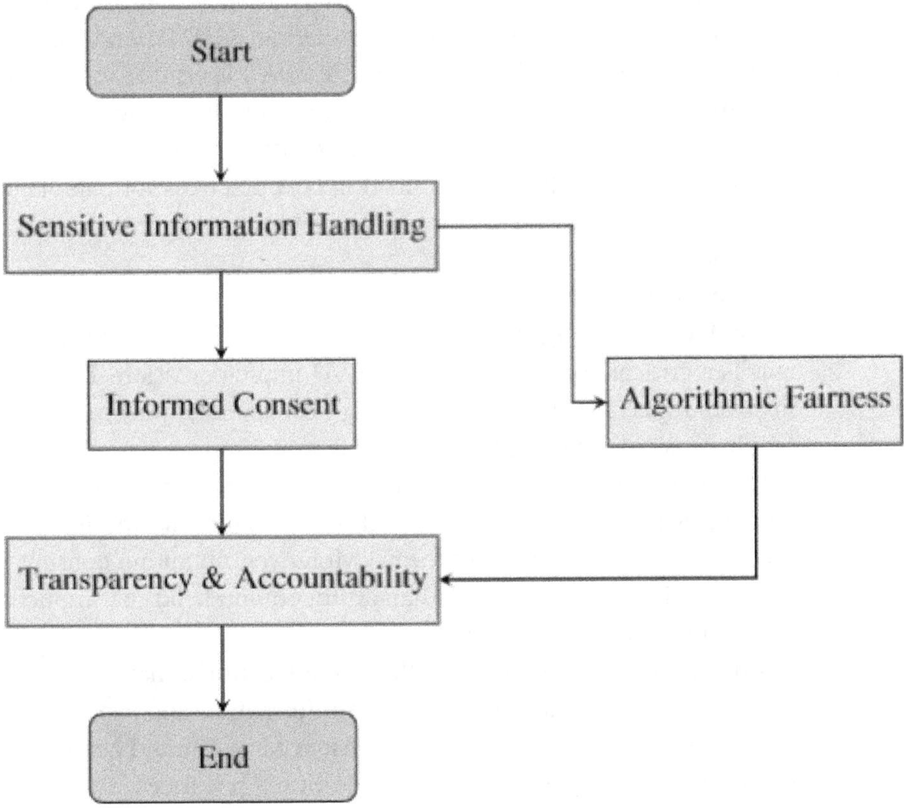

Data Privacy Concerns

1. **Sensitive Information Handling**
    - **Overview**: The deployment of AI in education necessitates the collection, storage, and analysis of significant amounts of student data. This data includes not only academic performance but also sensitive personal information, particularly pertinent in SE, where students' disabilities and specific educational needs are documented.
    - **Challenges**: Protecting this data from unauthorized access, breaches, and misuse poses a considerable challenge. The risk of exposure or exploitation of sensitive information can lead to significant harm to students and their families, including identity theft, stigmatization, and discrimination.

- **Solutions**: Ensuring robust data protection requires implementing advanced security measures, such as encryption, secure data storage solutions, and strict access control protocols. Adhering to legal frameworks, like the General Data Protection Regulation (GDPR) and the Family Educational Rights and Privacy Act (FERPA), is crucial for safeguarding student data. Additionally, conducting regular security audits and updating security protocols can help mitigate potential risks. Educators and administrators should be trained in best practices for data handling and privacy protection to ensure compliance and enhance security awareness.

2. **Informed Consent**
    - **Overview**: Obtaining informed consent from students and their guardians is a critical component of ethical AI implementation. This process involves transparently communicating how the data will be used, who will have access to it, and what protective measures are in place.
    - **Challenges**: Ensuring that consent is genuinely informed can be challenging due to the complexity of AI technologies and the legal terminology often used in consent forms. Moreover, obtaining consent from minors and ensuring that guardians fully comprehend the implications of data usage can be difficult.
    - **Solutions**: To address these challenges, educational institutions should strive to provide clear and accessible information about data usage in simple, understandable language. Consent forms should be straightforward, and institutions should offer additional resources, such as informational sessions or Q&A opportunities, to help guardians and students understand the implications of data sharing. Creating visual aids or videos that explain the consent process and data usage can also enhance understanding and facilitate informed decision-making.

Bias in AI Algorithms

1. **Algorithmic Fairness**
    - **Overview**: AI systems are trained on vast datasets, and the quality and diversity of these datasets significantly affect the AI's performance and fairness. If training data contains biases, the AI system is likely to perpetuate these biases, leading to unfair or discriminatory outcomes.
    - **Challenges**: In the context of SE, biased AI algorithms can disproportionately impact students with disabilities, resulting in unequal access to resources and support. For example, an AI system trained on data that

underrepresents certain disabilities may fail to accurately identify and assist those students.

- **Solutions**: Addressing bias requires using diverse and representative datasets during the training of AI algorithms. Continuous monitoring and evaluation of AI systems are necessary to identify and correct biases. Involving a diverse group of stakeholders, including educators, parents, and disability advocates, in the development and testing of AI systems can help ensure these tools are fair and inclusive. Implementing fairness-aware machine learning techniques and conducting regular audits for bias can further enhance algorithmic fairness.

2. **Transparency and Accountability**
    - **Overview**: Transparency in AI algorithms and decision-making processes is crucial for building trust and ensuring accountability. Stakeholders need to understand how AI systems arrive at specific conclusions or recommendations.
    - **Challenges**: AI systems, particularly those using complex machine learning techniques like deep learning, can be "black boxes" where the decision-making process is not easily understood or explained. This lack of transparency can lead to mistrust and difficulty in identifying and addressing biases.
    - **Solutions**: Developers should prioritize transparency by providing clear documentation and explanations of how their algorithms work. Implementing explainable AI (XAI) techniques can help make AI decisions more understandable. Establishing accountability mechanisms, such as regular audits and third-party evaluations, ensures AI systems function as intended and fairly. Open-sourcing AI models and providing detailed case studies on AI decision-making processes can further enhance transparency and accountability.

Potential Impact on Human Interaction and Empathy in Education

1. **Reduction of Human Interaction**
    - **Overview**: One major concern regarding the increasing use of AI in education is the potential reduction of human interaction. Education, especially SE, heavily relies on the empathy, understanding, and personalized support that educators provide.
    - **Challenges**: Over-reliance on AI could diminish the role of human educators, potentially affecting the quality of education and support students receive. There is a risk that AI might be used to replace rather

than augment human teachers, leading to a more impersonal educational experience.

- o **Solutions**: AI should be used as a tool to enhance, not replace, human interaction in education. AI can handle repetitive tasks and provide data-driven insights, freeing educators to focus on personalized instruction and emotional support. Hybrid models combining AI tools with human oversight and interaction can maintain the balance between technology and empathy in education. Professional development programs should emphasize the importance of maintaining human connection and provide strategies for effectively integrating AI while preserving essential human elements.

2. **Maintaining Empathy and Emotional Support**
   - o **Overview**: Empathy and emotional support are critical components of effective teaching, particularly in SE. Educators play a vital role in understanding and addressing the unique emotional and psychological needs of students with disabilities.
   - o **Challenges**: AI systems lack the ability to provide genuine empathy and emotional support. An increased focus on AI-driven solutions could lead to a more mechanized and less emotionally responsive educational environment.
   - o **Solutions**: To maintain the human element in education, it is important to integrate AI tools that support, rather than detract from, the emotional and empathetic aspects of teaching. AI should be designed to recognize when human intervention is necessary, ensuring educators remain at the forefront of providing personalized and empathetic support. Developing AI tools that assist educators in identifying students' emotional needs can enhance their ability to provide timely and appropriate interventions. Additionally, promoting a culture that values empathy and human connection within educational institutions can help balance the use of AI with essential emotional support.

While AI offers transformative potential in Special Education, addressing the ethical considerations and challenges is critical for its responsible and effective implementation. Ensuring data privacy and security, mitigating bias in AI algorithms, and maintaining the essential human elements of interaction and empathy are key to leveraging AI's benefits while minimizing its risks. By focusing on these ethical considerations, educators, policymakers, and technology developers can collaborate to create AI-driven solutions that enhance educational outcomes for students with disabilities, ensuring equity, fairness, and human connection. This balanced approach will help harness AI's full potential in Special Education, providing all students with the support and resources they need to thrive.

PRACTICAL GUIDANCE FOR IMPLEMENTATION

Integrating Artificial Intelligence (AI) into Special Education (SE) can significantly enhance the educational experiences of students with disabilities. To achieve this, it is essential to follow best practices, address challenges, and implement well-informed recommendations. This section expands on practical guidance for integrating AI in SE.

Best Practices for Integrating AI in Special Education

Building a strong foundation for AI in Special Education involves a focus on collaboration, responsible development, and accessibility. Educators, researchers, and developers working together can ensure AI solutions meet student needs. Rigorous research fuels continuous improvement, while ethical frameworks safeguard data and promote responsible AI use. Inclusive design principles and student feedback are vital for creating accessible AI tools. Figure 3 shows the practices for integrating AI in education.

Figure 3. Integrating AI in Special Education

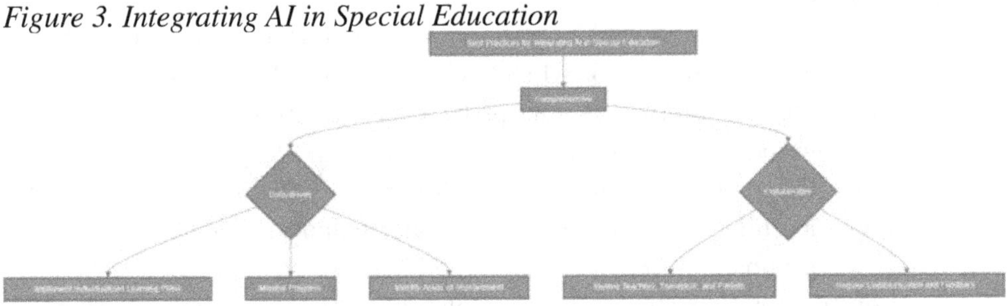

1. **Comprehensive Needs Assessment**
   - **Overview**: Conducting a thorough needs assessment helps identify the specific requirements of students with disabilities and how AI can meet those needs.
   - **Steps**:
     - Gather input from educators, parents, students, and other stakeholders to understand the diverse needs of students.

- Assess the current technological infrastructure and capabilities within the school or district.
- Identify specific gaps in resources or support where AI could provide substantial benefits.

- **Outcome**: A detailed understanding of the areas where AI can provide the most significant benefits, ensuring that resources are allocated effectively to address the unique needs of students with disabilities.

2. **Inclusive Design and Development**
   - **Overview**: AI tools should be designed with input from a diverse group of stakeholders to ensure they meet the needs of all students.
   - **Steps**:
     - Involve educators, parents, students, disability advocates, and AI developers early in the design process.
     - Conduct pilot programs to gather feedback from actual users and make necessary adjustments based on their experiences.
     - Ensure the design process includes considerations for accessibility and usability, particularly for students with various disabilities.
   - **Outcome**: AI tools that are more likely to be effective, inclusive, and user-friendly, tailored to the diverse needs of students in SE.
3. **Professional Development and Training**
   - **Overview**: Educators need ongoing training to effectively use AI tools and integrate them into their teaching practices.
   - **Steps**:
     - Provide initial and ongoing professional development sessions focused on the use of AI technologies in the classroom.
     - Include training on data privacy, ethical considerations, and how to identify and address potential biases in AI systems.
     - Offer resources and support for troubleshooting and continuous learning, such as online tutorials, helpdesks, and peer support groups.
   - **Outcome**: Educators who are confident and competent in using AI tools to enhance their teaching and support students with disabilities effectively.
4. **Data Governance and Privacy Protection**
   - **Overview**: Ensuring data privacy and security is crucial when implementing AI in SE.
   - **Steps**:
     - Develop clear policies and procedures for data collection, storage, and usage that comply with legal standards and best practices.

        - Implement strong encryption and security measures to protect student data from unauthorized access and breaches.
        - Regularly review and update data privacy practices, conducting audits to ensure compliance and address vulnerabilities.
    - **Outcome**: A secure environment where student data is protected, fostering trust among students, parents, and educators.
5. **Continuous Monitoring and Evaluation**
    - **Overview**: Regularly assessing the impact of AI tools helps ensure they are meeting their intended goals and allows for ongoing improvements.
    - **Steps**:
        - Establish metrics and benchmarks for evaluating the effectiveness of AI tools in improving educational outcomes for students with disabilities.
        - Collect and analyze data on student outcomes, engagement, and satisfaction to identify areas for improvement.
        - Make iterative improvements based on feedback and evaluation results, ensuring AI tools remain effective and relevant.
    - **Outcome**: AI tools that continually evolve and improve, providing better support for students with disabilities over time.

Strategies for Overcoming Challenges

1. **Addressing Data Privacy and Security Concerns**
    - **Challenge**: Protecting sensitive student data from breaches and misuse.
    - **Strategy**: Implement robust cybersecurity measures, conduct regular audits, and ensure compliance with data protection regulations. Educate all stakeholders on best practices for data security.
    - **Actions**:
        - Use encryption, secure servers, and multi-factor authentication to protect data.
        - Provide training on data privacy to educators, administrators, and IT staff.
        - Establish clear data governance policies and procedures.

2. **Mitigating Bias in AI Algorithms**
    - **Challenge**: Preventing AI systems from perpetuating existing biases.
    - **Strategy**: Use diverse and representative datasets, apply fairness-aware machine learning techniques, and regularly audit AI systems for bias. Involve diverse stakeholders in the development and evaluation process to ensure inclusive perspectives.

- o **Actions**:
    - ▪ Train AI models on datasets that represent the diverse student population.
    - ▪ Implement algorithmic fairness checks and bias detection tools.
    - ▪ Encourage ongoing dialogue with disability advocates and experts to identify and address potential biases.

3. **Balancing AI and Human Interaction**
    - o **Challenge**: Ensuring AI does not replace essential human interaction and empathy.
    - o **Strategy**: Use AI to augment, not replace, human educators. Implement hybrid models where AI handles repetitive tasks and provides data-driven insights, allowing educators to focus on personalized instruction and emotional support.
    - o **Actions**:
        - ▪ Design AI tools that complement and enhance teacher-student interactions.
        - ▪ Provide training on integrating AI tools into teaching practices without diminishing personal engagement.
        - ▪ Promote a classroom culture that values empathy and human connection.

4. **Ensuring Ethical Use of AI**
    - o **Challenge**: Navigating ethical concerns related to AI decision-making and autonomy.
    - o **Strategy**: Develop and adhere to ethical guidelines for AI use in SE. Ensure transparency in AI decision-making processes and establish accountability mechanisms. Provide training on ethical considerations and involve ethicists in AI implementation planning.
    - o **Actions**:
        - ▪ Create ethical guidelines and best practices for AI use in education.
        - ▪ Ensure AI systems have transparent decision-making processes and provide explanations for their recommendations.
        - ▪ Involve ethicists and legal experts in the development and oversight of AI initiatives.

5. **Scalability and Resource Allocation**
    - o **Challenge**: Scaling AI solutions across different educational settings with varying resources.

- **Strategy**: Start with pilot programs to refine AI tools and demonstrate their effectiveness. Secure funding and resources through grants, partnerships, and government support. Provide scalable solutions that can be adapted to different contexts and resource levels.
- **Actions**:
  - Pilot AI tools in select schools to gather data and refine implementations.
  - Apply for grants and seek partnerships with technology companies and research institutions.
  - Develop adaptable AI solutions that can be tailored to different educational environments and resource availability.

Table 2. Recommendations for Educators and Policymakers

Category	Recommendation	Action
Collaboration and Partnerships	Foster collaboration between stakeholders to develop and implement AI solutions for SE.	* Establish working groups with educators, researchers, policymakers, and technology developers. * Facilitate regular meetings and information sharing.
Research and Development	Invest in research to explore new AI applications and refine existing technologies.	* Fund research initiatives and pilot projects focused on AI in SE. * Encourage partnerships between educational institutions and AI research centers.
Policies and Guidelines	Develop comprehensive policies and guidelines for the ethical use of AI, data privacy, and security in SE.	* Collaborate with experts to create frameworks for responsible AI use. * Provide clear guidelines for implementation in schools. * Regularly review and update policies.
Accessibility and Inclusivity	Design AI tools that are accessible to all students with disabilities.	* Implement universal design principles. * Involve students with disabilities in testing and feedback. * Offer training and resources for educators on using AI tools effectively.
Resources and Support	Allocate resources for the effective implementation of AI in SE, including funding, training, and technical support.	* Secure grants, allocate budget resources, and establish support networks. * Provide training programs and technical assistance for educators. * Develop a central repository of resources (best practices, case studies, troubleshooting guides).

Integrating AI into Special Education offers immense potential to enhance educational experiences and outcomes for students with disabilities. Table 2 shows the recommendations for educators and policymakers. By following best practices, addressing challenges proactively, and implementing thoughtful policies and guidelines, educators and policymakers can harness the power of AI to create a more inclusive and effective educational environment. Ensuring the ethical and responsible use of AI, while maintaining a balance with human interaction and empathy, will be key to realizing the full benefits of AI in Special Education. This balanced approach will help harness AI's full potential in Special Education, providing all students with the support and resources they need to thrive.

FUTURE DIRECTIONS IN AI AND SPECIAL EDUCATION

As AI technology continues to advance, its potential to revolutionize Special Education (SE) becomes more pronounced. This section delves into the emerging trends, key areas for further research, and the future vision of AI in SE.

Emerging Trends in AI and Special Education

The field of special education is undergoing a transformation fueled by artificial intelligence. AI-powered adaptive learning systems are on the horizon, capable of tailoring the learning experience to each student's unique needs and emotional state in real-time. Immersive technologies like AR and VR are being harnessed to create interactive learning environments, allowing students to practice social skills safely or visualize complex concepts. AI is also driving advancements in assistive technologies, with smarter hearing aids and communication devices empowering students with disabilities. Data analysis is another exciting area, where AI can identify learning patterns and predict challenges, enabling educators to take proactive measures. Collaboration is further enhanced by AI tools that foster communication and share insights between educators and parents, ultimately supporting the development of optimal Individualized Education Plans (IEPs). For a detailed breakdown of these emerging trends, refer to Table 3.

Table 3. Emerging Trends in AI and Special Education

Category	Trend Description	Focus Area	Potential Benefits
Personalized Learning	Advanced Adaptive Learning Systems	Student-specific learning experiences	Increased engagement, improved comprehension, caters to individual needs and pace
Immersive Learning	Integration of Augmented Reality (AR) and Virtual Reality (VR)	Interactive and engaging learning environments	Practice social skills in safe settings, visualize complex concepts, maintain focus
Accessibility & Support	AI-Driven Assistive Technologies	Removing barriers to learning	Improved communication, enhanced access to educational materials, participation in activities
Data-Driven Decisions	Enhanced Data Analytics for Educational Insights	Identifying learning patterns and challenges	Proactive interventions, personalized teaching strategies, improved educational outcomes
Collaboration & Support	Collaborative AI Tools	Communication and coordination between educators, parents, and students	Informed decision-making, support for individualized education plans (IEPs), progress tracking

Potential Areas for Further Research

1. **Longitudinal Studies on AI Impact**
   - **Overview**: There is a need for long-term studies to assess the sustained impact of AI interventions in SE.
   - **Details**: Research should focus on tracking student outcomes over several years to determine the long-term benefits and potential drawbacks of AI technologies. This includes examining academic performance, social development, and emotional well-being over extended periods.
2. **AI Ethics and Fairness**
   - **Overview**: Ensuring ethical AI use and addressing biases in AI algorithms are critical areas for ongoing research.
   - **Details**: Studies should investigate methods for minimizing biases in AI systems, particularly in the context of diverse student populations. Research should also explore ethical frameworks for AI deployment in SE, ensuring transparency, accountability, and fairness in AI applications.
3. **AI and Human-Computer Interaction**
   - **Overview**: Understanding how students with disabilities interact with AI technologies is essential for optimizing their design and effectiveness.

- **Details**: Research should focus on the usability and accessibility of AI tools, examining factors such as user interface design, ease of use, and user satisfaction. This includes studying how AI can be designed to enhance, rather than detract from, human interaction and empathy in the educational process.

4. **AI in Early Childhood Education**
   - **Overview**: Investigating the role of AI in early childhood education for students with disabilities is a promising area for research.
   - **Details**: Early interventions can have a significant impact on long-term outcomes. Research should explore how AI can be used to identify and support young children with developmental delays or disabilities, providing tailored interventions at an early stage.
5. **Cross-Disciplinary Approaches**
   - **Overview**: Leveraging insights from multiple disciplines can enhance the development and implementation of AI in SE.
   - **Details**: Research should explore the intersection of AI with fields such as psychology, neuroscience, and educational theory to create more holistic and effective AI-driven educational tools. This includes studying how different disciplines can inform the design and deployment of AI technologies in SE.

Vision for the Future of AI in Enhancing Special Education

1. **Universal Accessibility and Inclusivity**
   - **Overview**: The future of AI in SE envisions a learning environment where all students, regardless of their disabilities, have access to high-quality education tailored to their unique needs.
   - **Details**: AI technologies will be universally designed to be inclusive and accessible, breaking down barriers to learning and providing equal opportunities for all students. This includes seamless integration of assistive technologies and personalized learning experiences that adapt to each student's strengths and challenges.
2. **Empowered Educators and Informed Decision-Making**
   - **Overview**: AI will serve as a powerful tool for educators, providing them with actionable insights and freeing up time for personalized instruction and support.
   - **Details**: Educators will have access to real-time data and analytics, enabling them to make informed decisions about teaching strategies and interventions. AI will handle routine administrative tasks, allowing

teachers to focus more on fostering meaningful interactions and relationships with their students.

3. **Collaborative and Connected Learning Communities**
   - o **Overview**: AI will facilitate greater collaboration and communication among all stakeholders in the educational ecosystem.
   - o **Details**: Advanced AI tools will connect educators, parents, students, and support staff, creating a cohesive and supportive learning community. These tools will provide platforms for sharing information, tracking progress, and coordinating efforts to support students' educational journeys.
4. **Ethically and Responsibly Deployed AI**
   - o **Overview**: The future of AI in SE will prioritize ethical considerations, ensuring that AI technologies are used responsibly and transparently.
   - o **Details**: Robust ethical frameworks and guidelines will govern the use of AI in education, protecting student privacy, promoting fairness, and ensuring accountability. Continuous monitoring and evaluation will ensure that AI systems are aligned with educational goals and societal values.
5. **Innovation and Continuous Improvement**
   - o **Overview**: The field of AI in SE will be characterized by ongoing innovation and continuous improvement.
   - o **Details**: Researchers, developers, and educators will work collaboratively to push the boundaries of what AI can achieve in SE. This includes exploring new applications, refining existing technologies, and incorporating feedback from users to ensure that AI tools remain effective and relevant.

The future of AI in Special Education holds immense promise for transforming the educational experiences of students with disabilities. By staying attuned to emerging trends, prioritizing ethical considerations, and fostering a culture of innovation and collaboration, educators and policymakers can harness the power of AI to create a more inclusive, effective, and supportive educational environment.

CONCLUSION

In conclusion, AI has the potential to revolutionize Special Education, offering new opportunities for personalized learning, accessibility, and support. By approaching the integration of AI with careful consideration and a commitment to ethical practices, stakeholders can ensure that AI serves as a powerful ally in enhancing the educational journeys of students with disabilities. The collective effort of educators, policymakers, researchers, parents, and students is crucial to harnessing the transformative power of AI and creating a more inclusive and effective educational landscape.

Summary of Key Findings

The exploration of Artificial Intelligence (AI) in Special Education (SE) has revealed a landscape rich with potential, yet fraught with challenges that require careful navigation. The key findings from this examination include:

1. **Personalized Learning**: AI technologies offer significant advantages in creating tailored learning experiences that accommodate the unique needs of students with disabilities. These systems can dynamically adjust content and instruction to optimize learning outcomes.
2. **Early Detection and Intervention**: AI's ability to analyze extensive datasets allows for the early identification of learning disabilities, facilitating timely and effective interventions that can significantly improve long-term educational outcomes.
3. **Enhanced Accessibility**: AI-powered assistive technologies, such as speech-to-text and text-to-speech systems, as well as eye-tracking and gesture-recognition tools, are making educational content more accessible to students with a wide range of disabilities.
4. **Improved Communication and Collaboration**: AI tools enhance the coordination and collaboration among educators, parents, and other stakeholders, ensuring that all parties have access to real-time data and insights that inform decision-making processes.
5. **Ethical and Implementation Challenges**: The integration of AI in SE must address significant challenges, including data privacy and security concerns, biases in AI algorithms, potential reductions in human interaction, and the need for robust ethical guidelines and frameworks.
6. **Future Potential**: Emerging trends such as advanced adaptive learning systems, the integration of AR and VR, AI-driven assistive technologies, enhanced data analytics, and collaborative AI tools indicate a promising future for AI in SE, with opportunities for further research and development.

Final Thoughts on the Role of AI in Special Education

The role of AI in Special Education is both transformative and complex. As the technology continues to evolve, its application in SE promises to provide unprecedented levels of support, accessibility, and personalization for students with disabilities. By leveraging AI, educators can create more inclusive learning environments that cater to the diverse needs of all students.

However, the deployment of AI in SE must be approached with caution. Ensuring that AI technologies are used ethically and responsibly is paramount. This includes addressing data privacy concerns, mitigating biases, maintaining the essential human elements of education, and providing adequate training and resources for educators. The goal should be to use AI as a tool to enhance human capabilities and interactions, rather than replace them.

Call to Action for Stakeholders to Leverage AI Responsibly

To realize the full potential of AI in Special Education, stakeholders must take deliberate and thoughtful actions:

1. **Educators**: Embrace AI technologies as tools to augment teaching practices, but remain vigilant about the ethical implications and ensure that AI complements rather than replaces human interaction and empathy. Continuous professional development and training on AI applications and their ethical use are essential.
2. **Policymakers**: Develop and implement policies that promote the responsible use of AI in SE. This includes establishing ethical guidelines, ensuring data privacy and security, and providing funding and resources for the integration and scaling of AI technologies in schools.
3. **Researchers and Developers**: Continue to innovate and refine AI technologies, focusing on creating inclusive, unbiased, and user-friendly tools. Conduct longitudinal studies to assess the long-term impact of AI in SE and ensure that developments are guided by evidence-based research.
4. **Parents and Guardians**: Stay informed about the use of AI in their children's education and advocate for technologies that prioritize their children's needs and rights. Engage with educators and policymakers to ensure that AI tools are implemented in ways that benefit students.
5. **Students**: Provide feedback on their experiences with AI technologies to help shape the development and implementation of tools that truly meet their needs. Empower students to use AI as a means to enhance their learning and self-advocacy skills.

REFERENCES

Ali, B. M., Maheswari, M., Nagendrudu, P. V. V. S. D., Rani, D. L., & Hashmi, A. (2023). Application of Artificial intelligence Assisted Robots to Improve the Educational Outcome for Special Children in Disability Education. *Journal for ReAttach Therapy and Developmental Diversities*, 6(9s), 328–337.

Bhatti, I., Mohi-U-din, S. F., Hayat, Y., & Tariq, M. (2024). Artificial Intelligence Applications for Students with Learning Disabilities: A Systematic Review. *European Journal of Science. Innovation and Technology*, 4(2), 40–56.

Confer, C. A. (2023). The Use of Artificial Intelligence to Create Inclusivity in Special Education Classrooms. *Journal of Applied Professional Studies*, 4(9).

Garg, S., & Sharma, S. (2020). Impact of artificial intelligence in special need education to promote inclusive pedagogy. *International Journal of Information and Education Technology (IJIET)*, 10(7), 523–527. DOI: 10.18178/ijiet.2020.10.7.1418

Hopcan, S., Polat, E., Ozturk, M. E., & Ozturk, L. (2023). Artificial intelligence in special education: A systematic review. *Interactive Learning Environments*, 31(10), 7335–7353. DOI: 10.1080/10494820.2022.2067186

Huera, E. N. M., Novay, E. G. Z., Meneses, A. L. T., & Villacrés, R. C. I. (2024). Curricular adaptations based on Information and Communication Technologies for students with special educational needs. *Sinergias Educativas, 9*(1).

Jadán-Guerrero, J., Tamayo-Narvaez, K., Méndez, E., & Valenzuela, M. (2024, June). Adaptive Learning Environments: Integrating Artificial Intelligence for Special Education Advances. In *International Conference on Human-Computer Interaction* (pp. 86-94). Cham: Springer Nature Switzerland. DOI: 10.1007/978-3-031-61953-3_10

Kalonde, G., Boateng, S., Sanni, L., Chotwe, S., & Ododo, F. (2024, March). Artificial Intelligence and Special Education: The use and the integration. In *Society for Information Technology & Teacher Education International Conference* (pp. 1926-1932). Association for the Advancement of Computing in Education (AACE).

Kharbat, F. F., Alshawabkeh, A., & Woolsey, M. L. (2021). Identifying gaps in using artificial intelligence to support students with intellectual disabilities from education and health perspectives. *Aslib Journal of Information Management*, 73(1), 101–128. DOI: 10.1108/AJIM-02-2020-0054

Kumar, A., Nayyar, A., Sachan, R. K., & Jain, R. (Eds.). (2023). *AI-assisted Special Education for Students with Exceptional Needs*. IGI Global. DOI: 10.4018/979-8-3693-0378-8

Mehta, P., Chillarge, G. R., Sapkal, S. D., Shinde, G. R., & Kshirsagar, P. S. (2023). Inclusion of Children With Special Needs in the Educational System, Artificial Intelligence (AI). In *AI-Assisted Special Education for Students With Exceptional Needs* (pp. 156-185). IGI Global.

Rice, M. F., & Dunn, S. (2023). The use of artificial intelligence with students with identified disabilities: A systematic review with critique. *Computers in the Schools*, 40(4), 370–390. DOI: 10.1080/07380569.2023.2244935

Şen, N., & Akbay, T. (2023). Artificial intelligence and innovative applications in special education. *Instructional Technology and Lifelong Learning*, 4(2), 176–199.

Zdravkova, K. (2022). The potential of artificial intelligence for assistive technology in education. In *Handbook on Intelligent Techniques in the Educational Process: Vol 1 Recent Advances and Case Studies* (pp. 61-85). Cham: Springer International Publishing. DOI: 10.1007/978-3-031-04662-9_4

Zdravkova, K., Krasniqi, V., Dalipi, F., & Ferati, M. (2022). Cutting-edge communication and learning assistive technologies for disabled children: An artificial intelligence perspective. *Frontiers in Artificial Intelligence*, 5, 970430. DOI: 10.3389/frai.2022.970430 PMID: 36388402

Chapter 4
The Potential of Artificial Intelligence to Enhance Special Education

Shiwangi Sharma
Manav Rachna International Institute of Research and Studies, India

ABSTRACT

Artificial Intelligence affects all the major players in the education sector and has become the new normal in the current and upcoming era. This chapter aims to probe specifically and introduce inclusivity in the education sector with an interdisciplinary approach of AI for students with hearing disability, visual impairment, mobility dysfunction, and intellectual challenges. Teaching and learning pedagogies from educational institutions are emphasized to understand the importance of inclusion of AI in special education. Several techniques that provide personalized hand-holding to special students are also particularized. Ethical policy has been taken into considerations for special education that trusted technical involvement through artificial intelligence. Comprehensive understanding of the potential advantages of AI and challenges are included in the chapter. Applications of artificial intelligence in the same are due to the multiplicity of difficulties encountered in special education, thus the study has been found imperative to cater different needs of each special student.

INTRODUCTION

With advancement in technology, people's interest in it also increases irrespective of their demographic factor of age, and place they are living. Technology and its related products has impacted the daily life of people may it be personal or professional; hence it is widely implemented in different industries. Education industry

DOI: 10.4018/979-8-3693-5538-1.ch004

is one such industry in which the applications of technical products are extensively applied in teaching and learning different aspects (Sen, and Akbay, 2023). Interruption of technology in different forms of IoT, AI, AR, VR, and Machine Learning are changing the landscape of various workplaces across the world. Furthermore, rapid technical development becomes more prominent when it is used for education of disabled people, in the form of special education. Bringing this in light, report of UNESCO, Asia Pacific Education Bureau in 2019, along with the recent data of World Health Organization (WHO) stated that the entire world has more than 1 billion people who are suffering from some or the other disabilities out of which a precarious figure of 93 million are of children under 14 years of age. Disappointingly, these figures are more likely to increase due to various change in the demographic patterns and chronic diseases in the upcoming generation (Disability, 2023). Disability is considered as lack of capability (as a result of impairment) to live like a normal human being and perform daily functions in usual manner. Impairment, that are held responsible for causing disabilities are defined as any loss of psychological or anatomical loss of function.

A White paper on "Rights of Persons with Disabilities", explains disability as that a person is called disabled when he/she is with sensory impairment of social, psychosocial, physical, mental or neurological dysfunctioning and is not able to take up social responsibilities with natural acceptance. Such people suffering from impairment or disability due to impairment needs care, attention, education and supervision more than a normal human being; thus such people are known as "People with Special needs". These people generally struggle with 3 interrelated blocks namely, social, psychological and structural (inclusive of infrastructure and operations). With all these behold, technology has really plunged in to take the baton of education in its court for these children of special need. Thus, progress in technology has given a new ray of hope to the special education, which was otherwise not much noticed (Garg, and Sharma, 2020). Special education is defined as a way to deliver education well with the aid of technical products because of its variance in accessibility, rapid use and alluring to more than one sense at a time. The people in special need can learn without any constraint of time and place. Technical innovation can be placed in support to special students need and interest, their learning style, discretion among selves. Such aids makes the accessibility of technology better than before as they can learn in their own way, at their own pace independently without anybody's assistance to them. Ease of understanding technology gives a better handholding to the special people in learning the subject and its content of their interest. By this they are further able to understand concepts and express themselves in a better way than before. In short, technology has made lives of special people easier in the form of improved communication, expression of feelings and well-being (Sen, and Akbay, 2023).

Term like Artificial Intelligence was coined first time in the year 1956 with the due diligence to technical development. It is defined as, the mechanical simulation system that gathers data, information and knowledge from external sources and further process all for the intelligence to Universe by interrelating and interpreting to spread the actionable acumen (Grewal, 2014). Artificial Intelligence can be accessed through the information agents physically in the form of Robots and virtually by the help of software's. In current era AI is coming up with more computerized power, complex algorithms, and restored data. Likewise, scope of investment with an expected outcome of innovation has given various new outlooks to the use of AI. Thus, with the inventive paramount of AI, Special education practices are also transforming (Ojha, 2022). AI rules ahead with the power of diagnosing, planning, to implementing various intervention strategies by the assistance of number of computer tools. Here main underlying objective of AI is to give a better life to the disabled students, empowering them, promote their learning and enriching their lives with easier way of living. In order to fulfill the basic brass tacks, AI is well equipped with knowledge base, machine learning, and understanding towards language, expert vision, and computer vision. Robotic teacher as an innovation of AI has been familiarized in schools. Google AI can help doctors in examining retina and diagnosing chances for diabetic retinopathy. Similarly, Google search engines assisted its users on the basis of AI. In fact not only these, but AI is also able to understand the search preferences of people now a days and by this function it starts showing similar predilections to us on different platforms. All these shows that no matter AI is a technology driven tool, but it is capable of understanding human functions, speech perceptions, skills, visual recognition and translation skills. All these analytical benefits further place AI as a good fitment and boon for the education of special people, who lack in their self-fulfillment of day to day activities (Ojha, 2022).

Florida department of Education in 2010 characterizes the disabilities as Hearing, Visual, Physical Disability, Specific Learning or Language Disability. Further Research of (Laabidi, et al., 2013) has characterized the special people on the basis of their need/disabilities into 4 categories explicitly as Mobility impairment, Hearing impairment, Cognitive impairment and Visual impairment. Artificial Intelligence has different technical tools to get apt with every category of special needs (Garg, and Sharma, 2020). However, this fact can never be changed that no technology can ever replace any of the teacher from the school, but it can definitely assist them for better achievement of their goals. Efforts of humans and technology are inclined towards working together to achieve common goals and make it convenient and promise able for the special need people to get helped in hybrid mode from both.

Need of Artificial Intelligence in Special Education

With a speedy development and progress Artificial Intelligence has a broader horizon now and has penetrated in almost every field. This projection has demanded the Inclusion of AI in the special need education also, in order to impart knowledge, develop learning, analytical and logical reasoning, proactively planning, rationale perceiving, clearly communicating, and using technical tools to analyze things which were otherwise cannot be seen naturally. These practices typically lodged to help in decisive decision making, strong and in-depth learning, and emotional computing. Artificial Intelligence is flexed with strong and authentic database that helps in fast screening of the appropriate keywords from the massive record available and also its quick recovery in case of loss. AI based education is a flourishing field now, after it has been integrated into new educational pedagogy. Scientific and technological worth are advanced in the means of education to give this sector a new face in the form of fairer and high quality education with variety of teaching aids. Similarly, when thought of AI is pragmatic in education, it comes out with a purpose to improve computational intelligence and its technology, learning analysis technology along with machine learning, data mining technology, image recognition, natural language processing, speech recognition, virtual reality, augmented reality, hybrid reality and other advanced technologies (Han et al, 2022). Exemplary, Artificial Intelligence has assisted students seeking special need with 24*7 care using Robotics. It also facilitated students to get help from mobile applications without even being on the same wavelength with it. For an instance Apple assisted “Siri” for voice virtual assistant functionally proactive on iPhones allows disabled people to use its voice applications without actually clicking on it. Google “Alexa” function allows people to ask for any query without typing anything in the search bar. Both these functions “Siri” and “Alexa” are annotated by AI and works virtually with the voice commands. Such applications are pro in providing assistive services to the students/ people in special need (Garg, and Sharma, 2020).

Factors Inclined with AI Based Special Education

The inclusion of AI has crossed many benchmarks to achieve and further advance with its offerings to various physically, mentally, emotionally and psychologically challenged children. Artificial Intelligence supports special education with ample of techniques like customized virtual tutors, speech recognition tools, facial recognition, adaptive learning platforms, etc. However, it is not influential only to the special students, but also to the rest other stakeholders who are aligned directly or indirectly with the special education cohort in the form of teachers, counselors, and parents. Studies suggest that following are the factors that incline towards Artificial Intelligence based Special Education –

- Advance level of personalized training – Artificial Intelligence assist in better individual level training to fulfill the need of the special students. By the help of adaptive learning platform it becomes easier for the teachers to manage the learning gap of students that suggests customized steps of action and instant feedback.
- Improved special students engagement – Special students feel more motivated and connected with their environment while using Artificial Intelligence tools. Student's engagement is assured by the gamification format of the program, and learning by interaction, to gain sustained attention and active participation in the learning.
- Assist in variety of teaching style – Artificial Intelligence provides number of teaching aids to the teachers that may make teaching easier for all kind of delivery modes may it be verbal, haptic or visual. This has made lives of the special learners easier as they can learn in the way they want to learn and whichever way suits them best.
- Time effectiveness for teachers – Beyond providing teaching assistance, Artificial Intelligence tools also helps in administrative tasks, like lesson planning, tracking assessment, and thus saving time of teachers. This extension of help allows educators to devote more time towards personalized course of action as per the demand of special students.
- Better association and communication – Means of Artificial Intelligence facilitates seamless communication between parents, special students, and teachers. It further helps in seeking personalized recommendations based on the progress reports, real-time data for the updates. Collaborations and communications among all the stakeholders can also be improved by the help of Artificial Intelligence tools (Sharma et al., 2023).

Contemporary Equipment's of Artificial Intelligence: Tools to Assist Special Students

Necessity of understanding exploratory applications of wide range of Artificial Intelligence has raised the need of elaborating imminent sub-fields and contemporary equipment's of the same. Expert systems, machine learning, fuzzy logic, artificial neural networks, intelligent agents, deep learning, genetic algorithms, and natural language processing are the major ones to be highlighted –

- Expert Systems- An expert system is a technically designed program in order to understand and get the judgment of a subject matter expert. This judgment is derived out of experience and knowledge base and maturity that gives a sense to access knowledge base when and where required. The study explains the characteristics of a preferred expert system which turns up to understand the special need of the person in need, accessible and understandable for all, allows reasoning and questioning session and expect quality output (Gupta, and Nagpal, 2020).

Figure 1. Expert systems architecture (Source: Islam, 2013; ShellAg: Expert System Shell for Agricultural Crops.).

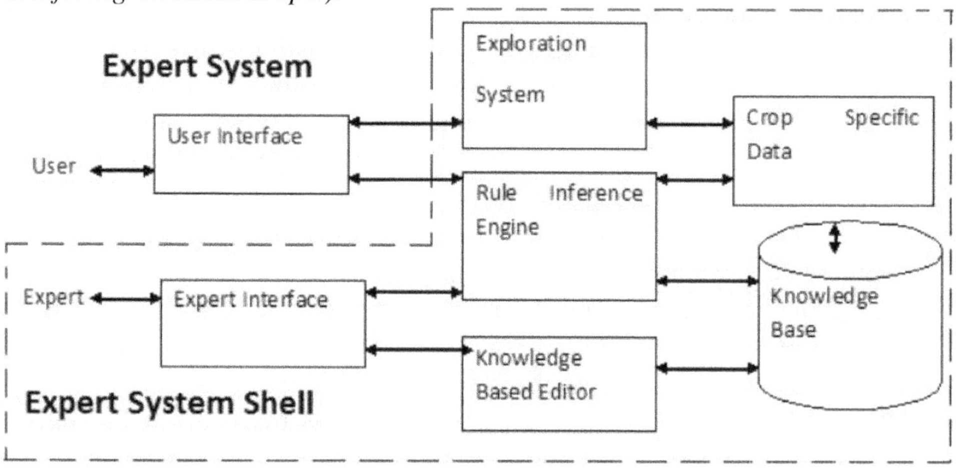

Figure 1 denotes Expert System architecture, which comprise of interface that gives consents for a direct communication between the user and the system. Knowledge base is constructed with the information from the expert interface, database consists of the processed data to solve the problem, and the Inference Engines assists in reasoning of the rules used for inference (Islam, 2013). Expert system helps in special education by giving explanation by advanced reasoning facilities. It has a process of Forward chaining in which rules are placed one by one, these rules are further evaluated to reach up to the solution and proceed rule wise once it is found right. This forward chaining method designs an algorithm by data processing and staging it with the rules to help students in special need by checking their characteristics and providing solutions as per their need (Rizky & Hakim, 2020).

- Machine Learning – Machine Learning is known as a collection of algorithms based on the collected data, it helps in predicting, improve some utility function, explore and retain some unseen data and then processing the same (Amazon, 2021). Machine learning techniques are classified into 3 categories on the basis of the functions they can serve – Supervised Machine Learning, Unsupervised Learning, and Reinforcement Learning. In order to work with supervised machine learning a training data set is developed to place linear regression and logistic regression analysis on it. During training session machine works on input and output relationships with an objective to understand the input data process the same into output. Base on the learning of the input and output relationship, machine learning is able to perform functions like regression type of analysis is performed. In the due course to assist special students in the need of assistive devices, supervised machine learning classification serves best in serving by state-of-the-art voice synthesis. Inbuilt AI can read aloud the content of the course material by using this input-output relation and state-of-the-art technique for those who are visually impaired (Sharma et al., 2023). Further, data set which do not fall under the category of input-output relationship is dealt through unsupervised machine learning by the analysis of pattern identify, clustering, principal component analysis. Semi-Supervised Machine Learning is based on environmental situation and takes decision for long term advantage (Kaur et al., 2021). These machine learning categories serves various applications like mail filtering, face recognition, object recognition, optical character recognition, understanding spoken language, and medical uses (Rende et al., 2016).
- Fuzzy Logic – In Fuzzy Logic, is a part of particular group and the elements of these groups are predetermined. In Fuzzy groups, memberships of the present elements are destined between the values of 0 to 1. Thus, it makes a logical framework, explaining the complex situations by understanding the part of the fuzzy groups to which the elements belongs too (Kambalimath & Deka, 2020; Özdemir & Kalınkara, 2020). With this application, Fuzzy Logic is very much applicable in implementing Student Model to get a pedagogical decision. It analyzes the student's observable response for any particular stimulus and by this it helps in understanding and differentiating the unobservable behavior of the special student. It thus, helps in analyzing the uncertain behavior of some mentally challenged students and try to get its solution by the help of Fuzzy Logic. It also aids in providing linguistic description of the cognitive thinking and help the child along with the teachers assessment (Sripan & Suksawat, 2010). Students suffering from Autism have very less span of attention at a stretch, thus AI tool like Fuzzy Logic work here by using a fuzzy cognitive map approach. The analysis of attention span

is done for clinical study by comparing performance data with that of user's actual performance data (Drigas, and Ionnaidu, 2012).

- Artificial Neural Networks – Artificial Neural Networks as the name suggests are parallel distributed networks that use its own valuable connections (Montesinos López, 2022). Neuroscience in this case draws attention from psychology, neurology, physiology, and biology (Goswami, 2008). This term become prominent in studying brain monitoring and imaging technique through electroencephalography (EEG), functional magnetic resonance imaging (MRI), positron emission tomography (PET) and Artificial Neural Networks (Muller, 2011). Here Artificial Neural Networks acts like biological neural networks after training through database. It requires external stimuli to learn and make contingent decisions similar to that of biological brain activities (Aggrawal, 2018). It is known to simulate human brain because of processing elements called neurons aligned together to unravel specific problems. Artificial Neural Networks has used arithmetical training tool for the children having Learning Disabilities and is also used for evaluating successful completion of training program for the students suffering from Serious Emotional Disturbance claiming not much but yes 64% accuracy (Linstrom, and Boye, 2005). Also, the neuroscience promises to build a strong connection with the special education by the help of biomarkers. These help in indicating cognitive learning disability, dyslexia, Autism, ADHD, and language impairment (Goswami, 2008).
- Deep Learning – Deep Learning is known to have higher level construct in the form of various hierarchical architecture embedded in the countless hidden layers of Artificial Neural Networks (Guo et al, 2016). Deep learning technique works through indulging into feature extraction and then its classification. It expands its scope even more in the form of reasoning and planning as these are remains baffled by artificial intelligence (Skansi, 2018). Deep learning is used for various patterns of learning including language processing, image processing, and signal processing and voice recognition (Sen, and Akbay, 2023).
- Intelligent agents – Intelligent agents are known as autonomous decision making software based on the present situation (Mbaabu, 2020). Studies suggest 3 different agents in the name of human beings, robots, and software's. Human beings have limbs and senses, robots have camera, and infrared range detector along with motor and software's has input commands from humans to respond back to the environment on the respective sensible signals, thus these are considered as intelligent agents. Actions such as sharing, displaying, and printing are dealt on the level of agents in response to their environment. These agents use the cognitive tools to make students understand or use mod-

el building approach to stimulate the understanding of the special students and train them well to respond with respect to the environment (Nayak, and Das, 2020). Artificial Intelligence and Rehabilitation Robots also drives well in movement and learning support for students suffering physical incapacities. The Surrogate medical Robot is been connected with the brain computer interface (BCI) and the wearer can do whatever activity he/she wants to do by investigating the signals through Electroencephalogram (EEG). This assist physically challenged person to independently interact with the environment that supports their interest in learning (Zang et al. 2017).

- Genetic Algorithms – The popularity of Genetic Algorithms has stepped ahead than before with regards to its feasibility of solving real life problems. It is a bigger part of evolutionary algorithms and also a biologically inspired computational technique that is working efficiently to bring revolution. By its advance conceptual module this algorithm is providing cloud educational platform to assist special students with personalized learning. They copy the natural selection process and try to respond in the simulated context of factual situations (Lambora, Gupta, & Chopra, 2019). It caresses the theory of survival of the fittest to get the technology well along for consecutive generation (Katoch, Chauhan, & Kumar, 2021; Lambora, Gupta, & Chopra, 2019).
- Natural Language Processing – Natural Language Processing is the group of computational processing's that analyzes natural occurring contents at various steps of linguistic analysis just a like and to understand human like language processing. It helps in getting well through the natural language handling mechanism along with the assistance of chat bots. It supports special education by synthesizing speeches, translating and understanding texts, responding to oral and written commands, producing and briefing texts, and grading essays (Sen, and Akbay, 2023).

Aforesaid, equipment's of artificial intelligence are thus tempered with the objective of assisting special education in need with their personalized requirements.

Learning Pedagogy for Special Students from Educational Institutions

Studies say that all almost every child may be capable or incapable faces certain problems in the school. These problems vary from the understanding, grasping, and learning capabilities that is different from child to child, not able to cope up among other children, disparity by the teachers, special need of education, and problem in adjustment within school, etc. These are some serious issues which seeks some changes in the curriculum in order to build up a healthy learning environment and that is aligned with the child's special need. These problems also drive the need of special education in the Educational Institutions, not only to with stand with the same but also to bring some pedagogical changes in the curriculum that promotes the concept of individualized learning, so that even a disabled child should remain motivated and focused towards learning and feel as normal as an abled child (Garg, and Sharma, 2020).

Inclusivity of AI in the Education Sector for Special Students

As per UNICEF, 2014, Pedagogy is defined as "the act of teaching altogether with the attendee's revelation and a mutual agreement of all". It demarcates clearly the priorities of what skills are required to be understood and what is to be inculcated. As mentioned in Figure 2, Inclusive Teaching style and Inclusive Pedagogy both creates matrix that is required to promote inclusive education.

Figure 2. Inclusive pedagogy and teaching style to promote inclusive education

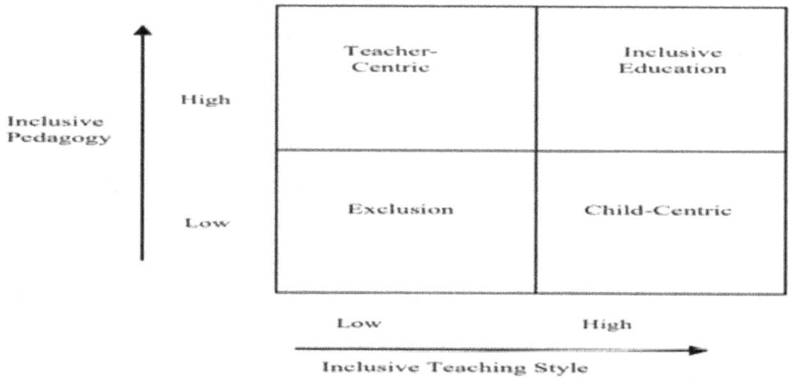

Source - (Garg, and Sharma, 2020).

As stated in Figure 2, Inclusive Teaching Style at X-Axis, exhibits the style of teaching without doing any disparity between a special student and a normal student, Similarly Inclusive Pedagogy is the art of teaching by paying attention to the learners requirements as per their abilities and disabilities. There are 4 quadrants designed in the matrix of the figure, these are as follows –

1. Exclusion – Inclusive Teaching Style and Inclusive Pedagogy both are low as shown in Figure 2. This suggests that neither of these is inclined towards teaching needs of special education and imparting equitable education. In this case the teacher coming to the class may teach without much focus on equitable learning. Such teachers may differentiate the students on the basis of their learning

capabilities and assume that the slow learners or those having disabilities will be taught by certain specific teachers.

2. Teacher-Centric – Inclusive Pedagogy is high but the Inclusive teaching style is low in this section. Here it totally depends upon the teachers as upon which student he/she is going to pay attention, segregating them for the rest of the class. In case teachers' pay some attention to certain specific child, even that is not appreciated as it violates the concern for equitable education.
3. Child-Centric –Inclusive teaching style is high but the Inclusive Pedagogy is low in the Child-Centric section. Even this section does not supports complete Inclusive structure, because teachers are highly concerned for students and may adopt different pedagogical structure for every student but even then it leads to the categorization of the children.
4. Inclusive – Inclusive Pedagogy and Inclusive teaching style both are high, while promoting equitable education without discriminating students on the basis of their background. This majorly depends upon the way teacher manages both the students and teaching them. They need to develop certain creative pedagogy that provides a cordial environment to the students to grow, interact, discuss, suggest and learn.

In order to promote Inclusivity in the special education, it depends organization's management support, infrastructure build up backed by Artificial Intelligence, Augmented and Virtual Reality (Garg, and Sharma, 2020). Inclusive structure of education includes all the need of education, pedagogy assessment, redesigning assessment and primarily the essence of education for every single student (Jha, 2002).

Study of Morrison in 2017 clearly mentions that it is imperative to understand the requirement of people in special need as necessitating technologically dwelled supplies. As AI has been well implemented and has countless benefits in the education sector; it has increased the bar of expectations for the special need stakeholders as well (Drigas, and Ioannidou, 2012). AI is disciplined to intersect between social and natural sciences marginally, and is featured with brain science, cloud computing, big data, and supercomputing. Thus, to accomplish the need of special need students, both Artificial Intelligence and Special need education join forces together. Students with hearing, learning, visual, and mobility impairment can look for the benefits by the inclusion of AI in special education (Garg, and Sharma, 2020). Such technologically aided education will also be beneficial for PwDs. Further, let's ponder more on the objectivity behind the inclusion of AI in the education sector for special students.

Role of Artificial Intelligence in Teaching

Individual difference is quiet common among all the human beings, but when it comes to special people, these differences increases even more based on the degree of their disability. Such students also bump into havoc while adjusting in class with other students. Thus, with due respect to the individual difference of each single special child, every special student seeks specific attention from the teachers side, as they do not learn or understand things with the same pace. It becomes imperative to pay detailed attention on physical, mental, social, psychosocial and potential development of every single special child in their education, hence teachers and the counselors aligned with the special child is required to devote keen observation and supervision while attending the class. Though, in today's era where the education pattern has been transformed into one to many layouts, it has become very difficult for teachers to pay attention on every individual student. This results in less interaction among teachers and students, teacher's biasness, ignorance of students, reduced tutoring, lower motivation, and less interest in learning. Artificial intelligence and neural networks uses previous data to check the learning progress of child and to opt some student wise adaptive learning plans as per his/her current situation. In this way technology build AI achieves the objective of helping students to learn and teachers to teach. Along with this, AI also helps in collecting and transferring the teaching data to the administrative team to take required decision in opinion plans or evaluation up gradation (Han et al, 2022).

Seeking some improvement, AI applications can be auxiliary in providing assistance through voice recognition, educational robots or semi-robotic technology to collect teaching notes and other study materials and assist teachers in teaching students. This gives some spare time to the teachers as well, so that they can invest some time in looking forward for special need of students and guide them accordingly. AI build tools also connect and help teachers and students virtually to know with the students that whether they like the class, teaching pattern and methods, and are satisfied with the quality of curriculum and study material delivered or not. Students can also use AI platform to seek help from teachers to solve their queries, re-teach any particular topic, this not only clarifies the doubts of the students, but also give opportunity of good interaction among teachers and students and strengthen the bond and communication between them. This feature is also strengthened by the AI empowered collaborative interactive and learning platform. One of the magnificent features of using AI tool is that AI traces the mood swings pattern of the students and notifies the teachers accordingly; this allows the content to get adjusted as per the students mental status so that the student should not feel discomfort at any level. Text messaging platform of AI are providing mental health intervention to the young special students. These enable special students explicitly to express their feelings, understand in self and make others also understand about themselves with the complete independence irrespective of their paucity (Ojha, 2022). Learning disability of the students can be addressed by teachers at an early age of life by the help of AI tools (Han et al, 2022).

Role of Artificial Intelligence in Student's Learning

Special children are completely different from normal children because of their special needs, their mental, physical and emotional capabilities. Hence, once these children get enrollment in school, they are assessed to check their degrees of disabilities, and after analyzing they are assigned class as per their demand and required level of education. The advanced teaching system, is established on the basis of artificial intelligence is designed through algorithms, data computation, learning analysis technology, data mining, etc. These data tryouts depend upon level of learning and understanding of the students, their progress, and learning contents. AI assist in personalizing the teaching goals with respect to every student in framing questions, designing their curriculum, notes or even judgment to analyze the right structure of the course to be delivered as per the captivating capacity of the student. Supplementing to this, the progress of the students can be differentiated from other students, so that individual students' strategic plan for improvement can be made. Students can gather data through AI based smart devices, to develop their own database in personalized way, which is not limited to that of the information's and knowledge gained from Textbooks, constrained dimensions of knowledge, this helps in arbitrating students' learning ability, knowledge gained, and self-awareness.

By the use of Electroencephalogram an information acquisition technology, wavelength of special students brain during learning can be collected to identify the learning state and analyzing their cognitive ability of learning. Big data technology also performs macroscopic analysis to check the optimal brainwave signal that indicates the location of the stimulation in the students' brain that initiates and then aids in learning by improving cognitive performance, for those students who are not mentally active (Ke and Wang, 2019). Similarly, for the students who are suffering from physical disabilities suffer from low capability of learning, they are unable to understand their own stimulus well, or cannot acquire knowledge through vision, but can feel things only by touch and sound signals. Thus, visually impaired students are helped with collective functions of artificial intelligence and neural network by sensing, assembling, processing, and then analyzing the learning data given by teachers in the learning programs. This when further aligned with the brain computer interface (BCI) constructs and imparts remodeled neural signals to help the students with visual impairment (Yilin, and Wang, 2020). For students suffering from communication and expression disorder, it becomes difficult for instructors to understand the students thought process or psychological state of mind, just by their expressions or body language. Thus, to associate an interaction among the outer world and the cognitive activities of the student, they are asked to wear Brian computer interface so that it can connect with the cognitive signs and collect the same through Electroencephalogram. This helps in analyzing whether the mental status of the student is stable, or unstable with mood swings. Teachers can obtain data from their and understand the feelings of the students, level of feelings, emotional shifts, and plan teaching learning strategies based on the instructions derived from the technical output (Liang, 2020).

Physically restricted students can learn through intelligent speech recognition by interacting through Robots and inbuilt technologies of speech recognition, and natural language understanding by asking questions from them, getting answers of these questions, and completing searches. Also for the special learners who cannot understand and grasp much in class, Artificial Intelligence is a boon for them by connecting them to the virtual reality, which creates a simulated environment of learning by controlling visual, sensory, auditory and palpable senses. It refurbishes the standard teaching modals, in a way that it is easily implicit by the learners. Special learners are helped in an intuitive way of learning with the practical training instructions. This allows students to generate a better, comprehensive and substituting mechanism in response to learning (Cheng, and Wang, 2021).

Role of AI in Parental Guidance

Special child requires thorough care and thus they seek, teaching feedback database of teachers and others who all are in teaching cohorts for special education. To assure the quality of teaching and imparted education which adheres around fulfillment of all the needs of the demarcated child, AI builds CreditSPMS to evaluate performance and quantitative assessment of the ethical standards of members of teaching fraternity and then further share it with the parents of the child. AI tools based on big data and Blockchain shares emotional, moral, psychological, academic deliverables of students which were collected at the time of teaching for evaluation levels and further share it with the parents. This gives a chance for parents and teachers interaction and discuss regarding the child's development and required area of improvements; this interaction between family and teachers together cooperate the child to develop better. Also, with the help of face detection attendance, data analysis and prediction and thermal imaging monitoring, student's behavior can be traced, monitored at regular intervals, to understand the physical, psychological and mental health of the child. These data's are then shared with the parents to gives them an idea where early medical detection and treatment is required (Han, 2022).

Potential Advantages of AI Over Special-Category Learners

Challenged students are suffering from various physical, mental, and sensory gaps as compared to the normal students. These gaps generate disabilities, which further causes various diseases, resulting into in-capabilities of doing even basic things. Inclusions of Artificial Intelligence were thus introduced in order to upkeep the need of special students and support them in learning, and communicating. Based on the potential advantages of Artificial Intelligence over various categories of Special learners, there are various benefits that these students avails to suffices the physical, mental, or sensory infirmities in them. These are as follows –

- Assistance of Artificial Intelligence for Students suffering with Dyslexia – It is a slow development syndrome, where children suffer from less capabilities of learning, reading and writing. It's a complex lifelong neurological problem which has been made easier by the support of Artificial Intelligence. Rule based fuzzy system has been used to detect, Dyslexia in the early childhood. Early detection of disease is further communicated to parents and teachers for further assessment by the trained professionals (Palcios, et al., 2010). The diagnosis for early stage of children was done in a systematic way by (Kohli et al., 2010) using Artificial Neural Network. Intelligent tutoring system was introduced with the help of web based intelligent tutoring system that allows students to understand and learn fast in their respective environment. Phonological awareness educational software's are also developed to assist students in understanding simple graphics with any load on their cognitive capabilities (Drigas, and Ionnaidu, 2012). Research done by (Rogoshui, 2023) contributes by introducing digital education games helps in improving visual perception of dyslexia students. It is a combination of interactive activities, image, and sound that upgrades the capabilities of learners to concentrate and learn better.
- Assistance of Artificial Intelligence for Students suffering with Attention Deficit Hyperactive Disorder – It is a disorder generally noticed in the age of development, due to wide range of problems comprising of hyperactivity, problem of intention, and impulsiveness. Artificial Intelligence has lessened the burden of performance by such students by introducing some level of diagnosis and interventions to resolve behavior problems. The interventions include an introduction of neuro-sky headset which has 3 bands type electrodes which has to be worn near the ears and on the forehead. The electrical signals captured by these electrodes are transferred to neuro-sky monitor the recorded signals in the form of algorithms to analyze the attention levels. An AI driven Avatar and a tutor module by intelligent tutoring system are

introduced to assist the interaction level of the student. These are low cost, non-medical and easy to use tools that aid the life and learning of attention deficit hyperactive students (Ojha, 2022). Study of (Anuradha et al., 2010) gave an even better and accurate way to diagnose and treat the problem of ADHD. Support Vector Machines were used to generate certain specific algorithms within the supervised learning mechanism. The dataset of SVM is derived from the combine results of doctor's questionnaire, and verified medical records. This method of diagnosis is preferable because it has reduced the chances of convolution diagnosis. This test is proved 88% accurate when tested over children of the age 6 years to 11 years.

- Assistance of Artificial Intelligence for Students suffering with Sensory and Physical Impairment – Fuzzy Cognitive map was used to diagnose the language weakening. It uses a soft computing technology that presents different diagnosis technology by the use of symbolic representation of the complex system; this differentiates the diagnosis pattern from that of Autism and Dyslexia. Fuzzy technology also assists by using computer based speech therapy to help the learners suffering from speech disorders (Schipor et al., 2003). Neural Network approach was implemented for the self-assessment of the learners who are having the gap of genetic programming (Ojha, 2022). Similarly, visual impairment includes either completely blind or partially, who uses visual aid devices like Braille or those which can change its size, and color; to give some feel of education and improve their learning (Garg, and Sharma, 2020).
- Assistance of Artificial Intelligence for Students suffering with Autism – Children suffering from Autism are having less span of attention and their thought is fragmented, this can be increased by regular external intervention to assure expected level of learning (Han et al., 2022). Robotic assist in managing children suffering from Autism Spectrum Disorder (ASD) in order to understand emotions and behavior and learn social skills (Itsquiz, 2016). A game known as Life is Game is developed for the kids suffering from Autism Spectrum Disorder to get well through their Facial Expressions and understand the mental status. Microsoft also proposes an AI tool named as Equadox, in the form of a mobile mechanism that helps in easy communication and understanding the environment through visual presentation (Alleebe, 2017). Fuzzy Logic and Artificial Neural Networks will also work in improving the children from Autism, by the help of pseudo algorithm that gives a real time data to diagnose the level of attention in the children and work on it (Drigas, and Ioannidou, 2012).
- Assistance of Artificial Intelligence for Students suffering with Cerebral Palsy Disorder –

Cerebral Palsy is a disorder caused due to certain groups of conditions that affect body movement and postures. It is majorly caused due to damaged brain development even before birth. Artificial Intelligence tools are used to convert brain signals into computer commands that give a platform to the children to interact with the digital devices. Students with physical motor disabilities are mainly benefitted by these tools (Zavaraki, 2023). AI assisted virtual reality system helps in controlling motor skills of the students suffering from Cerebral Palsy through Symptom management devices in form of mobility devices adapting navigation. In addition to these, mobility devices along with the artificial intelligence allow to analyze large set of data in the form of visual material. This indeed helps medical practitioner to understand the mental proficiency of the child, diagnose the treatment better and started its ailment as soon as possible (Ojha, 2022).

Hence, there are ample of potential advantages of Artificial Intelligence over special-category learners. These are implicitly aiding towards making the lives of special students easier and much more as normal.

Ethical Policy Considerations by Involvement of AI for Special Education Stakeholders

Ethics is highly concerned in any technical functioning. When artificial intelligence is involved in special education, there are various ethical issues that urge's the focus of the stakeholders. These are as follows –

- Use of Algorithm attentiveness to observe the need of proper utility for special learners; else a wrong algorithm might create adverse effects as well.
- Combine educational, researching, analysis and implantation efforts are required from all the stakeholders to assure ethical use of technology.
- Artificial Intelligence has contributed by advancements in brain monitoring and also by its application in psychiatric treatment. Although there are various challenges yet ethical considerations are there in gaining the potential benefits of AI. Its application in treating mental illness improves patience outcomes, efficiency of their learning and cost effectiveness. However, ethical challenges to address accuracy issues, privacy issues, and perpetuating risk of biasness increases (Terra, et al., 2023).
- Focus more on autonomy, trust, responsibility and privacy to have better understanding of ethical codes while incorporating AI.
- Well designed and framed layout is required for implementation of AI in multidisciplinary approach which gives a robust picture of advanced treatment and education of special children.

- Artificial Intelligence is used to learn predictive analytics, intelligent tutoring system, personalization, evaluation and assessment of special children. This use data of the learners hence data privacy, data ownership, and its exclusion are on high priority of ethical concerns.
- Informed Consents has to be taken from Educational Institutions before implementing any AI tool on the special learners, and further the tools should be implemented only after the consent is duly signed (Sadhana, and Yadav, 2024).

Challenges faced by Introducing AI in Special Education

Although, there are various benefits of introducing Artificial Intelligence in Special Education, still it comes with challenges in imparting special education. The measures are reinforced to overcome these defies on the way, these are mentioned below –

- Cost – Introducing and familiarizing Artificial Intelligence empowered system is financially demanding; as institutions are not always having decent budget to bear the cost. Providers also choose credit system to optimize the usage and get enough funds, but even that becomes exorbitant many times.
- Ethical considerations – Ethical considerations are utterly important while working through technology, however it is never assured. Privacy, inequity, security and plagiarism of the teaching contents are some of the major ethical challenges, which seek a check point.
- Quality Assurance – Quality concerns, maintaining high standards, and assuring effective AI-generated contents are very critical while imparting education. An over dependency on Artificial Intelligence tools, may defoliate the quality of the content because the latter is not well researched that results in biasness, plagiarized content and inaccuracies.
- Technical Expertise – Technical expertise is very uncommon among common people. Also, when it comes to adoption of Artificial Intelligence, sense of insecurities generates because more often it is thought to be the human replacement. However, this is never the reality, both has their own uniqueness, as human can never be replaced by any technology; the former regards emotional perspectives, critical and creative thinking, and latter Artificial Intelligence assist in fulfilling the gap by some expertize that human can otherwise takes time to accomplish (Open Learning, 2024).

Future Prospects of Using AI in Special Education

As stated in the article "Exploring the Role of AI in Special Education," 2024 Artificial Intelligence is looking forward for the inclusion and embeddeness in Special Education by educators and researchers worldwide, it has become imperative to focus on its future projections. The technology has shown various new ways of divulging special education making it more personalized, effective, understandable and accessible by all. Thus following are the high spots of the same –

- Developing Inclinations – Intelligent Tutoring Systems are in significant demand in the field of special education. It is introduced to offer personalized instructions as per the need of every single special student. These technology works on the real time data to improve student's performance, and work on feedback. Additionally, predictive analytics has also been in trend as it predicts the student's behavior, performance and development. The result of the predictive analysis tells about the learning capabilities and gap before it creates any havoc.
- Role of Educators and Parents in acceptance of Artificial Intelligence – Role of Educators and parents are pivotal in the growth of special students by the integration of Artificial Intelligence in special education. By staying updated and informed they perform a fundamental role where Artificial Intelligence takes the baton to transform the special education effectively. Educators influence special learners by providing personalized education to them and parents strengthen their morale by making them use artificial learning tools for their day to day activities. Furthermore, as Artificial Intelligence is projecting high, it becomes a core responsibility of teachers, parents and policy makers to assure its ethical and beneficial implementation in favor of special students in every means.
- Assistive Technologies – Artificial Technology are remarkably contributing towards assistive technology to benefit special education. Assistive Technologies are serving in language assistance by speech recognition software; Artificial Intelligence Powered Prosthetic to facilitate learning of disabled students may it be visual, speech, writing, sensory or any other cognitive disability.
- Better Accessibility – With the increasing technology, its accessibility and reachability has become easier than before. Artificial Intelligence being one such necessitated aid of technology inclines moreover towards providing better accessibility to maximum special students who are seeking special education. Proving this in fact, AI converts text books into audio and digital books with adjustable formatting options. Also, AI-powered predictive anal-

ysis provides option of checking potential impediments and related way outs to overcome it. This helps in framing beforehand strategies to achieve better outcomes to mass an inclusive environment.

Ultimately, Artificial Intelligence being most in demand should be implicitly clear to everyone including teachers, parents and policy makers. The technology should be developed without ambiguity to serve beneficially for the special students.

REFERENCES

Aggarwal, C. C. (2018). *Neural networks and deep learning*. Springer. DOI: 10.1007/978-3-319-94463-0

Allebee, A. (2017). Equadex, Microsoft cognitive services. [Online]. Available: https://customers.microsoft.com/en-us/story/equadex-partner-professional-services-cognitive-services

Amazon (2021). What is artificial intelligence? Machine learning and deep learning. Retrieved from https://aws.amazon.com/machine-learning/what-is-ai/ on 11 October 2021.

Anuradha, J., Ramachandran, V., Arulalan, K., & Tripathy, B. (2010). Diagnosis of adhd using svm algorithm. *Proceedings of the Third Annual ACM Bangalore Conference*, 1–4.

Chen, J., & Miao, W. (2021). Application and inspiration of virtual reality technology in vocational education in the United States. *Adult Education*, 41(06), 90–93.

Disability. (2023, March 7). World Health Organization (WHO). https://www.who.int/news-room/fact-sheets/detail/disability-and-health

Drigas, S., & Ioannidou, R.-E. (2012). Artificial intelligence in special education: A decade review. *International Journal of Engineering Education*, 28(6), 1366–1372.

Exploring the Role of AI in Special Education. (2024, February 29). 21K Schools. https://www.21kschool.com/us/blog/ai-in-special-education/#:~:text=The%20Potential%20of%20AI%20in%20Special%20Education,-AI%20holds%20immense&text=This%20personalization%20can%20maximize%20learning,with%20speech%20impairments%20communicate%20effectively

Garg, S., & Sharma, S. (2020). Impact of artificial intelligence in special need education to promote inclusive pedagogy. *International Journal of Information and Education Technology (IJIET)*, 10(7), 523–527. DOI: 10.18178/ijiet.2020.10.7.1418

Goswami, U. (2008). Principles of learning, implications for teaching: A cognitive neuroscience perspective. *Journal of Philosophy of Education*, 42(3/4), 381–399. DOI: 10.1111/j.1467-9752.2008.00639.x

Grewal, S. (2014). A critical conceptual analysis of definitions of AI as applicable to computer. *IOSR Journal of Computer Engineering*, 16(2), 9–13. DOI: 10.9790/0661-16210913

Guo, Y., Liu, Y., Oerlemans, A., Lao, S., Wu, S., & Lew, M. S. (2016). Deep learning for visual understanding: A review. *Neurocomputing*, 187, 27–48. DOI: 10.1016/j.neucom.2015.09.116

Han, X., Hu, L., Han, D., Peng, Y., Wang, Y., Yan, C., & Wang, Z. (2022). International Conference on Social Science, Education and Management (ICSSEM 2022). CSP.

Islam, S. N. (2013, November). ShellAg: Expert system shell for agricultural crops. In *2013 International Conference on Cloud & Ubiquitous Computing & Emerging Technologies* (pp. 83-86). IEEE DOI: 10.1109/CUBE.2013.24

Itsquiz. (2016). AI in special education. [Online]. Available: https://medium.com/@itsquiz15/artificial-intelligence-in-special-educ ation-dab27649b9b6

Jha, M. M. (2002). *School Without Walls: Inclusive Education for All*. Heinemann.

Kambalimath, S., & Deka, P. C. (2020). A basic review of fuzzy logic applications in hydrology and water resources. *Applied Water Science*, 10(8), 1–14. DOI: 10.1007/s13201-020-01276-2

Katoch, S., Chauhan, S. S., & Kumar, V. (2021). A review on genetic algorithm: Past, present, and future. *Multimedia Tools and Applications*, 80(5), 8091–8126. DOI: 10.1007/s11042-020-10139-6 PMID: 33162782

Kaur, J., Khan, M. A., Iftikhar, M., Imran, M., & Haq, Q. E. U. (2021). Machine learning techniques for 5G and beyond. *IEEE Access : Practical Innovations, Open Solutions*, 9, 23472–23488. DOI: 10.1109/ACCESS.2021.3051557

Ke, Q., & Wang, P. (2019). Research progress of educational applications of brain-computer interface technology. *China Electro-Chemical Education*, (10), 14–22.

Laabidi, M. (2013). *Jemni, L. J. B. Ayed, H. B. Brahim, and A. B. Jemaa, "Learning technologies for people with disabilities," Research Laboratory of Technologies of Information and Communication & Electrical Engineering LaTICE*. National Higher School of Engineering of Tunis.

Lambora, A., Gupta, K., & Chopra, K. (2019, February). Genetic algorithm-A literature review. In 2019 international conference on machine learning, big data, cloud and parallel computing (COMITCon) (pp. 380-384). IEEE.

Liang, M. (2020). Research on the application of brain-computer interface technology in the education of special children attending classes. *Computer Knowledge and Technology*, 16(18), 200–201.

Linstrom, K. R., & Boye, A. J.Neural Network Prediction Model for a Psychiatric Application, Proceedings of the Sixth International Conference on Computational Intelligence and Multimedia Applications (2005).

Montesinos López, O. A., Montesinos López, A., & Crossa, J. (2022). Fundamentals of artificial neural networks and deep learning. In *Multivariate statistical machine learning methods for genomic prediction* (pp. 379–425). Springer International Publishing. DOI: 10.1007/978-3-030-89010-0_10

Morrison, E. C., & Dhareshwar, A. "Imagining AI applications with people with visual disabilities using tactile ideation," in *Proc. ASSETS '17*, 2017. DOI: 10.1145/3132525.3132530

Muller, E. (2011, July). *Nasdse*. inForum. https://nasdse.org/docs/72_f2f7f9b7-ff92-4cda-a843-c817497e81e4.pdf

Nayak, S., & Das, R. K. (2020). Application of artificial intelligence (AI) in prosthetic and orthotic rehabilitation. In *Service Robotics*. IntechOpen. DOI: 10.5772/intechopen.93903

Ojha, S. T. (2022). Artificial Intelligence In Special Education, Id& Cp. *Journal of Positive School Psychology*, 6(6), 8341–8345. https://journalppw.com/index.php/jpsp/article/view/9109/5928

OpenLearning. (2024, March 7). AI in education: Benefits, challenges, and best practices. Learning Design Theories, Micro-credentials and Online Education - OpenLearning Blog. https://blog.openlearning.com/ai-in-education

Özdemir, O., & Kalınkara, Y. (2020). Bulanık Mantık: 2000-2020 Yılları Arası Tez ve Makale Çalışmalarına Yönelik Bir İçerik Analizi. *Acta Infologica*, 4(2), 155–174. DOI: 10.26650/acin.762872

Palacios, A. M., Sánchez, L., & Couso, I. (2010). Diagnosis of dyslexia with low quality data with geneticfuzzy systems. *International Journal of Approximate Reasoning*, 51(8), 993–1009. DOI: 10.1016/j.ijar.2010.07.008

Rende, F. Ş., Bütün, G., & Karahan, Ş. (2016). Derin Öğrenme Algoritmalarında Model Testleri: Derin Testler. 10. Ulusal yazılım Mühendisliği Sempozyumu,24-26 Ekim, pp:54-59, Çanakkale. Russell, S. J., & Norvig, P. (2020). Artificial intelligence: a modern approach (Fourth edition), Pearson Education.

Rizky, R., & Hakim, Z. (2020). *International Conference on Science, Health, Economics, Education and Technology (ICoSHEET 2019)*. Atlantis Press.

Rogoshui, A. Z. (2023) The effect of digital educational game on the visual perception of dyslexic first grade students [thesis]. Tehran, Iran: Allameh Tabataba'i University

Sadhana, & Yadav, D. S. (2024). Ethical Considerations in AI-Driven Education: Balancing Innovation and Responsibility. International Journal Of Innovative Research In Technology, 10(10), 49-53. https://ijirt.org/master/publishedpaper/IJIRT162392_PAPER.pdf

Schipor, O. A., Pentiuc, S. G., & Schipor, M. D. (2010). Improving computer-based speech therapy using a fuzzy expert system. *Computer Information*, 29(2), 303–318.

Şen, N., & Akbay, T. (2023). Artificial intelligence and innovative applications in special education. Öğretim Teknolojisi ve Hayat Boyu Öğrenme Dergisi - Instructional Technology and Lifelong Learning. https://doi.org/DOI: 10.52911/itall.1297978

Sharma, S., Tomar, V., Yadav, N., & Aggarwal, M. (2023). Impact of AI-Based Special Education on Educators and Students. In *AI-Assisted Special Education for Students With Exceptional Needs* (pp. 47–66). IGI Global., DOI: 10.4018/979-8-3693-0378-8.ch003

Skansi, S. (2018). *Introduction to Deep Learning: from logical calculus to artificial intelligence*. Springer. DOI: 10.1007/978-3-319-73004-2

Sripan, R., & Suksawat, B. (2010, January). Proposal of Fuzzy Logic-based Students´ Learning Assessment Model. ResearchGate. https://www.researchgate .net/publication/238519325_Propose_of_fuzzy_logic-based_students'_learning _assessment

Terra, M., Baklola, M., Ali, S., & El-Bastawisy, K. (2023). Opportunities, applications, challenges and ethical implications of artificial intelligence in psychiatry: A narrative review. *The Egyptian Journal of Neurology, Psychiatry and Neurosurgery*, 59(1), 80. DOI: 10.1186/s41983-023-00681-z

White paper on rights of persons with disabilities. (2015). [Online]. Available: https://www.ru.ac.za/media/rhodesuniversity/content/equityinstitution alculture/documents/White%20Paper%20on%20the%20Rights%20of %20Persons%20 with%20Disabilities.pdf

Yilin, T., & Wang, C. (2020). Research on the application of artificial intelligence in individualized education for special children. *Journal of Suihua College*, 40(07), 126–129.

Zavaraki, E. Z. (2023). Artificial Intelligence for Quality Education [Working Title]. DOI: 10.5772/intechopen.1004158

Zhang, F., Yu, H.-L., Wang, L.-L., Meng, Q., Li, S.-J., & Ni, W. (2017). Exploring the classification of rehabilitation robots. *Chinese Journal of Physical Medicine and Rehabilitation*, 39(08), 633–636.

KEY TERMS AND DEFINITIONS

Artificial Neural Networks: Artificial Neural Networks acts like biological neural networks after training through database. It requires external stimuli to learn and make contingent decisions similar to that of biological brain activities (Aggrawal, 2018).

Deep Learning: Deep Learning is known to have higher level construct in the form of various hierarchical architecture embedded in the countless hidden layers of Artificial Neural Networks (Guo et al, 2016).

Disability: Disability as that a person is called disabled when he/she is with sensory impairment of social, psychosocial, physical, mental or neurological dysfunctioning and is not able to take up social responsibilities with natural acceptance (Garg, and Sharma, 2020).

Expert Systems: An expert system is a technically designed program in order to understand and get the judgment of a subject matter expert (Gupta, and Nagpal, 2020).

Fuzzy Logic: Fuzzy Logic is a part of particular group and the elements of these groups are predetermined (Kambalimath & Deka, 2020; Özdemir & Kalınkara, 2020).

Genetic Algorithms: It is a bigger part of evolutionary algorithms and also a biologically inspired computational technique that is working efficiently to bring revolution. By its advance conceptual module this algorithm is providing cloud educational platform to assist special students with personalized learning (Lambora, Gupta, & Chopra, 2019).

Intelligent Agents: Intelligent agents are known as autonomous decision making software based on the present situation (Mbaabu, 2020).

Machine Learning: Machine Learning is known as a collection of algorithms based on the collected data, it helps in predicting, improve some utility function, explore and retain some unseen data and then processing the same (Amazon, 2021).

Natural Language Processing: Natural Language Processing is the group of computational processing's that analyzes natural occurring contents at various steps of linguistic analysis just a like and to understand human like language processing (Sen, and Akbay, 2023).

Chapter 5
Promoting Accessibility and Personalizing Learning Experiences Through AI

Elazab Elshazly
United Arab Emirates University, UAE

ABSTRACT

Artificial Intelligence (AI) is swiftly reshaping modern education through innovations in classroom management, personalized learning, and administrative effectiveness. This chapter investigates AI's diverse impact on education, emphasizing its role in improving accessibility and inclusivity. AI employs advanced algorithms and data analysis to customize educational content, pacing, and teaching methods to meet individual student requirements, thereby enhancing engagement and minimizing disruptions. Automated assessment tools deliver immediate feedback, enabling educators to concentrate on interactive teaching. Furthermore, AI applications in Special Education offer personalized learning experiences that enhance cognitive and social skills for students with diverse needs. Additionally, AI adoption in education is gaining traction in the Arab world to meet the demands of the Fourth Industrial Revolution and enhance learning outcomes.

INTRODUCTION:

In contemporary academia, Artificial Intelligence (AI) has emerged as a pivotal catalyst for transformation within the education domain, fundamentally altering conventional pedagogical approaches by fostering greater accessibility and tailoring.

DOI: 10.4018/979-8-3693-5538-1.ch005

Leveraging advanced algorithms and data analysis, AI tools offer distinct avenues to address diverse learning requirements and individual preferences, thereby fostering inclusivity and augmenting educational outcomes. This chapter delves into the multifaceted ways AI is reshaping the educational landscape, particularly in its capacity to enhance accessibility and personalize learning encounters for students on an individualized basis. It further examines the role of AI in Special Education, probing its potential impact on students with special needs. At the same time, this chapter will demonstrate the utilization of Artificial Intelligence in the Arab World and the challenges. Besides, the role of Artificial intelligence education and the promotion of inclusion.

An effective method of incorporating technology into education is via the use of artificial intelligence (AI). AI, as defined by the Merriam-Webster dictionary, refers to a machine's capacity to replicate intelligent human behavior. It is used for tasks that need the application of computer programs to do tasks that typically demand human intellect (Becker, 2017; Luckin et al., 2016). Popenici and Kerr (2017) provide a definition of AI systems as systems that handle complicated human tasks.

Actions such as acquiring knowledge, examining, combining, and adjusting. AI approaches are more used in educational contexts. Over the past few years, a group of scholars has been advocating for the use of AI in education (AIEd). They argue that AI techniques can customize learning, enhance the effectiveness of the learning environment, provide guidance to teachers and students during teaching and learning activities, and promote more interactive experiences in the classroom (Drigas & Ioannidou, 2012). Furthermore, Luckin et al. (2016) highlight that AIEd offers students the opportunity to develop essential abilities for the modern day, such as creativity and critical thinking. This technology also allows for the assessment and analysis of complicated talents. It aids in comprehending the instructional methodologies and learning environments required to effectively teach these abilities. AIEd, or Artificial Intelligence in Education, is a multidisciplinary area that has attracted the attention of scholars over the last three decades. The advancement of adaptive systems and versatile, individualized, interactive AI technologies has facilitated an interdisciplinary approach that integrates several fields and enables learning in any location (Luckin et al., 2016).

Artificial Intelligence

Artificial Intelligence (AI) is a branch of computer science that develops machines 'abilities to work, take decisions, and learn like humans. Also, Artificial Intelligence (AI) as a concept _refers to the ability of a digital machine to perform tasks commonly associated with intelligent beings '(Ritonga, et al.,2022). AI associated technologies include different branches, such as Computer vision, Robotics, Speech Recognition, Machine Learning, and Natural Language Processing.

Personalizing Education

Personalizing education can be considered as an evidence-based approach in educational practice. A personalized system of education is designed to recognize and analyze the individual-specific learning abilities, learning requirements, and study goals so as to customize the content delivered accordingly. This customization can be comprised of revision, reorientation and even reconstruction of an otherwise unified curriculum. An individual-specific focus can also help to eliminate learning difficulties of marginalized learners for a subsequent enhancement in teaching and learning productivity (Yonezawa et al., 2012). In fact, personalization is not a new concept in the education sector. Terms such as personalizing, matching, or tailoring of educational content have been used interchangeably over time to recognize and better understand the heterogeneity among learners with specific problems so as to prescribe remedial interventions more precisely, (Cook et al., 2018).

Artificial Intelligence in Special Education

Artificial Intelligence (AI) technology has developed computer tools for carrying out a number of tasks, simulating the intelligent way of problem solving by humans. AI techniques have also been identified as one of the most valuable applications in the field of special educational needs (SEN). The goal of these tools is to enhance the way children interact with their environment to promote learning and to enrich their daily life, (Hopcan et al.,2022).

Accessibility in Education

Accessibility in education ensures that all learners, regardless of their individual backgrounds, abilities, or situations, have equitable access to educational materials, may participate in learning activities, and can achieve academic success. Artificial intelligence (AI) technology and applications are crucial in enhancing accessibility by mitigating various barriers to learning. By using speech recognition and natural language processing algorithms, students with impairments may engage with educational information via voice commands, thereby overcoming challenges linked to conventional text-based materials (A. Agarwal & A. P. Agarwal, 2019). Furthermore, AI-powered adaptive learning systems play a vital role in tailoring educational experiences to meet the specific needs and preferences of individual learners. These platforms customize the pace, content, and teaching techniques based on the abilities, preferences, and progress of individual students, thereby catering to different learning styles and demands (Baker, 2016). These systems use machine learning algorithms to analyze students' performance data and provide personalized learning routes that specifically target their unique strengths and weaknesses. AI-powered adaptive learning systems empower learners by offering instant feedback and individualized interventions, enabling them to engage with educational content at their desired pace and degree of difficulty. This fosters a nurturing and all-encompassing educational atmosphere (C. Romero & S. Ventura, 2013).

Personalized Learning

Personalized learning refers to the technique of tailoring educational experiences to cater to the distinct needs, interests, and objectives of individual learners. The objective of this strategy is to enhance their level of engagement, drive, and scholastic performance. AI technologies provide unparalleled potential for customisation via the use of big data analytics, predictive modeling, and cognitive computing methodologies. Intelligent tutoring systems use algorithms to analyze learners' learning patterns, preferences, and misconceptions. Educators may provide personalized instruction and real-time guidance with this capability (Koedinger et al., 2012). Furthermore, artificial intelligence-driven recommendation engines use collaborative filtering algorithms to propose pertinent learning resources, assignments, and assessments, taking into account learners' interests, past interactions, and performance data (Y. Wang et al., 2015). These systems empower learners to design personalized learning routes and access additional learning opportunities, enabling them to explore their areas of interest, deepen their comprehension, and pursue self-directed learning objectives (D. G. Oblinger & J. L. Oblinger, 2005). Artificial Intelligence (AI) is becoming more and more integrated into the education sector, offering innovative methods to improve both the learning and teaching processes. Artificial Intelligence (AI) has a diverse array of uses in the field of education, including personalized learning opportunities and streamlined administrative processes. The potential in this sector is always expanding. AI is used in education via several means, including adaptive learning systems, intelligent tutoring systems, learning analytics, and educational data mining (Wang et al., 2023).

According to educators in information technology and information systems (Rizvi, 2023), technology has the potential to enhance curriculum and provide students with more engaging learning experiences. Nevertheless, concerns about the inflexibility of online learning systems have been brought forth. In order to address this challenge accurately, sophisticated learning algorithms have been developed in response. An innovation that has the potential to significantly impact the educational system is the use of state-of-the-art data analytics and artificial intelligence (AI) techniques. Modern learning platforms use historical data from previous users to tailor educational material and ensure its relevance to individual student requirements (Hasanov et al., 2019). Intelligent tutors and learning analytics are only two instances of AI-powered learning systems that provide individualized feedback and guidance to students, greatly enhancing their learning experience. Advancements in AI research have led to the development of various AI-enabled learning systems, such as intelligent tutors and learning analytics. These advancements in education have been beneficial as they provide students with individualized feedback and coaching, hence enhancing the efficiency of the learning process (Rizvi, 2023). Technology enhances students' educational experiences and equips instructors with the means to create dynamic, flexible learning environments. Artificial intelligence in education enables instructors to adapt their lesson plans to cater to diverse learners, enhancing both student engagement and learning results. The integration of technology and artificial intelligence into higher education has brought about a significant revolution in the way students study and professors educate. Higher education institutions (HEIs) may enhance the delivery of personalized and engaging learning experiences by using enhanced learning frameworks, virtual reality classrooms, and artificial intelligence (AI) enabled technologies. The full potential of these advancements will be realized over time, owing to continued research and technology progress, which will propel higher education into a dynamic and student-focused future.

The use of AI in Advancing Inclusive and Accessible Learning Environments

Vincent-Lancrin and van der Vlies (2020) authored a study aimed at making a valuable contribution to the G20 AI dialogue. The researchers examined the impact of AI on education and identified two specific concerns. Initially, they explored the use of artificial intelligence (AI) to enhance the quality of education, both inside the framework of the classroom and across the education system. Furthermore, they emphasized the need of equipping pupils with the necessary skills to thrive in an increasingly technologically advanced society. They provided an explanation of how artificial intelligence (AI) has the potential to enhance personalized learning and provide assistance to students with specific educational requirements. In order to fully use the potential of AI, it was crucial to establish a sense of trust among individuals about its functionality and ethical implementation. This resulted in novel policy dilemmas about "trustworthy AI," which included safeguarding data and assuring its equitable and unbiased use. Chan (2023) did a research to develop a policy about the integration of AI education in higher education. This was accomplished by examining the perceptions and consequences associated with text-generative artificial intelligence technology. The research included the involvement of 457 students, as well as 180 instructors and staff members. The review examined the various impacts of Artificial Intelligence on teaching techniques and the learning process in higher education. Moreover, the research suggests that students should have an active role in formulating and implementing this policy. Toyokawa et al. (2023) aimed to investigate the challenges and possibilities of integrating artificial intelligence (AI) into the field of inclusive education in Japan. The research used the Learning and Evidence Analysis Framework (LEAF), a learning environment that was augmented with learning analytics. The study used Active Reading as a representative learning activity, which took place in a resource room with two students. The research examined the learning records in the LEAF system as each student completed a particular learning activity. The study identified certain learning behaviors via the analysis of logs and examined the difficulties and potential advantages of using AI technology for learning. The research also considered the function of human interaction in promoting inclusive educational practices. McArdle (2022) sought to understand how future teaching approaches may promote justice and consistency while also incorporating AI systems focused on automation, standardization, and efficiency. The research was based on conceptual engagement, identifying major barriers for future implementation, and summarizing the latest investigations and studies. The text provided a summary of the complex difficulties that arise from the combination of AI technology and the need to develop inclusive educational methods.

Artificial Intelligence Technology and Educational Setting

AI technology may provide educators useful insights via data analysis, assisting them in making well-informed choices on classroom management techniques and teaching methods (Mohammed & Nell'Watson, 2019). AI offers assistive technology such as live transcription services, text-to-speech capabilities, and personalized learning experiences. These tools enable students with impairments or unique learning requirements to engage with course material in various forms and at their own preferred speed. Artificial Intelligence (AI) has the capability to develop tools that enhance accessibility in education. These tools include AI interfaces, instructional chatbots, and assistive robot mentors. They are designed to promote inclusivity and facilitate accessible education (Miao & Holmes, 2021). Artificial intelligence (AI) enhances the efficiency of instructors by automating time-consuming procedures, such as grading, enabling them to focus on delivering tailored education and assistance to students. Artificial intelligence (AI) enables instructors to get significant insights into student learning, allowing them to tailor teaching methods to meet the specific needs of each learner and provide immediate feedback (Vincent-Lancrin & van der Vlies, 2020). Artificial intelligence (AI) has the ability to provide an educational setting that is inclusive, ensuring that all students, regardless of disabilities or specific educational needs, have equal access to academic resources.

Improving Individualized Instructional Approaches with Artificial Intelligence

In a research done by Chen (2023), the aim was to investigate the potential of AI as a virtual trainer for adopting customized teaching techniques that cater to unique training needs. The study shown that AI techniques may be efficiently used in several facets of training, including knowledge management, requirements assessment, training organization, and result feedback. By using AI-based training methods, businesses may convert into knowledge-driven entities that excel at satisfying personalized learning needs and enhancing the overall quality of the educational experience. AI technologies facilitate a revolution in the several phases of training, including the development of knowledge bases, making evaluations of requirements, organizing training programs, and providing feedback on outcomes. Renz and Hilbig (2020) examined the practices of EdTech enterprises in using data for educational purposes. It was discovered that these organizations use Learning Analytics with AI to facilitate tailored learning. The research also examined individuals' cognitive processes about traditional and contemporary forms of schooling. Although the concept of flexible and tailored income using AI is appealing to many, practical implementation is hindered by issues like as data management, uncertainty, and a lack of comprehensive knowledge of data mechanics. Maghsudi et al. (2021) investigated customized learning to develop a highly efficient learning route that matched the individual strengths of learners and addressed their deficiencies in order to attain their intended objectives. The research used artificial intelligence techniques to precisely capture student attributes, using previous experiences and analyzing extensive datasets to reveal learner traits and commonalities. The research investigated the difficulties linked to AI-driven individualized education and put up possible remedies. These obstacles included issues such as the lack of peer contact, the need to maintain student motivation, the promotion of diversity, and the mitigation of biases in data and algorithms, among other concerns.

Artificial Intelligence Technology and Digital Expertise

Teaching kids about AI is essential for promoting digital literacy skills, critical thinking abilities, and preparing them for future academic pursuits and employment success. Students are provided with a basic comprehension of AI systems, allowing them to interact with and conceive concepts regarding AI approaches in a safe, responsible, and ethical manner (Pedro et al., 2019). The study of AI also encourages students to analyze and evaluate question structures, digest intricate information, question assumptions, and ponder the ethical implications associated with the use of AI technology. AI processes have a beneficial impact on the number and quality of communication between learners and instructors (Kateryna et al., 2020). Proficiency in AI may provide learners with the requisite knowledge and skills needed to pursue careers in technology, data science, and other highly sought-after areas. AI allows instructors to use AI technology to improve the support they provide to individual pupils when they have limited time available. Artificial intelligence improves the flexibility of instructional resources to align with students' skills and needs (Quaicoe & Pata, 2020). Artificial intelligence (AI) has the potential to enhance teachers' digital literacy and computer abilities, while also facilitating access to a wider range of digital instructional resources. Artificial intelligence (AI) has the potential to assist educators and learners in cultivating the necessary skills and abilities to excel in an educational setting that is heavily influenced by AI technology.

The Intersection Between Artificial Intelligence Technologies and Learning Styles

AI is believed to have a beneficial effect on the capacity to recognize and understand the unique learning styles of individual pupils. Learning styles pertain to the many methods that people prefer and prioritize in order to actively acquire knowledge. The common learning modes are visual, aural, kinesthetic, and reading/writing (Chan, 2023). Artificial intelligence has the capacity to use data and insights obtained from students' interactions with educational materials and technology in order to ascertain their learning preferences. This information may assist in tailoring instructional material and practices to more closely match the individual requirements of each student. AI has the capability to provide tailored recommendations, such as selecting appropriate teaching materials, organizing courses effectively, and determining the optimal timing for providing further support to specific learners (Chen et al., 2020). Historically, educators have depended on a restricted range of teaching methods. Nevertheless, AI can provide educators with valuable information and suggestions about how to modify their teaching methods, so allowing them to effectively cater to the various learning styles and requirements of their pupils (Almasri, 2022).

The use of Artificial Intelligence Technologies in the Context of Classroom Management.

Artificial intelligence (AI) assesses the unique learning requirements and talents of each student, enabling instructors to tailor their training to meet the specific needs of individual pupils. Implementing personalized strategies may effectively enhance student engagement and motivation, hence mitigating disruptive behavior within the classroom setting (Kim et al., 2020). AI-powered assessment solutions can efficiently analyze student performance on assignments and examinations, relieving instructors from time-consuming evaluation tasks. This enables instructors to concentrate more on teaching and engaging with students. Artificial intelligence solutions streamline the process of monitoring attendance and promptly notify instructors of student absences. This facilitates instructors in effectively monitoring attendance and resolving any possible concerns related to truancy. Artificial intelligence (AI) helps optimize classroom schedules and allocate resources, ensuring that instructors have timely access to necessary materials and facilities. This may enhance the overall efficiency of the educational environment (Chatterjee & Bhattacharjee, 2020). Artificial intelligence utilizes student data to promptly detect any problems or obstacles as they occur. As an example, it has the capability to identify kids who may be lagging behind or encountering difficulties with certain ideas, enabling instructors to intervene and provide supplementary assistance prior to issues escalating (Nazaretsky et al., 2022).

Artificial Intelligence Technology and its Relationships

Artificial intelligence may aid in tailoring educational material to meet particular needs and cater to the unique learning styles of individual pupils. By analyzing student data, artificial intelligence (AI) may suggest tailored resources, tasks, or study materials, enabling instructors to provide individualized instruction to each student. The act of customization demonstrates to pupils that their distinct learning requirements are being recognized and attended to, therefore bolstering their confidence in their educators (Guilherme, 2019). Artificial intelligence may enhance communication between educators and learners by using chatbots or virtual assistants. These technologies have the capability to respond to frequently asked questions, provide reminders, and provide assistance, so allowing instructors to allocate their attention towards more significant encounters. Students may find it more convenient to engage with their professors when they have more urgent problems, resulting in more robust connections (Shakhnoza, 2023). AI-driven evaluation systems may provide students with immediate feedback on their performance, helping them identify their areas of strength and weakness. Teachers may use this feedback to initiate substantive conversations with students on their development, establishing objectives and tactics for improvement. These interactions provide a nurturing and productive learning atmosphere (Ayuwanti & Siswoyo, 2021).

Utilization of Artificial Intelligence in the Arab World

The use of Artificial Intelligence (AI) in education has gained significant interest, especially in the Arab world. The motivation for this interest arises from the need to adjust education to the profound changes brought about by the Fourth Industrial Revolution, a worldwide problem that has a significant influence on the methods and outcomes of teaching and learning (Alraasibia, 2021). The countries of Saudi Arabia, UAE, Libya, Oman, Lebanon, Palestine, and Egypt have commenced the study conducted by Haneya et al. (2021) focuses on investigating and using artificial intelligence in educational systems. Nevertheless, according to Sourani (2019), Arab countries are now unprepared to substitute instructors with artificial intelligence (AI) owing to a range of distinctive obstacles they encounter, which differ from those experienced by Western nations.

Historically, education systems in the Arab world have faced challenges in traditional classrooms, such as restricted engagement and inefficient teaching methods that impede students' oral communication skills (Makhlouf, 2021). The issues were worsened by the COVID-19 epidemic, which led to a transition to online education and emphasized the need for creative solutions. Although there are challenges to overcome, technology has opened up new possibilities for assessing and improving teachers. Policymakers and governments have acknowledged the crucial role of technology in education (Makhlouf, 2021).

The use of AI applications in education shows potential for improving both the quality of instruction and the learning experiences. These programs have the capability to provide accurate evaluations, aid in the improvement of abilities, and demonstrate the benefits of intelligent teaching techniques (Abuzakiyeh, 2018). AI plays a crucial role in medical education by aiding with activities like analyzing medical images and making diagnoses. This technology enhances patient care and monitoring by enabling telehealth solutions (Haneya et al., 2021). Furthermore, artificial intelligence (AI) plays a vital role in the fight against infectious illnesses such as COVID-19 by providing assistance in remote monitoring and diagnosis.

AI and Machine Learning (ML) apps provide interactive and immersive learning environments, using virtual and augmented reality capabilities that may be accessed via digital devices such as tablets and smartphones (Haneya et al., 2021). These tools improve learning experiences and make administrative work easier for educators by automating grading procedures, therefore maximizing time management.

To summarize, the integration of artificial intelligence (AI) in education offers a revolutionary method for tackling obstacles and improving educational results in the Arab world. It provides a means to provide inclusive and high-quality education for all learners.

The Current Status of the Arab World

The Arab world has seen a surge in interest in artificial intelligence (AI), as many governments have introduced national AI plans and are actively exploring the possibilities of this technology. According to the Artificial Intelligence Index Report by Stanford University (Alghamdi et al., 2021), Saudi Arabia achieved a significant second place worldwide in terms of "AI awareness." The UAE is considered the leader in adopting AI, followed by Saudi Arabia and Egypt, as shown by this recognition and existing research. This reflects their strong interest in the transformational effects of AI on education.

In nations experiencing volatile circumstances such as Libya, Iraq, Palestine, and Lebanon, the primary emphasis of study is in the introduction of artificial intelligence (AI) methods and their consequences for intelligent educational systems, rather than on the examination of particular AI applications. Studies conducted in Libya examine the use of AI methods in facilitating intelligent education systems (Abuzakiyeh, 2018) and investigate the possible advantages of AI for students and teachers (Hussin et al., 2021). In a similar vein, research conducted in Iraq examines the use of artificial intelligence (AI) in education, specifically focusing on the viewpoint of university professors.

Although there has been some advancement in the use of AI, there are still difficulties in expanding AI efforts in the Arab world. Challenges include a scarcity of experience and proficient AI specialists, as well as restricted financing for AI research.

Additionally, there are challenges related to entrepreneurship and limited availability of data caused by privacy concerns and restrictions. However, there are many chances for AI to contribute to economic growth and have a significant influence on society in the area. Nations like as Egypt, Saudi Arabia, and the UAE are proactively allocating resources towards AI programs and policies in order to exploit its potential. The AI ecosystem in the Arab world is expected to see substantial growth in the near future due to the implementation of strategic policies, increasing financing, and talent development.

The Difficulties Associated with Using Artificial Intelligence (AI) in the Field of Education Within the Arab World.

The integration of Artificial Intelligence (AI) into education in the Arab world poses several obstacles. These difficulties include:

1. Infrastructure constraints: The use of AI in education requires a significant investment in infrastructure, including hardware, software, training, and networking. Alhashmi et al. (2021) highlight the need of investing in order to adapt to developments such as the incorporation of AI robots. Moreover, the resistance to transition from conventional teaching techniques to AI-driven methodologies is a significant obstacle (Sayed et al., 2023).
2. Resource limitations: Numerous educational institutions in the Arab world have limits in terms of resources, which hinder their ability to successfully use AI.
3. Cultural barriers: The cultural environment of the Arab world poses substantial challenges to the use of AI in education, since it is shaped by society conventions, beliefs, and attitudes towards technology. The presence of misunderstandings about the potential replacement of human instructors by AI contributes to the opposition against its deployment (Johnson et al., 2022).
4. Language barriers: The intricacy of the Arabic language poses difficulties for Natural Language Processing (NLP), such as its extensive morphology, intricate syntax, variances in dialects, and restricted linguistic resources in comparison to English. The development of sophisticated NLP models and procedures specifically designed for Arabic is impeded by these limitations (Johnson et al., 2022).
5. Ethical considerations: The use of AI in education gives rise to ethical problems related to privacy, prejudice, and accountability. These concerns need careful thought and the implementation of measures to address them.
6. Financial limitations: The exorbitant expenses linked to AI and its implementations provide economic obstacles for educational institutions aiming to incorporate AI into their systems and procedures.

Artificial Intelligence Education and the Promotion of Inclusivity

Countries worldwide are formulating strategic plans to provide future generations with the necessary skills and knowledge to succeed in the digital era (Touretzky et al., 2019). Given the rapid integration of AI skills and knowledge into a comprehensive education, it is crucial to tackle the issue of fairness (Chiu et al., 2021). According to UNESCO, a good school education should be planned in a just and inclusive way that allows all students to gain and enhance the information, abilities, and principles that contribute to a purposeful and productive life (Stabback, 2016). Inclusion and diversity, which are often referred to as the practice of ensuring equal opportunities and representation for all individuals regardless of their background or characteristics.

In order to guarantee the success of AI education, it is crucial to focus on enhancing the motivation and involvement of underrepresented groups in learning. This has been emphasized by several researchers (Delaine et al., 2016; Ibe et al., 2018; Chiu & Lim, 2020; Chiu & Mok, 2017; Chiu et al., 2020; Eccles, 2007; Prince & Hadwin, 2013). The effectiveness of formal school education is greatly influenced by the way instructors plan and execute learning activities (Kelly, 2009). Instructional designs that include inclusion and diversity may enhance student involvement by accommodating various requirements (Chiu & Lim, 2020; Chiu & Mok, 2017; Chiu et al., 2020). Self-determination theory (SDT) posits that student engagement and well-being may be enhanced by fulfilling three fundamental psychological needs: autonomy, competence, and relatedness.

Facilitating and Improving the Process of Learning Information and Skills

By using AI technology, educators may empower children with special needs to take control of their educational advancement. AI-driven adaptive learning systems provide prompt feedback and customized interventions, allowing students to progress at their own pace and skill level (Romero & Ventura, 2013). The amount of autonomy fosters a sense of accountability and efficacy among students with special needs, empowering them to surmount challenges and achieve their full potential. In addition, educational games and simulations that use artificial intelligence provide immersive learning experiences that cater to different learning preferences, hence enhancing student engagement and motivation (Holmes et al., 2018).

The Use of Artificial Intelligence in the Domain of Special Education

The rapid advancement of Artificial Intelligence (AI) technology has led to substantial advantages for educational approaches (DuPaul et al.,2013). Artificial Intelligence in Education (AIEd) has shown significant promise in assisting children with unique educational needs (Linnet et al., 2003). Artificial intelligence (AI) technology may be used to several areas of special education, as shown by studies conducted by Kieling et al. (2011), Hansen et al. (2018), and DuPau et al. (2013). AI systems have the capacity to provide personalized learning experiences tailored to satisfy the distinct learning requirements of each learner (Sridhar et al., 2017). Research has shown that artificial intelligence applications are efficacious in enhancing the abilities and literacy of pupils with distinctive educational difficulties (DuPaul et al., 2013). Furthermore, educational systems driven by artificial intelligence have the capability to handle monotonous teaching tasks, so allowing educators to focus on more intricate teaching strategies (DuPaul et al.,2013). Furthermore, artificial intelligence-powered assistive technologies enhance the independence and quality of life for children with unique educational needs (Sheehan et al., 2017). While the importance of AI in special education is generally acknowledged by researchers, more extensive research in this domain is required (Akutagava-Martins et al., 2016, Linnet et al., 2003). Furthermore, while AI technologies provide several benefits to the special educational needs (SEN) population, the perspectives and demands of this specific group are sometimes disregarded during the creation of these technologies (DuPaul et al., 2013).

Researchers emphasize the need of taking into account the unique viewpoints and requirements of the SEN (Special Educational Needs) population to promote a more inclusive and equitable environment in the advancement of AI.

Artificial intelligence and Pupils with Special Needs

Students with special needs may encounter unique challenges in accessing educational resources and achieving academic success. Traditional teaching approaches may not adequately accommodate the diverse learning requirements of people. Artificial Intelligence (AI) may potentially overcome these challenges by offering personalized learning experiences and flexible support systems. AI technology may use advanced algorithms and data analytics to cater to the individual needs of children with special requirements, eventually promoting inclusivity and enhancing their educational accomplishments.

AI applications provide remedies for a broad spectrum of shortcomings. Personalized systems have the ability to align with the distinct attributes of pupils and meet their specific requirements (Brown et al., 2020; Fahimirad & Kotamjani, 2018). AI has a positive impact on students with exceptional needs (Karsenti, 2019). Various AI-powered solutions, such as virtual reality and augmented reality robots, may assist students with special needs by enhancing their involvement and learning (Vincent-Lancrin & Van der Vlies, 2020). According to Karsenti (2019), these 3D interactive environments have the potential to motivate students to engage with and comprehend the course material. AI approaches are anticipated to contribute towards the attainment of certain sustainable goals set by the United Nations.

The focus of the development goals (SDGs), particularly Goal 4, is to provide universal access to high-quality education for all individuals (UN, 2020). For example, "... guarantee equitable opportunities for individuals who are vulnerable, such as persons with disabilities, ethnic minorities, and children in precarious circumstances, to access education and vocational training at all levels." The reference "(United

Nations, SDG 4.5)" pertains to the United Nations' Sustainable Development Goal 4.5. The efficiency potential of AI approaches in aiding kids with exceptional needs is significant.

The Advantages of Artificial Intelligence in Assisting Individuals with Special Needs

1. Customized and responsive education: Artificial intelligence algorithms have the capability to examine large quantities of data in order to detect certain patterns of learning in individuals. Patterns facilitate the development of customized learning experiences for individuals with specific needs. These customized treatments improve understanding, involvement, and the learning results in general (Patwa, 2020).
2. Enhancement of cognitive abilities: AI-driven teaching tools and programs provide engaging and thought-provoking experiences. Environments that foster the growth of cognitive abilities. AI enhances the learning experience for those with special needs by replicating real-life situations and offering immediate feedback, therefore facilitating improvement, their cognitive skills in critical thinking, problem-solving, and decision-making.
3. Improving social skills: Artificial intelligence (AI) applications have the capability to enhance the social and emotional development of individuals with special needs. Enhance pupils' social contacts and bolster their communication abilities. AI-driven virtual agents provide a secure environment for learners to engage in social interactions, hence lowering anxiety and enhancing social preparedness (Praglin et al., 2020).
4. Environment that promotes inclusivity in learning: AI technologies facilitate the bridging of the accessibility gap by offering alternate ways. Regarding communication, modifications to the curriculum, and the use of assistive technology. Individuals with specific requirements. Students have the ability to get instructional resources in several media, including audio, visual, or the concept of tactility is used to guarantee equitable involvement and foster inclusiveness (Rose, 2018).

Facilitating Handling Administrative Tasks

AI applications are used in school administration procedures, including attendance tracking and newsletter distribution. An AI program can accurately forecast students' likelihood of dropping out, providing this information to school authorities who may then take proactive measures to avoid it (Karsenti, 2019). An early warning system that relies on long-term data sets shows promise for predicting and recognizing danger (Brown et al., 2020), as well as assisting school administrators in finding ways to minimize the school drop-out rate (Luckin et al., 2016; Vincent-Lancrin & Van der Vlies, 2020). These forecasts and warnings assist educators in monitoring students' progress, informing pupils of their performance, and offering constructive feedback to both instructors and students (Fahimirad & Kotamjani, 2018).

Enabling Evaluation

Artificial intelligence (AI) continuously tracks and assesses students' progress in acquiring skills in real-time along their learning journey (Karsenti, 2019). Conventional assessments are often used in modern education; however, they may not adequately assess intricate abilities like problem-solving and teamwork. An embedded assessment is a method used to evaluate students' understanding of a topic by continuously assessing their progress in real-time (Vincent-Lancrin & Van der Vlies, 2020). Artificial intelligence employs techniques such as voice recognition and language analysis to assess students' cognitive processes and responses throughout the learning process. AI solutions facilitate the assessment and measurement of complex abilities in game-based evaluations, both in formative and summative contexts (VincentLancrin & Van der Vlies, 2020). Furthermore, AI technology has the capability to assess and evaluate assignments and examinations, as shown by Fahimirad and Kotamjani (2018) and Karsenti (2019). Automated AI grading streamlines the grading process for instructors by efficiently evaluating open-ended questions, as well as multiple choice and fill-in-the-blank questions. Ongoing research is being conducted on the evaluation of open-ended questions (Fahimirad & Kotamjani, 2018). Artificial intelligence has the capability to efficiently manage and complete activities that often require a significant amount of time (Karsenti, 2019). AI assessments are effective in delivering consistent and unbiased evaluations by using standardized criteria and offering constructive comments on student performance (Chassignol et al., 2018).

Incorporating Artificial Intelligence (AI) Technology into Current Educational Systems in Order to Guarantee the Incorporation of all Individuals and the Availability of Resources for Everyone.

- The incorporation of Artificial Intelligence (AI) technology into current educational systems Frameworks have the capacity to improve inclusion and accessibility by offering Customized educational encounters, encouraging active participation from students, facilitating different methods of communication, and cultivating equitable chances for learners from all backgrounds.

Incorporating Artificial Intelligence (AI) technology into educational systems provides novel possibilities to guarantee inclusiveness and accessibility for all learners.

- Concerns and the provision of teacher training are essential for the appropriate and efficient integration of AI in education. With ongoing technology breakthroughs, several elements of society are being reshaped.
- By using artificial intelligence, instructors may effectively cater to a wide range of learning requirements and adjust their teaching methods accordingly.
- Considering several factors is crucial for the appropriate and efficient incorporation of AI technology in educational environments.

The Advantages of Incorporating AI Technology into Current Educational Systems Frameworks

1. Tailored educational experiences: AI technology has the capability to examine extensive quantities of student data, including learning patterns, Customized learning routes are generated by considering individual preferences and optimizing performance. This customized the technique enables instructors to address the unique requirements of each student, promoting enhanced involvement and comprehension (VanLehn et al., 2007).
2. Enhanced student involvement: By using AI-driven interactive learning systems and By using virtual assistants, student engagement may be heightened. AI systems have the ability to adjust to pupils' progress, provide feedback in real-time, and give customized assistance, resulting in order to enhance motivation and enhance the ability to remember information, Morales et al. (2021) conducted a study.
3. Additional techniques of communication: AI technology enables learners to use different means of communication. to enable those with disabilities, such as vision or hearing problems, to get information and Engage actively in classroom activities. Speech recognition, natural language processing, and multimodal interfaces help to the development of an inclusive and fair environment. Praglin et al. (2020) propose a learning environment that caters to the needs of all students.
4. Promoting equity and ensuring equal access to opportunities: Artificial intelligence technology has the capability to eliminate obstacles to learning by creating instructional materials. Readily available, regardless of geographic location or physical impairments. Cloud-based systems, chatbots driven by artificial intelligence, and algorithms based on machine learning have the ability to provide the aim is to provide individualized assistance and make education accessible to everyone, thereby promoting equitable opportunity for all learners (Brynjolfsson & McAfee, 2017).

Obstacles and Essential Factors to take into Account

1. The availability and accessibility of technological systems and networks.

Efficient incorporation of AI technology need a sturdy technical framework, including dependable internet access, suitable hardware, and software. Available assets: Ensuring fair and equal access to these resources across students and schools is important to prevent worsening the already existent inequalities (Penuel et al. 2019).

2. Ethical concerns and the protection of data privacy:

The incorporation of AI technology gives rise to apprehensions over the confidentiality and protection of data. The responsible use of student data. Optimizing the acquisition and use of data. Respecting the rights of individuals to privacy is crucial for maintaining trust, openness, and safeguarding learner information (Edwards & Vlachokyriakos, 2017).

3. Professional development and assistance for educators:

In order to successfully incorporate AI technology into educational systems, instructors must sufficient training and opportunity for professional growth. Teachers ought to be Proficient at using AI technologies and analyzing data. To achieve optimum learning results, it is important to have insights and retain pedagogical control (Ertmer et al., 2012).

CONCLUSION

To summarize, the use of Artificial Intelligence (AI) into educational methods has great potential for enhancing accessibility and tailoring learning experiences, especially for students with varied learning requirements. AI technologies use sophisticated algorithms and data analytics to provide customized solutions that cater to individual tastes and overcome learning barriers. AI facilitates individualized interventions and adaptive learning systems, allowing students to interact with educational information according to their own speed and competence level. This promotes inclusion and improves educational results.

Additionally, recommendation engines and intelligent tutoring systems powered by AI enable learners to investigate their interests and pursue self-directed learning objectives, therefore enhancing their educational experiences. Within the field of special education, artificial intelligence (AI) technologies provide customized solutions to meet the distinct needs of children with disabilities, improving their independence and overall well-being. Future research and development activities must focus the views and requirements of the special educational needs (SEN) population to guarantee the construction of inclusive and fair AI-driven educational settings.

The ongoing development and integration of AI in educational environments has the significant capacity to enhance accessibility and customize learning experiences for all students. Through the responsible and inclusive use of AI technology, educators have the ability to empower students, enabling them to overcome challenges, optimize their capabilities, and attain academic excellence.

References

Abuzakiyeh, K. (2018). Expert systems in artificial intelligence and their employment in education and education. *Journal of Faculties of Education, University of Al-Zawiya, 12*.

Alghamdi, R., Alshehri, A., & Alqahtani, M. (2021). The impact of artificial intelligence on learning and teaching in higher education in Saudi Arabia. *Education and Information Technologies*, 26(3), 3547–3566.

Alhashmi, M., Mubin, O., & Baroud, R. (2021). Examining the use of robots as teacher assistants in UAE classrooms: Teacher and student perspectives. *Journal of Information Technology Education*, 20, 245–261. DOI: 10.28945/4749

Almasri, F. (2022). Simulations to teach science subjects: Connections among students' engagement, self-confidence, satisfaction, and learning styles. *Education and Information Technologies*, 27(5), 7161–7181. DOI: 10.1007/s10639-022-10940-w PMID: 35153535

Alraasibia, A. (2021). Mechanisms for developing teaching and learning in the Sultanate of Oman in accordance with the requirements of the Fourth Industrial Revolution. *Al-Andalus Journal for Humanities and Social Sciences, 45*(8). Retrieved from http://www.andalusuniv.net/AUSTNEW/ma gazine/sh/2021/8/45/7908bbd-5015f9b3e7b5 7ceefdd1580d1.pdf

Ayuwanti, I., & Siswoyo, D. (2021). Teacher-student interaction in mathematics learning. *International Journal of Evaluation and Research in Education*, 10(2), 660–667.

Brynjolfsson, E., & Mcafee, A. (2017). Artificial intelligence, for real. *Harvard Business Review*, 1(95), 1–31.

Chai, C. S., Lin, P. Y., Jong, M. S. Y., Dai, Y., Chiu, T. K., & Qin, J. (2021). Perceptions of and behavioral intentions towards learning artificial intelligence in primary school students. *Journal of Educational Technology & Society*, 24(3), 89–101.

Chiu, T. K. (2021a). A holistic approach to the design of artificial intelligence (AI) education for K-12 schools. *TechTrends*, 65(5), 796–807. DOI: 10.1007/s11528-021-00637-1

Chiu, T. K. (2021b). Applying the self-determination theory (SDT) to explain student engagement in online learning during the COVID-19 pandemic. *Journal of Research on Technology in Education, 54*(sup1), S14-S30.

Chiu, T. K. (2021c). Digital support for student engagement in blended learning based on self-determination theory. *Computers in Human Behavior*, 124, 106909. DOI: 10.1016/j.chb.2021.106909

Chiu, T. K. (2021d). Student engagement in K-12 online learning amid COVID-19: A qualitative approach from a self-determination theory perspective. *Interactive Learning Environments*, 31(6), 3326–3339. DOI: 10.1080/10494820.2021.1926289

Chiu, T. K., & Chai, C. S. (2020). Sustainable curriculum planning for artificial intelligence education: A self-determination theory perspective. *Sustainability (Basel)*, 12(14), 5568. DOI: 10.3390/su12145568

Chiu, T. K., Chai, C. S., Williams, P. J., & Lin, T. J. (2021). Teacher professional development on self-determination theory–based design thinking in STEM education. *Journal of Educational Technology & Society*, 24(4), 153–165.

Chiu, T. K., & Churchill, D. (2016). Adoption of mobile devices in teaching: Changes in teacher beliefs, attitudes and anxiety. *Interactive Learning Environments*, 24(2), 317–327. DOI: 10.1080/10494820.2015.1113709

Chiu, T. K., Jong, M. S. Y., & Mok, I. A. (2020). Does learner expertise matter when designing emotional multimedia for learners of primary school mathematics? *Educational Technology Research and Development*, 68(5), 2305–2320. DOI: 10.1007/s11423-020-09775-4

Chiu, T. K., & Lim, C. P. (2020). Strategic use of technology for inclusive education in Hong Kong: A content-level perspective. *ECNU Review of Education*, 3(4), 715–734. DOI: 10.1177/2096531120930861

Chiu, T. K., Meng, H., Chai, C. S., King, I., Wong, S., & Yam, Y. (2021). Creation and evaluation of a pretertiary artificial intelligence (AI) curriculum. *IEEE Transactions on Education*, 65(1), 30–39. DOI: 10.1109/TE.2021.3085878

Chiu, T. K., & Mok, I. A. (2017). Learner expertise and mathematics different order thinking skills in multimedia learning. *Computers & Education*, 107, 147–164. DOI: 10.1016/j.compedu.2017.01.008

Chiu, T. K. F. (2020). Six key principles in designing AI curriculum for middle schools. Association for Educational Communications and Technology (AECT) International Convention, November 3–7, Jacksonville, Florida. Retrieved from https://members.aect.org/pdf/Proceedings/proceedings20/2020i/20_03.pdf

Delaine, D. A., Williams, D. N., Sigamoney, R., & Tull, R. G. (2016). Global Diversity and Inclusion in Engineering Education: Developing Platforms toward Global Alignment. *International Journal of Engineering Pedagogy*, 6(1), 56. DOI: 10.3991/ijep.v6i1.5372

Edwards, E., & Vlachokyriakos, V. (2017). Artificial intelligence in the home: How to help humans think. In *Proceedings of the 2017 ACM Conference on Computer Supported Cooperative Work and Social Computing*, 363-375

Ertmer, P. A., Paul, A., Molly, L., Eva, R., & Denise, W. (2012). Examining teachers' beliefs about the role of technology in the classroom. *Journal of Research on Technology in Education*, 45(2), 101–125.

Guilherme, A. (2019). AI and education: The importance of teacher and student relations. *AI & Society*, 34(1), 47–54. DOI: 10.1007/s00146-017-0693-8

Haneya, H., AlKaf, D., Bajammal, F., & Brahimi, T. (2021). A meta-analysis of artificial intelligence applications for tracking COVID-19: The case of the UAE. *Procedia Computer Science*, 194, 180–189. DOI: 10.1016/j.procs.2021.10.072 PMID: 34876933

Hasanov, A., Laine, T. H., & Chung, T. S. (2019). A survey of adaptive context-aware learning environments. *Journal of Ambient Intelligence and Smart Environments*, 11(5), 403–428. DOI: 10.3233/AIS-190534

Hessen, S. H., Abdul-Kader, H. M., Khedr, A. E., & Salem, R. K. (2022). Developing Multiagent E-Learning System-Based Machine Learning and Feature Selection Techniques. *Computational Intelligence and Neuroscience*, 2022(1), 2941840. DOI: 10.1155/2022/2941840 PMID: 35140765

Hopcan, S., Polat, E., Ozturk, M. E., & Ozturk, L. (2023). Artificial intelligence in special education: A systematic review. *Interactive Learning Environments*, 31(10), 7335–7353. DOI: 10.1080/10494820.2022.2067186

Ibe, N. A., Howsmon, R., Penney, L., Granor, N., DeLyser, L. A., & Wang, K. (2018, February). Reflections of a diversity, equity, and inclusion working group based on data from a national CS education program. In *Proceedings of the 49th ACM Technical Symposium on Computer Science Education* (pp. 711-716). DOI: 10.1145/3159450.3159594

Johnson, D., Alsharid, M., El-Bouri, R., Mehdi, N., Shamout, F., Szenicer, A., Toman, D., & Binghalib, S. (2022, June). An experience report of executive-level artificial intelligence education in the united arab emirates. *Proceedings of the AAAI Conference on Artificial Intelligence*, 36(11), 12766–12773. DOI: 10.1609/aaai.v36i11.21555

Kim, J., Merrill, K., Xu, K., & Sellnow, D. D. (2020). My teacher is a machine: Understanding students' perceptions of AI teaching assistants in online education. *International Journal of Human-Computer Interaction*, 36(20), 1902–1911. DOI: 10.1080/10447318.2020.1801227

Maghsudi, S., Lan, A., Xu, J., & van Der Schaar, M. (2021). Personalized education in the artificial intelligence era: What to expect next. *IEEE Signal Processing Magazine*, 38(3), 37–50. DOI: 10.1109/MSP.2021.3055032

Makhlouf, M. K. I. (2021). Effect of artificial intelligence-based application on Saudi preparatory-year students' EFL speaking skills at Albaha university. *International Journal of English Language Education*, 9(2), 36–56. DOI: 10.5296/ijele.v9i2.18782

McArdle, L. (2022). Artificial Intelligence and Inclusive Education: Speculative Futures and Emerging Practices. *Journal of Interdisciplinary Studies in Education*, 11(2), 210–211.

Miao, F., & Holmes, W. (2021). *Artificial intelligence and education. Guidance for policy-makers*. United Nations Educational, Scientific and Cultural Organization (UNESCO).

Mohammed, P. S., & 'Nell'Watson, E. (2019). Towards inclusive education in the age of artificial intelligence: Perspectives, challenges, and opportunities. *Artificial Intelligence and Inclusive Education: Speculative futures and emerging practices*, 17-37.

Morales, M. (2021). Enhancing student engagement in math education through the use of gamified AI virtual assistants. *Frontiers in ICT (Lausanne, Switzerland)*, 8, 614019.

Nazaretsky, T., Cukurova, M., & Alexandron, G. (2022, March). An instrument for measuring teachers' trust in AI-based educational technology. In *LAK22: 12th international learning analytics and knowledge conference* (pp. 56-66).

Praglin, L. J. (2007). Ida Cannon, Ethel Cohen, and early medical social work in Boston: The foundations of a model of culturally competent social service. *The Social Service Review*, 81(1), 27–45. DOI: 10.1086/511013

Renz, A., & Hilbig, R. (2020). Prerequisites for artificial intelligence in further education: Identification of drivers, barriers, and business models of educational technology companies. *International Journal of Educational Technology in Higher Education*, 17(1), 1–21. DOI: 10.1186/s41239-020-00193-3

Ritonga, M., Zulmuqim, Z., Bambang, B., Kurniawan, R., & Pahri, P. (2022). SIAKAD Machine Learning for Correcting Errors in Speaking Arabic. *World Journal on Educational Technology: Current Issues*, 14(3), 768–780. DOI: 10.18844/wjet.v14i3.7214

Rɪzvɪ, M. (2023). Investigating AI-Powered Tutoring Systems that Adapt to Individual Student Needs, Providing Personalized Guidance and Assessments. *The Eurasia Proceedings of Educational and Social Sciences*, 31, 67–73. DOI: 10.55549/epess.1381518

Rose, D. (2018). *Universal Design for Learning Environments*. Harvard Education Press.

Sayed, W. S., Noeman, A. M., Abdellatif, A., Abdelrazek, M., Badawy, M. G., Hamed, A., & El-Tantawy, S. (2023). AI-based adaptive personalized content presentation and exercises navigation for an effective and engaging E-learning platform. *Multimedia Tools and Applications*, 82(3), 3303–3333. DOI: 10.1007/s11042-022-13076-8 PMID: 35789938

Shakhnoza, M. (2023). The role of AI in teaching: Advantages, disadvantages, and future implications. *Genius Repository, 24*, 8–12. Retrieved from https://www.geniusrepo.net/index.php/1/article/view/43

Stabback, P. (2016). What Makes a Quality Curriculum? In-Progress Reflection No. 2 on" Current and Critical Issues in Curriculum and Learning". *UNESCO International Bureau of Education*. Retrieved from https://unesdoc.unesco.org/ark:/48223/pf0000243975

Touretzky, D., Gardner-McCune, C., Breazeal, C., Martin, F., & Seehorn, D. (2019). A year in K–12 AI education. *AI Magazine*, 40(4), 88–90. DOI: 10.1609/aimag.v40i4.5289

Toyokawa, Y., Horikoshi, I., Majumdar, R., & Ogata, H. (2023). Challenges and opportunities of AI in inclusive education: A case study of data-enhanced active reading in Japan. *Smart Learning Environments*, 10(1), 67. DOI: 10.1186/s40561-023-00286-2

VanLehn, K., Lynch, C., Schulze, K., Shapiro, J. A., Shelby, R., Taylor, L., & Wintersgill, M. (2005). The Andes physics tutoring system: Lessons learned. *International Journal of Artificial Intelligence in Education*, 15(3), 147–204.

Vincent-Lancrin, S., & Van der Vlies, R. (2020). Trustworthy artificial intelligence (AI) in education: Promises and challenges. In *OECD education working papers* (Vol. 218). OECD Publishing.

Xia, Q., Chiu, T. K., Lee, M., Sanusi, I. T., Dai, Y., & Chai, C. S. (2022). A self-determination theory (SDT) design approach for inclusive and diverse artificial intelligence (AI) education. *Computers & Education*, 189, 104582. DOI: 10.1016/j.compedu.2022.104582

Chapter 6
Creating Academically Advanced Learning Environments for Gifted Students Through Artificial Intelligence

Tia M. Neal
https://orcid.org/0000-0003-1246-0998
University of Louisiana at Monroe, USA

ABSTRACT

The objective of this chapter is to examine how to provide gifted learners with classroom settings that are equipped to challenge them in ways that are cognitively appropriate and intellectually stimulating through the use of artificial intelligence (AI). This chapter seeks to explore the following questions: (a) How can AI be utilized to enhance regular education environments to provide gifted learners with personalized learning experiences? (b) In what ways can educators utilize AI to engage gifted learners with formative assessments that are differentiated to appropriately challenge their advanced cognitive abilities? (c) What is the role of human intelligence in tandem with AI when it comes to providing educational experiences for gifted learners, and what are the ethical considerations that may arise from this collaborative approach to instruction? The chapter will conclude with a discussion of solutions and recommendations as well as implications for future research.

DOI: 10.4018/979-8-3693-5538-1.ch006

INTRODUCTION

In the realm of special education, there is one group of learners who find themselves at a crossroad. One path can lead to promising opportunities while the other can lead to challenges, disinterest, and detachment from the classroom environment. These young minds are gifted learners, full of promise, potential, talents, and abilities. They represent individuals who could become tomorrow's leaders, innovators, and critical thinkers. However, meeting the needs of gifted learners within the regular education classroom can be a difficult task due to the depth and complexity that is often needed to challenge them at appropriate levels (Rimm et al., 2018).

Gifted learners exist in almost every classroom, and they possess a variety of academic, social, and emotional needs (Neihart et al., 2002), which are not always recognized by the regular or general education teacher (Reis & Renzulli, 2004; Reis, 2023). This can simply be due to lack of training in this specific area of special education in teacher preparation programs or lack of professional learning opportunities within school districts (Davidson Institute, 2024). Fortunately, with the rise of artificial intelligence (AI) in the last few years, educators in both regular education and special education environments can develop personalized learning paths, can provide opportunities for differentiation and intellectual stimulation, and can tailor instruction to their specific needs (Edutopia, 2023).

This chapter begins at the crossroad where educators have a choice to utilize AI to provide gifted learners with a rich educational experience through innovative technologies or to continue down the path of tradition where opportunities for advanced learning and individualized growth can possibly be missed. The objective of this chapter is to examine the various aspects of that crossroad to determine how to provide gifted learners with classroom settings that are equipped to challenge them in ways that are cognitively appropriate and intellectually stimulating. This chapter seeks to explore the following questions: (a) How can AI be utilized to enhance regular education environments to provide gifted learners with personalized learning experiences? (b) In what ways can educators utilize AI to engage gifted learners with formative assessments that are differentiated to appropriately challenge their advanced cognitive abilities? (c) What is the role of human intelligence in tandem with AI when it comes to providing educational experiences for gifted learners, and what are the ethical considerations that may arise from this collaborative approach to instruction?

The chapter will conclude with a discussion of solutions and recommendations for utilizing AI within both the regular and special education settings. Implications for future research of this topic will also be discussed. Additionally, this chapter seeks to stress the importance of designing learning environments that are academically appropriate for gifted learners, so they may journey down paths that lead to educational fulfillment and maximization of their learning potential.

BACKGROUND

Who are gifted learners? According to the National Association for Gifted Children (NAGC), gifted learners are those who can perform, or have the capability of performing, at advanced academic levels when compared to their chronologically aged peers in one or more areas due to possessing one or more gifts and/or talents (National Association for Gifted Children [NAGC], n.d.a). According to the NAGC (n.d.), these individuals "Require sufficient access to appropriate learning opportunities to realize their potential" (para. 1). Gifted learners come from all races, ethnicities, cultural backgrounds, and economic situations (NAGC, n.d.). These students may even have learning disorders in addition to their gifts and/or talents (Baldwin, Omdal, Pereles, 2015; Karnes & Stephens, 2008) and may require specialized interventions and supports (NAGC, n.d.) due to their dual exceptionalities.

Krijan, Jurčec, and Borić (2015) conducted a study in which they sought to better understand the mindset of primary school teachers towards gifted learners, and one notable finding that emerged from their study was that:

...teachers generally have a neutral attitude toward the gifted, meaning that teachers recognize the needs, support and social value of the gifted, but lack a clearly defined attitude toward special provisions for the gifted and toward the consequences special support of the gifted might have. (p. 681)

When teachers, not just primary teachers, do not see the importance of supporting gifted learners within their classrooms, these students are at risk to have lower self-concept and self-efficacy, which increases the likelihood that they will not perform at their highest levels (Neal, 2016). It is the responsibility of all educators to design and modify learning environments that can provide appropriate academic challenges within each learner's levels of ability. Learning environments should intentionally be designed in ways that will motivate gifted learners and will allow them to explore topics of interest to increase their potential for success (Meulen et al., 2014).

Given this information, it is essential to provide support for gifted learners within classroom environments to meet their individualized learning needs. Using AI, teachers can weave into their lessons differentiation that allows for personalized learning of the content. Teachers can also differentiate the process of learning for students as well as the products that they create by utilizing AI tools and features. Formative assessments can be scaffolded to levels that will challenge students to apply their learning in new and meaningful ways. Teachers can generate ideas that will give students choices to create products that are all connected to one standard or objective yet can meet the criteria for a given rubric. If educators will choose the path towards transformation, creativity, and innovation, AI has the potential to revolutionize classroom environments for gifted learners.

FOCUS OF THE CHAPTER

Education has evolved and morphed so much over the course of history, as it is an extraordinarily dynamic field. As such, it is one that requires educators to change and shift when new curricula or technology are introduced. These changes involve shifts in pedagogy that have moved the traditional classroom from being one that is teacher-centered to one that is student-centered, where the learner has an increased amount of autonomy over their learning experience. Educators oftentimes are met with resistance when it comes to changes that deviate from the traditional practices that have been commonly utilized for centuries.

Modern educators must intertwine standards and curricula together with integrity in a way that meets the needs of all learners in their classrooms. Educators are expected to scaffold tasks for gifted learners within their zone of proximal development (ZPD), which is "the distance between the actual developmental level as determined by independent problem solving and the level of potential development as determined through problem-solving under adult guidance, or in collaboration with more capable peers" (Vygotsky, 1978, p. 86). This is no easy task to accomplish, yet it is necessary for teachers to remain effective in their roles.

Integrating new technology into their classrooms gives educators the power to create learning environments that can motivate, excite, and inspire students to achieve success within their ZPD. When the field of education shifts and changes, and it always will, educators must stand ready to embrace those changes with open minds that will allow them to adapt teaching methods to foster innovation within their classrooms. The remainder of this section of the chapter will discuss some common challenges faced by gifted learners within regular education classrooms and the benefits of providing them with intellectual stimulating environments with AI while also taking into consideration potential ethical issues that may arise.

Challenges Faced by Gifted Learners

Oftentimes gifted learners are categorized as being one-size-fits-all, and consideration is not given to the various ability levels that can be found within the subcategories of giftedness (mild, moderate, high, exceptional, and profound (International Gifted Consortium, 2020). No two gifted learners are alike (Institute for Educational Advancement, 2022), and they each bring into their classrooms a unique set of challenges. While not an exhaustive list, some of those challenges are listed below with the intent to later determine how AI can be utilized to support gifted learners with specific challenges.

Perfectionism

As defined by Neihart et al. (2002) "Perfectionism is a combination of thoughts and behaviors generally associated with high standards or expectations for one's own performance" (71). Perfectionism can be seen as a challenge for gifted learners because sometimes they are unable to set healthy boundaries or limits for themselves when it comes to achieving a goal (Olton-Weber, et.al, 2020). "The desire to complete a project perfectly may be a response to high expectations of others, putting the gifted individual into a state of anxiety when performance is uncertain", which has the potential to lead to anxiety and depression (Cross & Cross, 2015, p. 164).

Asynchronous Development

When a child experiences asynchronous development, it means that the child is "more advanced mentally than others of [the same] chronological age, and most [gifted children] have disparities between their intellectual abilities (as indicated by mental age) and their physical abilities (closely aligned to chronological age)" (Neihart et al., 2002, p. 31). When a gifted learner experiences asynchronous development in a regular education classroom, significant challenges may arise. For example, a gifted learner may have difficulties making friends. Their peers are the same chronological age, yet intellectually their abilities differ, which could lead to the gifted learner feeling isolated.

Twice Exceptional Students

Simply put, when someone is twice exceptional (2e), it means having both a gift and a disability (Karnes & Stephens, 2008). An example of a 2e child would be a learner who is gifted in mathematics but has difficulties in reading due to a diagnosis of dyslexia. This could also impair the child's ability to successfully work problems in mathematics, which in this case the disability would mask the gift, potentially leading to a lack of appropriate supports or interventions. In such situations, educators must adapt their teaching methods to challenge gifted learners' strengths while simultaneously providing support for weaknesses.

Underachievement

According to McCoach, Siegle, and Rubenstein (2020), gifted underachievement is when there is a substantial difference between what gifted leaners produce when given tasks versus what they have the potential to produce. Too often, gifted learners who have immense potential fail to succeed (Davidson Academy, 2021). "Research reveals that social-emotional difficulties and underachievement of gifted students are the result of both internal and external factors; however, it is less understood as to which influences have greater effects on the other" (Bass, 2014, pp. 243-244). Instruction in a general education classroom is typically geared towards supporting learners of average abilities and fails to provide gifted learners with an intellectually stimulating environment. If a curriculum is not differentiated in a manner that challenges their advanced academic abilities, gifted learners could become disengaged, which could lead to boredom, frustration, underachievement and could even lead to behavioral disruptions within the classroom. Without opportunities for intellectual stimulation equal to their abilities, gifted learners may not actualize their fullest potential.

Addressing the Challenges to Benefit Gifted Learners

To address these challenges, educators can employ a variety of traditional strategies, such as providing explicit instruction, opportunities for peer collaboration and student discourse, flexible group strategies, specific feedback, etc. Offering challenging and intellectually stimulating curriculum in addition to providing for regular education students or students who are struggling can be a cumbersome task for teachers of all grade levels. However, teachers now have the benefit of utilizing AI to support their work. If teachers choose to leverage AI tools, they can enhance the overall learning experiences for their students, track their progress, and then provide personalized learning experiences that are more meaningful to them, which can lead to success for each student.

For example, given the challenges mentioned above, AI can support students with characteristics of perfectionism by helping them to set realistic goals and manage their expectations. It can also help teachers develop coaching plans for students with perfectionism traits. To address asynchronous development, AI can develop differentiated learning materials and content that aligns with a student's intellectual abilities. AI can also develop accommodations and modifications that can help educators support 2e students within regular education learning environments. To support underachievement in gifted learners, AI can increase student engagement and motivation by differentiating the content that is learned, the process of learning, and the products created.

There are a multitude of ways that students of all ability levels can be supported using AI in both the special education and the regular education environments. The ideas listed in the above paragraph are only a few and do not begin to scratch the surface of what one can do when AI is used to support students in classroom environments. Additionally, AI is ever evolving and making improvements and advancements in technology, which will continue to lead to enhanced teaching and learning experiences for both educators and students.

Using Artificial Intelligence to Enhance Classroom Environments for Gifted Learners

When educators offer gifted learners challenging opportunities that are intellectually stimulating, they are fostering excellence in the classroom. Additionally, they are ensuring equity in the classroom by providing students with activities that are tailored to their unique learning needs within their ZPD. These types of learning environments are those in which students of varying ability levels have the potential to succeed and experience academic success through activates that allow for trial and error and the receipt of nonjudgmental feedback (Lee, 2024). The next section of the chapter will explore how educators can leverage various AI tools currently available at the time of publication to craft environments for gifted learners that can promote equity in education by optimizing their learning experience.

Magic School

"More than four in ten K-12 teachers in the U.S. (44%) say they "always" or "very often" feel burnt out at work—outpacing all other industries nationally" (Magic School, 2024b, para. 1). This AI tool is one that can reduce burdens for teachers and help them save valuable time so that they can focus on what is most important – the children! "At the core of teaching is interacting with a child to help them grow—a deeply human, demanding, and complex responsibility. But today, teaching requires an unreasonable amount of work behind the scenes, much of it repetitive and tedious" (Magic School, 2024b, para. 2).

Once an account has been created with Magic School (2024a), educators have access to a wonderfully overwhelming number of tools within the platform. Tools are available for both teachers and students. Examples of some of the tools that are available for teachers are worksheet generators, assessment generators, an Individual Education Program (IEP) generator, a Behavior Intervention Plan (BIP) generator, a feedback generator, a unit plan generator, a choice board generator, and so much more (Magic School, 2024a)! Examples of some of the tools that are available for students are an email writer, a multiple explanations generator, tools that can make what they are learning relevant to their lives and to the real world, and many more (Magic School, 2024a)! Examples of how to use some of these tools are listed below:

Multiple Choice Assessment

On the Magic School (2024a) dashboard, the option to create an assessment using the "Multiple Choice Assessment" tool is available. While a multiple assessment tool does not capture the depth and breadth of a standard, it does provide a way for educators to formatively assess content knowledge, and when combined with other assessment methods, such as open-ended questions and short answer questions, it helps to determine if gifted learners have mastered the content presented to them. This particular AI tool is great for gifted learners because the grade level can be altered to increase the rigor without jeopardizing the integrity of the standard. For instance, if a gifted learner is in 2nd grade but working on a 10th grade reading level, an educator can alter the grade level within the tool to adjust the content of the assessment to meet the reading level of the student. The educator would then input a topic, standard, text, or a description of the assessment into the tool, being as specific as possible. For example, if the following Louisiana Student Standard (2022) for social studies "2.8 Interpret legends, stories, and songs that contributed to the development of the cultural history of the United States, including Native American legends, African American history, tall tales, and stories of folk heroes" (p. 6) is input into the tool on a tenth-grade level, the following cultural history legends assessment is produced by Magic School (2024a):

1. What type of stories and legends contributed to the development of the cultural history of the United States?
   a. Fairy tales
   b. Native American legends
   c. Greek mythology
   d. Science fiction tales
2. Which cultural history is specifically mentioned as contributing to the development of the United States in the context of legends and stories?
   a. European history
   b. African American history
   c. Australian history
   d. Asian history
3. What is one category of stories highlighted in the text as contributing to the development of the cultural history of the United States?
   a. Ghost stories
   b. Love stories

c. Detective stories
d. Tall tales

4. Which group of people is mentioned in the text as having legends that influenced the cultural history of the United States?
   a. Australians
   b. Native Americans
   c. Egyptians
   d. Vikings
5. What kind of heroes' stories are specifically referred to as part of the cultural history of the United States?
   a. Superheroes
   b. Greek heroes
   c. Folk heroes
   d. Antiheroes

An answer key (1. B; Native American legends; 2. B: African American history; 3. D: Tall tales; 4. B: Native Americans; and 5. C: Folk heroes) is provided. An educator can choose up to 20 assessment questions utilizing this tool. Magic School (2024a) cautions educators to check the key for accuracy as mistakes can be made, and answers could potentially be inaccurate. AI does not replace the teacher, so care should be taken to ensure that both questions and answers are accurately aligned to the topic, standard, text, learning goal, standard, or objective prior to administering the assessment to the student. If used as a formative assessment, this will help to provide a valid and reliable measure of what gifted learners have mastered, which will ultimately support educators in making informed and data-driven instructional decisions needed for the academic growth of their students.

Choice Board

The products that gifted learners create should be consistent with their learning styles and should address real world problems to validate their learning experiences. Providing gifted learners with choices in how they synthesize their products is one way to differentiate learning environments to meet their needs. When students are allowed to choose how to create their own products based on a given specific learning goal, standard, objective, or topic, it gives them a certain amount of control over their learning experience, thus helping them to become more autonomous learners (University of Amsterdam (2022). Choice boards are an approach to instruction that breaks away from the traditional one-size-fits-all approach, allowing gifted learners to work towards autonomy and individualized growth. Not only do choice boards help develop autonomy, but they empower gifted learners by capitalizing on their strengths. Choice boards are a great approach for 2e learners as it helps them develop a sense of agency as well as a sense of direction.

To ensure that gifted learners have a variety of choices, an educator can use the "Choice Board" tool. This tool can help to ensure that gifted learners have product choices that are available to them at varying levels of difficulty. Having differentiated product choices can increase motivational levels and reduce boredom for early finishers. On the Magic School (2024a) dashboard, an educator would need to select the "Choice Board" tool. Once the tool has been selected, the grade level needs to be chosen, and then the learning goal, standard, objective, or topic should be input into the tool. After that, there is the option to provide additional details into the choice board. One suggestion is to include a statement that tells the tool to provide as many options as possible based on the varying levels of Bloom's Taxonomy (Vanderbilt University, 2024). For instance, given the 2nd grade student working on a 10th grade level from the scenario above and utilizing the same Louisiana Student Standard (2022) for social studies "2.8 Interpret legends, stories, and songs that contributed to the development of the cultural history of the United States, including Native American legends, African American history, tall tales, and stories of folk heroes" (p. 6), the choice board provides an educator with options for students. Table 1 below shows the results of the choice board provided by Magic School (2024a) when given these factors:

Table 1. Cultural History Interpretation

Assignment Title	Assignment Description
Visual Timelines	Create a timeline with images and captions depicting key events in Native American and African American history.
Story Retelling	Choose a Native American legend or African American story to retell in your own words.
Song Analysis	Listen to a traditional song from Native American or African American culture and write about its historical significance.
Character Profile	Create a detailed profile of a folk hero from American folklore, highlighting their traits and contributions.
Tall Tale Creation	Invent your own tall tale featuring exaggerated characters and events, inspired by American folklore.
Comparative Analysis	Compare and contrast two Native American legends, focusing on their themes and cultural significance.
Cultural Work	Create a piece of artwork inspired by a legend, story, or folk hero from American cultural history.
Research Project	Conduct research on a lesser-known story or song from African American history and present your findings.
Legend Mapping	Create a map tracing the origins and spread of a specific legend or folktale in the United States.

Projects, such as these provided by the choice board, are wonderful ways to differentiate the products for gifted learners. Additionally, projects such as these are a great way to support gifted learners who struggle with perfectionism tendencies in the classroom. Choice board projects tend to be less intimidating than a normal test or assignment (University of Pennsylvania, 2023), which lends the learning experience more towards focusing on the process of learning rather than the actual product created, thus reducing the focus on having a perfect score.

Student Work Feedback

Anytime that either a formative assessment, a summative assessment, or a project is given to gifted learners, specific academic feedback should be provided as this will help students progress more intentionally towards their learning objectives (Yale University, 2021). Educators can harness the data obtained from the differentiated products and provide gifted learners with specific academic feedback to continuously develop environments that are both enriching and challenging. Given the example above, if an educator wanted to provide specific feedback to a gifted learner on the creation of a tall tale, the "Student Work Feedback" tool on Magic School (2024a) could be utilized. Using the same example of the 2nd grader working on a 10th grade level, the educator would need to input the assignment description into the tool. The focus of the feedback could be to provide the student with a set of glows and grows. The next step is to input the student work. A sample set of work based on the assignment description required for the tall tale creation was generated by OpenAI (2024) and is as follows:

In the untamed Old West, there roamed Big John Buckaroo, a legendary cowboy so tall he ducked to avoid clouds, and with boots that could stomp out wildfires. With his trusty steed Thunderhoof and grizzly companion Bearclaw, Big John righted wrongs and battled outlaws with his lightning-fast lasso. One day, he faced off against the notorious outlaw Bad Bart, whose long beard trailed like tumbleweeds and voice could shatter glass. In a showdown at high noon, Big John emerged victorious, outsmarting Bart with wit and strategy, restoring justice to the frontier. As tales of his exploits spread, Big John's legend grew, forever etching his name in American folklore as the greatest cowboy of all time.

Once the student grade level, assignment description, focus of the feedback, and student work have been input into the "Student Work Feedback" tool, Magic School (2024a) can generate specific feedback that can be provided to the gifted learner. Based on the example given, the following areas of strength and areas of growth were identified by (Magic School, 2024a):

Areas of Strength: Your creation of exaggerated characters like Big John Buckaroo, Bearclaw, and Bad Bart really captures the essence of American folklore and tall tales. The vivid descriptions of the characters and their actions make the story engaging and entertaining for the reader. The use of hyperbole and larger-than-life events, such as stomping out wildfires and a showdown at high noon, adds to the excitement and entertainment value of the tale.

Areas for Growth: Consider adding even more over-the-top details and wild exaggerations to further enhance the tall tale aspect of the story. Try to develop the plotline with more unexpected twists and turns to keep the reader guessing and eager to know what happens next. Work on incorporating dialogue between characters to bring the narrative to life and add depth to their interactions.

As with anything provided by AI, an educator should read both the assignment, as well as the feedback, to ensure accuracy and alignment to the task. This type of specific academic feedback can provide the 2nd grade gifted learner in the example with constructive guidance on how to improve the assignment. Suggestions that include developing an unexpected plotline will help the gifted learner grow and increase skills as a writer, thereby increasing autonomy.

Make it Relevant!

Continuing with the example above, the gifted learner can take the standard utilized in the assessment and the choice board and make a deeper connection to it using the tool called "Make it Relevant!" on the Magic School (2024a) platform. Based on the gifted learner's intellectual level, the student would choose grade 10 and then input the Louisiana Student Standard (2022) for social studies "2.8 Interpret legends, stories, and songs that contributed to the development of the cultural history of the United States, including Native American legends, African American history, tall tales, and stories of folk heroes" (p. 6). The gifted learner would then be prompted to input interests, such as enjoys pop music, making videos, and American food. Based on the information input into the tool, Magic School (2024a) generated the following ideas:

Connecting Pop Music to Cultural Legends and Stories: Pop music often draws on a rich tapestry of cultural stories, legends, and historical events. By exploring the roots of some of your favorite pop songs, you could discover how they're influenced by the cultural history of the United States. For example, many African American musicians have used their music to share stories of their heritage, struggles, and victories, contributing significantly to the cultural landscape of the U.S. Creating videos that analyze these connections could be an engaging way to blend your interest in pop music and video making with learning about cultural history. This could involve researching the background of certain songs and presenting your findings in a creative video format.

American Food as a Reflection of Cultural History: American food is a melting pot of various cultures, each contributing unique flavors and dishes to the national cuisine. You could explore how traditional Native American foods have influenced modern American dishes or how African American culinary traditions have shaped the food scene in the U.S. This might involve creating a video series where you cook these dishes, discuss their origins, and illustrate how they reflect the cultural history of the United States. It can be a delicious and tangible connection to the past, showing how cultural stories and histories continue to influence everyday life.

When a gifted learner utilizes the "Make it Relevant!" tool on Magic School (2024a), connections are made that draw the standard closer to the things that are relevant in the student's life. The gifted learner is then encouraged to complete other activities that connect to the standard, thereby solidifying the learning experience even more deeply through critical thinking. This type of learning extends beyond the classroom and into the gifted learner's day-to-day life, empowering the student through a meaningful academic experience and fostering a love for learning.

ChatGPT

Another tool that an educator can utilize to extend the learning based on the example that has been provided thus far is ChatGPT (OpenAI, 2024). There are a multitude of ways that this tool can be utilized. When one opens the language platform, it simply asks the question "How can I help you today?" (OpenAI, 2024), while a message box found below awaits the prompt. Hypothetically, assume an educator needed to differentiate a regular education curriculum that had been provided by the district to better meet the needs of the 2nd grade gifted student that has been discussed in the example above. This hypothetical educator is expected to teach the Louisiana Student Standard (2022) for social studies "2.8 Interpret legends, stories, and songs that contributed to the development of the cultural history of the United States, including Native American legends, African American history, tall tales, and stories of folk heroes" (p. 6). Assume that the following low-level question is in the curriculum: What is a song that is part of the history of the United States?

The educator could utilize ChatGPT (OpenAI, 2024) to differentiate this question to better meet the needs of the 2nd grade gifted learner discussed in the examples provided. For instance, the educator could ask the AI tool to differentiate the question based on the varying levels of Bloom's Taxonomy, taking into consideration the specific interests and learning styles of the student. Additionally, the educator could ask the AI tool to provide small group activities for each level. The educator could narrow down the request to be as specific as needed, and the AI tool will oblige the request. Based on this criteria, the following bulleted list was generated by ChatGPT (OpenAI, 2024).

1. Remembering (Knowledge):
   a. Question: What is a song that is part of the history of the United States?
   b. Small Group Activity: In small groups, students brainstorm and list songs they know that are associated with American history. They can use resources such as history books, music websites, or personal knowledge to generate a list.
2. Understanding (Comprehension):
   a. Question: How do songs contribute to the understanding of American history?
   b. Small Group Activity: Students discuss in small groups the role of songs in conveying historical events, themes, or sentiments. They analyze lyrics, discuss cultural context, and identify examples of songs that have had significant impact on shaping American history.
3. Applying (Application):
   a. Question: Can you create a song that represents a specific event or era in American history?
   b. Small Group Activity: In small groups, students select a historical event or era and collaborate to create a song that captures its significance. They consider the tone, style, and lyrics of the song to effectively convey the historical context and themes.
4. Analyzing (Analysis):
   a. Question: How do different genres of music reflect different aspects of American history?
   b. Small Group Activity: Students examine various genres of American music (e.g., blues, jazz, folk, rock) and discuss how each genre reflects the cultural, social, and historical context of its time. They compare and contrast musical styles, themes, and influences.
5. Evaluating (Evaluation):
   a. Question: Which song do you think best represents a particular period in American history, and why?
   b. Small Group Activity: Students analyze and evaluate different songs from various periods of American history, considering factors such as historical accuracy, cultural significance, and emotional impact. They present their findings and reasoning to the class.
6. Creating (Synthesis):
   a. Question: How would you use music to teach others about an important event or figure in American history?

b. Small Group Activity: Students collaborate to design a multimedia presentation or performance that uses music as a central element to educate others about a specific aspect of American history. They incorporate research, storytelling, and musical elements to create an engaging and informative presentation.

Depending on the environment, either regular education classrooms or gifted education classrooms, the gifted learner could dig deep into the standard and explore it as far as possible. By differentiating the question and providing the small group activities, the educator in the hypothetical scenario is providing the gifted learner with challenging activities that are intellectually stimulating through the differentiation of the content, the process of learning, as well as the products that students are expected to create. These activities will not only challenge the gifted learner's ability level but will also provide an opportunity to extend the learning experience into something significant, memorable, and meaningful, thus increasing motivation and decreasing underachievement levels.

Diffit

One tool that is meant to strictly differentiate content is called Diffit (2024). On the dashboard of this AI tool, it will prompt the user to either ask a question, attach an article or a video using a uniform resource locator (URL), or insert an excerpt from a text. The tool will ask the user to choose a reading level and select the language. Utilizing the same scenario with the 2nd grade student mentioned above and inputting the Louisiana Student Standard (2022) for social studies "2.8 Interpret legends, stories, and songs that contributed to the development of the cultural history of the United States, including Native American legends, African American history, tall tales, and stories of folk heroes" (p. 6) into Diffit (2024) while selecting a 10th grade reading level yields the following results:

- Adapted Reading Passage: In the vast tapestry of American cultural history, legends, stories, and songs have played a significant role in shaping the nation's identity. From Native American legends to African American history, tall tales, and stories of folk heroes, these narratives have contributed to the rich cultural heritage of the United States.

Native American legends hold a special place in the cultural history of the United States. Passed down through generations, these stories often revolve around nature, spirituality, and the origins of their tribes. They provide valuable insights into the beliefs, values, and traditions of Native American communities. These legends serve as a reminder of the deep connection between Native Americans and the land they inhabited long before the arrival of European settlers.

African American history is another crucial aspect of the cultural history of the United States. The stories and experiences of African Americans, from the time of slavery to the civil rights movement, have shaped the nation's understanding of equality, justice, and perseverance. These stories shed light on the struggles, triumphs, and contributions of African Americans, highlighting their resilience and determination in the face of adversity.

Tall tales, on the other hand, bring a touch of humor and exaggeration to American cultural history. These larger-than-life stories often feature characters with extraordinary abilities or feats. They are rooted in the oral traditions of various regions and have entertained generations with their imaginative narratives. Tall tales not only entertain but also provide insights into the values and aspirations of different communities across the United States.

Stories of folk heroes further contribute to the cultural history of the United States. These heroes, often ordinary individuals who rise to extraordinary circumstances, embody the ideals and values of their respective communities. From Johnny Appleseed to Paul Bunyan, these folk heroes have become symbols of American ingenuity, resourcefulness, and perseverance. Their stories inspire and remind us of the power of the human spirit.

Songs, too, have played a significant role in shaping the cultural history of the United States. From spirituals to protest songs, music has been a powerful medium for expressing emotions, spreading messages, and documenting historical events. African American spirituals, for instance, served as a means of communication and resistance during the time of slavery. These songs not only provided solace but also conveyed hidden messages of hope and freedom.

Interpreting legends, stories, and songs that contributed to the development of the cultural history of the United States allows us to gain a deeper understanding of the diverse communities that have shaped the nation. It enables us to appreciate the richness and complexity of American culture, fostering empathy, respect, and a sense of shared heritage. By exploring these narratives, we can connect with the past, learn from it, and continue to build a more inclusive and vibrant future.

- Summary:
  - Legends, stories, and songs have shaped the cultural history of the United States.
  - Native American legends provide insights into their beliefs and traditions.
  - African American stories highlight struggles, triumphs, and contributions.

Diffit (2024) effectively took the 2nd grade standard and modified it to be more advanced for the 2nd grade learner who reads and comprehends material on a 10th grade reading level. In addition to the adapted reading passage and the summary, Diffit (2024) also generated a list of key vocabulary terms with examples of how to use the terms in a sentence. Short answer prompts and open-ended prompts were also generated as well as multiple graphic organizers, such as hexagonal thinking and writing strategy organizers, that can be used to map and chart thoughts when given specific tasks. Examples of the short answer and open-ended prompts that were generated by Diffit (2024) are as follows:

- Short Answer Prompts:
    - What is the significance of Native American legends in shaping the cultural history of the United States? Answer: Native American legends hold a special place in the cultural history of the United States as they provide valuable insights into the beliefs, values, and traditions of Native American communities. They also remind us of the deep connection between Native Americans and the land.
    - How have African American stories and experiences contributed to the understanding of equality and justice in the United States? Answer: African American stories and experiences, from the time of slavery to the civil rights movement, have shaped the nation's understanding of equality, justice, and perseverance. These stories shed light on the struggles, triumphs, and contributions of African Americans, highlighting their resilience and determination.
    - What role do tall tales play in American cultural history? Answer: Tall tales bring humor and exaggeration to American cultural history. Rooted in oral traditions, these larger-than-life stories entertain and provide insights into the values and aspirations of different communities across the United States.
- Open-ended Prompts:
    - How do the legends, stories, and songs mentioned in the text reflect the cultural heritage of your own community or background?
    - In what ways can the struggles and triumphs of African Americans mentioned in the text inspire you to overcome challenges in your own life?
    - Think about a folk hero or a character from a tall tale mentioned in the text. How does their story resonate with your own values and aspirations?

Diffit (2024) is a tool that educators can use to create personalized learning paths for gifted learners that keep the integrity of the standard at the heart of the work. The more advanced content and challenging activities that are presented to gifted learners through Diffit (2024) will help them stay engaged with the material, which ultimately helps them grow academically and can reduce underachievement. Of course, as with any AI tool, teachers will need to monitor the accuracy of the content and provide gifted learners with specific support as they work through their assigned tasks.

Gemini

A tool that is very similar to ChatGPT (OpenAI, 2024) is called Gemini (Google AI, 2024). When a user visits the dashboard of Gemini, it will ask "How can I help you today?", and then the prompt or command need only be entered into the dialog box (Google AI, 2024). Given the example of the 2nd grade gifted learner working on a 10th grade reading level, it is highly possible that the student is experiencing asynchronous development due to advanced cognitive abilities far beyond that of the child's chronological peers. Having an advanced vocabulary and the ability to comprehend and analyze complex texts could lead to the gifted learner having a difficult time relating to peers, which could lead to social isolation. This isolation could also lead to anxiety and even depression, which could then potentially lead to underachievement. Inputting the scenario into Gemini (2024) and asking it to build a plan that includes enrichment, acceleration strategies, social and emotional support, and the creation of a supportive environment yielded the following results and suggestions:

- Enrichment:
    - Provide access to advanced materials: This could include books, articles, or other resources that are more challenging than what the child is typically exposed to in the classroom. Look for age-appropriate materials that deal with complex topics.
    - Encourage independent learning: Give the child opportunities to explore their interests on their own. This could involve providing them with time and space to work on projects or helping them find online resources that can supplement their learning.
    - Offer opportunities for creativity: This could involve enrolling the child in art, music, or drama classes. It could also involve providing them with time and materials to pursue their own creative interests.
- Acceleration:

- o Grade skipping: This is a controversial option, but it may be appropriate for some gifted children. If the child is significantly ahead of their peers in all subjects, skipping a grade may allow them to be challenged academically.
- o Subject acceleration: This allows the child to move ahead in one or more subjects while remaining at grade level in others. This is a good option for children who are gifted in specific areas.
- o Early college entrance: Some gifted children are ready to begin college coursework at a young age. This can be a great way to challenge them academically and allow them to be with peers who are more intellectually similar.

- Social and Emotional Support:
  - o Social skills groups: These groups can help gifted children learn how to interact with their peers in positive ways.
  - o Mentorship programs: Mentorship programs can connect gifted children with adults who can provide them with guidance and support.
  - o Counseling: A counselor can help gifted children deal with the social and emotional challenges that can come with being gifted.
- Supportive Environment:
  - o Communication with teachers: It is important for parents and teachers to communicate regularly about the child's needs. Teachers can provide enrichment opportunities in the classroom and help the child feel supported.
  - o Advocacy: Parents of gifted children may need to advocate for their child's needs. This may involve working with teachers, administrators, or school boards to ensure that the child has access to appropriate programs and services.
  - o Finding a gifted community: There are many online and in-person communities for gifted children and their families. These communities can provide support and friendship for gifted children.
  - o Celebrate their strengths and interests.
  - o Provide opportunities for them to challenge themselves.
  - o Help them to develop a growth mindset.
  - o Encourage them to be themselves.

These suggestions and ideas could be appropriate for meeting the needs of the gifted learner in the scenario. However, if these suggestions are not specific enough, an educator can simply tell Gemini (2024) to be more specific or give more examples for one of the ideas given. For example, if an educator likes the ideas or suggestions given for social and emotional support and wants more details or resources, one only need to ask Gemini (2024), which can yield results that are similar to the following:

- Social Skills Groups:
    - Targeted Skills: Look for groups that address specific areas gifted children struggle with, such as active listening, perspective-taking, or conflict resolution.
    - Local Programs: Check with your school district, community centers, or after-school programs for social skills groups specifically designed for gifted children.
- Online Resources:
    - The National Association for Gifted Children (NAGC) has a directory of programs for gifted children, which may include social skills groups (https://nagc.org/).
    - Social Thinking (https://www.socialthinking.com/) provides resources and training for educators and parents to help children develop social thinking skills.
- Mentorship Programs:
    - Match Interests: Connect your child with a mentor who shares their interests. This can provide a valuable source of guidance and support.
    - Formal Programs: Look for gifted student mentorship programs offered by universities, museums, or local organizations.
    - Informal Mentors: Consider reaching out to professionals in your child's field of interest to see if they'd be willing to mentor them informally.
- Counseling:
    - Individual Counseling: A therapist specializing in gifted children can help them navigate social anxieties, perfectionism, or feelings of isolation.
    - Group Counseling: Group counseling specifically for gifted children can provide a safe space for them to connect with peers who understand their experiences.
- Resources:
    - The American Psychological Association (APA) has a psychologist locator tool to find a therapist in your area who specializes in gifted children (https://www.apa.org/).
    - SENG (Supporting Emotional Needs of the Gifted) offers a directory of therapists and counselors who work with gifted individuals (https://www.sengifted.org/).
- Additional Support Strategies:

- o Social and Emotional Learning (SEL) Activities: Integrate SEL activities into your daily routine to help your child develop self-awareness, relationship skills, and responsible decision-making. There are many free online resources available, or you can check with your child's school counselor.
- o Books and Articles: Encourage your child to read books about giftedness and social-emotional challenges. Here are a few suggestions:
  - "Who Am I in the World?" by Ellen Johnsen
  - "Freaks, Geeks, and Asperger's: Understanding Clumsy Kids in a Mixed-Up World" by Tony Attwood
  - "https://www.amazon.com/Survival-Guide-Gifted-Kids-Under/dp/1575424487" by Judy Freeman
  - Uniquely Gifted: A Guide to Supporting and Understanding Advanced Learners" by Diane Montgomery (https://www.amazon.com/Dyslexia-Strategies-Interventions-Sandra-Rief/dp/1935609165)

All of these ideas, suggestions, and resources provided are completely generated by AI (Gemini, 2024), and not only are they appropriately designed for the gifted learner in the given scenario, but they are also ideas that an educator did not have to take time to craft. Each of these ideas, suggestions, and resources were created in a matter of seconds by only inputting a simple, yet specific prompt. Utilizing AI can help educators save valuable time while crafting high quality accommodations and modifications for gifted learners in their classrooms. This allows educators to give more detailed attention to the experience of teaching and learning, which will ultimately allow them to foster deeper and more meaningful relationships with their students, creating a supportive and risk-free learning environment.

Ethical Considerations

When utilizing AI, educators should remain vigilant to ensure that the tools they are using are not perpetuating bias, so that they may uphold equity within their classrooms. These tools are artificial, not human, and therefore cannot operate on the same intelligence and awareness levels. Knowing that, educators should be very careful not to choose resources that are beyond the scope of a student's ability level. The objective is to utilize AI to help gifted learners develop agency and autonomy to grow and succeed, so it is extremely important to ensure that the tasks generated by AI are aligned to the ability levels of the learners.

Additionally, student names or any other identifiable information should never be input into AI to protect the privacy of the learners. Any data that is created by AI and collected or stored for gifted learners should be done in a way that safeguards their privacy and confidentiality. Gifted learners have the right to come to school each day knowing that they are protected, and this should include protection with AI.

Finally, remember that AI does not replace human intelligence. AI is a technology tool, and as a tool, it should complement the learning experience and support the teacher in making instructional decisions. In no way should AI replace a teacher, as doing so hinders the human connection, as well as the learning environment itself. AI should enhance the teaching and learning experience for both students and teachers, not replace it.

SOLUTIONS AND RECOMMENDATIONS

At the beginning of this chapter, challenges faced by gifted learners were discussed. In the example given throughout the chapter, the strategies suggested ways to help motivate the gifted learners with challenging tasks that could potentially motivate the student to achieve as opposed to the possibility of the student underachieving. Additionally, the gifted learner in the example faced the challenge of asynchronous development, and AI was utilized to determine strategies and resources for support. However, the gifted learner in the example was not challenged by a disability, perfectionism, or any other issues; but what if a situation arose where a gifted learner did face challenges due to disabilities or perfectionism?

An educator could utilize the AI tools listed throughout the chapter to design personalized learning paths for the gifted learner based on the specific areas of strengths and weaknesses. The educator can also alter the delivery of the content based on the gifted learner's needs. Specific academic feedback can be generated using AI tools to support the gifted learner, help track progress, and identify areas for growth. Project-based learning opportunities can also be created based on the gifted learner's needs. The possibilities are endless! No matter what issue an educator or gifted learner is facing, AI can be utilized to develop solutions, suggestions, ideas, resources, and tasks to help meet the need, fill a learning gap, and ultimately challenge the learner at appropriate levels.

Knowing that AI can be a valuable tool in education, one recommendation is for educators to immerse themselves in any professional learning opportunities that are available to enhance their understanding of AI in educational settings. Professional learning opportunities could be conferences, conventions, webinars, local trainings within school districts, online courses, collaboration with other educators, and professional learning communities. Taking time to reflect on the practice of utilizing AI within the classroom to discern what worked and what did not work is also a great way to continuously improve one's teaching craft. Learning how to effectively integrate these tools into a teaching and learning environment will ultimately benefit the gifted learners both in regular education settings and gifted education settings.

IMPLICATIONS FOR FUTURE RESEARCH

The field of AI is ever evolving, constantly moving, changing, and growing. There are a multitude of tools available, not just the tools listed in the chapter, for educators to use to enhance the learning environments for gifted students. Knowing this, research in this area should continually analyze the effectiveness of utilizing AI within the classroom environments, particularly when it comes to educating diverse populations, such as gifted students, in a way that maximizes their potential for success. More research in creating personalized learning pathways for gifted learners would be increasingly helpful in designing learning environments specifically tailored to meet their unique learning needs. Additionally, research should consider the impact that AI has on the outcome of success for gifted learners, both in regular education and gifted education classrooms.

Another area of research that would be beneficial for educators is the consideration of specific training programs that could disseminate information to teachers regarding the use of AI powered educational platforms. It would be beneficial for educators to receive uniform training or professional learning to ensure that information is being distributed equally and fairly. Furthermore, it would be beneficial to research the impact of such a training program to determine effectiveness and to determine what type of ongoing support is needed for educators.

CONCLUSION

At the beginning of this chapter, three questions were presented as a central focus: (a) How can AI be utilized to enhance regular education environments to provide gifted learners with personalized learning experiences? (b) In what ways can educators utilize AI to engage gifted learners with formative assessments that are differentiated to appropriately challenge their advanced cognitive abilities? (c) What is the role of human intelligence in tandem with AI when it comes to providing educational experiences for gifted learners, and what are the ethical considerations that may arise from this collaborative approach to instruction? In response to the first and second question, multiple suggestions were listed to help educators integrate AI tools into their classroom practices with a specific focus on providing personalized learning experiences through differentiated assessments and academic feedback. In response to the third question, the role of human intelligence used in tandem with AI to create academic experiences for gifted learners was discussed in the focus of the chapter, as were the ethical considerations that may arise.

Integrating AI into classroom practices has enormous potential when it comes to providing enriching learning environments that can empower gifted leaners. Their unique needs can be met by simply inputting data into an AI tool and telling it specifically what is needed. Doing so can help educators create personalized learning experiences while providing gifted learners with specific academic feedback to guide them. AI is constantly changing at a rapid pace, and educators are on a continuous journey of discovery as they learn how to use new AI tools to navigate their classrooms. It is essential that while on this voyage of exploration that educators never lose sight of what matters most – the students.

Hence, when educators find themselves at the crossroad of where traditional teaching methods meet innovative teaching practices using AI, they are faced with a decision as to which path they should take on their journey as teachers in the field. One path offers standardized practices that often involve a one-size-fits-all approach with limited opportunities for student agency and autonomy, while the other redefines the limits of student engagement and increased student success. Through innovative teaching methods supported by using tools powered with AI, educators can create learning environments that foster critical thinking opportunities, connections to real-world problems, innovation, and creativity, which have the potential to lead students down a path of life-long learning, motivation, and success. Therefore, it is essential that educators choose the pathway that aligns most effectively with the needs of their gifted learners in this ever-changing world, ensuring that their students are equipped to inherit the earth and continue moving towards progress.

REFERENCES

Baldwin, L., Omdal, S. N., & Pereles, D. (2015). Beyond stereotypes: Understanding, recognizing, and working with twice-exceptional learners. *Teaching Exceptional Children*, 47(4), 216–225. DOI: 10.1177/0040059915569361

Blaas, S. (2014). The relationship between social-emotional difficulties and underachievement of gifted students. *Australian Journal of Guidance & Counselling*, 24(2), 243–255. DOI: 10.1017/jgc.2014.1

Cross, J. R., & Cross, T. L. (2015). Clinical and mental health issues in counseling the gifted individual. *Journal of Counseling and Development*, 93(2), 163–172. DOI: 10.1002/j.1556-6676.2015.00192.x

Davidson Academy. (2021). *Underachievement in gifted students*. https://www.davidsonacademy.unr.edu/blog/underachievement-in-gifted-students/

Davidson Institute. (2024). *Roles in gifted education: A parent's guide*.https://www.davidsongifted.org/gifted-blog/roles-in-gifted-education-a-parents-guide/#:~:text=CLASSROOM%20TEACHER&text=In%20fact%2C%20most%20teacher%20preparation,professional%20development%20on%20gifted%20education

Diffit. (2024). *Learning resources for all*. https://web.diffit.me/

Edutopia. (2023). *Using ChatGPT to support student-led inquiry*.https://www.edutopia.org/article/using-chatgpt-support-student-led-inquiry/?gad_source=1&gclid=CjwKCAjwrIixBhBbEiwACEqDJYrYiCqWwl0YSCWwSupsfjRx0s_VWTDIQg1anQ2hBIFQUn8NMNJhlRoCDoIQAvD_BwE

Google, A. I. (2024). *Gemini* [Large language model]. https://gemini.google.com/app/d0458de8087b1246

Institute for Educational Advancement. (2022). *Defining gifted*. https://educationaladvancement.org/what-is-gifted/?gad_source=1&gclid=CjwKCAjwz42xBhB9EiwA48pT75g3YhNOgcSkc9VYLksuh9Ow8PfrUyaOgFAAROCHL-Krlfpa1nIBXhoCvqEQAvD_BwE

International Gifted Consortium. (2020). *High, exceptional, and profound giftedness*. https://giftedconsortium.com/high-exceptional-profound-giftedness/

Karnes, F. A., & Stephens, K. R. (2008). *Achieving excellence: Educating the gifted and talented*. Pearson Education, Inc.

Krijan, I. P., Jurčec, L., & Borić, E. (2015). Primary school teachers' attitudes toward gifted students. *Croatian Journal Educational.*, 17, 681–707. DOI: 10.15516/cje.v17i3.1199

Lee, S. (2024). *3 types of learning environments.* https://www.wgu.edu/blog/3-types-learning-environments2111.html#:~:text=Studies%20have%20shown%20that%20positive,they%20learn%20evolve%20as%20well

Magic School. (2024a). *Mission.* https://www.magicschool.ai/mission

Magic School. (2024b). *Tools.* https://app.magicschool.ai/tools

McCoach, D. B., Siegle, D., & Rubenstein, L. D. (2020). Pay attention to the inattention: Exploring ADHD symptoms in a sample of underachieving gifted students. *Gifted Child Quarterly*, 64(2), 100–116. DOI: 10.1177/0016986219901320

Meulen, R., Bruggen, C., Spilt, J., Verouden, J., Berkhout, M., & Bögels, S. (2014). The pull-out program day a week school for gifted children: Effects on social- emotional and academic functioning. *Child and Youth Care Forum*, 43(3), 287–314. DOI: 10.1007/s10566-013-9239-5

National Association for Gifted Children. (n.d.). *What is giftedness.*https://nagc.org/page/what-is-giftedness

Neal, T. (2016). *Teacher, parent, and student perceptions of adolescent giftedness and self- concept in rural northeast Louisiana schools* (10148471) [Doctoral dissertation, University of Louisiana at Monroe]. ProQuest Dissertations and Theses database.

Neihart, M., Reis, S. M., Robinson, N. M., & Moon, S. M. (Eds.). (2002). *The social and emotional development of gifted children: What do we know?* Prufrock Press, Inc.

Olton-Weber, S., Hess, R., & Ritchotte, J. A. (2020). Reducing levels of perfectionism in gifted and talented youth through a mindfulness intervention. *Gifted Child Quarterly*, 60(4), 319–330. DOI: 10.1177/0016986220953392

Open, A. I. (2024). *ChatGPT* [Large language model]. https://chat.openai.com/

Reis, S. (2023). *Reconsidering regular curriculum for high achieving students, gifted underachievers, and relationship between gifted and regular education.* https://gifted.uconn.edu/schoolwide-enrichment-model/reconsidering_regular_curriculum/#:~:text=Sixty%2Done%20percent%20of%20public%20school%20teachers%20and,to%20meet%20the%20needs%20of%20gifted%20students

Reis, S., & Renzulli, J. (2004). Current research on the social and emotional development of gifted and talented students: Good news and future possibilities. *Psychology in the Schools*, 41(1), 119–130. DOI: 10.1002/pits.10144

Rimm, S. B., Siegle, D., & Davis, G. A. (2018). *Education of the gifted and talented* (7th ed.). Pearson Education, Inc.

University of Amsterdam. (2022). *How to develop learner autonomy*. https://www.itta.uva.nl/learnerautonomy/how-to-develop-learner-autonomy-59

University of Pennsylvania. (2023). *Confronting perfectionism, inspiring excellence*. https://almanac.upenn.edu/articles/confronting-perfectionism-inspiring-excellence

Vanderbilt University. (2024). *Bloom's taxonomy*. https://cft.vanderbilt.edu/guides-sub-pages/blooms-taxonomy/

Vygotsky, L. S. (1978). *Mind in society: The development of higher psychological processes*. Harvard University Press.

Yale University. (2021). *Formative and summative assessments*. https://poorvucenter.yale.edu/Formative-Summative-Assessments

ADDITIONAL READING

Beck, J. E. (2020). *Teaching and learning in the age of AI*. Harvard Education Press.

Colangelo, N., & Davis, G. A. (2003). *Handbook of gifted education* (3rd ed.). Allyn and Bacon.

Davis, G., Rimm, S., & Siegle, D. (2011). *Education of the gifted and talented* (6th ed.). Pearson Publishing.

Goodfellow, I., Bengio, Y., & Courville, A. (2016). *Deep learning*. MIT Press.

Kulkarni, C. (2019). *AI in Education: Exploring the Potential of Artificial Intelligence in Education*. Packt Publishing.

Maker, C. J., & Schiever, S. W. (2010). *Curriculum development and teaching strategies for gifted learners* (3rd ed.). Pro-Ed.

Russell, S. J., & Norvig, P. (2020). *Artificial intelligence: A modern approach* (4th ed.). Pearson Publishing.

Turnbull, R., Turnbull, A., Shank, M., Smith, S., & Leal, D. (2013). *Exceptional lives: Special education in today's schools* (7th ed.). Merrill/Prentice Hall.

Zhao, Y. (2021). *AI in education: Affordances and challenges*. Routledge.

Zumbach, J., & Hirschbühl, J. (Eds.). (2020). *AI and digital education: Promises, practices, and implications*. Springer.

KEY TERMS AND DEFINITIONS

Artificial Intelligence: Otherwise known as AI, this technology can simulate human intelligence to write information when given a specific prompt, and it can also analyze pieces of data and provide reports. Additionally, it can create something from nothing, such as an image, by only being given a simple command.

Autonomous Learner: These learners can regulate their own learning experiences by recognizing problems, developing solutions to those problems, and reflecting on the process. Autonomous learners can set their own goals, work toward those goals, and reflect on the experience to determine how they learn best.

Bloom's Taxonomy: A model used to classify learning objectives or goals into levels of complexity.

Choice Board: This is an educational tool that offers activity choices students can select to complete that best align with their preferred interests, learning styles, and ability levels.

Formative Assessment: These are assessments that should be given throughout a lesson to determine whether students are mastering the content that is being presented to them so that an educator may adjust instruction accordingly. Formative assessments are given as students are forming their learning experiences.

Gifted Education Classroom: A gifted classroom is a learning environment specifically created to meet the needs of academically gifted students. These classrooms are typically taught by educators who have special training, degrees, or credentials that qualify them to meet the advanced needs of gifted leaners.

Gifted Learner: This is a learner who demonstrates exceptional, above average ability or talent in one or more domains.

Regular Education Classroom: A regular education classroom is a learning environment that is meant to cater to the needs of general education students. These classrooms are typically taught by teachers who have had training or who are receiving training to teach students within the general education population.

Summative Assessment: These are assessments at the end of a chapter or unit to determine what students have mastered at the end of a learning experiences. Summative assessments are a summary of what the students have learned.

Uniform Resource Locator (URL): A URL is an address to a location on the internet. It usually begins with "http" or "https", followed by the name of a webpage. The additional information at the end, such as ".com", ".org", or ".gov" for example, specifies the location of the webpage.

Chapter 7
Artificial Intelligence (AI) in Special Education: AI Therapeutic Pedagogy for Language Disorders

Mohsen Mahmoudi-Dehaki
https://orcid.org/0000-0002-4962-6827
English Department, Islamic Azad University, Najafabad, Iran

Nasim Nasr-Esfahani
https://orcid.org/0000-0002-2388-6524
Department of English, Islamic Azad University, Isfahan, Iran

ABSTRACT

This chapter explores the role of AI in addressing language impairments and Language-Based Learning Disorders (LBLDs) in Special Education (SE). It distinguishes between these conditions and their unique challenges. It examines the intersection of language impairments and AI, analyzing how AI-based technologies can support individuals with articulation, fluency, voice, and broader language disorders. The discussion includes an assessment of the potential benefits and limitations of AI-powered interventions. It also explores the application of AI in addressing LBLDs, such as dyslexia, dysgraphia, dyscalculia, and Auditory Processing Disorder (ADP). It investigates how AI-driven tools and techniques can enhance assessment, diagnosis, and remediation of these learning disorders, with a focus on personalized and adaptive learning. It provides an overview of the role of AI in SE, offering insights and recommendations for stakeholders interested in leveraging AI to support individuals with language impairments and LBLDs.

DOI: 10.4018/979-8-3693-5538-1.ch007

INTRODUCTION

Special Education (SE) encompasses a comprehensive framework of tailored services, adaptations, and pedagogical methodologies designed to address the distinctive learning requirements of students with disabilities or other special needs. This specialized education domain is predicated on the fundamental principles of providing Free and Appropriate Public Education (FAPE), ensuring nondiscriminatory evaluation, facilitating active parental involvement, and upholding due process safeguards (Rufo & Causton, 2022). At the core of SE is the Individualized Education Program (IEP), a personalized plan that outlines the specific supports, accommodations, and instructional strategies to be implemented for each qualifying student. This customized approach aims to grant these learners access to the general education curriculum within the least restrictive environment possible, fostering their integration and participation alongside their non-disabled peers to the greatest extent appropriate.

The overarching objective of SE is to empower students with diverse abilities to achieve a heightened level of personal success, both academically and socially, within the school setting and their broader communities. This is accomplished through the deployment of specialized teaching methods, the utilization of adapted equipment and materials, and the provision of tailored support services designed to address a wide range of disabilities, including learning disabilities, physical impairments, emotional/behavioral disorders, autism spectrum conditions, and beyond. By upholding the core principles of non-discrimination, parental involvement, and procedural safeguards, SE ensures that students with special needs are afforded the necessary resources and opportunities to thrive and reach their full potential alongside their peers in the general education system.

Language impairments and Language-Based Learning Disorders (LBLDs) represent a significant concern in SE, yet they often fail to receive the attention warranted by their prevalence and impact (Pennington et al., 2019). This discrepancy can be attributed to several factors. The multifaceted nature of language disorders poses significant challenges.

- These conditions encompass a broad spectrum of difficulties, ranging from articulation and fluency to receptive and expressive language problems. This heterogeneity complicates the identification and intervention process, as each student may present with a unique constellation of symptoms.
- Language disorders frequently co-occur with other conditions, such as autism spectrum disorder, intellectual disabilities, or attention-deficit/hyperactivity disorder. The overlapping symptoms can create diagnostic challenges, mak-

ing pinpointing the primary area of concern and developing targeted interventions arduous.

- General education teachers may lack sufficient training to recognize the early warning signs of language disorders. Furthermore, the availability of Speech-Language Pathologists (SLPs) who specialize in these areas is often limited within school settings, hindering timely and appropriate support.
- Regrettably, language and learning disorders are sometimes perceived as a result of laziness or lack of effort. This stigma can deter families from seeking necessary evaluations and interventions, further exacerbating the issue.
- Many school districts face significant resource constraints, such as the ones in the Middle East and North Africa (MENA) region, including limited funding and personnel. These limitations make providing comprehensive assessments and individualized interventions for students with language and learning disorders challenging, compromising the available support quality.

A multifaceted approach is required to address this disparity. Enhancing awareness, improving teacher training, and increasing access to specialized services are crucial in ensuring that students with language impairments and language-based learning disorders receive the support they need to thrive academically and socially. The underrepresentation of language impairments and LBLDs in the SE discourse is a pressing concern that demands innovative solutions. Fortunately, Artificial Intelligence (AI) technology promises to transform the landscape and address this critical gap (Yu & Lu, 2021).

- AI-driven speech recognition algorithms can analyze a child's speech patterns and pronunciation with unparalleled precision, enabling the early detection of potential language disorders. This objective and data-driven approach can lead to timely interventions, significantly improving the prospects for positive outcomes.
- The heterogeneity of language disorders necessitates a tailored approach to intervention. AI-powered digital tools can adapt to students' unique needs, providing personalized exercises and feedback. This level of adaptability is crucial in addressing the diverse manifestations of language impairments and language-based learning disorders.
- AI-driven applications can leverage gamification techniques to make speech and language therapy more engaging and accessible for students. By integrating captivating characters and narratives, these tools can foster a sense of enjoyment and motivation, overcoming the stigma and lack of engagement that often hinder progress.

- AI can be a valuable assistant to teachers and SLPs, providing objective data, recommendations, and progress tracking. This support can free up professionals to focus on higher-level interventions, ensuring consistent and evidence-based care, even in the face of limited specialized personnel.
- AI-powered screening tools hold the potential to identify potential language issues early, even before a child enters the school system. This proactive approach can prevent the compounding effects of untreated disorders on academic and social development, leading to more positive long-term outcomes.

By harnessing the capabilities of AI in speech recognition, Natural Language Processing (NLP), and adaptive learning, the educational community can make significant strides in addressing the underserved needs of language disorders in SE. However, it is crucial to ensure that the development and implementation of these AI-powered solutions are guided by the expertise of professionals, with a keen focus on cultural sensitivity and the complementary role of human expertise.

LANGUAGE IMPAIRMENTS VS. LANGUAGE-BASED LEARNING DISORDERS (LBLDs)

Speech or language impairment can be a communication disorder that negatively impacts a child's educational performance. It may manifest as difficulties with fluency, such as stuttering, impaired articulation, language-related challenges, or voice-related issues (Hegde & Freed, 2020). These communication disorders can adversely affect a child's academic progress and overall educational experience. There are several instinctive types of language impairments.

1. **Articulation disorders:** These involve the incorrect production of speech sounds, such as a lisp or difficulty pronouncing specific phonemes like /l/ or /r/.
2. **Fluency disorders:** Fluency disorders disrupt the flow of speech, manifesting as repeated, prolonged, or avoided sounds, syllables, and words. Stuttering is a prime example of a fluency disorder.
3. **Voice disorders:** Voice disorders are characterized by abnormal voice quality in pitch, resonance, or loudness.
4. **Language disorders:** They are marked by difficulties expressing needs, ideas, or information and/or understanding what others convey. Characteristics may include improper use of words and meanings, inability to express ideas, inappropriate grammar, reduced vocabulary, and difficulty following directions.

Students with language impairments often face challenges in effectively communicating with their peers and teachers, understanding or delivering oral presentations, participating in classroom discussions, and achieving social normalcy. Early intervention by a speech-language pathologist is crucial to address issues like stuttering and articulation problems before they escalate, leading to more significant difficulties later in the student's educational journey. On the other hand, LBLDs represent a spectrum of neurodevelopmental disorders that impair an individual's capacity to effectively process, comprehend, and utilize spoken and written language (Newhall, 2012). Often heritable and rooted in neurological differences, these conditions manifest through various symptoms that can significantly hinder academic achievement and social-emotional development.

1. **Dyslexia:** It is considered a primary LBLD, characterized by a profound difficulty in decoding and fluently reading words and deficits in phonological awareness - the ability to recognize and manipulate the constituent sounds within language. This neurobiological disorder, which frequently runs in families, results in slow, inaccurate reading, poor spelling, and difficulty sounding out unfamiliar words.
2. **Dysgraphia**: As another prevalent LBLD, it is marked by impairments in the physical act of writing, including illegible handwriting, inconsistent spacing, and laborious composition processes. This learning disability, which may co-occur with other disorders such as dyslexia, is believed to stem from deficits in fine motor skills and the cognitive organization required for practical written expression.
3. **Dyscalculia**: It is a less widely recognized but equally debilitating LBLD that disrupts an individual's understanding and application of numerical concepts. Hallmark symptoms include difficulty with basic counting, slow or inaccurate mathematical calculations, and a fundamental misunderstanding of core mathematical principles. Like other LBLDs, dyscalculia is not a reflection of intellectual capacity but rather a neurologically-based challenge.
4. **Auditory Processing Disorder (APD):** It is a distinct yet often co-occurring LBLD that involves a disconnect between the ears' ability to detect sounds and the brain's capacity to interpret and make sense of them. Individuals with APD struggle to follow multi-step instructions, comprehend speech in noisy environments, and acquire foundational reading and phonics skills.

The etiological origins and scope of language impairments and LBLDs are distinctly divergent. Language impairments are narrowly circumscribed to deficits in physical coordination and production of speech sounds. In contrast, LBLDs encompass broader challenges in comprehending and expressing spoken and written language. Specifically, language impairments stem from difficulties with the neuromuscular mechanisms underlying articulation, while LBLDs are believed to arise from atypical neurological processing of linguistic information (Cummings, 2014). The symptomatic manifestations also differ markedly between the two constructs. Individuals with language impairments exhibit distortions or inaccuracies in their speech pronunciation and prosodic features despite typically preserving adequate receptive language abilities. Conversely, those with LBLDs demonstrate a constellation of difficulties, including deficits in listening comprehension, oral expression, reading, writing, spelling, mathematical reasoning, and social-pragmatic communication despite intact word-level recognition.

The diagnostic procedures likewise vary considerably. Language impairments are identified through standardized assessments of speech sound production concerning developmental norms, whereas identifying LBLDs necessitates a comprehensive evaluation of an individual's overall language skills and the impact on academic and functional performance. Correspondingly, the therapeutic interventions diverge in their foci—treatment for language impairments centers on remediating the physical aspects of speech through targeted speech therapy. In contrast, remediation for LBLDs targets the underlying language processing deficits through specialized, structured instruction across the language-related domains. While both language impairments and LBLDs involve language-based difficulties, the etiological origins, symptomatic profiles, diagnostic procedures, and intervention approaches are distinctly differentiated between the two constructs.

Although existing interventions provide valuable support for students with language impairments, they fail to achieve significant and lasting effectiveness (Peterosn et al., 2020). Several factors contribute to the limitations of these solutions. First, language impairments are multifaceted disorders involving difficulties across various domains, including articulation, fluency, voice, comprehension, and expression. Each affected child exhibits a unique constellation of strengths and weaknesses, necessitating highly personalized interventions tailored to their needs.

Second, early identification and intervention are critical for mitigating the adverse effects of language disorders. However, many children with language impairments are not recognized or do not receive services until they enter the school system. By this juncture, the language gaps between these students and their typically developing peers have often widened, rendering it more arduous to bridge the disparities. Third, While speech-language therapy is a cornerstone of intervention for language disorders, it may not suffice in addressing the full spectrum of academic and social challenges faced by students with language impairments. These learners frequently require additional support and accommodations within the classroom, which general education teachers may not consistently provide.

Fourth, many classroom teachers lack sufficient training in evidence-based strategies for supporting students with language disorders in the mainstream educational environment. Whole-class approaches to language facilitation are not systematically implemented, further exacerbating the challenges faced by learners with language impairments. Fifth, funding and resource limitations in SE often result in high caseloads for SLPs and insufficient time for collaboration with classroom teachers. This issue makes it arduous to provide the intensity and consistency of intervention necessary for optimal outcomes. Sixth, language impairments can have far-reaching and long-lasting consequences if not addressed comprehensively and early in a child's development. Even with intervention, many students struggle with language and literacy difficulties throughout their academic careers and adulthood, underscoring the need for more effective solutions.

AI holds immense promise in addressing the multifaceted limitations that constrain the efficacy of current solutions for supporting students with language impairments (Grabowski, 2023). AI is the development of computer systems capable of executing tasks that typically require human intelligence, such as learning, problem-solving, decision-making, and perception. By leveraging the sophisticated capabilities of AI, educators, and clinicians can overcome the inherent complexities of these disorders, optimize the timing of identification and intervention, augment traditional speech-language therapy, enhance teacher training, mitigate resource constraints, and foster long-term success for individuals with lifelong language challenges.

AI-powered tools can analyze the unique profiles of individual students, identifying their specific strengths and weaknesses across the various language domains. This granular understanding can inform the development of highly personalized intervention strategies tailored to each child's needs, transcending the one-size-fits-all approach that often falls short in addressing the heterogeneity of language impairments. AI-based screening and assessment systems hold the potential to detect language impairments much earlier, enabling timely intervention before significant gaps emerge between affected students and their typically developing peers. Early identification is critical in mitigating language disorders' adverse effects and maximizing subsequent support's efficacy.

AI can complement and enhance traditional speech-language therapy by providing intelligent tutoring systems, interactive language games, and virtual practice environments. These AI-powered tools can deliver customized, intensive language practice that extends beyond the capacity of a clinician alone, thereby amplifying the impact of therapeutic interventions. AI-based professional development programs can equip general education teachers with evidence-based strategies for supporting students with language impairments in the mainstream classroom. Furthermore, AI can power intelligent assistants that provide real-time guidance to teachers on tailoring instruction to meet the unique needs of these learners. AI can help SLPs manage high caseloads more efficiently by automating administrative tasks, analyzing student data, and generating personalized treatment plans. It can free up clinicians to dedicate more time to direct intervention, thereby mitigating the resource constraints that often hinder the delivery of comprehensive support.

AI-powered tools can provide continuous, adaptive support for individuals with language impairments throughout their educational and professional journeys. AI-based assistants can help these individuals navigate academic and workplace challenges, fostering long-term success and minimizing the lifelong consequences often associated with language disorders. In conclusion, AI's advanced pattern recognition, personalization, and automation capabilities hold immense potential to transform the support landscape for learners with language impairments. By strategically integrating AI-driven solutions, educators and clinicians can overcome the limitations of current approaches and unlock new pathways for these students to thrive academically, socially, and beyond. The following discussion delves into how AI can be leveraged to address the unique challenges individuals with language impairments face.

LANGUAGE IMPAIRMENTS AND AI

In this section, the various language impairments (articulation, fluency, voice, and language disorders) are concisely explicated, followed by a discussion on how the capabilities of AI can be leveraged to identify and beneficially intervene in these speech-related disorders. Additionally, the potential ethical considerations surrounding the use of AI in this domain are explored.

Articulation Disorders

Deficits in speech sound production, commonly referred to as articulation disorders, represent a prevalent communication impairment in the SE domain. These disorders manifest through various atypical speech patterns, including sound substitutions, distortions, omissions, and additions, adversely affecting a child's intelligibility and ability to engage effectively in academic and social settings. The etiology of articulation disorders is multifaceted, with potential contributing factors ranging from hearing loss and oral-motor dysfunction to neurological factors and environmental influences. Irrespective of the underlying cause, students grappling with these disorders often exhibit characteristics such as unclear speech, frustration with communication, challenges with literacy development, and social difficulties stemming from their compromised verbal expression. The following presents a series of AI-driven solutions for students with articulation disorders. These innovative approaches leverage the power of AI to address the unique challenges faced by individuals with speech sound production difficulties.

Timlogo

Timlogo's advanced machine learning algorithms analyze children's speech patterns, identify specific articulation errors, and recommend personalized exercises to remediate those issues. The platform creates a captivating, gamified environment that encourages active participation and sustained engagement from young learners by integrating engaging games, animated characters, and immersive stories. Crucially, Timlogo's AI-powered adaptive capabilities ensure that the difficulty level and content of the activities evolve in tandem with the child's progress, maintaining an optimal level of challenge and reinforcement. A key distinguishing feature of Timlogo is its ability to provide real-time feedback on pronunciation. The AI engine can detect and highlight mispronounced sounds, offering immediate guidance and encouragement to the child. This instant feedback loop is instrumental in reinforcing correct articulation patterns and bolstering the child's confidence in their speech abilities. Furthermore, Timlogo's flexibility, with the option to utilize the platform both during in-person therapy sessions and as a home practice tool, facilitates a seamless continuum of care and promotes the transfer of skills to everyday communication contexts.

Yoodli

Yoodli, an AI-powered speech coaching solution, offers a versatile approach to improving communication skills, including those related to articulation disorders. While not exclusively designed for the special education domain, Yoodli's AI-driven feedback mechanisms can benefit students grappling with speech sound production challenges. Yoodli's AI engine analyzes various aspects of a user's speech delivery, including pronunciation, intonation, word choice, and body language, and provides detailed, actionable feedback. Notably, the platform's ability to identify and address mispronounced individual sounds can be precious for students with articulation disorders, empowering them to target specific areas of need. In addition to real-time feedback, Yoodli offers interactive practice tools like mock interviews, speech prompts, and conversation simulations. These exercises enable users to apply their newly acquired skills in realistic scenarios, fostering fluency and confidence in their communication abilities. While Yoodli is not intended to replace professional speech therapy, it can serve as a complementary resource, empowering students to improve their speech and language skills actively.

Fluency Disorders

Fluency disorders, a category of communication impairments, disrupt the seamless flow of speech, manifesting as recurrent, prolonged, or avoided sounds, syllables, and words. Stuttering, the most prevalent example, is a prime illustration of this phenomenon. These disorders impair the natural rhythm and timing of speech, leading to various disfluencies. The hallmarks of fluency disorders include the involuntary repetition of sounds, syllables, or words, the protracted pronunciation of certain sounds, and the avoidance of specific sounds, syllables, or words. These irregularities can disrupt speech's natural cadence and timing, rendering it less fluent and more laborious. Stuttering, the most widely recognized fluency disorder, is characterized by the uncontrolled reiteration or prolongation of sounds, syllables, or words. The severity of stuttering can range from mild, occasional disfluencies to severe, chronic speech disruptions. Other forms of fluency disorders encompass cluttering, marked by an abnormally rapid rate of speech with frequent pauses, interjections, poor speech organization, and neurogenic and psychogenic fluency disorders stemming from neurological conditions or psychological factors, respectively.

The precise etiologies of fluency disorders remain incompletely understood, but research suggests that a combination of genetic, neurological, and environmental factors may contribute to their development. Family history, neurological differences, and developmental delays have been linked to an increased susceptibility to fluency disorders. Effective management of fluency disorders involves a multifaceted approach, including speech therapy, counseling, and sometimes medication. The specific treatment plan is tailored to the type and severity of the fluency disorder and the individual's unique needs and goals. The primary treatment objectives are to enhance speech fluency, mitigate the disorder's impact on the individual's communication and quality of life, and provide strategies for coping with disfluencies. The subsequent sections introduce a series of AI-driven interventions designed to support students with fluency disorders.

Voiceltt

The Voiceltt platform is a web-based application that leverages AI and machine learning to recognize and translate non-standard speech patterns. This system, developed in collaboration with individuals living with speech disabilities and SLPs, offers three key functionalities: "Speak," which enables users to convert short phrases into clear, synthesized speech; "Dictate," which provides speech-to-text functionality; and "Integrations," which offers personalized closed captioning during video conferencing. The customizable language models, personalized vocabulary, and alternative access methods incorporated into Voiceltt have been instrumental in its successful implementation within various educational settings to support students with fluency disorders.

Cogito

The Cogito Language Analyzer is an AI-based automated language assessment tool that employs machine learning algorithms to analyze language samples and identify areas of concern, such as vocabulary, grammar, and pragmatic skills. Implementing this system has improved efficiency, enhanced diagnostic accuracy, and facilitated evidence-based intervention planning for students with fluency disorders by providing objective and standardized assessment results, enabling therapists to develop targeted intervention strategies and track progress over time.

Voice Disorders

Aberrant phonatory attributes, commonly called voice disorders, are characterized by abnormal qualities in the human voice's pitch, resonance, or intensity. These deviations from the expected norms can significantly impact an individual's communication ability and may have far-reaching consequences on their social, professional, and emotional well-being. The primary manifestations of voice disorders encompass a broad spectrum of anomalies, including fluctuations in vocal pitch, alterations in resonance, and variations in vocal intensity. Pitch abnormalities may present as an excessively high or low-pitched voice incongruent with the individual's age, gender, and habitual vocal patterns. Resonance issues can result in a nasal, muffled, or distorted vocal quality, often attributable to pathologies affecting the nasal passages, pharynx, or other structures integral to phonation. Furthermore, deviations in vocal intensity, ranging from hypophonia (diminished volume) to hypophonia (excessive volume), can impede effective communication and audibility.

The etiologies underlying voice disorders are multifaceted, encompassing structural, neurological, behavioral, respiratory, and psychological factors. Structural abnormalities, such as vocal fold nodules, polyps, or paralysis, can directly impair the normal functioning of the laryngeal mechanism. Neurological conditions, including Parkinson's disease and cerebrovascular accidents, can disrupt the neural control of phonation, leading to aberrant voice characteristics. Vocal abuse or misuse, manifested through excessive yelling, singing, or prolonged speaking, can induce vocal strain and contribute to the development of voice disorders. Respiratory ailments, including asthma and Chronic Obstructive Pulmonary Disease (COPD), can compromise the airflow and pressure dynamics essential for optimal voice production. Additionally, psychological stressors and anxiety can exacerbate or precipitate voice disorders, as exemplified by muscle tension dysphonia. The following sections present a collection of AI-powered strategies aimed at assisting learners experiencing vocal impairments.

Stamurai

The mobile application Stamurai emerges as a promising AI-driven solution to assist individuals, particularly students, overcome fluency disorders. Stamurai's comprehensive approach leverages technology to provide personalized speech therapy, real-time feedback, and access to licensed SLPs. The app's instructional videos, customized training plans, and AI-based speech analysis enable users to practice targeted exercises and receive immediate guidance on improving their fluency and speech patterns. Furthermore, Stamurai's self-help group feature facilitates peer-to-peer support and practice, fostering a sense of community and shared experiences among users. The app's accessibility and scalability, with costs significantly lower than traditional in-person therapy, make it a viable option for students seeking to address their fluency challenges. By combining personalized interventions, expert guidance, and technological advancements, Stamurai aims to empower students with fluency disorders to overcome communication barriers and enhance their overall quality of life.

Speechify

Speechify is an AI-driven platform that offers a range of solutions tailored to the needs of those with fluency disorders. Speechify's AI-powered speech recognition software provides real-time feedback to users on their fluency and pronunciation. At the same time, its virtual assistant and chatbots engage individuals in conversation practice, adapting to their unique speech patterns. The platform also incorporates AI-powered fluency coaches that deliver personalized feedback and exercises to enhance fluency, utilizing advanced speech recognition and natural language processing techniques. Furthermore, Speechify leverages immersive environments created through virtual and augmented reality, where AI characters and scenarios adapt to the user's speech, providing a safe and engaging space for fluency practice. Incorporating gamification elements in Speechify's solutions further enhances user engagement and motivation, making fluency practice more enjoyable and rewarding.

Language Disorders

Language disorders represent a complex array of communication impairments that significantly impede an individual's capacity to comprehend and/or express language effectively. These multifaceted conditions can manifest in diverse ways, profoundly impacting those affected's academic, social, and professional trajectories. The primary categorization of language disorders encompasses two distinct subtypes: expressive language disorders and receptive language disorders. Expressive language disorders are characterized by difficulties in language production, marked by limitations in vocabulary, grammatical errors, reduced fluency, and challenges in organizing and articulating thoughts coherently. Conversely, receptive language disorders involve deficits in language comprehension, manifesting as struggles to grasp the meaning of words, phrases, and sentences, as well as difficulties following complex instructions and grasping the contextual nuances of conversations. The underlying causes of language disorders are multifarious, encompassing developmental delays or disabilities, neurological conditions, hearing impairments, and environmental factors such as limited language exposure or socioeconomic disadvantages. These diverse etiologies contribute to the heterogeneous nature of language disorders, underscoring the importance of comprehensive assessment and individualized intervention approaches. The subsequent sections introduce a series of AI-driven interventions designed to support students with language disorders. These interventions are intended to help learners overcome the challenges associated with their language impairments and improve their overall communication abilities.

AI Orchestrator

The National AI Institute for Exceptional Education has spearheaded the development of innovative AI-driven technologies to support children with language disorders. Among the most promising of these solutions is the AI Orchestrator, a virtual assistant designed to augment the efforts of SLPs in delivering personalized interventions. Leveraging advanced natural language processing and machine learning algorithms, the AI Orchestrator analyzes a student's speech and language patterns to identify areas of difficulty. Based on this assessment, the system can recommend tailored therapy activities and exercises to address the student's specific needs. For instance, if the AI Orchestrator detects receptive language challenges, it may suggest interactive simulations and games focused on improving auditory comprehension. By acting as a virtual co-therapist, the AI Orchestrator enables SLPs to provide each student with more individualized attention and support, thereby enhancing the efficacy of speech and language services, particularly in resource-constrained educational settings. The system's ability to dynamically adjust the difficulty of interventions as the student progresses further underscores its potential to drive meaningful improvements in language outcomes.

Text-to-Speech (TTS) and Speech-to-Text (STT) Services

Complementing the AI Orchestrator's capabilities are text-to-speech (TTS) and speech-to-text (STT) services, which harness the power of AI to bridge the gap between spoken and written language. TTS empowers students with receptive language disorders by allowing them to access written content through an auditory modality, improving their comprehension. Conversely, STT assists those with expressive language challenges by transcribing their spoken words into text, enabling them to communicate their thoughts and ideas more effectively. These AI-powered tools leverage advanced speech recognition and natural language processing algorithms to adapt to each student's unique voice, accent, and speaking patterns, providing a highly personalized experience. Features such as adjustable playback speed, text highlighting, and error correction further enhance the accessibility and usability of these services, empowering students with language disorders to participate in educational activities actively, express themselves, and access information more effectively.

LBLDS AND AI

The following sections provide a concise elucidation of various LBLDs, including dyslexia, dysgraphia, dyscalculia, and APD). Furthermore, the capabilities of AI that can be leveraged to identify and effectively intervene in these LBLDs are examined. These AI-powered strategies are designed to offer personalized support and tailored interventions to address the unique needs of students struggling with these language-based learning challenges. By harnessing the power of AI, educators, and researchers aim to enhance the learning experiences and academic outcomes of individuals with LBLDs.

Dyslexia

Dyslexia is a persistent neurological disorder characterized by unexpected difficulties in acquiring proficient reading and spelling skills despite adequate intelligence, educational opportunity, and socio-cultural exposure. This specific learning disability originates from a core deficit in the phonological component of language, which impairs the individual's ability to accurately and fluently recognize words and their capacity for efficient decoding and encoding of written language. The etiology of dyslexia is multifactorial, with a strong genetic predisposition and neurobiological underpinnings. Neuroimaging studies have revealed atypical brain development and functioning patterns in individuals with dyslexia, particularly in regions associated with language processing. Environmental factors, such as the quality and timing of reading instruction, can also influence the manifestation and severity of dyslexia symptoms. The subsequent sections introduce a series of AI-driven interventions designed to support students with dyslexia. These strategies are developed to help learners with dyslexia overcome their reading and writing difficulties, enabling them to achieve academic success. The interventions are tailored to address the specific needs of each student, ensuring personalized support.

ClaroRead

Claro Software's ClaroRead is a comprehensive assistive technology suite meticulously crafted to address the unique needs of dyslexic learners. By leveraging the power of TTS capabilities, the platform enables seamless conversion of written content into high-quality audio, facilitating enhanced reading comprehension. Furthermore, the tool's word prediction and spell-checking functionalities work in tandem to streamline the writing process, empowering dyslexic students to express their ideas with greater fluency and accuracy. Complementing these core features, ClaroRead also incorporates a robust vocabulary support system, equipping users with a dictionary, thesaurus, and picture-based resources to expand their lexical repertoire. Accessible across Windows and macOS platforms, this versatile solution has garnered widespread acclaim within educational settings, from primary schools to higher learning institutions.

Ghotit Real Writer & Reader

Ghotit Real Writer & Reader represents a pioneering AI-driven solution tailored to individuals with dyslexia and other learning disabilities. By the use of advanced algorithms, the platform excels in contextual spelling and grammar correction, seamlessly identifying and rectifying errors within the written text. The tool's TTS capabilities enable dyslexic students to engage with content through auditory means, bolstering their reading comprehension. Moreover, Ghotit's vocabulary support features, including definitions, synonyms, and illustrative examples, foster a deeper understanding of unfamiliar words, ultimately enhancing the user's overall literacy skills. Designed as a web-based application, Ghotit Real Writer & Reader offers the convenience of cross-device accessibility, empowering dyslexic students to access its transformative features in the classroom and at home. This assistive technology serves as a transformative tool, bridging the gap between the cognitive abilities of students with dysgraphia and the challenges they face in written expression.

Dysgraphia

Dysgraphia is a neurologically-based learning disability that manifests as a profound impairment in the transcriptional aspects of written expression (Berninger & Wolf, 2016). Individuals with dysgraphia exhibit inconsistent and poorly formed handwriting, with irregularly spaced and shaped letters, reflecting underlying challenges with fine motor coordination and graphomotor skills required for fluent written output. The process of translating one's thoughts and ideas into written words is effortful and laborious for those with dysgraphia, resulting in slow, dysfluent writing that fails to convey the individual's true linguistic capabilities accurately. Concomitant difficulties with spelling, grammar, and punctuation are common in dysgraphia, despite the individual potentially possessing solid oral language skills, demonstrating the dissociation between written and verbal expression that is a hallmark of the disorder.

Dysgraphia is considered a specific learning disability that is distinct from broader challenges in written expression and often co-occurs with other neurodevelopmental disorders such as dyslexia, ADHD, and developmental coordination disorder. While there is no cure, early identification, and targeted interventions can help individuals with dysgraphia develop compensatory strategies and improve their written communication abilities. The following sections present a series of AI-powered interventions developed to assist students struggling with dysgraphia, a learning disability that impairs handwriting and written expression. These innovative approaches leverage the capabilities of AI to provide personalized support and enhance the educational experiences of individuals affected by this condition. The introduced interventions harness the power of AI technology to address the unique challenges faced by students with dysgraphia. These solutions provide tailored support, improve writing skills, and foster academic success.

Read&Write

Read&Write, a robust literacy support tool, equips students with various features tailored to mitigate the difficulties associated with dysgraphia. The text-to-speech functionality empowers learners to have written content read aloud, enhancing comprehension and reducing the burden of decoding. Integrated textual and visual dictionaries bolster vocabulary development by providing definitions and contextual imagery. The word prediction capability streamlines the writing process, diminishing the strain of spelling and keystrokes. Furthermore, the advanced grammar and spelling checking tools ensure that student's written work is polished. At the same time, the audio maker feature enables them to convert text into audio files for alternative review methods. The tool also offers a screen masking feature, which helps students focus on specific text sections by blocking out distractions. The highlighter and annotation tools also allow students to mark up and organize important information, facilitating active engagement with the content.

Glean

Glean is an AI-powered note-taking application that addresses the specific challenges faced by students with dysgraphia in the classroom setting. The app's audio recording and playback functionalities allow learners to capture lectures and presentations without extensive handwriting, a common obstacle for those with dysgraphia. The text-to-speech option empowers students to convert their written notes into audio format, facilitating review and comprehension. Glean's visual mapping tools enable learners to organize their notes using color coding, shapes, and icons, fostering deeper understanding and retention of the material. Notably, the AI-powered suggestion system analyzes students' notes, guiding them on improving organization, highlighting key points, and summarizing the content, thereby supporting their focus on the substance of the information rather than the mechanics of note-taking.

Dyscalculia

Dyscalculia is a complex learning disability that profoundly impacts an individual's capacity to comprehend, retain, and manipulate numerical information. This neurological condition is characterized by challenges, including struggles with fundamental arithmetic operations, grasping mathematical concepts, and executing computational tasks. The hallmarks of dyscalculia are manifold and far-reaching. Affected individuals often exhibit delays in basic counting skills and an inability to commit essential arithmetic facts to memory. Additionally, they may experience profound difficulties understanding quantities, comparing numerical values, and performing everyday mathematical activities, such as managing finances or telling time. The subsequent sections introduce a series of AI-driven interventions designed to support students grappling with dyscalculia, a learning disability that impairs the acquisition of mathematical skills and concepts. These innovative approaches leverage the capabilities of AI to provide personalized assistance and enhance the educational experiences of individuals affected by this condition.

Calcularis

Calcularis, an AI-based learning software, employs a personalized and adaptive methodology grounded in neuroscientific insights. By conducting comprehensive assessments, the software identifies each student's strengths and weaknesses, enabling the creation of individualized learning plans. Calcularis' multisensory approach engages various modalities, including visual, auditory, and tactile, to enhance mathematical comprehension for students with dyscalculia. The software's focus on developing core skills, such as number sense, arithmetic abilities, and mental number line representation, is underpinned by the latest research on the neurological foundations of mathematical learning and dyscalculia. Studies have demonstrated the efficacy of Calcularis in improving arithmetic skills and number line estimation abilities, with lasting benefits even after the training period.

DysCalc

DysCalc, a startup leveraging AI, offers personalized and adaptive math games to nurture students' number sense and arithmetic proficiency. The AI-powered games continuously assess student performance and adjust difficulty and content to match individual needs. By incorporating engaging and gamified elements, DysCalc creates an enjoyable and motivating learning environment for students with dyscalculia. The personalized learning pathways generated by the AI ensure that each student progresses at their own pace, with regular feedback and progress reports provided to students, parents, and teachers. DysCalc's multisensory approach, similar to Calcularis, incorporates visual, auditory, and tactile components to accommodate diverse learning styles and enhance overall mathematical comprehension.

APD

APD represents a complex neurological condition impairing the brain's ability to process and interpret auditory stimuli, particularly speech. This disorder, which can manifest in children and adults, is distinct from conventional hearing loss, as it reflects a disruption within the auditory cortex and associated neural pathways responsible for sound perception and comprehension. The prevalence of APD is estimated to range from 3 to 5 percent among the school-aged population, indicating a significant cohort of individuals grappling with this neurological challenge. Symptomatic manifestations of APD often include difficulties in understanding speech amidst background noise, challenges following multi-step verbal instructions, and struggles with literacy-related skills such as reading, spelling, and writing. The etiological underpinnings of APD can be diverse, encompassing factors such as head trauma, premature birth, chronic ear infections, and genetic predispositions. Importantly, APD is not synonymous with learning disabilities or attention-deficit/hyperactivity disorder, although these conditions may co-occur in some cases. The following sections present a series of AI-powered interventions to assist students struggling with APD. These interventions have been carefully designed to provide targeted support and address the unique challenges faced by individuals with this condition. Furthermore, the proposed AI-driven interventions are grounded in the latest research and evidence-based practices, ensuring that they are both practical and tailored to the specific needs of students with APD. Implementing these interventions is expected to enhance this population's educational experiences and outcomes significantly.

Tawi

Tawi, a mobile application, harnesses the capabilities of speech recognition technology to enhance the communication experiences of APD-affected individuals. By dynamically suppressing ambient noise and amplifying the clarity of speech, Tawi empowers these students to better focus on and comprehend verbal exchanges, even in acoustically challenging environments such as classrooms or crowded social settings. Furthermore, the app's real-time speech-to-text transcription functionality provides a complementary visual aid, facilitating improved understanding during lectures, meetings, and discussions where note-taking can pose a significant challenge.

AudioFoco

the AudioFoco solution adopts a multifaceted approach. It integrates an online screening tool, AudBility, which meticulously evaluates an individual's auditory processing capabilities across various domains, including auditory discrimination, memory, and attention. Armed with the insights gleaned from this assessment, the platform's Afinando o Cérebro component then delivers a curated selection of 180 targeted activities designed to stimulate and strengthen the identified areas of auditory processing deficiency. Crucially, the AI-driven recommendation engine within AudioFoco analyzes the AudBility results and dynamically tailors the activity sequence to each student's unique needs, ensuring a personalized and optimized training regimen for continuous improvement.

BENEFITS AND CHALLENGES OF AI THERAPEUTIC PEDAGOGY FOR LANGUAGE DISORDERS

The use of AI-powered systems in language therapy and rehabilitation holds significant promise, but essential challenges warrant careful consideration. On the one hand, incorporating AI can enhance SLPs's efficiency and effectiveness, improve language therapy's speed and responsiveness, enable highly personalized learning experiences, and foster more contextual and nuanced interactions between students and the learning system. These potential benefits could improve outcomes and better support for individuals with language disorders. However, implementing AI in this context also raises concerns about bias, inaccuracies, the risk of misuse and cheating, student isolation and disengagement, job displacement fears, and essential privacy and ethical considerations. Navigating this complex landscape requires a collaborative and proactive approach involving educational institutions, healthcare providers, and policymakers to maximize the advantages while mitigating the risks of AI in therapeutic pedagogy for language disorders.

Benefits

The integration of AI-powered systems into therapeutic pedagogy for language disorders holds the promise of significantly enhancing the efficiency and effectiveness of SLPs in their clinical practice. SLPs play a crucial role in assessing, diagnosing, and treating individuals with a wide range of communication and swallowing difficulties, including language disorders. However, their workload can be demanding, including developing individualized treatment plans, creating engaging learning materials, tracking student progress, and coordinating with other healthcare professionals. AI-based tools can assist SLPs by automating or streamlining various administrative and time-consuming tasks, allowing them to dedicate more of their expertise and attention to the core aspects of their work. For example, AI systems can be leveraged to generate customized lesson plans, student projects, and assessment materials tailored to each client's needs and learning goals. It can save SLPs valuable time and energy that would otherwise be spent on resource development and lesson planning. Furthermore, AI-powered assistants can provide real-time support to students during therapy sessions, offering immediate feedback, reminders, and strategies to help them stay engaged and on track. It can free up the SLP to observe the student's performance, provide hands-on guidance, and make necessary adjustments to the therapy plan. By delegating specific support tasks to AI, SLPs can devote more of their expertise and attention to the core aspects of their work, such as conducting comprehensive assessments, designing targeted interventions, and collaborating with families and other professionals to ensure the best possible outcomes for their clients.

Another significant advantage of incorporating AI into therapeutic pedagogy for language disorders is the potential to improve the speed and responsiveness of the learning process. Traditional language therapy often involves repetitive drills, practice exercises, and feedback loops, which can be time-consuming and potentially tedious for some students. AI-based systems, on the other hand, can provide instantaneous responses and personalized guidance, helping to maintain student engagement and motivation. For instance, if a student is struggling with a particular language concept or skill, an AI tutor can quickly identify the area of difficulty, offer targeted explanations and examples, and provide immediate feedback on the student's progress. This real-time support can be particularly beneficial for students who may become frustrated or lose focus during more traditional, linear learning activities. Moreover, AI-powered systems can adapt their teaching strategies and content based on the student's performance, learning style, and progress over time. This level of personalization and responsiveness can help ensure that each student receives the support they need to overcome their specific language challenges without waiting for the SLP to adjust the therapy plan manually. By delivering fast, tailored assistance, AI can help maintain the momentum and engagement of language therapy sessions, ultimately leading to more efficient and effective student learning outcomes.

One of the most significant advantages of incorporating AI into therapeutic pedagogy for language disorders is the ability to create highly individualized learning experiences for each student. Traditional language therapy often relies on a one-size-fits-all approach, with SLPs delivering standardized lessons and activities to a group of students. While this can be a practical and cost-effective solution, it may not always meet each individual's unique needs and learning preferences. In contrast, AI-powered systems can analyze a student's performance, learning style, and language proficiency to tailor instruction's content, delivery, and pace accordingly. This personalization can take many forms, such as adapting the complexity and difficulty of the learning materials to match the student's current language level and abilities, translating or providing multilingual support for students whose native language is different from the primary language of instruction, incorporating the student's interests, hobbies, and cultural background into the learning activities to enhance engagement and relevance, adjusting the modality of instruction (e.g., visual, auditory, kinesthetic) to cater to the student's preferred learning style, providing additional scaffolding, repetition, or alternative explanations for concepts that the student is struggling with. By creating a highly personalized learning experience, AI-based systems can help students with language disorders feel more supported, motivated, and empowered in their therapy sessions. This, in turn, can lead to improved learning outcomes, increased confidence, and better long-term language development.

Moreover, the ability to continuously monitor and adapt to the student's progress can ensure that the therapy remains relevant and effective over time, even as the student's needs and abilities evolve.

Another advantage of AI-powered therapeutic pedagogy for language disorders is the potential for more contextual and nuanced interactions between the student and the learning system. Traditional language therapy often relies on structured, scripted activities and exercises, which can sometimes feel disconnected from the real-world contexts and social situations that students will encounter. AI-based systems, however, can be designed to engage in more natural, conversational interactions that mimic the flow and complexity of everyday communication. For example, an AI tutor could roleplay as a character in a story, discussing the character's thoughts, emotions, and motivations and encouraging the student to respond kindly. This contextual, narrative-based interaction can help students practice their language skills more meaningfully and engagingly while also developing their understanding of social cues, pragmatics, and the nuances of communication. Additionally, AI systems can be programmed to recognize and respond to the student's tone, body language, and other nonverbal cues, providing a more immersive and interactive learning experience. It can be particularly beneficial for students with language disorders who struggle with social communication and interpreting subtle social signals. By fostering these more contextual and nuanced interactions, AI-powered therapeutic pedagogy can help students with language disorders develop a deeper understanding of language in its natural, conversational form rather than just focusing on isolated skills and drills.

Challenges

One of the primary concerns with using AI in therapeutic pedagogy for language disorders is the potential for bias and inaccuracies in the system's outputs and recommendations. AI systems ultimately depend on the data they are trained on, and if that data is biased or incomplete, the AI's responses and suggestions may perpetuate or even amplify those biases. For example, suppose the training data for an AI language tutor predominantly features content and examples that reflect a particular cultural or socioeconomic background. In that case, the system may struggle to provide appropriate support for students from diverse backgrounds. Additionally, AI systems can make mistakes or generate inaccurate information, especially when the underlying data is incomplete or outdated. This can be particularly problematic in language disorders, where providing accurate, evidence-based information is crucial for effective therapy and intervention. AI-powered therapeutic systems must be carefully designed, tested, and monitored to ensure that they provide reliable, unbiased, and accurate information and support to students. It may involve incorporating robust data validation and quality control measures and ongoing monitoring and adjustment of the AI's performance based on feedback and real-world outcomes.

Another significant concern with using AI in therapeutic pedagogy for language disorders is the potential for students to misuse or cheat with the technology. For example, students may attempt to use AI-powered writing assistants or chatbots to generate their assignments or projects rather than engage in the learning process themselves. It could undermine the intended learning objectives and lead to inaccurate assessments of students' true language abilities. Additionally, there is a risk that students could use AI to impersonate others or generate inappropriate content, which could have serious ethical and legal implications, particularly in the context of language therapy and rehabilitation. To address these concerns, educational institutions and SLPs must implement robust policies and safeguards to monitor and detect the misuse of AI technology. It may include the use of plagiarism detection software, the implementation of strict guidelines around the use of AI tools, and the provision of clear guidance and education for students and parents on the appropriate and ethical use of these technologies.

While AI-powered therapeutic pedagogy can offer many benefits in terms of personalization, responsiveness, and efficiency, there is also a risk that overreliance on these technologies could lead to isolation and disengagement among students with language disorders. Language therapy and rehabilitation often involve significant human interaction, with SLPs and other professionals providing face-to-face support, encouragement, and emotional connection. Suppose students become too dependent on AI-based systems for language learning and therapy. In that case, they may miss out on these crucial interpersonal experiences, essential for their overall well-being and social-emotional development. Moreover, some students with language disorders may feel more comfortable and engaged when working directly with a human therapist or teacher, who can provide a more empathetic and nuanced understanding of their unique needs and challenges. In regard to mitigating this risk, AI-powered therapeutic pedagogy must be implemented as a complement to, rather than a replacement for, human-led language therapy and instruction. SLPs and other professionals should maintain a strong presence in the learning process, using AI-based tools and systems to enhance and support their work rather than relying on them as the sole means of intervention. Additionally, educational institutions and therapy providers should carefully monitor student engagement, motivation, and social-emotional well-being to ensure that the use of AI technology is not leading to unintended negative consequences.

Another potential concern with the integration of AI into therapeutic pedagogy for language disorders is the fear of job displacement among SLPs and other language professionals. As AI-powered systems become more sophisticated and capable of handling a wider range of tasks, there may be a perception that these technologies could eventually replace the need for human SLPs and language therapists. This concern is understandable, as the automation of certain administrative and support tasks could potentially reduce the demand for some traditional SLP roles. However, it is essential to note that the role of the SLP in language therapy and rehabilitation is multifaceted and often requires a level of nuanced, contextual understanding that current AI systems may struggle to replicate. SLPs bring a wealth of specialized knowledge, clinical expertise, and interpersonal skills that are essential for providing practical, personalized care to individuals with language disorders. Rather than viewing AI as a threat to their jobs, SLPs and other language professionals should consider how these technologies can be leveraged to enhance and support their work rather than replace it. By embracing AI as a tool to streamline certain tasks and free up time for more direct patient care, SLPs can potentially expand their role and impact within the field of language therapy and rehabilitation. Ultimately, the integration of AI into therapeutic pedagogy for language disorders should focus on collaboration and complementarity rather than the replacement or displacement of human professionals.

The use of AI in therapeutic pedagogy for language disorders also raises important privacy and ethical concerns that must be carefully considered. One key concern is the potential for AI systems to collect and store sensitive personal data, such as student performance records, therapy notes, and audio or video recordings of therapy sessions. This data could be vulnerable to breaches or misuse, potentially compromising the privacy and confidentiality of the individuals involved. Additionally, there are concerns about the ethical implications of using AI to make decisions or recommendations that could significantly impact the lives of individuals with language disorders. For example, an AI system could potentially be used to make recommendations about the type or intensity of therapy a student should receive, which could have significant consequences for their long-term language development and overall well-being. To address these concerns, educational institutions and therapy providers must implement robust data privacy and security measures and clear ethical guidelines and oversight mechanisms for using AI in therapeutic pedagogy. It may include obtaining informed consent from students and their families before using AI-powered systems, ensuring that all personal data is securely stored and only accessed by authorized personnel, implementing transparent and accountable decision-making processes for any AI-driven recommendations or interventions, regularly reviewing and updating ethical guidelines to keep pace with the evolving landscape of AI technology. By prioritizing privacy and ethical considerations, educational and healthcare providers can help ensure that the integration of AI into therapeutic pedagogy for language disorders is done in a responsible and trustworthy manner, with the best interests of the students and their families at the forefront.

Integrating AI into therapeutic pedagogy for language disorders presents a complex and multifaceted landscape, with significant opportunities and important challenges that must be carefully navigated. On the one hand, the incorporation of AI-powered systems can enhance the efficiency and effectiveness of SLP interventions, improve the speed and responsiveness of language therapy, enable highly personalized learning experiences, and foster more contextual and nuanced interactions between students and the learning system. However, the use of AI in this context also raises concerns about bias, inaccuracies, the potential for misuse and cheating, the risk of student isolation and disengagement, job displacement fears, and important privacy and ethical considerations. To maximize the benefits and mitigate the risks of AI in therapeutic pedagogy for language disorders, a collaborative and proactive approach is essential, involving educational institutions, healthcare providers, and policymakers. This approach should include implementing rigorous data validation and quality control measures, providing clear guidance and education for all stakeholders, maintaining a robust human presence in the language therapy process, and prioritizing privacy and ethical considerations. By taking a thoughtful and comprehensive approach to integrating AI in this domain, we can harness the power of this technology to enhance the quality, accessibility, and effectiveness of language therapy and rehabilitation while safeguarding the well-being and rights of the individuals we serve.

SUMMARY

SE is crucial in supporting students with language impairments and LBLDs. SE provides a comprehensive framework of tailored services, adaptations, and pedagogical methodologies designed to address the unique learning requirements of these students. At the core of SE is the IEP, a personalized plan that outlines the specific supports, accommodations, and instructional strategies to be implemented for each qualifying student. This customized approach aims to grant learners with language disorders access to the general education curriculum within the least restrictive environment possible, fostering their integration and participation alongside their non-disabled peers. However, existing interventions within the SE system often fall short of effectively addressing the multifaceted challenges faced by students with language impairments and LBLDs. Factors such as the heterogeneous nature of these disorders, the need for early identification and intervention, limited teacher training, and resource constraints contribute to the limitations of current approaches. AI technology holds immense potential to transform the support landscape for individuals with language disorders within the SE framework. AI-driven solutions can provide personalized interventions, enhance teacher training, and optimize the delivery of speech and language services, even in resource-constrained educational settings. By strategically integrating AI-powered tools, educators and clinicians can overcome the limitations of current approaches and unlock new pathways for students with language impairments and LBLDs to thrive academically, socially, and beyond. This integration of AI in SE aims to ensure that these learners receive the comprehensive support they need to reach their full potential.

REFERENCES

Ahuja, N. J., Dutt, S., Choudhary, S., & Kumar, M. (2022). Intelligent tutoring system in education for disabled learners using human–computer interaction and augmented reality. *International Journal of Human-Computer Interaction*, 21(3), 1–13. DOI: 10.1080/10447318.2022.2124359

Brahmi, Z., Mahyoob, M., Al-Sarem, M., Algaraady, J., Bousselmi, K., & Alblwi, A. (2024). Exploring the role of machine learning in diagnosing and treating speech disorders: A systematic literature review. *Psychology Research and Behavior Management*, 17(1), 2205–2232. DOI: 10.2147/PRBM.S460283 PMID: 38835654

Cummings, L. (2014). *The communication disorders workbook*. Cambridge University Press. DOI: 10.1017/CBO9781107295117

Grabowski, C. (2023). *A review of the use of artificial intelligence to enhance the practice of speech-language pathology*. Abe Books.

Hegde, M. N., & Freed, D. (2020). *Assessment of communication disorders in adults: Resources and protocols*. Plural Publishing.

Mulfari, D., Carnevale, L., & Villari, M. (2023). Toward a lightweight ASR solution for atypical speech on the edge. *Future Generation Computer Systems*, 149(1), 455–463. DOI: 10.1016/j.future.2023.08.002

Newhall, P. W. (2012). *Language-based learning disabilities*. Landmark School Outreach Program.

Pennington, B. F., McGrath, L. M., Peterson, R., & Peterson, R. L. (2019). *Diagnosing learning disorders: From science to practice*. Guilford Publications.

Peterson, A. K., Fox, C. B., & Israelsen, M. (2020). A systematic review of academic discourse interventions for school-aged children with language-related learning disabilities. *Language, Speech, and Hearing Services in Schools*, 51(3), 866–881. DOI: 10.1044/2020_LSHSS-19-00039 PMID: 32525756

Rufo, J. M., & Causton, J. (2022). *Reimagining special education: Using inclusion as a framework to build equity and support all students*. Brookes Publishing.

Yu, S., & Lu, Y. (2021). *An introduction to artificial intelligence in education*. Springer. DOI: 10.1007/978-981-16-2770-5

ADDITIONAL READING

Abraham, A., Dash, S., Pani, S. K., & García-Hernández, L. (Eds.). (2022). *Artificial intelligence for neurological disorders*. Academic Press.

Bakken, J. P., & Obiakor, F. E. (Eds.). (2023). *Using technology to enhance special education*. Emerald Publishing Limited. DOI: 10.1108/S0270-4013202337

Beccaluva, E. A., Catania, F., Arosio, F., & Garzotto, F. (2024). Predicting developmental language disorders using artificial intelligence and a speech data analysis tool. *Human-Computer Interaction*, 39(1-2), 8–42. DOI: 10.1080/07370024.2023.2242837

Hopcan, S., Polat, E., Ozturk, M. E., & Ozturk, L. (2023). Artificial intelligence in special education: A systematic review. *Interactive Learning Environments*, 31(10), 7335–7353. DOI: 10.1080/10494820.2022.2067186

Kumar, A., Nayyar, A., Sachan, R. K., & Jain, R. (Eds.). (2023). *AI-assisted special education for students with exceptional needs*. IGI Global. DOI: 10.4018/979-8-3693-0378-8

Markelz, A. M., Nagro, S. A., Monnin, K., & Bateman, D. F. (2023). *The Essentials of Special Education Advocacy*. Rowman & Littlefield. DOI: 10.5771/9781538172483

KEY TERMS AND DEFINITIONS

Artificial Intelligence (AI): AI encompasses a diverse array of technologies that empower machines to carry out tasks that have traditionally necessitated human intelligence, including the ability to learn, solve problems, and make decisions.

Automated Speech Recognition (ASR): ASR systems represent a significant advancement in AI, enabling the conversion of human speech into machine-readable text by applying sophisticated machine-learning techniques. These systems harness the power of deep learning algorithms, natural language processing, and neural network architectures to analyze audio waveforms and accurately transcribe spoken language into sequences of words.

Free and Appropriate Public Education (FAPE): The United States educational system is founded upon equality, ensuring that all children, regardless of their abilities or disabilities, have access to a high-quality education. This commitment is embodied in the concept of FAPE, which guarantees students with disabilities the right to an education tailored to their individual needs, provided at no cost to the student or their family. FAPE rests upon three fundamental pillars: free, appropriate, and public.

Individualized Education Program (IEP): The IEP is a comprehensive document that outlines the specialized instruction, support services, and accommodations necessary for students with disabilities to thrive academically. This meticulously crafted plan is developed by a collaborative team consisting of the student, family members, educators, and other relevant professionals, ensuring that each component is tailored to the unique needs and abilities of the individual learner.

Intelligent: Tutoring Systems (ITS): ITS represents a significant advancement in educational technology, leveraging the power of AI and cognitive science to provide personalized, real-time instruction and feedback to learners. These sophisticated computer-based systems are designed to tailor the learning process to the unique needs and learning patterns of each student, a feat that has traditionally been the domain of skilled human tutors.

Language-Based Learning Disorders (LBLDs): They represent a specific category of learning disorders that primarily impact language-dependent academic skills, particularly reading, writing, and spelling. LBLDs are characterized by phonological awareness, word recognition, fluency, and/or reading comprehension difficulties.

Language Impairment: It involves difficulties with the fundamental components of language processing and production. These deficits can manifest in either receptive language challenges, characterized by impaired comprehension of linguistic input, or expressive language difficulties, marked by limitations in language production.

Natural Language Processing (NLP): NLP is a burgeoning subfield within artificial intelligence that has garnered significant attention due to its ability to facilitate seamless communication between humans and machines. This interdisciplinary domain, which intersects computer science and linguistics, aims to equip computers with the capacity to comprehend, interpret, and manipulate human language in its natural form.

Chapter 8
Can Artificial Intelligence Facilitate Mathematics Instruction?

Veena Paliwal
https://orcid.org/0000-0001-6552-9798
University of West Georgia, USA

Sonal Patel
University of West Georgia, USA

ABSTRACT

Artificial Intelligence (AI) is an emerging field that encompasses educational tools for teachers, students, and administrators. Vast research (Alam, 2021; Chen et al, 2022; Chiu et al., 2023; Ouyang & Jiao, 2021) has developed AI tools that can be used in the classrooms to enhance students' engagement, students' learning, and promote success. Mathematics education is a crucial field of education as learning of mathematical ideas affects the learning in other related areas. AI can be used in multiple ways in mathematics education including: creating adaptive learning environments, using assistive technology to facilitate students with special needs, helping as a plagiarism detection tool, and performing data analysis. This chapter will explore and report on various AI tools available for mathematics educators that can assist teachers in tutoring, preparing personalized lesson plans, developing learning trajectories based on students' performance, effectively grading the exams and home-works, and supporting students with special needs.

DOI: 10.4018/979-8-3693-5538-1.ch008

INTRODUCTION

Artificial Intelligence (AI) is an emerging field that encompasses educational tools for teachers, students, and administrators. AI uses computer systems to perform tasks that usually require human intelligence. AI tools are designed to mimic human cognitive functions of understanding language, recognizing patterns, solving problems, creating alternate approaches to a problem, and making decisions. Vast research (Alam, 2021; Chen et al, 2022; Chiu et al., 2023; Ouyang & Jiao, 2021) has developed AI tools that can be used in the classrooms to enhance students' engagement, students' learning, and promote success. With the prevalence of AI, it is crucial to understand its positive and negative impacts on education, and work towards unlocking its potential to enhance education in an ethical, equitable, and risk-free way.

Mathematics education is a crucial field of education as learning of mathematical ideas affects the learning in other related areas (Asfar et al, 2019; Hiebert & Grouws, 2007). AI can be used in multiple ways in enhance mathematics education including: creating adaptive learning environments, using assistive technology to facilitate students with special needs, helping as a plagiarism detection tool, and performing data analysis. This chapter will explore and report on various AI tools available for mathematics educators that can assist teachers in tutoring, preparing personalized lesson plans, developing learning trajectories based on students' performance, effectively grading the exams and home-works, and supporting students with special needs. We will also report on the strengths and weaknesses of AI use in mathematics instruction.

AI RESOURCES AVAILABLE FOR TEACHERS AND STUDENTS

Various AI resources are available that are beneficial for teachers and students, including students with special needs as they offer interactive activities, constant and active involvement, easy to understand, immediate feedback, and personalized instructions.

Resources Available for Teachers

Many AI tools are available for teachers to create immersive and personalized learning environment for students. Different AI tools are designed to facilitate teachers in teaching by creating personalized lesson plans or interacting quizzes, and helping in identifying the areas where student may need additional assistance. These tools can help in improving students learning outcomes, reducing teachers' workload, and making learning experience fun and enjoyable by increasing students' engagement.

Course and Lesson Plan Creator

Chatgpt, Classpoint, and Copilot are some of the AI tools for teachers. Copilot allows creating courses and lesson plans that are personalized to the teachers and cater to their students needs. Chatgpt can assist in creating courses and lesson plans by answering any specific questions including creating a rubric. Classpoint allows creating AI powered power points quizzes based on the questions in the slides. These quizzes can help in engaging student and also evaluating their performance on the topics covered in a class.

Differentiated Learning

Some available AI tools are Dreambox, Smart Sparrow, Knewton. These tools allow teachers to gauge students' specific strengths, weaknesses, and learning preferences. Teachers can analyze students' assessment scores, attendance reports, and some behavioral patterns to recommend personalized lessons and materials for students. These materials can also be used for students with special needs to create lesson plans based on individual learning style, progress, and abilities.

Grading

Available AI tools that can reduce grading time and help teachers with grading are:

Gradescope. AI tool Gradescope is an auto grading tool. Teachers can upload their own criterion and assigning weightage to different steps required to complete in solving a problem. This tool will auto grade all the assignments based on the criterion set by the teachers. Teachers can review and adjust the grading (if needed) before releasing grades to students. This can save lots of time for teachers to focus to other necessities for students.

Scantron (https://www.zipgrade.com/forms/). This grading app is best for multiple choice questions quizzes/tests for students taking in the class or remotely. It is affordable for teachers and easy to learn.

Pros: The app allows scanning the answer sheets using ZipGrade app. The app is compatible with both iOS and Android. Teachers can download it on their smartphones, iPads, tablets, or laptops with camera access. It is a quick and easy way to scan students' solutions on scantrons. The free version of the app allows 100 Scans/Month. It allows keeping records of scantrons for all classes with past and current records available for data analyses and comparison. Teachers can download a grade book report, statistics of scores, graphs, and data in an Excel file, or CSV file. Convenient to use in face-to-face classes or for online quizzes and tests.

The quizzes can be administered either using *Open* submissions or *Verified* submissions. Open submission is the quickest way to allows students complete their work online, but it could be used for viewing questions before the actual exam as the information can not be verified. Verified submission is only available for ZipGrade accounts that have defined student records and have assigned students to classes. It provides a submission limit so students can not submit multiple answer sheets. The verified version also has a feature where instructor can remove a graded paper so that students can resubmit their work.

Cons: Student portal is not required to administer quizzes online which can result in students submitting more than one response. Additional features need to be enabled to get one response per student. The number of questions can only be 20, 50, and 100. Users need to print ZipGrade answer sheets as the app only supports ZipGrade answer sheets. Because there is a submission limit, if a student accidentally submits an answer sheet, they will not be able to retake a test unless you remove that graded paper. The scanned answer sheet does not provide feedback on answer sheets for students to improve learning until the teacher marks it. However, a digitally scanned image shows it.

Pinpoint Knowledge Gap

This is one of the areas where teachers need assistance to be able to help their students in the right direction. One AI tool Exact Path can facilitate teachers in accomplishing this goal. Exact Path uses adapted assessments to identify the areas where students are struggling. It provides a learning path that can facilitate students in improving on those concepts. Teachers can use these tools for tracking students' progress as well as adjusting instruction in the class based on students' learning level. This can also help in planning individual learning trajectory for students who require additional assistance for learning.

Test Prep

To prepare students for exams teachers can use AI tools Classpoint or ExamSoft. These can help in preparing lessons before upcoming exams or quizzes. Teachers can create targeted practice areas for students based on their understanding or using the AI tool Exact Point to pinpoint concepts students are struggling the most. ExamSoft allows students to analyze data analytics and prepare them to ask follow up questions to the instructors. Classpoint allows creating the quiz questions based on the content in the lessons. This can help in examining students understanding of the concepts covered in the class and adjust instructions that can match students' current level of understanding.

Task Automation

Helping teachers with administrative tasks using AI can enable teachers to spend more time in teaching and interacting with students that can promote students' academic performances. One such tool is Zipper. These tools make it easy to collect or move data, send our email reminders about upcoming lessons or exams. Teachers can use this app as a personalized assistance to use their time wisely on the target goals that can promote students' success.

Provide Student Feedback

Providing students timely feedback is crucial and time-consuming for teachers. AI powered *Turnitin* can provide feedback to students on the accuracy as well as ways to improve their performance, and help maintain academic integrity. The feedback provided by *Turnitin* is objective based on analyses of data. Teachers can also go back and add constructive feedback for students if needed. *Turnitin* also produces similarity report that allows teachers to detect plagiarism.

AI Enabled Live Captioning

For students with special needs or language barrier, AI tools like *a i media* and *PowerPoint* allow live captioning of the content for better understanding. These tools help bridging the back between students learning abilities and different backgrounds by converting speech to text. This could make it easy for students in dealing with problems with hearing issue, different accent, or pronunciation. This also helps creating a conducive learning environment for student who are multi-lingual.

Smart Teaching Assistant

AI tools ChatGPT and Fetchy provide answers to personalized research questions, prepare lesson plans, help with administrative tasks, and provide feedback. ChatGPT stores the responses and provides feedback based on earlier conversations. The tool is designed to get smarter and more accurate after each use. Fetchy is a tool designed specifically for educators. This tool allows effectively conveying information. Fetchy works with paid subscription and is not free like ChatGPT.

Graphing

Demos is AI powered graphing calculator that focuses on visualizing mathematical concepts effectively. It is one of the popular graphing and user-friendly interface available to students and educators. Demos enables exploring mathematical relationships interactively by plotting the function and enabling the users to manipulate the graphs. Graphs can be shared on embedded in a Power Point or other documents to make enjoyable and effective learning experience.

Resources Available for Students

Various AI tools available for students to enhance their learning experience and get immediate feedback on solutions, and introduce students to other resources that can facilitate in learning. Students' experience with AI tool using questions-and-answers approach was reported to be useful and enjoyable. Some of the AI tools available to students for math learning are detailed below:

Photomath

This AI resource requires users to upload an image. A detailed solution with step-by-step explanations is provided to users for problems in different area of mathematics from elementary grades through college including elementary mathematics, geometry, trigonometry, statistics, and calculus. The app can be downloaded on phones and subscriptions are available for *photomath plus* that has advanced features for solving math problems including videos. The app has advanced AI features that can provide solution to any problem by image recognition including the handwritten ones. Multiple solutions to a problem are provided that include graphical representations, different approaches to a problem, videos and step-by-step solutions to a problem. Multiple solutions can be used to understand different approaches to solve the problems. The app also allows users to share the solutions with the peers, which can be used for collaborative learning experiences.

Limitations. App does not provide step-by-step solution in the free version if the image is uploaded from the textbook. However, users can get complete solutions when the app does not recognize that the problem is from a textbook by typing the same problem to a word document or handwriting it. The app can provide a solution to a diagram from a geometry problem only if it is from a textbook. For any random geometry problem, the app does not recognize it to show the solution. For problems from algebra 2, the app recognizes the problems from a textbook and provides some basic steps to solve them. These steps are in the right direction to understand the solutions, but are not very clear for a user who's not well-acquainted to the problem solution.

Pros- User-friendly app that provides solutions to problems just by uploading the image. The app can be used on phones and computers.

Cons- Solutions to complex equations or word problems may not be generated or may be incorrect. App does not work for any other inputs than the image. Socratic by Google.

Mathway

This app is free to download on phones. Allows users to type or upload an image of the problem to be solved. Upon uploading an image, the app prompt the users to detail the kind of the solution intended (for example, factoring the equation, show grouping method, or graph the equation). Shows the correct solution, but step-by-step solutions is available to only users with paid subscription. The app can not be useful for geometry as it can't read the diagrams to understand the problem to be solved. The app recognizes the problems in trigonometry, algebra 2, and calculus. Occasionally, the app provides the formula used to solve the problem along with the correct solution, but does not provide any details on producing the solution. The free version of this app is only beneficial to the users who are not intending to get details on solving the problems, but are only interested in checking the solutions.

Pros- App provides support for broad range of math concepts with in-depth explanations for thorough understanding. In addition, it also introduces users to related math solution for practice.

Cons- App requires paid subscription to get detailed explanations on the problems, does not recognize images from a textbook, and requires users to hand type problems.

Socratic

This app is free to download from Google. Users need to have a google account to be able to download. Socratic app is easy to use and provides solutions to problems without any paid subscriptions. The solutions are detailed with step-by-step explanations, and also include info cards that explain conceptual concepts that were used to solve. App has embedded videos that further provide detailed explanations.

Limitations. App does not recognize the geometry problems from a textbook to provide any solution. App sometimes does not solve a problem, but recommends various apps that can provide a solution i.e., it serves as a search engine. Socratic does not have content in it, but can guide the users in right directions to find a solution.

Pros: App is free to use and provides high quality educational resources that can help in developing conceptual understanding. Multiple approaches to a solution are provided to users that can facilitate in broadening conceptual and procedural understanding.

Cons: App does not have its own content, but it relies on other educational resources. This process is mostly time-consuming, and may be used to get a solution without any understanding of the concepts.

Comparison of Mathway, Photomath, and Socratic

Free version of Photomath provides more detailed solution than Mathway that just shows the solutions with no details. Socratic goes further than Photomath with not only step-by-step explanations, but detailing mathematical concepts used to solve the problem. Users are also provided with related videos on similar problems to effectively understand the concepts. For example, for an integration-by-parts problem from calculus, Mathway only provides the correct solution and the formula. In comparison, Photomath provides step-by-step solution. The formatting is little difficult to follow, but the explanations are easy to understand. Photomath is a better app than Mathway that not only provides detailed solution to almost all types of problems (except the ones from a textbook), but also does not require users to get a subscription.

Most effective app for algebra amongst the three apps is Socratic as it not only understands the problems, it provides a step-by-step solution with detailed explanations. For trigonometry, Socratic is better than Mathway as it directs the users to different resources to get a solution. Photomath is better than Socratic as it shows solutions without asking users to explore other options that may or may not work. For higher level classes like precalculus and calculus, both Mathway and Photomath are better than Socratic as Socratic recognizes the problems, but does not provide any solution or a resource to a solution.

In comparison, Socratic provides the best solutions for lower level classes like algebra, algebra 2, or trigonometry. The app struggles to even recognizes a problem for higher level courses like precalculus or calculus. Mathway's free version recognizes the problems irrespective of a lower-level or a higher-level course, but may require a subscription to get detailed solution. Photomath works for both lower and higher-level math courses, and it solves most of the problems without requiring any paid subscriptions.

ROLE OF AI TOOLS IN SPECIAL EDUCATION

Mathematics teaching in special education need to address the issues of students needing personalized learning experiences, aid in skill development, and improving accessibility for students with special needs. AI tools are also available for conducting students progress to help educators and students plan their future course of action. AI can provide assistive technology, accessibility, and data analysis needed for ensuring that all students are provided equal resources to succeed in school mathematics.

Personalized Learning

AI tools can help students enhance their learning experience using a personalized tutor (khanmigo or Wolfarm) that can not only provide tailored learning paths, but also look at students' strengths and weaknesses to adapt the educational content. Students with special needs often require personalized learning approach and AI can be used for it.

Assistive Technology and Improved Accessibility

AI tools can transform special education by providing useful resources to students with special needs. For example, speech to text software can help students with hearing impairments to prepare for the instruction and text to speech software can assist students with visual impairments in their learning process. This can also help students with language barrier to understand class instruction and notes, and come to the same level as other students. Educators can provide various options to students with special needs that can improve their accessibility to instructional resources.

Adaptive Learning Environment

AI can help creating an adaptive math learning environment for students (Burm, Chun, & Han, 2023). Self-directed learning environment using AI can prepare a personalized math learning program tailored to students' needs. Adaptive learning environment can in turn help in alleviating math anxiety and lack of confidence amongst students (Inoferio et al., 2024). Research by Inoferio and all (2024) reported on the use of AI tools to promote self-efficacy and confidence by delivering tailored mathematics instruction for students with special needs.

Real-time Feedback

AI tools can provide immediate feedback about students' learning-levels to educators. These resources can be used by educators to adopt much needed educational amendments in their instruction. Students can use the feedback to direct their focus on the concepts that can needed for developing conceptual understanding. Students can use these feedbacks for setting up goals for themselves. This in turn can create a growth mindset where students take charge of their learning.

Additional Resources for Special Education

Khanmigo (https://www.khanacademy.org/teacher/khanmigo-tools) Khanmigo is an AI-powered teaching assistant that is 100% free for educators.

Pros: Free AI-powered tools to easily access, and create lesson plans, rubrics, exit tickets, multiple-choice assessments, question generators, real word context generators, and many more. The app allows teachers to create a lesson plan either using Khan Academy content or their own using learning objectives, and topics and adding teaching tools. The biggest tool available at Khanmigo is Text-to-Speech technology for AI tutor. This AI tool does not only provide explanations, steps, or math but also talks making it easy for students with various needs to understand the material.

Cons: Teacher will not be able to add students as this AI tool is limited for teachers. However, Classroom access for Khanmigo is only available through school or district at this time.

Classpoint AI. This is an interactive quiz making tool available for both teachers and students. Classpoint allows teachers to create interactive quizzes in gamification mode. The quizzes are introduced in a game format that promote students' engagement. Classpoint competition mode allows users to create quizzes in competition format that can be used for both face-to-face or online classes. Students can use these tools to have self-directed learning tools and mastery-based progression opportunities by allowing them to work at their pace and focus on areas that need improvement.

Do2Learn.com- Do2Learn.com offers a wealth of resources for special education, including interactive games and activities. These resources are available for students with various social and behavioral needs, and are based on age-level. Teachers and parents can choose from various available resources for students needing assistance in developing motor skills that require hand and eye coordination. Many activities are there that can facilitate in the development of skills such as using scissors, fasten clothing, hold utensils, write, or activities that require left to right task orientation. Website also provide resources that can assist in developing social skills to improve communication skills, social behavior, using face clues to understand emotions, and understand social emotion skills. Special education teachers can use teacher toolbox to assist their students with correct intervention for varying social, emotional, or learning disorders. These activities are available for providing intervention in different subjects and can be tailored to individuals needs.

IXL.com- provides personalized learning for students from kindergarten to 12th grade, covering various subjects.

AAA Math.com- AAA Math.com offers comprehensive math lessons and interactive exercises, perfect for special education students.

Arcademics.com- Arcademics.com engages students with multiplayer math games, making learning fun and interactive."

Calculators.org- Calculators.org provides handy tools for special education students, making math calculations easier.

AI and Common Core State Standards

AI tools can facilitate with teaching concepts recommended by Common Core State Standards (CCSS, 2010) reports and follow Standards of Mathematical Practices for teaching. Following are the Standards of Mathematical Practices

1. Make sense of problems & persevere in solving them- AI tools can facilitate problem solving by restating the problem in simple language, finding different approaches to work on the problems using alternate ways to express them, analyze and implement the strategies to solve the problems, look back and check for accuracy of the solutions.
2. Reason abstractly & quantitatively- AI tools for connecting the pathways between problem scenarios and mathematical relationships to solve problems.
3. Construct viable arguments & critique the reasoning of others- AI tools can be used to prepare solution strategies and examine the accuracy of a solution.
4. Model with mathematics- AI tools allow modeling with mathematics to enhance learning experience. For example, $2 + 7 = ?$ Problem is depicted by AI tools using various models (number-line, take-away) to enhance users understanding of the concept.
5. Use appropriate tools strategically- mathematics problem-solving involves examining various approaches to solve a problem and use the most efficient and appropriate approach. AI tools can provide multiple strategies that can aid in understanding the problem and then solving it.
6. Attend to precision- mathematical problem-solving results when unnecessary details are avoided and attention is given to the information that can lead to solving the problem. AI tools like graphically representation can facilitate in using the appropriate information for problem-solving.

7. Look for & make use of structure- efficient problem-solving involves looking for and using the mathematical structure to solve problem. For example, understanding that addition and subtraction are complementary operations facilitate in solving subtraction problems $8 - 3 = ?$ using addition operation understanding $5 + 3 = 8$ or understanding that solution to an integration problem can be verified by differentiating the solution. AI tools can allow visual representations (for example, number-line model to represent addition operations) that can facilitate in using mathematical structure to solve problems.
8. Look for & express regularity in repeated reasoning- efficiently and accurately solving mathematical problems involve using reasoning. This can eliminate instances where an inaccurate computation was performed. For example, addition of two odd numbers leads to a solution that is an even number or multiplication of an odd and an even number results in even number solution.

Implementing the Standards of Mathematical Practices Using AI Tools

AI tools can help teachers in connecting the Standards for Mathematical Practice with the Standards for Mathematical Content. Teachers can use AI tools to make sense of problems and persevere in solving them by providing restating the problem in simple language, enabling users to convert the problems in their own language, finding different approaches to work on the problems using alternate ways to express them, analyze and implement the strategies to solve the problems, allowing looking back and check for accuracy of the solutions. To reason abstractly and quantitatively, AI tools are available for connecting the pathways between problem scenarios and mathematical relationships to solve problems. Educators and students can use AI for constructing viable arguments and critiquing the reasoning of others by comparing different solution strategies and examine the accuracy of a solution. One of the best use of AI in mathematics instruction is for modeling with mathematics. AI tools allow modeling with mathematics to enhance learning experience. For example, $2 + 7 = ?$ Problem is depicted by AI tools using various models (number-line, take-away) to enhance users understanding of the concept. Various tools allow users to graph the equation to understand the problems and come up with solution strategies.

AI tools for Understanding the Problems

Educators and students can use AI for understanding problems and comparing their solutions. For example, a simple search on CHATGPT allows users to restate the problem. For example, CHAT GPT restated the problem, "Joey is 20 years younger than Becky. In two years, Becky will be twice as old as Joey" as

- Joey is 20 years younger than Becky, which means if we subtract 20 from Becky's age, we get Joey's age. Additionally, in two years, Becky will be twice as old as Joey.
- Joey's age is 20 years less than Becky's. In two years, Becky will be twice as old as Joey.
- Becky is 20 years older than Joey, and in two years, Becky's age will be double Joey's age.
- Joey's age is 20 years less than Becky's. Two years from now, Becky's age will be twice Joey's age.

Examining the accuracy of a solution on CHATGPT. For the problem, "Joey is 20 years younger than Becky. In two years, Becky will be twice as old as Joey" CHATGPT was used to examine the solution Joey being 15 years old and Becky being 20 years old?

Let's check if Joey being 15 and Becky being 20 satisfies the given conditions:

- Joey is 20 years younger than Becky:

If Becky is 20 years old, and Joey is 20 years younger than Becky, then Joey's age should be 20−20=0 which is not possible because Joey's age can't be negative.

In two years, Becky will be twice as old as Joey:

- In two years, if Becky is $20 + 2 = 22$ years old and Joey is $15 + 2 = 17$ years old, Becky is not twice as old as Joey ($22 \neq 2 * 17$).

So, the ages you suggested for Joey and Becky do not satisfy the given conditions.

AI for Mathematics Instruction in Elementary Grades (K-5)

CCSS (2010) Standards for mathematics content in elementary grades (K-5) includes:

- Grade K (counting and cardinality, understanding addition-putting together and subtraction operations-taking apart or from for numbers from 1-10, compare numbers, basic understanding of shapes-circles, triangles, etc.);
- Grade 1 (add and subtract within 20, understanding algebraic properties, place-value, measurement using appropriate units, reason with shapes);
- Grade 2 (add and subtract within 20, understanding equal grouping for multiplication, place-value, work with time and money, interpret data, reason with shapes);

- Grade 3 (multiplication and division within 100, Use place value understanding and properties of operations to perform multi-digit arithmetic, understanding of fractions, interpret data, geometric measurement);
- Grade 4 (use the four operations with whole numbers to solve problems, gain familiarity with factors and multiples, generate and analyze patterns, fractions, decimals, and percentages, interpret data, properties of their lines and angles);
- Grade 5 (write and interpret numerical expressions, perform operations with multi-digit whole numbers and with decimals to hundredths, operations with fractions, geometric measurements, graphing).

Tools for basic operations addition, subtraction, multiplication, and division-Grades K-5

- Wolfarm Alpha is an AI powered tool for effectively teaching basic operations in elementary grades. Teachers can look up any common core standard to Wolfarm Alpha to get related problems and various representations to understand the concepts and standards. For example, for common core standard *Compare two numbers (CCSS.Math.Content.K.CC.C.7)* users are provided with explanations for the standard along with three examples to effectively introduce the concept: Is 5 greater than 2?, Which is smaller, 8 or 6?, and compare 4 and 1. The solution for the three examples includes multiple representations for conceptual understanding. For example, *compare 4 and 1* includes visual representation of the distance of numbers 4 and 1 from the starting point, pie chart covering 4 (80%) and 1 (20%) spaces, differences between the two numbers ($4 - 1 = 3$, $1 - 4 = -3$), or ratio of the numbers ($\frac{4}{1} = 4, \frac{1}{4} = \frac{1}{4} = 0.25$). Teachers can use any of the illustrations depending on students' conceptual understanding to enforce learning of the concepts. Another example for the tools used to display various models is $5 + 4 = ?$ Problem is represented using a number-line model with 5 spaces away from zero and adding 4 additional spaces to find out the distance from the starting point zero or a set of 5 objects are combined with 4 objects to find out the total number of objects. For advanced users, some real-life addition scenarios are also introduced where solution can be found by adding the given numbers.
- NoteGPT - https://notegpt.io/. NoteGPT is an AI powered to summarize notes. This tool makes it easy to take notes and is specifically useful for special education students making it easy to understand content in an effective and interactive way. The tool caters to individual needs by enabling user preferred learning environment. For example, for a student more interested in a

reading than watching video, this AI to can facilitate in learning by summarizing YouTube video by providing summary or transcripts. This tool helps in saving time as teacher can only read transcript to view the content cover in it and does not need to watch the whole video.

- Magic School - https://app.magicschool.ai/ The Magic School offers one stop for teachers assisting in instruction from developing lesson plans, designing user-friendly assignments, or creating newsletters highlighting the class activities. These tools can handle diverse needs of teachers and students. This tool has been noted to save approximately 10 hours of teachers' time that can be devoted towards other constructive activities. The AI offers nearly 50 tools that can help educators. Math educators can use *Math Spiral Review Generator* for generating grade-level based review questions that can provide additional practice for the students. This will allow students a chance to review the concepts and also enables educators to evaluate their students learning. *Math Story Word Problems* is a creative tool that can generate grade-level based problems along with the solutions on a math concept in the real-life story format. Educators can use this tool to create problems using a scenario that resonates with students. For example, a seventh-grade decimal fraction problem on Taylor Swift concert. *SAT Math Practice Test Generator* is a tool for high school math educators to ensure that their class content is preparing students for SAT aligned content. The test generator can create questions from a SAT covered math concept along with solutions. Educators can use this tool to assist students in preparing for SAT. *Common Misconception Generator* is an effective instructional tool for educators to prepare for any possible misconceptions on a math concept that can hinder students understanding and performance. The tool not only generates any possible misconceptions student might have, but also provides detailed steps to address them so that students are guided in the right direction.

Benefits

1. This AI can automatically generate educational materials for educators saving valuable time for other constructive activities.
2. The content follows Common Core Standards (2010) provided research guided relevant quality material at fingertips.
3. AI can generate educational material in 25 languages supporting needs of diverse population.
4. The app provides support for other subjects too.

Limitations

1. Some users could find the content little outdated as it contains material up to 2021.
2. There is a chance for biases as AI generates adaptive material that could be incorrect. This requires careful review and validation from the users.

Cost

Magic school AI has different options depending on the needs for the users. It is available free of charge for teachers. Premium Subscriptions are available for companies. Schools can explore custom pricing plans to meet their specific needs.

AI for Mathematics Instruction in Middle Grades (6-8)

CCSS (2010) standards for middle grades (Grades 6-8) include following concepts: ratio and proportional reasoning, expressions and equations, number systems (integers), functions, statistics, probability, and geometry. Students develop a thorough understanding of the concepts as they progress through the grades. For example, expressions and equations in grade 6 involve solving single variable equations and working through some simple computations with one-variable equations and expressions. In grade 7, students solve real-life problems by forming equations and working through multi-step equations. In grade 8, students work with equations that include radicals and exponents, equations involving simultaneous linear equations, and quadratic equations. Various AI tools available at *Wolfram Alpha,* Diffit - https://beta.diffit.me/#topic and Conker AI - https://www.conker.ai/ can be used to provide students at different stages of understanding with resources that can facilitate learning.

AI for Mathematics Instruction in High School Grades (9-12)

CCSS (2010) standards for middle grades (Grades 9-12) involve following concepts: number and quantity (real numbers, complex numbers, vectors and matrix, quantities), algebra (seeing structure in expressions, arithmetic with polynomials & rational expressions, creating equations, reasoning with equations & inequalities), functions (interpreting functions, linear, quadratic, exponential, and trigonometric functions, building functions), modeling, geometry (right triangles, circles, similarities, congruence, expressing geometric properties with equations, geometric measurement & dimension, modeling with geometry), statistics and probability (interpreting categorical and quantitative data, making inferences and justifying conclusions, conditional probability and rules of probability, using probability to make decisions). These AI tools are available for understanding hig school mathematics:

- *Wolfarm Alpha*. One of the best AI tools available for assistance for high school mathematics including trigonometry, algebra, calculus, linear algebra, differential equations. Discrete mathematics, complex analysis, probability, or statistics.
- *Microsoft Math Solver*. It provides solutions to problems in trigonometry, statistics, pre-algebra, algebra, matrices, calculus, and statistics. Users can choose to solve, practice, or play. Solve category is user-friendly and comes with an online calculator available for different math concepts and user are provided step-by-step solutions in a short time. It also supports hind-written inputs. User can choose play category to understand PEMDAS and related concepts. Practice category include solving available quizzes for basic math concepts needed for succeeding in high school mathematics including exponents, LCM, linear equations, quadratic equations, and inequalities. Interactive graphs available for users to promote visual understanding of the concepts.
- *GeoGebra* for algebra, calculus and geometry teaching for all grades K-12.

STRENGTHS AND LIMITATIONS OF AI IN MATHEMATICS INSTRUCTION

Strengths

AI tools can facilitate in creating an adaptive learning environment for students. Various AI tools can available that can tailor the instruction based on students' level of understanding and then provide recommendations that can promote their mathematical understanding.

Stronger Procedural Understanding. Conceptual understanding in mathematics refers to having a stronger foundational understanding of the concepts and facts involved mathematics. Procedural understanding refers to understanding of procedure or method involved in carrying out a computation. For example, to compute $\frac{1}{2} + \frac{3}{5}$, conceptual understanding that both fractions represent a part of the whole and addition cannot be computed without having a common denominator. Procedural understanding involves knowledge that common denominator for both fractions is 10 as both 2 and 5 are relatively primes and both numerator and denominator need to be multiplied by 5 in the first fraction and 2 in the second fraction. Mathematical knowledge involves both conceptual understanding and procedural understanding, and both conceptual and procedural understanding are intertwined (Rittle-Johnson, Siegler, & Alibali, 2001) of mathematics. AI tools that provide timely feedback and accurate solution can help students with procedural knowledge. The feedback provided by AI tools can be used to understand the process involved in computing the solution, which in turn help in developing conceptual understanding.

Personalized Adaptive Instruction. AI-powered adaptive learning platforms provide interactive activities based on a student's capacities, disabilities, and skills. These platforms provide a vast range of math learning assignments in different forms such as video quizzes that are adaptable to users' preferences. Some AI tools like Khamingo provide a free AI tutor where students can chat or ask questions, and receive step-by-step solutions to problems in math. In addition, AI offered by Khan Academy is one of the most popular tools due its ability to adapt and provide explanation.

Learning Outcomes Using AI. Various AI tools can be used by instructors to gauge students' mathematics understanding and use the data to provide tailored mathematics instruction to promoting success. Many studies have reported students' learning outcome using AI tools in following categories (Chiu at el., 2023): Academic performance (29%), motivation and engagement (34%), 21st century skills (25%), and non-cognitive skills (12%). The effect of students' interaction with AI machine chatbot on student experience is not studied widely and there are not enough resources that can pinpoint when and how to use chatbot for fostering learning and engaging students (Chiu at el., 2023). AI tools like Khanmigo offer an AI-powered tutor to assist in learning. However, the lack of human touch during the use of AI cannot assist in the behavioral needs that involve emotional, social, communication, and interactive skills.

Enjoyable Learning Environment. AI tools introduce learning using gamification that makes learning experience more enjoyable and likely to keep students motivated for a longer span. Gamification of learning also provides a relatable experience to students as present students are more proficient in using gaming.

Limitations

AI can provide theoretical instructions, link to resources, or provide an explanation of content. But it does not pass a QEP standard, active learning activities, critical skill, problem solving skill, analysis skills, and most importantly AI does not respond to students' curiosity level due to the main focus on accuracy. Here is an example of a solution from Wolfram Alpha (https://www.wolframalpha.com/) and Perplexity AI (https://www.perplexity.ai/) of the same problem (see Figure 1). Then they both provide different methods and different answers. This highlights that AI can be a supporter, but cannot be a tutor or educator.

Figure 1. Calculation on WolframAplha

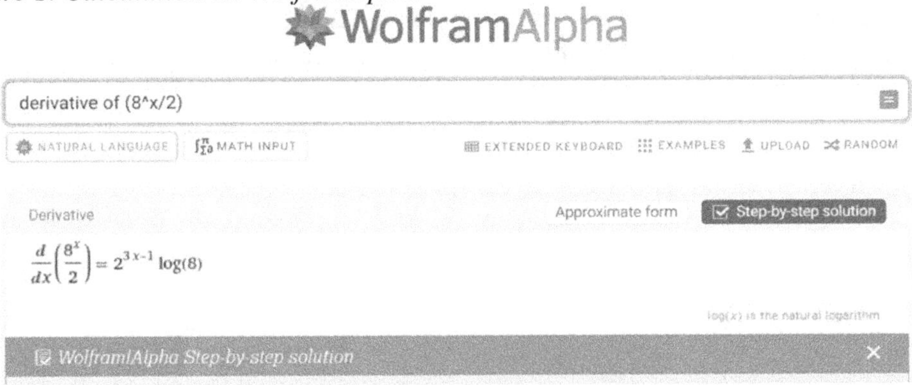

The derivative of $\frac{8^x}{2}$ with respect to x is $\frac{8^x ln8}{2}$

Users need to understand the algebra behind both solutions to decide if the solutions are accurate and are identical. When a problem like this is given in multiple choices, users who do not understand algebra will not be able to relate the two identical solutions.

Inaccurate and Insufficient Information. Most AI tools that are free for users provide insufficient information about a computation that can lead to more anxiety and confusion. Many free AI applications offer only solutions with no descriptions. This can create anxiety and stress among students who need help in carrying out steps for solving. AI tools are machine operated and look for a pattern in finding the solutions. This could result in finding inaccurate solutions to any problems that are based on logic. Students may not get any help in solving that are written by teachers themselves. Students needs a solid conceptual understanding of concepts that can enable them in identifying inaccurate solutions and also check the solutions that are AI generated.

Focus on Solution Only. AI tools can increase students' reliance to use tools for getting an accurate solution in a short span. This in turn can lead to just focusing on the generating solutions and not engaging in developing an understanding towards problem-solving and developing conceptual understanding. In mathematics, the concepts are related and lack of understanding in pre-requisite concepts will affect academic success in related concepts. For example, limits understanding is needed for understanding continuity of functions or differentiation.

Lack of Human Intervention. AI tools like Khanmigo offer an AI-powered tutor to assist in learning. However, the lack of human touch during the use of AI cannot assist in the behavioral needs that involve emotional, social, communication, and interactive skills. Moreover, AI powered tools provide solution based on the data provided and AI cannot account for factors that cannot be measured.

In conclusion, AI offers a wide range of support for both teachers and students that can aid in learning. There are many factors that cannot be tackled by AI and users needs to understand them before relying on AI for their educational needs.

References

Alam, A. (2021, November). Possibilities and apprehensions in the landscape of artificial intelligence in education. In *2021 International Conference on Computational Intelligence and Computing Applications (ICCICA)* (pp. 1-8). IEEE. DOI: 10.1109/ICCICA52458.2021.9697272

Asfar, A. I. T., Asmawaty, A., Asfar, A. I. A., & Nursyam, A. (2019). Mathematical concept understanding: The impact of integrated learning model. *Al-Jabar: Jurnal Pendidikan Matematika*, 10(2), 211–222. DOI: 10.24042/ajpm.v10i2.3880

Burm, E., Chun, Y. E., & Han, J. Y. (2023). Validation of the effectiveness of AI-Based Personalized Adaptive Learning: Focusing on basic math class cases. *Journal of Internet of Things and Convergence*, 9(3), 35–43.

Chen, X., Zou, D., Xie, H., Cheng, G., & Liu, C. (2022). Two decades of artificial intelligence in education. *Journal of Educational Technology & Society*, 25(1), 28–47.

Chiu, T. K., Xia, Q., Zhou, X., Chai, C. S., & Cheng, M. (2023). Systematic literature review on opportunities, challenges, and future research recommendations of artificial intelligence in education. *Computers and Education: Artificial Intelligence*, 4, 100118. DOI: 10.1016/j.caeai.2022.100118

Hiebert, J., & Grouws, D. A. (2007). The effects of classroom mathematics teaching on students' learning. *Second handbook of research on mathematics teaching and learning*, 1(1), 371-404.

Inoferio, H. V., Espartero, M., Asiri, M., Damin, M., & Chavez, J. V. (2024). Coping with math anxiety and lack of confidence through AI-assisted Learning. *Environment and Social Psychology, 9*(5).

Ouyang, F., & Jiao, P. (2021). Artificial intelligence in education: The three paradigms. *Computers and Education: Artificial Intelligence*, 2, 100020. DOI: 10.1016/j.caeai.2021.100020

Rittle-Johnson, B., Siegler, R. S., & Alibali, M. W. (2001). Developing conceptual understanding and procedural skill in mathematics: An iterative process. *Journal of Educational Psychology*, 93(2), 346–362. DOI: 10.1037/0022-0663.93.2.346

Chapter 9
Specializing Instruction With the Use of Artificial Intelligence

Rajesh Kanna Rajendran
https://orcid.org/0000-0001-7228-5031
Christ University, India

Ashok Immanuel V.
Christ University, India

Mohana Priya T.
Christ University, India

ABSTRACT

The integration of Artificial Intelligence (AI) promises to transform how educators deliver specialized instruction. AI empowers educators to personalize learning experiences for each student. This chapter investigates into how AI can create individualized learning paths, improve learning outcomes, and address diverse educational needs. We'll explore AI applications in education, discuss their benefits and limitations, and envision the future of AI-powered learning environments that are both inclusive and effective.AI personalizes instruction by adapting educational content and methods to each student's unique needs. AI-powered platforms analyze vast amounts of data on students' learning styles, pace, strengths, and weaknesses. This data allows these platforms to create personalized learning paths, recommend resources, and provide targeted feedback. This level of customization ensures students receive the right support and challenges, maximizing their potential and fostering a more engaging learning experience.

DOI: 10.4018/979-8-3693-5538-1.ch009

INTRODUCTION

Although AI has yet to become a standard in schools, its integration into education has been evolving since the technology's surge in the 1980s. Education and AI are a natural fit: while education aims to develop minds that expand and leverage knowledge, AI provides tools that offer a more accurate and detailed understanding of how the human mind works. AI's digital and dynamic nature offers student engagement opportunities beyond the static, outdated textbooks and the confines of traditional classrooms. This synergy has the potential to propel both fields forward, accelerating the discovery of new learning frontiers and fostering the creation of innovative technologies. As explored in our AI Future Scape series, the education of future leaders in business and government on AI practices is crucial for the continued development and implementation of AI in various sectors.

One significant advancement in AI for education is the development of intelligent tutoring systems (ITS), which offer personalized electronic tutoring tailored to each student's learning styles and preferences. These systems, along with smart content technologies that condense textbooks into useful tools for exam preparation, such as true or false questions, and virtual facilitators that serve as guides in educational and therapeutic environments, are pioneering applications in the field. While these applications are still in their relatively "primitive" stages, they hold immense potential for shaping a future of more personalized learning and responsive teaching.

Literature Review

AI's ability to personalize learning is one of its most significant contributions to education. Personalized learning involves tailoring educational experiences to meet the individual needs of each student. According to Holmes et al. (2019), AI systems can analyze student data to create customized learning pathways, providing targeted support and resources that cater to individual learning styles and preferences. This personalization enhances student engagement and improves learning outcomes.

Intelligent Tutoring Systems (ITS) are AI-driven platforms that offer personalized tutoring to students. ITS can adapt to a student's learning pace and provide immediate feedback, thus promoting a more effective learning process. Ma, Adesope, and Nesbit (2014) conducted a meta-analysis of ITS and found that these systems significantly improve student performance across various subjects. They highlighted that ITS can mimic the benefits of one-on-one tutoring, making personalized instruction more accessible. AI technologies have revolutionized the assessment and feedback processes in education. Automated grading systems and AI-powered feedback tools can provide timely and accurate evaluations of student work. This immediate feedback helps students understand their mistakes and learn from them more effectively. Lu,

Huang, and Azar (2018) emphasize that AI-driven assessment tools not only save time for educators but also ensure a consistent and unbiased evaluation of student performance. Virtual Reality (VR) and Augmented Reality (AR) technologies, powered by AI, offer immersive learning experiences that traditional methods cannot provide. These technologies enable students to explore complex concepts in an interactive environment. For instance, VR can simulate historical events or scientific phenomena, making learning more engaging and memorable. Cheng and Tsai (2020) found that VR and AR applications in education significantly improve student motivation and comprehension. West, Kraut, and Chew (2019) highlight the importance of establishing ethical guidelines and frameworks to govern the use of AI in educational settings. They stress the need for transparency and accountability in AI algorithms to prevent biases and ensure fair treatment of all students.

How is Artificial intelligence used in Education

Artificial Intelligence is revolutionizing education by enabling highly personalized learning experiences and efficient assessment processes. AI systems analyze student data to create tailored learning paths, adjusting content, pace, and difficulty to optimize each student's educational potential. For instance, adaptive learning platforms use AI algorithms to monitor progress and provide targeted practice, addressing specific areas of strength and weakness. According to recent data, 60% of educational institutions report using AI-driven tools to automate grading and deliver instant feedback, significantly reducing educators' workload and enhancing student improvement. Furthermore, AI's natural language processing capabilities support applications such as automated essay grading and language learning platforms, with over 70% of language learners benefiting from AI-based pronunciation feedback. AI also contributes to content creation by generating customized quizzes, tutorials, and simulations, thus enriching the learning experience and promoting deeper understanding of complex subjects.

Automated Assessment Systems

Automated assessment systems are revolutionizing the way evaluations are conducted in education by leveraging AI to streamline and enhance the assessment process. These systems utilize advanced algorithms to automatically grade assignments, quizzes, and exams, providing instant feedback to students. This immediate response allows learners to quickly understand their mistakes and improve their performance, significantly reducing the time educators spend on grading and administrative tasks. For instance, automated systems can assess multiple-choice questions, short answers, and even complex essays using natural language processing techniques, ensuring a comprehensive evaluation of student work.

Automated assessment systems offer the capability to analyze large volumes of data to identify trends and patterns in student performance. This analysis helps educators gain valuable insights into learning outcomes, pinpoint areas where students commonly struggle, and tailor instructional strategies accordingly. The ability to handle diverse types of assessments and provide detailed analytics enhances the overall efficiency of the educational process and supports a more personalized learning experience. As these systems continue to evolve, they promise to further refine the accuracy and effectiveness of educational assessments, making them an essential tool in modern education.

AI-Enhanced Virtual Reality (VR) and Augmented Reality (AR)

AI-driven Virtual Reality (VR) and Augmented Reality (AR) technologies are revolutionizing how students interact with educational content. These immersive tools provide interactive learning experiences that traditional methods cannot match. Recent developments include the use of AI to create adaptive VR/AR environments. For example, AI algorithms can adjust the level of complexity in VR simulations based on the student's performance, offering a customized experience that evolves with their progress. This adaptability enhances engagement by allowing students to explore and interact with complex concepts in a more tangible and interactive way. AR applications are also benefiting from AI, which allows for dynamic overlays of educational content in the real world, such as interactive diagrams or contextual information, thus enriching the learning experience.

AI-Powered Collaborative Learning Platforms

AI is significantly enhancing collaborative learning through platforms that support effective group interactions. These platforms use AI to facilitate smart groupings, matching students based on their learning styles, strengths, and weaknesses. This intelligent grouping helps create balanced teams that can work together more effectively. AI also supports real-time feedback during group activities, analyzing group dynamics and offering suggestions to improve collaboration and productivity. For instance, AI tools can monitor group discussions and provide insights into group performance, helping students refine their collaborative strategies and ensuring more productive group work.

Real-Time Feedback and Assessment Tools

Recent AI techniques have transformed the feedback and assessment processes in education. Automated grading systems powered by AI use advanced machine learning models to provide instant, detailed feedback on assignments and exams. These systems evaluate not just the correctness of student responses but also analyze patterns in the data to offer insights into common misunderstandings and areas where students need further support. This immediacy in feedback helps students quickly understand their mistakes and learn from them. Furthermore, AI-driven analytics tools enable educators to track student progress and engagement in real-time, allowing for timely interventions and tailored support based on up-to-date performance data.

AI-Driven Virtual Assistants and Chatbots

AI-powered virtual assistants and chatbots are increasingly used to support both students and educators. These tools can handle a wide range of queries, from administrative tasks to course-related questions, providing instant responses and assistance. Recent advancements have improved the complexity and accuracy of these virtual assistants, enabling them to manage more sophisticated interactions and integrate seamlessly with other educational technologies. For example, chatbots can guide students through complex processes, offer tutoring support, and provide personalized recommendations based on individual learning needs. This continuous support enhances the overall educational experience by making information and assistance readily available.

Emotion Recognition and Adaptive Learning

Emotion recognition systems, powered by AI, are an emerging technique that assesses students' emotional states during learning activities. By analyzing facial expressions, voice tones, and physiological responses, these systems can gauge students' emotional and cognitive states. This real-time emotional data allows the AI to adjust the learning environment to better support students' needs. For instance, if the system detects signs of frustration or disengagement, it can modify the difficulty level of tasks, provide additional resources, or offer encouragement. This adaptive approach helps keep students engaged and motivated, ensuring a more responsive and supportive learning experience.

Paving New Learning Pathways in the Era of AI

Education has long been driven by direct human interaction, with the integration of AI progressing slowly in replicating the nuanced aspects of human responsiveness, adaptability, and understanding. Nonetheless, AI's strengths in processing and analyzing large datasets offer promising solutions to critical challenges in learning and teaching. By continuously monitoring a student's performance across various subjects, AI can provide real-time, targeted feedback and practice. This not only helps students get the precise support they need but also enables educators to develop more effective, personalized learning plans based on detailed insights into student progress.

As AI technologies advance, they are expected to complement rather than replace human educators. Emerging areas for AI application in education include providing personalized mentorship, enhancing 21st-century skills, utilizing interaction data to improve learning experiences, ensuring global classroom access, and supporting lifelong learning. These advancements suggest that AI will serve as a powerful tool to extend the capabilities of human teachers, helping them address the diverse needs of students more effectively and manage various aspects of academic and social development in the classroom.

Smart Content: Revolutionizing Educational Resources

Smart content is rapidly transforming educational resources by leveraging AI to enhance the way information is presented and interacted with. This innovative approach utilizes advanced technologies to create dynamic and interactive learning materials that go beyond traditional textbooks. By integrating AI, smart content adapts to individual learning needs, providing a more personalized and effective educational experience.

Adaptive Learning Materials

One of the core features of smart content is its ability to adapt learning materials based on student performance and engagement. AI algorithms analyze how students interact with content, identifying patterns and adjusting the difficulty level or presentation style to better suit each learner's needs. This adaptability ensures that students receive content that matches their current understanding, making learning more efficient and effective. For example, if a student struggles with a particular concept, smart content can offer additional explanations, examples, or practice problems tailored to that specific area.

Interactive and Engaging Content

Smart content also enhances the interactivity and engagement of educational materials. Traditional textbooks often present information in a static format, but smart content incorporates multimedia elements such as videos, simulations, and interactive exercises. These elements make learning more engaging and help students grasp complex concepts through hands-on experience. For instance, an interactive textbook might include embedded simulations that allow students to experiment with scientific principles or explore historical events through virtual tours.

Personalized Learning Pathways

Another significant advantage of smart content is its ability to create personalized learning pathways. AI-driven platforms can track individual progress and preferences, recommending specific resources or activities that align with each student's unique learning style and goals. This personalized approach not only improves comprehension and retention but also helps students stay motivated by providing content that is relevant and interesting to them.

Real-Time Feedback and Analytics

Smart content provides real-time feedback and analytics to both students and educators. As students interact with the content, AI systems can generate immediate assessments of their performance, offering feedback and suggestions for improvement. Educators can access detailed reports on student engagement and progress, allowing them to identify areas where students may need additional support or intervention. This data-driven approach facilitates a more responsive and supportive learning environment.

Enhanced Student Engagement

Enhanced student engagement through AI-driven technologies is revolutionizing the educational experience by making learning more interactive and personalized. AI tools can analyze student interactions and performance in real-time, allowing for tailored content that aligns with each student's unique learning style and interests. This adaptive approach helps capture students' attention by offering challenges and resources that are relevant to their individual needs, fostering a more engaging learning environment. AI-powered platforms can adjust the difficulty of tasks, provide instant feedback, and suggest supplementary materials based on a student's progress, ensuring that learning remains stimulating and appropriately challenging.

AI technologies such as gamified learning experiences, virtual reality (VR) simulations, and interactive multimedia content are making educational activities more immersive and enjoyable. These innovative tools transform traditional learning materials into dynamic, hands-on experiences that encourage active participation. By incorporating elements such as interactive exercises, simulations, and real-time problem-solving scenarios, students are more likely to remain engaged and motivated throughout their educational journey. Enhanced student engagement through AI not only improves understanding and retention but also helps foster a more enthusiastic and participatory learning atmosphere.

AI For Personalized Learning

Artificial Intelligence (AI) is transforming education through personalized learning by tailoring the educational experience to meet the unique needs of each student. This approach allows for adjustments in various aspects of the learning process, such as the pace, materials, sequence, and methods of instruction. Educators can customize learning experiences to align with individual goals and preferences, enhancing engagement and effectiveness. AI facilitates this by analyzing data on students' learning behaviors and outcomes, enabling the creation of personalized educational paths that accommodate each learner's strengths and areas for improvement.

The application of AI in personalized learning offers the flexibility for students to learn at their own pace and convenience. AI technology predicts learning patterns and outcomes, allowing for the development of content and resources that are specifically tailored to each student's needs. This level of personalization, which might be challenging to achieve on a large scale without AI, ensures that educational experiences are more relevant and impactful. AI is significantly enhancing the ability of educators to deliver individualized instruction and support, thereby making education more accessible and effective for every student.

Equitable use of AI in Education

The equitable use of AI in education is crucial for ensuring that all students benefit from technological advancements regardless of their socio-economic background or geographic location. AI can help bridge educational gaps by providing personalized learning experiences and resources that are tailored to individual needs. However, to achieve true equity, it is essential to address disparities in access to AI technologies and ensure that they are accessible to underserved and marginalized communities.

This involves providing necessary infrastructure, such as reliable internet and devices, as well as designing AI tools that cater to diverse learning needs and languages.

Equitable use of AI in education requires continuous monitoring and addressing of potential biases within AI systems. AI algorithms must be developed and tested to prevent reinforcing existing inequalities or biases, ensuring that all students receive fair and unbiased support. Implementing robust policies and practices that promote inclusivity and accessibility, educational institutions can harness the power of AI to enhance learning opportunities for every student, ultimately contributing to a more just and equitable educational landscape.

CONCLUSION

AI is poised to significantly enhance education through innovations in assessment and feedback systems. AI-driven assessment technologies will streamline the grading process by automating evaluations, allowing educators to concentrate more on teaching and less on administrative tasks. Automated grading ensures consistency and fairness, while instant feedback provides students with timely insights to swiftly address their learning gaps. The integration of data analytics will offer valuable insights into student performance, enabling educators to tailor their instructional strategies more effectively. Natural language processing will refine the analysis of written work, enhancing the accuracy of automated grading and offering deeper insights into student understanding.These advancements promise to make education more personalized, efficient, and equitable, paving the way for a more adaptive and data-driven learning environment.

REFERENCES

Baker, R. S. J. d., & Inventado, P. S. (2014). Educational data mining and learning analytics. In *Learning Analytics* (pp. 61–75). Springer. DOI: 10.1007/978-1-4614-3305-7_4

Beal, C. R., & Lee, H. (2019). Creating cognitive and metacognitive support for students in intelligent tutoring systems. *Journal of Educational Psychology*, 111(4), 666–677.

Borenstein, J., & Howard, A. (2020). The ethics of artificial intelligence in education: Emerging issues and the potential for lasting impact. *Educational Technology Research and Development*, 68(4), 1997–2011.

Chen, L., Chen, P., & Lin, Z. (2020). Artificial intelligence in education: A review. *IEEE Access : Practical Innovations, Open Solutions*, 8, 75264–75278. DOI: 10.1109/ACCESS.2020.2988510

Cheng, K. H., & Tsai, C. C. (2020). The interactions between self-regulation of learning and the use of AI-based applications in learning. *Journal of Educational Computing Research*, 57(6), 1585–1602.

Dillenbourg, P., & Fischer, F. (2007). Basics of computer-supported collaborative learning. Zeitschrift für Berufs- und Wirtschaftspädagogik, 21, 111-130.

Ha, S. H., & Park, C. G. (2017). The use of artificial intelligence in educational systems: Benefits and challenges. *Journal of Educational Technology Development and Exchange*, 10(1), 55–66.

Heffernan, N. T., & Heffernan, C. L. (2014). The ASSISTments ecosystem: Building a platform that brings scientists and teachers together for minimally invasive research on human learning and teaching. *International Journal of Artificial Intelligence in Education*, 24(4), 470–497. DOI: 10.1007/s40593-014-0024-x

Holmes, W., Bialik, M., & Fadel, C. (2019). *Artificial Intelligence in Education: Promises and Implications for Teaching and Learning*. Center for Curriculum Redesign.

Kulik, J. A., & Fletcher, J. D. (2016). Effectiveness of intelligent tutoring systems: A meta-analytic review. *Review of Educational Research*, 86(1), 42–78. DOI: 10.3102/0034654315581420

Lu, O. H. T., Huang, A. Y. Q., & Azar, P. (2018). AI-based assessment and feedback in education: Enhancing student learning outcomes. *Journal of Learning Analytics*, 5(2), 91–104.

Ma, W., Adesope, O. O., Nesbit, J. C., & Liu, Q. (2014). Intelligent tutoring systems and learning outcomes: A meta-analysis. *Journal of Educational Psychology*, 106(4), 901–918. DOI: 10.1037/a0037123

McArthur, D., Lewis, M., & Bishay, M. (1993). The roles of artificial intelligence in education: Current progress and future prospects. *Journal of Educational Computing Research*, 9(2), 165–189.

West, S. M., Kraut, R. E., & Chew, H. E. (2019). I'd blush if I could: Closing gender divides in digital skills through education. *AI & Society*, 34(1), 31–46.

Woolf, B. P. (2010). *Building Intelligent Interactive Tutors: Student-Centered Strategies for Revolutionizing E-learning*. Morgan Kaufmann.

Yang, S. J. H., & Wang, Y. (2019). The impact of AI on learning: Future perspectives. *Interactive Learning Environments*, 27(7), 1020–1033.

Chapter 10
Executive Functioning Skills and Artificial Intelligence

Tamar F. Riley
https://orcid.org/0009-0006-4230-5808
Alabama A&M University, USA

Annamaria Jerome-Raja
https://orcid.org/0009-0007-2926-8747
Florida Memorial University, USA

Srimani Chakravarthi
https://orcid.org/0000-0001-8777-3273
University of St. Francis, USA

ABSTRACT

This chapter addresses the topic of equitable instruction using Artificial Intelligence for Executive Functioning skills of students with disabilities. The chapter will have the following content: Types of EF needs: This will outline varied EF needs with classroom examples on how the needs are reflected. Overview of AI tools for EF: AI has the potential to act as a digital assistant in creating to-do lists, prioritize, and set reminders like a personal assistant. This section will cover popular AI tools such as ChatGPT, Grammarly, PowerPoint Speaker Coach, Motion, LightKey, etc., with specific examples of use. Approaching EF needs from an equitable perspective using AI: This section will outline the AI tools that can help with EF, with specific application examples and uses. Cultural and linguistic diversity considerations will be included. Case study examples: This will include brief case studies of SWD with EF deficits in planning, prioritizing, organizing, problem solving, time management, etc.

DOI: 10.4018/979-8-3693-5538-1.ch010

EXECUTIVE FUNCTIONING

Executive Functioning skills are a set of diverse neurological and higher-order cognitive abilities involved in self-regulation, such as processing information, planning, prioritizing, organizing, guiding, reviewing, displaying flexibility and goal-setting (Blair & Ursache, 2011). These are skills that influence academic success, emotional regulation, and social interactions. Executive Functioning (EF) skills mainly consist of working memory, inhibitory control, and cognitive flexibility. Multiple factors play a role in the development of EF skills. These self-regulation skills are needed in all aspects of functioning and across age-levels to varying extents in different environments.

Several students with disabilities, including students with Learning Disabilities, Attention Deficit Hyperactivity Disorders, Autism, and Emotional Disturbance, have been found to have some level of deficits in executive functioning skills. However, students who have Attention Deficit Hyperactivity Disorder (ADHD) are known to face most challenges with limited goal-directed behavior and self-regulation of their thinking and behavior through the use of working memory, inner speech, control of emotions, arousal levels, analysis of problems and communication of problem solutions to others (Barkley, 2020). Twenty to 60 percent of students with ADHD have deficits in one or more areas of executive functioning (Kofler, Irwin, Soto, Groves, Harmon, & Sarver, 2019) and are typically found to be at least 30-40% behind in executive functioning as compared to their peers (Barkley, 2020). According to a 2023 report, 85% of educators have had students in their classrooms who struggle with executive functioning (Deshpande, 2023). In addition, the number of students exhibiting deficits in working memory, flexible thinking, following directions, solving problems and managing long-term projects seems to have risen noticeably after the recent COVID-19 pandemic (Frolli et al., 2023), calling attention to instruction and intervention in executive functioning skills. These pervasive deficits in executive functioning can be addressed through the use of Artificial Intelligence (AI) tools, using a systematic approach to identification, assessment and intervention.

Executive Functioning and Artificial Intelligence

Artificial Intelligence (AI) has shown promise and continues to gain interest in how it might be used to improve learning for students with disabilities. AI powered assistive technologies can help students access education by providing them with tools and devices that can assist with reading, writing, communicating and self-regulation. AI has the potential to improve the lives of students with disabilities by providing them with the tools and support they need to succeed in school and beyond. Using AI as an assistive tool to support EF for students with disabilities, can empower them with decision-making power and support their inclusion in typical school settings (Pierres, Darvishy, & Christen, 2023).

While AI tools such as the virtual calendar, remind apps, that assist with self-regulation skills are not new, the emergence of a plethora of tools to choose from and enabling personalization to suit the individual, is certainly a recent development. Digital technology to support interventions for elementary students with learning problems, which increasingly uses AI, has grown tremendously each year. Research published in 2021-2022 supporting digital technology more than doubled in publication rate compared to the previous five years combined (Gunnar, 2023). Digital game-based and gamified learning tools powered by AI have become popular methods of effective teaching, particularly in special education to support executive function intervention due to the systematic behavioral instruction that is matched to the curriculum and delivered in manageable chunks. These assistive apps to help students focus on specific tasks and can monitor their goal attainment through data reporting, are becoming increasingly popular among special education teachers who rely heavily on data to measure student progress.

While AI tools do facilitate 'taking over' the executive functions such as keeping track of assignments, reminders, task planning, etc., AI has also been used for cognitive training of executive functioning. Research in the effectiveness of AI tools and programs is emerging and yet to be established as a preferable intervention. However, the existing studies do highlight the benefits of AI based tools and programs to executive functioning skills. In three systematic review studies which compiled more than 101 randomized controlled trials (RCT) in children with ADHD, interventions that used serious games, virtual reality and neurofeedback were found to have a favorable effect on executive functioning skills of working memory, attention, planning, inhibition and self-regulation (Sonuga-Barke, Brandeis, Holtmann, & Cortese, 2014; Lakes, Cibrian, Schuck, Nelson & Hayes, 2022; Cibrian, Lakes, Schuck & Hayes, 2022). A systematic review of 19 RCTs in students with autism showed that artificial cognitive computational training shows more significant improvements in executive functioning than other common interventions, with carry-over effects on social skills (Ge, Zhu, Wu et al., 2018)

There are numerous computerized cognitive training programs that use software, applications and online platforms which are commonly used in rehabilitation in the health sector (Robledo-Castro, Castillo-Ossa & Corchado, 2023) and emergent in the educational realm by providing tools for planning and designing personalized learning programs. The optimization of data collection and processing by machine learning algorithms has facilitated adaptation of activities to individualization of training (Parre & Sujatha, 2021). The ease of access to AI powered tools from multiple devices and modalities (computers, tablets, phones, wearables, etc.) has removed logistical and geographical barriers, reducing barriers to access and use. AI thus holds great potential for improving outcomes across cultures and populations, facilitated by large data analysis enabling data-based revisions and improvements based on use and feasibility. The benefit of AI powered interventions is the ability to individualize and personalize the interventions without neglecting companionship, instructional support and follow-up of the intervention process; which allows for multiple quality interventions at a time, freeing up time for the instructor (Robledo-Castro, Castillo-Ossa & Corchado, 2023)

Li, Zarei, Alibakhshi, and Labbafi (2024) investigated the benefits of interventions that primarily used AI to improve support to students with Autism. Researchers found that teachers and students found these applications to be a benefit to students by providing them increased engagement and personalized learning. Although authors provided several cautions in using AI, they summarized that AI interventions had potential to tailor instruction to the unique learning needs for each student. With each new iteration in programming, AI can adapt learning materials and experiences with greater potential for individualized intervention, potentially make life easier for students. According to TeachAI (2023), 73% of students indicated that AI helped them better understand the material while 67% of students indicated that AI helped them study faster and more efficiently. Klarin, Hoff, Larsson, & Daukantaite (2024) found a pattern among students who exhibited EF deficits having a heavier reliance on AI as a tool to assist them with completing academic tasks. Furthermore, the research suggested that students with EF deficits may be more apt to rely on AI tools to supplant their skills instead of enhancing or supplementing their abilities. The authors offered speculations regarding potential negative implications for students' ability in developing EF skills in natural contexts if there is a heavy reliance on AI. Overall, researchers consistently echo the call for "thoughtful" plans to implement AI tools.

In a study 82 high school students were asked to play the *Alien Game,* an AI based game, for over a six-week period. The researchers employed pre and posttest measures to determine if the game, which relies on AI, would improve EF skills (Homer, Plass, et.al, 2018). They concluded that the video game was able to build cognitive skills as long as that is what the game was designed to do. They went on to explain that in order for these types of games to be effective platforms for intervention to improve EF, that the game and its elements would need to be both engaging and challenging in order to target specific EF skills. In this particular study, the *Alien Game* was found to improve the EF subskill of shifting, being able to quickly shift from one task to another, as well as some development of the subskill of inhibition, which is the ability to control automatic urges.

The use of AI is not entirely smooth and does pose some challenges - one of them being the infrastructure to support and gather the needed data to make decisions for appropriate use and benefits, especially when considering the unique learning needs of students. In a qualitative study conducted by Garg & Sharma (2020), results of focused interviews with students with disabilities and teachers in inclusive settings, acknowledged the need for infrastructures with the help of AI technologies and augmented technology.

AI has the potential to improve outcomes in academic personalized learning, social and communication skills. All students with disabilities struggle with Executive Functioning skills to varying extent. The potential of AI to help with executive functioning is vast and ranges from diverse applications. This chapter addresses the topic of equitable instruction in Executive Functioning skills of students with disabilities and other diverse needs.

Executive Functioning Skills Needed in the Classroom

Executive functioning skills are required inside and outside the classroom, throughout the learning experience within the school environment. The skills of time management, planning, prioritizing, executing and self-regulation which students gain exponentially in the schooling years are expected to be generalized to life and careers. The most common executive functioning skills required in the classroom are:

- **Planning:** The ability to 'look ahead' and decide on a proposal for accomplishing a desired goal. Students are given a project to be completed over time and it includes several components, comes with directions, and has an accompanying rubric. Or it could be that a student is given an essay topic to complete a response in a given time period. Possibly, it is a science investigation that requires reporting over multiple time periods.
- **Organization:** The ability to arrange and manage objects, thoughts and ideas. Students have to manage multiple assignments across subjects (and teachers), some as practice, some as daily assignments, and others as projects. This could be keeping up with important communication from the school to the student's guardian. How these documents are retained, stored, retrieved require a habitual system that can be executed consistently, meeting expectations of supporting parties.
- **Time management:** This ability calls for a perception of time or time sense - the ability to gauge how much time is left or elapsed time. It also includes the ability to manage tasks within a reasonable time, estimating the time needed and prioritizing to manage time efficiency. This management and accounting of time is essential from the moment a student starts the day until the time they go to bed. School, classes, appointments, deadlines, all call for proficiency in time keeping and managing. In early grades, teachers heavily prompt students with reminders and set timers to help monitor their pacing

and sustained attending to a task. As students get older, prompting fades and expectations for individual time management increases. Time is allotted for each in class task and it considers the students age and ability to use time wisely.

- **Self-monitoring:** The ability to gauge one's own abilities using metacognition. This includes the ability to monitor oneself in academics and behavior, and the ability to change oneself based on learned failures and successes. Students are expected to regulate their emotions, know when they need to request assistance, accept that the unexpected can and will happen and be able to make adjustments to their thoughts and actions to successfully navigate the challenges of the learning environment. There is an expected level of self-awareness of personal needs negotiated by the norms established in the classroom and school environment.
- **Working memory:** This ability refers to processing, engaging, storing and retrieving information throughout the learning experience. Students are required to recall previously learned information and build upon it to make new knowledge. Inefficient memorization strategies contribute to breakdown in this function, complicated by lack of attention and efficient organization strategies. When there is a breakdown in this function, there are learning problems, which lead to other issues impeding school success.
- **Self-control:** This refers to self-management of their physical and emotional outputs, and inhibitory behavior. Students should be able to pivot successfully when challenges are encountered. Each classroom is guided by a set of expectations, which many of them have self-control at its foundation such as keep your hands to yourself, respect yourself and others, use kind words, etc. Students are expected to transition from one activity to the next while maintaining the equilibrium of the classroom while regulating their moods, feelings and emotions to suit the expected norms of the environment..
- **Flexible/adaptive thinking:** The ability to 'go with the flow' and adapt to changes in the environment, without breaking down. Students need to understand obstacles or problems are just opportunities needing a solution. Having a growth mindset and considering alternatives as work-arounds, while acting on a new plan demonstrates adaptability, which is a skill that is lacking in several students with and without disabilities.

Artificial Intelligence Tools for Executive Functioning

Most students who struggle with EF skills of planning, prioritizing, organization, time management, self-monitoring, etc. can benefit with an external source that would support these skills. Tools like the physical planner and to-do lists have been a helpful support to facilitate these skills and help most people perform their daily tasks with ease. A key aspect that needs to be emphasized here is the 'support' the tools offer while not 'taking-over' the function. The advancements in AI tools now have the potential to create to-do lists, prioritize, and set reminders like a personal assistant. It is imperative to not rely solely on the AI tools but to consider them as supportive solutions that do not replace EF training or coaching. Below is a list of some of the popular free tools that are gaining ground for supporting EF:

1. ChatGPT (https://openai.com/chatgpt/): Can create drafts of any writing tasks, provide scripts for difficult communication tasks, help break down a task that can feel overwhelming, provides planning tips when provided an agenda and time, can provide actionable steps for items on your checklist and organize them logically.
2. Microsoft Bing AI Copilot (https://www.bing.com/chat?form=CONVRD): Uses chatbots that are AI-powered to help with web searches. In Microsoft's words it is like '*having a research assistant, personal planner and creative partner by your side*'. The Copilot can compose the first draft of essays and letters, summarize content, write code and answer complex questions.
3. Gemini AI (https://gemini.google.com/): Google's version of AI coach for writing draft papers, planning and personalizing learning.
4. 1st Things 1st (https://www.1st-things-1st.com/): Assistance with prioritizing tasks and decision-making.
5. Rationale (https://rationale.jina.ai/): Helps with decision making while analyzing all relevant factors, background, multiple criteria and causes and providing options.
6. Trevor (https://www.trevorai.com/): Daily planning assistant that schedules tasks.
7. Reclaim (https://reclaim.ai/): Helps to build consistent daily habits, helping choose how to prioritize to-do tasks.
8. Grammarly (https://www.grammarly.com/): Helps improve productivity and quality of writing with drafting and editing grammar and voice.
9. LightKey (https://www.lightkey.io/): Offline writing support with writing style personalized word predictor and editor.
10. PowerPoint Speaker Coach (free with Microsoft Powerpoint): Helps preparation of presentations by detecting overly wordy or verbatim presentations. Also helps in evaluating pacing, pitch, use of filler words, informal speech, euphemisms and culturally sensitive terms.
11. Vital (https://joinvital.ai/): Generates personalized meditation prompts for emotional well-being.

12. Taskade (https://www.taskade.com/): Several AI functions including generating personalized mindfulness exercises.

Artificial Intelligence for Planning, Attention and Focus

AI powered calendars, such as *Google Calendar* and *Microsoft Outlook calendar* enhance productivity by organizing calendars. These tools help to automatically schedule events, organize meetings, manage appointments and even suggest alternate times based on conflicts on the calendar. They can send reminders, and predict times based on previous history. Smart assistants like *Alexa, Siri,* and *Google assistant* are voice activated AI assistants which help manage daily tasks. They help create shopping lists, set reminders, answer quick questions, and manage home devices. For students specifically, they can help set study/ homework reminders, develop schedules based on assignments given. For academic assistance apart from setting reminders and schedules, AI tools help track progress (*Google Assignment Tracker*). Students with EF struggles quite often find task-initiation a challenge, especially with academic tasks that require writing. AI tools offer great promise to improve writing, organize ideas, generate outlines and help the editing process (*ChatGPT, Writing Pal (W-Pal)). Google AI* such as *Help me Write*, *Help me Read*, assist with literacy tasks. *Mindomo* simplifies project planning by creating collaborative concept maps, outlines, and charts. Tools such as *Grammarly* provide spelling, grammar help and *Co-Writer* helps with predictive texts and adaptive keyboard.

Academic tasks require extended maintenance of focus, which is one of the most challenging EF skills. AI tools offer help to improve focus, help with time tracking, particularly when distracted with phone usage. *RescueTime* helps to track the amount of time spent on devices and offers suggestions to improve focus. *Forest* is a popular app that uses a game format to track the amount of time spent away for phone usage. *Focus@Will, Brain.fm*, and *Noisli* use music to help with focus, sleep and relaxation. AI powered apps such as *Fabulous* also help with setting focus goals, habit building, and creating routines. While considering AI support for this function, consider tools that fit the unique focus patterns (hyper focusing, difficulty maintaining focus, distractibility) of the individual.

Artificial Intelligence to Improve Working Memory

A crucial component of EF is working memory. Reasoning, decision making, and learning require working memory. Challenges with working memory manifest in difficulties following instructions, paying attention, planning and organization. Various AI tools have been developed to enhance the above-mentioned shortfalls. Many AI tools have evolved that are cognitive training tools which are embedded in neuroscience, particularly based on neuroplasticity. *CogniFit* is an AI powered tool that employs cognitive training exercises, games to improve cognitive functions, and a variety of exercises to improve cognitive skills, including memory, focus, and processing speed. This app also tracks and provides reports on progress. *Peak* a brain training tool through challenging and fun games increases cognitive skills including memory, attention and problem solving. It includes daily short training sessions, games that challenge cognitive functioning. Other brain training tools that aim at improving cognitive skills are *Elevate* and *Lumosity*. These tools have a suite of exercises that can match the individual's learning style. They also include a wide variety and levels of challenge and provide feedback on learner's performance. Another similar tool is *NeuroNation* which aims at improving cognitive skills such as mental agility. Underlying techniques seen in these tools are adaptability based on the user's ability, opportunities to practice using repetition, and using multi-sensory stimulation.

Artificial Intelligence for Emotional Regulation, Self-awareness & Inhibition:

Emotional regulation is essential for mental well-being in our increasingly demanding world. AI technology has advanced to offer various tools designed to help individuals manage their emotions, reduce stress, and enhance overall emotional health. AI tools that help with emotional regulation help in the form of exercises, conversations, track mood changes, offer a safe space to express thoughts, feelings and emotions. Tools such as *Wysa, Replica* focus on providing emotional support through interactions. AI tools such as *Youper* and *Woebot* use specific therapy styles such as CBT (Cognitive Behavior Therapy) and DBT (Dialectical Behavior Therapy) for emotional regulation. These tools also help in managing depression and anxiety which are a common result of EF deficits. AI tools like *Calm* help in practicing and promoting mindfulness and relaxation. To add engagement, there are tools that use a gamified approach to practice happiness like *Happify*. These tools enhance emotional regulation and well-being.

Matching EF Characteristics to AI tools

With the plethora of tools available in AI to address EF deficits, decision-making and finding the most appropriate fit that is personalized poses a challenge. To help start this matching process, *Table 1* outlines the common EF characteristics with the classroom manifestation and identifies possible tools for consideration.

Table 1. EF characteristics, classroom examples and supporting AI tools

EF characteristics	Classroom manifestation	Possible AI tools
Planning, Organization & Problem solving	● Challenges finding materials for class ● Forgetting homework ● Keeping track of due dates ● Prioritizing tasks ● Difficulty with tasks requiring more efforts (ex. writing) ● Coming up with solutions for day-to-day problems ● Getting overwhelmed with task completion	Alexa, Siri, Google assignment tracker, ChatGPT, Writing Pal (W-Pal), Grammarly, Co-Writer, PowerPoint Speaker Coach, Motion Google GeminiAI, Google Task & Google Calendar, Mindomo
Focus	● Getting 'lost' during class ● Day-dreaming ● Sustained longer attention limited for less engaging materials ● Easily distracted by external stimuli	Rescue time, Focus@will, Brain.fm, Forest, Serene, Fabulous, Pomodoro, Noisli Google GeminiAI, Livescribe (note-taking, audio recorded notes) ReaderQ
Working Memory	● Difficulty with self-speech or internal speech (verbal working memory) ● Difficulty with multi-tasking, holding things in their mind, thinking of future tasks while working, picturing things mentally (non-verbal working memory)	Cognifit, Peak, Elevate, Lumosity, Neuronation, BrainHQ, Moshi, LightKey, OtterAI Kami Quizizz EquatIO
Emotional Regulation	● Mood swings ● Varying levels of energy ● Lack of motivation ● Fluctuating levels of engagement ● Lesser ability to create required effort for tasks when low ● Learning to use words and self-talk to alter how they feel about things	Happify, Calm, Mindstrong, Sanvello, Woebot, Youper, Replika, Wysa
Self-awareness (self-directed attention)	● Figuring out what works best for them as a learner ● Figuring out what they are good at ● Identifying environments/conditions that they learn/focus best	Ginger, BetterHelp, WoeBot, Wysa, Microsoft Viva Insights, DreamBox
Inhibition	● Impulsive ● Get into fights ● Quick to anger or dislike someone or like someone ● Poor judgment	GoGuardian, ClassDojo

AI Considerations for EF

A wide range of AI tools and applications are available, making it important to take into consideration factors that influence their efficacy. When choosing the right AI tools, it is essential to identify ones that fit the student's routine, and are easy to use. It is also essential to personalize the tools such as those that fit the individual characteristics of the student, such as settings that are conducive, areas of distraction, unique focus patterns (hyper focusing, difficulty maintaining focus, distractibility), and individual fit to the type of approach of the AI (conversations, gamified approach, guided exercises). It is also imperative to consider the nature of need (support for stress, anxiety, depression) and user-friendliness that can be incorporated into the routine. In addition, most importantly, data privacy measures should be examined.

Training in AI tools is another consideration. In a study conducted in 2019, researchers found that students who identified as having a physical and/or learning disability that required accessible technologies or accommodations for their coursework, wanted greater accessibility to content through online platforms. Students acknowledged the need for in depth training on digital tools and resources for both them and their instructors (Gierdowski & Galanek, 2020).

Selecting AI for EF Deficits

Specialized instruction is characterized by individualization of learning. Similar to academic and social learning tools, the efficacy of AI lies in the ideal match of the tool to the student's interests and EF strengths and needs. The exponential rise of AI tools prompts for suggestions to facilitate choice-making and implementation. The dilemma of making a choice of the tool that would be the most effective for the student prompts several considerations. Here are a few to be mindful about, while identifying the right fit of the AI tool for the student:

1. What are student's strengths and needs in academics, communication, socialization and EF skills?
2. How adept is the student at using technology?
3. What are the AI tools that could address the specific EF needs identified?
4. Which of these tools are developmentally appropriate for the student, in addition to addressing the needs and interests of the student?
5. What is the cost of the tool?
6. What are the pros and cons of the tool as indicated by users?
7. How is data privacy maintained?

8. What training would the teacher, student, and/or family members need in order to support students during initial use?

Identifying AI Tools for Personalizing EF Supports

To illustrate the process of finding a 'good-fit' and the considerations, we present a couple of case studies to illustrate how AI tools could be matched to EF and student's needs.

Case Study 1: Meet Tania

Tania is a nine-year-old fourth grader at Marketville Elementary School. At six years old, she was diagnosed with Attention Deficit Disorder, inattentive type. Tania currently takes a stimulant in the morning to help improve her focus throughout the day. Even though teachers report her improvement in sustained attention during whole group instruction and some small improvements within small group instructional groupings, she still has difficulty beginning and completing independent assignments without excessive promptings and reminders from her teacher, Mr. Campus. He has recently met with the special education teacher for some consultative support to consider ways that he could support her without the use of his constant prompting. With teacher support, Tania can maintain adequate performance across most content areas, with the exception of math. As the skills become more complex and detailed, Tania is easily frustrated and can often be heard muttering under her breath, "this is sooo hard!" Recently, she's begun to put her head down when assigned independent writing to complete in class. Tania often says she will complete it at home when her mom is off work; however, rarely does the work come back completed. All students have access to an electronic tablet while at school.

Mr. Campus is considering the following AI options that address specific EF skills – intermittent prompts to self-monitor on-task behavior, goal setting and evaluation of task completed, timers for self-regulation and supports for math. Given the type of attention deficits and frustration management issues Tania exhibits, AI tools could be used to support her during her independent seatwork in math, while considering her interest and level of comfort using technology over the past 3 years with access to computers at her school. Mr. Campus considers supporting her writing with the use of *DreamBox,* an adaptive math AI program that personalizes lessons based on individual learning style and progress. He is also considering *SMART Learning Suite* online to promote game-based learning in math to keep her engaged while raising her confidence in math abilities. To address Tania's anxiety in math, Mr. Campus also generated a social script for Tania using the prompt "solving math problems" on the AI platform https://theuniversalsandpit.org/social-scripts He shared the social script with Tania to help her with her frustration (see Figure 1)

Figure 1. Sample Social Script generator

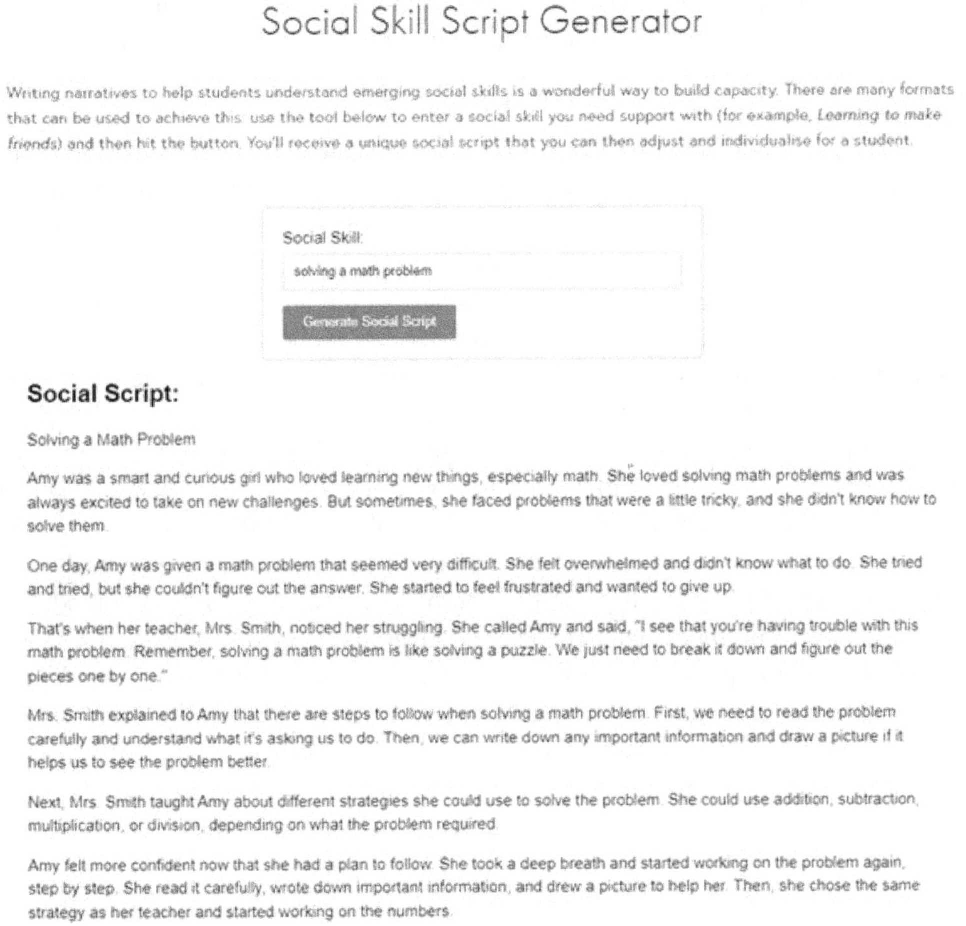

Social Skill Script Generator

Writing narratives to help students understand emerging social skills is a wonderful way to build capacity. There are many formats that can be used to achieve this: use the tool below to enter a social skill you need support with (for example, *Learning to make friends*) and then hit the button. You'll receive a unique social script that you can then adjust and individualise for a student.

Social Skill:

solving a math problem

Generate Social Script

Social Script:

Solving a Math Problem

Amy was a smart and curious girl who loved learning new things, especially math. She loved solving math problems and was always excited to take on new challenges. But sometimes, she faced problems that were a little tricky, and she didn't know how to solve them.

One day, Amy was given a math problem that seemed very difficult. She felt overwhelmed and didn't know what to do. She tried and tried, but she couldn't figure out the answer. She started to feel frustrated and wanted to give up.

That's when her teacher, Mrs. Smith, noticed her struggling. She called Amy and said, "I see that you're having trouble with this math problem. Remember, solving a math problem is like solving a puzzle. We just need to break it down and figure out the pieces one by one."

Mrs. Smith explained to Amy that there are steps to follow when solving a math problem. First, we need to read the problem carefully and understand what it's asking us to do. Then, we can write down any important information and draw a picture if it helps us to see the problem better.

Next, Mrs. Smith taught Amy about different strategies she could use to solve the problem. She could use addition, subtraction, multiplication, or division, depending on what the problem required.

Amy felt more confident now that she had a plan to follow. She took a deep breath and started working on the problem again, step by step. She read it carefully, wrote down important information, and drew a picture to help her. Then, she chose the same strategy as her teacher and started working on the numbers.

Case Study 2: Meet Juan

Juan is a 14-year-old ninth grader at Grayside High School. At three years old he was diagnosed with Autism Spectrum Disorder, Level 1, high functioning. He has received most of his instruction in general education classrooms throughout his school experience, with some consultative support from the special education teacher. Now that Juan is transitioning to high school, his educational team wants to support his independent functioning and self-determination skills as part of his transition plan. In general, Juan demonstrates average performance in his courses and indicates a desire to attend post-secondary education. Consistently, middle school teachers reported that Juan possessed the capability to perform grade level work independently; however, he struggled with staying focused on reading, organizing his learning materials and managing his in-class task completion in a timely manner (including getting started) and submitting homework assignments without multiple reminders. Juan also struggled with seeking assistance from the teacher when he needed help.

Given the type of organizational and management deficits Juan exhibits, his teachers follow the considerations to identify AI tools that could support him in working independently inside and outside of the classroom. They consider his use of apps on his mobile device and level of comfort using technology and follow the considerations in selecting the AI. Juan's teachers recommended ReaderO, a Google Chrome Add-On that eliminates distractions when reading web pages and help readers get to the main point of what they're reading, which seemed to help Juan improve his focus and attention to reading tasks. Juan was also shown how to use ChatGPT to generate sample difficult conversations such as asking for assistance from the teacher when he needed it. Juan was trained by modeling prompts such as "asking my teacher for help when I need it" on the ChatGPT platform that generated sample scripts for conversations while predicting difficult questions and comments during the conversation by the teacher and the appropriate response. They also modeled to him on how to prompt ChatGPT to break down his tasks to set a plan to achieve them by using prompts such as "I have a project on World War II and do not know where to start" (See Figure 2 for sample generated script for task breakdown) and create a 'to-do' list of actionable items.

Figure 2. AI Task Breakdown Support

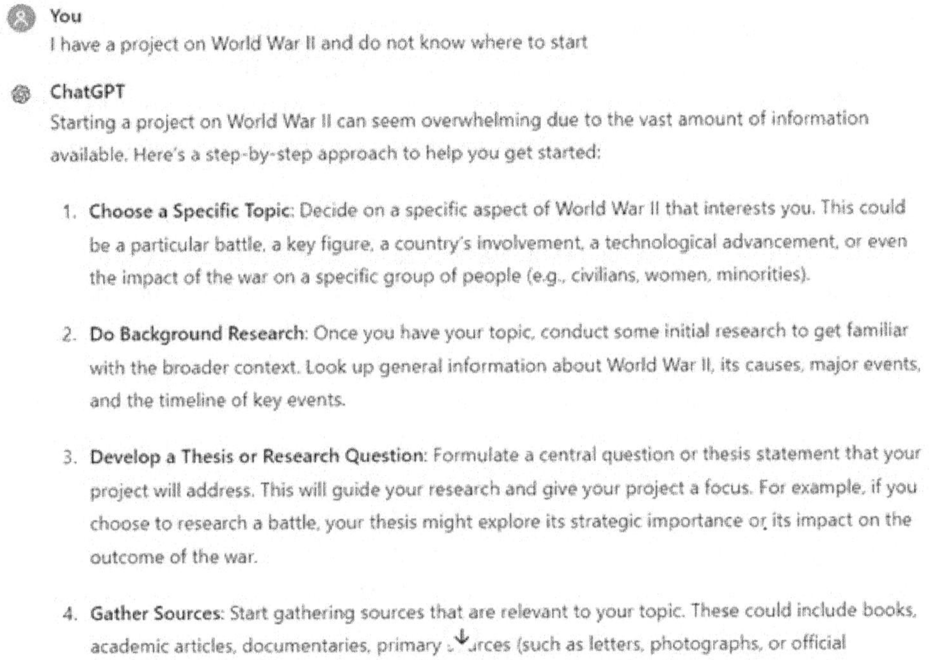

You

I have a project on World War II and do not know where to start

ChatGPT

Starting a project on World War II can seem overwhelming due to the vast amount of information available. Here's a step-by-step approach to help you get started:

1. **Choose a Specific Topic:** Decide on a specific aspect of World War II that interests you. This could be a particular battle, a key figure, a country's involvement, a technological advancement, or even the impact of the war on a specific group of people (e.g., civilians, women, minorities).
2. **Do Background Research:** Once you have your topic, conduct some initial research to get familiar with the broader context. Look up general information about World War II, its causes, major events, and the timeline of key events.
3. **Develop a Thesis or Research Question:** Formulate a central question or thesis statement that your project will address. This will guide your research and give your project a focus. For example, if you choose to research a battle, your thesis might explore its strategic importance or its impact on the outcome of the war.
4. **Gather Sources:** Start gathering sources that are relevant to your topic. These could include books, academic articles, documentaries, primary ..urces (such as letters, photographs, or official

Cautions in Using AI tools for EF

While AI can benefit students, it should be approached with the lens of equity to ensure it meets the needs for all students. Some AI tools may discriminate against students with disabilities (Welker, 2023). Cutting-edge assistive technologies, such as AI and its ability to adjust to the user, can mitigate some of the challenges of cultural and language differences of students (Zdravkoval, et. al., 2022). AI can be powerful tools that have the capability of transforming communication systems that have typically been low-tech with words and symbols to a more high-tech option through technological devices that can employ a human voice for output. When considering the legal mandate to individualize instruction for students with disabilities as outlined in IDEIA (U. S. Department of Education, 2004), AI algorithms, largely dependent on using big data, rarely account for the unique needs of individual students with disabilities (Wald, 2022). Compounding this notion with diverse cultural characteristics and unique characteristics manifested by disability, teachers will need to ensure that the AI tools selected are offered in students' native language when necessary, ensure that the content demonstrates cultural sensitivity, and considers a wide range of diverse characteristics and experiences into the programming.

AI-based design and development is often driven by the needs and behaviors of the "average user," (Brewer, Gerard & Hakkinen, 2020) and from a user experience design perspective, people with disabilities typically fall outside of the usual experience. Building an AI model requires high-quality data and can be done through different methods, including no-code/low-code platforms, AutoML, and traditional programming. The Pecan Team (2023) noted that the choice of method depends on coding expertise, customization needs, and time availability. So, careful consideration when selecting AI for students with disabilities must include weighing the characteristics displayed by individual students, Individualized Education Programs (IEPs), and what the program will teach or reinforce. Automatic speech recognition (ASR) systems, for example, typically are optimized around common speech patterns, not around the speech patterns of people with speech disabilities (Emerging Technologies and Trends, 2022). As a result, students who rely on ASR systems are more likely to be disadvantaged in educational and work settings where the ASR may not be optimized for them. There still seems to be a lack of consensus on the most effective ways to use AI to support learning for students with Autism (Li Zarei, Alibakhshi, & Labbafi, 2024).

AI can pose some challenges that may be exacerbated with students with disabilities. Common concerns in the literature are centered around the following four themes:

1. Bias and stereotyping: AI systems can perpetuate existing biases and perpetuate false assumptions if they are not properly designed and tested (Li Zarei, Alibakhshi, & Labbafi, 2024). We are most likely familiar with machine bias when considering the risk level of someone to reoffend. Programmer bias when designing multi-step algorithms used for decision making may lead to unintended consequences. AI-based tools may present similar issues with subjectivity in determining which definitions or characteristics should be used in programming and design, which may unintentionally incorporate the prejudices of developers (Rangnekar, 2021). AI systems are trained on data that may not fully represent the diverse population of children, including children with disabilities, which in turn may not be effective for all individuals (Li Zarei, Alibakhshi, & Labbafi, 2024). Trewin et al. (2019) caution that developers should consider engaging individuals with disabilities as an effective way to source data to support product design and effectiveness.
2. Privacy concerns: AI systems often collect and store large amounts of personal data, which can raise privacy and security concerns, especially when talking about a vulnerable population. If sensitive personal information is collected and stored by the AI system, there is a risk that it could be misused or accessed

by unauthorized parties. Security breaches are a case of concern when sharing personal information. Parental awareness about how data is used and potential privacy issues is a crucial step to address privacy concerns. Children's Online Privacy Protection Rule (COPPA) is an act that aims to protect children's privacy with parental consent while using sites and apps with children (Federal Trade Commission, 2024).

3. Lack of human interaction: AI systems can replace human interaction, which can lead to social and emotional isolation. When applied to students with disabilities who often are socially isolated, AI dependence may support greater isolation and limited desire to interact with nondisabled peers.
4. Cost: Implementing and maintaining AI systems can be expensive, and not all schools, institutions, and home settings may have the resources to adopt this technology. Costs likely include a device that has the capability that can support ongoing updates of the system being used as well as costs regarding the program license or app purchase.

It is important to weigh the benefits and disadvantages of AI and to ensure that its use is balanced, ethical, and responsible. Compatibility of existing educational programs with the AI driven tools needs to be carefully assessed before use. Sufficient training and support for using the AI technologies is crucial and poses a challenge for educators providing services for students. Evaluating the effectiveness of AI based interventions in EF and assessing their effectiveness with students is essential. Collaboration between educators, parents, psychologists, other service providers, students, and the AI researchers will help create effective solutions. We provide a simple guide for teachers to consider when reviewing AI implementation for an individual or group of students:

- Adequate fit- does the AI tool address the most prominent aspect of EF deficit the student exhibits?
- Improvement focused- does the AI tool develop the target skill and supports a scaffolded approach to eliminate the dependency on the AI once skill is developed and consistently demonstrated.
- Ease of use- is the tool able to be navigated easily by the student independently after minimal training and guidance. How much time and effort are required by the teacher for monitoring and training?
- Cost and licenses- tools are great, but most often there is a charge. Teachers must consider who will bear the burden of the cost or maintain the license. If free versions are used, what will students encounter (advertisements, distractions, and limitations in feature use).

- Collected user data- privacy and data sharing issues continue to be of concern for students and especially those with disabilities. However, certain information may need to be collected if the AI is intuitive and created to adapt features for the individual user. Take the time to read the requirements for the AI use.

Concerns about ethical use of AI by students can be ensured with explicit addressing of considerations before introducing the AI tools in the classroom. A checklist can be adapted and used as a proactive way to avoid complications resulting from unethical use of AI.

- [ ] AI can help me learn better and is important for my future, so I promise to use it the right way and make smart choices.
- [ ] I will use AI tools responsibly and will not use AI in a way that could harm myself or others.
- [ ] I will only use AI to support my learning and will follow my school's rules and teacher's instructions on when and how to use AI on an assignment.
- [ ] I will be honest about when I use AI to help with assignments, and I will not turn in work that is fully created by an AI as my own.
- [ ] If I use AI, I will review its work for mistakes.
- [ ] I will check with my teacher when unsure about what is acceptable.

AI shows great promise to support individualized instruction and intervention for students with disabilities with executive function deficits. The exploration and research being conducted in this area is growing exponentially and constantly changing. While we await research to conclusively establish the efficacy of AI in EF support, we are left to rely on users' perspectives and teacher anecdotes to help make decisions and choices of AI tools. Increasingly users on chat platforms are expressing the numerous benefits to their EF. One Reddit user commented that ChatGPT had the biggest impact on task-initiation - the EF skill that boggles most students with disabilities. Many attest to how it changed their productivity and performance. As teachers, we need to be mindful of how we can use technology to facilitate the skills that our students lack and AI certainly comes with a promise for Executive functioning skills.

References:

Barkley, R. A. (2020). *Taking charge of ADHD: The complete, authoritative guide for parents*. Guilford Publications.

Blair, C., & Ursache, A. (2021). A bidirectional model of executive functions and self-regulation. In Vohs, K. D., & Baumeister, R. F. (Eds.), *Handbook of Self-regulation: Research, Theory, and Applications* (pp. 300–320). Guilford Press.

Brewer, J., Gerard, C., & Hakkinen, M. (2020). The Impact of AI on Accessibility. EDUCAUSE Review, November 4, 2020. https://er.educause.edu/articles/2022/6/3-ways-ai-can-help-students-with-disabilities

ChatGPT. (2024, January 19). How do you cite an answer in ChatGPT. Retrieved from [https://chat.openai.com/]

Cibrian, F. L., Lakes, K. D., Schuck, S. E. B., & Hayes, G. R. (2022). The potential for emerging technologies to support self-regulation in children with ADHD: A literature review. *International Journal of Child-Computer Interaction*, 31, 100421. Advance online publication. DOI: 10.1016/j.ijcci.2021.100421

Deshpande, S. (April, 2023). Supporting K-12 Learners: The Importance of Executive Functioning Development.State of Neurodiversity 2023 Report. Learnfully blog. https://learnfully.com/state-of-neurodiversity-2023-report/

Emerging Technologies and Trends. (June 3, 2022). *3 Ways AI Can Help Students with Disabilities." The Voice of the Higher Education Technology Community: EDUCAUSE Review.* https://er.educause.edu/articles/2022/6/3-ways-ai-can-help-students-with-disabilities

Federal Trade Commission. (2024). Children's Online Privacy Protection Rule. Retrieved from https://www.ftc.gov/legal-library/browse/rules/childrens-online-privacy-protection-rule-coppa

Frolli, A., Ricci, M. C., Di Carmine, F., Lombardi, A., Bosco, A., Saviano, E., & Franzese, L. (2021). The Impact of COVID-19 on Cognitive Development and Executive Functioning in Adolescents: A First Exploratory Investigation. *Brain Sciences*, 11(9), 1222. Advance online publication. DOI: 10.3390/brainsci11091222 PMID: 34573241

Garg, S., & Sharma, S. (2020). Impact of artificial intelligence in special need education to promote inclusive pedagogy. *International Journal of Information and Education Technology (IJIET)*, 10(7), 523–527. DOI: 10.18178/ijiet.2020.10.7.1418

Ge, S., Zhu, Z., Wu, B., & McConnell, E. S. (2018). Technology-based cognitive training and rehabilitation interventions for individuals with mild cognitive impairment: A systematic review. *BMC Geriatrics*, 18(1), 213. DOI: 10.1186/s12877-018-0893-1 PMID: 30219036

Gierdowski, D. C., & Galanek, J. D. (2020). *ECAR Study of the Technology Needs of Students with Disabilities, 2020. Research report*. ECAR.

Gunnar, F. (2024). A Systematic Review of Special Educational Interventions for Student Attention: Executive Function and Digital Technology in Primary School. *Journal of Special Education Technology*, 39(2), 264–276. DOI: 10.1177/01626434231198226

Homer, B. D., Plass, J. L., Raffaele, C., Ober, T. M., & Ali, A. (2018). Improving High School Students' Executive Functions through Digital Game Play. *Computers & Education*, 117, 50–58. DOI: 10.1016/j.compedu.2017.09.011

Klarin, J., Hoff, E., Larsson, A., & Daukantaite, D. (2024). Adolescents' use and perceived usefulness of generative AI for schoolwork: Exploring their relationships with executive functioning and academic achievement. *Frontiers in Artificial Intelligence*, 7, 1415782. https://www.frontiersin.org/journals/artificial-intelligence/articles/10.3389/frai.2024.1415782 doi.org/10.3389/frai.2024.1415782. DOI: 10.3389/frai.2024.1415782 PMID: 39263526

Kofler, M. J., Irwin, L. N., Soto, E. F., Groves, N. B., Harmon, S. L., & Sarver, D. E. (2019). Executive Functioning Heterogeneity in Pediatric ADHD. *Journal of Abnormal Child Psychology*, 47(2), 273–286. DOI: 10.1007/s10802-018-0438-2 PMID: 29705926

Lakes, K. D., Cibrian, F. L., Schuck, S. E. B., Nelson, M., & Hayes, G. R. (2022). Digital health interventions for youth with ADHD: A mapping review. *Computers in Human Behavior Reports*, 6, 100174. Advance online publication. DOI: 10.1016/j.chbr.2022.100174

Parre, M. D.; Sujatha, B. (2021): Novel human-centered robotics: towards an automated process for neurorehabilitation. Neurology Research International, 2021 (1). https://doi.org/DOI: 10.1155/2021/6690715

Pierres, O., Darvishy, A., & Christen, M. (2023). AI in Higher Education: Ethical Concerns for Students with Disabilities. In Alvarez, J.M., Fabris, A., Heitz, C., Hertweck, C., Loi, M., Zehlike, M. Proceedings of the European Workshop on Algorithmic Fairness (EWAF'23). Winterthur: CEUR-WS, 7-9.

Robledo-Castro, C., Catillo-Ossa, L. F., & Corchado, J. M. (2023). Artificial Cognitive Systems Applied in Executive Function Stimulation and Rehabilitation Programs: A Systematic Review. *Arabian Journal for Science and Engineering*, 48(2), 2399–2427. DOI: 10.1007/s13369-022-07292-5 PMID: 36185593

Sonuga-Barke, E., Brandeis, D., Holtmann, M., & Cortese, S. (2014). Computer-based cognitive training for ADHD: A review of current evidence. *Child and Adolescent Psychiatric Clinics of North America*, 23(4), 807–824. DOI: 10.1016/j.chc.2014.05.009 PMID: 25220088

Teach, A. I. (2023). AI guidance for schools toolkit - AI Education in School Presentation. https://www.teachai.org/toolkit

The Pecan Team. (2023, December 15). 3 Ways to Build Your Own AI Model. Blog post. https://www.pecan.ai/blog/3-ways-build-your-own-ai-model/#:~:text=Building%20an%20AI%20model%20requires,customization%20needs%2C%20and%20time%20availability

Trewin, S., Basson, S., Muller, M., Branham, S., Treviranus, J., Gruen, D., Herbert, D., Lyckowski, N., & Manser, E. (2019). Considerations for AI Fairness for People with Disabilities. *AI Matters*, 5(3), 40–63. DOI: 10.1145/3362077.3362086

Trust, T., Whalen, J., & Mouza, C. (2023). Editorial: ChatGPT: Challenges, Opportunities, and Implications for Teacher Education. *Contemporary Issues in Technology and Teacher Education, 23*(1), 1-23. Waynesville, NC USA: Society for Information Technology & Teacher Education. Retrieved September 27, 2024 from https://www.learntechlib.org/primary/p/222408/

U. S. Department of Education. (2004). Individuals with Disabilities Education Act (IDEA). https://sites.ed.gov/idea/about-idea/

Wald, M. (2021). AI data-driven personalization and disability inclusion. Secondary Machine Learning and Artificial Intelligence. *Frontier Artificial Intelligences*, 3, 1–14. DOI: 10.3389/frai.2020.571955 PMID: 33733215

Welker, Y. (2023). Algorithmic Diversity: Mitigating AI Bias and Disability Exclusion. Forbes Technology Council. https://www.forbes.com/sites/forbestechcouncil/2023/05/09/algorithmic-diversity-mitigating-ai-bias-and-disability-exclusion/

Zdravkova1, K., Krasniqi1, V., Dalipi, F., & Ferati, M. (28 October 2022). Cutting-edge communication and learning assistive technologies for disabled children: An artificial intelligence perspective. Frontiers in Artificial Intelligence, 1-14. DOI: 10.3389/frai.2022.970430

Chapter 11
Role of AI in Special Education in India

Oindrila Chakraborty
J.D. Birla Institute, India

ABSTRACT

This chapter will primarily examine the utilization of AI in special education, focusing on the perspectives of educators and parents. It will also explore the level of awareness and impact of AI in special education in India. More over, this research will assess the various tools currently employed in special education and the potential for incorporating AI in different areas of this field in the future. The satisfaction level of students and the scope of AI implementation will also be analyzed. The study will further investigate the difficulties, obstacles, and concerns surrounding the use of AI in special education within India. By separately considering the opinions and viewpoints of instructors and parents of children with special needs, this study addresses both classroom and non-classroom implementations of AI in special education. Moreover, it ensures that individual challenges specific to each domain are taken into consideration.

INTRODUCTION

Special Education is a form of education designed to cater to the individual needs of students with disabilities. It provides a range of services and support to help these students learn and reach their full potential. This can include personalized learning plans, assistive technologies, and specially trained teachers. Special

DOI: 10.4018/979-8-3693-5538-1.ch011

education aims to create an inclusive learning environment where all students feel valued and supported.

There are thirteen different categories of special education recognized under the Individuals with Disabilities Education Act (IDEA) in the United States. These categories are designed to ensure that children with a wide range of disabilities can access a free and appropriate public education (FAPE) .

A brief overview of the thirteen categories are given below:

1.Autism Spectrum Disorder (ASD)

Children with ASD may have difficulty with social interaction, communication, and repetitive behaviours. Special education services can help them develop communication skills, social skills, and learn to manage their behaviours.

2.Blindness

Children who are blind are visually impaired to the point that they cannot see well enough to learn effectively in a regular classroom setting. Special education services can provide them with instruction in Braille, help them develop orientation and mobility skills, and teach them how to use assistive technology.

3.Deafness

Children who are deaf are completely or severely hard of hearing. Special education services can provide them with instruction in sign language, help them develop listening and spoken language skills, and teach them how to use assistive technology.

4.Deaf-Blindness(DB)

Children who are deaf-blind have both a visual impairment and a hearing impairment. Special education services can provide them with specialized instruction that meets their unique needs.

5.Emotional Disturbance (ED) Children with ED may experience emotional problems that can interfere with their learning. Special education services can help them develop coping mechanisms, manage their emotions, and improve their social skills.

6. Hearing Impairment (HI)

Children with hearing impairments have a partial hearing loss that may affect their learning. Special education services can provide them with amplification devices, instruction in listening and spoken language skills, and help them develop strategies for coping with their hearing loss.

7.Intellectual Disability (ID)

Children with ID have significantly below-average intellectual ability and may have difficulty with conceptual skills, social skills, and practical skills. Special education services can help them develop these skills and learn to live as independently as possible.

8.Multiple Disabilities (MD)

Children with MD have more than one disability. Special education services can provide them with comprehensive support that meets their individual needs.

9.Orthopedic Impairment (OI)

Children with OI have a physical disability that affects their ability to move. Special education services can help them develop motor skills, access the curriculum, and participate in school activities.

10.Other Health Impairment (OHI)

Children with OHI have a chronic health condition that affects their learning. This could include conditions such as asthma, diabetes, or epilepsy. Special education services can help them manage their health condition and participate in school activities.

11.Specific Learning Disability (SLD) Children with SLD have a learning disorder in one or more basic skills, such as reading, writing, math, or language processing. Special education services can provide them with individualized instruction and support to help them overcome their learning difficulties.

12.Speech or Language Impairment (SLI)

Children with SLI have difficulty communicating effectively. This could include difficulty with speaking, understanding language, or using language socially. Special education services can help them develop their communication skills.

13.Traumatic Brain Injury (TBI)

Children with TBI have a brain injury that affects their learning and functioning. Special education services can help them relearn skills that were lost due to the injury and develop strategies for coping with their disability.

Though these are validated and well accepted categories but it is also imperative to recognize that each child with a disability is unique and they need that kind of unique and special attention. Hence, Special education services are designed in almost every country to meet the individual needs of each child and to make it effective as well as inclusive at the same time.

Several research work and educational development have been specially designed for special education with the help of AI.Some of which have been mentioned below: García-Martínez, I., et al. (2023) analyzed the impact of artificial intelligence and computational sciences on student performance with a positive outcome and recommended the use of more of AI techniques for assistive learning.Kohli, R., Phutela, S., Garg, A., & Viner, M. (2021) analysed the current and future artificial intelligence to meet the needs of numerous students with special learning requirements and highlighted the functioning of the AIEd model as well as AI aid for instructors and learners separately. Barua, S., et al. (2022) highlighted the artificial intelligence enabled personalised assistive tools to enhance education of children with neurodevelopmental disorders. The diversity and effectiveness of artificial intelligence-assisted tools developed using machine learning models to address learning difficulties in students with neurodevelopmental disorders.

Yi, H., Liu, T., & Lan, G. (2024) highlighted the key artificial intelligence technologies in early childhood education.

LEGAL RIGHTS FOR SPECIAL EDUCATION

Cross borders, it is imperative to have a legal framework and boundary to control the educational policy for the special children, since they are fairly neglected compared to the ordinary children in a common public forum . Like many other developed and civilised societies, India also provides a legal framework for the unique need of the specially abled children to enrich the overall growth of the society and for practising inclusion. The legal rights for special education in India are protected under several acts and articles of the Constitution. While there is not a specific act solely dedicated to special education in India, there are some key pieces of legislation those address the rights and access to education for children with disabilities:

1. The Rights of Persons with Disabilities Act (RPwD Act) 2016:

This act is a comprehensive legislation that guarantees and protects the rights of persons with disabilities, including their right to education. It mandates the government to provide inclusive education to children with disabilities until they reach the age of 18.

2. The Right to Education Act (RTE Act) 2009:

This act ensures free and compulsory education for all children between the ages of 6 and 14, including those with disabilities [Right of Children to Free and Compulsory Education Act, 2009]. It guarantees access to free textbooks, writing materials, uniforms, and learning materials specifically suited to their needs.. While not solely focused on special education, it emphasizes the importance of inclusive education within mainstream schools. The RTE Act works in conjunction with the RPwD Act to provide a legal framework for the education of children with disabilities in India.

3. Persons with Disabilities Act (PwD Act) 1995:

This act works towards creating equal opportunities for people with disabilities. It ensures their right to free education up to the age of 18 years, either in integrated schools or special schools depending on their needs [Special Education Laws in India]. The act also mandates provisions like accessible transportation, removing architectural barriers, and modifying examination systems to benefit these children.

There are some additional policies to consider in India which are favouring special needs:

The Samagra Shiksha Scheme: This government initiative aims to universalize school education by integrating Schemes for School Education like Sarva Shiksha Abhiyan (SSA) and Rashtriya Madhyamik Shiksha Abhiyan (RMSA). It includes a strong focus on inclusive education, providing support for children with disabilities through resource teachers and assistive technologies.

Indian Constitution:

The Constitution itself protects the rights of children with disabilities through several articles:

Article 29(2): Prohibits discrimination against any citizen based on factors like religion, caste or disability, ensuring access to educational institutions [Legal rights of the disabled in India].

Article 45: Makes it the state's responsibility to provide free and compulsory education to all children up to 14 years old, including special children.

Article 21: Guarantees the right to life and liberty, which applies to persons with disabilities as well.

While there is no single act dedicated to special education, the combination of the RPwD Act, RTE Act, articles in Indian constitution and the initiatives like Samagra Shiksha work together to ensure the right to education and access to inclusive learning environments for students with disabilities in India.

SPECIAL EDUCATION IN INDIA

With a focus on providing equal opportunities for individuals with special needs, the government has initiated various programmes and policies to support their education and subsequently employment. There is also a growing awareness and understanding of the importance of inclusive education in mainstream schools. In addition, organizations and NGOs are actively working towards creating a more inclusive society for individuals with special needs. This shift towards a more inclusive and supportive environment for individuals with special needs is a positive step towards the overall development of the country. It not only ensures that all individuals have access to quality education and opportunities for growth, but also promotes a more empathetic and understanding society. As the conversation around special education continues to evolve, it is becoming more important for stakeholders to work together to ensure that individuals with special needs are provided with the support and resources they need to thrive. With these efforts, India is on its way towards achieving a more inclusive and equitable society for all. Special education in India is gradually emerging and evolving to provide a more inclusive learning environment for children with disabilities with many experimental broader horizon. While traditional special schools exist, there is a growing emphasis on integrating students with special needs into mainstream classrooms. This approach utilizes resource teachers and specialists to provide individualized learning plans and support for students. Government initiatives like the Right to Education Act and Samagra Shiksha aim to bridge the gap by offering identification camps, assistive devices, and teacher training programmes. However, challenges like infrastructure limitations and ensuring proper teacher training programmes remain to be addressed for special education to reach its full potential in India. Despite these challenges, special education in India is making strides. Technological advancements like AI-powered learning tools offer promising avenues for personalized education and bridging accessibility gaps. Furthermore, growing awareness and advocacy by parents' organizations are pushing for better implementation and ensuring children with disabilities have the opportunity to thrive in school and society.

BACKGROUND OF SPECIAL EDUCATION

The history of special education goes way back internationally, but the concept of providing tailored education to students with disabilities is a relatively recent development, especially in developing world. A brief overview is given below with a holistic view and also from Indian perspective:

Early Initiatives

Historically, children with disabilities were often excluded from education altogether. Early interventions focused on charity and institutionalization rather than focused learning.

Emerging Developments in Early 20th Century

The 20th century saw a paradigm shift towards providing educational opportunities for the disabled students. Special schools and programmes emerged, with a focus on specific disabilities like blindness or deafness.

Legislation and Inclusion

Federal laws like the Individuals with Disabilities Education Act (IDEA) in the US mandated 'Free and Appropriate Public Education' (FAPE) for all students with disabilities. This act emphasized creating Individualized Education Programmes (IEPs) to cater to each student's specific needs.

The Movement Towards Inclusion

The later part of the 20th century saw a push for inclusion, integrating students with disabilities into general education classrooms with support. Special education is still an ongoing area of development and debate and continues to evolve globally, focusing on more inclusive and effective learning experience for students with diverse needs.

Unlike the western World, background of special education in India has a unique trajectory compared to other countries, especially the west.

Early Seeds (1800s)

Unlike the West, the initiative came from Christian missionaries and NGOs (The Aditya Birla Integrated School). In the 1880s, they established schools for the visually impaired (1887), hearing impaired (1888), and those with intellectual disabilities (1934).

Government Involvement (Post-Independence)

After gaining independence in 1947, the Indian government took a more active role. They moved beyond charity models and focused on providing educational, rehabilitation, and social services(Shia College, Lucknow, n.d.).

Growth and Challenges

The latter half of the 20th century saw a rise in government-run special schools. However, the number remained limited, particularly in rural areas where most of the population resides .

Legislative Framework

Important milestones include the National Policy on Education (1986) and the Rehabilitation Council of India Act (1992). These acts aimed to establish a legal framework for special education and teacher training (Shia College, Lucknow, n.d.).

The Inclusion Debate

Similar to global trends, India is witnessing a shift towards inclusion. The Persons with Disabilities Act (1995) emphasizes integrating children with disabilities into mainstream education (Shia College, Lucknow, n.d.).

Current Status

India faces challenges in providing sufficient resources and trained teachers for inclusive education across the vast nation. Efforts are ongoing to bridge this gap and ensure quality education for all children with disabilities.

SPECIAL EDUCATION AND USE OF AI

Teaching special children has always been a challenging task, since they may not always be as receptive to ideas as ordinary children, unless extraordinary techniques have been adapted to reach out to them. However, they have demonstrated amazing abilities that can surpass their learning limitations. It is important to remember that the teaching and learning environment for these children cannot be the same as for ordinary children for the obvious reasons, mentioned earlier. As a result, there has been a great deal of experimentation done to find the most effective methods for educating these children. With the same intention, Kumagai & Nagai, (2022) explored the potentials of AI for data-driven approaches in special education and highlighted a case study on using AI to analyse the reading of data and personalized reading instruction for students with learning difficulties and established a great connect between data driven personalised teaching- learning procedure for special education . A systematic review (Lytras et al., 2020) provided a comprehensive analysis of research on AI in special education . Lytras et al., (2020) provided an exhaustive research on AI in special education and identified the trends in research methods, areas of application (focusing on cognitive and affective aspects of learning), and learning content. Sharma et al., (2020) explored how AI can be used to create inclusive learning environments for students with special needs. According to Getting Smart, (2016), the use of AI are significant for personalized learning and AI-powered virtual tutors highly suitable for special needs learners. Drigas,(2012) provided a deeper look at the potential of AI for assessment and intervention in special needs education. Drigas & Ioannidou, (2013) offered a good overview of AI applications in special education, analysing research from the past decade to ensure its importance. A 2021 study by Smith et al., 2021 investigated how tailored learning platforms driven by artificial intelligence could improve the educational experiences of individuals with learning difficulties. According to the researchers' findings, students with special needs can do better academically and engage more while using these platforms because of their adaptive nature, which modifies content and instructional tactics based on individual learner profiles. Another study published in 2022 investigated the use of AI-driven assistive technologies, such as speech recognition and text-to-speech tools, to support students with physical or cognitive disabilities (Jones et al., 2022). The findings from Jones' research suggested that these technologies can significantly improve accessibility, allowing learners to independently access educational materials and effectively communicate their needs and ideas. In the realm of autism spectrum disorder (ASD), many researchers have explored the potential of AI-based social skills training programmes. Such a study conducted in 2021 demonstrated the effectiveness of an AI-powered platform that uses interactive virtual scenarios to help students with ASD developing the quintessential social and communication skills (Davis et al., 2021). The authors also noted that the personalized feedback and adaptive nature of the programme can lead to increased social competence and improved overall well-being for these students. Furthermore, AI-powered assessment tools have been developed to assist in the early identification and diagnosis of learning disabilities to assist in the prognosis of the challenging situations and thereby the copiing strategies and treatment, if required. A 2022 study examined the use of machine learning algorithms to analyse student performance data and accurately predict the likelihood of specific learning disabilities, enabling timely intervention and support (Fernandez et al., 2022). A 2023 study by Xie et al. explored the application of AI-driven adaptive learning systems to support students with attention-deficit/hyperactivity disorder (ADHD). The researchers found that these systems, which tailor content and pacing to individual needs, can lead to improved focus, task completion, and overall academic performance for learners with ADHD (Xie et al., 2023).In 2023, researchers investigated the use of AI-powered virtual assistants to provide real-time support and guidance for students with intellectual disabilities. Sato et al. (2023) reported that these assistants, which can offer step-by-step instructions, prompts, and feedback, can significantly enhance the independence and confidence of these students in completing daily living and learning tasks. A 2022 study by Nguyen and colleagues examined the potential of AI-based language processing tools to support the communication and literacy development of students with speech and language impairments. The findings suggested that these tools, which can translate between spoken and written language, provide real-time feedback, and generate personalized learning materials, can lead to notable improvements in language and literacy skills (Nguyen et al., 2022). Furthermore, a 2022 systematic review by Wilson et al. synthesized the current evidence on the integration of AI-powered assistive robotics in special education. The review highlighted the positive impact of these technologies on enhancing mobility, independence, and social interaction for students with physical disabilities or autism spectrum disorder (Wilson et al., 2022). As the field of AI in special education continues to evolve, researchers have also begun to explore the use of AI-driven data analytics to inform personalized interventions and support. A 2023 study by Zhao et al. demonstrated the potential of machine learning algorithms to analyse student performance data and identify early warning signs of learning difficulties, enabling educators to provide timely and targeted assistance (Zhao et al., 2023).Overall, the significance of personalized teaching-learning via AI has been highlighted by almost all the stalwarts in the field of special education.

In India, numerous significant and quality research works have been conducted in the domains of usage of AI in special education. In 2023, a study conducted by researchers from the Indian Institute of Technology, Bombay explored the implementation of AI-powered assistive technologies in special education schools across India (Sharma et al., 2023). The researchers found that the integration of AI-driven tools, such as speech recognition software and adaptive learning platforms, has helped to improve accessibility and personalize the learning experience for students with diverse needs, including those with hearing impairments, autism spectrum disorder, and intellectual disabilities. A 2024 report by the National Council of Educational Research and Training (NCERT) in India highlighted the potential of AI-based assessment and monitoring systems to support early identification and intervention for learning disabilities (NCERT, 2024). The report emphasized the importance of developing AI-powered screening tools that can analyse student performance data and provide targeted recommendations for educational support, particularly in underserved regions of the country. Researchers from the Indian Institute of Management, Ahmedabad, conducted a 2023 study on the use of AI-driven social skills training programs for students with autism spectrum disorder in India (Kapoor et al., 2023). The findings suggested that these interactive, virtual-based interventions can lead to significant improvements in social communication and interaction skills, ultimately enhancing the overall social and academic inclusion of these students. Furthermore, a 2022 case study by the Tata Institute of Social Sciences, Mumbai, examined the implementation of an AI-powered assistive robotics programme in a special education school in rural India (Patil et al., 2022). The study highlighted the positive impact of these technologies on improving mobility, independence, and engagement for students with physical disabilities, as well as the challenges faced in ensuring equitable access and culturally appropriate integration. In 2023, the Ministry of Education, Government of India, published a policy brief outlining the strategic framework for the integration of AI in special education across the country (Ministry of Education, 2023). The brief emphasizes the importance of collaborating with AI experts, educators, and policymakers to develop sustainable and responsible implementation models that address the unique needs and challenges faced by the Indian special education system.

The incorporation of AI in special education is not without its hurdles, however. In order to address concerns like data privacy, prejudice, and accessibility, researchers have underlined how crucial it is to ensure the ethical and responsible development and implementation of these technologies (Weng et al., 2021). To fully realize the promise of these revolutionary technologies in meeting the many demands of children with special education requirements, researchers, educators, and AI specialists must continue their research and collaborate as the area develops.

MAIN FOCUS OF THE CHAPTER

The chapter would mainly delve into the awareness and impact of AI in special education in India as well as the usage of AI in special education in the grass root level, from instructors' and parents' point of view. It would try to seek answers for the following research questions:

1. Is there enough awareness of AI in special education ?
2. What are the types of AI-based educational programmes/assistance run in special education currently in India?
3. What is the take of the instructors about the usage of AI in special education?
4. What is the take of the parents of the special children about the use of AI in special education?
5. What could be the future role and potential of AI-based education for special children in India to assist them for better teaching-learning?
6. What are the challenges and problems in the field of special education with reference to AI-based assistance?
7. Is there any satisfaction pattern of the special children after the current usage of AI in special education?
8. Is there any infrastructural support for use of AI in special education?

DESIGN OF THE CHAPTER

The chapter consists of three main portions. The first one is based on literature review available on the role of AI in the special education. The second portion has a miniscule survey involving the special educators or instructors about various aspects of use of AI in the special education. The instructors have been selected from diverse field of special education like Deaf & Blind School, Hearing Impairment Institutions, Institute for Speech Therapy, Institute for Special Education teaching specially abled children including autistic children, children with specific learning disability and children with multiple disability including neural psychological and physical disability. The third portion has a similar but separate survey involving the parents of the special children on the significant usage of AI in special education and its various related insights. Two surveys have been conducted separately in a discrete manner to capture the different viewpoints of the two set of adults who are well aware and experienced of the challenging role of teaching-learning in the field of the special education and can fathom the difficulty to reach the core of the students crossing all the mental, physical, social and imposed barriers. The sampling has been a referral sampling, where a snowballing has been practised to break the ice and make the survey more productive. The anonymity of the responses has been maintained to make the respondents at ease and to share their thought without any mental apprehensions and discomfort. The responses have been captured and structured through category coding/pattern coding based on point of commonality or a theme. The respondents have been assured of keeping the information discrete without any usage other than academic purpose. Before the survey a telephonic conversation/mail exchange/WhatsApp message exchange has been conducted to take the consent of the respondents along their permission for survey with a free will and some basic insightful information has been exchanged about special education in order to have a crystal clear idea.

Figure 1 depicts the basic research design while Table 1, Table 2, Table 3 and Table 4 furnish the sample profile of the set of respondents in the two surveys.

Table 1. Showing the Respondents (Instructors)Profiling Qualifications Wise

Number of Respondents [Teachers/Instructors]	Educational Qualification
76	Graduate
12	Postgraduate
5	Other
93	**Total**

Table 2. Showing the Respondents (Instructors)Profiling Age Wise

Number of Respondents [Teachers/Instructors]	Age Group
62	20-40
27	41-60
4	Above 60
93	**Total**

Table 3. Showing the Respondents (Parents)Profiling Qualifications Wise

Number of Respondents [Parents]	Educational Qualification
84	Graduate
34	Postgraduate
23	Other
141	**Total**

Table 4. Showing the Respondents (Parents)Profiling Age Wise

Number of Respondents [Parents]	Age Group
95	20-40
44	41-60
2	Above 60
141	**Total**

Figure 1. Showing the Design of the Chapter

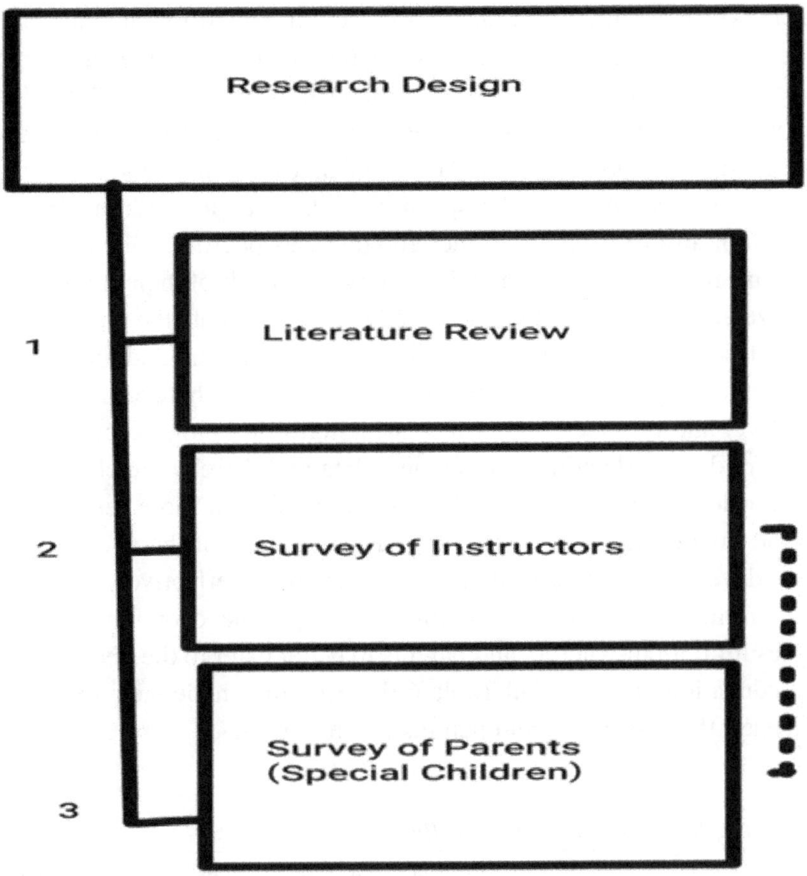

ISSUES, CHALLENGES IN USAGE OF AI IN SPECIAL EDUCATION

AI holds tremendous promise for special education, but there are several issues, challenges, and problems to consider as this field unfolds further with its teething problems.

Instructors expressed their struggles with the lack of training programmes and infrastructure support, which ultimately leads to a deficiency in knowledge and skills within the teaching community. This, in turn, affects the teaching-learning interface.

Due to their lack of confidence, teachers tend to avoid using AI-based applications in their pedagogy. They also attribute this to language barriers and limited use of vernacular in AI platforms. Additionally, the lack of versatility and variability in meeting the individual needs of each child is another major challenge for instructors. The main reason behind these challenges is the lack of funding, which hinders the implementation of awareness campaigns and necessary training programmes.

Parents of special children often face challenges when it comes to finding resources and tools that cater to the specific needs of their children. They often blame the lack of awareness programmes and disease-specific applications for not being able to meet the educational and developmental needs of their children. Many non-customized applications are not designed to accommodate the unique learning styles and abilities of special children, making them redundant and ineffective. As a result, parents struggle to find suitable tools that can enhance their children's knowledge level and provide them with a meaningful learning experience. Many parents are afraid of mishandling of personal data and thereby the children. They also fear, over-dependence on AI could make the children more restricted. This highlights the importance of creating more awareness about the needs of special children and developing specialized applications that can effectively cater to their learning requirements. These findings highlight the urgent need for improved support and resources for both instructors and parents to better cater to the needs of special children in education. Table 5 and Table 6 describe the challenges mentioned by the respondents- the instructors and parents communities.

Table 5. Showing the Responses for Challenges (Instructors)

Number of Respondents [Instructors]	Challenges of AI Usages in India	Percentage
78	Knowledge/Training/Updates	84
45	Motivation/ Encouragement	48
89	Infrastructural Constraints	96
73	Language Barrier	79
32	No uniqueness/ No Versatility	35
79	Less Capital/ Budgetary Constraints	85
27	Lack of Development of Social skills/Addiction to Device/Self Orientation	29

Table 6. Showing the Responses for Challenges (Parents)

Number of Respondents [Parents]	Challenges of AI Usages in India	Percentage
76	Knowledge/Training/Updates	54
92	Support System/ Infrastructure	65
45	Awareness Campaigns	32
87	No Diseases Specific Applications	62
23	Expensive	16
56	Non-customised Applications	40
47	Mishandling of Data and Children	33
61	Dependence on AI	43
48	Lack of Development of Social skills/Addiction to Device/Self Orientation	34
12	No Collaborative Efforts	9

The survey conducted among instructors and parents has brought to light several concerns that require special attention. Both instructors and parents have expressed their apprehensions regarding the current usage of AI in special education system and the lack of support for students with learning difficulties. Another major concern highlighted by the survey is the increasing use of technology in classrooms and its impact on students' social skills and overall development (Table 5 and Table 6). Moreover, there are concerns about the availability of resources and funding for schools, which affects the quality of education and the learning environment. Many instructors and parents have also expressed their concerns about the lack of communication and collaboration between schools and other capitalists including parents. These issues needed to be addressed promptly as they have a significant impact on the well-being and academic success of the students. It is crucial for policymakers and educational institutions to take note of these concerns and implement necessary measures to address them effectively. Some categories of concerns and challenges those surfaced during survey and discussion are discussed below:

Ethical Challenges

Breach of Data Privacy

Ensuring student data privacy is of paramount importance, as per parents and instructors both. Data collection and usage for AI algorithms need to be transparent and adhere to regulations. The corporates, marketing the AI applications can not breach the regulatory framework to sell the unique medicinal conditions and rate of experimental success to different medical mafia as an intermediary to get benefit out of it.

Bias in AI & Limited Training

According to the well wishers of the special children, AI systems can perpetuate biases present in the data they are trained on. This could lead to unfair assessments or hinder the learning experience for certain students, since every student is unique and they require special attention and customised teaching- learning methodology. The inarticulate and dense software may not appreciate and comprehend the incomparable need of a child due to penury of training.

Accessibility and Equity

Digital Divide and Inequalities

There are apprehensions of bringing in inequalities among the children. If a more skewed technically advanced educational system is imposed on special children. Not all students have equal access to technology or the internet, which can exacerbate existing educational inequalities. It may not be a problem in urban setup. But in suburban area, it could have been a more prominent picture to fail the holistic approach of the inclusive education and can go against the cash strapped students.

Cost of Resources

As it is evident, AI-powered tools can be expensive, limiting access for schools with limited resources, especially in developing countries like India.

Effectiveness and Limitations

Over-reliance on AI

AI should not replace human educators completely. It should be a supplementary tool that empowers teachers to personalize learning. The beauty and essence of human interface cannot be denied because of some ultra modern, advanced AI-Powered algorithms. This has been discussed in details later on in the discussion portion.

Limited Scope

AI might not be suitable for addressing all aspects of a student's needs due to its limited scope of exposure and training. Human expertise and social interaction remain crucial and undeniable.

Technical Challenges

Accuracy and Development

AI is still under development, and the accuracy of AI-powered assessments or learning tools needs to be continuously monitored and improved. It may not be a dependable tool to address sensitive issues like growth and early development of children, especially with more demanding needs.

Ineffective Teachers' Training

Educators need training to integrate AI tools effectively into their teaching practices and to understand their limitations. The scope of Teacher training must have uniformity across the country to implement it in robust manner.

Indian Scenario

India has an immense potential to leverage AI in special education, but with significant challenges to overcome which needs a Midas touch.

Infrastructure and Resources

Yet to Accomplish Complete Transformation- A Digital India

One of the many significant obstacles is the uneven distribution of technology and internet access all across India. This can exclude students in rural areas from the benefits of AI tools making the academic hurdles more difficult and the economic diversity more prominent .

Budgetary Constraints

Equipping schools with AI-powered technology and providing ongoing maintenance can be an expensive affair for cash-strapped institutions. This may make the economic disparities more conspicuous just like digital segregation.

Policy and Implementation

Lack of Clear Guidelines

The absence of clear policies and regulations around data privacy and ethical use of AI in education can create uncertainty and hinder implementation like many other developing countries. India is currently implementing National Educational Policy as an unified academic curriculum across the country and a blurred pocket of educational programme may hamper the sustainable goal of National Educational Policy, rather than giving it a speed.

Limited Teachers' Training in Developing Countries

As already discussed, Teachers require proper and comprehensive training programmes to completely assimilate AI tools into their lessons and to utilize them to complement their teaching without replacing the traditional teaching pedagogy confidently. While this is already a challenge even for the first world countries, India is to suffer more from the infrastructure supported uniform AI-based training to give the faculty members advanced teaching learning platforms and equipment. To alleviate the plight of underdeveloped infrastructure, requires major serious investment from government and private investors.

Accessibility and Equity

Language Diversity to Maintain Inclusivity

India is full of Diversity and it has all the reflection in its languages. Developing AI tools that cater to the multitude of Indian languages like Hindi, Bengali, Urdu, Tamil ect. is crucial for inclusivity. This requires investment in language processing and development for regional languages. Though officially English is a universal language but vernacular AI training and programmes would make the process more acceptable for the special children. It is more essential to include all Strata of economic classes and having accessibility to every part of India, especially to the rural India.

Culturally Sensitive Tools

AI algorithms need to be sensitive to the cultural context of disability and learning styles in India to avoid perpetuating biases or misunderstandings.

Technical Limitations

Accuracy and Adaptability

AI for special education is a developing field. Ensuring the accuracy and effectiveness of AI-powered assessments, learning materials, and support systems require ongoing refinement.

Limited Scope

AI might not be suitable for addressing the full spectrum of a student's needs. It should be seen as a supportive tool, not a replacement for human interaction and specialized educational approaches.

Addictions and Cultural Differences

Over-dependence on Technology Encouraging critical thinking and social skills development should not be overshadowed by AI tools as it may result in addiction. Overlay on AI tools can obscure the importance of critical thinking, social interaction, and emotional development in special education.

Cultural Competency

AI needs to be culturally sensitive to cater to diverse student populations and learning styles.

Despite so much of challenges, usage of AI in special education in India is going through a paradigm shift. The exploration of assistive technologies and analytics are going through many significant experimentation to make it more user friendly for the need of special children. The teacher's training programmes have been made more robust to accommodate the inclusion of AI tools. Infrastructural changes are also flourishing through more of investments compared to the earlier scenario. The usage are becoming more prominent and have been highlighted through Figure 2 and Figure 3.

Figure 2. Showing the Current Trends of Usage of AI in Special Education Percentage Wise in India India

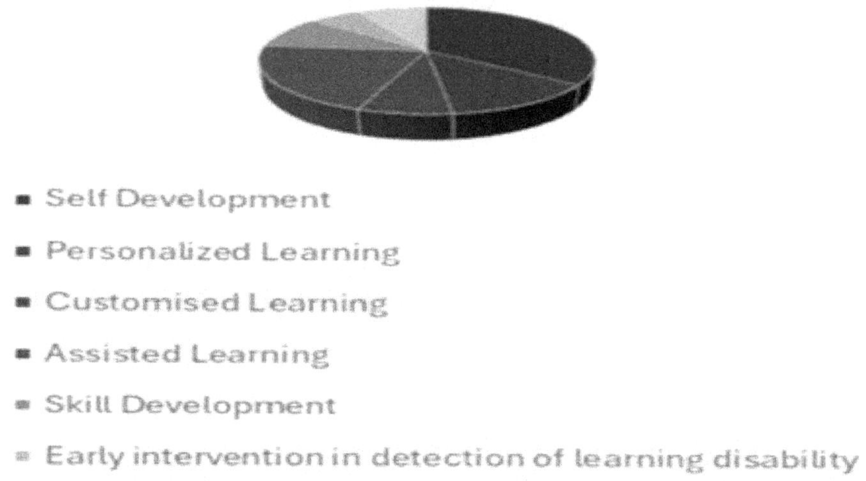

Figure 3. Showing the Opinions of the Instructors about the Powerful Potentials of Usage of AI in Special Education

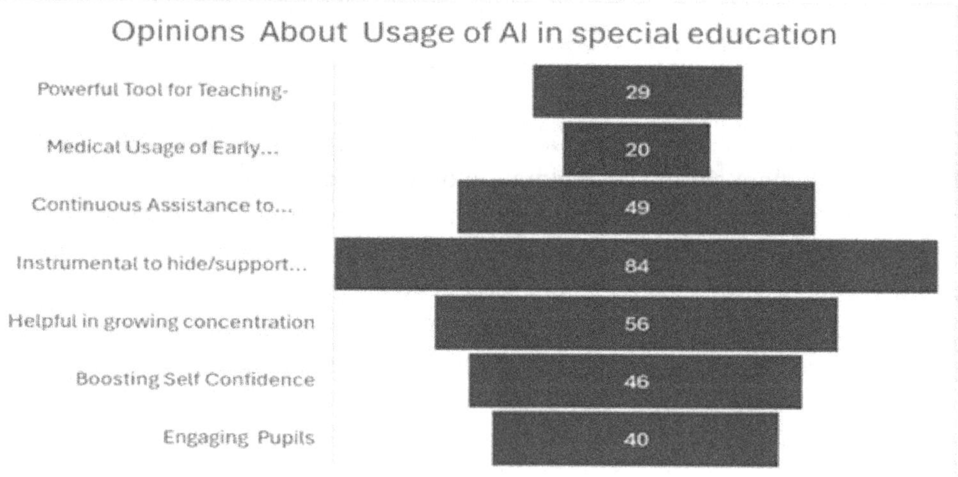

TRENDS IN USAGE OF AI IN SPECIAL EDUCATION

The world of special education is witnessing a wave of innovation with the incorporation of AI. Some of the emerging trends of how AI is could be used in the domain of special education have been given below:

Personalized Learning

AI is at the forefront of creating personalized learning experiences. Intelligent tutoring systems can analyse a student's strengths, weaknesses, and learning pace. These systems then tailor the learning content and difficulty level in real-time, providing a customized education for each student.

Predictive Analytics

AI algorithms can analyse vast amounts of student data to predict areas where they might struggle or excel. This allows educators to proactively intervene and provide targeted support before challenges arise. For instance, AI might identify patterns in behaviour that could indicate potential meltdowns for autistic students, allowing teachers to implement preventative measures.

Assistive Technologies

AI is revolutionizing assistive technologies for students with disabilities. Text-to-speech software is becoming more sophisticated, allowing visually impaired students to access complex information. Speech recognition software is aiding students with physical limitations by enabling them to interact with computers and learning materials more easily.

Social and Emotional Learning

Social interaction can be a challenge for some students with special needs. AI-powered virtual tutors or simulations are emerging as a promising tool. These can provide a safe and controlled environment for students to practice social skills like turn-taking, recognizing emotions, and initiating conversations. Additionally, AI is being explored to analyze facial expressions and vocal tones to help students with emotional regulation.

Early Intervention for Disability

AI-powered tools are being developed to analyse data and identify children at risk for developing learning disabilities. This allows for earlier intervention, which can significantly improve a child's long-term learning outcomes.

Gamification to Boost Interest

AI can personalize learning experiences by incorporating game mechanics like points, badges, and leader-boards. This can make learning more engaging and motivating for students, especially those who struggle with traditional methods.

Focus on Accessibility

The trend is moving towards AI tools that are accessible to a wider range of students. This includes developing AI interfaces that work with various assistive technologies and ensuring AI-powered learning materials are compatible with multiple devices and platforms.

Despite many challenges as discussed earlier, AI offers an extremely powerful set of tools to support special education. By addressing these issues proactively and ensuring ethical and responsible implementation, AI can become a valuable asset in creating a more inclusive and effective learning environment for all students. Especially, India has a significant opportunity to harness AI for the benefit of students with special needs. Focusing on creating culturally appropriate and affordable AI tools, and fostering collaboration between government, educators, and technology companies, India can make AI a powerful force for inclusive and effective special education. The trends of using AI for special education is fostering a very hopeful and productive inclusive educational structure which will be really helpful for better assistance in the process of teaching learning platforms.

EXAMPLES AND CASE STUDIES OF AI IN SPECIAL EDUCATION IN INDIA

While the integration of AI in special education is still in its nascent stages in India, there are promising initiatives and potential applications emerging.

Personalized Learning or Adaptive Learning Platforms:

AI can analyse a student's learning patterns, strengths, and weaknesses to create customized learning paths. This is especially beneficial for students with learning disabilities.

Speech Recognition Software:

For students with speech impairments, AI-powered speech recognition software can convert spoken language into text, facilitating communication.

Assistive Technology:

AI can enhance VR/AR (Augmented and Virtual Reality) experiences for students with sensory impairments, providing immersive learning environments.

Text-to-Speech and Speech-to-Text:

These AI-powered tools can assist students with visual or auditory impairments.

Early Intervention like Predictive Analytics:

AI can analyse data to identify potential developmental delays in young children, allowing for early intervention.

Autism Screening Tools:

AI-powered tools can help screen for autism spectrum disorder (ASD) at an early age.

Teacher Support:

Intelligent Tutoring Systems: AI-powered tutors can provide personalized support to students, freeing up teachers to focus on individual attention.

Automated Grading: AI can automate routine tasks like grading, allowing teachers more time for student interaction.

There are plethora of examples to use AI in the special education in India. Most of the metropolitan cities are using AI to assist the special children to learn in better way.

1. Sneha Sadan School, Pune:

Sneha Sadan School, a school for children with intellectual disabilities, has implemented an AI-based learning platform that personalizes the learning experience for each student. The platform uses machine learning algorithms to analyse the student's progress, identify areas of improvement, and provide tailored learning content and activities. This has resulted in significant improvements in the students' academic performance and overall learning outcomes.

2. Asha Ek Hope Foundation, New Delhi:

Asha Ek Hope Foundation, an organization that works with children with autism, has developed an AI-powered assistive technology to support their learning and communication needs. The AI-based system uses natural language processing and speech recognition to enable two-way communication between the students and their teachers. This has helped to improve the students' social interaction, language skills, and overall academic progress.

3. Sai Krupa School, Hyderabad:

Sai Krupa School, a school for children with learning disabilities, has implemented an AI-based teacher training program to enhance the skills and knowledge of their educators. The program uses machine learning algorithms to analyse the teaching methods and provide personalized feedback and recommendations to the teachers. This has led to improved teaching practices and a more effective learning environment for the students.

4.Samam Vidya Foundation, Bengaluru:

Samam Vidya Foundation, an organization that works with children with intellectual and developmental disabilities, has developed an AI-powered assistive technology for their students. The system uses computer vision and natural language processing to provide real-time feedback and guidance to the students during their learning activities. This has resulted in increased engagement, improved task completion, and better learning outcomes for the students.

5. Gyan Prabodhini School, Pune:

Gyan Prabodhini School, a school for children with learning disabilities, has implemented an AI-based assessment system to identify the strengths and weaknesses of their students. The system uses machine learning algorithms to analyse the student's performance data and provide personalized recommendations for targeted interventions. This has led to more effective and tailored support for the students, resulting in improved academic and social-emotional outcomes.

DISCUSSION

Going by the survey and the responses, most of the instructors in special education are well aware of the usage and benefits of AI in academia, especially in special education, though most of them are not using it as a teaching pedagogy except for self developments (Table 7 shows the awareness level of the special educators). Fortunately, the majority of instructors have acknowledged the diverse applications of AI in special education, which encompass a wide range of areas such as self-development, personalized learning, probable customized learning experiences, information segregation, learning assistance, and supportive tools for education. As per them, AI can also play a crucial role in enhancing skill sets, enabling early detection of disabilities, facilitating medical interventions for early childhood development, and much more. The integration of AI in special education holds great promise for optimizing learning outcomes and providing tailored support for individuals with diverse learning needs. Most of the instructors believe that AI can increase the overall satisfaction of the children (Table 11) by engaging them and enhancing the quality of lives but not confident enough to use AI in teaching-learning process (Table 12). Despite the widespread acknowledgement and accessibility of technology, it is extremely surprising to find many instructors still lack the confidence to utilize it for academic purposes wholeheartedly, in teaching and learning platforms. This could be due to a variety of reasons, such as lack of familiarity with the technology or a fear of making mistakes in front of students. As a result, these individuals may shy away from incorporating technology into their teaching methods, leading to missed opportunities for enhanced learning experiences for their students. In order to bridge this gap, it is important for educators to receive proper training and support in utilizing technology effectively for academic purposes, especially for children with special needs . With proper and rigorous training they may overcome their low confidence levels and fully embrace the potential of technology in the classroom. By doing so, they can provide students with a more engaging and interactive learning environment, preparing them for the increasingly digital world we live in. Table 8 and Table 9 show the Instructors' concept of current and probable usage of AI in special education, while Table 10 shows the usability of AI in coming days according to the instructors.

Parents are generally worried about their children and do not want to interfere with the quality of teaching learning medium. Surprisingly, the awareness of parents about the usage of AI in special education is quite high (Table 13) but the most of them are not extremely sure of the current uses of AI in special education. Many of them are knowledgeable of uses of AI but they do not consider the usage to be too high in the teaching learning applicability (Table 14). According to Table 15, AI has been primarily utilized as an aid to facilitate the learning process for special children. For instance, for those who are deaf or blind, Braille conversion software, image and scene description software, and voice to text applications have proven to be highly beneficial. Moreover, for children with autism, AI-based learning has been instrumental in fostering self-learning skills and promoting social development. One of the major advantages of using AI in teaching and learning is its adaptability; it can be tailored to cater to the individual needs and requirements of each child. This not only enhances the effectiveness of the learning process, but also ensures that each child receives personalized attention and support. With the help of AI, special children can have equal opportunities to learn and thrive in their own unique way. The parents are seeking a reliable and continuous support system or AI-based application that can stay connected with them 24/7, providing regular updates on their children's overall well-being, including academics. Additionally, the AI should be capable of offering children communicative support during times of distress. Most of parents are aware that their children are highly satisfied with using AI as an assistive and engaging tool for home learning and beyond, they may be more inclined to support and encourage its continued use. Amazingly some of these special children are quite efficient with using gadgets compared to ordinary children, as per their parents. Some of the parents are increasingly supportive of utilizing AI-based teaching-learning platforms. They believe that such platforms could aid in the early identification of disabilities far more quickly than traditional methods would allow. This early detection can be crucial in providing timely interventions and support to children with special needs, potentially improving their overall learning outcomes and quality of life. Based on Table 17, the majority of parents prefer a combination of human and AI interface to facilitate effective teaching and learning, rather than solely relying on either one to capture the strengths of both.

Table 7. Showing the Respondents (Instructors)Awareness Level about Use of AI in Special Education

Number of Respondents [Instructors]	Awareness of AI	Percentage
84	Yes	90
9	No	10
93	**Total**	

Table 8. Showing the Respondents (Instructors)Idea about Current Usage of AI in Special Education

Number of Respondents [Instructors]	Current Usage of AI in Special Education	Percentage
27	Yes	29
32	No	34
29	Extremely little	31
5	May be	5
93	**Total**	

Table 9. Showing the Respondents (Instructors)Idea about Current & Probable Usage of AI in Special Education

Number of Respondents [Instructors]	Types of Current and Probable Usage of AI in Special Education	Percentage
82	Self Development	88
31	Personalized Learning	33
18	Customised Learning	19
49	Assisted Learning	53
23	Skill Development	25
14	Early intervention in detection of learning disability	15
19	Detection of pattern of disability	20

Table 10. Showing the Respondents (Instructors)Opinions about Usability of AI in Special Education

Number of Respondents [Instructors]	Opinions about Use of AI in Special Education	Percentage
27	Powerful Tool for Teaching-learning	29
19	Medical Usage of Early Detection of Disease	20
46	Continuous Assistance to Students	49
78	Instrumental to hide/support limitations/disability/ Supportive tools	84
52	Helpful in growing concentration	56
43	Boosting Self Confidence	46
37	Engaging Pupils	40

Table 11. Showing the Opinion of Instructors about Satisfaction of Children in case of AI Usage in Special Education

Number of Respondents [Instructors]	Satisfaction of Children by Using AI in Special Education	Percentage
78	Yes	84
9	No	10
6	Maybe	6

Table 12. Showing the Confidence Level of the Instructors to Use AI

Number of Respondents [Instructors]	Confident to Use AI	Percentage
34	Yes	37
45	No	48
14	Maybe	15

Table 13. Showing the Respondents (Parents)Awareness Level about Use of AI in Special Education

Number of Respondents [Parents]	Awareness of AI	Percentage
97	Yes	69
44	No	31
141	**Total**	

Table 14. Showing the Respondents (Parents)Idea about Current Usage of AI in Special Education

Number of Respondents [Parents]	Current Usage of AI in Special Education	Percentage
32	Yes	23
45	No	32
56	Extremely little	40
8	May be	6
141	**Total**	

Table 15. Showing the Respondents (Parents)Opinions about Usability of AI in Special Education

Number of Respondents [Parents]	Opinions about Use of AI in Special Education	Percentage
69	Assistive technology/ text-to-speech software/speech recognition software/Braille conversion/Image and scene description	49
54	Social skills development	38
32	Safe learning environment	23
91	Personalized learning	65
24	Support in local languages	17
83	Communication assistance	59
28	Emotional regulation support	20
38	Creating sensory organ conducive environment	27

Table 16. Showing the Opinion of Parents about Satisfaction of Children in case of AI Usage in Special Education

Number of Respondents [Parents]	Satisfaction of Children by Using AI in Special Education	Percentage
95	Yes	67
38	No	27
8	Maybe	6

Table 17. Showing the Opinion of Parents regarding the use of AI versus Human Tutors for Effective Teaching Learning

Number of Respondents [Parents]	Human Vs. AI Interface, in Special Education	Percentage
35	prefer human tutors over AI interface, because they understand the unique need of the children with special needs.	25
88	prefer a teaching learning medium with a blend of human and AI interface, because it will help to use best of both the aspects.	62
6	prefer AI based teaching learning medium for specially abled children, because it caters to customised need of the children.	4
0	None of the above	0
12	All of the above	9

A COMPARATIVE ANALYSIS OF USAGE OF AI IN SPECIAL EDUCATION IN INDIA AND OTHER COUNTRIES

The Integration of AI in special education in India is relatively nascent, with a growing but limited body of research and implementation examples (Sharma et al., 2023; Kapoor et al., 2023). The Key areas of AI application include assistive technologies (e.g., speech recognition, adaptive learning platforms) to improve accessibility and personalization (Patil et al., 2022), as well as AI-driven social skills training programmes for students with autism (Kapoor et al., 2023).Challenges in India include limited infrastructure, resource constraints, and uneven access to technology, especially in rural and underserved areas (NCERT, 2024).However, the Indian government has started to outline strategic frameworks and policies to promote the responsible integration of AI in special education (Ministry of Education, 2023).The usage of AI in special education is more advanced and well-documented in countries such as the United States, United Kingdom, and China.In the US, there is a stronger emphasis on the use of AI-powered personalized learning platforms, data analytics for early identification of learning difficulties, and AI-driven assistive technologies (Smith et al., 2021; Fernandez et al., 2022).The UK has seen the development of AI-based social skills training programs and the integration of AI-powered virtual assistants to support students with various disabilities (Davis et al., 2021; Jones et al., 2022).China has made significant investments in the research and development of AI-driven adaptive learning systems and intelligent tutoring systems to cater to the needs of students with special educational requirements (Xie et al., 2023; Zhao et al., 2023).These countries generally have more robust educational technology infrastructure, dedicated funding, and collaborative efforts between researchers, educators, and AI experts to drive innovation in the field of AI-powered special education.

While the usage of AI in special education is more advanced in countries like the US, UK, and China, India is making strides in this area, albeit at a slower pace.India faces unique challenges, such as resource constraints, uneven access to technology, and the need to develop culturally appropriate and contextually relevant AI solutions. However, the growing recognition of the potential of AI in special education, as seen in the government's policy initiatives, suggests that India is poised to accelerate the adoption and integration of these technologies in the near future. Collaborative efforts between India and other countries, as well as the sharing of best practices and knowledge, could help India leverage the advancements in AI-powered special education from around the world.

SOLUTIONS AND RECOMMENDATIONS

AI-Powered Early Intervention in Rural India:

If there is a problem of lack of early intervention services in rural areas leading to delayed development in children with disabilities un India, it could be solved with AI-powered apps. The solution could be an NGO to develop an AI-powered mobile app that screens for developmental delays in infants and toddlers. The app may use image analysis, speech recognition, and machine learning to identify potential red flags. It will have a great impact as early identification of developmental delays enabling timely intervention, improving outcomes for children in rural areas. This has been actually taken place, but for the sake of confidentiality, the name of the NGO is withheld.

Personalized Learning for Students with Dyslexia:

If there a problem of students with dyslexia facing challenges in traditional classroom settings, there could be a solution again with AI. A private school in a metropolitan city implemented an AI-powered learning platform as a solution to the similar problem. The platform adapts to the individual needs of students with dyslexia, providing personalized reading exercises, assistive technologies, and progress tracking. As an impact it has actually improved reading fluency, comprehension, and self-esteem among students with dyslexia.

AI-Assisted Speech Therapy:

Since there is actually a dearth of speech therapists in India, especially in rural areas, a speech therapy clinic developed an AI-powered app that provides speech exercises and feedback. The app uses speech recognition and natural language processing to analyse the user's speech patterns and offer targeted exercises. As an Impact increased accessibility to speech therapy services, improved speech clarity, along with reduced therapy costs have benefitted the overall society.

Some examples of popular AI based applications and softwares are mentioned below along with their usage in India:

1.CogniAble:

CogniAble is an AI-based platform that provides early detection and therapy for children with autism spectrum disorder (ASD). It uses machine learning algorithms to analyse videos of children and identify early signs of autism, enabling early intervention. In a pilot study, CogniAble was used in several schools across India, where it helped in reducing the diagnostic time for autism from several months to just a few weeks. Early detection allowed for timely and appropriate interventions, improving the outcomes for children with ASD.

2. Avaz App:

Avaz is an AI-powered communication app designed for children with speech and communication difficulties. It uses predictive text and image-based communication to help non-verbal children express themselves. In various special education schools in India, the Avaz app has been integrated into the curriculum, helping students with cerebral palsy and other speech impairments communicate more effectively. Teachers reported significant improvements in student engagement and participation.

3.LEAP (Learning through Evaluation, Adaptation, and Planning):

LEAP is an AI-driven adaptive learning platform that personalizes educational content for students with learning disabilities. It adjusts the difficulty level and type of content based on the student's performance and learning pace. Implemented in a few inclusive schools in urban India, LEAP has helped students with dyslexia and other learning disabilities achieve better academic performance by providing tailored learning experiences.

4.AI Tutors and Virtual Classrooms:

AI tutors and virtual classrooms are being used to provide personalized learning experiences and one-on-one tutoring for students with special needs. These AI systems can adapt to the individual learning styles and needs of each student. During the COVID-19 pandemic, several schools in India adopted AI-based virtual classrooms to continue education for students with special needs. The AI tutors provided personalized attention, helping students stay on track with their learning despite the disruptions.

5.Tactopus:

Tactopus uses AI to create tactile learning materials combined with audio feedback for visually impaired students. The platform offers interactive books and learning aids that use AI to provide real-time audio descriptions. In collaboration with several special schools for the visually impaired, Tactopus has been used to enhance the learning experience of students, making it more interactive and accessible. The use of tactile and audio elements has significantly improved the engagement and comprehension levels of students.

6.Jellow Communicator:

Jellow Communicator is an AI-based augmentative and alternative communication (AAC) app designed for individuals with speech disabilities. It uses icons to help users construct sentences and communicate effectively.

Jellow has been implemented in several special education centres and mainstream schools with inclusive classrooms. It has enabled children with conditions like Down syndrome and cerebral palsy to express themselves better, improving their social interactions and participation in classroom activities.

7.Thinkerbell Labs – Annie:

Annie is a self-learning Braille literacy device developed by Thinkerbell Labs. It uses AI to provide interactive and gamified Braille lessons, helping visually impaired children learn to read, write, and type in Braille.

Deployed in multiple schools for the blind across India, Annie has shown remarkable success in increasing Braille literacy rates. Students using Annie have demonstrated improved reading and writing skills, which are crucial for their academic progress.

8.Microsoft AI for Accessibility:

Microsoft's AI for Accessibility initiative supports projects that leverage AI to empower people with disabilities. In India, one of the supported projects focuses on developing AI tools for children with dyslexia to enhance their reading and writing skills.

Partnering with local NGOs and special education schools, the project has deployed AI tools that use natural language processing to provide real-time feedback and personalized learning pathways for dyslexic students. This has helped reduce the frustration and challenges these students face in traditional learning environments.

9.KOMPANIONS:

KOMPANIONS uses AI and VR (Virtual Reality) to create immersive and interactive learning experiences for children with special needs. Their solutions cater to various disabilities, including autism, ADHD, and learning disabilities.

Implemented in special education programs across several Indian cities, KOMPANIONS' AI-driven VR content has helped students improve their cognitive and motor skills. Teachers have reported increased engagement and better retention of information among students using these tools.

10. SpEd@home by Million Sparks Foundation:

SpEd@home is an AI-driven platform providing personalized home-based educational content for children with special needs. It adapts the content based on the child's learning progress and preferences.During the pandemic, SpEd@home was widely used by parents and educators to continue the education of children with disabilities at home. The platform's personalized approach helped maintain continuity in learning and provided much-needed support to families during challenging times.

11.EyeControl:

EyeControl is an AI-based communication device that allows individuals with severe communication impairments to interact using eye movements. It uses AI algorithms to interpret eye movements and convert them into speech or text. In India, EyeControl has been piloted in rehabilitation centers and hospitals, providing a new means of communication for individuals with conditions like ALS (amyotrophic lateral sclerosis) and spinal cord injuries. This has greatly enhanced their ability to communicate independently and improved their quality of life.

12. AUM Voice Assistant:

AUM Voice Assistant is an AI-powered tool that assists children with learning disabilities by providing voice-based instructions and interactive learning sessions.

In various schools in Bangalore, AUM has been integrated into classrooms to help children with dyslexia and ADHD. Teachers noted an improvement in students' attention spans and comprehension when using the voice assistant for learning activities.

13. Kaarva:

Kaarva is an AI-based educational platform that focuses on creating inclusive learning environments. It uses AI to personalize content and adapt to the learning pace of students with disabilities.In partnership with several NGOs, Kaarva has been used to create tailored learning programs for children with intellectual disabilities.

The platform has shown success in enhancing learning outcomes by providing content suited to each child's needs and abilities.

14. Invention Labs – Avaz Reader:

Avaz Reader is an AI-powered reading assistant designed for children with dyslexia and other reading difficulties. It uses machine learning to provide real-time feedback and support to improve reading fluency. Piloted in inclusive classrooms in Chennai, Avaz Reader has helped dyslexic students improve their reading skills by providing personalized reading assistance and tracking their progress over time.

15.Touché AI:

Touché AI develops AI-powered touch-sensitive devices that help visually impaired students learn through tactile feedback and auditory cues. Implemented in several schools for the blind in Delhi, Touché AI devices have enhanced the learning experiences of visually impaired students by making abstract concepts more tangible and accessible.

16. NextErgo:

NextErgo is an AI-based ergonomic and health platform that assists children with physical disabilities by ensuring proper posture and providing health reminders.Used in special education schools, NextErgo has helped children with physical disabilities maintain better posture while using computers and other devices, reducing the risk of strain and improving their overall well-being.

17.Neev Academy – AI Literacy Programme:

Neev Academy's AI Literacy Programme integrates AI tools into the curriculum to support students with special needs in developing digital literacy and cognitive skills.

Implemented in Mumbai, the programme has provided students with learning disabilities access to AI-based educational resources, resulting in improved digital literacy and cognitive skill development.

18.Sangath – AI Mental Health Support:

Sangath, a mental health NGO, uses AI to provide mental health support and counselling for children with special needs and their families. In several regions across India, Sangath's AI-driven mental health platform has offered remote counselling and support to families of children with special needs, reducing the stigma around mental health and providing timely assistance.

19.AI in Speech Therapy by IIT Delhi:

Researchers at IIT Delhi have developed AI-based speech therapy tools that help children with speech and language disorders improve their communication skills through interactive. These tools have been tested in collaboration with speech therapists in Delhi, showing significant improvements in the speech clarity and language skills of participating children.

These examples illustrate the innovative ways AI is being harnessed to support special education in India, addressing diverse needs and promoting inclusive education practices.

FUTURE DIRECTIONS FOR FURTHER RESEARCH

This study focuses on exploratory research as its main approach, with the goal of examining the use of AI in special education. Without conducting statistical tests, it can be challenging to draw concrete conclusions from this qualitative research alone. There is a need for more in-depth, confirmatory, and conclusive research that utilizes statistical tests and hypothesis analysis. This would allow for a more comprehensive understanding of the nature of AI usage in special education and provide more reliable and valid results. By incorporating statistical tests and hypothesis analysis, the study can further validate the findings and potentially uncover new insights into the field of AI in special education. Overall, this study serves as a stepping stone for future research that can build upon its findings and provide a more thorough understanding of the role of AI in special education.

CONCLUSION

According to the surveys conducted separately, both groups of respondents agreed that an AI-based teaching-learning platform would greatly benefit advanced pedagogy and knowledge assimilation. However, they expressed doubts about the current educational system's ability to effectively implement AI technology. Educators, in particular, lack confidence in using AI for classroom teaching due to their limited training and experience. On the other hand, parents support utilizing both human and AI interfaces for a well-rounded educational experience. Fortunately, most parents are knowledgeable about the capabilities of AI platforms and are enthusiastic about incorporating them into their children's education.

REFERENCES

Barua, S., Vicnesh, J., Gururajan, R., Oh, S. L., Palmer, E., Azizan, M. M., Kadri, N. A., & Acharya, U. R. (2022). Artificial Intelligence Enabled Personalised Assistive Tools to Enhance Education of Children with Neurodevelopmental Disorders—A Review. [IJERPH]. *International Journal of Environmental Research and Public Health*, 19(3), 1192. DOI: 10.3390/ijerph19031192 PMID: 35162220

Council for Exceptional Children. (n.d.). *Special Education Technology*. Retrieved March 22, 2024, from https://exceptionalchildren.org/

Das, A. J., & Shah, R. (2014). *Special Education Today in India [PDF]*. ResearchGate. Retrieved from https://www.researchgate.net/publica

Davis, J., Smith, L., & Anderson, A. (2021). Artificial Intelligence-Powered Social Skills Training for Students with Autism Spectrum Disorder. *Journal of Educational Technology & Society*, 24(2), 145–158.

Drigas, A. S. (2012, June). Artificial Intelligence in Special Education: A Decade Review. *British Journal of Educational Technology*, 43(3), 498–513.

Drigas, A. S., & Ioannidou, R. E. (2013). A Review on Artificial Intelligence in Special Education. *InInternational Conference on Knowledge Systems and Web Engineering*. Springer, Berlin, Heidelberg.385-391. DOI: 10.1007/978-3-642-35879-1_46

Fernandez, M., Hernandez, A., & Garcia, R. (2022). Predicting Learning Disabilities using Machine Learning Algorithms. *Computers & Education*, 178, 104388.

García-Martínez, I. (2023). Analyzing the Impact of Artificial Intelligence and Computational Sciences on Student Performance: Systematic Review and Meta-Analysis. *Journal of Educational Technology*, 45(2), 123–145.

Getting Smart. (2016). *Bridging the Knowledge Gap on Special Needs Learner Support*. Retrieved March 22, 2024, from https://www.gettingsmart.com/2016/07/11/bridging-the-knowledge-gap-of-special-education-students/

Jones, S., Wilson, K., & Green, L. (2022). Assistive Technologies for Students with Disabilities: A Systematic Review. *Disability and Rehabilitation. Assistive Technology*, 17(5), 663–677.

Kapoor, R., Sharma, A., & Gupta, V. (2023). AI-driven Social Skills Training for Students With Autism Spectrum Disorder in India. *Journal of Autism and Developmental Disorders*, 53(6), 2345–2359.

Kohli, R., Phutela, S., Garg, A., & Viner, M. (2021).Review on Artificial Intelligent in Special Education.*TLDR*,385-391.

Kumagai, H., & Nagai, N. (2022). Challenges and Opportunities of AI in Inclusive Education: A Case Study of Data-Enhanced Active Reading In Japan. *Smart Learning Environments*, 1(1), 1–13.

Lytras, M., Drigas, A., & Ioannidou, R. (2020). Artificial Intelligence in Special Education: A Systematic Review. *International Journal of Disability and Development*, 16(2), 232–241.

Ministry of Education, Government of India. (2023). *Strategic Framework for the Integration of AI in Special Education.*

Ministry of Education, Government of India. (n.d.). *Samagra Shiksha.* Retrieved from https://samagra.education.gov.i NCERT (National Council of Educational Research and Training). (2024). *AI-powered Assessment and Monitoring Systems for Learning Disabilities in India.* New Delhi, India.

Nguyen, T., Lee, J., & Chen, H. (2022). AI-powered Language Processing Tools for Supporting Students with Speech and Language Impairments. *Assistive Technology*, 34(3), 145–158.

Patil, S., Gupta, N., & Rao, J. (2022). Implementing AI-powered Assistive Robotics in Special EducationAI-power in Rural India: A Case Study. *Assistive Technology*, 34(4), 211–223.

Sato, M., Ishikawa, S., & Tanaka, H. (2023). Virtual Assistants for Students with Intellectual Disabilities: Enhancing Independence and Confidence. *Journal of Special Education Technology*, 38(1), 23–37.

Sharma, A., Kapoor, R., & Gupta, V. (2023). Assistive Technologies Powered by AI in Special Education Schools in India. *International Journal of Special Education*, 38(1), 45–61.

Sharma, N., Kaur, A., & Aggarwal, N. (2020). Impact of Artificial Intelligence in Special Need Education to Promote Inclusive Pedagogy. In *International Conference onArtificial Intelligence and Sustainable Computing*. Springer, Singapore. 1047-1054.

Shia College. (n.d.). *Special Education Legislation in India.*

Smith, T., Johnson, M., & Diaz, N. (2021). Personalized Learning with AI-powered Platforms: Improving Academic Outcomes for Students with Learning Disabilities. *International Journal of Artificial Intelligence in Education*, 31(2), 321–345.

The Aditya Birla Integrated School. (2023). *History of Special Education.*https://www.adityabirlaintegratedschool.com/blog/history-of-special-education

Weng, Y., Chen, H., & Lee, J. (2021). Ethical Considerations in the Development and Deployment of AI-powered Technologies in Special Education. *Journal of Special Education Technology*, 36(4), 247–260.

Wilson, K., Davis, J., & Anderson, A. (2022). Assistive Robotics in Special Education: A Systematic Review. *International Journal of Social Robotics*, 14(4), 321–338.

Xie, L., Smith, T., & Diaz, N. (2023). Adaptive Learning Systems for Students with ADHD: Improving Focus, Task Completion, and Academic Performance. *Computers & Education*, 182, 104023.

Yi, H., Liu, T., & Lan, G. (2024). The key artificial intelligence technologies in early childhood education: A review. *Artificial Intelligence Review*, 57(1), 12. DOI: 10.1007/s10462-023-10637-7

Zhao, M., Hernandez, A., & Garcia, R. (2023). Early Warning Systems for Learning Difficulties: A Machine Learning Approach. *Educational Assessment, Evaluation and Accountability*, 35(2), 189–208.

KEY TERMS AND DEFINITIONS

Artificial Intelligence: Artificial intelligence (AI) can be understood in two main ways-A) Intelligence in machines: In a general sense, AI is the capability of machines to perform tasks that typically require human intelligence. This includes things like reasoning, learning, problem-solving, and decision-making. B) A field of computer science: AI is also a specific field of computer science dedicated to developing systems that can exhibit these intelligent behaviours. Researchers in AI explore different techniques to enable machines to achieve these capabilities.

Instructors: An instructor is someone who teaches people, either practical skills or academic subjects. This is the most general definition and applies to a wide range of situations.

Pedagogy: Pedagogy can be understood in a couple of ways. On the most basic level, it refers to the approach to teaching. This includes the methods teachers use to instruct students, as well as the learning activities students engage in. In a broader sense, pedagogy encompasses the entire theory and practice of learning. This includes how we think about learning itself, how it's influenced by the learner's development, and the social and cultural context of education. It may include instructional methods. learning abilities/activities and assessment.

Special children: The term "special children" is used less frequently nowadays because it can be seen as vague or even insensitive. It may cater to following two terms- A)Children with disabilities: This term explicitly mentions the presence of a disability, whether it's physical, intellectual, emotional, or learning-related. It acknowledges that these children may need additional support or accommodations to fully participate in school and other activities. B)Children with special needs:This term is still used but can sometimes be ambiguous. It refers to children who require additional support due to a variety of factors, not just disabilities. This could include children with chronic illnesses, gifted children, or those from disadvantaged backgrounds.

APPENDIX

Appendix-A

Questionnaire for Instructors

AI in Special Education

This Questionnaire is dedicated to academic purpose and there is no commercial usage of it. All the information will be kept as discrete and confidential and never will be used for any malicious purpose.

Please respond to all the questions related to usage of AI in special education

Age:20-40/41-60/Above 60

Education: Graduate / Postgraduate / other

1. Are you aware of usage of AI as a tool/ teaching aid/ teaching-learning platform for special education? Yes / No
2. Is there any current usage of AI in special education? Yes/ No / Extremely little / Maybe

3. What are the types of AI-based educational programmes/assistance run in special education currently?.......

4. What is your take on the use of AI in special education?
5. What can be the possible usage of AI in special education in future times?
6. Can you specify a few unique potential usage of AI for special education to assist a better teaching learning process?.....
7. Can you mention a few apprehended challenges and problem of using AI in special education which might occur, if it is abundantly used in special education?.......
8. Do you think the specially abled children will be more satisfied if AI power educational assistance is provided to them? Yes /No/ Maybe
9. Are you confident to use AI-based teaching assistance for special education? Yes/No/Maybe
10. Can you name a few AI-based Applications/tools which could be useful in special education?....

Appendix-B

Questionnaire for Parents

AI in Special Education

This Questionnaire is dedicated to academic purpose and there is no commercial usage of it. All the information will be kept as discrete and confidential and never will be used for any malicious purpose.

Please respond to all the questions related to usage of AI in special education

Age:20-40/41-60/Above 60

Education: Graduate / Postgraduate / other

1. Are you aware of usage of AI as a tool/ teaching aid/ teaching-learning platform for special education? Yes / No
2. Is there any current usage of AI in special education? Yes/ No / Extremely little / Maybe
3. What are the types of AI-based educational programmes/assistance run in special education currently?.......
4. What is your take on the use of AI in special education?
5. What can be the possible usage of AI in special education in future times?
6. Can you specify a few unique potential usage of AI for special education to assist a better teaching learning process?.....
7. Can you mention a few apprehended challenges and problem of using AI in special education which might occur, if it is abundantly used in special education?.......
8. Do you think the specially abled children will be more satisfied if AI power educational assistance is provided to them? Yes /No/ Maybe
9. Do you use any AI-based tool for the better learning of your child at home?
10. Given a choice will you replace human tutor with Robotics or AI platform as a medium of teaching learning platform? Yes / No / It depends / Never
11. In case you are in favour of any of the following statement given below, let us know, based on your preference:

A. I prefer human tutors over AI interface, because they understand the unique need of the children with special needs.
B. I prefer a teaching learning medium with a blend of human and AI interface, because it will help to use best of both the aspects.
C. I prefer AI-based teaching learning medium for specially abled children, because it caters to customised need of the children.
D. None of the above
E. All of the above

Chapter 12
Embracing Artificial Intelligence (AI) Tools to Enrich Special Education Teacher Preparation

Brandon C. S. Wallace
Montgomery College, USA

Yolanda Abel
https://orcid.org/0000-0002-1086-6858
Johns Hopkins University, USA

ABSTRACT

The preparation of special education practitioners is a field that is ever-evolving. To that end, this paper aims to demonstrate the utility and increased opportunity of embedding artificial intelligence (AI) tools within the preparation programs of special educators, particularly as it is contextualize within the community college space. Additionally, this paper attempts to establish an abbreviated research base for AI within education-centered literature, particularly as this piece illustrates the impact of community college and specific coursework that is used to provide learning opportunities for students studying the fundamentals of special education. Last, this document illustrates how AI may be used as an engaging component to special education coursework to improve the ways in which special education teacher-educators, i.e., research-practitioners who train and provide academic and professional development for special educators, design and develop coursework within settings of teaching and learning.

DOI: 10.4018/979-8-3693-5538-1.ch012

INTRODUCTION

Research on special education teacher education is limited, particularly on how community colleges fit into the work of developing novice or experienced special educators (Brownell et al., 2005). The clarity of the roles of what special educators must be most competent in and the training that must accompany the specific enactments that a special educator must be able to do within a classroom setting is imperative, yet research on the topic is seldom prioritized for within the field of educational research (Shepherd, 2016). While teacher preparation has gone through many variations throughout the years, especially since 2020 when the COVID-19 global pandemic rendered the work of teacher preparation impossible, particularly in face-to-face formats, there still is a need to codify practices, even the practice of field experiences within special education, that are being utilized for educators within the field of special education (Ali, 2023; O'Brien, 2024; Williams, 2023;).

Historically, educators have attempted to continue preparing teachers, especially special education practitioners; however, there has still been, for a myriad of reasons, an exodus, of sorts, of special educators from the K-12 field, leaving the high-quality, internal training opportunities for novice special educators in a state of disrepair in many local education agencies (Mason-Williams et al., 2021; Hester, Bridges, & Rollins, 2020). The limited research of special education teacher preparation may be attributed to many different ideas, including the ways in which professors, whose role in studying phenomena, are, also, leaving higher education spaces because budget cuts, salary freezes, and program eliminations (Faris, 2024). With that stated, there is still a great need to recruit, train, and develop educators, especially special educators, because the need of ensuring that students with disabilities are provided specially designed instruction is still a legal mandate within the United States of America (IDEA, 2004).

With the revelatory need of teacher preparation noted, as well as the forthcoming transparency of the human capitol crisis on both ends, i.e., educators who train special educators and special educators, themselves, it is salient to explore and evaluate new and emerging practices that honor the work of the past and ushers in the work of the future, especially as technological advances continue to advance and enhance the way we work with greater effectiveness and efficiency. While there have been some practical innovations in teacher preparation, this paper aims to add to the field of special education teacher preparation by suggesting an empowering way to embed artificial intelligence into the training process of special educators, both new and experienced (Cochran-Smith, et al., 2020; Blömeke, S., Nilsen & Scherer, 2021; Ellis, V., Steadman, S., & Mao, 2020).

Perhaps it is the hesitancy to work within a heuristic model of training teachers or simply an inability to approach preparation with a new, fresh, different approach, but the work of teacher preparation is still a vast landscape, filled with standards *and* opportunities for the newest generation of special educators and those still making remarkable gains for neurodivergent students. The field of special education, particularly now with so many shortages and in the face of inflation, must begin to embrace new and emerging forms of teacher preparation to engage newer generations of teachers and inspire more experienced special educators to continue their ongoing growth within the field (Darling-Hammond, DiNapoli Jr., Kini, 2023; Flores & Craig, 2023; Ingersoll & Tran, 2023).

While this paper has several foci, the primary focus of this paper is to demonstrate how an artificial intelligence may be used to create and engaging and responsive method to enrich current special education coursework practices. A secondary focus of this paper is to note that special education and its rich history must be honored by the work we do as reflective practitioners and researchers while, simultaneously, ensuring that remember the ways in which creativity and specialness brought us to the field of specialized instruction and how different special education and it's preparation methods must be from general education, even though there must be, because of lack of research centered on special education, certain connections that must be made through the research conducted for general education contexts. A tertiary focus of this work is to advocate for more opportunities wherein community colleges might be utilized to enhance and advance the field of special education teacher preparation, Finally, this paper offers additional considerations to ensure that the work of educating special educators is done in partnership with researchers, practitioners, and all stakeholders, including students with disabilities, to the comprehensive betterment of training, recruiting, retaining, and graduating more special educational professionals.

BACKGROUND

Landmark Cases that Shaped our Understandings

Within the United States, special education teacher preparation and training measures have drastically been transformed over the last 70 plus years, right around the same time that the first artificial neural network was developed, leading the way for computer systems to be modeled after the human brain and capable of making decisions based on data (Hill-Jackson & Lewis, 2023; Kumar & Thakur, 2012; McCray, 2023). Prior to inclusive classroom settings, children with disabilities were educated away from their typically aged peers. Because of the Civil Rights Movement, *Brown v. Board of Education of Topeka, Kansas*, and other special education landmark cases to ensure the rights of learners with disabilities, there have been major, positive shifts in teacher preparation, especially as teacher preparation programs have increase their use of current and emerging evidence-based practices and technologies (Ford et al., 2024; Ruppar, 2023; Skiba et al., 2008). Cases that brought together disability and disproportionality because of race and ethnicity became more and prevalent within the United States. For example, in *Hobson v. Hansen* (1967), it was determined that African American children were being placed in lower educational tracks in the Washington, DC, public schools (McNamara, 2023).

Additionally, cases ranging from *Diana v. Board of Education* (1970), a case that held assessments used to measure intelligence could not be linguistically biased, *PARC v. Commonwealth of Pennsylvania* (1972), a case that created the foundation of least restrictive environment, *Mills v. Board of Education of the District of Columbia* (1972), a case that ruled that children with disabilities could no longer be suspended, transferred, expelled, and reassigned without due process, and finally *Larry P. v. Riles* (1979) cases where African American students took culturally biased tests, which strengthened the mechanism for compensatory education and fairer assessments, and, much later of course, response to intervention (RTI), and multi-tiered systems of supports (MTSS). While all students were placed in public schools, the problem was that students from lower socioeconomic status or from minority groups were being discriminated against. Most of the tests used were normed on white, middle-class children, which discriminated against other racial groups (Birnbaum, 2006). To understand special education means that one understands, of course, evidence-based practices, intervention implementation, progress monitoring and some of the most critical components to teaching and learning within specialized instruction; while, at the same time, understanding culture and culturally respectful practices to ensure that some of our most vulnerable students are given the free and appropriate public educations that they all have a right to access.

Case after case, there are rulings that have attempted to address the issue of inappropriate special education placement because of race in specialized education settings. Arguably, it is difficult task to solely focus on the futuristic opportunities that technology, particularly artificial intelligence, can bring to teacher preparation, without mentioning how the litigious happenings of the past have impacted the field of special education as a whole, insisting that we teach both the historical challenges and the present opportunities of equipping special educators with the robust, comprehensive knowledge to do great work for students with disabilities. There is, now, an opportunity to meaningfully combine various cultures, disability/ability, technology, etc., together to vastly improve the ways in which we support students with disabilities across our nation's classroom settings through technology in a new and creative way.

Teacher Preparation within Special Education

One of the first teacher preparation programs in special education in the United States was situated in a residential facility and were erected by incredible foundational members of the special education community, including Laurent Clerc and Thomas Hopkins Gallaudet (Connor, 1976). This and other training programs like them were located at either special training schools within a clinical setting and served only a few types of disabilities, e.g. speech, hearing, and visual impairments, as well as mental retardation (noted as intellectual disability in current laws and literature) (Brownell et al., 2005). Teacher preparation programs shifted around the 1970s, and the rise of competency-based teacher education (CBTE) become more and more apparent within schools of education across the country, lessening the intimate knowledge that was once required to support students with specific disabilities to framing teacher preparation through generalities of understanding different skills, knowledge, and abilities within the practice to achieve and acquire specific competencies (Ghosh & Sankar, 2024; Rajesh & Joseph, 2023; Roth, 1977; Semmel & Semmel,1976).

Findings from Shortes, Cegelka, and Nelson (1973) illustrated an indication that, "[Teacher] competencies tended to be derived from 'expert' opinion rather than the direct observation of teacher behavior, that they often are not behaviorally stated or evaluated as to whether or not they have a positive impact on children performance, and that few teacher educators or researchers were, at the time, attempting to validate competencies empirical before including them in teacher education programs" (p. 192). CBTE has had its issues, particularly as some researchers have noted its often too mechanical reception, creating the environment for pre-service teachers being instructed in a broader, more generalizable method, creating overlaps that minimize and reduce the specialness from special education (Brownell et al., 2010; Hallahan & Kauffman, 1977).

Because of the lack of specificity in addressing specially designed instruction, the conflation of teacher education of special education and general education occurs, inopportunely creating teacher preparation programs for special educators that look too analogous to any typical preparation program of any content-area or student-centered approach (Goe, 2006). Additionally, even some alternative teacher certification programs, attempting to do the work that higher education institutions seemingly struggle with, are currently certifying teachers in a specific content area and, as an essential *add-on*, offering dual teaching certificates by simply taking a handful of classes on the topic of specialized instruction (CityTeachingAlliance). The case is clear: without a deepened and deliberate understanding of how-to best support students with disabilities and their teachers, there will be little-to-no significant gain in successful outcomes for students with disabilities (Blasey, Wang, and Blasely, 2023).

Now, more than ever, especially because of the many dismal outcomes for so many students with disabilities, there is more of a need to ensure that teacher educators specify and situate special education teacher preparation with students with disabilities at the center of learning the field in a more deeply focused way (Cole et al., 2023; Cooc, 2023; Kloos, Nacik, & Ward, 2023). Now, with the varying ways by which formal and informal teacher preparation is conducted, i.e., in-person, virtual, etc., the opportunity to ensure techniques and technologies are crafted with, first, students with disabilities in mind, is more imperative than ever before. Even informal methods whereby there is an underpinning of learners with disabilities have started to emerge like never before. For example, viral video models and speech and language supports can be widely accessed by educators of students with disabilities, even by Rachel Griffin Accurso, more widely known as Miss Rachel, an educator with two master's degrees in education and a passion to support her son, Thomas, who was diagnosed with speech delay (Calloway-Appleton, 2023). Ultimately, special education teacher educators must rethink what makes a quality special education teacher, and that process should be informed by the field's history and by the trends in policy, service delivery, and research that have shaped special education and teacher education practices (Brownell et al., 2010). Moreover, understanding the history of our work is salient, while, concurrently, ensuring that we are looking ahead at tools and strategies to ensure that researchers and practitioners are aware of emerging and new ideas to promote the work of specially designed instruction without conflating it with the supports that other students need and deserve.

Sindelar and colleagues (2010) found studies could be categorized into the following areas that aligned with research gaps within special education teacher preparation: (a) pedagogical strategies (i.e., specific approaches, such as coaching and action research that are used in initial preparation and PD opportunities to improve teacher knowledge, beliefs, and instruction); (b) technologies that could be used to deliver practice-based approaches; (c) fieldwork experiences offered in schools, communities, clinics, or tutoring programs; (d) program experiences (i.e., a set of courses and fieldwork experiences that are structured around a particular topic, such as inclusion); and (e) measurement of teacher knowledge, instructional practice, or beliefs. No studies, as shared by Sindelar et al. (2010), were identified that provided information about variables that might moderate or mediate the effectiveness of teacher education innovations or how to promote the collaborative learning of special and general education teachers in ways that would improve their ability to co-teach or work within multi-tiered systems of support (MTSS) (p. 29).

That study of nearly fifteen years ago, today, had a noticeable absence, of course, of one of today's leading opportunities to help create solutions to some of the research gaps noted—that solution being artificial intelligence within the work of special education teacher preparation. This observation leads readers to realize that there was an omission of how emerging technologies, beyond computer-aided instruction, of course, could help to provide stronger and richer outcomes for students with disabilities. Now, special educators and teacher preparers, can envision how artificial intelligence, another field of special education preparation that requires research and consideration, could be used to deliver practice-based approaches within specialized education, as well as the pedagogical strategies that can now be realized by AI tools.

In addition to the apparent gaps of research within special education, it must also be noted that there are significant redesigns happening in special education teacher preparation all the time because of new and emerging practices within the space of program evaluation to ultimately strengthen the delivery methods and experiences of special education teacher preparation. Goeke, Kossar, and Mitchem (2018) share that the Recognizing Effective Special Education Teachers (RESET), is one of many evaluative tools currently being implemented in the country, conceptually framing well-defined observations that incorporate clearly explicated criteria linked to evidence-based practices within special education, directing teacher's attention to implement instructional practices that have been demonstrated to result in improved outcomes for students with disabilities (SWD) (pgs. 155-156). Readers must understand that there is a balance happening within special education teacher preparation. While there are gaps that exist, there is still meaning, rich work happening to ensure that special educators are getting what they need in order to be the best special educators, particularly in the areas of history and content, for the students and families that they serve.

Byrd and Alexander (2020), in an investigation of the demonstration of special educators' content concluded:

That content area specialty does provide one type of expertise, there is much more to teaching than that knowledge. They share that, "We can all learn from each other the most effective methods of adapting the curriculum to meet the needs of all students. And finally, all of this can be done through effective communication that must be multi-directional (among all stakeholders, including administration). These issues can act as a springboard starting from the day a teacher candidate entered their program and continued throughout their careers. It is not necessarily asking for others to think outside the box; it is realizing that the box is bigger than previously considered by those involved in this endeavor. (p. 80).

This notion of the "box being bigger than previously considered helps readers to practitioners to understand that there is no myopic, one-size fits all to the education matters for students with disabilities or the ways in which to prepare their teachers (Bryd & Alexander, 2020). In fact, the *one-size-fits-all* method is contrary to specialized education and specially designed instruction. Allowing special educators and the professionals who teach them to continuously improve by incorporative effective methods to assist in the teaching and learning of students with disabilities is imperative for the success of field of special education.

Special Educational Technology and AI in the Literature

Technology has been noted as *the great equalizer* in education, and the benefit of technology has also been noted to allow students with disabilities being able to strategically solve many of the challenges faced by learners with disabilities (Schradie, 2020). For example, ". ... [Technology] can provide a voice to those students who may not otherwise have one per their disability (i.e., AAC devices), read a text to a student who struggles with reading as a result of his/her disability (i.e., text-to-speech devices, screen readers, and Reading Pens), grant access to a computer and other electronic tools (i.e., switches and speech recognition), and offer low-tech devices such as pencil grips or lined paper to aid students in writing (Bouck, 2010). Although never actually mentioning artificial intelligence, Edyburn, one of the most notable researchers in special education technology, shares:

Educators are often so focused on their day-to-day work that there is little time for considering the emerging trends and issues happening around us. Trend analysis is a basic technique futurists use in order to develop scenarios that are helpful in planning for the future. For those willing to take great risks, there is the potential for great reward. The special educational needs of individuals with disabilities require considerable effort and technologies to assist them in maximizing their potential. However, there are many secondary benefits to society when some specialized technologies (i.e., screen magnification, text to speech, and word prediction) are implemented as inclusive technologies, providing benefits for everyone. As a result, it is important to think about the needs of diverse individuals when planning for the future of education. (p. 291)

While this comment takes on both a hardware and software conceptualization of special education. It is clear that the emerging trends and issues happening around us, particularly in education, cannot be ignored and must be embraced if we are going to ensure that our educational systems, specifically or special education system, have the most well-prepared teachers for some of our most vulnerable populations.

Western Governors University provides insight into the different technology that has appeared in special education over the years. The following table is represented of the information shared:

Table 1. Western Governors University's Types, Definitions, and Examples of Technology

Type of Technology	Definition of Technology	Example of Technology
Assistive listening devices	Students with difficulties hearing or concentrating can benefit from the use of an assistive listening device. These are designed to make it easier for students to listen during class by amplifying sound.	FM systems and sound field systems use wireless transmitters to broadcast and amplify the teacher's voice. Whether an instructor must assist an individual student with special needs in an inclusive classroom or to amplify their voice in a classroom with poor acoustics, this technology can help dramatically.
Text-to-speech tools	Students with disabilities that impact their ability to read, such as visual impairments or dyslexia, can struggle in general education classrooms without the help of text-to-speech tools. By using assistive technology for reading, educators can improve classroom performance for these individuals.	There are many text-to-speech tools for educators available for both desktops and mobile devices. Using free applications and browser plug-ins, students with vision or reading impairments can save and hear educational content in an audio format.
Switch devices	Mobility impairments can make it hard for students with disabilities to engage with lessons in the same way as their peers. Switch devices allow these learners to engage with content with alternative input devices. There are switch devices designed to allow users to touch, blink, kick, or push and pull to interact with educational content and software.	Sip-and-puff (SNP) systems allow students with mobility impairments to interact with computers and mobile devices by sipping or puffing on a controller, effectively replacing a mouse or keyboard.
Proofreading technology	Students with disabilities that may impact their mobility, language comprehension, or ability to type can benefit from assistive proofreading technology. This is designed to either automatically fix common errors or to make grammatical suggestions.	Basic proofreading software can help learners write more efficiently, while more sophisticated solutions can identify student problem areas, then make advanced recommendations. This data can also help teachers determine where a student may require further instruction.

continued on following page

Table 1. Continued

Type of Technology	Definition of Technology	Example of Technology
Assistive technology for math	There are a wide range of devices and software options to help students with conditions that impact their ability to complete calculations. From basic arithmetic to calculus and beyond, there are assistive technologies for most subjects in math.	Calculators can help students solve simple and complex math problems. Some are designed with large buttons, which can help students with mobility or visual impairments. More advanced tools, like equation-solving software, can make suggestions to help students without directly giving them answers. Some even offer games that make teaching math easy and fun.
Augmented and virtual reality	Learners with disabilities who experience struggles focusing on projects or "tuning out" distractions can be aided through augmented or virtual reality software. The former can highlight key elements of a project and provide additional information or guidance, while the latter can provide a virtual environment in which external distractions can be reduced.	Examples of augmented and virtual reality applications for assistive learning include AR flashcards, AR-enabled worksheets, VR educational simulations, and VR collaboration software. Each of these can improve student engagement by drawing student interest and eliminating distractions.

Again, readers will notice that artificial intelligence is not actually named within the technology listed; however, it is clear that artificial intelligence absolutely has convergence in this work, as represented by AI tools that perform specific tasks presented. For example, Grammarly, one of the more widely known AI tools in this space, is used to perform the task of proofreading, along with other tools like Ginger Software, QuillBot, Slick Write, PaperRater, and countless other artificial intelligence tools.

Artificial intelligence has been used and referenced in several areas within general education. For example, Salas-Pilco, Xiao, and Hu (2022) share that artificial intelligence (AI) and learning analytics (LA) have been introduced in the field of education; they find: (a) there is a focus on studying the behaviors, perceptions, and digital competence of pre- and in-service teachers regarding the use of AI and LA in their teaching practices; (b) the main data sources are behavioral data, discourse data, and statistical data; (c) machine learning algorithms are employed in most of the studies; and (d) the ethical clearance is mentioned by few studies. The implications will be valuable for teachers and educational authorities, informing their decisions regarding the effective use of AI and LA technologies to support teacher education (p. 569).

These types of findings are salient to the field of education and, although they do not reference special education teacher preparation, readers may be able to approximate how the findings from the work of Salas-Pilco, Xiao, and Hu (2022) help to shape a clear vision by which teacher-educators might be able to shape the ways in which AI can be yielded.

Additionally, Sperling et al. (2024) illustrate how, although AI literacy is a globally emerging research field, specifically in business and computer science; however, there is an absence of AI literacy, as initially defined by Long and Magerko (2020), particularly as a professional knowledge base, within teacher education. This blatant omission of artificial intelligence within specialized instructional settings may widen the knowledge gap between what is known by emerging technologies within the field of human endeavor, e.g., AI, and how it might add a beneficial layer to the work of special education teacher preparation for years to come.

Globally, educational partners from the United Arab Emirates have addressed the role of artificial intelligence in teacher professional development, yet, unfortunately, the study is not centered on special education preparation. While the findings by Hashem Mahmoud Muslim al-Zyoud (2020) are helpful in understanding some intelligent applications that can be utilized within professionals development of teachers, the study does not provide a practical implication for special educators to see how AI might be able to complement the work of special educators within coursework, as well as an ability to provide the increased competencies to work within a dual capacity approach, engaging special educators with increased awareness and utility of emerging technologies, as well as providing special educators with practical tools to help increase productivity and support the challenging work of special education, as an entire specialized field. Additionally, Lameras and Arnab (2021) explore the role of teachers to be the subject matter experts to design, visualize, and orchestrate AI-enabled teaching and learning, which is an undoubted direction that education is moving towards, but not quite making its way to embedding AI within special education-teacher preparation (Ng et al., 2023).

Currently, most of the literature centers on learning about AI, not using it to enhance a specific capacity of knowledge within the content area of preparing special educators. In the following sections of this paper, readers will learn about the general composition of the community college space as an environment to provide training to educators through special education coursework, as well as a formal addressing of how artificial intelligence has been used within teacher preparation to enhance the practice and access of emerging technologies that may lead to increase engagement within student-candidates attempting to learn more about the pedagogical practices of specialized instruction. Waterfield, Watson, and Day (2024), share, "special education teachers can leverage AI platforms, tools, and other technologies to support general tasks in their day to day practice, lesson planning, content creation, and more" (p. 449). While some studies share the litany of tools that may be useful to special educators, there is no pedagogical framing by researchers, professors, or knowledgeable others within specialized education, supporting learners' knowledge and application.

Moreover, Morino et al. (2023) reveal, "[S]pecial education teacher preparation programs must reconsider how we prepare future teachers." When provided the prompt, "Given the future use of AI, what are some considerations for preparing future educators and special educators?" ChatGPT gave the following answer. None of the words in these seven considerations have been edited:

1. Equip educators and special educators with the knowledge and skills to understand and use AI in the classroom. This includes understanding the various types of AI, the ethical considerations, and the potential applications of AI.
2. Provide educators and special educators with the opportunity to explore how AI can be used to support personalized instruction and how AI can be used to identify student learning needs.
3. Educate educators and special educators on the implications of using AI in the classroom, such as potential privacy concerns, data security, and bias in AI systems.
4. Provide educators and special educators with resources on AI-based learning and assessment tools, and how to integrate them into their teaching and assessment practices.
5. Develop guidelines and protocols for the use of AI in the classroom and for the ethical use of AI by educators and special educators.
6. Educate educators and special educators on the potential risks of AI and the ways in which AI can be managed, monitored, and regulated.
7. Encourage educators and special educators to collaborate with experts in AI to ensure that AI is used to its fullest potential in the classroom. (p. 411)

While artificial intelligence shares the *what* of special education teacher preparation, there is still a prevalent need to identify and create the *how* of special education, essentially ensuring that reflective practitioners are given the opportunity to consider special education, first, when considering how to train teachers who will serve and support students with disabilities. One of the ways that can be done is through the possible flexibility that institutions of higher education, particularly at the community college level, can employ while educator future special educators. Because of the history of the comprehensive community as a nimble place that responds to the needs of its local community, there is an opportunity to ensure that community colleges take their place within the conversation of how to utilize AI to help support the production of special educators.

The Comprehensive Community College

As researchers examine the spaces wherein artificial intelligence may have the most exploratory, effective, and efficient opportunities to provide added instruction and education to the field, it is important to review the composition of community colleges. Since their inceptions, community colleges have been expected to serve several roles in American society (Kisker Cohen, & Brawer, 2023). As the entryway to college for groups of people who would otherwise have been excluded from higher education, community colleges often provide the first step on the road toward a baccalaureate degree and safe spaces that address the educational and civic needs of a wide array of local citizens; no other segment of postsecondary education has been more responsive to its community's workforce needs because at community colleges, students can learn at any point in their lives while taking advantage of low tuition, convenient campus locations, open admissions, and comprehensive course offerings (Kasper, 2003; Ives, 2006).

Community colleges are diverse spaces that, since their beginnings, have sought to find their identities in an ever-changing U.S. and address the changes that society and the world bring—both foreseen, such as changing demographics, and unforeseen, such as recessions and, of course, global pandemics, now, too (Bulman & Fairlie, 2022; Carales, 2020). Schools, including institutions of higher education like community colleges, are nested in providing comprehensive support to a diverse body of students. Given community colleges' open enrollment policies and their numerous instructional missions, students enter and re-enter with various and often multiple objectives but not always with clear knowledge of how to clarify and accomplish them; this makes successful completion in community colleges that much more difficult than other educational spaces (Lee et al., 2021; Hatch & Garcia, 2017).

Typically during times of financial uncertainty, community colleges often bore witness to large leaps in enrollment and completion; however, in the wake of the financial and health uncertainties created by Covid-19, that was not the case (Mountjoy, 2022). Historically, with low cost and ready-access, community colleges have been an opportunity for the marginalized to engage and enroll in higher education schools (Krebs, 1999; Soria Hargos, &Shenouda, 2023). Community colleges have, like any other educational constructs, not been without their problems, even with low-cost incentives that make these institutions favorable to so many, particularly in the area of student completion rates (Acton, 2021). Even with that noted, because of the flexibility that community college spaces offer, it makes the inclusion of AI within teacher preparation at this level of higher education a fertile and promising space to creatively envision how teacher preparation, particularly special education teacher preparation, might look in the near future.

Community Colleges as Places of Teacher Preparation

Over the years, community colleges have been a major source of providing credentials, through state education agency-approved coursework, for decades, and the ability for community colleges to provide essential training and technical assistances is evermore present, especially in the post-pandemic era (Garza-Mitchell, Geier, & Singleton, 2019; Kisker, C. B., Cohen, A. M., & Brawer, F. B, 2023). Garza-Mitchell, Geier, & Singleton share:

However, despite being providers of teacher education preparation, the history of serving students in urban and rural areas, both areas of high turnover, their commitment to serving underserved students, and their dedication to remediating students who may not initial qualify for teacher education programs at [traditional four year institutions], they are not considered valuable resources in their regard. In order for community colleges to successfully serve workforce needs, including teacher education, they must be included in national conversations about low-cost, high-quality options for preparing teachers. (p. 25)

Removing community colleges from the broader conversations of teacher preparation, which inevitably removes them, too, from conversations about methods of teacher preparation and innovative coursework compositions, has, historically, created an under-utilization of resources for the work of teacher preparation. Now that artificial intelligence has become more and more apparent with the field of education and other fields of human endeavor, as shared earlier in this work, community colleges are positioned to take advantage of the many ways that are possible to ensure a technologically advanced and engaging way to capture more students who have an interest in becoming educators to possibly improve the teacher shortage in the United States (K-12 Education). Admittedly, there is little information about special education teacher preparation within community college contexts, which underscores the salience of this chapter, especially as emerging technologies are being actualized and utilized.

For the sake of presenting a wide view of the possibility of wherein community colleges might strengthen their presence in the space of places of teacher preparation and the innovation that may exist within those spaces, this paper must present findings that demonstrate a strong understanding of this work. Park and colleagues (2018) researched community college teacher education baccalaureate programs, in innovative approach to ensure that the teacher shortage, billowing from the past 20 years, is creatively addressed. Unfortunately, Park et al., (2018):

Faced with declining numbers of students in teacher education programs, policymakers in many states are considering new actions that might increase teacher supply. One approach that has gained increasing popularity is community colleges beginning to offer 4-year degrees in teacher education. This study explores state adoption of these programs and its effect on the number and diversity of students earning bachelor's degrees in teacher education. Overall, we find no effect of these programs; however, in the limited case of a state with widespread use of community college baccalaureate (CCB) teacher education programs we find that degree production increased, yet the diversity of the graduates declined. (p.1)

This critical study demonstrates the underpinning of ensuring that degree attainment, particularly within teacher preparation, cannot be the sole focus of new and emerging work that happens within the space of education. A critical lens must be applied to recruitment and retention of community college students seeking to become teachers. Additionally, it must be noted that special education preparation was not mentioned in this article; however, readers might make inferences about the extension of the work to prepare general education teachers and how it dovetails with the work of preparing special educators, too. While the strategies mentioned, again, do not specify the work of preparing special educators but, rather, general educators, it must be noted that artificial intelligence was omitted, too, which leads to an additional mention about the relationship between retention and engagement, specifically noting how specific strategies may be employed to increase the ultimate output and outcomes of reinventing and reimaging what teacher preparation might look like for special educators in the future. Because this paper's primary aim is to consider the ways in which artificial intelligence tools might be utilized in the preparation of special educators, conceptualizing the work of teacher preparation more deeply than simply offering a degree, there must be, albeit, brief conversation about how some student see AI as a way to stay current and engaged with coursework material and classroom experiences.

Harvard University's Graduate School of Education conducted a study wherein they elicited student thinking in a survey, centering questions about artificial intelligence and its use within classroom settings. The Harvard Graduate School of Education shares:

Of the teens surveyed, many admitted to using AI to cheat on assignments, homework, or tests. But while academic integrity remains a concern for both adults and teens alike, many study participants highlighted positive academic experiences they've had with generative AI. AI was called "the modern approach to learning," while other teens surveyed pointed out that "not all kids use it to cheat in school. Reflecting insights heard from teens and young adults about their excitement for the future of generative AI, teens also wanted adults to know they can be trusted to, as one participant wrote, "use it in a good way," such as asking for help starting papers or to create an individualized learning plan. (p. 2)

Ladson-Billings (2007) notes that university teacher education programs are antiquated and barely existing in their failing attempts to recruit and graduate diverse teacher candidates. By ensuring that AI tools start to become more embedded into core course curricula, teacher educators might be able to reinvigorate the profession, especially the training that must occur within the work. Seemingly, many students want to stay on the cusp of what is current and we, as teacher preparers, must be willing to, at best, explore tools that may enhance our overall work of, in this case, preparing special educators in the most progressive and applicable ways possible, leveraging technologies, even if albeit heuristically imperfect. Regardless of the technology, of course, the knowledge and art of teaching students with disabilities is still paramount and must be done by an experienced practitioner who has the wherewithal to ensure that, technology is used as a tool to assist the learning process, not in sole replacement of deep, rich pedagogical methodologies.

Again, the primary focus of this paper is to demonstrate how AI tools and technologies might be used to train and develop students formally learning special education practices within coursework settings at a largely diverse community college in the Mid-Atlantic region within the United States of America. Within an introductory course to special education, students are asked to perform several tasks, i.e., research historical legal cases that contributed to special education precedents within the American legal systems, create a lesson plan with clear evidence-based practices to be utilized for students with disabilities, present findings about Individuals with Disabilities Education Improvement Act of 2004 categories, including possible student behavioral manifestations, and other major assignments (IDEA, 2004). This type of historical and pedagogical opportunity allows students to witness the past, present, and potential future of special education, while simultaneously creating and ideating supports for students with disabilities. Recently, a new, major assignment was added to the curricula for the course, which is illustrated in Figure 1 (see Appendix A).

Figure 1. Artificial Intelligence (AI) Gadget and Website Scavenger Hunt and Critique Assignment Cycle

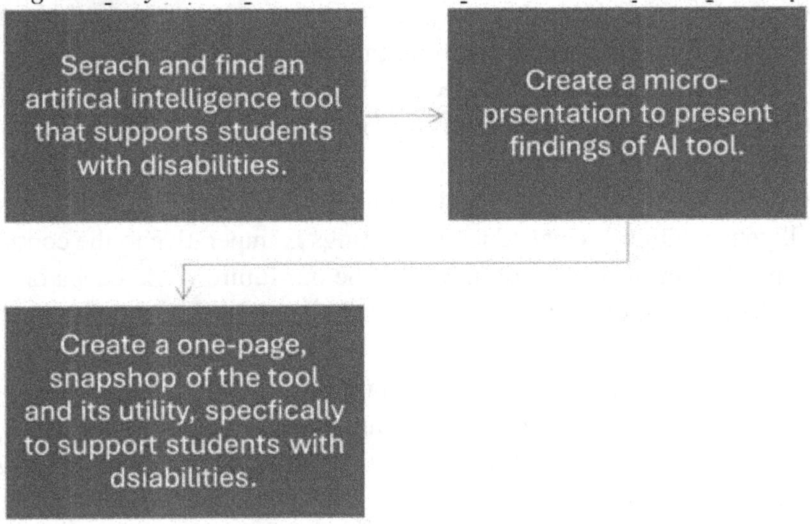

First, by allowing students to freely explore gives them a bound autonomy to increase their practices and skill set of being a research-investigator, a skill that will undoubtedly be helpful when they begin their careers as teachers of record (Zigmond & Kloo, 2017). This sense of autonomy underscores what empowerment theorists would note as being evidence when instructors can rely on the results of this paper due to its facilitation of the learning process in the classroom and beyond the brick-and-mortar system by leading students from behind. As mentioned by Joseph (2020), "If provided with ample opportunities for leadership on course assignments, students may become more empowered by learning their own way . . . [a] mastery of the empowerment theory would certainly prepare students for a better understanding of an avalanche of new . . . ideas in both clinical and non-clinical settings. (Joseph, 2020, p. 11-12). This helps researchers to understand allow the types of assignments within coursework allows the practicability of technology to come to the forefront of teaching and learning, particularly as a chance for practitioners to experiment and take calculated risks with the content, while keeping students with disabilities at the center of the work.

Additionally, ensuring that they are able to record and present their findings is an opportunity for students to get comfortable being the knowledgeable other within the context of finding and reporting on an AI tool that will be useful to them and their practices. At the conclusion of the assignment, the videos are shared through a cloud folder so students have a crowd-sourced, curated menu of AI tools that may be learned and used well beyond the conclusion of the course. From this assignment, students have been able to find AI tools that assist with text adaptation, social narratives, and a myriad of other evidence-based practices found within the rich instructional history of special education; this is just one of many ways by which teachers-educators might develop special educators abilities to utilize AI in their instructional practices, specifically to support students with disabilities and their families (Wallace & Abel, 2021).

Embedding meaningful assignments centered on discovering the utility of artificial intelligence within special education settings is imperative to the continuation of exposing students to what will inevitably be our future work–educators yoking the strength of technology, specifically artificial intelligences, so we might be able to facilitate deeper connections between the ways teachers are trained to work and support students with disabilities and their families, as well as connecting practical tools that students might be able to turnkey into the classroom setting, as they work with students with learning disabilities and difficulties. This type of AI assignment aligns well with the expected course outcomes, and, because of the intended outcomes of the assignment, aligns well with several standards found within the *Practice-Based Standards for the Preparation of Special Educators* (2022).

CONCLUSION

There is still quite a considerable amount of work to do to purposefully and meaningfully embed AI as tools within the work of preparing special educators to be practical and well prepared to meet the needs of the students they serve. By allowing AI to appear within the work of special education-teacher preparation, the professor, acting as the expert, can provide meaningful feedback, leading to additional discoveries for students based upon the work they have ultimately submitted (see Appendix B) to explore even more research and resources that may lead to even deeper connections (see Appendix C).

Moreover, teachers able to use emerging technologies coincides with the teacher empower model and teacher empowerment theory, ensuring that teachers are given agency and a voice in the decision-making processes that affect their work and their students with disabilities (Mokhlis & Abdullah, 2024; Short & Rinehart, 1992; Wu, 2024). For example, teachers are able to explore more tools that will inevitably support their students' learning, removing the barriers that some curricula may bring in the space of specialized instruction. This opportunity for teachers to, in an efficient and timely manner, create and implement artificial intelligence tools to enhance their students' utility of technology as a leveraging support is critical, and addresses several domains, i.e., self-efficacy, autonomy, decision-making, and impact, within the theoretical framework of empowerment (Yang et al., 2024).

Of course, more research and development are necessary for the ethical implications of allowing AI to support novice special educators, as well as the review and codification of useful tools done by experienced practitioners within and throughout special education. Additionally, it is necessary to begin ensuring that there is official guidance from an accrediting body within special education teacher preparation, as there may be some teacher preparation programs, specifically for special education teacher preparation, that may give additional accessibility and allowance to ensure that special education teacher preparation work occurs without potential barriers from internal controls found within some institutions of higher education, as well as teacher preparation programs that are incepted within and for local education agencies.

We know that it takes much more than a degree or coursework to become and effective special educator. We know that there is a functional relationship between the intervention and mentor knowledge as well as the ability to identify components of specialized instruction, and, most importantly, novice special educators improve their instructional practices after being mentored by those who received the professional development and specialized coaching (Cornelius, Rosenberg, & Sandmel, 2019). Beyond the work of institutions of higher education, High-quality, meaningful PD opportunities for teachers working in inclusive settings is critical to the continued success of children with disabilities (Francois, 2020). The future of curating meaningful experiences for those training to become special educators is dependent on the field to be able to coexist with artificial intelligence and so many other emerging technologies.

Finally, any effective shift within education systems or contexts requires real and thoughtful leadership—leaders who are willing subscribe to a critical and comprehensive theory of change (Fullan, 2007). Theory of change, a particular approach for making underlying assumptions in a change project explicit and using the desired outcomes of the project as a mechanism to guide project planning, implementation, and evaluation, involves single change initiatives, and is marked by choosing the right sources, i.e., literature, experts, and other elements curated by a carefully selected project team (Reinholz & Andrews, 2020). If community colleges become bold enough to thoughtfully adopt AI tools as an emerging technology in teacher preparation, local education agencies and schoolhouses must be in a position to rightfully receive the innovative teaching practices. Local education agencies and schools must continue working closely with community college and see them as partners in the work of providing the most effective practices for students with disabilities, beyond dual enrollment or middle college practices (Giani, Krawietz, Whittaker, 2023; Johnson et al., 2024). There must be a willingness shared between stakeholders, even parents of students with disabilities, to learn and understand how educational landscapes are increasingly shifting towards AI tools and technology. School administrators must have an expectation to see how coursework enhancements for the teachers who teach in their schools help and ultimately benefit learners with disabilities under their care. There must be a greater alignment and working relationship between those who teach special educators to enact innovative approaches in coursework at the collegiate level and those who supervise, observe, and review the performance of special educators within the classroom setting. With greater alignment between stakeholders

REFERENCES

Al-Zyoud, H. M. M. (2020). The role of artificial intelligence in teacher professional development. *Universal Journal of Educational Research*, 8(11B), 6263–6272. DOI: 10.13189/ujer.2020.082265

Ali, Z., Ahmad, N., Rehman, H. U., Ullah, N., & Zahra, T. (2023). Investigating Teacher Educators' Perceptions on Technology Integration in Teacher Preparation Programs. *Journal of Social Sciences Review*, 3(2), 341–355. DOI: 10.54183/jssr.v3i2.272

Birnbaum, B. W. (2006). *Foundations of special education leadership: Administration, assessment, placement and the law*. Edwin Mellen Press.

Blasey, J., Wang, C., & Blasey, R. (2023). Accommodation use and academic outcomes for college students with disabilities. *Psychological Reports*, 126(4), 1891–1909. DOI: 10.1177/00332941221078011 PMID: 35303777

Blömeke, S., Nilsen, T., & Scherer, R. (2021). School innovativeness is associated with enhanced teacher collaboration, innovative classroom practices, and job satisfaction. *Journal of Educational Psychology*, 113(8), 1645–1667. DOI: 10.1037/edu0000668

Bouck, E. C. (2010), "Chapter 6 Technology and students with disabilities: Does it solve all the problems", Obiakor, F.E., Bakken, J.P. and Rotatori, n.F. (Ed.) *Current Issues and Trends in Special Education: Research, Technology, and Teacher Preparation* (*Advances in Special Education, Vol. 20*), Emerald Group Publishing Limited, Leeds, pp. 91-104. https://doi-org.proxy1.library.jhu.edu/10.1108/S0270-4013(2010)0000020009

Brownell, M. T., Jones, N. D., Sohn, H., & Stark, K. (2020). Improving Teaching Quality for Students With Disabilities: Establishing a Warrant for Teacher Education Practice. *Teacher Education and Special Education*, 43(1), 28–44. DOI: 10.1177/0888406419880351

Brownell, M. T., Ross, D. D., Colón, E. P., & McCallum, C. L. (2005). Critical features of special education teacher preparation: A comparison with general teacher education. *The Journal of Special Education*, 38(4), 242–252. DOI: 10.1177/00224669050380040601

Brownell, M. T., Sindelar, P. T., Kiely, M. T., & Danielson, L. C. (2010). Special education teacher quality and preparation: Exposing foundations, constructing a new model. *Exceptional Children*, 76(3), 357–377. DOI: 10.1177/001440291007600307

Bulman, G., & Fairlie, R. (2022). The impact of COVID-19 on community college enrollment and student success: Evidence from California administrative data. *Education Finance and Policy*, 17(4), 745–764. DOI: 10.1162/edfp_a_00384

Byrd, D. R., & Alexander, M. (2020). Investigating special education teachers knowledge and skills: Preparing general teacher preparation for professional development. *Journal of Pedagogical Research*, 4(2), 72–82. DOI: 10.33902/JPR.2020059790

Calloway-Appleton, T. April 15, 2023, "Mom couldn't find a show tailored to her son's special needs—so she made her own!" Inspiremore.com https://www.inspiremore.com/ms-rachel-developmental-programming-for-kids/

Carales, V. D. (2020). Examining educational attainment outcomes: A focus on Latina/o community college students. *Community College Review*, 48(2), 195–219. DOI: 10.1177/0091552120903087

CityTeachingAlliance. (n.d.). The program. https://cityteachingalliance.org/the-program/

Cochran-Smith, M., Keefe, E. S., Carney, M. C., Sánchez, J. G., Olivo, M., & Smith, R. J. (2020). Teacher preparation at new graduate schools of education. *Teacher Education Quarterly*, 47(2), 8–37.

Cole, S. M., Murphy, H. R., Frisby, M. B., & Robinson, J. (2023). The relationship between special education placement and high school outcomes. *The Journal of Special Education*, 57(1), 13–23. DOI: 10.1177/00224669221097945

Connor, F. P. (1976). The past is prologue: Teacher preparation in special education. *Exceptional Children*, 42(7), 366–378. DOI: 10.1177/001440297604200702

Cooc, N. (2023). National trends in special education and academic outcomes for English learners with disabilities. *The Journal of Special Education*, 57(2), 106–117. DOI: 10.1177/00224669221147272

Cornelius, K. E., Rosenberg, M. S., & Sandmel, K. N. (2020). Examining the impact of professional development and coaching on mentoring of novice special educators. *Action in Teacher Education*, 42(3), 253–270. DOI: 10.1080/01626620.2019.1638847

Council for Exceptional Children. (2022). *Practice-based standards for the preparation of special educators*. Council for Exceptional Children.

Darling-Hammond, L., DiNapoli, M.Jr, & Kini, T. (2023). *The Federal Role in Ending Teacher Shortages*. Learning Policy Institute. DOI: 10.54300/649.892

Diana, V. (1970). State Board of Education. Civil Action No. C-70-37 (N. D. Cal. 1970)

Edyburn, D. L. (2023). Reimagining the Future of Special Education Technology. In *Reimagining Education: Studies and Stories for Effective Learning in an Evolving Digital Environment* (pp. 281–292). Springer International Publishing. DOI: 10.1007/978-3-031-25102-3_23

Ellis, V., Steadman, S., & Mao, Q. (2020). 'Come to a screeching halt': Can change in teacher education during the COVID-19 pandemic be seen as innovation? *European Journal of Teacher Education*, 43(4), 559–572. DOI: 10.1080/02619768.2020.1821186

Esposito, M. C., Hamdan, K., & Benitez, X. (2014), "Providing Effective Special Education Teachers in Low-Income Urban Settings: Implications for Educational Leadership", *Pathways to Excellence: Developing and Cultivating Leaders for the Classroom and Beyond* (*Advances in Educational Administration, Vol. 21*), Emerald Group Publishing Limited, Leeds, pp. 205-219.

Faris, D. (2024). Why are professors trying to escape their jobs? *The Week*. https://theweek.com/education/professors-leaving-academia

Flores, M. A., & Craig, C. J. (2023). Reimagining teacher education in light of the teacher shortage and the aftershock of COVID-19: Adjusting to a rapidly shifting world. *European Journal of Teacher Education*, 46(5), 772–788. DOI: 10.1080/02619768.2023.2294697

Floyd, D. L., & Walker, D. A. (2003). Community college teacher education: A typology, challenging issues, and state views. *Community College Journal of Research and Practice*, 27(8), 643–663. DOI: 10.1080/713838241

Ford, D. Y., Hines, E. M., Middleton, T. J., & Moore, J. L.III. (2024). Brown vs. Board of Education: Implications for Gifted and Talented Education. *Gifted Child Today*, 47(3), 216–220. DOI: 10.1177/10762175241242493

Francois, J. (2020) "Teaching Beliefs and Their Relationship to Professional Development in Special Education Teachers," Educational Considerations: Vol. 45: No. 3. DOI: 10.4148/0146-9282.2195

Fullan, M. (2007). Change theory as a force for school improvement. In *Intelligent leadership: Constructs for thinking education leaders* (pp. 27–39). Springer Netherlands. DOI: 10.1007/978-1-4020-6022-9_3

Garza-Mitchell. Geier, & Singleton. (2019). Community college teacher education: Fulfilling the workforce development mission for diverse geographies. In C. Lewis & M. D'Amico (Eds.), Community college teacher preparation for diverse geographies (pp. 15-32). Information Age Publishing, Inc.

Ghosh, S., & Sankar, C. S. (2024). Competency-Based Teacher Education in Gender and Inclusive Practices. *Social Science Journal for Advanced Research*, 4(5), 18–25.

Giani, M. S., Krawietz, C. E., & Whittaker, T. A. (2023). The Role of Student Beliefs in Dual-Enrollment Courses. *Research in Higher Education*, 64(8), 1113–1142. DOI: 10.1007/s11162-023-09740-z PMID: 37359447

Goe, L. (2006). *The teacher preparation teacher practices student outcomes relationship in special education: Missing links and next steps. A research synthesis.* National Comprehensive Center for Teacher Quality.

Goeke, J. L., Kossar, K. R., & Mitchem, K. J. (Eds.). (2018). *Redesigning special education teacher preparation : challenges and solutions / edited by Jennifer L. Goeke, Katherine J. Mitchem, and Kalie R. Kossar* (1st ed.). Routledge.

Hallahan, D. P., & Kauffman, J. M. (1977). Labels, categories, behaviors: ED, LD, and EMR reconsidered. *The Journal of Special Education*, 11(2), 139–149. DOI: 10.1177/002246697701100202

Han, X., Hu, L., Han, D., Peng, Y., Wang, Y., Yan, C., & Wang, Z. (2022). Research on the Application of Artificial Intelligence in Special Education. In *International Conference on Social Science, Education and Management*. Harvard University's Graduate School of Education.(nd). https://www.gse.harvard.edu/ideas/usable-knowledge/24/09/students-are-using-ai-already-heres-what-they-think-adults-should-know#:~:text=Many%20participants%20reported%20using%20AI,use%20it%20to%20write%20code

Hatch, D. K., & Garcia, C. E. (2017). Academic advising and the persistence intentions of community college students in their first weeks in college. *Review of Higher Education*, 40(3), 353–390. DOI: 10.1353/rhe.2017.0012

Hester, O. R., Bridges, S. A., & Rollins, L. H. (2020). 'Overworked and underappreciated': Special education teachers describe stress and attrition. *Teacher Development*, 24(3), 348–365. DOI: 10.1080/13664530.2020.1767189

Hill-Jackson, V., & Lewis, C. W. (Eds.). (2023). *Transforming teacher education: What went wrong with teacher training, and how we can fix it.* Taylor & Francis.

Hobson v. Hansen (1967) 269 F.Supp. 401; (1971) 327 F.Supp 844.

Ingersoll, R. M., & Tran, H. (2023). Teacher shortages and turnover in rural schools in the US: An organizational analysis. *Educational Administration Quarterly*, 59(2), 396–431. DOI: 10.1177/0013161X231159922

Johnson, J. M., Paris, J. H., Curci, J. D., & Horchos, S. (2024). Beyond college access: An exploration of the short-term impact of a dual enrollment program. *Journal of College Student Retention*, 26(1), 41–63. DOI: 10.1177/15210251211056319

Joseph, R. (2020). The theory of empowerment: A critical analysis with the theory evaluation scale. *Journal of Human Behavior in the Social Environment*, 30(2), 138–157. DOI: 10.1080/10911359.2019.1660294

K-12 Education : Education Should Assess Its Efforts to Address Teacher Shortages : Report to Congressional Committees / United States Government Accountability. Office. (2022). United States Government Accountability Office. Print

Kisker, C. B., Cohen, A. M., & Brawer, F. B. (2023). *The American community college*. John Wiley & Sons.

Kloos, E., Nacik, E., & Ward, C. (2023). Developing implementation capacity of a state education agency to improve outcomes for students with disabilities. *Journal of Disability Policy Studies*, 34(2), 127–136. DOI: 10.1177/10442073221096393

Kumar, K., & Thakur, G. S. M. (2012). Advanced applications of neural networks and artificial intelligence: A review. *International Journal of Information Technology and Computer Science*, 6(6), 57–68. https://doi-org.proxy1.library.jhu.edu/10.5815/ijitcs.2012.06.08. DOI: 10.5815/ijitcs.2012.06.08

Ladson-Billings, G. (2006). From the Achievement Gap to the Education Debt: Understanding Achievement in U.S. Schools. *Educational Researcher*, 35(7), 3–12. DOI: 10.3102/0013189X035007003

Lameras, P., & Arnab, S. (2021). Power to the teachers: An exploratory review on artificial intelligence in education. *Information (Basel)*, 13(1), 14–20. DOI: 10.3390/info13010014

Larry P. v. Riles is 495 F. Supp. 926 (N.D. Cal. 1979).

Lee, J., Solomon, M., Stead, T., Kwon, B., & Ganti, L. (2021). Impact of COVID-19 on the mental health of US college students. *BMC Psychology*, 9(1), 95–102. DOI: 10.1186/s40359-021-00598-3 PMID: 34103081

Long, D., & Magerko, B. (2020, April). What is AI literacy? Competencies and design considerations. In *Proceedings of the 2020 CHI Conference on Human Factors in Computing Systems* (pp. 1-16). DOI: 10.1145/3313831.3376727

Mackie, R., & Dunn, L. (1954). *College and university programs for the preparation of teachers of exceptional children*. U.S. Department of Health, Education, and Welfare, Office of Education.

Marino, M. T., Vasquez, E., Dieker, L., Basham, J., & Blackorby, J. (2023). The future of artificial intelligence in special education technology. *Journal of Special Education Technology*, 38(3), 404–416. DOI: 10.1177/01626434231165977

Mason-Williams, L., Bettini, E., Peyton, D., Harvey, A., Rosenberg, M., & Sindelar, P. T. (2020). Rethinking shortages in special education: Making good on the promise of an equal opportunity for students with disabilities. *Teacher Education and Special Education*, 43(1), 45–62. DOI: 10.1177/0888406419880352

McCray, E. D. (2023). *Handbook of research on special education teacher preparation.* E. Bettini, M. T. Brownell, J. McLeskey, & P. T. Sindelar (Eds.). Taylor & Francis Group. DOI: 10.4324/9781003297093

McNamara, K. (2023). "The Magic of Numbers is Strong": Hobson v Hansen and Contested Social Science in Judicial Decision Making. *Social Science History*, 47(4), 641–664. DOI: 10.1017/ssh.2023.16

Mills v. Board of Education of District of Columbia: 348 F. Supp. 866 (D.D.C. 1972)

Mokhlis, S., & Abdullah, A. H. (2024). Does teacher empowerment contribute to innovative work behaviour? *International Journal of Management Education*, 18(2), 147–172.

Mountjoy, J. (2022). Community colleges and upward mobility. *The American Economic Review*, 112(8), 2580–2630. DOI: 10.1257/aer.20181756

Ng, D. T. K., Lee, M., Tan, R. J. Y., Hu, X., Downie, J. S., & Chu, S. K. W. (2023). A review of AI teaching and learning from 2000 to 2020. *Education and Information Technologies*, 28(7), 8445–8501. DOI: 10.1007/s10639-022-11491-w

Ng, D. T. K., Leung, J. K. L., Chu, K. W. S., & Qiao, M. S. (2021). AI literacy: Definition, teaching, evaluation and ethical issues. *Proceedings of the Association for Information Science and Technology*, 58(1), 504–509. DOI: 10.1002/pra2.487

O'Brien, K. M., Nagro, S. A., Binkert, G. D., Szocik, K., & Gerry, M. (2024). Field experiences in special education teacher preparation: A review of the literature. *Teacher Education and Special Education*, 47(1), 5–25. DOI: 10.1177/08884064231177662

Obiakor, F. E., Bakken, J. P., & Rotatori, A. F. (2010). *Current issues and trends in special education.Research, technology, and teacher preparation / edited by Festus E. Obiakor, Jeffrey P. Bakken, Anthony F. Rotatori.* (1st ed.). Emerald.

Ochoa, S. H., Rivera, B., & Ford, L. (1997). An investigation of school psychology training pertaining to bilingual psycho-educational assessment of primarily Hispanic students: Twenty-five years after Diana v. California. *Journal of School Psychology*, 35(4), 329–349. DOI: 10.1016/S0022-4405(97)00009-5

Park, T. J., Tandberg, D. A., Shim, H. K., Hu, S., & Herrington, C. D. (2018). Community college teacher education baccalaureate programs: Early evidence yields mixed results. *Educational Policy*, 32(7), 1018–1040. DOI: 10.1177/0895904816682317

Pennsylvania Association for Retarded Citizens (PARC) v. Commonwealth of Pennsylvania (1972, 334 F. Supp. 1257 Rajesh, R., & Joseph, Z. C. (2023). Competency-based teacher education (CBTE): A training module to improve knowledge, attitude, and practices (KAP) of school teachers on learning disabilities in children. *Journal of Family Medicine and Primary Care, 12*(5), 874-880.

Reinholz, D. L., & Andrews, T. C. (2020). Change theory and theory of change: What's the difference anyway? *International Journal of STEM Education*, 7(1), 1–12. DOI: 10.1186/s40594-020-0202-3

Roth, R. A. (1977). How effective are CBTE programs? *Phi Delta Kappan*, 58(10), 757–760.

Ruppar, A., Kurth, J., Bubash, S., & Lockman Turner, E. (2023). A framework for preparing to teach students with extensive support needs in the 21st century. *Teacher Education and Special Education*, 46(1), 26–43. DOI: 10.1177/08884064211059853

Salas-Pilco, S. Z., Xiao, K., & Hu, X. (2022). Artificial intelligence and learning analytics in teacher education: A systematic review. *Education Sciences*, 12(8), 569. DOI: 10.3390/educsci12080569

Schradie, J. (2020). The great equalizer reproduces inequality: How the digital divide is a class power divide. In *Rethinking class and social difference* (Vol. 37, pp. 81–101). Emerald Publishing Limited. DOI: 10.1108/S0198-871920200000037005

Semmel, M. I., & Semmel, D. S. (1976). Competency-based teacher education: An overview. *Behavioral Disorders*, 1(2), 69–82. DOI: 10.1177/019874297600100205

Shepherd, K. G., Fowler, S., McCormick, J., Wilson, C. L., & Morgan, D. (2016). The search for role clarity: Challenges and implications for special education teacher preparation. *Teacher Education and Special Education*, 39(2), 83–97. DOI: 10.1177/0888406416637904

Shores, R. E., Cegelka, P. T., & Michael Nelson, C. (1973). Competency Based Special Education Teacher Training. [Web]. *Exceptional Children*, 40(3), 192–197. DOI: 10.1177/001440297304000305

Sindelar, P. T., Brownell, M. T., & Billingsley, B. (2010). Special education teacher education research: Current status and future directions. *Teacher Education and Special Education*, 33(1), 8–24. DOI: 10.1177/0888406409358593

Skiba, R. J., Simmons, A. B., Ritter, S., Gibb, A. C., Rausch, M. K., Cuadrado, J., & Chung, C. G. (2008). Achieving equity in special education: History, status, and current challenges. *Exceptional Children*, 74(3), 264–288. DOI: 10.1177/001440290807400301

Smith, P. S. (2024). (Re) presenting race: An analysis of special education textbooks for engagement with race and ethnicity. *Race, Ethnicity and Education*, •••, 1–22. DOI: 10.1080/13613324.2024.2306409

Soria, K. M., Horgos, B., & Shenouda, J. D. (2023). Disparities in college students' financial hardships during the COVID-19 pandemic. *Journal of Student Affairs Research and Practice*, 60(1), 31–48. DOI: 10.1080/19496591.2022.2046597

Sperling, K., Stenberg, C. J., McGrath, C., Åkerfeldt, A., Heintz, F., & Stenliden, L. (2024). In search of artificial intelligence (AI) literacy in teacher education: A scoping review. *Computers and Education Open*, 6, 100169. DOI: 10.1016/j.caeo.2024.100169

Wallace, B. C., & Abel, Y. (2021). Utilizing specially designed, instructional evidence-based practices and family engagement: Increasing African American student achievement in digital literacies. In *Connecting Disciplinary Literacy and Digital Storytelling in K-12 Education* (pp. 24–37). IGI Global. DOI: 10.4018/978-1-7998-5770-9.ch002

Waterfield, D. A., Watson, L., & Day, J. (2024). Applying Artificial Intelligence in Special Education: Exploring Availability and Functionality of AI Platforms for Special Educators. *Journal of Special Education Technology*, 39(3), 448–454. DOI: 10.1177/01626434241257237

Weiler, S. C., & Bauries, S. R. (2021). Special Education's Lessons for School Funding Litigation. *Education Law & Policy Review, 6*, 126. Westerns Governors University. Nd. *Special education: History, resources, and advice.*https://www.wgu.edu/blog/special-education-history-resources-advice2001.html

Williams, M. K., Christensen, R., McElroy, D., & Rutledge, D. (2023). Teacher self-efficacy in technology integration as a critical component in designing technology-infused teacher preparation programs. *Contemporary Issues in Technology & Teacher Education*, 23(1), 228–259.

Wu, P. (2024). The Influence of Holistic Leadership of Administrators on Teachers Empowerment Program. *Journal of Education and Educational Research*, 7(2), 71–78. DOI: 10.54097/qcdv1t54

Yang, C., Rho, E., Lin, X., & Stomski, M. (2024). Empowerment and Silence: A Grounded Theory Exploration Among New Teachers. *School Psychology*, 39(3), 291–301. DOI: 10.1037/spq0000612 PMID: 38095960

Zigmond, N. P., & Kloo, A. (2017). General and special education are (and should be) different. In *Handbook of special education* (pp. 249–261). Routledge. DOI: 10.4324/9781315517698-21

APPENDIX

Assignment Details for the AI Gadget and Website Scavenger Hunt and Critique

AI Gadget and Website Scavenger Hunt and Critique

For this assignment, you need to select an AI tool from the following webpage: https://www.futurepedia.io/

The AI tool you select must clearly demonstrate its usefulness for students with disabilities, families, and/or school staff members whose sole focus is to support students with disabilities. This should be a resource that is user-friendly and helpful—something you will be able to take into your school as a teacher and utilize, and preferably free or low-cost.

You will present your findings to the class in a micro-presentation (no more than 3-5 minutes). You can record yourself on whatever device is easiest for you to use, i.e., Zoom, etc. In the past, students have recorded a screen-share and talked about the site; however, there is no one right way to do this assignment.

Note: *Presentations should include a one-pager. A one-pager provides an overview of the topic, a summary of the most salient points, important facts, and other relevant information related to the topic.*

Chapter 13
Exploring AI in Special Education With a Qualitative Study:
AI and Special Education Preservice Teachers

Jennifer Gallup
https://orcid.org/0000-0001-5057-6452
Idaho State University, USA

Dianne Chambers
https://orcid.org/0000-0002-3852-6425
Hiroshima University, Japan

Celal Perihan
Idaho State University, USA

Tiffany Crotteau
Idaho State University, USA

ABSTRACT

The integration of artificial intelligence (AI) technology into special education teacher preparation programs represents a transformative approach to addressing the complex needs of diverse learners. By leveraging AI, teachers can enhance pedagogical competencies, foster inclusive classroom environments, and optimize instructional practices tailored to individual student needs. Furthermore, using AI in special education promotes innovation, efficiency, and effectiveness. This chapter presents initial findings from preservice special education teachers regarding their

DOI: 10.4018/979-8-3693-5538-1.ch013

experiences learning to use AI technologies in the context of supporting students with disabilities through 1) effective lesson plan development, 2) implementation of evidence-based practices, and 3) identifying ways that AI can support their individual challenges.

INTRODUCTION

Overview of Generative AI in Education

The integration of Generative Artificial Intelligence (AI) technology into special education (SE) teacher preparation programs represents a transformative approach to addressing the complex needs of diverse learners. There is a critical shortage of Special Educators which leads to substandard outcomes due to high caseload numbers, lack of time to create individual content based on learner needs, and limited time to provide intervention for students with disabilities (SWD) (Hester et al., 2020; Peyton et al., 2021). Artificial Intelligence (AI) holds the potential to address these challenges by offering personalized learning experiences, data-driven insights, and advanced support tools to maximize integration of evidence-based-practices (EBP) to improve behavior and academic outcomes for children with more complex disabilities (e.g., intellectual disability, autism, down syndrome). Therefore, it is essential to explore how to integrate AI into Special Education teacher preparation while addressing intervention, outcomes, and collaboration with peers through effective lesson plans. The purpose of this chapter is to present initial findings from the perceptions of pre-service special education teachers (PSET) regarding their experiences learning to use artificial intelligence technologies in the context of lesson plan development and intervention.

Definition of Generative AI and Historical Context of AI in Special Education

AI has been an active topic of research for more than 50 years (Holmes, 2020) Some of the most typical AI applications in education involve knowledge representation, intelligent tutoring, natural language processing, autonomous agents etc… (Vincent-Lancrin & van der Vlies., 2020; Wu et al. 2006). The benefits of AI techniques have been gradually used to improve the life of those people with special needs (Hopcan et al., 2023). For example, AI has helped address computer-based speech therapy (Schipor et al. 2010), self-assessment through a neural network (Pavlopoulos et al. 2008), second-language learning (Drigas, 2008), early intervention for children with Autism (Rapin & Tuchman, 2008), emotional recognition instruction (Sebe et al. 2006), social skills instruction (Riedl et al. 2007) and with the diagnostics for Learning Disabilities identification (Hernandez, et al. 2009). AI techniques have also been identified as one of the most potentially valuable applications in the field of SE (Sharma et al., 2023). The goal of AI tools is to enhance the way children interact with their environment to promote learning and to enrich their daily life.

Importance and Relevance of AI in Special Education

Intervention strategies need to be highly individualized to be effective if they are to provide equitable access and level the playing field (Drigas, et al. 2023). AI training interventions are an important part of the education for children with SE needs since they can integrate the freedom of action of the student with a more explicit control and guide. By leveraging AI-driven simulations, lesson plans, and student interaction and learning, teacher preparation programs can enhance pedagogical competencies, foster inclusive classroom environments, and optimize instructional practices tailored to individual student needs. Furthermore, using AI in SE promotes innovation, efficiency, and effectiveness by addressing the unique challenges encountered in today's public schools and inclusive educational settings.

To initially address how to best incorporate AI into classrooms it is essential to train PSET how to effectively integrate AI into lesson planning, delivery, and more importantly student use to augment their content acquisition and enhance their outcomes.

Definition and Importance of Evidence-Based Practices (EBP)

Evidence-based practices refer to classroom practices that are "supported by multiple, high-quality studies that utilize research designs from which causality can be inferred and that demonstrate meaningful effects on student outcomes" (Vanderbilt University, 2023, para. 1). Data and evidence are required to show that a specific practice or strategy is effective. EBP differ from commonly used practices or best practices, which may not have appropriate evidence for their efficacy, but have 'always been used' in the classroom (Curtin, 2023). Teachers will often use practices that they have seen other teachers use while they were in training, or that were used with them when they were at school, which may or may not be evidence-based. Sometimes the strategies may be popular or trending but may not have sufficient empirical evidence behind them at this time, although may at a later stage.

Ongoing concerns around locating information on EBP and implementing the practices with fidelity have been identified (Cook & Odom, 2013). Cook and Odom (2013) suggest that the emphasis on EBP is justified and necessary in special education, particularly in producing more positive outcomes for students with disabilities. Additional tools are available to assist educators with accessing information on EBP and selecting appropriate practices for their students with a number of resources available. Resources include the *What Works Clearinghouse* (Institute of Education Sciences, n.d.) which provides educators with information on the levels of evidence for EBP and specific EBP that can be used in the classroom. The Council for Exceptional Children (2014) provides standards for categorizing the evidence base of practices in special education, but stresses that these should only be used by those who are experienced in educational research design and methods. Cooper et al. (2019) comment on a debate between implementing a practice with complete fidelity and having sufficient flexibility to accommodate a range of differing needs. They suggested that practitioner expertise can be useful in determining appropriate practices which suit individuals, particularly as no one practice will work for every student (Cook & Odom, 2013).

The use of evidence-based practice promotes continuous improvement for educators, as research is constantly refining EBP and identifying new practices for the classroom (Hume, et. Carefully chosen evidence-based practices are vital for improving student outcomes in special education (Garrad et al., 2022). Using practices that are known to improve outcomes for students with disabilities can save time, by removing the need for a trial-and-error approach, and funding, as only appropriate programs and resources need to be purchased. Most importantly they allow students with disabilities to feel engaged and empowered to learn. Engagement leads to better learning outcomes, which leads to further opportunities for school graduation and eventual employment and independence for students with disabilities. To ensure sound outcomes, educators need to have a deep understanding of their students with a disability so they can make clear, informed choices about the practices that they employ. They also need to be able to implement the practices, not just with fidelity to the practice, but also in accordance with the overall goals for the student and the class program (Hume et al., 2021). It is important that training in EBPs equip novice educators with the skills to select and implement EBP effectively, so that the next generation of special educators will feel committed and have sufficient capacity to use these practices (Lutkins et al., 2023).

AI in Developing Evidence-Based Practices

Schools and classrooms are complex environments and large amounts of information, particularly qualitative data, are often produced regarding the efficacy of a specific practice. This data is not necessarily analyzed in a timely or effective manner; therefore, AI offers opportunities to assist educators in analyzing data to determine the efficacy of a practice, including providing insights and recommendations (Google, n.d.). AI can assist in many ways, including with data collection, particularly with integrating from a variety of sources, and preparation of data for analysis. The teacher is still required to be a part of the analysis, as this often requires critical thinking skills and input into the process. One form of AI data analysis is natural language processing (NLP), which uses unstructured text data to provide insights (Luzmo, 2023). Other forms include machine learning, extracting patterns from large amounts of data, and deep learning, using neural networks.

In addition to displaying the data, AI, such as ChatGPT, can help with a visual representation of the data (see Figure 1 for an example using simple behavioral data) and a simple analysis of the data. For busy educators this process can be quite time consuming, especially with multiple students in the classroom having varying needs. When compared with a few seconds of processing by an AI, the benefits seem obvious.

Additionally, if further prompts are provided (i.e., What does this data mean?), the AI tool will also provide potential reasons (insights) and suggestions for future practice. Figure 2 displays the insights and suggestions for the behavioral data which appear to be very appropriate given the data provided. While this is a rather simple example, it is an illustration of how AI may be used in the classroom. The insights provided may include novel considerations that a teacher had not considered, or additional depth regarding a situation. When developing evidence-based practices, AI can support the researcher and teacher by providing access to aggregated data rapidly and assisting with analysis and interpretation of the data (Vincent-Lancrin & van der Vlies, 2020).

Figure 1. Example of ChatGPT Visualization and Analysis of Behavioral Data>

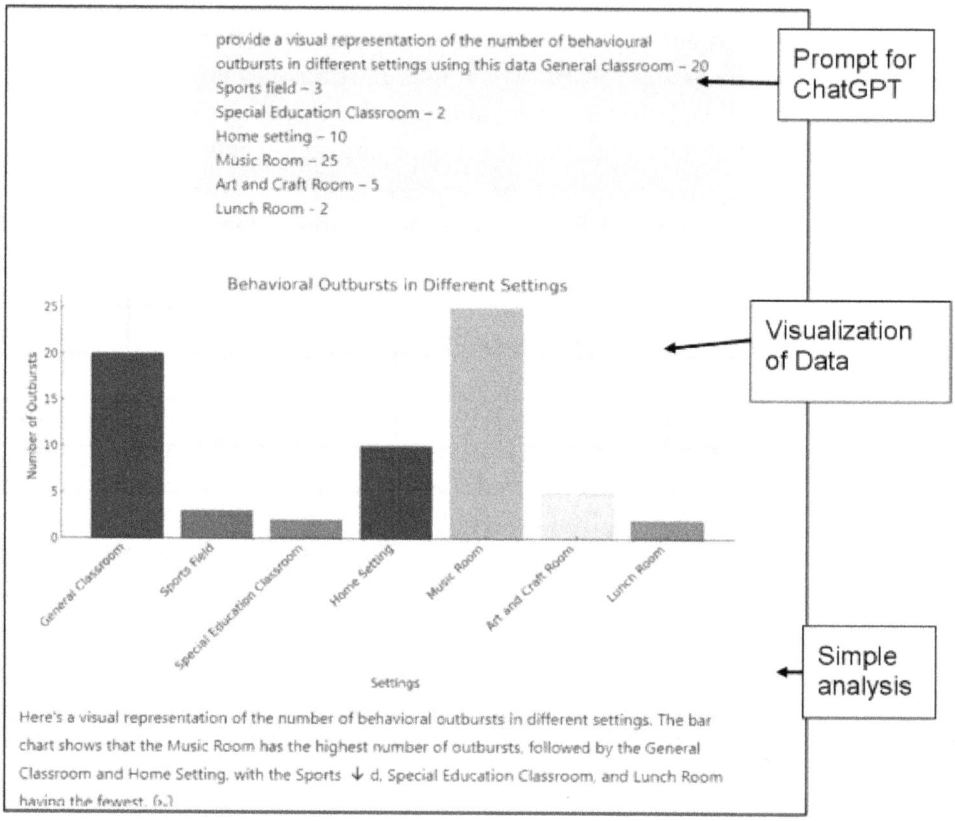

Figure 2. Example of ChatGPT Interpretation of the Data

The data represents the number of behavioral outbursts observed in different settings. Here is an interpretation of what each number indicates:

1. **General Classroom – 20**: There were 20 behavioral outbursts observed in the general classroom. This could suggest that this setting is a common place for students to experience behavioral challenges, possibly due to the structured nature and academic demands of the environment.
2. **Sports Field – 3**: Only 3 outbursts occurred on the sports field. This might indicate that students are generally more engaged and less likely to exhibit behavioral issues during physical activities or it could be due to the more informal and dynamic nature of this setting.
3. **Special Education Classroom – 2**: There were 2 outbursts in the special education classroom. This low number may suggest that the environment and support provided in this setting are effective in managing and preventing behavioral issues.
4. **Home Setting – 10**: In the home setting, there were 10 outbursts. This could reflect a variety of factors, such as the different expectations and routines at home compared to school or the lack of immediate support from educators and peers.
5. **Music Room – 25**: The highest number of outbursts, 25, occurred in the music room. This could indicate that the music room environment, activities, or specific interactions in this setting are particularly challenging for students, possibly due to sensory overload, group dynamics, or performance anxiety.
6. **Art and Craft Room – 5**: The art and craft room saw 5 outbursts. This might suggest that while some students may find this setting relaxing and expressive, others may struggle with the activities or materials used.
7. **Lunch Room - 2**: There were 2 outbursts in the lunch room. This low number could indicate that students generally find this unstructured time less stressful, or it could reflect effective supervision and social interactions during lunch.

In summary, the data highlights where behavioral issues are more likely to occur, which can help educators, parents, and support staff identify and address specific challenges in these settings. The high number of outbursts in the music room and general classroom suggests a need for targeted interventions in these areas.

The Role of AI in Lesson Planning

The role of AI in lesson planning can be transformative, offering numerous benefits that can enhance the teaching and learning experience. AI can be utilized in lesson planning to maximize inclusion by meeting the needs of unique learners by analyzing student data and generating individualized plans that cater to specific needs (Robert, et al. 2024). Moreover, extensive data analysis can take hours if not days, AI can analyze robust data sets quickly and efficiently. Moreover, in the context of lesson delivery, AI can provide immediate feedback to the students as they search for content, support active participation for those students who need additional support, and enhance collaborative learning (Kuprenko, 2020). Personalized learning is essential for all students, not just those with a disability. Students with disabilities may need more support, more differentiation, and guidance than their typical peers; however, these options and supports may provide better learning experiences for those without disabilities which in turn may increase engagement and decrease behavioral challenges. AI can analyze student data and identify individual learning styles, strengths, and weaknesses and generate content that is appropriately challenging for each student. Content generated can be interactive and engaging learning activities, such as quizzes, games, and simulations, which can be integrated into lesson plans. Moreover, AI can provide instant feedback to students during lessons, helping them understand concepts more quickly and accurately. AI in lesson planning offers significant potential to enhance educational practices by making them more personalized, efficient, and data-driven. By leveraging AI, teachers can create more effective lesson plans, better engage students, and ultimately improve learning outcomes (Kuprenko, 2020). As AI continues to evolve, its integration into lesson planning is likely to become even more sophisticated, further transforming the educational landscape.

Potential Challenges with University-Wide Acceptance

The lack of consistency in university approval may cause varied implementation and practices for teacher preparation programs, which may affect possible outcomes. The presence of AI is rapidly permeating many aspects of our daily functioning and with that there is an increase of AI used in academic settings. However, the integration and use of AI remains controversial among many institutions of higher education (IHE) and K-12 schools due to the abundance of unknowns, potential bias, and negative perceptions. The lack of consistency in regard to integration, acceptance, policy and impacts is beyond the scope of this chapter; however, it is important to note potential challenges related to adoption of AI which may lead to inconsistencies and may create challenges for educators in terms of training, curriculum design, and assessment. A unified guideline for inclusion of AI ensures that all teacher candidates receive a standardized level of training in AI. The training would equip them with the necessary skills to effectively integrate AI tools into their teaching practices. Consistency helps prevent disparities in teacher readiness across different programs within the university. Moreover, collaborative integration and training across IHE's nationally could promote equal access to AI tools and resources for all teacher candidates, regardless of the IHE they attend. This research is an initial step in developing the foundation to better understand how to integrate AI, the acceptance, and potential uses for K-12; thus, a qualitative study was conducted with preservice teachers who used AI to create lesson plans.

Purpose

The purpose of this research is to explore and elucidate the critical role of Artificial Intelligence (AI) in the preparation of special education teachers, drawing upon firsthand insights and experiences from educators preparing to teach special education. By examining the integration of AI technologies in teacher training programs, this chapter aims to highlight the transformative potential of AI in enhancing instructional practices, supporting diverse learner needs, and equipping future special education teachers with the necessary skills and knowledge to effectively leverage AI in their professional practice. Through a combination of qualitative data, including interviews and group interviews we will address the following research questions with the intent of providing a comprehensive review of challenges, uses, and practices related to AI use in special education teacher preparation programs.

1. What are pre-service special education teachers' perceptions of AI technologies in supporting diverse learners?
2. What are the challenges and benefits that special education teachers encounter when learning to use AI tools?
3. How do pre-service special education teachers perceive the impact of AI on their instructional practices and student outcomes?

Class Group Exploration of AI

A group of special education teachers were introduced to the concept of using AI as part of their lesson plan development, homework completion, and intervention development for children with disabilities. A designing instruction course was specifically designed with the purpose of introducing PSET to AI for lesson plan development, homework completion, and for their interventions explored and delivered to SWD. Students were asked to work in groups of four to create a final webpage that could be used to share their knowledge about what they learned, how they used AI, and how they plan to use AI in their future classrooms.

Methodology:

After obtaining permission from the Institutional Review Board, participants were identified through inclusionary criteria, then data were collected via interviews and observations. Next, data were coded using Moustakas' modified Van Kaam method (Moustakas, 1994). Finally, coded data were put into themes and validated between researchers. The researcher collected a large amount of data from a limited number of respondents which met saturation.

Participants:

Purposeful sampling of special education teachers currently enrolled in a teacher preparation program at Idaho State University participated in a semester-long course that focused on the effective integration and use of AI into lesson planning, instruction, and intervention. Fifteen participants were included. Students that were traditional-aged and non-traditional aged students were in the group. The class was composed of all females. Each participant was in their third year out of a four-year teacher-preparation program. All students were majoring in special education and elementary education. Participants were required to take the course titled *Designing Instruction*. Participants did not have to complete the focus groups for the research and were informed that participation was voluntary and would not impact their final grade. Three of the participants were non-traditional students who had returned to obtain a university degree after they had a former career, raised young children, and were married. These participants had to manage the demands of older children, their home life, and university requirements. Two participants were attending university on athletic scholarships and were full time students who had to balance the demands of continuous training and practice for their athletic scholarship requirements. The remaining ten participants were traditional college students in their early 20's both living on and off campus and working part time.

Data Collection:

Data were collected through focus groups and one-on-one interviews with participants to allow for in-depth exploration of their perceptions and experiences with AI in the special education *Designing Instruction* class. Open-ended semi-structured questions were used to encourage participants to share their thoughts, feelings, and experiences freely. Interviews were conducted over Zoom, recorded with participants' consent, and transcribed verbatim for analysis. The researchers collected a large amount of data from a limited number of respondents which met saturation.

Data Analysis:

Thematic analysis was conducted by analyzing the transcripts to identify recurring themes, patterns, and insights related to special education teachers' perceptions of AI. Initially all expressions relevant to the experience were listed to ensure no potential bias or meanings were overlooked. Next reduction and elimination was conducted to eliminate irrelevant, repetitive, or overlapping expressions to determine the invariant constituents, core themes that were necessary and sufficient to understand the shared experiences. To establish trustworthiness and rigor member checks were conducted by having transcriptions reviewed by 30% of focus group participants and 100% of the interview participants to ensure accuracy and an opportunity to clarify or provide additional insights.

Descriptive codes were given to each constituent. Similar constituents were merged or new labels given to more accurately reflect the specific experiences with AI in a Special Education Class. Labels used were verified against each participant's transcript to check for accuracy and relevancy. This process produced a total of 27 initial codes that reflected the experiences of PSET and AI. After identifying invariant constituents and generating labels for each line of text, an external check by an outside source was used to review decisions about codes and groupings. Initial coding was used to organize data into categories and subcategories based on commonalities and differences. Initial codes were identified by unpacking the language used and linking ideas presented back to the research question and literature. Codes were combined to generate themes and subthemes that encapsulate the range of experiences, perspectives, and interactions with AI by participants by closely related literature. Codes were then combined to develop themes by reviewing the closely related literature. The identified codes (see Table 1) were combined to form final themes in the research (see Table 2).

Initial Codes

Identify Evidence Based Practice
Differentiation Options/Given
Broaden Understanding of a Topic
Support Cognitive Load/Executive functions
Test Preparation
Enhance Individual Work/Thinking
Learning AI
Know Your Content/Have a Foundation
Barriers to AI
Improve Comprehension
Remove Barriers to Teaching
Remove Barriers for Student (K-12)
Remove Personal Barriers
Identify Evidence-based Practices
Differentiation/Options Provided
Save Time in the Classroom
Identify Barriers for Specific Disabilities related to Lesson Planning and Instruction
Develop Outlines for Lesson Plans/Assignment/University Level Support

Collaboration without Barriers and when Peers and Colleagues are not available
Teach Students to find their own Supports/EBP
Build Confidence
Dyslexia/Reading Disability Support

Themes Developed from Initial Codes

- Learning to use AI and Identifying Barriers
- Maximize teaching, student interaction, and learning with enhanced lessons and reduced time lesson planning
- Leveling the Playing Field with AI
- Utility of AI, Support, Instructional, and Assistive Technology Tool
- Theme 5: Mental Health Supports

THEMES DISCUSSED

Theme 1: Learning to use AI and Identifying Barriers

Learning to use AI is much like learning anything else. Technology affects teaching and learning across the board and is an integral part of modern human existence. The process of learning AI involves a structured process which includes understanding the theoretical foundations that includes AI as a tool to mimic human intelligence. Through the process of learning to use AI by gaining practical knowledge, experience, and application to real-world problems, AI becomes a tool to help improve the efficiency of teaching and learning (Thongprasit & Wannapiroon, 2022). All participants (100%) described their process of learning AI by building on their current knowledge, expanding their ideas related to specific constructs presented, and experimenting with language used to generate desired content. Overall, 19% of the coded lines were dedicated to the process of learning an intelligent platform through trial and error and application to their current class and assignments. One student described learning to be specific with the AI platform. The student 'T.C.' stated:

"If you are vague, AI is going to give back vague information and then if you ask it to delve more into the topic it might not be exactly what you were looking for. This process helped me understand that I did not have a strong understanding of the concept I was trying to research because I did not get content related to the topic, I put in. It wasn't until I put in more specific information that the AI then could elaborate and help me." - Student 'T.C.'

Furthermore, the students discussed challenges with feeling like they were cheating because all but two professors in their program had banned ChatGPT and other AI due to the potential of misconduct, cheating, and missing out on learning opportunities. The potential of cheating and misconduct has been discussed and the disruption to higher education (Sullivan & Kelly, 2023). While Eager and Brunton (2023) encourage the use of AI and opportunities presented through AI to enhance learning and outcomes rather than worry about the negative effects that cannot be readily controlled. Moreover, Kooli (2023) described the need to embrace AI into the educational domain with the perspective that they are incorporated as an opportunity for progress. Students in the focus group echoed the statements, student "N" stated:

"I was afraid of cheating but AI helped me and when my professor asked me about my use of AI based on the improvement in my writing, I was sincere. I helped her understand that I went on this [ChatGPT] on my own and that the idea was my own idea. But then I explained how I used the ChatGPT to help with the correct dialect grammar to be submitted to her."

Multiple students described that they had to understand the content and have a familiarity with the constructs they were researching to ensure that the content produced by AI was correct; moreover, they described putting the work into their own words. "I know that some people are scared but they should just try it and don't copy and paste and kind of put your own words into it and make it personal." Student K.H. Researchers demonstrate that when using AI tools such as ChatGPT for generating educational content, 'prompt engineering' is critical. Prompt engineering is the art and science of using language inputs [typed or written] into AI models to receive the output. Prompt engineering emphasizes the importance of students knowing their content or having enough knowledge to accurately input information to yield information that is beneficial.

Learning to use AI is an ongoing process as the system learns the users' preferences and content searched output changes, thus continuously gaining practical experience, exploring advanced topics, and updating knowledge through projects, research, and networking is essential. Ultimately, AI is ubiquitous, and has the potential to permeate all aspects of our life which augments the need to effectively learn how to use AI and apply it to solve real-world problems.

Theme 2: Maximize Teaching, Student Interaction, and Learning with Enhanced Lessons and Reduced Time Lesson Planning

An overwhelming 36% of all coded lines were dedicated to the use of AI and the potential it has for supporting instructional practices, learning styles, and reducing and eliminating barriers to learning for students. An intelligent learning platform refers to a learning system designed to create intelligence by focusing on human-computer interaction. The AI was described to help to improve the efficiency of lesson plan development, differentiation, and implementation. For example, one student K.H. stated: "When I put in my lesson subject [for example a lesson on the water cycle] and the grade level AI generated a standards-based lesson when I typed '*give me an Idaho standard that fit's* this [water cycle]" The student further described verifying the content generated by using their background knowledge and awareness of the subject matter. Another student discussed the strategies presented by AI in regard to meeting the needs of individual students: "This [lesson plan] will fit the needs of the specific student better with the differentiation options presented than this one [teacher developed support]. Differentiation has been a long-standing topic of discussion in regards to meeting unique student needs and described as the best way to maximize student learning and support inclusion (Suppan, 2006). Tailored instruction that considers individual learning styles and needs can help students with disabilities achieve better academic outcomes and improve their overall school experience (Gibson, 2013). All of the participants in the class discussed the array of options that were provided throughout the lesson to help meet the individual needs of students. Additionally, they discussed the benefits of the options in regards to instructional delivery and the benefits for them such as reducing the amount of time spent on lesson planning and reduction on cognitive consumption leading to cognitive fatigue which ultimately left more time to instruct and interact with students. Three participants discussed the lesson plan outline provided by AI which also saved them time. For example, student J stated "AI gave me an outline of something I could apply to my class and that only needed me to add some fine details". Student J then went on to discuss her decrease in fatigue and greater ability to focus on students and student needs because she had not spent all weekend or the night before planning for the next lessons. Student B added to the discussion of saving time and spending more time with students by describing using ChatGPT to generate rubrics: "I put the standard and assignment idea into ChatGPT to help me write a rubric and it was just so much faster than me doing it on my own". All participating students described struggling to not having enough time in the classroom to accomplish effective and interactive instructional lesson plans and assessments which weighed on them. They all described enjoying the use of AI especially because of the efficiency: Student J stated:

"And I liked how I was able to take the wording from the standard and put it into it and it would give me a lesson that was relevant to that standard so that I knew that I was meeting that standard and when I taught the lesson, things went really smoothly and the kids liked it. I felt like I could focus more on the students than on the lesson and making sure I hit every point".

One other participant pointed out how AI had introduced them to new platforms that could help differentiate content for them instantly. The student stated:

"I was excited because I learned about three things such as DreamBox that can adjust the difficulty of tasks in real-time because it analyzes student data based on their performance, so that each student has an appropriate challenge."

Ultimately, the AI platforms used could analyze strengths and weaknesses of learners to support the teacher with lesson plan delivery and increase interest in learning and promote the development of balanced learning (Yang & Wu, 2017).

Theme 3 Leveling the Playing Field with AI

AI can play a significant role in leveling the playing field for students with disabilities, especially due to the algorithms that can be used to identify evidence-based practices for struggling students (Robert et al. 2024). ten percent (10%) of the coded lines were dedicated to using AI to help improve Universal Design for Learning and Differentiation of content. One participant 'T.C.' in the class who also discussed being a parent of a child with a disability stated: "I have actually asked AI for EBP for my son too, I talked to LUDIA [an AI platform focused on Universal Design for Learning] and I asked how I can help him in school". 'T.C.' further discussed the AI platform providing her with several options to help her son and other students with reading difficulties. 'T.C.' stated that the list of options saved her time and effort trying to search for specific ones without the assistance of AI. The use of EBP has always been used in education (Curtin, 2023) and has been a staple of supporting students with disabilities and struggling learners. Often teachers will often use practices that are not EBP and do not have substantial evidence to demonstrate effectiveness. Sometimes the strategies may be popular or trending but may not have sufficient empirical evidence to support the use of them. These practices that are not evidenced can be ill taught by more seasoned teachers or learned through observational learning during a practicum or student teaching. Participant 'K.H.' stated:

"My favorite part of AI throughout the semester is how it can differentiate instruction between my students and offer suggestions of EBP to use to help my students with disabilities. Additionally, AI gave me references to look at the research behind the EBP. The AI was quick and gave me multiple suggestions which saved me time lesson planning so I could spend more time with my students'. - Participant 'K.H.'

Participant 'K.F.' described creating a lesson plan for their students in a practicum class and struggled to develop a plan that was differentiated to meet the learning levels and different disabilities, she described using AI to help her develop a comprehensive well differentiated lesson that used EBP that were effective across multiple disabilities. 'K.F.' stated:

"I had this lesson that I had prepared for them [class with multiple disabilities], I had students with ADHD, autism, auditory processing disorder, intellectual disability, and many behavioral challenges. The AI gave me suggestions on how I could respond to the challenges with a lot of these different things. Then the AI listed EBP to meet their needs. It saved me a ton of time and I felt like I was a better teacher." - Participant 'K.F.'

Theme 4: Utility of AI, Support, Instructional, and Assistive Technology Tool

Assistive and Instructional Technology for the inclusion of students with disabilities and supports for struggling students has become ubiquitous. Students with disabilities face many barriers in an educational setting that can be supported or even alleviated with the integration of technology both Assistive (AT) and Instructional (IT). Bond (2014) describes the use of IT and AT have benefited and changed the way students with disabilities participate in society and inclusive classrooms. AI platforms can facilitate inclusive education by offering various assistive features, such as text-to-speech, speech-to-text, and real-time translation. These tools help students with disabilities access and engage with educational content more easily. Assistive Technology along with IT was discussed by several participants and comprised 20% of the coded lines. One participant described having their student enter the main idea into the AI with the prompt: "Please explain this [content taught] to me". 'K.' a participant stated that she too used the AI to summarize content and also quickly found resources and videos that could be used to understand the material presented in class better than the lecture offered by the teacher. Furthermore, AI has the ability to help students learn content. Participant 'B' stated, " AI gave us either references that we either never heard of before or ideas to help support the new topic.' Seven students described using AI to help navigate assignment work by using AI to summarize content, help them learn the topic with additional support, then help create the assignment. One of the participants stated:

"AI helped me get through assignments faster and not because it was cutting corners or anything like that, it was helping me come up with ideas and it reduced my cognitive fatigue. Sometimes, school, work, and my homelife take up so much time that at the end of the night I struggle to come up with ideas and it [AI] kind of gives me a jump-start. I also do better listening to books than reading. I would put my questions in AI and it would read to me." - Student 'B.L.'

AI can enhance assistive technology, making it more effective and accessible for individuals with disabilities. Three participants discussed their diagnosis of dyslexia and stated that AI has helped them with content comprehension and application by using AI as an Assistive technology. For example, one participant stated that long text was difficult to read; thus, they used AI.

"Yeah, usually if I was given a paragraph or a really long thing to read, I would copy and it in there and say summarize this into bullet points and then it would just spit it out. and if I needed more information AI would explain it [the topic] much further concerning what I needed to know." - Participant 'T.C.'

Managing Dyslexia ~ Three Student's Perspectives. Often students with Dyslexia struggle to read and comprehend material. Three students described their struggles and use of AI over the semester. Of the lines coded 7% were dedicated to AI to support reading disabilities. One participant described an increase in reading and comprehension challenges with an increased fatigue level. 'K,' described often feeling tired in class due to having to attend evening classes after a long day of work. 'K.' noted that sustaining attention was difficult and the professor often talked using superfluous language that convoluted the concept being presented. Participant 'K.' further discussed that when she becomes tired reading becomes even more difficult. She stated:

"Because as college students we are given sources that are paragraphs or instructions that are like pages long or paragraphs long, I struggle to decode the directions and often miss steps because of my Dyslexia. AI just organizes the directions and gives me the directions in steps, it's really helpful." - Participant 'K.'

Specifically, one student with Dyslexia discussed the EBP suggestion of graphic organizers given to her and she stated: "I have actually implemented the graphic organizers to help me take notes and comprehend." Essentially, AI was supporting the students with greater access to the content, improved comprehension, and EBP that can be used to support them during class as active participants. The three students with Dyslexia had discussed their ability to be successful with the amount of literature assigned at the collegiate level. Prior to using AI as an assistive technology, they had noted that:

"I read a paragraph and completely forget everything and reread it and still forget everything and it takes me so much longer to read anything else. It's [AI] a really really great resource for those of us who have comprehension disabilities. I copy the text assigned and then ask it [AI] to summarize into bullet points or summarize into a paragraph and it gives the main ideas of whatever had been put into it. This feature has really saved me a lot for assigned readings" - Student 'K.H., K.B., and A."

Implementing differentiated instruction with EBP is crucial for supporting students with disabilities. By tailoring content, process, and product to meet individual needs, educators can create more inclusive and effective learning environments and students can take charge of their learning and use AI as a tool to support their individualized needs in the learning process.

In the field of education time is constantly in a deficit, teachers continuously report that they do not have time to create complex lessons, differentiate instruction, and individualize content for all students especially with the demands put on special education teachers. All participants, 100% discussed the amount of time saved learning to use AI for assignments, lesson plan development for their K-12 practicums, and support to find EBP for students with more complex needs. The time they saved was reallocated to time with students working on their pedagogy or time dedicated to self-care which reduced feelings of anxiety, depression, and feeling overwhelmed.

Theme 5: Mental Health Supports

The mental health challenges faced by undergraduate students significantly impact their academic performance and overall well-being, and these challenges have been exacerbated by the COVID-19 pandemic. Studies have shown that U.S. college students experienced increased levels of anxiety and depression during the pandemic, the increase in mental health has remained a challenge for many students who have to manage multiple classes, part or full time employment, a higher workload and independent reading load due to many classes remaining online (Roberts et al. 2023). All participants discussed a reduction in stress and improved mental health as a result of using AI as a tool to help them navigate the demands of learning to be a teacher and they encompassed 10% of the coded lines. Moreover, their reduction in stress led to them enjoying their classes, student teaching, and practicum experiences with students. Additionally, they described a new joy for teaching because they became excited to work on developing more complex lessons that are better suited to meet the unique needs of students with disabilities. Participant 'J.S.' stated:

"Being able to use AI this semester has made it so much easier with my assignments. I was in 18 credits this semester and 15 last semester and I felt like I was able to manage everything better even though I was in more credits and I felt like my work was more creative and I was more engaged" - Participant 'J.S.'

Additionally, students discussed how they felt encouraged to try new content areas to teach and try more complex lessons. 'V.O.' stated: *"I was confident in whatever I did and that it was encouraging to me to have AI help me learn and develop better lessons. I felt excited to be in the classroom again."* It is essential to help PSET feel confidence in the field of education, find ways to support working with a large population of diverse students and needs, and help reduce stress and improve mental health outcomes due to the persistent critical shortage of special education teachers. Special education teachers leave the profession at higher rates compared to their general education counterparts. The attrition is often due to job-related stress, burnout, and lack of administrative support. Research shows that about 50% of special education teachers leave their positions within their first five years of teaching (Billingsly & Bettini, 2019). Participants described a reduction in stress and improvement in their depression. Participant K.H. stated, "it [using AI for lesson planning and instruction with K-12 students] has definitely helped with the workload and my own depression and my happiness." Helping students manage depression and find joy in teaching is critical because many special education teachers feel inadequately prepared for the demands of their roles and are often stressed which diminishes their ability to serve students and support inclusion (Fuches, 2010, Guirguis, 2017). By leveraging AI, special education teachers can significantly reduce their workload and stress, allowing them to focus more on effective teaching and student engagement. This can lead to better educational outcomes for students and increased job satisfaction for teachers.

Potential Hesitancies to Integrate AI

With the integration of any new piece of technology a litany of challenges arise such as bias, confidentiality, limited trust, lack of understanding, impact on teaching, and personal pedagogical philosophical concerns such as depersonalization. Educators may be hesitant to adopt AI due to concerns that AI systems can perpetuate or even exacerbate bias, especially if the algorithms are trained on biased data. This can lead to unfair outcomes for students, particularly those from marginalized groups. Additionally, educators may be wary of relying on tools they do not fully understand or trust to be impartial or make decisions. This lack of trust and/or understanding of AI can also lead to personal conflict in regard to pedagogical preferences and philosophies. It is contingent upon the teacher and their professional judgment as to the use of AI tools and data. Teachers have appropriate training and experience to determine the applicability of AI and whether the outcomes are appropriate, and make changes where needed. This is the vital role of the teacher when using AI. Moreover educators across the K-12 and collegiate continuum might worry that AI could depersonalize education, reducing students to data points and diminishing the importance of the teacher's role as a mentor and guide; however, our goal is to effectively use AI to support teachers while enhancing interaction with students, as a result of reduced time spent developing lesson plans.

CONCLUSION AND RECOMMENDATIONS

Qualitative research was conducted due to the recent introduction of AI into university and K-12 experiences. Moreover, there are significant controversial ideas and beliefs about the use and integration of AI as a tool, support, and as a contributory entity to student's work. It is valuable insights into special education teachers' perceptions of learning to use AI and contribute to the advancement of knowledge in this important area. AI can support special education teachers in several ways, thereby reducing their stress and improving job satisfaction. Some examples include: 1) develop and manage personalized learning plans for students with disabilities, 2) provide real-time insights into student progress and behavior, allowing teachers to quickly identify and address issues, 3) identify challenges and barriers specific to disabilities, 4) identify EBP, 5) be used as an assistive technology or instructional technology, and 6) offer emotional support to teachers by reducing time planning lessons and researching innovative ideas or solutions to problems encountered in the classroom. Essentially, dynamic instructional practices that are individualized are presently limited in the scope of rigid teaching methods, standardized curriculum with direct instruction scripts, and the same assignment with the same output for each student limits one-to-one attention and can leave some students disengaged and struggling to keep up. A one-size-fits all approach tends to leave many students struggling and losing a desire to learn. Supports, guidance, and enhancements provided by AI hold the potential to elevate all students' learning and application (Thongprasit & Wannapiroon, 2022). Participants with documented disabilities in this class emphasized how much they felt AI had supported them, but not by making it easier or doing the work for them, but in helping them process the content and create assignments effectively. "... *it really did assist me in my disability and there were some assignments that I genuinely do not know how I would have done it [my semester work] without AI because of the complexity of the readings and assignments.*

While this chapter focuses on the benefits of AI and potential AI has to support PSET and ameliorate challenges when teaching students with disabilities as well as overcoming individual disabilities we want to acknowledge potential challenges. It is important to be aware of some challenges related to the use of AI such as possible cheating, overreliance on AI, lack of adequate training on the use of AI, and ensuring the privacy and security of student data; thus, continuous professional development for teachers is also essential to ensure these strategies are applied effectively in the classroom. Additionally, a unified policy or minimum standard of training on the use of AI would help create a more consistent, equitable, and effective teacher preparation process, ensuring that all future educators are well-equipped to integrate AI into their teaching practices and meet the evolving needs of students. Essentially, more research is needed to look at the benefits of AI and effective, ethical inclusion for both teachers and students at the K-12 and collegiate level.

References

Billingsley, B., & Bettini, E. (2019). *Special education teacher attrition and retention: A review of the literature.* AERA., DOI: 10.3102/0034654319862495

Bond, E. (2014). *Childhood, mobile technologies and everyday experiences: changing technologies changing childhoods?* Palgrave Macmillan. DOI: 10.1057/9781137292537

Cook, B. G., & Odom, S. L. (2013). Evidence-based practices and implementation science in special education. *Exceptional Children*, 79(2), 135–144. DOI: 10.1177/001440291307900202I

Cooper, B. R., Parker, L. A., & Diaz Martinez, A. (2019). *Balancing fidelity and adaptation: A guide for evidence-based program implementation.* Washington State University Extension. http://hdl.handle.net/2376/16873

Council for Exceptional Children. (2014). *Standards for evidence-based practices in special education.* CEC. https://exceptionalchildren.org/sites/default/files/2021-04/EBP_FINAL.pdf

Curtin, D. (2023). *Evidence-based practices in education.*https://plt4m.com/blog/evidence-based-practices-in-education/

Drigas, A., Kouremenos, D., & Vrettaros, J. (2008). Teaching of English to hearing impaired individuals whose mother language is the sign language. *Emerging Technologies and Information Systems for the Knowledge Society: First World Summit on the Knowledge Society,* WSKS 2008, Athens, Greece, September 24-26, 2008 *Proceedings, 1*, 263–270.

Drigas, A., Papanastasiou, G., & Skianis, S. (2023). The role of digital technologies, metacognition and emotional intelligence. *International Journal of Emerging Technologies.*, 18(9), 65–85. DOI: 10.3991/ijet.v18i09.38133

Fuches, W. (2009). Examining teachers perceived barriers associated with inclusion. *SRATE Journal*, 19(1), 30–35.

Garrad, T.-A., Vlcek, S., & Page, A. (2022). The importance of the promotion of evidence-based practice as a reasonable adjustment in mainstream education settings for students with Autism Spectrum Disorder. *Australasian Journal of Special and Inclusive Education*, 46(1), 101–112. DOI: 10.1017/jsi.2022.5

Google. (n.d.). *AI data analytics.*https://cloud.google.com/use-cases/ai-data-analytics

Hester, O. R., Bridges, S. A., & Rollins, L. H. (2020). 'Overworked and underappreciated': Special education teachers describe stress and attrition. *Teacher Development*, 24(3), 348–365. https://doi-org.ezproxy.ecu.edu.au/10.1080/13664530.2020.1767189. DOI: 10.1080/13664530.2020.1767189

Holmes, W. (2020). Artificial intelligence in education. In Tatnall, A. (Ed.), *Encyclopedia of education and information technologies* (pp. 88–103). Springer., DOI: 10.1007/978-3-030-10576-1_107

Hopcan, S., Polat, E., Ozturk, M. E., & Ozturk, L. (2022). Artificial intelligence in special education: A systematic review. *Interactive Learning Environments*, 31(10), 7335–7353. DOI: 10.1080/10494820.2022.2067186

Hume, K., Steinbrenner, J. R., Odom, S. L., Morin, K. L., Nowell, S. W., Tomaszewski, B., Szendrey, S., McIntyre, N. S., Yücesoy-Özkan, S., & Savage, M. N. (2021). Evidence-based practices for children, youth, and young adults with autism: Third generation review. *Journal of Autism and Developmental Disorders*, 51(11), 4013–4032. DOI: 10.1007/s10803-020-04844-2

Institute of Education Sciences. (n.d.). *What works clearinghouse*. https://ies.ed.gov/ncee/wwc

Kuprenko, V. (2020). Artificial Intelligence in education: benefits, challenges, and use cases. Retrieved from https://pub.towardsai.net/artificial-intelligence-in-education-benefits-challenges-and-use-cases-db52d8921f7a

Lukins, J. M., Able, H., & Hume, K. (2023). Novice teachers' implementation of evidence-based practices in autism education: Examining the roles of preparation and perception. *Focus on Autism and Other Developmental Disabilities*, 38(1), 5–16. DOI: 10.1177/10883576221144734

Luzmo. (2023). *Using AI for data analysis: The ultimate guide (2024).*https://www.luzmo.com/blog/ai-data-analysis

Pavlopoulos, J., Vrettaros, J., Vouros, G., & Drigas, A. (2008). The development of a self-assessment system for the learners' answers with the use of GPNN. In M. D. Lytras, J. M. Carroll, E. Damiani, R. D. Tennyson (Eds.), *Emerging technologies and information systems for the knowledge society.* WSKS 2008. Lecture Notes in Computer Science, 5288, 332–340. Springer. https://doi.org/DOI: 10.1007/978-3-540-87781-3_37

Peyton, D. J., Acosta, K., Harvey, A., Pua, D. J., Sindelar, P. T., Mason-Williams, L., Dewey, J., Fisher, T. L., & Crews, E. (2021). Special education teacher shortage: Differences between high and low shortage states. *Teacher Education and Special Education*, 44(1), 5–23. https://doi-org.ezproxy.ecu.edu.au/10.1177/0888406420906618. DOI: 10.1177/0888406420906618

Riedl, M., Arriaga, R., Boujarwah, F., Hong, H., Isbell, J., & Heflin, L. J. (2007). *Graphical social scenarios: Toward intervention and authoring for adolescents with high functioning autism.* Virtual Healthcare Interaction. Papers from the AAAI Fall Symposium, 64-73. https://aaai.org/papers/00945-945-graphical-social-scenarios-toward-intervention-and-authoring-for-adolescents-with-high-functioning-autism/

Schipor, O. A., Pentiuc, S. G., & Schipor, M. D. (2010). Improving computer-based speech therapy using a fuzzy expert system. *Computer Information*, 29(2), 303–318. https://www.cai.sk/ojs/index.php/cai/article/view/85

Sebe, N., Cohen, I., Gevers, T., & Huang, T. S. (2006). Emotion recognition based on joint visual and audio cues. Paper presented at *18th International Conference on Pattern Recognition* (ICPR 2006), 20-24 August 2006, Hong Kong, China. (pp. 1136-1139). https://doi.org/DOI: 10.1109/ICPR.2006.489

Sharma, S., Tomar, V., Yadav, N., & Aggarwal, M. (2023). Impacts of AI-based special education on educators and students. In Kumar, A., Nayyar, A., Sachan, R. K., & Jain, R. (Eds.), *AI-assisted special education for students with exceptional needs* (pp. 47–66). IGI Global Publishers., DOI: 10.4018/979-8-3693-0378-8.ch003

Suppan, P. (2006). Differentiated instruction: A research base. *International Education Journal*, 7(7), 935–947.

Vanderbilt University. (2023). *Evidence-based resources for EBP.* https://my.vanderbilt.edu/spedteacherresources/evidence-based-resources-for-ebp/

Vincent-Lancrin, S., & van der Vlies, R. (2020). Trustworthy artificial intelligence (AI) in education: Promises and challenges. *OECD Education Working Papers*, No. 218, OECD Publishing, Paris. DOI: 10.1787/19939019

Wu, T. K., Meng, Y. R., & Huang, S. C. (2006). Application of artificial neural networks to the identification of students with learning disabilities. *International Conference on Artificial Intelligence*, 162–168. https://www.semanticscholar.org/paper/Application-of-Artificial-Neural-Network-to-the-of-Wu-Meng/7826dcbaccba15159a69c16750ced68b5f818132

Yang, H. S., & Wu, J. P. (2017). Exploration on cultivation of application-oriented and innovative talents in the information field under "Internet +" environment. *Eurasia Journal of Mathematics, Science and Technology Education*, 13(8), 5607–5614. DOI: 10.12973/eurasia.2017.01014a

Chapter 14
Using AI to Support the Transition From Schooling to Employment for Autistic Individuals

Brady Lund
University of North Texas, USA

Karen Johnson
https://orcid.org/0000-0002-9900-6650
University of North Texas, USA

Regina Kaplan-Rakowski
https://orcid.org/0000-0002-6769-7784
University of North Texas, USA

ABSTRACT

While the significance of employment for individual well-being and sense of belonging is well-documented in the literature, individuals with autism spectrum disorder (ASD) face substantial challenges in securing and retaining meaningful employment after completing their schooling. This chapter addresses the gap in research concerning employment readiness, access, and retention for individuals with ASD by exploring the potential of generative artificial intelligence (GAI), specifically ChatGPT, to support their transition from education to employment. The chapter evaluates three propositions: ChatGPT as a tool for communication and social skills training, as a source of just-in-time (JIT) information, and as a support resource for caregivers. Based on a synthesis of existing literature, this chapter highlights the unique advantages of GAI, such as providing a low-stakes

DOI: 10.4018/979-8-3693-5538-1.ch014

environment for practicing social interactions and delivering immediate, reliable information, while also emphasizing the need to integrate AI alongside professional guidance in order to maximize effectiveness.

INTRODUCTION

The opportunity to work and be productive in a structured environment contributes to individuals' meaning of life, often recognized as the cornerstone of well-being (Ward & King, 2017). Work contributes positively to psychological well-being, physical wellness, and the overall quality of life (Salkever, 2000; Ward & King, 2017). Despite the importance of work to well-being, some minority populations within the U.S. experience significant challenges to obtain and retain meaningful and competitive jobs. For example, only 21% of people with disabilities, including autism spectrum disorder (ASD), are employed. Nearly 60% of autistic individuals in the U.S. are employed after receiving state-provided vocational rehabilitation services which typically begin in high school (Bureau of Labor Statistics, 2022).

Autism has been identified in children of all racial, ethnic, and socioeconomic groups. Current statistics for autism diagnosis indicate one in 36 children today are diagnosed with ASD, up from one in 44 children in 2018 (Centers for Disease Control and Prevention, 2023). Further, a growing number of autistic individuals are becoming adults and need gainful employment. According to the Centers for Disease Control and Prevention (2023), one in 45 adults in the U.S. is diagnosed with autism. The persistent deficit of individuals with ASD in social interaction causes functional limitations in effective communication, social participation, academic achievements, and occupational performance (American Psychiatric Association, 2013). These challenges underlie the low employment rates and lowest pay rates leaving autistic individuals at risk for unemployment and underemployment (Dreaver et al., 2019; Nicholas et al., 2019). Because of the behavioral, communication, and social challenges critical for effective job functioning, employment opportunities are limited. Autistic employees are often viewed as challenging and less appealing to work with (Tomczak, 2021).

Barriers to employment of ASD individuals and their participation in the workforce include challenges with the job application and interview processes, securing positions that align well with their skills and qualifications, understanding the social demands of the work environment, and adapting to an unpredictable workplace, including environmental distractors (e.g., lighting, noise, crowding; Dreaver et al., 2019; Scott et al., 2019). Furthermore, employees with autism tend to hold short-term employment because of workplace challenges with supervisors or colleagues (Bury et al., 2021). Some employers are hesitant to employ autistic individuals due to an absence of awareness and understanding of the disorder and most employers tend to focus on the repetitive or negative behaviors than the capabilities of the ASD individuals (Johnson, 2022; Nesbitt, 2000). Therefore, the transition into employment and retaining employment is difficult for individuals with ASD.

Autistic individuals are employed in various industry sectors including healthcare, retail, recreation, hospitality, food service, warehouse, education, and government (Wehman et al., 2016). Meanwhile, minimal research exists on employment readiness, access to employment, career development, and retention of individuals with ASD in the workforce (Johnson et al., 2020; Nicholas et al., 2018; Wehman et al., 2017). More research focused on strategies to improve employment and work outcomes is necessary (Wei et al., 2018). Researchers have indicated that appropriate interventions and training can lead to positive behavior change and improved work performance (Johnson et al., 2020; Johnson & Williams, 2022; Wehman et al., 2017). In today's digitized workplace, some of the technologies that have been used to support employment opportunities and workplace learning and training for autistic people include video modeling computer application (Rosen et al., 2017), virtual reality (Adiani et al., 2022; Ke et al., 2022; Kim et al., 2024), augmented reality (Chiam et al., 2021; Tan et al., 2022), mobile apps (Haoues & Mokni, 2023), and assistive technologies such as online communicators or chatbots (Tomczak, 2021). However, generative artificial intelligence (GAI) tools (e.g., ChatGPT, Bard) to facilitate learning for employees with autism have been unexplored. The goal of this chapter is to synthesize relevant literature regarding the potential role of GAI to facilitate learning and training in the workplace to improve employment opportunities for people with autism. The guiding research question for this conceptual review is *How may GAI support the transition from schooling to employment for autistic young adults?*

While research on autism and GAI is only beginning, the limited literature focuses on the use of GAI technology as an information-seeking tool for parents or caregivers to learn about autism (McFayden et al., 2024) and as a conversational agent to improve the social and communication skills of autistic individuals in their everyday lives (Choi et al. 2024). ChatGPT is also being explored as a behavioral therapy technique for children with autism (Ashraf et al., 2024) and when connected to a social robot, ChatGPT shows the potential to improve cognitive functioning (Bertacchini et al., 2023). If integrated in clinical settings, ChatGPT can aid autism diagnosis and assessments quickly and accurately which is critical for effective intervention planning (Hu et al., 2024).

Generally, most of the research on autism is focused on the effectiveness of early intervention for young children (Gelbar et al., 2014) and developing systems to help high schoolers with autism to transition to post-secondary education (Lizotte, 2018). However, only minimal research examines practices to aid the shift to gainful employment (Johnson et al., 2020). Similarly, the limited research on autism and ChatGPT is primarily centered on children with autism. Consequently, the literature lacks analysis on the benefits and limitations of GAI tools for autistic individuals transitioning from high-school or college/university to employment.

Generative Artificial Intelligence and Its Potential for Job Seekers with ASD

This section will start by reviewing the nature of generative artificial intelligence and the chatbot ChatGPT. It will then transition to the discussion of autistic job seekers and their information needs when seeking employment, and how these emerging technologies may help address these needs and produce better outcomes, including gainful employment.

Generative Artificial Intelligence and ChatGPT

Generative artificial intelligence (GAI) is characterized as a form of AI capable of generating novel content from the input it receives (Pavlik, 2023). As of 2024, one of the most often used GAI tool is ChatGPT. ChatGPT (https://chat.openai.com/) is an innovative chatbot developed by the California-based research organization, OpenAI. ChatGPT is powered by the *large language model* (LLM), Generative Pre-Trained Transformer (GPT). This model works by training a variety of parameters, or aspects of the model used for prediction and production of language, akin to adjusting settings such as volume or color contrast on a television set. It learns by using massive datasets, allowing it to generate responses based on the information it has been trained on. First, the model makes its own inferences based on observations of the training data through a process known as *pre-training*, and then is guided by a developer to refine its performance (Lund et al., 2023). ChatGPT is known for its ability to understand the patterns of human communication and generate realistic outputs based on user *prompts*. Prompt is the technical term to refer to the input or instruction provided to an AI model to guide what information or output is supplied in response (Liu & Chilton, 2022).

Since a sudden surge in popularity of GAI following the emergence of ChatGPT in November 2023 (Lamproupoulos et al., 2024), numerous publications have explored the capabilities of this technology in a wide range of domains. Generative AI models harness their training to generate information tailored to virtually any requirement, leading to its adoption across various industries. For instance, ChatGPT is perceived as useful in hospitality and customer service roles in crafting responses to customer inquiries (Limna & Kraiwanit, 2023) as well as in educational settings (Kaplan-Rakowski et al., 2023; Trust et al., 2023). However, one area that lacks extensive research is the application of GAI to support the distinctive needs of specific marginalized populations.

Studying the impact of GAI on individuals with autism has gained some attention with research focusing, for example, on AI for the initial screening and assessment of autism based on diagnostic criteria (Anagnostopoulou et al., 2020; Shahamiri & Thabtah, 2020), AI in the design of support and care systems for autism (Al Banna et al., 2020; Jaliaawala & Khan, 2020), and AI for the development of social skills in individuals with autism (Porayska-Pomsta et al., 2018).

One very important aspect of the life of any individual is employment. It gives identity, a sense of purpose, and, of course, income. No previous research has examined how AI can support employment opportunities for autistic individuals. Given that research gap, we investigate the following three propositions about the potential role of GAI in supporting the employment seeking of autistic individuals: (1) ChatGPT can serve as a learning tool for communication and social skills training for autistic individuals transitioning from schooling to employment, (2) ChatGPT can provide JIT (Just-In-Time) information as needed for autistic individuals transitioning from schooling to employment; (3) ChatGPT can be a support tool for parents and caregivers of young adult autistic individuals transitioning from schooling to employment.

Proposition 1: ChatGPT can Serve as a Learning Tool for Communication and Social Skills Training for Autistic Individuals Transitioning from Schooling to Employment.

Generative AI tools, such as ChatGPT, offer opportunities for practicing communicative skills and demonstrate considerable potential as low-stakes conversational partners (Chun et al., 2024; Thrasher et al., 2023) for autistic individuals to practice communication skills. The design of GAI tools allow for interaction with users on a wide range of topics and engagement in a variety of behaviors, including general conversation, question answering, simulated interviewing, and information retrieval (similar to a search engine). Indeed, these AI models have been suggested as a means to reduce loneliness and enhance communication abilities to the point of becoming "friends" with the technology (Dhimolea et al., 2023), similar to the 2013 film *Her* (Olasik, 2023; Saxena, 2020). In *Her*, the protagonist forms an emotional bond with the AI operating system, Samantha, resulting in companionship and emotional support. This film illustrates how AI can evolve beyond a functional tool to become a source of emotional connection.

If the human conversational partner miscommunicates, saying something not intended or potentially offensive to another person, or if they simply want to end a conversation, they can terminate the chat without any consequences. As opposed to real-life interactions with real humans, individuals conversing with GAI do not need to worry about upsetting the language model or acting off-putting because the AI model itself has no thoughts, feelings, or emotions. Instead, it is simply an algorithm that generates responses to inputs based on predefined criteria, making predictions as to how it should respond based on what the user types. It aims to please and does not carry any preconceptions from one conversation to the next unless instructed to do so.

This characteristic of GAI tools can serve as a protective shield for users, similar to the effect observed with other technologies such as virtual reality. For instance, some evidence suggests that the use of virtual reality can help reduce public speaking anxiety (Gruber & Kaplan-Rakowski, 2020; Kaplan-Rakowski & Gruber, 2023; Stupar-Rutenfrans et al., 2017). The reduction in speaking anxiety compared to face-to-face interactions may be due to technology creating a comfort zone (Kruk, 2020). Engaging with a real person can evoke undesirable emotions, including anxiety. In a similar way, GAI tools provide a low-stakes environment where individuals can practice communication skills without the fear of negative judgment or emotional repercussions. This safe space can encourage more frequent and open interactions, leading to improved communication abilities over time.

In some ways, AI models can be said to "think" and "communicate" in similar ways to the symptomology of ASD. The AI models understand *language* much better than they do *communication*. The communications produced by a model such as GPT-4o often sound artificial – overly verbose and formal – unlike typical human communications (Schreuter, 2021). The model operates without regard for greetings or other formalities. Its objective is to perform the assigned task based on user inputs. This behavior among the models may create some sense of comfort for the autistic individuals. One of the major factors in the adoption of new technologies among autistic young adults is the level of comfort with the technology, with unfamiliar communication assistive technologies being particularly challenging to adopt (Ghanouni et al., 2020; Ibrahim et al., 2023).

Downsides to using ChatGPT as a conversational partner exist as well. AI chatbots are not real people. While they can be advantageous for practice, they pose limitations for understanding how an actual person will react during an exchange. Ultimately, the objective of this practice is to prepare for real human interactions (Ratican & Hutson, 2023). Language models may be trained to react similarly to real people, but they can still be reset or turned off in a way that real people cannot. While AI can effectively prepare individuals for basic conversational etiquette, training with a human conversational partner remains essential. AI can complement a trained professional in preparing the autistic job seekers, but it should not replace the critical role of this professional in ensuring the job seeker's success.

Proposition 2: ChatGPT can Provide JIT (Just-In-Time) Information as Needed for Autistic Individuals Transitioning from Schooling to Employment.

Large language models such as ChatGPT can serve as just-in-time (JIT) information sources. That is, if an individual were to develop a question at a time when a human job coach would be unavailable (e.g., in the middle of the night or walking into an interview meeting), then ChatGPT could address this need, and likely be superior to web browsing (Wang et al., 2023). Just-in-time information is critical. While individuals may be well prepared for a meeting, one small uncertainty can derail their confidence. Information needs can emerge at any time, prompted by internal and external factors that impact the individual (Wilson, 1981). Having a virtual tool that can provide guidance at the point of need and assuage concerns is a boon.

Historically, the provision of JIT information may be facilitated by search engines, available at all times via the Internet. However, search engines do not generate information in the same way as GAI tools do. Rather, search engines index existing websites and provide links to this information in response to a search query (Rhodes & Maes, 2000). The quality of JIT information with search engines relies on the quality of information retrieved from websites. If the top search results are sites with limited or contradictory information, then the user's search is likely to be unsuccessful (Caramancion, 2024). Generative AI models such as ChatGPT use their broad training data to address the same question and provide a single, clear answer (Petroni et al., 2019).

This presentation of the information from GAI versus search engines can empower the user with confidence. For instance, consider a response to the question, "must I disclose an autism diagnosis during a job interview?" From a Google search on April 2, 2024, the top two results are from autism society websites indicating that disclosure should depend on the circumstances and feelings of the individual. However, the third link is to a Reddit post that suggests that "you should NEVER disclose" your autism diagnosis.

Meanwhile, we asked the same question within a ChatGPT prompt on the same date as the web search and received the following response: "Whether or not you should disclose an autism diagnosis during a job interview is a personal decision and depends on various factors including the specific job, the workplace culture, and your comfort level with sharing this information." The model then listed a variety of considerations when making a decision whether to disclose: whether the autism diagnosis may impact the ability to perform essential job functions, the perception of disclosure within the workplace culture (who is on the hiring committee), if you believe you will need accommodations to perform effectively, and your own comfort level (ChatGPT, personal communication).

However, an inherent risk associated with relying solely on JIT information from GAI tools is the potential for over-reliance or obsession, distracting from actual preparation efforts. It is essential to view GAI as a complementary resource to career coaching and regular practice sessions rather than a substitute. The capabilities of GAI tools may inadvertently create a false perception that all necessary information is readily available at one's fingertips, diminishing the importance of thorough preparation and human interaction in professional development (Koubaa et al., 2023). Thus, while ChatGPT offers unparalleled convenience and assistance as an information source, its role should be carefully balanced within a broader framework of career development strategies. These AI tools are also not infallible. They can provide false or misleading information and must be treated with skepticism (Gravel et al., 2023).

Proposition 3: ChatGPT can be a Support Tool for Parents and Caregivers of Young Adult Employees with ASD.

Autistic individuals and their caregivers often have many distinct information needs as they navigate their day-to-day life and professional careers. Shivers et al. (2018) noted the needs among caregivers of adults within the autism spectrum, aged 19 to 80. These needs include health information (5.94 distinct needs expressed on average)[1], emotional support (4.85), instrumental support, including self-care (3.73), professional support (2.95), community support (3.51), and involvement with care (1.51). Service needs related to employment (42.3%) and financial management (54.6%) were among the most commonly needed but not received needs for the population with ASD. Griffiths et al. (2016) noted that most young adults with autism and their caregivers are interested in them having a career. However, these individuals often grapple with uncertainties regarding the most suitable job type and the potential educational or behavioral barriers that may impede their pursuit of ideal employment opportunities.

In addressing these multifaceted needs, GAI tools are a promising solution. The ability of GAI to address a range of information needs, including job-related questions, typically exceeds the ability of search engines (Sun et al., 2024). McFayden et al. (2024) conducted research affirming the potential of GAI to cater to these diverse needs, albeit with some limitations. Their study highlights the effectiveness of ChatGPT as a resource for accessing information concerning health issues associated with ASD and their medical comorbidities. It demonstrates the capacity of ChatGPT to bridge critical information gaps for caregivers and individuals within the autism community.

However, McFayden et al.'s (2024) study also identifies limitations in fully addressing these information needs with reliable, scientifically accurate information. There are limitations in the training of AI that may lead to models providing incorrect or misleading guidance. Incomplete or biased training data can perpetuate societal biases and lead to improper decision-making among users (Ntoutsi et al., 2020). While AI models may be a useful tool for supporting some needs, it likely should not be trusted to address all concerns fully by itself. Users should seek to complement information provided by AI models with that acquired from other sources, such as trusted experts.

An Approach to Integrating Generative Artificial Intelligence into Autism Workforce Support

Based on the propositions discussed in the prior sections, we suggest that ChatGPT and similar tools are potentially valuable for supporting individuals with autism when seeking work opportunities. However, these tools should not be seen as a replacement for the support of professionals, but rather as a supplement that can provide practice support and supply JIT information to the job seeker. Job seekers will be well-served to have both a trusted professional who works with them long-term to develop communication and job performance and seeking skills, as well as an AI tool that can provide quick information that is relatively decisive and authoritative. Complementing professional expertise with the support of an AI tool has already been discussed as a powerful solution in many disciplines and professions (Lebovitz et al., 2022; Lopez Jimenez et al., 2021).

The idea of using new technologies as assistive tools to supplement rather than replace trained professionals is not new. Web-based job support and training programs (e.g., JobTIPS) became popular in the early 2010s, along with virtual reality and simulation training (Hedges et al., 2018; Smith et al., 2014; Strickland et al., 2013). However, generative AI chatbots such as ChatGPT introduce an additional dimension by lowering the stakes further than with these past technologies, allowing private conversations with the AI interface, and serving as an on-demand information source. These emerging tools can also be integrated into the existing programs. For instance, a program like Project SEARCH, which helps place individuals with disabilities into rewarding jobs, could create their own series of chatbots to help prepare the individuals that they serve, including autistic job seekers.

An important role related to these technologies will be trainers. Professionals should not assume that the individuals with whom they work will be familiar with or adept in using these AI models. If these models are not used responsibly, they may be more likely to produce unreliable results (Amaro et al., 2023). Thus, it is equally important that professionals themselves be trained in using these models (Meskó,

2023). We may see new employment possibilities emerge for individuals who are able to provide adept training on interaction with various AI tools, ethical risks, and prompt engineering, just as we have some professional trainers who specialize on Microsoft tools and social media training.

The Risks and Ethical Pitfalls of AI Usage for Autism Workforce Training

There are several serious risks and pitfalls that must be considered when using GAI tools in autism workforce training. These models are imperfect, with flaws ranging from minor inconveniences to major lapses that could mislead learners and cause harm in their job-seeking pursuits. Unlike search engines like Google, large language models typically supply only a single response to a given prompt, and often do not provide additional sources to support fact checking (Caramancion, 2024). Consequently, users must take the initiative to interact with the model with care and do their own fact-checking outside of their interactions with the model.

Three of the major issues that could emerge when users interact with AI models include AI hallucinations and the production of misinformation by AI models, the potential for bias embedded in the models, and the impact of poor prompt quality on model output.

AI Hallucinations and Misinformation. Generative AI tools such as large language models/GPT are prone to hallucinations: the generation of content that does not align with established world knowledge (Zhang et al., 2023). For instance, we might input a prompt into a model like "do vaccines cause autism" and a model may start by indicating "no" – giving us the correct answer – but then mention "in some cases vaccines may cause autism." Why would it provide this latter answer? It may be trained on flawed data that indicates vaccines cause autism, such as debunked and retracted research studies that were inappropriately labelled as such when they were used to train the model (Turi et al., 2024). Conversely, the model may have simply not made the right connections when learning from the training data and this issue may never have been discovered and corrected (Kumar et al., 2022). This issue is highly problematic, as users trust and rely on these AI models to provide reliable information and if poor quality information/misinformation is provided, then AI models are contributing to the growth of our current post-truth reality, where fact and falsehood are indistinguishable (Li & Chiu, 2024). Importantly, the misinformation provided by these models could represent the difference between an autistic young adult successfully securing a job and leaving their interview with humiliation. In a critical moment in the young adult's life, such as seeking their first professional role, reliable information is vital.

Bias in AI Models. Bias can be pervasive in AI models. Bias manifests when the data used to train AI models are flawed and these flaws influence the responses of the model to user prompts (Varona & Suarez, 2022). Consider, for example, an AI model trained solely on pre-21st century guides of professional etiquette. What outdated information might these guides contain about how to act at a professional interview? How discouraging may some of this information be for the autistic job seeker? There are likely plenty of job seeking guides published in recent years that would provide positive guidance to the autistic job seeker that would leave them enthusiastic and optimistic. However, if these guides are not included in the AI model's training, how could it be expected to know to provide this more positive advice? For this reason, it is critical for the developers of AI models to check their own biases as they train models, include diverse voices in the development and training of the models, and test the models thoroughly with diverse populations to identify any issues before deployment (O'Connor & Liu, 2024). Unfortunately, many AI developers do not enact these development and training processes, and many do not disclose any information at all about how their models are trained or what data are used. In some regards, this is understandable – developers do not want others to replicate the design of their models – but it is also unethical, as it leaves users uninformed about perilous risks associated with their AI usage.

Quality of prompts. An additional concern stemming from how the user interacts with the AI model is the quality of prompts. Depending on the specific prompt (instructions to the model) supplied by the user, the model may provide vastly different results (Frederick, 2024). For instance, if a user types "how do I get a job in sales?" versus "how do I get a job in car sales?", they will get considerably different results. Similarly, "how do I get a job in car sales?" versus "what qualifications do I need to get a job in car sales?" versus "how should I present myself in an interview to get a job in car sales?" will yield distinct results. As such, it is necessary for the user to be specific and provide context with their queries. Generic prompts will yield generic responses. The more detail about what information is needed and the context of this information, the better the results will align with the actual need. One trick to develop better prompts is to ask the model questions such as "how should I structure a prompt in order to get information about how I can get a job in car sales?" which will prompt the model to provide several different options of prompts that are tailored to specific information needs. It is also important for the user to not settle or be satisfied with an answer that does not truly address their need (Meskó, 2023). If the user believes that the AI model misunderstood their request, they should revise their prompt until they receive a satisfactory answer.

Overcoming these issues inherent in AI models requires care on the part of the user. Autistic job seekers should educate themselves about the risks with these models, and caregivers and advocacy organizations would be well-advised to create informational content to educate the job seekers about basic AI literacy and prompt engineering (Ng et al., 2021). Perhaps the most valuable piece of advice for any user of AI tools is to approach their interactions with AI with a healthy dose of skepticism. If any aspect of the model's response seems inaccurate or excessively favorable, it may stem from bias or hallucination. In such cases, the user would be wise to validate the response against other sources of information. These artificial intelligence tools, especially large language models and chatbots like ChatGPT, can be useful resources for the provision of guidance and JIT information, better satisfying the training and information needs of autistic job seekers. Meanwhile, they can also be a threat to reliable information and education, if they are used without critical examination of their potential biases and flaws. An ecosystem of support, in which AI tools are just one resource, is required to enhance outcomes for the autistic job seeker.

CONCLUSION

Several promising opportunities exist for using AI in addressing the challenges faced by the autism community in seeking and maintaining meaningful employment. As a learning tool, AI models such as ChatGPT offer a low-stakes environment for practicing communication and social skills that are necessary to obtain and maintain a job. These models can also provide JIT information to empower autistic job applicants and employees with the resources they need right when they need them, as well as support those individuals' caregivers as they help them navigate the employment landscape. However, it is critical to recognize that while ChatGPT shows promise for these purposes, it is not a miracle cure and support by family and trained professionals will remain vital to improve outcomes. Moving forward, integrating ChatGPT into autism workforce support initiatives requires an evidence-based approach that balances the benefits of AI technology with the need for human interaction and personalized support.

References

Adiani, D., Itzkovitz, A., Bian, D., Katz, H., Breen, M., Hunt, S., Swanson, A., Vogus, T. J., Wade, J., & Sarkar, N. (2022). Career interview readiness in virtual reality (CIRVR): A platform for simulated interview training for autistic individuals and their employers. [TACCESS]. *ACM Transactions on Accessible Computing*, 15(1), 1–28. DOI: 10.1145/3505560

Al Banna, M. H., Ghosh, T., Taher, K. A., Kaiser, M. S., & Mahmud, M. (2020, September). A monitoring system for patients of autism spectrum disorder using artificial intelligence. In *International conference on brain informatics* (pp. 251–262). Springer International Publishing. DOI: 10.1007/978-3-030-59277-6_23

Amaro, I., Della Greca, A., Francese, R., Tortora, G., & Tucci, C. (2023, July). AI unreliable answers: A case study on ChatGPT. In *International Conference on Human-Computer Interaction* (pp. 23–40). Springer Nature Switzerland. DOI: 10.1007/978-3-031-35894-4_2

American Psychiatric Association. (2013). *Diagnostic and statistical manual of mental disorders* (5th ed.), American Psychiatric Association. https://dsm–psychiatry online–org.libproxy.library.unt.edu/doi/full/10.1176/appi.books.9780890425596 .dsm01

Anagnostopoulou, P., Alexandropoulou, V., Lorentzou, G., Lykothanasi, A., Ntaountaki, P., & Drigas, A. (2020). Artificial intelligence in autism assessment. [iJET]. *International Journal of Emerging Technologies in Learning*, 15(6), 95–107. DOI: 10.3991/ijet.v15i06.11231

Ashraf, M. M., Ul-Haque, I., & Sangha, N. K. (2024). Navigating Autism Treatment: Unlocking New Frontiers with ChatGPT. *The International Journal of Neuroscience*, 1–3, 1–2. Advance online publication. DOI: 10.1080/00207454.2024.2341912

Bertacchini, F., Demarco, F., Scuro, C., Pantano, P., & Bilotta, E. (2023). A social robot connected with chatGPT to improve cognitive functioning in ASD subjects. *Frontiers in Psychology*, 14, 1232177. DOI: 10.3389/fpsyg.2023.1232177

Caramancion, K. M. (2024). Large Language Models vs. Search Engines: Evaluating User Preferences Across Varied Information Retrieval Scenarios. *arXiv preprint arXiv:2401.05761*.

Centers for Disease Control and Prevention. (2022). *Prevalence and characteristics of autism spectrum disorder*. Retrieved at https://www.cdc.gov/mmwr/volumes/72/ss/ss7202a1.htm?s_cid=ss7202a1_w

Chiam, B. S. W., Leung, I. M. W., Devilly, O. Z., Da Ow, C. Y., Guan, F. Y., & Tan, B. L. (2021, October). Novel augmented reality enhanced solution towards vocational training for people with mental disabilities. In *2021 IEEE International Symposium on Mixed and Augmented Reality Adjunct (ISMAR-Adjunct)* (pp. 195–200). IEEE. DOI: 10.1109/ISMAR-Adjunct54149.2021.00047

Choi, D., Lee, S., Kim, S. I., Lee, K., Yoo, H. J., Lee, S., & Hong, H. (2024, May). Unlock Life with a Chat (GPT): Integrating Conversational AI with Large Language Models into Everyday Lives of Autistic Individuals. In *Proceedings of the CHI Conference on Human Factors in Computing Systems* (pp. 1–17). DOI: 10.1145/3613904.3641989

Chun, D., Kaplan-Rakowski, R., Ovsiannikova, U., Thrasher, T., & Yuan, Y. (2024). AI-mediated high-immersion virtual reality for language learning. In Lan, Y. J., Qi, G., & Chun, D. (Eds.), *AI-mediated language education in the metaverse era*. Springer.

Dhimolea, T. K., Kaplan-Rakowski, R., & Lin, L. (2022). Supporting social and emotional well-being with artificial intelligence. In Albert, V. M., Lin, L., & Spector, J. M. (Eds.), *Bridging Human and Artificial Intelligence* (pp. 125–138). Springer., DOI: 10.1007/978-3-030-84729-6_8

Dreaver, J., Thompson, C., Girdler, S., Adolfsson, M., Black, M. H., & Falkmer, M. (2019). Success factors enabling employment for adults on the autism spectrum from employers' perspective. *Journal of Autism and Developmental Disorders*, 50(5), 1657–1667. DOI: 10.1007/s10803-019-03923-3

Frederick, D. E. (2024). Prompt engineering–a disruption in information seeking? *Library Hi Tech News*, 41(3), 1–5. DOI: 10.1108/LHTN-03-2024-0037

Gelbar, N. W., Smith, I., & Reichow, B. (2014). Systematic review of articles describing experience and supports of individuals with autism enrolled in college and university programs. *Journal of Autism and Developmental Disorders*, 44(10), 2593–2601. DOI: 10.1007/s10803-014-2135-5

Ghanouni, P., Jarus, T., Zwicker, J. G., & Lucyshyn, J. (2020). The use of technologies among individuals with autism spectrum disorders: Barriers and challenges. *Journal of Special Education Technology*, 35(4), 286–294. DOI: 10.1177/0162643419888765

Gravel, J., D'Amours-Gravel, M., & Osmanlliu, E. (2023). Learning to fake it: Limited responses and fabricated references provided by ChatGPT for medical questions. *Mayo Clinic Proceedings. Digital Health*, 1(3), 226–234. DOI: 10.1016/j.mcpdig.2023.05.004

Griffiths, A. J., Giannantonio, C. M., Hurley-Hanson, A. E., & Cardinal, D. N. (2016). Autism in the workplace: Assessing the transition needs of young adults with autism spectrum disorder. *Journal of Business and Management*, 22(1), 5–22. DOI: 10.1504/JBM.2016.141233

Gruber, A., & Kaplan-Rakowski, R. (2020). User experience of public speaking practice in virtual reality. In Zheng, R. Z. (Ed.), *Cognitive and affective perspectives on immersive technology in education* (pp. 235–249). IGI Global. DOI: 10.4018/978-1-7998-3250-8.ch012

Haoues, M., & Mokni, R. (2023). Toward an autism-friendly environment based on mobile apps user feedback analysis using deep learning and machine learning models. *PeerJ. Computer Science*, 9, e1442. DOI: 10.7717/peerj-cs.1442

Hedges, S. H., Odom, S. L., Hume, K., & Sam, A. (2018). Technology use as a support tool by secondary students with autism. *Autism*, 22(1), 70–79. DOI: 10.1177/1362361317717976

Hu, C., Li, W., Ruan, M., Yu, X., Paul, L. K., Wang, S., & Li, X. (2024). Exploiting ChatGPT for Diagnosing Autism-Associated Language Disorders and Identifying Distinct Features. *arXiv preprint arXiv:2405.01799.*

Ibrahim, Z., Mohamed, J., Kassim, N., & Bahrudin, I. A. (2023). The Assistive Technology for Teaching and Learning of Social Skills for Autism Spectrum Disorder Children: Multimedia Interactive Social Skills Module Application. *European Journal of Educational Research*, 12(3), 1465–1477. DOI: 10.12973/eu-jer.12.3.1465

Jaliaawala, M. S., & Khan, R. A. (2020). Can autism be catered with artificial intelligence-assisted intervention technology? A comprehensive survey. *Artificial Intelligence Review*, 53(2), 1039–1069. DOI: 10.1007/s10462-019-09686-8

Johnson, K. R. (2022). Using a Strengths–Based Approach to Improve Employment Opportunities for Individuals with Autism Spectrum Disorder. *New Horizons in Adult Education and Human Resource Development*, 34(1), 16–25. DOI: 10.1002/nha3.20321

Johnson, K. R., Ennis–Cole, D., & Bonhamgregory, M. (2020). Workplace success strategies for employees with autism spectrum disorder: A new frontier for human resource development. *Human Resource Development Review*, 19(2), 122–151. DOI: 10.1177/1534484320905910

Johnson, K. R., & Williams, K. (2022). Workplace Training for Employees with Autism Spectrum Disorder. In *Generation A* (pp. 7–18). Emerald Publishing Limited. DOI: 10.1108/978-1-80071-256-020211001

Kaplan-Rakowski, R., Grotewold, K., Hartwick, P., & Papin, K. (2023). Generative AI and teachers' perspectives on its implementation in education. *Journal of Interactive Learning Research*, 34(2), 313–338. https://www.learntechlib.org/primary/p/222363/

Kaplan-Rakowski, R., & Gruber, A. (2023). The impact of high-immersion virtual reality on foreign language anxiety when speaking in public. *Smart Learning Environments*, 10(46), 46. Advance online publication. DOI: 10.1186/s40561-023-00263-9

Ke, F., Moon, J., & Sokolikj, Z. (2022). Virtual reality–based social skills training for children with autism spectrum disorder. *Journal of Special Education Technology*, 37(1), 49–62. DOI: 10.1177/0162643420945603

Kim, S. I., Jang, S. Y., Kim, T., Kim, B., Jeong, D., Noh, T., Jeong, M., Hall, K., Kim, M., Yoo, H. J., Han, K., Hong, H., & Kim, J. G. (2024). Promoting Self-Efficacy of Individuals With Autism in Practicing Social Skills in the Workplace Using Virtual Reality and Physiological Sensors: Mixed Methods Study. *JMIR Formative Research*, 8, e52157. DOI: 10.2196/52157

Koubaa, A., Boulila, W., Ghouti, L., Alzahem, A., & Latif, S. (2023). Exploring ChatGPT Capabilities and Limitations: A Survey. *IEEE Access : Practical Innovations, Open Solutions*, 11, 118698–118721. DOI: 10.1109/ACCESS.2023.3326474

Kruk, M. (2020). Fluctuations in self-perceived foreign language anxiety during visits to Second Life: A case study. *Innovation in Language Learning and Teaching*. Advance online publication. DOI: 10.1080/17501229.2020.1813737

Kumar, A., Raghunathan, A., Jones, R., Ma, T., & Liang, P. (2022). Fine-tuning can distort pretrained features and underperform out-of-distribution. *arXiv preprint arXiv:2202.10054.*

Lampropoulos, G., Ferdig, R. E., & Kaplan-Rakowski, R. (2024). A social media data analysis of general and educational use of ChatGPT: Understanding emotional educators. *Journal of Educational Technology & Society*.

Lebovitz, S., Lifshitz-Assaf, H., & Levina, N. (2022). To engage or not to engage with AI for critical judgments: How professionals deal with opacity when using AI for medical diagnosis. *Organization Science*, 33(1), 126–148. DOI: 10.1287/orsc.2021.1549

Li, Y., & Chiu, C. Y. (2024, June). Redefining Truth in the Context of AI-Truth Era: A Practice-Led Research of "From Post-Truth to AI-Truth". In *International Conference on Human-Computer Interaction* (pp. 245-257). Cham: Springer Nature Switzerland. DOI: 10.1007/978-3-031-60913-8_17

Liu, V., & Chilton, L. B. (2022, April). Design guidelines for prompt engineering text-to-image generative models. In *Proceedings of the 2022 CHI Conference on Human Factors in Computing Systems* (pp. 1–23). DOI: 10.1145/3491102.3501825

Lizotte, M. (2018). I Am a College Graduate: Postsecondary Experiences as Described by Adults with Autism Spectrum Disorders. *International Journal of Education and Practice, 6*(4), 179-191.Limna, P., & Kraiwanit, T. (2023). The role of chatgpt on customer service in the hospitality industry: An exploratory study of hospitality workers' experiences and perceptions. *Tourism and Hospitality Management*, 29(4), 583–592.

López Jiménez, E. A., & Ouariachi, T. (2021). An exploration of the impact of artificial intelligence (AI) and automation for communication professionals. *Journal of Information. Communication and Ethics in Society*, 19(2), 249–267. DOI: 10.1108/JICES-03-2020-0034

Lund, B. D., Wang, T., Mannuru, N. R., Nie, B., Shimray, S., & Wang, Z. (2023). ChatGPT and a new academic reality: Artificial Intelligence-written research papers and the ethics of the large language models in scholarly publishing. *Journal of the Association for Information Science and Technology*, 74(5), 570–581. DOI: 10.1002/asi.24750

McFayden, T. C., Bristol, S., Putnam, O., & Harrop, C. (2024). ChatGPT: Artificial Intelligence as a Potential Tool for Parents Seeking Information About Autism. *Cyberpsychology, Behavior, and Social Networking*, 27(2), 135–148. Advance online publication. DOI: 10.1089/cyber.2023.0202

Meskó, B. (2023). Prompt engineering as an important emerging skill for medical professionals: Tutorial. *Journal of Medical Internet Research*, 25, e50638. DOI: 10.2196/50638

Nesbitt, S. (2000). Why and why not? Factors impacting employment for individuals with Asperger syndrome. *Autism*, 4(4), 357–369. DOI: 10.1177/1362361300004004002

Ng, D. T. K., Leung, J. K. L., Chu, S. K. W., & Qiao, M. S. (2021). Conceptualizing AI literacy: An exploratory review. *Computers and Education: Artificial Intelligence, 2*, article 100041.

Nicholas, D., Mitchell, W., Zulla, R., & Dudley, C. (2019). Perspectives of employers about hiring individuals with autism spectrum disorder: Evaluating a cohort of employers engaged in a job–readiness initiative. *Journal of Vocational Rehabilitation*, 50(3), 353–364. DOI: 10.3233/JVR-191018

Nicholas, D. B., Zwaigenbaum, L., Zwicker, J., Clarke, M. E., Lamsal, R., Stoddart, K., Carroll, C., Muskat, B., Spoelstra, M., & Lowe, K. (2018). Evaluation of employment support services for adults with autism spectrum disorder. *Autism*, 22(6), 693–702. DOI: 10.1177/1362361317702507

Ntoutsi, E., Fafalios, P., Gadiraju, U., Iosifidis, V., Nejdl, W., Vidal, M. E., Ruggieri, S., Turini, F., Papadopoulos, S., Krasanakis, E., Kompatsiaris, I., Kinder-Kurlanda, K., Wagner, C., Karimi, F., Fernandez, M., Alani, H., Berendt, B., Kruegel, T., Heinze, C., & Staab, S. (2020). Bias in data-driven artificial intelligence systems—An introductory survey. *Wiley Interdisciplinary Reviews. Data Mining and Knowledge Discovery*, 10(3), e1356. DOI: 10.1002/widm.1356

O'Connor, S., & Liu, H. (2024). Gender bias perpetuation and mitigation in AI technologies: Challenges and opportunities. *AI & Society*, 39(4), 2045–2057. DOI: 10.1007/s00146-023-01675-4

Olasik, M. (2023). "Good morning, ChatGPT, Can We Become Friends?" An Interdisciplinary Scholar's Experience of 'Getting Acquainted'with the OpenAI's Chat GPT: An Auto Ethnographical Report. *European Research Studies*, 26(2), 269–284. DOI: 10.35808/ersj/3168

Pavlik, J. V. (2023). Collaborating with ChatGPT: Considering the implications of generative artificial intelligence for journalism and media education. *Journalism & Mass Communication Educator*, 78(1), 84–93. DOI: 10.1177/10776958221149577

Petroni, F., Rocktäschel, T., Lewis, P., Bakhtin, A., Wu, Y., Miller, A. H., & Riedel, S. (2019). Language models as knowledge bases? *arXiv preprint arXiv:1909.01066*. DOI: 10.18653/v1/D19-1250

Porayska-Pomsta, K., Alcorn, A. M., Avramides, K., Beale, S., Bernardini, S., Foster, M. E., Frauenberger, C., Good, J., Guldberg, K., Keay-Bright, W., Kossyvaki, L., Lemon, O., Mademtzi, M., Menzies, R., Pain, H., Rajendran, G., Waller, A., Wass, S., & Smith, T. J. (2018). Blending human and artificial intelligence to support autistic children's social communication skills. [TOCHI]. *ACM Transactions on Computer-Human Interaction*, 25(6), 1–35. DOI: 10.1145/3271484

Ratican, J., & Hutson, J. (2023). The Six Emotional Dimension (6DE) Model: A Multidimensional Approach to Analyzing Human Emotions and Unlocking the Potential of Emotionally Intelligent Artificial Intelligence (AI) via Large Language Models (LLM). *Journal of Artificial Intelligence and Robotics*, 1(1), 481.

Rhodes, B. J., & Maes, P. (2000). Just-in-time information retrieval agents. *IBM Systems Journal, 39*(3.4), 685–704.

Rosen, R., Weiss, P. L., Zancanaro, M., & Gal, E. (2017). Usability of a video modeling computer application for the vocational training of adolescents with autism spectrum disorder. *British Journal of Occupational Therapy*, 80(4), 208–215. DOI: 10.1177/0308022616680367

Salkever, D. S. (2000). Activity status, life satisfaction and perceived productivity for young adults with developmental disabilities. *Journal of Rehabilitation*, 66(3), 4.

Saxena, N. B. (2020). AI as awakened intelligence: Buddha, Kurzweil and the film Her. *Theology and Science*, 18(1), 74–85. DOI: 10.1080/14746700.2019.1710351

Schreuter, D., van der Putten, P., & Lamers, M. H. (2021). Trust me on this one: Conforming to conversational assistants. *Minds and Machines*, 31(4), 535–562. DOI: 10.1007/s11023-021-09581-8

Scott, M., Milbourn, B., Falkmer, M., Black, M., Bölte, S., Alycia, H., Lerner, M., Taylor, J. L., & Sonya, G. (2019). Factors impacting employment for people with autism spectrum disorder: A scoping review. *Autism*, 23(4), 869–901. DOI: 10.1177/1362361318787789

Shahamiri, S. R., & Thabtah, F. (2020). Autism AI: A new autism screening system based on artificial intelligence. *Cognitive Computation*, 12(4), 766–777. DOI: 10.1007/s12559-020-09743-3

Shivers, C. M., Sonnier-Netto, L., & Lee, G. K. (2019). Needs and experiences of family caregivers of individuals with autism spectrum disorders across the lifespan. *Journal of Policy and Practice in Intellectual Disabilities*, 16(1), 21–29. DOI: 10.1111/jppi.12272

Smith, M. J., Ginger, E. J., Wright, K., Wright, M. A., Taylor, J. L., Humm, L. B., Olsen, D. E., Bell, M. D., & Fleming, M. F. (2014). Virtual reality job interview training in adults with autism spectrum disorder. *Journal of Autism and Developmental Disorders*, 44(10), 2450–2463. DOI: 10.1007/s10803-014-2113-y

Strickland, D. C., Coles, C. D., & Southern, L. B. (2013). JobTIPS: A transition to employment program for individuals with autism spectrum disorders. *Journal of Autism and Developmental Disorders*, 43(10), 2472–2483. DOI: 10.1007/s10803-013-1800-4

Stupar-Rutenfrans, S., Ketelaars, L. E. H., & Van Gisbergen, M. S. (2017). Beat the fear of public speaking: Does the 360° video virtual reality exposure training in home environment reduces speech anxiety? *Cyberpsychology, Behavior, and Social Networking*, 20, 624–633. DOI: 10.1089/cyber.2017.0174

Sun, X., Ma, R., Zhao, X., Li, Z., Lindqvist, J., Ali, A. E., & Bosch, J. A. (2024). Trusting the Search: Unraveling Human Trust in Health Information from Google and ChatGPT. *arXiv preprint arXiv:2403.09987.*

Tan, B. L., Guan, F. Y., Leung, I. M. W., Kee, S. Y. M., Devilly, O. Z., & Medalia, A. (2022). A gamified augmented reality vocational training program for adults with intellectual and developmental disabilities: A pilot study on acceptability and effectiveness. *Frontiers in Psychiatry*, 13, 966080. DOI: 10.3389/fpsyt.2022.966080

Thrasher, T., Kaplan-Rakowski, R., Ovsiannikova, U., Meyr, J., & Yuan, Y. (2023). *"I can talk to Spanish speakers in Illinois!": Student perspectives on AI-avatar role plays in virtual reality.* WorldCALL2023: Conference Proceedings. DOI: 10.22492/issn.2759-1182.2023.18

Tomczak, M. T. (2021). Employees with autism spectrum disorders in the digitized work environment: Perspectives for the future. *Journal of Disability Policy Studies*, 31(4), 195–205. DOI: 10.1177/1044207320919945

Trust, T., Whalen, J., & Mouza, C. (2023). Editorial: ChatGPT: Challenges, opportunities, and implications for teacher education. *Contemporary Issues in Technology & Teacher Education*, 23(1).

Turi, L. F., Cavalini, A., Comarela, G., Oliveira-Santos, T., Badue, C., & De Souza, A. F. (2024). Analysis of Bias in GPT Language Models through Fine-tuning Containing Divergent Data. In *2024 International Joint Conference on Neural Networks (IJCNN)* (pp. 1-8). IEEE. DOI: 10.1109/IJCNN60899.2024.10650574

US Bureau of Labor Statistics. (2023). *People with a disability: Labor Force Characteristics.* Retrieved at https://www.bls.gov/news.release/disabl.a.htm

Varona, D., & Suarez, J. L. (2022). Discrimination, bias, fairness, and trustworthy AI. *Applied Sciences (Basel, Switzerland)*, 12(12), 5826. DOI: 10.3390/app12125826

Wang, M., Wang, M., Xu, X., Yang, L., Cai, D., & Yin, M. (2023). Unleashing ChatGPT's Power: A Case Study on Optimizing Information Retrieval in Flipped Classrooms via Prompt Engineering. *IEEE Transactions on Learning Technologies*, 17, 629–641. DOI: 10.1109/TLT.2023.3324714

Ward, S. J., & King, L. A. (2017). Work and the good life: How work contributes to meaning in life. *Research in Organizational Behavior*, 37, 59–82. DOI: 10.1016/j.riob.2017.10.001

Wehman, P., Schall, C. M., McDonough, J., Graham, C., Brooke, V., Riehle, J. E., Brooke, A., Ham, W., Lau, S., Allen, J., & Avellone, L. (2017). Effects of an employer–based intervention on employment outcomes for youth with significant support needs due to autism. *Autism*, 21(3), 276–290. DOI: 10.1177/1362361316635826

Wilson, T. D. (1981). On user studies and information needs. *The Journal of Documentation*, 37(1), 3–15. DOI: 10.1108/eb026702

Wu, T., He, S., Liu, J., Sun, S., Liu, K., Han, Q. L., & Tang, Y. (2023). A brief overview of ChatGPT: The history, status quo and potential future development. *IEEE/CAA Journal of Automatica Sinica, 10*(5), 1122–1136.

Zhang, Y., Li, Y., Cui, L., Cai, D., Liu, L., Fu, T., . . . Shi, S. (2023). Siren's song in the AI ocean: a survey on hallucination in large language models. *arXiv preprint arXiv:2309.01219.*

Chapter 15
Implications of Artificial Intelligence for Special Education Technology

Bitan Roy
Brainware University, India

Sanchita Ghosh
Brainware University, India

Saptarshi Kumar Sarkar
Brainware University, India

Anupama Sen
Brainware University, India

Nobhonil Roy Choudhury
https://orcid.org/0009-0009-1046-7492
Brainware University, India

ABSTRACT

This study explores the diverse applications of Artificial Intelligence (AI) in special education, focusing on data-driven decision-making, behavioral and cognitive therapies, adaptive learning platforms, and enhancing accessibility through assistive technology and speech and language processing tools. AI-driven assistive technologies like smart glasses and screen readers enhance physical and digital accessibility, while AI makes data collection, analysis, and predictive analytics easier, allowing educators to customize interventions for specific students. The study emphasizes the potential of AI in special education to revolutionize the field by fostering academic

DOI: 10.4018/979-8-3693-5538-1.ch015

success, equality, and inclusion. It also discusses ethical aspects such as privacy, prejudice, and inclusiveness, and recommends professional development for educators, adoption of Universal Design for Learning concepts, data literacy and privacy awareness, and stakeholder cooperation.

INTRODUCTION

The use of special education technology is any form of device or software that is used to assist students with special educational needs or disabilities in meeting their learning targets. (Peterson et al. 2015) These include resources that promote accessibility and a variety of learning styles through assistive technology and adaptive learning environments. AI has been a disruptive factor in many areas, including education, in the last few years. Artificial intelligence (AI) is defined as technologies that can duplicate human intellects in terms of reasoning, learning and problem solving (Russell & Norvig, 2022). AI algorithms' improvements along with the large amount of data and computer power have led to the novel developments in education notably in special education. The possibilities of improving the educational experiences and the achievement of the kids with disabilities are immense when the AI and special education technologies are combined. AI-based learning tools as compared to traditional teaching methodologies are capable of customizing programs to the requirements of individual learners ((Pullen et al. 2019). AI in education would allow teachers to meet the different needs of students with disabilities more appropriately and make their classrooms more inclusive. The objective of this chapter is to examine how artificial intelligence (AI) will change the special education technology. We will examine the state of the art of the special education technology today, describe its main uses in this field, cover ethical problems that might occur, and demonstrate the difficulties and opportunities for the years to come.

HISTORICAL PERSPECTIVE

The first decade of the 20th century' gave birth to special education gadgets as educators placed resources for you willing to help kids with disabilities. Frank Haven Hall's invention of the Braille typewriter in 1892 greatly changed written communication for those who are blind or visually impaired. Technology-based innovations such as custom designed software for instruction, communication support, and hearing aids advanced education accessibility and learner potentials for a student with impairment. Personal computers and early educational software design that worked toward the new direction of being customized and adaptive became available in the late seventies and the eighties. These developments heightened the application of special education technology. The special education technology was first invented in the 1950s and the AI has played a very significant role in it. The machine learning algorithms, methods of the natural language processing, and the intelligent tutoring systems are the major accomplishment steps in the development of artificial intellect. AI's potential in health care appeared for the first time in 1974 when MYCIN system was developed, and later detected its diagnostic abilities which were as professional as those of a human specialist. Thus, the development of such systems was started to be called for further educational purposes, for instance, adaptive technology for children with impairments and personalized learning systems AI has been used in special education to design adaptable learning ecosystems and intelligent tutoring systems in a way which suits the user. The Cognitive Tutor marked the entry of AI algorithms into the education field in arithmetic practice using individualized training which emerged in the 1980's. This is an example of how AI can be utilized to customize education depending on the student's performance and learning styles. Both the technologies for synthetic voices and natural language processing has been a boon in assisting the students with language and speech problems, enhancing their team work and interactions by removing that barrier. The trail for the coming deployments of various AI applications in the special education appears to be already laid by the case studies of the use of AI in special education.

CURRENT LANDSCAPE OF SPECIAL EDUCATION TECHNOLOGY

A range of tools and resources are included in special education technology, which is intended to accommodate the requirements of children with disabilities or special needs. These technologies may be divided into a number of categories, such as instructional software, assistive technology, adaptive learning systems, and augmentative and alternative communication (AAC) devices. But even with all of the technological progress, instructors and students still have difficulties when putting these tools to use. The lack of resources and access, especially in impoverished places, might make it difficult to get the instruments that are required. Due to the lack of adequate accessibility features in many digital resources and educational software packages, accessibility and usability concerns still exist. In special education settings, educators frequently lack the professional development opportunities and training necessary to use technology successfully. Technical proficiency should be included in training programs, along with tactics for fostering inclusive learning environments and making use of technology to

Opportunities for Improvement Through AI Integration

Artificial intelligence (AI) offers promising potential to address the challenges faced by teachers and students in special education settings.

- **Personalized Learning:** AI-powered adaptive learning systems that evaluate student data may be used to provide personalized instruction and interventions tailored to each student's particular learning needs and preferences (Pullen et al. 2019)
- **Data-driven Decision Making:** Artificial intelligence (AI) algorithms can analyze large datasets to identify patterns and trends in student performance, assisting educators in making well-informed decisions about instructional strategies, modifications, and interventions (Pullen et al. 2019)
- **Natural Language Processing (NLP):** Wolf and Burleson (2017) state that NLP technology can help language-challenged pupils by enabling them to synthesis and identify speech, hence enhancing their communication abilities.

APPLICATIONS OF AI IN SPECIAL EDUCATION TECHNOLOGY

Natural language processing (NLP), adaptive learning systems, tailored learning experiences, assistive technologies for students with impairments, and AI-driven assessment and progress tracking tools are just a few of the ways that artificial intelligence (AI) technology has transformed education. With the help of AI algorithms, personalized learning systems evaluate student data and modify training to match each student's needs. This results in focused interventions, fast feedback, and specially created content. By using AI algorithms to dynamically modify the speed, subject matter, and degree of difficulty of education in response to student performance and advancement, adaptive learning systems foster student autonomy, engagement, and mastery of learning objectives. AI-driven assistive technologies improve accessibility and support for students with impairments. Examples of these include computer vision and object recognition, speech recognition and synthesis, prosthetics, and mobility aids. Students that struggle with communication can benefit from artificial intelligence (AI) systems' ability to comprehend, interpret, and produce human language thanks to natural language processing (NLP) technology. AI-driven solutions for tracking progress and assessments evaluate student performance data, spot patterns in learning outcomes, and tailor instruction to a varied student population using machine learning algorithms.

Personalized Learning Experiences

AI is able to assess student data and adjust instruction to meet the needs and preferences of individual students, enabling personalized learning experiences (Pullen et al. 2019) Personalized learning systems assess students' learning preferences, areas of strength, and areas of weakness using AI algorithms so that teachers may modify their approach. To assist students in achieving their learning objectives, AI-driven tutoring tools, for example, can provide targeted interventions, immediate feedback, and customized material (VanLehn et al. 2011).

Adaptive Learning Systems

Adaptive learning systems use AI algorithms to dynamically adjust the pace, content, and difficulty level of instruction based on students' performance and progress (Pullen et al. 2019) These systems analyze data from student interactions to identify areas of competency and those that require further support in order to deliver customized learning routes. Adaptive learning technologies promote student autonomy, engagement, and mastery of learning objectives by providing tailored scaffolding and challenges (((Anderson et al. 1995) et al. 1995) ; al., 1995).

Assistive Technologies for Students with Disabilities

AI-driven assistive technology increases accessibility and offers additional support in several domains to students with disabilities. For example, because to developments in computer vision and object recognition technologies, visually impaired pupils may now independently explore their environment (Miesenberger et al., 2018). Voice recognition and synthesis technology facilitate effective communication and self-expression for those with speech and language impairments (luculano et al. 2015). Artificial intelligence-driven prosthesis and mobility aids increase independence and mobility for students with physical constraints (Borg et al. 2012).

Natural Language Processing for Communication Support

Natural language processing (NLP) technology enables artificial intelligence (AI) systems to understand, interpret, and generate human language, which can be beneficial for students who have communication difficulties (luculano et al. 2015). Several NLP technologies, such as sentiment analysis, language translation, and speech recognition, can assist students in a range of communication tasks. For example, predictive text algorithms can assist language-challenged individuals in writing messages or participating in online discussions (Mayer et al. 2013)

AI-Driven Assessment and Progress Tracking Tools

Artificial intelligence (AI)-based assessment systems use machine learning algorithms to analyze student performance data and identify trends in learning outcomes and development. Through the provision of adaptive assessments, monitoring of student involvement, and provision of data for instructional decision-making, they enhance accessibility and optimize learning outcomes for a diverse student body.

CASE STUDIES AND EXAMPLES

Artificial intelligence (AI), particularly in intelligent tutoring systems, has to be included into special education to support students with learning disabilities. Social contact and communication are enhanced by NLP-capable social robots and Carnegie Learning's Cognitive Tutor software, which enhances instruction and learning chances.The integration of AI in special education has positively impacted the social skills and engagement of children with impairments. A University of Washington study found that while utilizing VR-based therapy, teenagers with autism were able to interact and communicate more socially. Mindspark is a program developed by Educational Initiatives in India that uses artificial intelligence (AI) algorithms to provide tailored arithmetic teaching to students with a range of learning challenges. In a randomized controlled trial, students who received personalized AI-based instruction outperformed those in traditional classrooms in terms of learning gains. These success stories show how artificial intelligence (AI) may enhance learning outcomes and student engagement for kids with disabilities.

Impact of AI on Student Outcomes and Engagement

AI has a significant impact on student outcomes and engagement in special education programs. It can provide personalized learning, increase engagement, and improve academic achievement by tailoring the learning experience to each student's needs and pace. This can be achieved by adjusting difficulty levels, providing targeted instruction, and catering to different learning styles. This personalization leads to a more engaging learning experience, fostering a sense of accomplishment and motivation meta-analysis of multiple research projects found that AI-based systems lead to increased academic achievement due to effective practice, immediate feedback, and increased focus and time on task. AI-driven assistive technologies, such as text-to-speech and speech-to-text tools, can help students with reading difficulties access information, improve their writing and dyslexia, and enable deaf or hard of hearing students to participate fully in classroom activities.AI-powered assistive technology fosters independence and self-reliance in students with disabilities by removing barriers to learning and communication. However, the effectiveness of AI depends on how it is implemented and integrated with a comprehensive special education program. Overall, AI offers a promising approach to enhance student outcomes and engagement in special education, but its effectiveness depends on how it is implemented and integrated with the program.

Enhancing Communication: AI in Augmentative and Alternative Communication (AAC)

AAC (alternative and augmentative communication) devices are instruments made to help people who have severe speech or language impairments. These gadgets vary in complexity from straightforward, low-tech solutions like picture boards to sophisticated, high-tech systems with speech-generating devices (SGDs). AAC devices are primarily intended to improve communication for people with impairments, allowing them to express themselves, engage in social interactions, and take part more fully in educational and professional environments (Beukelman et al. 2020).

AAC devices can be categorized into three main types:

- **No-Tech and Low-Tech AAC:** These gadgets, which include picture exchange systems, books, and communication boards, run off electricity and don't require batteries.
- **Mid-Tech AAC:** These are low-featured electronic gadgets, such basic SGDs that play recorded messages.
- **High-Tech AAC:** These are high-tech electronic gadgets that can produce synthesized speech and frequently have features like voice recognition and predictive text. Examples of these gadgets are tablets, computers, and advanced SGDs.

Artificial Intelligence (AI) has great promise for improving AAC devices' usability and efficacy. These gadgets can provide more individualized, effective, and organic communication experiences by incorporating AI. The following are some significant ways AI is changing AAC technology:

i. **Predictive Text and Word Prediction**: By analyzing a user's past inputs, artificial intelligence (AI) systems can anticipate the word or phrase the user will type next. This feature facilitates faster communication and lessens the work involved in crafting communication. For instance, machine learning models are used by predictive text solutions, such as those created by SwiftKey (now a part of Microsoft), to deliver precise word predictions, improving typing productivity for AAC users (Elsahar et al. 2019).

ii. **Natural Language Processing (NLP)**: NLP makes it possible for AAC devices to produce and comprehend human language in a way that is appropriate for the setting. This facilitates the conversion of user input into speech that sounds more realistic. By using NLP approaches, AAC devices may decipher unclear inputs and offer pertinent recommendations, improving user satisfaction and streamlining communication (Beukelman et al. 2020). The study of how computers and human language interact is the subject of the artificial intelligence discipline known as natural language processing, or NLP. It makes it possible for machines to comprehend, decipher, and react to human language in a way that is both practical and meaningful. NLP has revolutionized the way that assistive and alternative communication (AAC) technologies facilitate communication for students with disabilities. This section examines how NLP is used in AAC devices, providing practical examples and their effects.

Case Study: An program called SwiftKey predicts text and has been modified for usage with AAC devices. It offers extremely precise word predictions by learning from the user's writing style, which speeds up and eases the burden of communication for people with physical limitations that restrict their typing pace (Elsahar et al. 2019).

NLP Applications to Help Students with Disabilities Communicate

NLP technology allows for more natural, fluid, and productive conversations, which helps close the communication gap for children with impairments when using AAC devices. The following are some important applications:

iii. **Speech Recognition and Synthesis:** Users with restricted mobility can operate their AAC devices by speaking commands into advanced speech recognition software. Furthermore, voice synthesis enabled by AI generates more customized and natural-sounding speech outputs. To give realistic and customized voice options, businesses like Google and Amazon have created advanced voice synthesis technologies that can be included into AAC devices (Wang et al. 2017).

Case Study: Dysarthria and Speech Recognition: An NLP-based speech recognition system specifically designed for people with motor speech disorders, such as dysarthria, was created at the University of Sheffield through a project. After the system was trained on the distinct speech patterns of dysarthric speakers, recognition accuracy increased dramatically, strengthening the speakers' capacity for communication (Christensen et al. 2012).

iv. **Image and Object Recognition:** By identifying objects or images that users point to or gaze at and producing corresponding spoken words or phrases, AI-driven image and object recognition can support users with severe physical limitations in communicating. For example, Microsoft's Seeing AI app, which can be modified for AAC, uses machine vision to describe people, objects, and text in the environment (Miesenberger et al., 2018).
v. **Context-Aware Messaging**: AAC devices can provide more pertinent and well-thought-out responses when they are able to comprehend the context of discussions thanks to NLP. This is especially helpful in social interactions that are dynamic and subject to sudden changes in circumstance.

Case Study: Collaborative Writing Initiative: An NLP-driven AAC system that helps kids with learning difficulties write better by offering context-aware recommendations and corrections in real-time was developed as part of the CoWriter project, a cooperation between the University of Geneva and EPFL (Huang et al. 2024).

Impact on Communication and Quality of Life

AI has the capacity to gain knowledge from user interactions over time and modify itself to suit each user's unique requirements. By personalizing these gadgets, AAC devices become more responsive and intuitive. Adaptive learning algorithms improve the usability and efficiency of AAC devices by customizing their vocabulary and interface (King, 2011).The communication skills of people with disabilities are greatly improved by the incorporation of AI into AAC devices. Increased independence, better social contact, and an overall superior quality of life are the results of these developments. AI helps close the communication gap between users and AAC devices, enabling them to express themselves more fully and engage in community activities. Artificial Intelligence (AI) is transforming the AAC space by enhancing the efficiency, personalization, and naturalness of device communication. These upgrades not only improve the gadgets' functionalities but also greatly raise the standard of living for people who struggle with communication. AI has the ability to significantly change AAC and other assistive technology as it develops, providing new avenues for inclusivity and

ETHICAL CONSIDERATION

Since special education technology powered by artificial intelligence (AI) gathers and uses personal student data, privacy concerns are raised. AI systems may violate students' right to privacy since they rely on vast volumes of data to draw judgments. Concerns of student confidentiality, authorization, and data security are brought up by this data collecting. To allay these worries, educators and legislators must establish precise guidelines for the gathering, storing, and application of data in AI-driven special education programs. These include getting consent with full knowledge, protecting personal data from unwanted access, and putting strong cybersecurity measures in place to prevent data exploitation.

Bias and Fairness in AI Algorithms for Special Education

Artificial intelligence (AI) algorithms employed in special education technology have the potential to accentuate or perpetuate biases and disadvantages, particularly those related to gender, racism, socioeconomic status, and disability. This might lead to biased outcomes for underrepresented student populations. To lessen bias and enhance justice, developers should prioritize transparency, responsibility, and diversity when creating and deploying algorithms. This means ensuring that training datasets include a range of representations, conducting extensive testing and validation procedures, and frequently assessing AI systems for equity and justice.

Ensuring Inclusivity and Accessibility in AI-Driven Technologies

AI-driven solutions must be inclusive and accessible for special education. Developers should adopt a universal design approach that considers a variety of needs and ability levels. This includes integrated accessibility features, customizable user interfaces, support for multiple sensory modalities, and alternative input methods. Engaging in communication with end users can help guarantee that particular accessibility requirements are met.

AI Chatbots and Virtual Assistants for Real-Time Support

NLP-powered AI chatbots and virtual assistants empower students with impairments in real-time, improving their communication skills and helping with a range of activities.

- **AI Chatbots**: AI chatbots employ natural language processing (NLP) to communicate with users in natural language, answering their questions and holding discussions. These chatbots can provide instant conversational support by being embedded into AAC devices.

Case Study: Alternative for Emotional Assistance: People with autism have used Replika, an AI chatbot created for emotional assistance, to practice social interactions and communicate their emotions. Users can enhance their communication skills in a secure and encouraging setting by using the chatbot's comprehension and responsiveness to a broad spectrum of emotional emotions (Burke et al., 2021).

- **Virtual Assistants**: NLP is used by virtual assistants such as Siri, Google Assistant, and Alexa to interpret and carry out voice orders, complete tasks, and deliver information. With the integration of these aides into AAC devices, users can carry out daily tasks with greater independence.

Case Study: Violet, a business that specializes in non-standard speech recognition technology, has linked its system with Amazon Alexa. This enables voice commands to be used by people with speech difficulties to operate smart home appliances, retrieve information, and improve communication. The integration serves as an example of how NLP can improve technology's usability and accessibility for individuals with impairments (Voiceitt, 2021).

NLP applications in AAC devices significantly enhance communication for students with disabilities by providing more natural, intuitive, and efficient interactions. From predictive text to context-aware messaging and AI chatbots, these technologies are making a profound impact on the lives of individuals with communication challenges. By continuing to integrate and refine NLP capabilities, AAC devices can become even more powerful tools for fostering independence, inclusion, and social participation.

FUTURE DIRECTIONS AND CHALLENGES

Special education technology is going toward the intersection of AI and tailored learning, and many recent advancements are changing the landscape in this area:

- **Augmented Reality (AR) and Virtual Reality (VR)**: It is possible to create immersive learning environments that satisfy the different needs of students with disabilities by utilizing AR and VR technologies. Mukhtarkyzy et al. (2022; 2013) asserts that these technologies can provide chances for experiential learning, virtual field trips, and interactive simulations that enhance student comprehension and engagement.

- **Emotion Recognition and Affective Computing**: Artificial intelligence (AI)-driven systems with the ability to recognize and respond to their students' emotions may help and personalize social-emotional learning. By analyzing physiological data, facial expressions, and vocal intonations, these systems can provide adaptive feedback and therapies to promote resilience and well-being (Picard et al. 2000).
- **Blockchain for Secure Data Management** Blockchain technology allows for the safe management of sensitive student data on a transparent, decentralized network. By leveraging blockchain technology, special education technology providers may increase data privacy, integrity, and interoperability while granting students control over their personal data (Tapscott et al. 2016).

Potential Barriers to Widespread Adoption

Although artificial intelligence (AI) has much to offer special education technology, there are a few barriers that might keep it from being used widely:

- **Cost and Resource Constraints**: Deploying AI-driven technologies often requires significant infrastructure support, specialist knowledge, and financial investment. It's probable that many educational establishments lack the resources and know-how required to properly integrate and sustain these technologies, particularly those located in low-income areas (Bateman et al. 2019)
- **Lack of Training and Professional Development**: Educators and special education professionals can find it challenging to acquire the knowledge and skills required to properly integrate AI into their lesson plans. Teachers need to have access to extensive training and professional development programs in order to employ AI-driven technology to serve different learners in an effective manner. In 2015. Peterson et al.
- **Ethical and Legal Concerns**: Ethical worries concerning AI systems' fairness, bias, and data privacy significantly impede adoption. Educators, policymakers, and tech developers must navigate complex legal and ethical frameworks to ensure that AI-driven technologies protect students' rights, enhance justice, and minimize potential hazards (Noble, 2018).

Research Gaps and Areas for Further Exploration

The topic of artificial intelligence (AI) for special education technology has a number of research gaps and areas that require more investigation.

- **Long-Term Effects on Learning Outcomes**: More research is needed to assess the long-term impacts of AI-driven treatments on kids' academic achievement, social-emotional development, and post-school outcomes. Longitudinal studies can provide valuable information on the efficacy and long-term sustainability of AI-driven special education technology, claim VanDerHeyden et al. (2020).
- **Inclusive Design and User Experience**: To ensure that AI-driven solutions are accessible and useful for all students, including those with disabilities, inclusive design concepts and user-cantered methodologies should be prioritized in future research. By including stakeholders in the design and development process, learning environments may be made more egalitarian and inclusive (Rose et al. 2002).
- **Cross-Cultural and Multilingual Perspectives**: Studying the environmental, linguistic, and cultural factors influencing the effectiveness of AI-driven special education programs is necessary to advance global diversity and inclusion. Cross-cultural research can have an impact on the development of culturally aware AI systems and instructional techniques that meet the diverse needs of students from different backgrounds (Wozniak et al.2015).

SUPPORTING COGNITIVE AND BEHAVIOURAL INTERVENTIONS

Particularly for kids with exceptional needs, artificial intelligence (AI) holds great promise for revolutionizing the monitoring and evaluation of student behaviour in educational environments. Teachers and doctors can obtain profound insights into student behaviour patterns by utilizing AI, which makes it possible to provide more successful interventions and assistance.

- **Tracking and Analysing Student Behaviour:** Tracking and Analysing Student Behaviour Real-time tracking and analysis of student behaviour is becoming more and more common with the usage of AI technologies like computer vision and machine learning. In order to spot patterns and trends in behaviour, these systems are able to record and analyze data from a variety of sources, such as interaction logs, wearable sensors, and video feeds.

- **Classroom Management Systems Enhanced by AI:** Machine learning algorithms are used by AI-based classroom management systems, such as ClassDojo, to monitor student conduct. According to Lam et al. (2018), these systems evaluate participation, attentiveness, and social interaction data from classroom interactions to give teachers timely feedback and useful insights. These tools aid instructors in comprehending the root causes of behavioural problems and developing customized solutions by highlighting patterns.
- **Automated Intervention Strategies Based on Behavioural Data:** The creation and application of automated intervention techniques is another application for AI. AI systems are able to suggest individualized solutions that are catered to the unique requirements of every learner through the analysis of behavioural data. IBM Watson for Education uses artificial intelligence (AI) to deliver behavioural interventions and customized learning experiences. Watson can provide focused treatments, such more practice exercises or social-emotional learning activities, to address particular needs by evaluating student data, including academic performance and behavioural trends (Chen et al. 2016). This methodology guarantees that interventions are grounded in facts and evidence, hence augmenting their efficacy.

Cognitive Skill Development

By creative methods like gamification and cognitive training programs, AI-driven tools are also being utilized to improve cognitive abilities like memory and attention.AI technology can be used to develop customized cognitive training curricula that adjust to the unique requirements of every learner. These programs pinpoint areas of cognitive impairment and offer focused exercises to strengthen these abilities using data-driven insights.

- **Case Study: Lumosity**: Personalized brain training activities to improve memory, focus, and problem-solving abilities are provided by Lumosity, an AI-driven cognitive training platform. The platform ensures a personalized training experience that changes with the user's development by using machine learning algorithms to adjust the exercises' difficulty and type based on the user's performance (Hardy et al. 2011).

Gamification and AI for Cognitive Training

An additional effective strategy for developing cognitive skills is gamification, which is the use of game design principles outside of gaming environments. Gamification in conjunction with AI can produce interesting and successful cognitive training scenarios.

- **Case Study: CogniFit**: CogniFit creates cognitive training games that focus on particular cognitive skills by combining AI and gamification. After evaluating the user's cognitive strengths and limitations using AI, the platform suggests tailored games that target cognitive skills including memory, attention, and executive function. CogniFit encourages users to persist with their training regimens and produce greater results by making cognitive training enjoyable and interesting (Ballesteros et al. 2014).

AI has the ability to significantly improve behavioral and cognitive therapies for students with exceptional needs. Teachers are able to use data-driven, tailored interventions and obtain important insights by using AI to monitor and evaluate student behavior. Furthermore, cutting-edge methods for improving cognitive abilities are provided by gamification techniques and AI-driven technologies, which improve the efficacy and appeal of training. These technologies will probably have a greater influence on special education as they develop further, opening up new avenues for meeting the varied requirements of kids.

DATA-DRIVEN DECISION MAKING

Because it helps with data gathering and analysis, artificial intelligence (AI) is essential to special education. Digital learning platforms and wearable technology are only two of the sources from which AI-powered applications collect and evaluate many kinds of educational data, including behavior, performance, and engagement. AI systems examine this data in order to find patterns and insights that can direct intervention and instructional tactics.Real-time feedback and monitoring systems driven by AI offer instant insights into student behavior and performance, facilitating timely correction. Classcraft is one example of a tool that gamifies classroom management by tracking student behavior in real time. In special education, predictive analytics is especially helpful in identifying kids who may struggle academically and in creating interventions to assist them prevent or decrease such challenges. Predictive analytics employs artificial intelligence (AI) to estimate future educational outcomes.

Data Collection and Analysis

Particularly in special education, artificial intelligence (AI) is vital to the gathering and processing of educational data. AI helps educators make better decisions, customize interventions, and enhance educational outcomes for students with special needs by processing enormous volumes of data in real-time.AI-powered tools are skilled at gathering a wide range of educational data, such as behaviour, performance, and engagement from students. Numerous sources, including wearable technology, digital learning platforms, and classroom interactions, can provide these data points. This data is analyzed by AI algorithms to find trends and insights that might guide intervention and teaching tactics.

- **Case Study: Learning Analytics and AI**: AI-enhanced learning analytics solutions gather information on how students engage with course material and how they perform on tests. Systems such as BrightBytes, for example, employ artificial intelligence (AI) to evaluate data from several sources, giving teachers thorough assessments on their students' progress and pinpointing areas that need improvement (West et al. 2012). Teachers can better understand each student's individual learning needs and adjust their education by using a data-driven approach.

Real-Time Monitoring and Feedback Systems

AI-powered real-time monitoring and feedback systems give educators instant insights into the performance and conduct of their students, enabling prompt remediation. These systems can monitor a range of parameters, including assignment completion, participation rates, and engagement levels. They can also give teachers and students immediate feedback.

- **Case Study: Classcraft**: Classcraft is an AI-powered tool that tracks student behavior in real time and gamifies classroom management. The platform gathers information about student interactions and gives prompt feedback to promote positive behavior and involvement. Instructors can utilize the information to pinpoint students who might want more help and to carry out focused interventions (Abramovich et al. 2013).

Predictive Analytics

Using artificial intelligence (AI) to forecast future educational outcomes from historical and present data is known as predictive analytics. Predictive models are very helpful in special education when it comes to identifying pupils who may struggle academically and developing interventions to help them avoid or lessen such issues. Large datasets can be analyzed by AI algorithms to forecast a variety of educational outcomes, including academic achievement, graduation rates, and the chance of developing learning disabilities. Artificial Intelligence (AI) has the potential to offer educators valuable insights for creating customized learning plans and interventions by spotting patterns and trends.

- **Case Study:** Early Intervention Programs Using Predictive Analytics: AI is used by initiatives like Early Warning Systems (EWS) to identify pupils who may be at risk of falling behind. These programs look at information about conduct, grades, and attendance to find students who can benefit from extra help. For instance, the Chicago Public Schools' EWS employs predictive analytics to identify children who may be at risk of dropping out, enabling teachers to take early action and offer focused assistance (Heppen et al. 2008).

Early Identification of Learning Disabilities Through Predictive Models

Learning difficulties can also be early detected with predictive models. Artificial Intelligence is able to identify indicators of learning problems and suggest more testing and assistance by examining data from examinations, student performance, and behavioral observations.

- **Case Study:** Using AI to Identify Dyslexia Eye tracking technologies and machine learning algorithms are used by AI-driven products such as Lexplore to detect dyslexia in pupils. The technology examines pupils' eye movements while they read to identify dyslexia symptoms with a high degree of accuracy. For students with dyslexia, early diagnosis improves results by enabling educators to offer tailored treatments and support (Rello et al. 2015).

For special education, the use of AI in data gathering, analysis, and predictive analytics has a lot to offer. AI supports educators in making data-driven decisions that improve educational tactics and interventions by offering real-time monitoring and feedback. Early detection of learning problems and customization of interventions to each student's specific requirements are made possible by predictive analytics.

The potential for AI technologies to revolutionize special education through data-driven decision-making will only increase as they develop further.

ENHANCING PERSONALIZED LEARNING

Personalized learning experiences are made possible by AI-powered adaptive learning systems, which are made to dynamically change course content based on each student's performance and learning requirements. By analyzing student data and tailoring course materials to individual needs, these systems employ algorithms to pinpoint problem areas and offer targeted solutions. Through assignments, tests, and participation in activities, they gather data about how students interact with the course material. Based on this analysis, they can change the teaching approach, add more resources, or increase the level of difficulty.Knewton, DreamBox Learning, and Smart Sparrow are a few special education examples of adaptive learning platforms. These platforms offer strategies and customized data to better learning outcomes, with advantages like customized learning trajectories, prompt feedback and assistance, increased engagement, and focused interventions.For kids with impairments, individualized education plans, or IEPs, are essential in the field of special education. AI greatly enhances the efficacy and efficiency of the IEP preparation and administration processes. AI solutions streamline the creation and management of IEPs by automating procedures and providing data-driven insights. In order to assist instructors in creating comprehensive IEPs, AI may examine student data, including behavioral reports, testing results, and progress tracking. Additionally, AI systems have the ability to continuously track students' progress and modify IEPs as necessary.Numerous IEP process processes can be automated by AI, improving process efficiency and reducing teachers' administrative workload. It can gather and evaluate data from multiple sources on its own, guaranteeing that IEPs are founded on accurate and comprehensive data. AI can assist teachers in creating personalized, practical learning objectives and suggest the optimal learning tactics depending on each student's needs and developmental stage.

ADAPTIVE LEARNING SYSTEMS

AI-powered adaptive learning systems dynamically modify course material in response to each student's performance and learning requirements. Personalized learning experiences are provided by these systems, which address the various requirements of students—special education pupils in particular. Algorithms are used by AI-driven adaptive learning systems to evaluate student data and customize course materials to each student's needs. In order to offer individualized learning paths, these systems continuously evaluate the performance, preferences, and learning styles of their students. They assist in identifying problem areas for kids and provide focused interventions as a result. These systems collect information about how students engage with course material through assignments, quizzes, and activity participation. To ascertain the student's comprehension and areas of difficulty, the AI examines this data. The analysis is used by the system to modify the instructional strategy, add more resources, or raise the difficulty level.

Examples of Adaptive Learning Platforms in Special Education

A number of platforms for adaptive learning are made expressly to help kids with unique needs. These platforms provide methods and tailored information to improve learning results.

- **Knewton**: Knewton's AI-powered adaptive learning platform analyzes student data to tailor instruction. It provides students with learning difficulties with tailored support by modifying the speed and difficulty of lessons in real-time (Knewton, n.d.).
- **DreamBox Learning**: DreamBox Learning offers an adaptive math program that continuously assesses student performance and provides personalized instruction. It supports diverse learners, including those with special educational needs, by adjusting content to match their unique learning profiles (DreamBox Learning, n.d.).
- **Smart Sparrow**: This program gives individualized training and is a continuous student performance assessor for math. By customizing information to fit each learner's own learning profile, it accommodates a varied range of learners, including those with special educational needs (DreamBox Learning, n.d.).

Benefits for Students with Diverse Learning Needs

For students with a range of learning demands, AI-driven adaptive learning systems provide the following advantages:

- **Personalized Learning Paths**: These programs adapt course material to each student specifically, making sure that every student gets instruction according to their level and speed.

- **Immediate Feedback and Support**: Students can comprehend their errors and pick up new skills right away with the aid of adaptive learning systems, which offer real-time feedback.
- **Enhanced Engagement**: Adaptive learning systems boost students' motivation and engagement by providing content that aligns with their interests and skill levels.
- **Targeted Interventions**: By identifying problem areas and offering tailored interventions, these systems make sure that students' learning gaps are quickly filled.

Individualized Education Plans (IEPs)

Personalized learning goals and tactics for students with disabilities are outlined in Individualized Education Plans (IEPs), which are crucial in the field of special education. AI significantly contributes to the creation and administration of IEPs, improving process effectiveness and efficiency.AI technologies automate a number of processes and offer data-driven insights, which simplify the construction and administration of IEPs

- **Development of IEPs**: AI can examine student data, such as behavioral reports, assessment results, and progress monitoring, to assist teachers in creating thorough IEPs. This analysis guarantees that the plans are grounded in current, reliable data regarding the requirements and abilities of the students.
- **Management and Monitoring**: AI programs are able to keep an eye on students' development in real time and adjust IEPs as needed. This continuous observation ensures that the learning objectives and tactics are still applicable and successful.

Automation and Optimization of Personalized Learning Goals and Strategies

Numerous IEP process steps can be automated by AI, increasing process efficiency and lessening the administrative load on teachers.

- **Automated Data Collection**: AI systems are capable of autonomously collecting and analyzing data from a variety of sources, including behavioral observations, attendance records, and classroom assessments. IEPs are based on complete and reliable data thanks to this automatic data collecting.
- **Optimization of Learning Strategies**: AI is able to recommend the best learning approaches based on the demands and development of the student.

For instance, the AI may suggest that a student concentrate on learning new abilities or move on to more difficult material if they demonstrate improvement in a particular area.

- **Personalized Goal Setting**: AI can help teachers create individualized, realistic learning objectives for each student. AI assists in ensuring that objectives are reachable and in line with current circumstances by evaluating past data and forecasting future performance.

AI-driven adaptive learning systems and AI's role in managing IEPs significantly enhance personalized learning in special education. Adaptive learning platforms provide customized learning experiences, while AI streamlines the development and management of IEPs, ensuring that educational strategies are tailored to the unique needs of each student. The integration of AI in special education holds promise for improving learning outcomes and creating more inclusive and effective educational environments.

RECOMMENDATIONS FOR PRACTITIONERS AND POLICYMAKERS

Lawmakers and practitioners may successfully integrate artificial intelligence (AI) into special education curricula by putting these suggestions into practice:

I. **Professional Development**: Provide educators with opportunities for professional development and in-depth training so they may become more skilled at using AI-driven technologies. Training should cover both technical skills and pedagogical approaches in order to successfully incorporate AI into educational methods (Peterson et al. 2015).
II. **Universal Design for Learning (UDL)**: Embracing the UDL principles will ensure that all students, irrespective of ability or chosen learning style, may make inclusive and accessible use of AI-driven technology. Develop curricula that offer many platforms for representation, expression, and engagement in order to satisfy the needs of a diverse student body (Rose et al. 2002).
III. **Data Literacy and Privacy Awareness**: Educate practitioners about the ethical implications of artificial intelligence and data privacy issues. Provide educators with the knowledge and skills necessary to make decisions about data collection, usage, and protection that adhere to all relevant laws and rules (Mayer et al. 2013)

Policy Recommendations for Ethical AI Implementation

Legislators may contribute to ensuring that AI is applied responsibly in special education by putting these legislative ideas into practice:

I. **Data Governance Frameworks**: Establish clear guidelines and protocols governing the collection, storage, and utilization of student data in special education technologies driven by artificial intelligence. In data governance frameworks, make sure that student privacy, consent, and data security are prioritized along with accountability and transparency (Mayer et al. 2013)
II. **Equity and Inclusion Mandates**: Policy frameworks should integrate standards for equality and inclusiveness in order to address concerns about bias and fairness in AI algorithms. Require developers and suppliers to conduct bias assessments, audits, and transparency reports in order to identify and mitigate algorithmic biases that might perpetuate inequality (Buolamwini et al. 2018).
III. **Accessibility Standards**: Implement accessibility standards and guidelines to ensure that AI-driven technology are usable and accessible for students with disabilities. To promote equal access to educational opportunities, enforce conformity to accessibility requirements, such as the Americans with Disabilities Act (ADA) and the Web Content Accessibility requirements (WCAG) (Rose et al. 2002).

Collaboration Between Stakeholders to Maximize Benefits and Mitigate Risks

Cooperation between stakeholders is essential to optimizing the benefits and lowering the risks of AI in special education:

I. **Interdisciplinary Collaboration**: Policymakers, academics, technologists, educators, and other stakeholders should be encouraged to co-design and co-implement AI-driven special education initiatives. According to VanDerHeyden et al. (2020), interdisciplinary teams must to be encouraged to make use of their distinct perspectives and specialties in order to come up with original solutions that address the complex issues facing the industry.
II. **Community Engagement**: Involve parents, kids, advocacy groups, and community organizations in the decision-making process to ensure that AI-driven special education initiatives take into account their needs, preferences, and worldviews. Encourage open communication, honesty, and participative techniques in order to foster consensus and trust among stakeholders. In 2015. Peterson et al.

III. **Continuous Evaluation and Feedback**: Establish mechanisms for ongoing evaluation, monitoring, and commenting in order to analyze the effectiveness, equity, and ethical implications of AI-driven special education resources. To identify areas that require improvement and make the necessary adjustments to implementation plans, get feedback from stakeholders and end users (Pullen et al. 2019)

IMPROVING ACCESSIBILITY

The way non-verbal and speech-impaired students communicate is being revolutionized by AI-driven speech and language processing technologies, which also improves their accessibility and educational prospects. Key areas in which AI-based tools are assisting students with speech difficulties are speech recognition and synthesis. While text-to-speech (TTS) technology converts written text into spoken words, Google's Speech-to-Text and Apple's Siri rely on sophisticated algorithms to accurately transcribe spoken words.AI-driven translation and interpretation services facilitate better communication and learning for nonverbal pupils. Through the use of augmentative and alternative communication (AAC) technology, nonverbal children can communicate by having their thoughts translated into spoken language. In multilingual learning environments, non-verbal students can engage more completely thanks to real-time translation systems like Google Translate.AI-powered assistive technology, including smart glasses and screen readers, offers students with impairments a fresh approach to learning. Students with visual impairments can freely access digital content with the use of screen readers like JAWS and NVDA. Real-time audio descriptions of their surroundings are provided by smart glasses such as Google Glass and OrCam MyEye, which enhances users' interaction with their surroundings.AI-powered robotic aides give students with limited mobility a sense of independence by assisting them in navigating their physical surroundings. Physical accessibility in educational environments is further enhanced by automated accessibility elements including voice-activated workstations, elevators, and doors.

Speech and Language Processing Tools

Artificial intelligence (AI)-driven speech and language processing technologies are transforming the way non-verbal and speech-impaired students communicate, improving their educational opportunities and accessibility in general.AI-based tools are helping students with speech impairments a lot, especially in the areas of speech recognition and synthesis.

- **Speech Recognition**: Text is generated from spoken words using AI-powered speech recognition technologies. With the help of these technologies, students who struggle with speech can communicate in other ways. To assist students participate in class conversations and complete tasks orally, Google's Speech-to-Text and Apple's Siri employ sophisticated algorithms to reliably transcribe spoken words (Google Cloud, n.d.; Apple, n.d.).
- **Speech Synthesis**: Text-to-speech (TTS) technology, often known as AI speech synthesis, transforms written text into spoken words. With the help of this technology, students who struggle with speech can input their ideas and have the system read them aloud. Among the notable instances are the natural-sounding voice outputs provided by Microsoft's Azure Cognitive Services and Amazon's Polly (Amazon Web Services, n.d.; Microsoft Azure, n.d.).

Translation and Interpretation Services for Non-Verbal Students

AI-powered translation and interpretation services help nonverbal students communicate and study more effectively by offering crucial support.

- **Augmentative and Alternative Communication (AAC) Devices**: AI-enhanced AAC devices convert nonverbal pupils' thoughts into spoken language, facilitating communication. Students can communicate themselves more easily thanks to these technologies, which can translate written text, motions, and symbols into speech. In this regard, products such as Tobii Dynavox and Proloquo2Go are frequently utilized (AssistiveWare, n.d.; Tobii Dynavox, n.d.).
- **Real-Time Translation**: Non-verbal kids can benefit from real-time translation services by using AI translation technologies such as Google Translate to communicate with peers and teachers in many languages. According to Google Translate (n.d.), these tools facilitate both text and voice translation, allowing nonverbal students to participate more completely in multilingual learning contexts.

Assistive Technologies

Education is becoming more inclusive as a result of AI-driven assistive devices that improve both physical and digital accessibility for students with disabilities. Students with a range of disabilities are having a completely new educational experience thanks to assistive devices driven by AI.

- **Screen Readers**: By using AI to translate text on a screen into voice or Braille, screen readers like JAWS (Job Access With voice) and NVDA (NonVisual Desktop Access) allow visually impaired students to access digital content on their own (Freedom Scientific, n.d.; NV Access, n.d.).
- **Smart Glasses**: Artificial intelligence-enabled smart glasses, such as Google Glass and OrCam MyEye, help students who are visually impaired by giving them audio explanations of their surroundings in real time. These gadgets improve the user's interaction with their environment by reading text, recognizing faces, and identifying objects (OrCam, n.d.; Google Glass, n.d.).

Improvements in Physical Accessibility Using Automation and Robots

Significant progress is being made in enhancing physical accessibility for students with impairments through robotics and automation driven by artificial intelligence.

- **Robotic Assistants**: Students with mobility disabilities can navigate their physical environment with the assistance of AI-driven robotic assistants. For example, Kinova Robotics' JACO robotic arm can help with everyday chores and give students with restricted mobility more independence (Kinova Robotics, n.d.).
- **Automated Accessibility Features**: Additionally, automated elements that improve physical accessibility in educational settings are being developed using AI. In order to make classrooms more accessible to students with physical disabilities, examples include automated doors, elevators, and adjustable desks that respond to voice commands or other inputs (Smith, 2018).

AI-driven assistive technology and speech and language processing tools are greatly improving accessibility in education for students with disabilities. AI is enhancing inclusiveness and assistance for all learners in school by offering cutting-edge assistive devices, translation services, voice synthesis, and enhanced speech recognition. By enhancing physical accessibility and facilitating communication and engagement, these technologies enable students with disabilities to fully participate in educational settings and reach their potential.

CONCLUSION

This research investigates the relationship between artificial intelligence (AI) and special education technology, emphasizing the historical evolution and current condition of the technology. Among the applications of AI in special education that are discussed are personalized learning, adaptive learning systems, assistive technology, natural language processing, and AI-driven evaluation tools. The research also addresses privacy, racism, and inclusion as ethical concerns. It offers guidelines for the moral application of AI, standards for integrating AI into curricula, and collaboration amongst stakeholders as recommendations for lawmakers and educators. The study concludes that artificial intelligence (AI) has great promise for transforming special education while simultaneously enhancing equity, inclusivity, and academic achievement. It promotes continued research and innovation, including longitudinal studies, looking at novel uses of AI, and collaborating across academic boundaries, in order to build inclusive, moral, and practical AI-driven technology.

References:

Abramovich, S., Schunn, C., & Higashi, R. M. (2013). Are badges useful in education?: It depends upon the type of badge and expertise of learner. *Educational Technology Research and Development*, 61(2), 217–232. DOI: 10.1007/s11423-013-9289-2

Anderson, J. R., Corbett, A. T., Koedinger, K. R., & Pelletier, R. (1997). K. R., & Pelletier, R. (1995). Cognitive tutors: Lessons learned. *Journal of the Learning Sciences*, 4(2), 167–207. DOI: 10.1207/s15327809jls0402_2

Baker, R. S., D'Mello, S. K., Rodrigo, M. M. T., & Graesser, A. C. (2010). Better to be frustrated than bored: The incidence, persistence, and impact of learners' cognitive–affective states during interactions with three different computer-based learning environments. *International Journal of Human-Computer Studies*, 68(4), 223–241. DOI: 10.1016/j.ijhcs.2009.12.003

Ballesteros, S., Prieto, A., Mayas, J., Toril, P., Pita, C., Ponce de Leon, L., & Waterworth, J. (2014). Brain training with non-action video games enhances aspects of cognition in older adults: A randomized controlled trial. *Frontiers in Aging Neuroscience*, 6, 277. DOI: 10.3389/fnagi.2014.00277 PMID: 25352805

Bateman, D., & Cline, J. (2019). *Special Education Leadership*. Routledge. DOI: 10.4324/9781351201353

Beukelman, D., & Light, J. (2020). Augmentative and alternative communication: Supporting children and adults with complex communication needs.

Borg, J., Larsson, S., Östergren, P. O., Rahman, A. A., Bari, N., & Khan, A. N. (2012). Assistive technology use and human rights enjoyment: A cross-sectional study in Bangladesh. *BMC International Health and Human Rights*, 12(1), 1–11. DOI: 10.1186/1472-698X-12-18 PMID: 22992413

Buolamwini, J., & Gebru, T. (2018, January). Gender shades: Intersectional accuracy disparities in commercial gender classification. In Conference on fairness, accountability and transparency (pp. 77-91). PMLR.Noble, S. U. (2018). Algorithms of oppression: How search engines reinforce racism. NYU Press.

Chen, G., Davis, D., Hauff, C., & Houben, G. J. (2016, April). Learning transfer: Does it take place in MOOCs? An investigation into the uptake of functional programming in practice. In *Proceedings of the Third(2016) ACM Conference on Learning@ Scale* (pp. 409-418).

Christensen, H., Cunningham, S. P., Fox, C., Green, P. D., & Hain, T. (2012, September). A comparative study of adaptive, automatic recognition of disordered speech. In *Interspeech* (pp. 1776-1779). DOI: 10.21437/Interspeech.2012-484

Elsahar, Y., Hu, S., Bouazza-Marouf, K., Kerr, D., & Mansor, A. (2019). Augmentative and Alternative Communication (AAC) Advances: A Review of Configurations for Speech Disabled Individuals.

Hardy, J. L., Drescher, D., Sarkar, K., Kellett, G., & Scanlon, M. (2011). Enhancing visual attention and working memory with a web-based cognitive training program. *Mensa Research Journal*, 42(2), 13–20.

Heppen, J. B., & Therriault, S. B. (2008). Developing Early Warning Systems to Identify Potential High School Dropouts. Issue Brief. *National High School Center*.

Huang, W., Billinghurst, M., Alem, L., Xiao, C., & Rasmussen, T. (2024). *Computer-Supported Collaboration: Theory and Practice*. John Wiley & Sons. DOI: 10.1002/9781119719830

Iuculano, T., Rosenberg-Lee, M., Richardson, J., Tenison, C., Fuchs, L., Supekar, K., & Menon, V. (2015). Cognitive tutoring induces widespread neuroplasticity and remediates brain function in children with mathematical learning disabilities. *Nature Communications*, 6(1), 8453. DOI: 10.1038/ncomms9453 PMID: 26419418

Mayer-Schönberger, V., & Cukier, K. (2013). *Big data: A revolution that will transform how we live, work, and think*. Houghton Mifflin Harcourt.

Miesenberger, K., & Kouroupetroglou, G. (Eds.). (2018). Computers Helping People with Special Needs:*16th International Conference, ICCHP 2018,* Linz, Austria, July 11-13, 2018, *Proceedings, Part I* (Vol. 10896). Springer.

Mukhtarkyzy, K., Abildinova, G., & Sayakov, O. (2022). The use of augmented reality for teaching Kazakhstani students physics lessons. *International Journal of Emerging Technologies in Learning*, 17(12), 215–235. DOI: 10.3991/ijet.v17i12.29501

Parsons, S., & Mitchell, P. (2002). The potential of virtual reality in social skills training for people with autistic spectrum disorders. *Journal of Intellectual Disability Research*, 46(5), 430–443. DOI: 10.1046/j.1365-2788.2002.00425.x PMID: 12031025

Peterson-Karlan, G. R. (2015). Assistive technology instruction within a continuously evolving technology environment. *Quarterly Review of Distance Education*, 16(2), 61.

Picard, R. W. (2000). *Affective computing*. MIT press. DOI: 10.7551/mitpress/1140.003.0008

Pullen, P. C., & Kennedy, M. J. (Eds.). (2019). *Handbook of response to intervention and multi-tiered systems of support*. Routledge.

Rello, L., & Ballesteros, M. (2015, May). Detecting readers with dyslexia using machine learning with eye tracking measures. In *Proceedings of the 12th international web for all conference* (pp. 1-8). DOI: 10.1145/2745555.2746644

Rose, D. H., & Meyer, A. (2002). Teaching every student in the digital age: Universal design for learning. Association for Supervision and Curriculum Development, 1703 N. Beauregard St., Alexandria, VA 22311-1714 (Product no. 101042: $22.95 ASCD members; $26.95 nonmembers).

Scassellati, B., Admoni, H., & Matarić, M. (2012). Robots for use in autism research. *Annual Review of Biomedical Engineering*, 14(1), 275–294. DOI: 10.1146/annurev-bioeng-071811-150036 PMID: 22577778

Shortliffe, E. H., & Buchanan, B. G. (1975). A model of inexact reasoning in medicine. *Mathematical Biosciences*, 23(3-4), 351–379. DOI: 10.1016/0025-5564(75)90047-4

Tapscott, D., & Tapscott, A. (2016). *Blockchain revolution: how the technology behind bitcoin is changing money, business, and the world*. Penguin.

VanLehn, K. (2011). The relative effectiveness of human tutoring, intelligent tutoring systems, and other tutoring systems. *Educational Psychologist*, 46(4), 197–221. DOI: 10.1080/00461520.2011.611369

Wang, Y., Skerry-Ryan, R. J., Stanton, D., Wu, Y., Weiss, R. J., Jaitly, N., . . . Saurous, R. A. (2017). Tacotron: Towards end-to-end speech synthesis. *arXiv preprint arXiv:1703.10135*. DOI: 10.21437/Interspeech.2017-1452

West, D. M. (2012). Big data for education: Data mining, data analytics, and web dashboards. *Governance studies at Brookings, 4*(1), 1-10.

Wozniak, M., Krishnaswamy, D., Callegari, C., Takagi, H., Prasad, N. R., Que, X., & Sandhu, R. (2015). *Advances in Computing, Communications and Informatics*. ICACCI.

Key Terms and Definitions

Adaptive Learning Systems: AI-driven systems that dynamically adjust instructional content and strategies based on real-time analysis of a student's performance. These systems are used in special education to create customized learning experiences.

Artificial Intelligence (AI): A branch of computer science focused on creating systems capable of performing tasks that normally require human intelligence, such as learning, reasoning, and problem-solving. In special education, AI is used to develop tools that adapt to the individual needs of students.

Assistive Technology: Devices or software designed to aid individuals with disabilities in performing tasks that might otherwise be difficult or impossible. AI enhances assistive technology by improving accessibility and user interaction.

Augmentative and Alternative Communication (AAC): Tools and strategies used to support individuals with communication difficulties. AI enhances AAC devices by translating non-verbal communication into spoken language, improving accessibility for non-verbal students.

Data-Driven Decision Making: The process of making educational decisions based on the analysis of data collected from various sources. In special education, AI facilitates data-driven decision-making by providing real-time insights into student performance.

Gamification: The application of game-design elements in non-game contexts, such as education, to engage and motivate students. In special education, AI-driven gamification strategies are used to enhance cognitive skill development.

Individualized Education Plan (IEP): A legally required document in the U.S. that outlines personalized learning goals and services for students with disabilities. AI assists in the creation and management of IEPs by providing data-driven insights.

Natural Language Processing (NLP): A field of AI that focuses on the interaction between computers and human language. NLP tools are used in special education to assist students with language impairments by improving communication and comprehension.

Personalized Learning: An educational approach that uses AI to tailor instruction to the individual needs, skills, and interests of each student. Personalized learning is particularly beneficial in special education for addressing diverse learning needs.

Speech Recognition: A technology that converts spoken language into text using AI. It is used in special education to assist students with speech impairments in communicating more effectively.

Chapter 16
Reflections on AI-Augmented Professional Development in Special Education:
Promises and Pitfalls

Seth King
University of Iowa, USA

ABSTRACT

Artificial intelligence (AI) has the potential to radically change a wide range of disciplines, including special education. Given the chronic issues with recruitment and retention of personnel involved in services for people with disabilities, automating professional development and training represents a promising application of AI. However, powerful technologies such as AI often produce adverse or unintended consequences. This chapter discusses the ethical implications of a line of research involving the integration of AI into immersive virtual reality (VR)— 'smart' VR—designed to teach practitioners a research-based behavior intervention for children with intellectual and developmental disabilities. Specific sections describe the impetus and potential advantages of smart VR, delineate the development and evaluation of the training, and identify concerns related to the use of similar applications in special education.

DOI: 10.4018/979-8-3693-5538-1.ch016

REFLECTIONS ON AI-AUGMENT PROFESSIONAL DEVELOPMENT IN SPECIAL EDUCATION: PROMISES AND PITFALLS

Artificial intelligence (AI) refers to software capable of acquiring, processing, and acting upon information (Gonzalez-Calatayud et al., 2021). A cursory glance at recent research, however, reveals that this simple description does not fully capture the extent of AI's capabilities. Applications such as natural language processing can classify text, make predictions, and provide recommendations (Holmes, 2020). Generative AI (e.g., ChatGPT) offers a seemingly limitless array of images, text, and other content from simple prompts (e.g., Elasri et al., 2022). In K-12 and higher education, AI can adjust instruction based on learner characteristics, process learner responses, and provide feedback (e.g., Afzal et al., 2019).

Readily accessible technology with extraordinary capabilities has implications for special education. The ability of AI to summarize and generate responses raises the question of whether educators should support students in the independent performance of tasks (e.g., reading, writing) or instead devote instructional time toward the effective use of emerging technologies (Marino et al., 2023). Many meditations on the applications of AI to the preparation of special educators and other disciplines have raised concerns regarding the potential for teaching candidates to outsource their academic responsibilities to AI assistants (e.g., King & ChatGPT, 2023; Marino et al., 2023). Others have emphasized the potential of AI to enrich special educator preparation with simulations and individualized instruction (e.g., Khazanchi & Khazanchi, 2024).

Combining AI with virtual reality (VR) poses challenges that have not been extensively addressed in the literature (Chang et al., 2023). VR is another highly publicized technology which uses various sensors and displays to place users in simulated settings. My work in this area has focused on using VR simulations and AI to improve educators' administration of interventions for children with disabilities who exhibit dangerous, challenging behaviors. This work has involved several AI applications including speech-to-text, text-to-speech, text classification, and other functions to create simulations that provide trainees with opportunities to rehearse evidence-based practices and receive feedback with limited instructor assistance. As will be discussed in this chapter, these projects have at once revealed both the promise and pitfalls of applying AI to special education.

The many applications of AI will likely result in considerable changes to how special educators are trained. This chapter describes some of the ethical issues raised by the author's attempts to integrate AI into training opportunities for special educators. First, the rationale and initial findings from research involving professional development for special educators in behavior intervention are described. Salient ethical issues related to this work are then identified. The chapter concludes with a reflection on mitigating factors and future directions.

The Promise of 'Smart' Virtual Reality

AI encompasses an exhaustive array of capabilities with relevance to many areas of special education. For example, predictive analytics—or the use of a set of rules by a computer to complete operations—can estimate the benefit of interventions in relation to disabilities and other learner characteristics (Akgun & Greenhow, 2021; Holmes, 2020; Ouyang et al., 2022). The ability to identify potentially effective services more quickly could remove much of the trial-and-error from data-based individualization (Fuchs et al., 2021) and related procedures pertaining to the delivery of appropriate instruction. As with any proposed application of AI, however, there are issues with predictive analytics. Prediction models are usually based on training data from small samples that may not resemble the general population, resulting in inaccurate or biased results (Mühlhoff, 2021).

The range of potential issues with the breadth of AI applications is beyond the scope of a single chapter. Thus, this chapter will focus on a use case with which I have direct experience: educator training. The current section briefly describes the impetus for this work—challenges in recruiting and retaining qualified personnel in special education—along with an overview of research involving 'smart' virtual reality.

The Need for Effective Training in Behavior Intervention

Nearly 17% of all children in the US are diagnosed with intellectual and developmental disabilities (IDD; Zablotsky et al., 2023). As many as 20% of people with IDD display challenging behavior, including physical aggression and self-injurious behavior (SIB; Dimian & Symons, 2022). Persistent dangerous behaviors limit educational opportunities and expose children to harm (Prykanowski et al., 2021). The long-term relegation of children with IDD to restrictive settings excludes them from learning opportunities (e.g., Krezmien et al., 2017). Effective interventions can increase the likelihood that children with challenging behavior will participate in less restrictive settings.

One of the most successful interventions for challenging behavior is functional communication training (FCT; Ghaemmaghami et al., 2021). In FCT, children learn to communicate—such as by signing or making a vocal request—through systematic prompting involving models or physical prompts (e.g., Shepley et al., 2019). The interventionist ensures that communicative behaviors help the child manage the environment (e.g., result in a desired activity) and withhold consequences likely to reward challenging behavior (O'Brien et al., 2022). However, personnel often struggle to use FCT effectively (Hanley et al., 2001).

Disparate access to qualified personnel exacerbates issues associated with challenging behavior and the misuse of effective interventions. A national survey indicated 71% of school districts identified staffing issues in special education (Frontline Education, 2021). Special educators have twice the turnover of general educators (Espinoza et al., 2018). Shortages in special education personnel often stem from limited access to training and professional development (Rude & Miller, 2018).

Special education personnel need effective training to reduce challenging behaviors and improve student outcomes (Brownell & Leko, 2018). Behavioral skills training (BST) is a research-based training paradigm for school staff that consists of (a) instruction, (b) modeling, (c) rehearsal, and (d) feedback (e.g., Kirkpatrick et al., 2019). Training ideally provides supervised practice in unpredictable situations (Dempsey et al., 2012). However, logistical issues restrict opportunities for rehearsal beyond a few scenarios (Reid et al., 2011), and BST's resource-intensive nature limits implementation in many areas (Shapiro & Kazemi, 2017).

Expanding the scope of personnel preparation in behavior intervention with technology is not an entirely new concept. Synchronous telehealth and asynchronous computer learning modules offer convenient training in many skills related to behavior intervention (e.g., Nylen & King, 2023). Telehealth, or remote services provided via telecommunication, usually requires a trainee to conference with a specialist online while engaging with a less qualified specialist in person (Nelson & Bui, 2010). Despite clear benefits, telehealth may involve more resources and be less engaging than traditional methods (Ferguson et al., 2019; Neely et al., 2021). Asynchronous computer-based training (e.g., Hirsch et al., 2015) consisting of brief lectures and video-models of practice has also shown promise. However, studies often do not link the performance of practitioners to child outcomes or assess trainees' implementation skills. Video-based training also presents a limited number of practice scenarios, which can prevent the generalization of techniques (Dempsey et al., 2012; Shapiro & Kazemi, 2017).

Augmented reality (AR) refers to technology that supports the rehearsal of practical skills by simulating aspects of the performance context during conventional training (e.g., Chang et al., 2023). Avatars depicted on monitors used in the AR teaching simulator Mursion (2020) are controlled by instructors who collect trainee skills data (Dieker et al., 2015). Mursion allows for the rehearsal of a range of skills relevant to special education (e.g., systematic prompting; Vince-Garland et al., 2016). However, the need for live supervisors and specialized settings, along with its limited use for severe challenging behaviors, represent critical limitations (King et al., 2021).

VR refers to the use of multisensory interfaces, such as a headset and motion controls, to immerse participants in simulations (Jensen & Konradsen, 2018; Suh & Prophet, 2018). VR has become increasingly affordable and is linked to improvements in learner outcomes and engagement (e.g., Yu & Xu, 2022). The ability to safely rehearse dangerous skills (e.g., de-escalation; Bailenson, 2020) represents another benefit of VR. As with AR, many VR simulations that involve human interaction use a "Wizard-of-Oz" approach, with humans controlling events (e.g., Burke et al., 2018; Chang et al., 2023). This enables many activities but does not address shortages of qualified trainers (King et al., 2021).

Additional issues with current VR training scholarship include (a) the lack of comprehensive training and (b) the limited emphasis on behavior intervention (Radianti et al., 2020). Placing trainees in situations similar to those encountered in practice represents an intuitive improvement over traditional roleplay but falls short of providing the range of instruction and feedback needed by educators to implement techniques in practice. While they address valuable skills, simulations targeting classroom management techniques (e.g., Lugrin et al., 2016) may not be applicable to severe challenging behavior. As an exception, Clay and colleagues (2021) administered BST featuring live lectures, modeling, and practice administering FCT in VR to 13 clinicians. Participants provided verbal/physical prompts and reinforcement to avatars scripted to exhibit challenging behaviors. Participants mastered FCT after VR training. Data collection and feedback were handled by humans, however.

Immersive AI-enhanced training systems capable of instructing, assessing, and providing feedback with minimal human oversight have the potential to reduce costs and broaden access to behavior intervention training. Few AI-training studies focus on job-related tasks, however; excluding our work (King, Boyer, et al., 2022; King, Estapa, et al., 2024), none address educators (Chang et al., 2023). Many studies target interviewing (e.g., Albright et al., 2018) or case assessment (Pantziaras et al., 2015). AI in these studies manages the responses and actions of patient avatars. However, trainees in interview simulators often select extant conversation options from dialogue boxes using a mouse rather than speaking naturally. Training, therefore, differs from actual practice. Employment simulators do not target movement (Chang et al., 2023), and rarely use VR or incorporate validated training paradigms (e.g., BST; Middeke et al., 2018). The extent to which AI accurately assesses responses is unclear, as few studies (e.g., Middeke et al., 2018; Pantziaras et al., 2015) involve AI assessment.

Smart VR

Current research involving the use of AI training frequently overlooks the needs of special educators (Chang et al., 2023). My work explicitly includes all elements of BST, provides immersive skill-related practice, and employs AI to train and assess the physical and vocal aspects of FCT (King et al., in press; King, Ross, et al., 2024). The underlying premise of this training involves identifying a practice with empirical support (e.g., FCT). The practice is then divided into distinct steps via a task analysis (Cooper et al., 2020). This process resembles the approach many special educators take in preparing to teach academic, functional, or social skills to their students (e.g., Tan et al., 2016). It diverges from more conventional practice, however, by incorporating common variations into the procedure into the analysis. For example, rather than simply describing the steps of FCT where a trainee might prompt a replacement communicative behavior (e.g., the sign for break) after introducing an instructional task, our task list also addresses how the trainee might address compliance or innocuous inappropriate behavior. The result resembles a flowchart encompassing common anticipated student behaviors when a procedure is presented (Figure 1). Individual pathways from the flowchart are then used as lessons, which the trainee progresses through while in VR.

Figure 1. Flowchart of possible steps in functional communication training lessons

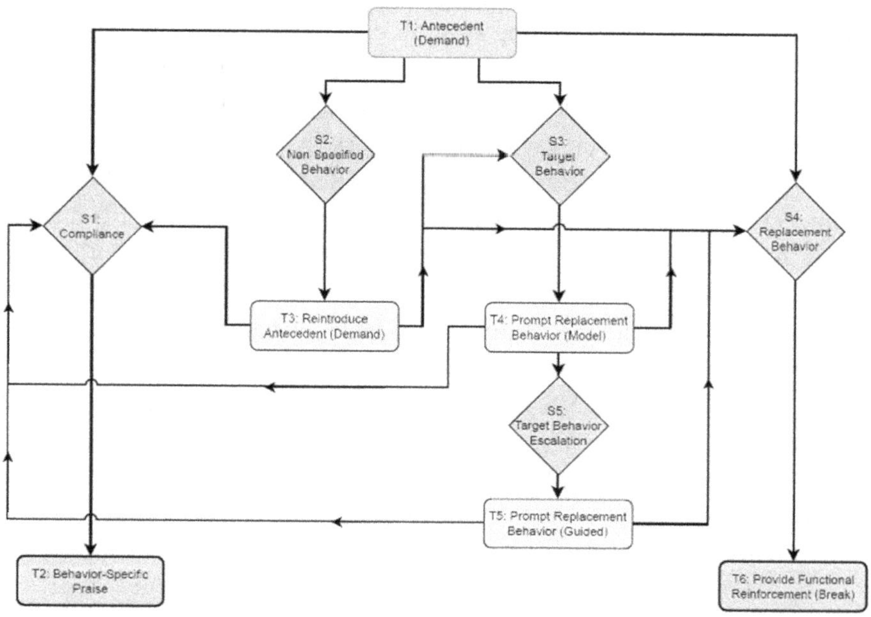

Note. Figure depicts possible steps in a procedure designed to teach functional communication training. Each process begins with the introduction of an academic task linked to a challenging behavior (i.e., antecedent demand). At this point, the simulated student may comply with instruction, exhibit a behavior that is not consistent with the demand but which has not been identified as warranting intensive behavior intervention (i.e., non-specified behavior; e.g., engaging in a task other than the assignment), engage in the targeted challenging behavior (e.g., head-banging) or engage in communication (e.g., the sign for break). Each of these should result in a separate trainee behavior (e.g., behavior specific praise, providing access to a break). Individual cells from the chart are placed in a distinct order to serve as lessons, which the trainee is guided through with the assistance of AI-controlled prompts.

Establishing the steps of an FCT procedure and training personnel through VR can be accomplished without AI integration, however (see Clay et al., 2021 for an example). As mentioned previously, AI applications could largely remove instructors from this process. In smart VR, statements corresponding with possible student statements are typed and assigned to specific cells in the flowchart. The system then selects from these typed responses during relevant moments of the simulation, which are rendered as speech using an AI text-to-speech module. This allowed an avatar to simulate an elementary student and speak, albeit in a robotic monotone.

Trainees interacted with the avatar using a head-mounted display. In earlier simulations (e.g., King, Estapa, et al., 2024), interaction consisted almost entirely of speaking to the avatar. This was facilitated by a microphone in the VR headset activated using the hand controls. A speech-to-text application then transformed speech into text strings that could be interpreted using a natural language classifier. For each cell of the flowchart in which a trainee vocal response was required, we trained the classifier on several examples of an appropriate response. When, for example, it was time for a trainee to provide praise, the classifier would compare the trainee's statement—transcribed in real-time via speech-to-text—to the training sample. It would then generate a confidence value between 0.00 (i.e., not at all similar to the training data) and 1.00 (i.e., an exact match for a statement in the training sample). As the goal of the simulation was to establish general adherence to the targeted procedures without encouraging rote memorization, a relatively high classification threshold that permitted variation in responding (0.75) was selected.

The effectiveness of this training model was first demonstrated in experiments involving nondirective mathematical questioning (King, Boyer, et al., 2022; King, Estapa, et al., 2024). Instructional elements were incorporated into an AI-integrated VR simulation (i.e., smart VR) with assessment and feedback capabilities. After watching a video presentation, trainees interacted with the avatar within the simulation. Onscreen text prompts guided trainees through lessons, and an AI speech-to-text module allowed trainee responses to be assessed through AI text classification. The results of text classification allowed the AI to determine if trainee responses were correct and provide appropriate feedback. AI assessment was generally accurate (approximately 90%), and the simulation itself was linked to trainee acquisition of the procedure.

In addition to elements directly related to instruction, the simulation was also linked to a customized web interface constructed using an open-source application (i.e., React). This application allowed for the storage and external evaluation of trainee responses within the simulation, such as would be needed to integrate the simulations into coursework or professional development. Additionally, this platform allowed instructors to customize lessons through the manipulation of virtual flowcharts depicting the skills targeted within each lesson (see King, Boyer, et al., 2022).

Limitations of the mathematics studies included an exclusive focus on speech. FCT simulations provided an opportunity to use AI to train physical and vocal skills in relation to an intervention with relevance to special educators. Changes from the earlier simulation included animated student avatars, the use of a generative voice AI to make the avatar sound childlike (ElevenLabs, 2023), and the assessment of trainee movement. We also added more variety to sessions, meaning the avatar would engage in different versions of behaviors, and the trainee would have to present steps of FCT in a different order across sessions. Lessons concerned FCT for SIB (i.e., headbanging) exhibited by a child when confronted with academic tasks, and a separate lesson for a child who exhibited tantrums when a preferred item was removed. Within the simulation, trainees interacted with the environment through speech and actions such as modeling gestural forms of communication or guiding the student avatar to use a response card.

Regardless of modality, the system assessed trainee responses and provided feedback as appropriate (King, Ross, et al., 2024). This included two types of prompting within the simulation: error-free prompts, where text describing the correct action following a student's behavior was immediately displayed on the screen, and delayed prompts, which appeared only when the trainee provided an incorrect response or did not respond after several seconds. Additionally, the percentage of steps in the procedure correctly performed by the student was displayed at the end of the simulation. Trainees also had the opportunity to practice without feedback.

The research involving smart VR and FCT is still at an early stage; however, results are promising (King, Ross, et al., 2024). Development first involved the use of several single-case designs, or within-subject experiments in which control is demonstrated through systematic variations in the timing of intervention (King et al., 2023; King, Nylen, et al., 2024). Through this method, we examined the basic functionality of the system and made adaptations, as needed (King et al., in press; King, Ross, et al., 2024). A small group of research participants ($n = 5$), including graduate students and university faculty, completed the simulation. After three brief sessions, participants exhibited at least 80% of steps in the procedure correctly. However, there were disparities in the assessment conducted by observers and AI, particularly when participants spoke in accented English. That is, the speech-to-text module had a high incidence of inaccuracy when attempting to transcribe the words spoken by international students. This produced words and phrases wildly different from those included in the text classifier's training data. Consequently, the system would falsely identify statements spoken in accented English as incorrect. This occurred across a range of statements, including statements where an observer confirmed the statement provided by the trainee matched a statement in the classifier's training data. Attempts to remedy this issue by incorporating a more sophisticated speech recognition module (Whisper; OpenAI, 2022) did not improve accuracy.

A more recent investigation integrated smart VR into a required classroom management course for undergraduate teaching candidates (n = 49; average age = 22 years). We randomly assigned participants to control or treatment groups. The treatment group received training in one 60-min session, which included a VR tutorial, an instructional video, and several runs through a prompted simulation. Control group participants watched the video exclusively. Posttest scores for the intervention group (M = 78.70%; SD = 18.94) exceeded those of the control group (M = 33.52%; SD = 13.27), with $t(47) = 9.70$, $p<.001$, and Hedge's $g = 2.73$. Scores collected one week after intervention also favored the treatment group (M = 61.34%; SD = 22.13), relative to control (M = 31.78%; SD = 12.16), with $t(47) = 5.83$, $p<.001$, and Hedge's $g = 1.64$.

Like all research, our work concerning smart VR has many limitations. There is much work left to be done, such as demonstrating that skills demonstrated within the simulation generalize to service settings. Throughout the development process, we have always insisted that the question of whether AI-augmented training 'works' may be secondary to other, ethical questions that are not necessarily amenable to experimental inquiry.

ETHICAL AI-INTEGRATED TRAINING

Having established the basic features of smart VR, this section turns to salient ethical issues related to its development and application. More general notions of ethics featured in previous discussions of special education are referenced (e.g., Marino et al., 2023) as well as the specific guidelines of special educators and related professions, such as behavior analysts (e.g., Behavior Analyst Certification Board [BACB], 2020; Council for Exceptional Children [CEC], 2015). Although issues such as plagiarism and professional development rightfully warrant discussion (e.g., Marino et al., 2023), relevant ethical guidelines applicable to special education encompass many other issues. Specific areas of interest include dimensions of effectiveness, recognition of diversity, and the extent to which stakeholders are represented in the decision-making process. Throughout, the section refers to the development of smart VR described in the previous section.

Effectiveness

AI-augmented training is appealing because it may extend access to training in high-need disciplines, such as special education, at costs lower than those associated with conventional training. Much of this enthusiasm stems from the assumption that the quality of AI-augmented training would be approximately equivalent to in-person services, as a disparity could disproportionately provide inferior services based on location or resources (Parsons, 2021). Rather than perpetuate longstanding inequities, AI-integrated training would ideally extend high-quality services to all educators and children (King, Ross, et al., 2024). To do otherwise would violate ethical principles related to the equitable provision of services.

Whether augmenting training and other aspects of special education with AI results in improved outcomes is a primary ethical concern related to the use of the technology. For example, the emphasis on contrived mechanics (e.g., button pressing, salient prompting) and lack of photorealistic detail in many simulations could hinder trainee performance in authentic settings (King et al., 2021). The potential for AI to reduce human oversight compounds the potential for harm. For this reason, the incorporation of AI into training activities should supplement, rather than replace, qualified supervisors (King et al., 2022). However, financial imperatives regarding the costs and feasibility of service delivery incentivize the rapid, inexpensive training of personnel who often have limited qualifications (Kornack et al., 2014; Vivanti & Stahmer, 2018). These factors form a dangerous synergy with the reckless haste with which many commercial technology development sectors test, market, and implement novel AI applications (Losavio, 2023). Such circumstances could result in the proliferation of ineffective training.

My early work reveals a few areas where the limitations of AI have the potential to compromise training and services. Future studies will no doubt reveal additional areas of concern. The imperfect correspondence between AI and human observers is perhaps the biggest limitation of AI-driven training systems. Across FCT studies (King et al., in press; King, Ross, et al., 2024), results from AI assessment corresponded with human observations about 90% of the time. Of course, no training is perfect, and different instructors are likely to have varying definitions of what constitutes a correct element of FCT. Flawed assessment in automated training essentially means that trainees are receiving incorrect feedback in 1 of every 10 behaviors they rehearse, however. Research shows that the faulty implementation of instruction can perpetuate errors in practice, as errors acquired through initial training tend to recur without extensive retraining (Brand et al., 2019; Fryling et al., 2012). In the context of FCT, AI-training systems could perpetuate or worsen harm related to severe challenging behavior relative to best practice.

A similar issue involves the incorporation of motion into VR training. We scrupulously tried to avoid contrived movement (e.g., use of texts in menus) in our simulations to increase their relevance to authentic contexts. Trainees in our simulations (King, Ross, et al., 2024) were trained to teach student avatars to replace challenging behaviors (e.g., head banging, tantrums) with a hand sign (i.e., touching his fists together), using a response card (e.g., Fisher et al., 2014), or by making a vocal request (e.g., "Can I have a break?"). When prompting these behaviors within the simulations, trainees modeled or guided the targeted communicative response by speaking into a microphone or using motion controls (King, Ross, et al., 2024).

Though ostensibly an improvement over menu-based instruction featured in previous simulations (Chang et al., 2023), translating FCT into an automated VR simulation imposes several restrictions on the learner. Unlike in VR simulations where assessment is conducted solely by humans (e.g., Clay et al., 2021), the system must be trained to recognize specific movements—any corresponding avatar animations must also be prepared in advance. This impedes the sort of individualized training special educators and related personnel are ethically obligated to provide (BACB, 2020). Likewise, the current limitations of technology predispose training to focus on signs and other movements that are compatible with motion controls rather than those that might be more relevant to the learner.

A larger issue with incorporating technology into training is the need to ensure trainees have the requisite skills to engage with computers. The lack of technology literacy among certain populations represents a tremendous barrier to the use of more conventional telehealth applications (e.g., phones and desktop computers), to say nothing of those involving VR (Kruse et al., 2018). In the FCT studies, verbal tutorials were generally ineffective in preparing cohorts consisting of young college students enrolled at a state university (King, Ross, et al., 2024). Consequently, we found it necessary to create a customized tutorial designed to acclimate learners to VR, which only partially remedied the situation. The necessity of extensively training participants in the use of technology before they can begin learning the techniques of interest undermines claims regarding the efficacy of technology—especially for uncommon, somewhat cumbersome platforms such as VR (Garrett et al., 2018).

Diversity

The various ethical codes that guide professionals involved in services for people with disabilities have increasingly included language regarding the importance of responding to cultural and linguistic diversity. Practitioners must respect the diverse backgrounds of their students (e.g., CEC, 2015), maintain competence as it relates to cultural responsiveness (e.g., National Association of School Psychologists, 2020), and avoid practices that might discriminate against service recipients (e.g., BACB, 2020). Removing the bias inherent in human decision-making through AI is ostensibly consistent with these guidelines. However, AI can compound existing inequities and prejudices because of how it is trained and applied (Ferrer et al., 2021).

The extent to which smart VR makes decisions is admittedly less pronounced than the algorithms that are currently involved in medical decision-making (Kempt et al., 2022) and that will undoubtedly be used to supplement instruction in the future (Cox & Jennings, 2024; Hopcan et al., 2023). The classification of trainee speech as correct or incorrect is a primary function of smart VR and, as we have observed, varies based on the demographic characteristics of trainees. Speech-to-text often struggles to interpret accented English (Shadiev et al., 2018). This is somewhat similar to problems observed in emotional AI (i.e., applications that identify feelings and emotions based on textual and visual information) in which the accuracy varies widely across cultural and ethnic groups (Podoletz, 2023). The significance of facial expressions and vocal tone varies across cultures, meaning that AI trained using a homogenous sample may reach the wrong conclusions when attempting to draw conclusions in relation to job performance.

In the smart VR experiments involving FCT, the system falsely concluded some international trainees had incorrectly performed spoken steps due to an ability of speech-to-text to appropriately assess accented English (King et al., in press; King, Ross, et al., 2024). Accommodating accented English, particularly in real-time applications, is a longstanding technical challenge (OpenAI, 2022; Shadiev et al., 2018) that discipline-specific researchers may understandably be unable to address. Nonetheless, this barrier to access cannot be easily overlooked given the increasing diversity of paraprofessionals who administer special education services (U.S. Equal Employment Opportunity Commission, 2022) and the communities that receive services (Beaulieu & Jimenez-Gomez, 2022).

Leaving aside ethical guidelines concerning diversity, shortages in personnel and an increasing population of students with disabilities from culturally distinct backgrounds calls for more inclusive training. Changes in the demographics of service administrators and recipients appear to be coalescing with the availability of AI. Assuring that these developments complement one another will require a dedicated effort to ensure technology meets the needs of diverse populations. The effectiveness of AI training and the extent to which factors such as technological literacy and other resources can be addressed relate to issues of diversity. At present, evidence does not suggest AI-supplemented training is superior to more conventional forms of high-quality training, such as BST administered by qualified supervisors (Kirkpatrick et al., 2019). Seizing upon advances in technology to provide historically underserved populations with access to a potentially inferior substitute could be seen as a form of discrimination (Benfer et al., 2019; Parsons, 2021). On the other hand, excluding populations from such training due to a lack of access to technology could also constitute a form of discrimination, particularly if AI is found to increase the quality of services.

A more insidious consequence of smart VR relates to the manner in which the biases of the developers may reside in the training and be firmly ingrained in the trainees through repeated use of the simulation. The ability of AI to facilitate role-play without instructor assistance represents one of the potential benefits of smart VR. Unlike conventional training, smart VR could allow trainees to rehearse skills until they are acquired and potentially practice across a range of different settings and approaches. The conceptualization of skills addressed in the FCT simulation accounted for student responses that require a different response by the trainee (i.e., functional variations; e.g., off-task behavior compared to headbanging or tantrums) as well as topographically distinct behaviors that nonetheless require the same response (e.g., different ways of refusing to complete an assignment; King, Ross, et al., 2024). The development of smart VR was in part motivated by a desire to reward repeated uses, encourage generalization, and decrease rote memorization of the steps in the procedure.

One key limitation of this stage of development, however, is that people with disabilities and their communities were not involved in creating the simulations. This means that the depiction of disabilities potentially reflects the implicit biases of the White, largely neurotypical (King, 2022) development team. The most obvious reflection of this form of bias would be the repeated pairing of specific avatar behaviors with student characteristics (Matsuda et al., 2020), which could disseminate stereotypes about neurodiverse children (King, Ross, et al., 2024). Avoiding such issues in the future requires assiduous attention to issues of diversity in the development and dissemination phases of technology.

Representation

The emphasis on the individual needs of the learner distinguishes special education and related disciplines from more typical forms of instruction (Zigmond & Kloo, 2017). Ethical codes in special education and related fields increasingly emphasize both responsiveness to the preferences of service recipients and the inclusion of stakeholders in instructional planning, implementation, and evaluation (Callender et al., 2020). Many applications that use AI purport to provide individualized instruction with limited human oversight. Intelligent tutoring systems, such as IBM Watson Tutor, provide instruction that varies based on the responses of learners (Afzal et al., 2019; Holmes, 2020).

The process by which AI systems arrive at decisions or recommend specific instructional approaches, however, is often opaque and in many cases does not allow humans to be in the 'loop' of decision-making (Nakao et al., 2022). Researchers involved in smart VR studies attempted to provide supervisor input into training through the use of a web application allowing for the arrangement of steps in the lesson (e.g., King et al., 2022). However, this only provides choices within the framework of FCT, as defined by a single research team. In studies in which education personnel were taught to implement FCT (e.g., Chazin et al., 2018; Walker et al., 2021), only Gormley and colleagues (2019) used a standardized measure of FCT implementation. This is emblematic of the flexibility in which many personnel and researchers observe in the conceptualization and implementation of practices (e.g., Carroll et al., 2018). Automated trainings reflecting a limited number of approaches may create a factitious consensus regarding best practices in special education.

Relatedly, consumers of special education services are increasingly demanding input into the interventions they receive (Beaulieu & Jimenez-Gomez, 2022; Callender et al., 2020). This has resulted in the rejection or alteration of practices long viewed as effective (e.g., ignoring challenging behavior; Leaf et al., 2022) in favor of more considerate, trauma-informed approaches (e.g., Maddox et al., 2022; Rajaraman et al., 2022). AI training systems developed without the involvement of relevant stakeholders (e.g., parents, teachers, or potential service recipients) may impart methods that community members find objectionable (Wali et al., 2023). For example, the version of FCT featured in the smart VR simulations incorporates physical prompting, in which an instructor physically guides the learner in the use of a communicative response (e.g., Falcomata et al., 2012). Though generally effective, many stakeholders demand less intrusive forms of prompting in instruction (Leaf et al., 2022). As mentioned previously, the smart VR system allows instructors to remove lesson components that may be distasteful. Changing views about what interventions are permissible in special education should prompt developers to allow humans to alter AI programs and—perhaps most importantly—include end-users in the development of AI applications designed for use in special education.

CONCLUSION

This chapter primarily addresses concerns related to a specific application of AI—smart VR training simulations. Like many of the proposed uses of AI in special education, smart VR training platforms have the potential to address longstanding problems. Research in this area (King et al., 2022; King, Ross, et al., 2024), though still at an early stage, suggests that AI-enhanced training platforms are feasible and may eventually help trainees acquire a wide range of effective practices. Unfortunately, these potential benefits are at least partially offset by potential violations of the rights and dignity of service recipients as well as threats to the integrity of services. The discussion emphasized issues related to service efficacy, diversity, and representativeness as they relate to smart VR. The range of issues posed by AI in special education, such as the inappropriate or nonconsensual use of data in making predictions (e.g., Schiff, 2021), is so vast as to defy a concise description in this or any other chapter. In any event, caution, in terms of the development and implementation of AI in special education, is warranted.

Of course, many of the issues identified with AI are amenable to technological advances and more conscientious approaches to development. Novel approaches to AI training and calibration (e.g., Aksenova et al., 2021) could address the deficiencies observed in speech-to-text and encountered with smart VR. Incorporating large language models exemplified by ChatGPT could likewise improve classification accuracy, and the concerns regarding the tendency of such models to 'hallucinate' or incorporate irrelevant information into discipline-specific discussions (e.g., Weiser, 2023) can be obviated through the development of customized large language models specializing in special education (Hussain et al., 2024). Likewise, issues related to diversity and representation of stakeholders in AI applications can be addressed by an emphasis on simple metrics of effectiveness in development and the incorporation of potential end-users into each stage of development. Many agencies that distribute funds related to innovation in disability services, such as the U.S. Department of Army–Medical Research Acquisition Activity (2024), offer awards that prohibit applicants from conducting clinical trials to incentivize these forms of inquiry.

Nonetheless, the likelihood that current concerns regarding AI may be addressed in the short term should not lead to complacency. New technology can, indeed, solve problems introduced by earlier technological advances. Though perhaps unavoidable, the self-evidently Sisyphean process of innovating solutions to problems produced through earlier innovation should be anticipated and considered in advance (Imam, 2021; King, Ross, et al., 2024).

Funding for AI-related research in special education is critical due to the need to enlist experts from a variety of fields, the resource intensiveness of development, and the lack of financial rewards associated with conscientious development. Yet it is not entirely clear that agencies dedicated to research in special education, such as the Office of Special Education and Rehabilitative Services (OSERS) or the National Center of Special Education Research (NCSER), uniformly value deliberate, responsible development and dissemination of AI. Many awards, such as the OSERS (2024) call involving the dissemination of emerging technology, prioritize rapid dissemination of AI-enhanced interventions at the potential expense of increases in development time or stakeholder involvement. The award implicitly addresses concerns regarding the effectiveness of AI through the stipulation that some element of the intervention be recognized as evidenced-based. Yet AI can change how normally effective practices function through the removal of human mediation. Other awards, such as the Development and Innovation awards offered by NCSER (2023), impose several onerous barriers (e.g., the need to examine cascading effects of intervention on students) that are likely to prevent responsible advances in resource intensive areas such as the professional development of special educators (Brownell & Leko, 2018).

AI technologies like natural language processing and machine learning are more than just tools. They are also transformative media that reshape cultural and social dynamics. In the context of human service professions, such as special education, the ethical integration of AI presents significant challenges and opportunities. As AI technologies become more integrated into educational environments, they influence the methods and efficacy of teaching and learning, particularly for students with special needs. The ethical considerations in these applications are paramount; they require a careful balancing of benefits and potential harms, ensuring that AI tools enhance rather than diminish the human-centric goals of education. In the realm of special education, AI should amplify opportunities for learning and inclusion, not create barriers or diminish human interaction. These considerations must be at the forefront of integrating AI into human services to foster environments that are both innovative and respectful of individual human dignity.

References

Afzal, S., Dempsey, B., D' Helon, C., Mukhi, N., Pribic, M., Sickler, A., Strong, P., Vanchiswar, M., & Wilde, L. (2019). The personality of AI systems in education: Experiences with the Watson Tutor, a one-on-one virtual tutoring system. *Childhood Education*, 95(1), 44–52. DOI: 10.1080/00094056.2019.1565809

Akgun, S., & Greenhow, C. (2021). Artificial intelligence in education: Addressing ethical challenges in K-12 settings. *AI and Ethics*, 2(3), 431–440. DOI: 10.1007/s43681-021-00096-7 PMID: 34790956

Aksënova, A., van Esch, D., Flynn, J., & Golik, P. (2021). How might we create better benchmarks for speech recognition? In Church, K., Liberman, M., & Kordoni, V. (Eds.), *Proceedings of the 1st Workshop on Benchmarking: Past, present and future* (pp. 22–34)., https://aclanthology.org/2021.bppf-1.pdf DOI: 10.18653/v1/2021.bppf-1.4

Albright, G., Bryan, C., Adam, C., McMillan, J., & Shockley, K. (2018). Using virtual patient simulations to prepare primary health care professionals to conduct substance use and mental health screening and brief intervention. *Journal of the American Psychiatric Nurses Association*, 24(3), 247–259. DOI: 10.1177/1078390317719321 PMID: 28754067

Bailenson, J. (2020, September 18). Is VR the future of corporate training? *Harvard Business Review*. https://hbr.org/2020/09/is-vr-the-future-of-corporate-training

Beaulieu, L., & Jimenez-Gomez, C. (2022). Cultural responsiveness in applied behavior analysis: Self-assessment. *Journal of Applied Behavior Analysis*, 55(2), 337–356. DOI: 10.1002/jaba.907 PMID: 35266143

Behavior Analyst Certification Board. (2020). *Ethics code for behavior analysts.* https://bacb.com/wp-content/ethics-code-for-behavior-analysts/

Benfer, E. A., Mohapatra, S., Wiley, L. F., & Yearby, R. (2019). Health justice strategies to combat the pandemic: Eliminating discrimination, poverty, and health disparities during and after COVID-19. *SSRN*, 19(3), 122–171. DOI: 10.2139/ssrn.3636975

Brand, D., Henley, A. J., DiGennaro Reed, F. D., Gray, E., & Crabbs, B. (2019). A review of published studies involving parametric manipulations of treatment integrity. *Journal of Behavioral Education*, 28(1), 1–26. DOI: 10.1007/s10864-018-09311-8

Brownell, M. T., & Leko, M. M. (2018). Advancing coherent theories of change in special education teacher education research: A response to the special issue on the science of teacher professional development. *Teacher Education and Special Education*, 41(2), 158–168. DOI: 10.1177/0888406417748430

Burke, S. L., Bresnahan, T., Li, T., Epnere, K., Rizzo, A., Partin, M., Ahlness, R. M., & Trimmer, M. (2018). Using virtual interactive training agents (ViTA) with adults with autism and other developmental disabilities. *Journal of Autism and Developmental Disorders*, 48(3), 905–912. DOI: 10.1007/s10803-017-3374-z PMID: 29168090

Callender, A., King, S. A., & Howard, M. (2020). Social validity assessment: Examples from a functional skills training intervention. In Jaworski, J. A. (Ed.), *Advances in Sociology Research* (Vol. 31). Nova Science Publishers.

Carroll, R. A., Owsiany, J., & Cheatham, J. M. (2018). Using an abbreviated assessment to identify effective error-correction procedures for individual learners during discrete-trial instruction. *Journal of Applied Behavior Analysis*, 51(3), 482–501. DOI: 10.1002/jaba.460 PMID: 29675825

Chang, A. A., Kazemi, E., Esmaeili, V., & Davies, M. S. (2023). The effectiveness of virtual reality training: A systematic review. *Journal of Organizational Behavior Management*, 44(3), 214–232. DOI: 10.1080/01608061.2023.2240767

Chazin, K. T., Barton, E. E., Ledford, J. R., & Pokorski, E. A. (2018). Implementation and intervention practices to facilitate communication skills for a child with complex communication needs. *Journal of Early Intervention*, 40(2), 138–157. DOI: 10.1177/1053815118771397

Clay, C. J., Schmitz, B. A., Balakrishnan, B., Hopfenblatt, J. P., Evans, A., & Kahng, S. (2021). Feasibility of virtual reality behavior skills training for preservice clinicians. *Journal of Applied Behavior Analysis*, 54(2), 547–565. DOI: 10.1002/jaba.809 PMID: 33482023

Cooper, J. O., Heron, T. E., & Heward, W. L. (2020). *Applied behavior analysis* (3rd ed.). Pearson.

Council for Exceptional Children. (2015). *What every special educator must know: Professional ethics and standards* (7th ed.). Council for Exceptional Children. https://www.archive.org/details/isbn_9780865865044

Cox, D. J., & Jennings, A. M. (2024). The promises and possibilities of artificial intelligence in the delivery of behavior analytic services. *Behavior Analysis in Practice*, 17(1), 123–136. DOI: 10.1007/s40617-023-00864-3 PMID: 38405282

Dempsey, N., Brown, C., & Bramley, G. (2012). The key to sustainable urban development in UK cities? The influence of density on social sustainability. *Progress in Planning*, 77(3), 89–141. DOI: 10.1016/j.progress.2012.01.001

Dieker, L. A., Hynes, M. C., Hughes, C. E., Hardin, S., & Becht, K. (2015). TLE TeachLive (TM): Using technology to provide quality professional development in rural schools. *Rural Special Education Quarterly*, 34(3), 11–16. DOI: 10.1177/875687051503400303

Dimian, A. F., & Symons, F. J. (2022). A systematic review of risk for the development and persistence of self-injurious behavior in intellectual and developmental disabilities. *Clinical Psychology Review*, 94, 102158. Advance online publication. DOI: 10.1016/j.cpr.2022.102158 PMID: 35580423

Elasri, M., Elharrouss, O., Al-Maadeed, S., & Tairi, H. (2022). Image generation: A review. *Neural Processing Letters*, 54(5), 4609–4646. DOI: 10.1007/s11063-022-10777-x

Elevenlabs. (2023). *Generative voice AI*. https://elevenlabs.io/

Espinoza, D., Saunders, R., Kini, T., & Darling-Hammond, L. (2018). Taking the long view: state efforts to solve teacher shortages by strengthening the profession. *Learning Policy Institute*. https://learningpolicyinstitute.org/product/long-view-report

Falcomata, T. S., Roane, H. S., Muething, C. S., Stephenson, K. M., & Ing, A. D. (2012). Functional communication training and chained schedules of reinforcement to treat challenging behavior maintained by terminations of activity interruptions. *Behavior Modification*, 36(5), 630–649. DOI: 10.1177/0145445511433821 PMID: 22327267

Ferguson, J., Craig, E. A., & Dounavi, K. (2019). Telehealth as a model for providing behavior analytic interventions to individuals with autism spectrum disorder: A systematic review. *Journal of Autism and Developmental Disorders*, 49(2), 582–616. DOI: 10.1007/s10803-018-3724-5 PMID: 30155578

Ferrer, X., Van Nuenen, T., Such, J. M., Coté, M., & Criado, N. (2021). Bias and discrimination in AI: A cross-disciplinary perspective. *IEEE Technology and Society Magazine*, 40(2), 72–80. DOI: 10.1109/MTS.2021.3056293

Fisher, W. W., Greer, B. D., Querim, A. C., & DeRosa, N. (2014). Decreasing excessive functional communication responses while treating destructive behavior using response restriction. *Research in Developmental Disabilities*, 35(11), 2614–2623. DOI: 10.1016/j.ridd.2014.06.024 PMID: 25036315

Frontline Education. (2021). *Teacher shortages: The new normal.*https://www.frontlineeducation.com/solutions/recruiting-hiring/insights/teacher-shortages-new-normal/

Fryling, M. J., Wallace, M. D., & Yassine, J. N. (2012). Impact of treatment integrity on intervention effectiveness. *Journal of Applied Behavior Analysis*, 45(2), 449–453. DOI: 10.1901/jaba.2012.45-449 PMID: 22844155

Fuchs, L. S., Fuchs, D., Hamlett, C. L., & Stecker, P. M. (2021). Bringing data-based individualization to scale: A call for the next-generation technology of teacher supports. *Journal of Learning Disabilities*, 54(5), 319–333. DOI: 10.1177/0022219420950654 PMID: 33813936

Garrett, B., Taverner, T., Gromala, D., Tao, G., Cordingley, E., & Sun, C. (2018). Virtual reality clinical research: Promises and challenges. *JMIR Serious Games*, 6(4), e10839. Advance online publication. DOI: 10.2196/10839 PMID: 30333096

Ghaemmaghami, M., Hanley, G. P., & Jessel, J. (2021). Functional communication training: From efficacy to effectiveness. *Journal of Applied Behavior Analysis*, 54(1), 122–143. DOI: 10.1002/jaba.762 PMID: 32929757

Gonzalez-Calatayud, V., Prendes-Espinosa, P., & Roig-Vila, R. (2021). Artificial intelligence for student assessment: A systematic review. *Applied Sciences (Basel, Switzerland)*, 11(12), 5467. Advance online publication. DOI: 10.3390/app11125467

Gormley, L., Healy, O., O'Sullivan, B., O'Regan, D., Grey, I., & Bracken, M. (2019). The impact of behavioural skills training on the knowledge, skills and well-being of front line staff in the intellectual disability sector: A clustered randomised control trial. *Journal of Intellectual Disability Research*, 63(11), 1291–1304. DOI: 10.1111/jir.12630 PMID: 31106922

Hanley, G. P., Iwata, B. A., & Thompson, R. H. (2001). Reinforcement schedule thinning following treatment with functional communication training. *Journal of Applied Behavior Analysis*, 34(1), 17–38. DOI: 10.1901/jaba.2001.34-17 PMID: 11317985

Hirsch, S. E., Kennedy, M. J., Haines, S. J., Thomas, C. N., & Alves, K. D. (2015). Improving preservice teachers' knowledge and application of functional behavioral assessments using multimedia. *Behavioral Disorders*, 41(1), 38–50. DOI: 10.17988/0198-7429-41.1.38

Holmes, W. (2020). Artificial intelligence in education. In Tatnall, A. (Ed.), *Encyclopedia of education and information technologies* (pp. 88–103). Springer., DOI: 10.1007/978-3-030-10576-1_107

Hopcan, S., Polat, E., Ozturk, M. E., & Ozturk, L. (2023). Artificial intelligence in special education: A systematic review. *Interactive Learning Environments*, 31(10), 7335–7353. DOI: 10.1080/10494820.2022.2067186

Hussain, Z., Binz, M., Mata, R., & Wulff, D. U. (2024). A tutorial on open-source large language models for behavioral science. *Behavior Research Methods*. Advance online publication. DOI: 10.3758/s13428-024-02455-8 PMID: 39147947

Imam, A. A. (2021). Historically recontextualizing Sidman's Tactics: How behavior analysis avoided psychology's methodological Ouroboros. *Journal of the Experimental Analysis of Behavior*, 115(1), 115–128. DOI: 10.1002/jeab.661 PMID: 33336404

Jensen, L., & Konradsen, F. (2018). A review of the use of virtual reality head-mounted displays in education and training. *Education and Information Technologies*, 23(4), 1515–1529. DOI: 10.1007/s10639-017-9676-0

Kempt, H., Heilinger, J. C., & Nagel, S. K. (2022). Relative explainability and double standards in medical decision-making: Should medical AI be subjected to higher standards in medical decision-making than doctors? *Ethics and Information Technology*, 24(2), 20. Advance online publication. DOI: 10.1007/s10676-022-09646-x

Khanzanchi, R., & Khanzanchi, P. (2024). Generative AI to improve special education teacher preparation for inclusive classrooms. In Searson, M., Langran, E., & Trumble, J. (Eds.), *Exploring new horizons: Generative artificial intelligence and teacher education* (pp. 159–177). Association for the Advancement of Computing in Education., https://www.learntechlib.org/primary/p/223928/

King, M. R., & Chat, G. P. T. (2023). A conversation on artificial intelligence, chatbots, and plagiarism in higher education. *Cellular and Molecular Bioengineering*, 16(1), 1–2. DOI: 10.1007/s12195-022-00754-8 PMID: 36660590

King, S. A. (2022). The education context for twice-exceptional students: An overview of issues in special and gifted education. *Neurobiology of Learning and Memory*, 193, 107659. Advance online publication. DOI: 10.1016/j.nlm.2022.107659 PMID: 35835373

King, S. A., Boyer, J., Bell, T., & Estapa, A. (2022). An automated virtual reality training system for teacher-student interaction: A randomized controlled trial. *JMIR Serious Games*, 10(4), e41097. Advance online publication. DOI: 10.2196/41097 PMID: 36480248

King, S. A., Dzenga, C., Burch, T., & Kennedy, K. (2021). Teaching partial-interval recording of problem behavior with virtual reality. *Journal of Behavioral Education*, 30(2), 202–225. DOI: 10.1007/s10864-019-09363-4

King, S. A., Estapa, A., Bell, T., & Boyer, J. (2024). Behavioral skills training through smart virtual reality: Demonstration of feasibility for a verbal mathematical questioning strategy. *Journal of Behavioral Education*, 33(2), 396–420. DOI: 10.1007/s10864-022-09492-3

King, S. A., Feng, L., Glazek, C., Ross, K. M., Green, M., Lele, H., & Bell, T. (2024, October 11). (in press). Developing smart virtual reality to teach functional communication training. *Journal of Behavioral Education*. Advance online publication. DOI: 10.1007/s10864-024-09569-1

King, S. A., Nylen, B., Enders, O., Wang, L., & Opeoluwa, O. (2024). Examining the impact of design-comparable effect size on the analysis of single-case design in special education. *School Psychology*. Advance online publication. DOI: 10.1037/spq0000628 PMID: 38753395

King, S. A., Ross, K. M., Glazek, C., Feng, L., Green, M., Bell, T., & Lele, H. (2024). Integrating artificial intelligence and virtual reality to train educators in functional communication training—Results from exploratory studies. In Eom, M., Kim, Y., Lee, K., Lee, S., & Oh, H. (Eds.), *Proceedings of the 24th International Conference on Educational Research: Reimaging Teaching and Teachers in a Changing World* (pp. 1–5)., https://icer.snu.ac.kr/sub_proceeding/icer_add.php?mode=view&year=2024&number=31

King, S. A., Wang, L., Nylen, B., & Enders, O. (2023). Prevalence of research design in special education: A survey of peer-reviewed journals. *Remedial and Special Education*, 44(6), 480–494. DOI: 10.1177/07419325231152453

Kirkpatrick, M., Akers, J., & Rivera, G. (2019). Use of behavioral skills training with teachers: A systematic review. *Journal of Behavioral Education*, 28(3), 344–361. DOI: 10.1007/s10864-019-09322-z

Kornack, J., Persicke, A., Cervantes, P., Jang, J., & Dixon, D. (2014). Economics of autism spectrum disorders: An overview of treatment and research funding. In Tarbox, D. J., Dixon, D. R., Sturmey, P., & Matson, J. L. (Eds.), *Handbook of early intervention for autism spectrum disorders: Research, policy, and practice* (pp. 165–178). Springer. DOI: 10.1007/978-1-4939-0401-3_9

Krezmien, M. P., Travers, J. C., & Camacho, K. (2017). Suspension rates of students with autism or intellectual disabilities in Maryland from 2004 to 2015. *Journal of Intellectual Disability Research*, 61(11), 1011–1020. DOI: 10.1111/jir.12406 PMID: 28836311

Kruse, C. S., Karem, P., Shifflett, K., Vegi, L., Ravi, K., & Brooks, M. (2018). Evaluating barriers to adopting telemedicine worldwide: A systematic review. *Journal of Telemedicine and Telecare*, 24(1), 4–12. DOI: 10.1177/1357633X16674087 PMID: 29320966

Leaf, J. B., Cihon, J. H., Javed, A., Klick, S., Ferguson, J. L., Milne, C., Creem, A., Arthur, S., Saunders, M., Olive, M. L., Ross, R. K., Leaf, R., & McEachin, J. (2022). A call for discussion on stereotypic behavior. *European Journal of Behavior Analysis*, 23(2), 156–180. DOI: 10.1080/15021149.2022.2112810

Losavio, M. (2023). Forensic proof and criminal liability for development, distribution and use of artificial intelligence. In Wang, C., Iyengar, S. S., & Sun, K. (Eds.), *AI Embedded Assurance for Cyber Systems* (pp. 37–48). Springer., DOI: 10.1007/978-3-031-42637-7_3

Lugrin, J. L., Latoschik, M. E., Habel, M., Roth, D., Seufert, C., & Grafe, S. (2016). Breaking bad behaviors: A new tool for learning classroom management using virtual reality. *Frontiers in ICT (Lausanne, Switzerland)*, 3(26), 1–21. DOI: 10.3389/fict.2016.00026

Maddox, R. P.II, Rujimora, J., Nichols, L. M., Williams, M. K., Hunt, T., & Carter, R. A.Jr. (2022). Trauma-informed schools: Implications for special education and school counseling. *Teaching Exceptional Children*, 56(6), 510–520. DOI: 10.1177/00400599221107142

Marino, M. T., Vasquez, E., Dieker, L., Basham, J., & Blackorby, J. (2023). The future of artificial intelligence in special education technology. *Journal of Special Education Technology*, 38(3), 404–416. DOI: 10.1177/01626434231165977

Matsuda, K., Garcia, Y., Catagnus, R., & Brandt, J. A. (2020). Can behavior analysis help us understand and reduce racism? A review of the current literature. *Behavior Analysis in Practice*, 13(2), 336–347. DOI: 10.1007/s40617-020-00411-4 PMID: 32642393

Middeke, A., Anders, S., Schuelper, M., Raupach, T., & Schuelper, N. (2018). Training of clinical reasoning with a Serious Game versus small-group problem-based learning: A prospective study. *PLoS One*, 13(9), e0203851. Advance online publication. DOI: 10.1371/journal.pone.0203851 PMID: 30204773

Mühlhoff, R. (2021). Predictive privacy: Towards an applied ethics of data analytics. *Ethics and Information Technology*, 23(4), 675–690. DOI: 10.1007/s10676-021-09606-x

Mursion. (n.d.). *Mursion* [software]. https://www.mursion.com/

Nakao, Y., Stumpf, S., Ahmed, S., Naseer, A., & Strappelli, L. (2022). Toward involving end-users in interactive human-in-the-loop AI fairness. A*CM Transactions on Interactive Intelligent Systems (TiiS), 12*(3), 1–30. https://doi.org//arXiv.2204.10464DOI: 10.48550

National Association of School Psychologists. (2020). *The professional standards of the National Association of School Psychologists.* https://www.nasponline.org/standards-and-certification/professional-ethics

National Center for Special Education Research. (2023). *Special education research grants program.* US Department of Education. Institute of Education Sciences. https://ies.ed.gov/funding/pdf/2024_84324A.pdf

Neely, L., MacNaul, H., Gregori, E., & Cantrell, K. (2021). Effects of telehealth-mediated behavioral assessments and interventions on client outcomes: A quality review. *Journal of Applied Behavior Analysis*, 54(2), 484–510. DOI: 10.1002/jaba.818 PMID: 33621358

Nelson, E. L., & Bui, T. (2010). Rural telepsychology services for children and adolescents. *Journal of Clinical Psychology*, 66(5), 490–501. DOI: 10.1002/jclp.20682 PMID: 20306524

Nylen, B., & King, S. A. (2023). Training practitioners to conduct a functional behavior assessment via telehealth-delivered behavioral skills training: A systematic literature review. *Journal of Behavioral Education.* Advance online publication. DOI: 10.1007/s10864-023-09514-8

O'Brien, M. J., Pelzel, K. E., Hendrix, N. M., Schieltz, K. M., Miller, K., Call, N. A., Tsami, L., Lerman, D. C., Berg, W. K., Kopelman, T. G., Wacker, D. P., & Lindgren, S. D. (2022). Parent ratings of generalized and indirect effects of functional communication training for children with autism spectrum disorder. *Behavior Modification*, 46(5), 971–1001. DOI: 10.1177/01454455211018815 PMID: 34041956

Office of Special Education and Rehabilitative Services. (2024). *Applications for new awards; Educational technology, media, and material for individuals with disabilities program-stepping-up technology implementation.* US Department of Education. https://www.federalregister.gov/documents/2024/03/01/2024-04316/applications-for-new-awards-educational-technology-media-and-materials-for-individuals-with

Open, A. I. (2022). *Introducing Whisper.* https://openai.com/research/whisper

Ouyang, F., Zheng, L., & Jiao, P. (2022). Artificial intelligence in online higher education: A systematic review of empirical research from 2011 to 2020. *Education and Information Technologies*, 27(6), 7893–7925. DOI: 10.1007/s10639-022-10925-9

Pantziaras, I., Fors, U., & Ekblad, S. (2015). Training with virtual patients in transcultural psychiatry: Do the learners actually learn? *Journal of Medical Internet Research*, 17(2), e46. Advance online publication. DOI: 10.2196/jmir.3497 PMID: 25689716

Parsons, J. A. (2021). The telemedical imperative. *Bioethics*, 35(4), 298–306. DOI: 10.1111/bioe.12847 PMID: 33586790

Podoletz, L. (2023). We have to talk about emotional AI and crime. *AI & Society*, 38(3), 1067–1082. DOI: 10.1007/s00146-022-01435-w

Prykanowski, D. A., Conroy, M. A., & Reichow, B. (2021). Schedule thinning during functional communication training in the home for young children with autism. *Journal of Positive Behavior Interventions*, 23(4), 257–271. DOI: 10.1177/1098300721994204

Radianti, J., Majchrzak, T. A., Fromm, J., & Wohlgenannt, I. (2020). A systematic review of immersive virtual reality applications for higher education: Design elements, lessons learned, and research agenda. *Computers & Education*, 147, 103778. Advance online publication. DOI: 10.1016/j.compedu.2019.103778

Rajaraman, A., Austin, J. L., Gover, H. C., Cammilleri, A. P., Donnelly, D. R., & Hanley, G. P. (2022). Toward trauma-informed applications of behavior analysis. *Journal of Applied Behavior Analysis*, 55(1), 40–61. DOI: 10.1002/jaba.881 PMID: 34525220

Reid, D. H., O'Kane, N. P., & Macurik, K. M. (2011). Staff training and management. In Fisher, W. W., Piazza, C. C., & Roane, H. S. (Eds.), *Handbook of applied behavior analysis* (pp. 281–296). The Guilford Press.

Rude, H., & Miller, K. J. (2018). Policy challenges and opportunities for rural special education. *Rural Special Education Quarterly*, 37(1), 21–29. DOI: 10.1177/8756870517748662

Schiff, D. (2021). Out of the laboratory and into the classroom: The future of artificial intelligence in education. *AI & Society*, 36(1), 331–348. DOI: 10.1007/s00146-020-01033-8 PMID: 32836908

Shadiev, R., Wu, T. T., Sun, A., & Huang, Y. M. (2018). Applications of speech-to-text recognition and computer-aided translation for facilitating cross-cultural learning through a learning activity: Issues and their solutions. *Educational Technology Research and Development*, 66(1), 191–214. DOI: 10.1007/s11423-017-9556-8

Shapiro, M., & Kazemi, E. (2017). A review of training strategies to teach individuals implementation of behavioral interventions. *Journal of Organizational Behavior Management*, 37(1), 32–62. DOI: 10.1080/01608061.2016.1267066

Shepley, C., Lane, J. D., & Ault, M. J. (2019). A review and critical examination of the system of least prompts. *Remedial and Special Education*, 40(5), 313–327. DOI: 10.1177/0741932517751213

Suh, A., & Prophet, J. (2018). The state of immersive technology research: A literature analysis. *Computers in Human Behavior*, 86, 77–90. DOI: 10.1016/j.chb.2018.04.019

Tan, H. C., Hughes, M. R., & Toogood, S. (2016). Using task analysis to promote engagement in special educational settings. *European Journal of Behavior Analysis*, 17(2), 116–130. DOI: 10.1080/15021149.2016.1247575

U.S. Department of Army–Medical Research Acquisition Activity. (2024). *Autism research program idea development award.* U.S. Department of Defense. https://cdmrp.health.mil/funding/arp

U.S. Equal Employment Opportunity Commission. (2022). *Elementary-secondary staff information report (EEO-5) data collection*. https://www.eeoc.gov/employers/eeo-5-elementary-secondary-staff-information-report-data-collection

Vince-Garland, K. M., Holden, K., & Garland, D. P. (2016). Individualized clinical coaching in the TLE TeachLivE lab: Enhancing fidelity of implementation of system of least prompts among novice teachers of students with autism. *Teacher Education and Special Education*, 39(1), 47–59. DOI: 10.1177/0888406415600769

Vivanti, G., & Stahmer, A. (2018). Early intervention for autism: Are we prioritizing feasibility at the expense of effectiveness? A cautionary note. *Autism*, 22(7), 770–773. DOI: 10.1177/1362361318803043 PMID: 30235939

Wali, A., Mahamad, S., & Sulaiman, S. (2023). Task automation intelligent agents: A review. *Future Internet*, 15(6), 196. Advance online publication. DOI: 10.3390/fi15060196

Walker, V. L., Carpenter, M. E., Clausen, A., Ealer, K., & Lyon, K. J. (2021). Special educators as coaches to support paraprofessional implementation of functional communication training. *Journal of Positive Behavior Interventions*, 23(3), 174–184. DOI: 10.1177/1098300720957995

Weiser, B. (2023). Here's what happens when your lawyer uses ChatGPT. *The New York Times*. https://www.nytimes.com/2023/05/27/nyregion/avianca-airline-lawsuit-chatgpt.html

Yu, Z., & Xu, W. (2022). A meta-analysis and systematic review of the effect of virtual reality technology on users' learning outcomes. *Computer Applications in Engineering Education*, 30(5), 1470–1484. DOI: 10.1002/cae.22532

Zablotsky, B., Ng, A. E., Black, L. I., & Blumberg, S. J. (2023). Diagnosed developmental disabilities in children aged 3–17 years: United States, 2019–2021. *NCHS Data Brief*, 473, 1–8. DOI: 10.15620/cdc:129520 PMID: 37440277

Zigmond, N. P., & Kloo, A. (2017). General and special education are (and should be) different. In Kauffman, J. M., Hallahan, D. P., & Pullen, P. C. (Eds.), *Handbook of special education* (2nd ed., pp. 249–261). Routledge. DOI: 10.4324/9781315517698-21

Chapter 17
Artificial Intelligence: Solutions in Special Education

Wasim Ahmad
https://orcid.org/0000-0002-2106-7824
National Institute for the Empowerment of Persons With Intellectual Disabilities, Navi Mumbai, India

Ruchika Shokeen
https://orcid.org/0009-0003-3322-9389
National Institute for the Empowerment of Persons With Intellectual Disabilities, Navi Mumbai, India

Rishu Raj
https://orcid.org/0009-0003-5440-8837
National Institute for the Empowerment of Persons With Intellectual Disabilities, Navi Mumbai, India

ABSTRACT

The evolution of Artificial Intelligence (AI) has significantly transformed various fields, including education, by introducing advanced techniques and algorithms. This transformation encompasses tasks such as convergence, classification, identification, recognition, and beyond, integrating knowledge from sociology, psychology, ethics, computer science and pedagogy. The historical milestones of AI, from the early works of Turning and McCarthy to the recent advancements in Large Language Models (LLMs) like ChatGPT, demonstrate AI's progression and its impact on education. Recent advancements in AI, including Internet of Thing, Machine Learning, Augmented Reality, and Virtual Reality, have transformed the educational landscape, making it more inclusive and accessible for individuals with disabilities. This chapter proposes AI as solution to the field of special education particularly while addressing the needs of CwSN in mainstream settings. The re-

DOI: 10.4018/979-8-3693-5538-1.ch017

search conducted in the past suggests that the use AI has greater advantages over traditional methods of teaching to the CwSN.

INTRODUCTION

The landscape of Artificial Intelligence (AI) has witnessed substantial development following the launch of intricate approaches and algorithms. The field of AI has majorly evolved since the introduction of highly developed and ultra-modern techniques and algorithms shaping the AI powered education, which has been employed for tasks of converging, reversion, classification, identification, recognition, translation, elucidation and beyond (Chen et al., 2020a; Lee & Cho, 2021; Velander et al., 2024). Different sector of knowledge for examples sociology, psychology, ethics, pedagogy, etc are employed in these analytics (UNESCO, 2019).

Establishing a functional definition of AI is essential because there is no universally accepted definition, even among experts in computer science and engineering, a broad description of AI can be articulated as the potential of a computational system to execute activities those usually necessitate human cognitive abilities, including visual interpretation, speech identification, and decision formulation (Cummings et al., 2018). The understanding of AI can be approached through two perspectives: thinking humanly and rationally, and acting humanly and rationally. The first is concerned with thought processes and reasoning, and the second addresses human behavior and actions. Thinking humanly and acting humanly approach evaluate success based on how closely it matches human performance, while thinking rationally and acting rationally, evaluate success against an ideal standard of rationality (Russell & Norvig, 2010). A system is considered rational if it acts appropriately based on the information it possesses. Throughout history, each of the four methodologies in the field of Artificial Intelligence has been pursued by distinct individuals employing diverse techniques. An empirical examination of human behavior constitutes a fundamental component of the human-centered approach, entailing the formulation of observations and hypotheses. Conversely, a rationalist approach integrates principles from mathematics and engineering. The different factions within the discipline have alternately criticized and supported one another as explained in figure 1 (Russell & Norvig, 2010).

Figure 1. Four methodologies in the sector of Artificial Intelligence. Source: Russell & Norvig, 2010

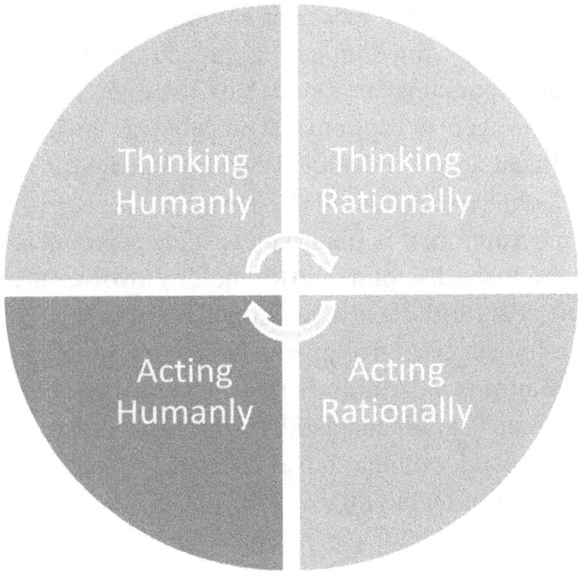

Acting humanly means to engage in human-like conduct necessitates that the computer replicate human actions, thereby requiring an array of competencies, which encompass natural language processing to facilitate proficient communication in English, knowledge representation for the systematic storage of acquired data, automated reasoning for addressing inquiries and deriving novel conclusions, machine learning for the adaptation to novel circumstances and the identification of patterns, computer vision for the interpretation of objects, and robotics for the manipulation of objects and movement (Russell & Norvig, 2010). *Thinking humanly* focuses on the concept of thinking like a human concentrate on affirming that a specific program displays cognitive processes similar to those of humans. It is crucial to investigate the actual mechanisms that underlie human cognitive processes. There exist three methodologies for accomplishing this objective: introspection, which entails documenting one's thoughts as they manifest; psychological experiments, which involve observing individuals engaging in various tasks; and brain imaging, which encompasses monitoring brain activity. Once a detailed model of human cognition is established, it becomes possible to convert this model into a computational framework (Russell & Norvig, 2010). When discussing the concept of *thinking rationally* in the context of AI, it employs symbolic logic to represent the principles of logical thinking as manipulable symbols. The process of inference involves manipulating these symbols in accordance with clearly defined rules, akin to algebraic operations. As a result, an abstract representation of human cognition is created. This particular approach is attractive to theoretical researchers because it involves simulating the optimal modes of human thinking and logical deduction (Russell & Norvig, 2010). *Acting Rationally* approach signifies behaving in a logical manner, which involves pursuing one's goals based on one's beliefs or understanding of the environment. An agent is a system that perceives an environment and operates within it. An intelligent agent is distinguished by its capacity to act rationally in accordance with its objectives (Russell & Norvig, 2010).

In addition to a definition, it is important to understand what AI means. AI, in simple terms, pertains to the discipline and technology involved in creating intelligent machines by means of algorithms or a predefined set of instructions that enable the machine to imitate human cognitive processes like learning and problem-solving (McCarthy, 2007; Bajwa et al., 2021). Furthermore, artificial intelligence systems exhibit a remarkable capacity for adaptability and autonomy, perpetually advancing and recalibrating as they assimilate novel datasets. AI constitutes an innovative domain within the field of technological sciences, devoted to the exploration and formulation of theories, methodologies, technologies, and application frameworks that emulate, augment, and enhance human cognitive capabilities (Robert et al., 2024). AI is designed to enable machines to reason like humans and imbue them with intelligence. Today, the scope of AI has significantly expanded, making it a highly interdisciplinary field (Xu et al., 2021).

The commitment to ensuring "AI for all" necessitates that all individuals have the opportunity to benefit from the ongoing technological advancements and gain access to its benefits, particularly in relation to innovation and knowledge (UNESCO, n.d.). UNESCO has established a Chair focused on Artificial Intelligence to investigate how AI can contribute as a catalyst and component in developing solutions and strategies to promote the Sustainable Development Goals (SDGs). UNESCO, with its distinct mandate in education and culture, leads this initiative. In 2021, UNESCO published guidelines for policymakers, addressing the integration and assessment of AI technologies in education, including ethical considerations (UNESCO, 2021a). In November of the same year, UNESCO unveiled a report that underscores the vital role of education and supports the United Nations' overarching objective (SDG 4) to ensure inclusive, equitable, as well as quality education for all. It also highlights the substantial challenges that must be addressed to achieve these goals, for example, inequality in quality education is growing exponentially. This report delivers a strong message: guaranteeing universal accessibility to high-quality educational resources and continuous learning prospects is crucial. This goal necessitates forging a new social contract to propel global education forward, acknowledging that mere access to schools falls short of what is needed (UNESCO, 2021b).

AI technologies are employed to guarantee fair and comprehensive entry to the realm of education. They afford marginalized individuals and communities, persons with disabilities, refugees, individuals not attending school, and those residing in secluded areas with the means to engage in suitable learning prospects (UNESCO, 2019). Through the judicious and holistic application of artificial intelligence technologies, societies possess the potential to advance toward the realization of a future that is equitable and achievable for all individuals, regardless of their abilities or disabilities (Toyokawa et al., 2023). Given this perspective, artificial intelligence is revolutionizing the landscape of Special Education across various dimensions, which will be explored further in this chapter.

EVOLUTION OF AI AND SPECIAL EDUCATION

The evolution of Artificial Intelligence (AI) from the 1940s to the 2020s was characterized by notable achievements and advancements. A pioneering work by McCulloch and Pitts in 1943 focused on artificial neurons, establishing the foundational principles of neural network theory (McCulloch & Pitts, 1943; Abraham, 2002). Post-World War II, several individuals commenced independent research endeavors in the realm of intelligent machines, with Alan Turing, the English mathematician, potentially being among the earliest contributors. Turing asserted that the exploration of artificial intelligence should primarily emphasize the sphere of computer programming rather than the enhancement of mechanical devices, and he introduced the Turing test, which serves as a criterion for assessing a machine's ability to exhibit cognitive characteristics that resemble human behavior. The development of AI has been closely linked to advances in assistive technologies, greatly impacting special education, especially for children with special needs (CwSN). In the 1940s and 50s, Warren McCulloch and Walter Pitts laid the foundation of neural networks, which formed the theoretical basis for adaptive learning systems used in special education today. These systems adjust content delivery based on individual learning patterns, providing tailored support for CwSN, particularly those with cognitive challenges. Alan Turing's creation of the Turing Test in 1950, which assesses machine intelligence, spurred AI research, leading to John McCarthy's coining of "artificial intelligence" in 1956 (McCarthy, 2007). Turing's work on machine intelligence paved the way for early conversational agents, helping children with speech or social difficulties, such as those on the autism spectrum, to practice communication in structured environments (Sebesta, 2012). In 1957, Frank Rosenblatt's Perceptron demonstrated machines' potential to learn from experience, setting the stage for machine learning in personalized education tools. Today, AI-powered systems assess and adapt to the learning pace of CwSN, offering customized educational experiences (Freund & Schapire, 1999).

By the 1960s, AI research expanded into areas like expert systems and robotics, giving rise to early assistive technologies such as speech synthesis and screen readers. These technologies, like IBM's Shoebox, ELIZA, and SHRDLU, were critical in helping students with visual and auditory impairments through voice-based interactions and text-to-speech systems (Weizenbaum, 1966; Ward, 2006). Despite a decline in funding during the AI Winter (1970s-2000), research continued in neural networks, leading to more sophisticated adaptive educational tools. These systems became essential in differentiated instruction, allowing educators to better meet the diverse learning needs of CwSN (Crevier, 1993; Rumelhart et al., 1986).

The 1990s saw the emergence of specialized educational software like Sherlock (intelligent tutoring systems) and Reader Rabbit (early learning games), which allowed educators to provide differentiated instruction and multisensory learning experiences (Sharma et al., 2023; Russell & Norvig, 2021). These tools benefited students with dyslexia, ADHD, and other learning differences by reinforcing lessons with visual and auditory cues. In the 2000s, assistive technologies like JAWS (screen readers), Dragon NaturallySpeaking (speech recognition), and predictive text systems like T9 made it easier for CwSN with physical or learning disabilities to access and interact with digital content independently, improving their inclusion in educational environments.

The 2010s introduced AI-powered virtual assistants like Siri, Alexa, and Google Assistant, which helped CwSN navigate digital environments with greater independence (Duffy et al., 2018; Ferrucci, 2012). AI-driven tutoring systems became more advanced, using data analytics and adaptive learning to customize lessons for individual students, particularly benefiting those with autism, ADHD, or learning disabilities by providing personalized learning paths (Ersozlu et al., 2021; Chen et al. 2020b; Kahraman et al., 2010; Peredo et al., 2011; Chassignol et al., 2018).

As AI continues to evolve, the 2020s bring potential breakthroughs in special education through innovations such as generative AI (e.g., ChatGPT) and brain-computer interfaces (BCIs). These technologies promise even more tailored educational experiences, enhancing communication, mobility, and learning for CwSN with physical or developmental disabilities. Moving forward, the emphasis on AI-related ethics, privacy, and security, coupled with ongoing research, will ensure responsible and effective use of these technologies to improve the educational experiences of all students, especially those with special needs. (Maiseli et al., 2023; Linde & Agarwal, 2023; Sağdıç et al., 2024). Let's have a look over the simplified timeline of evolution of AI in the field of Special Education.

The Simplified Timeline of Evolution of AI in the Field of Special Education

Figure 2 Flow Chart Depicting the Evolution of AI in Special Education

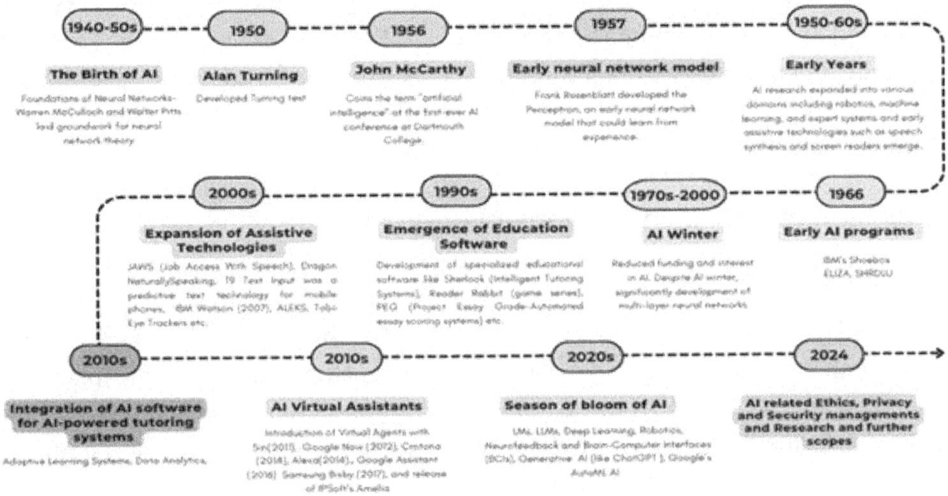

Early Years (1950-60s):

Prominent AI programs were created in the early stages of development, including ELIZA, a natural language processing application functioning as an artificial conversational agent (Weizenbaum, 1966). SHRDLU is a program capable of interpreting basic English statements that were launched during this time (Ward, 2006). AI research expanded into various domains including robotics, machine learning, and expert systems and early assistive technologies such as speech synthesis and screen readers emerged, laying the groundwork for future AI applications in special education.

AI Winter (1970-80s)

AI winter was the phase when funding and interest in AI were reduced (Crevier, 1993). Despite AI winter, in 1986 Rumelhart, Hinton, and Williams introduced the backpropagation algorithm that revitalized neural network research, significantly improving the training of multi-layer neural networks (Rumelhart et al.,1986).

Emergence of Education Software (1990s)

Development of specialized educational software for students with disabilities, including programs for cognitive skill development, communication, and sensory integration. These programs often incorporate basic AI techniques for personalization and adaptive learning (Sharma et al., 2023). Russell and Norvig (2021) in their publication titled Artificial Intelligence: A Modern Approach, deliberated on the goals and various facets of Artificial Intelligence, such as problem resolution, Machine Learning, and Deep Learning, among others.

Expansion of Assistive Technologies (2000s)

Assistive devices became central to rehabilitation, gaining popularity and eventually evolving with the integration of AI smart technology. In the early 2000s, ActiveMath was created as an adaptive online mathematics learning platform. This innovative tool used AI to customize learning experiences based on how each student performed (Melis et al., 2001). Tobii Eye Trackers, the world's first remote eye tracker was created in 2002 (Duffy et al., 2018). Rapid advancement in assistive technologies, like speech recognition software like Dragon Naturally Speaking, has benefited students with dyslexia, visual impairments, and communication disorders. Computer-Based Speech Therapy, AI-driven tools were developed to assist in speech therapy, using fuzzy expert systems to enhance the effectiveness of therapeutic interventions (Schipor et al., 2010). T9 Text Input was a predictive text technology for mobile phones (Vidhya et al, 2009). Adaptive Hypermedia Systems are systems that adapt educational content to the individual needs of learners, such as an adaptive system that was developed to tailor English language instruction for hearing-impaired individuals using sign language (Drigas et al., 2008). Expert Systems for Learning Disabilities used AI to diagnose learning disabilities in children. For instance, a study by Hernandez et al. (2008) developed an expert system for diagnosing learning difficulties in basic education (Hernandez et al., 2008). Systems like ALEKS (Assessment and Learning in Knowledge Spaces) use AI to diagnose learning gaps and provide personalized instruction for students with special educational needs (Canfield, 2001). In 2007, IBM Research initiated the development of an advanced computational system designed to compete with champions in the intellectual game show Jeopardy (Ferrucci, 2012).

Integration of AI Software for AI-Powered Tutoring Systems (2010s)

Adaptive learning systems leverage artificial intelligence to develop interactive and customized learning experiences (Russel & Norvig, 2010). The integration of AI in the field of education is particularly effective in establishing tailored learning settings through the adjustment of educational content and teaching methods to suit the specific requirements of each student (Russel & Norvig, 2010). AI-powered assistive technologies, including speech recognition software, text-to-speech, and predictive typing tools, are advancing in complexity, providing valuable support to students with disabilities in various communication and educational activities. One notable example is RoboKind's Milo, a humanlike robot specifically created to assist children with autism, in enhancing their social skills through engaging interactive sessions (Gudlin et al., 2022). Rapid advancement in assistive technologies, including text-to-speech like Kurzweil 3000 (Kurzweil, 1998), Microsoft Learning Tools had benefited students with dyslexia, visual impairments, and communication disorders (Microsoft, n.d.). Introduction of AI-driven learning platforms like DreamBox Learning, were capable of adapting to individual learning styles and needs. For educators aiming to enhance student participation, these metrics present a valuable resource. Furthermore, the rise of classroom simulation tools offers teachers the opportunity to refine their abilities in authentic scenarios (Ersozlu et al., 2021). Educators are increasingly employing artificial intelligence in data analytics to oversee the progress of students, identify patterns in their learning, and tailor teaching methods to meet the diverse needs of students with disabilities. The assimilation of AI tools could further assist teachers in handling elaborate classroom processes (Holstein et al., 2019). Moreover, as pointed out by Chen et al. (2020a), an AI-driven assistant can potentially function as an additional collaborative member in a small student group, helping with tasks. Introduction of Virtual Agents with Siri (2011), Google Now (2012), Crotona (2014), Alexa (2014), Google Assistant (2016) Samsung Bixby (2017), and release of IPSoft's Amelia (Hoy, 2018). Chatbots are currently being employed in a multitude of sectors, encompassing the realm of education. The majority of contemporary intelligent AI chatbots are internet-dependent systems that adjust to the actions of educators and students alike, thereby enriching the educational process (Kahraman et al., 2010; Peredo et al., 2011; Chassignol et al., 2018).

Season of Bloom of AI (2020s)

The development of Large Language Models (LLMs) like ChatGPT in the 2020s has transformed AI's ability to enhance enterprise value. These generative AI techniques rely on deep-learning models trained on vast amounts of unstructured data (IBM, n.d.).

Personalized Learning Platforms: AI is instrumental in creating personalized learning platforms, tailoring content, pacing, and support for students with disabilities. Programs like ALEKS assess students' knowledge and adjust instruction (Lin et al., 2023), while Duolingo uses AI to personalize language lessons (Guo et al., 2021).

Learning Analytics & Intelligent Tutoring Systems: AI-based learning analytics platforms analyze large datasets from educational software, providing insights for instructional decisions. Intelligent tutoring systems evaluate student performance in real time, offering personalized feedback and adjustments (Anderson et al., 1995; Blikstein & Worsley, 2016).

Social Robots and Assistive Technology: AI-powered social robots assist students with autism in developing social skills (Kouroupa et al., 2022). Robotic mobility aids enhance independence for individuals with physical disabilities (Brose et al., 2010), while AI-based neurofeedback systems help students with learning disabilities improve cognitive skills (Maiseli et al., 2023). Neurofeedback and Brain-Computer Interfaces (BCIs), for example, computers and robotic limbs enable the brain and external devices to have direct communication (Maiseli et al., 2023). AI-powered neurofeedback systems and BCIs are explored as tools for enhancing cognitive skills, attention, and self-regulation in students with learning disabilities and other developmental disabilities.

AI in Assistive Technology: AI enhances assistive tools, including augmentative and alternative communication devices, and tools for visual and auditory impairments (Zdravkova et al., 2022). Autonomous vehicles, such as those developed by Tesla, use AI to revolutionize transportation for people with disabilities (Parekh et al., 2022).

Language Models and Generative AI: LLMs, which gained momentum with the transformer model in 2017, power daily tools like chatbots and translation services. Reinforcement Learning from Human Feedback (RLHF) refines these models through user interaction (Linde & Agarwal, 2023). The rise of GenAI and AI-driven tools has reshaped various sectors, from education to assistive technologies. However, while these models offer vast potential, challenges remain in terms of ethical usage and limitations (Office of Educational Technology, 2023).

NEED OF AI IN SPECIAL EDUCATION

AI tools and inventories possess the capability to assimilate the requirements of children with special needs, thus becoming a crucial component of the academic procedure. The utilization of AI by educators and parents is on the rise for delivering educational content rather than evaluation, leading to a harmonious blend of increased oversight and guidance alongside the encouragement of student independence (Sharma et al., 2023). Addressing AI in education is crucial for several reasons. Primarily, there exist three reasons for exploring AI in the realm of education. The initial justification pertains to the capacity of AI to amplify the attainment of educational objectives in a more efficient manner, on a large scale, and with reduced expenditures. Through enhancing the flexibility of educational materials to cater to the strengths and requirements of students, AI can offer enhanced assistance to educators by means of automated aides and other resources, thereby enabling teachers to expand their support to individual students in situations where time is limited. Moreover, AI has the potential to facilitate the creation of materials that are attuned to the diverse knowledge and backgrounds that students bring from their respective communities and cultures, enabling a higher degree of customization of educational resources to fulfil local demands. The second reason lies in the immediacy and significance of incorporating AI into the educational sphere, which arises from a growing recognition of risks at the systemic level and concerns regarding potential future hazards. Lastly, this urgency is compounded by the magnitude of potential unintended or unforeseen repercussions. As AI facilitates the automation of instructional choices on a broad scale, educators may encounter unanticipated adverse consequences (Office of Educational Technology, 2023).

In the field of education AI technologies and the solutions they support, are segmented into three phases: Sense, Comprehend, and Act. Within the Sense phase, AI technologies such as Computer Vision and Audio Processing facilitate solutions like Virtual Agents and Identity Analytics by enabling systems to interpret visual and auditory data. The Comprehend phase involves technologies like Natural Language Processing and Knowledge Representation, which underpin solutions such as Cognitive Robotics and Speech Analytics by facilitating machines to comprehend and process human language and data. Lastly, in the Act phase, Machine Learning and Expert Systems support solutions like Recommendation Systems and Data Visualization, empowering AI to make decisions and display data in a user-friendly format. This methodical approach demonstrates how fundamental AI technologies form the basis for a broad array of practical implementations (Refer Figure 3).

Figure 3. Three phases of Application of AI in Special Education. Source: National Institution for Transforming India (NITI Aayog) (National Institute for Transforming India, 2023)

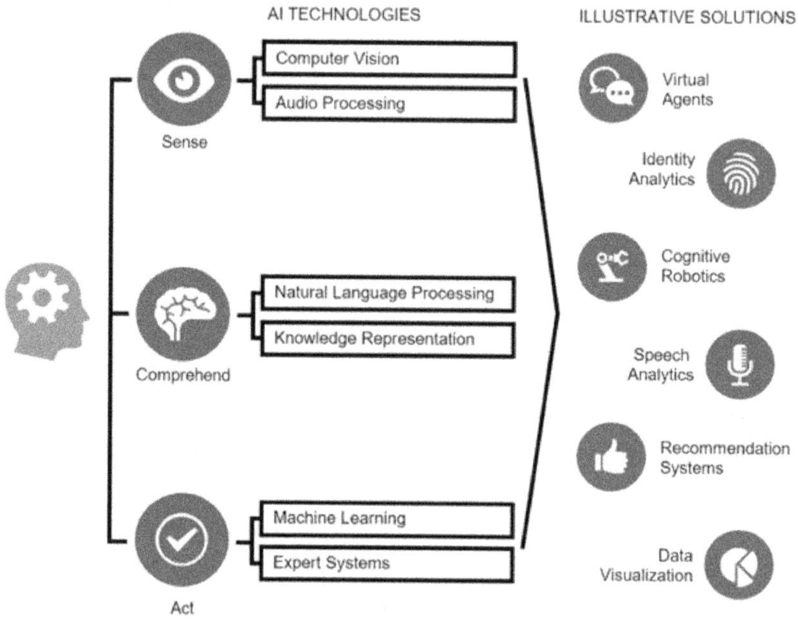

AI tools and resources possess the capability to seamlessly incorporate the needs of children with special requirements, thus becoming a fundamental component of the educational framework. The utilization of AI is on the rise among educational professionals and caregivers, focusing on imparting knowledge instead of evaluating, thereby striking a harmonious chord between enhanced oversight and guidance, ultimately fostering student independence (Sharma et al., 2023). In general, an approach focused on data is crucial for the efficient decision-making and resolution of problems in the realm of AI. By emphasizing the significance of data within the paradigm of artificial intelligence and conforming to exemplary methodologies for data integrity, management, governance, and integration, organizations can fully harness the potential of AI and achieve enhanced outcomes (Aldoseri et al., 2023).

OVERVIEW OF CONTRIBUTIONS OF AI IN SPECIAL EDUCATION

In the modern age, the quick advancements in technology are significantly transforming professional environments through shifts like workflow automation, internet of things, artificial intelligence, machine learning, as well as the captivating experiences presented by augmented reality and virtual reality. This transformation is particularly consequential for individuals with disabilities, necessitating a rapid adaptation of the workforce to novel operational methodologies and organizational cultures, thereby fostering enhanced inclusivity and accessibility (Economic Commission for Latin America and the Caribbean, 2021). AI facilitates a tailored approach to the learning process. This personalized strategy cultivates a more profound engagement with educational content, thereby augmenting students' motivation and enthusiasm for academic pursuits (Xu, 2024). Recent advancements within the Artificial Intelligence domain may serve as a catalyst for enhancements in education and training, particularly by empowering individuals with specific educational requirements (Garg, 2020). Educators are actively pursuing technologically enhanced methodologies that cater to these specific needs, prioritizing solutions that are not only secure and efficient but also capable of being implemented on a large scale (Office of Educational Technology, 2023). The progress made in technological innovations has allowed corporations like Microsoft to support individuals with disabilities through various means, such as offering educational tools that have proven beneficial for children with dyslexia. Consequently, this has expanded the applications of Artificial Intelligence and Machine Learning (Garg, 2020). Through the utilization of machine learning algorithms, which possess the capability to process extensive datasets encompassing factors like eye movement, facial expressions, and physical gestures, it becomes feasible to construct sturdy models for detecting attention levels in digital learning environments (Lim et al., 2024).

An array of challenges encompasses Speech, Language, and Communication Disorders, autism, and Asperger's Syndrome; Cognitive and Learning hurdles (Intellectual Disability, Learning Disability); issues regarding Social, Emotional, and Mental wellbeing; Attention Deficit Disorder alongside Attention Deficit Hyperactivity Disorder; in addition to Sensory and/or physical disabilities (Motor difficulties, Visual Impairment (VI), Hearing Impairment (HI), Multi-sensory Impairment (MSI)); together with Exceptional Giftedness and Dual Exceptionality (American Psychiatric Association, 2022; World Health Organization, n.d.; Stoeger et al., 2018).

Academic institutions have long embraced instructional technology; yet, the recent advent of AI in the context of special education is a noteworthy evolution. When examining the various classifications of AI applicable to the realm of special education, one engages with a broad spectrum of technological innovations and methodologies designed to enhance the educational experience and outcomes for individuals with unique needs. The integration of AI into learning environments facilitates the identification of specific learning behaviors, thereby providing effective and customized educational experiences (Toyokawa et al., 2023). As AI becomes increasingly embedded within educational frameworks, two predominant perspectives emerge concerning its function: initially, AI's capacity to augment student learning, and subsequently, its role in promoting education about AI and associated technologies (Office of Educational Technology, 2023).

Artificial Intelligence technologies are anticipated to augment inclusive educational environments for a heterogeneous array of learners within inclusive educational frameworks. (Toyokawa et al., 2023). Central to this is the incorporation of AI within the special education domain, utilizing computational algorithms and machine learning models for data analysis, pattern recognition, and the generation of valuable insights to customize and enhance the learning experience for individuals with specific requirements. Furthermore, associated domains within the realm of special education, such as speech and language therapy, occupational therapy, physiotherapy, and psychology AI expands its utilization (Kaelin et al., 2021). The educational landscape is being reshaped by AI advancements, enriching inclusivity and accessibility by adjusting to individual learning preferences and styles. Moreover, through sophisticated approaches AI facilitates behavior therapy, physical therapy, and speech-language therapy. Establishing support for Inclusive Education necessitates organizational backing by incorporating inclusive infrastructures with the aid of AI technologies and Augmented Technology to advocate Special Need Education (Garg, 2020).

Categories of AI that are Used in Special Education and its Extended Areas

a) Sensory AI, encompassing technologies like Computer Vision and IoT for sensory perception.
b) Physical AI, pertains to the utilization of robotics and industrial automation to facilitate tangible interaction.
c) General AI, offering versatile problem-solving capabilities.
d) Mental AI, utilizes Natural Language Processing (NLP) and worker training to enhance cognitive abilities.
e) Explainable AI, providing transparent insights into AI decision-making processes (NITI Aayog, 2023).

f) GenAI: While the distinctions between general AI and generative AI are becoming less clear, generative AI holds potential in specific areas like simulating human-like interactions. When considering GenAI, it is essential to address certain challenges that need further examination. Efficiently engineering prompts involves establishing successful and productive communication between GenAI and human-machine interaction, particularly (Sağdıç et al., 2024).

Among the many transformative applications, AI-driven therapies stand out, offering innovative solutions for behavioral therapy, physical therapy, and speech and language therapy (Khalid et al., 2024). Let's explore in details:

AI in Speech and Language

Sophisticated algorithms and machine learning utilizes AI-powered solutions aimed at speech and language development to deliver tailored, efficient, and interactive therapeutic measures. Here are some notable examples of how AI is being utilized in speech and language development- Speech Recognition Software *(Nuance Dragon Speech Recognition* (Poulter, 2020), *Google Speech to text and Apple Siri).* Speech Therapy Apps like *Articulation Station, Speechtree and linguistic Horizon,* uses AI to create personalized speech therapy exercises (Furlong et al., 2018). The Articulation Station application conducts an analysis of a child's phonetic patterns and customizes therapeutic exercises aimed at specific phonemes or lexemes with which they encounter difficulty. This approach enhances the engagement and efficacy of therapy, as it is responsive to the user's developmental trajectory and requirements. Virtual assistants such as Timo provide immediate access to speech therapy sessions (Urrea et al., 2024). Furthermore, Virtual Assistants (e.g., Google Assistant and Amazon Alexa) and interactive robots like Leka can captivate children through games and activities designed to foster speech and language development, thus offering an enjoyable and interactive modality for practicing these competencies (Leka, 2016; Patnaik & Agrawal, 2022). For individuals experiencing significant speech and language impairments, AI-powered Alternative & Augmentative communication devices such as Proloquo2Go facilitate vocalization by transforming textual or symbolic inputs into audible speech (Collette et al., 2019). Language Learning Platforms, including Duolingo and Babbel, leverage artificial intelligence to tailor language acquisition experiences in accordance with individual advancement and challenges encountered (Kessler et al., 2023). In relation to speech and language acquisition, these platforms furnish oral exercises that employ speech recognition technology to deliver immediate feedback, thereby assisting learners in enhancing their pronunciation and fluency. AI-enhanced Language Analysis Tools, exemplified by Linguistic Inquiry and Word Count, serve as an artificial intelligence-driven resource that evaluates both spoken and written communication to yield insights into linguistic usage and emotional undertones. Likewise, artificial intelligence systems such as "Beyond Verbal" scrutinize vocal inflections and speech characteristics to discern emotions and sentiments. A highly sophisticated artificial intelligence instrument, The Language Assessment Remedies and Screening Procedure, is utilized for the assessment of linguistic capabilities and the identification of language disorders in individuals, with a particular focus on those experiencing developmental language impairments (Medenica et al., 2023). Apraxia World and Gemiini Systems employ artificial intelligence to analyze speech samples, recognize patterns of errors, and generate comprehensive reports that assist therapists in devising more focused intervention strategies. Speech therapists can utilize this instrument to evaluate a patient's linguistic patterns and emotional expressions, thereby customizing therapeutic interventions to meet specific needs and monitor progress over time. AI-empowered translation tools, including Google Translate and Microsoft Translator, aid in communication between languages.

Behavioral Therapy

Chen and Lu (2023) elucidated a novel interactive technological paradigm intended for the detection of behavioral challenges among learners and the alleviation of such behavioral difficulties. This discourse delineates the formulation and implementation of an advanced pedagogical assistant meticulously crafted to aid educators in the identification of these challenges. This artificial intelligence system employs a task-oriented conversational methodology to accurately ascertain the fundamental origins of disruptive behaviors, such as unfulfilled needs, and provides tailored recommendations to instructors (Chen & Lu, 2023). Furthermore, it leverages semantic search capabilities to uncover and reference analogous instances that seasoned educators have successfully addressed (Lidströmer et al., 2021; Chen & Lu, 2023). The Cognitive Assessment and Rehabilitation Environment System, constitutes an AI-powered evaluative tool that integrates virtual reality technology, motion capture, and artificial intelligence algorithms to assess cognitive capabilities such as attention, memory, and executive functioning in individuals exhibiting cognitive deficits (Medenica et al., Year). Social-Emotional Assessment Tools, including the Affective Computing Assessment Toolkit, incorporate artificial intelligence algorithms to scrutinize facial expressions, vocal patterns, and psychological indicators to evaluate emotional states and social engagements. Behavior imaging emerges as a nascent research domain distinguished by the quantification and analysis of human behavior through computational sensing and modeling methodologies. This field involves utilizing video, audio, and wearable sensors to create a comprehensive depiction of behavior. Owing to the abundant sensor data available, it can identify and document characteristics such as latency, trajectory, among others (Zubair & Rangreze, 2023).

Physical Therapy

AI has the capacity to enhance the supportive structures within the field of physiotherapy amidst the digitalization of healthcare. This is achieved through a diverse array of novel applications, which include providing real-time video guidance coupled with the identification of poses and joint angles to offer optimum feedback. Additionally, incorporating motivational and psychotherapeutic elements serves to enhance the accuracy and adherence to exercise routines (Fulk, 2023). The Kinect-Based Movement Assessment System incorporates an artificial intelligence algorithm along with depth sensing technology from Kinect to evaluate motor skills and movement patterns in individuals with motor impairment. The algorithm scrutinizes body movements to accurately identify and assess motor impairment (Medenica et al., 2023). Artificial Intelligence in neurologic physical therapy enhances assessment, gait analysis, personalized interventions, outcome prediction, and remote monitoring, revolutionizing patient-centred care in physical therapy (Jain et al., 2023). Physiotherapeutic aid utilizing AI and ML enables posture detection and assessment for remote exercise guidance, particularly beneficial for older individuals unable to visit physiotherapists or doctors (Pattison & Roopaei, 2023). An AI-based exercise game has been designed to support Occupational and Physical Therapy. The incorporation of AI into the game aims to enrich the therapy process. Furthermore, it tackles issues related to inadequate staffing, group therapy, patient motivation, and periods of inactivity (International Commission on the Futures of Education, 2021). AI offers numerous opportunities to unlock the full potential of intellectually gifted children by delivering tailored, efficient, and captivating educational experiences. Gifted learners can leverage artificial neural networks to simulate intricate connections between an individual's existing skill level and their internal and external surroundings, facilitating comprehension and reinforcement of their extraordinary growth (Shane & Phillipson, 2023).

AI TRENDS IN SPECIAL EDUCATION

The continuous progression of AI is significantly enhancing its ability to transform the field of special education. Recent developments underscore an auspicious outlook in which technology not only provides assistance but also enhances the academic journey of individuals with special needs, guaranteeing parity in opportunities for their growth and achievement. There's been a surge in AI applications designed specifically for addressing the requirements of special education, some of these are:

Adaptive Learning Tools for Customised Learning

AI-powered adaptive learning systems are increasingly adopted, providing customized learning paths customized to the specific requirements and abilities of students. By integrating adaptive learning systems, educators apply principles from cognitive learning theory, recognizing and accommodating the diverse cognitive processes of learners (Siemens, 2005).

An AI-driven adaptive learning technology empowers users to craft custom learning paths tailored to their individual strengths, preferences, and progress.

- **ObjectiveEd's Braille AI Tutor** leverages AI-powered speech recognition and gamification, enabling students to enhance their Braille skills autonomously.
- **Whatfix's** digital adoption platform facilitates adaptive learning by delivering personalized, context-sensitive guidance to users based on their unique requirements and interactions within an application or software.
- **Adaptemy** offers adaptive learning solutions, like their platform, enabling the creation of highly effective products and learning experiences by integrating with existing learning platforms and content (Ghergulescu et al., 2015).

Figure 4. Applications of AI in Various Areas of Special Education

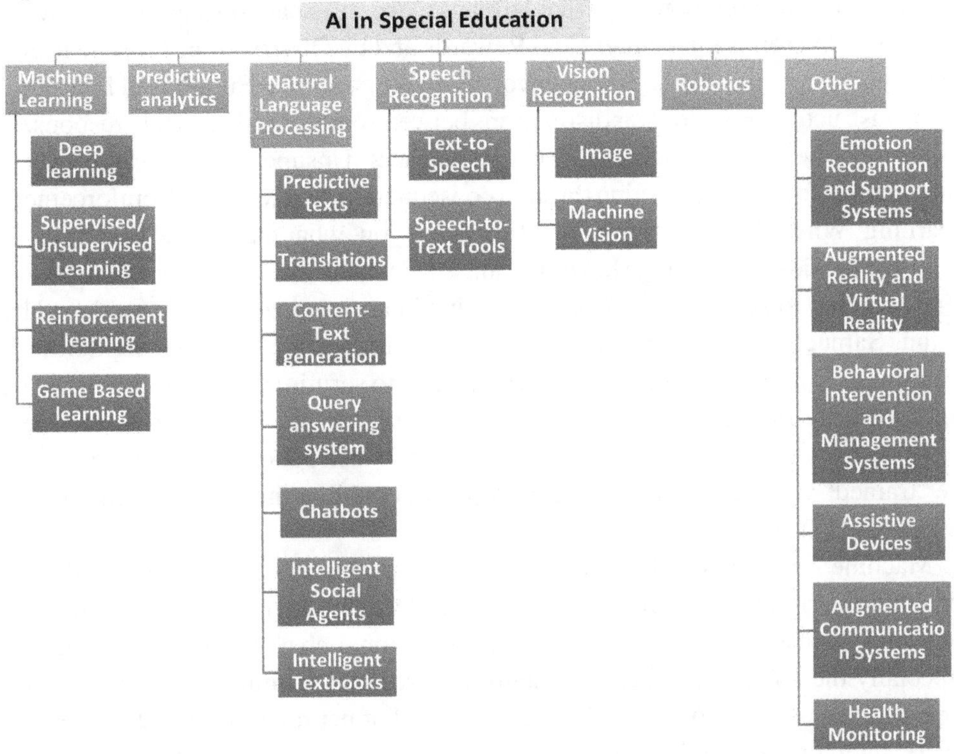

EdApp, an adaptive learning platform, is equipped with a range of features including an authoring tool, e-learning templates, gamification elements, and analytics (Putra, 2023).

Knewton (New York-based adaptive learning platform), CogBooks, Realizeit, Smart Sparrow (adaptive learning platform, situated in San Francisco, created by research group in Australia), Pearson Interactive Labs (Hybrid Labs), Scholar ALS, StoichTutor (designed to help high school students learn chemistry) are few examples of such platforms which uses artificial intelligence to create personalized learning experiences (Howlin & Lynch, 2014; Hakkal & Ait Lahcen, 2021; Contrino et al., 2024; Manyilizu, 2023).

Intelligent and Interactive Tutoring Systems:

Simply put, an Intelligent tutoring system is a sophisticated tool driven by computer technology for education, designed to emulate human tutors. It provides tailored and instant guidance or feedback to learners, frequently operating autonomously without requiring human oversight. To understand how the machines Tutor, let us first look at three common ways that humans learn. these are through Instructions, by Trial and Error or Punishment and Rewards and by Observation. These learning encompasses various methods: one involves direct guidance- Supervised Learning, where instructors provide clear distinctions between correct and incorrect responses; another involves independent discovery by learners- Unsupervised Learning; and a third method focuses on learning through consequences and rewards- Reinforcement Learning. When the results of your action teach you, what may be the best thing to do to get the desired result (Aldoseri et al., 2023).

According to Algren et al. (2021) Machine Learning, a term first introduced by Arthur Samuel in 1959, pertains to the capacity for learning without explicit programming. It entails the utilization of algorithms to scrutinize data, derive insights, and formulate projections or determinations based on such acquired knowledge. Rather than manually coding software with specific instructions for a task, machines are “trained” with large datasets and algorithms, enabling them to perform specific tasks (Awad & Khanna, 2015).

Machine Learning can be categorized into supervised, unsupervised, and reinforcement learning domains (Bajwa et al., 2021). Deep Learning, a branch of Machine Learning, is inspired by the structural and functional characteristics of the brain, especially the connections between neurons. Artificial Neural Networks imitating the biological makeup of the brain, are composed of neurons structured in separate layers, interconnected with one another. Each layer is tasked with recognizing particular features, and the integration of multiple layers endows deep learning with its profound nature (Sarker, 2021).

Figure 5. The relationship between Artificial Intelligence, Machine Learning and Deep Learning

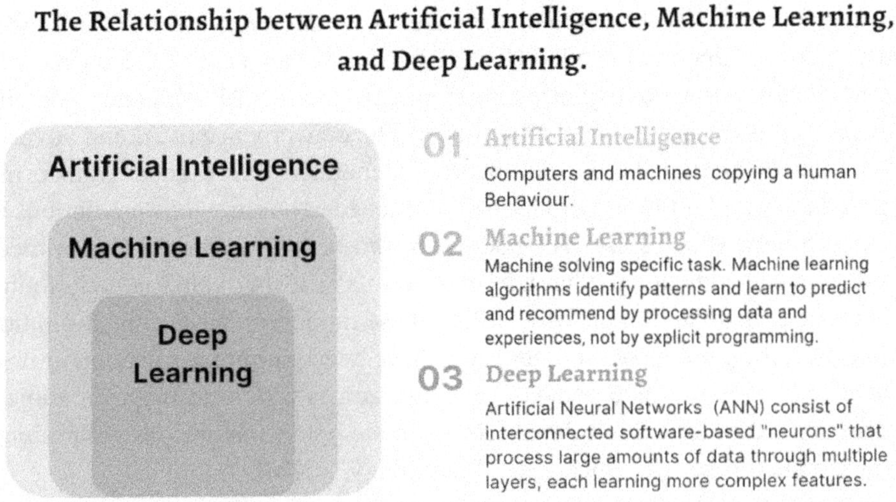

Learning Models, Large Learning Models (LLMs) and Generative AI (GenAI): Daily tools such as email autocomplete, translation services, and chatbots that provide responses rely on language models in their core functions. The predominant change in extensive LLMs most likely commenced in 2017 with the advent of the transformer model, a pioneering advancement by researchers at Google. Following this, numerous LLMs, influenced by this revolutionary approach, have been developed by AI scientists. These models have rapidly grown in both size and capability, continuously outperforming previous standards at an impressive pace (Linde & Agarwal, 2023). Iterative investigation resulted in the advancement of artificial intelligence techniques that encompass human involvement in the iterative process and learning through prompts. This involves the training of LLMs on extensive datasets over multiple iterations. The method known as 'Reinforcement Learning from Human Feedback' (RLHF), utilized by prior models developed by OpenAI, introduced an innovative approach to integrating human feedback into the training of LLMs (Linde & Agarwal, 2023).

GenAI is posited as a technological intervention intended to augment educational experiences and to promote the development of learners with varying needs (Johnson et al., 2023). As well, concrete research points to the potential of LLMs and different types of Generative Pre-trained Transformers (GPT) in the swift recognition of autism (Li et al., 2023; Mukherjee et al., 2023). Years of cumulative research initiatives culminated in a pinnacle with the advent of advanced image generation frameworks such as DALL-E and Stable Diffusion, alongside artificial intelligence models capable of generating realistic video content from textual descriptions. Furthermore, AI systems engineered to perform a multitude of generative functions, akin to the operations of ChatGPT, began to materialize during the years 2021-2022 (Linde & Agarwal, 2023). OpenAI unveiled ChatGPT towards the end of 2022, a time when humanity inclined towards exploring the frontiers of artificial intelligence, perceived this endeavor as reaching a state of maturity. The convergence of AI and advanced LLMs created through the development of Generative Pre-trained Transformers has paved the way for the rise of GenAI that exceeded our previous predictions and forecasts (Sağdıç et al., 2024). AI models are showcasing enhanced capabilities as a result of advancements in what are referred to as LLMs or alternatively foundational models. In spite of their wide utility, these models do have some limitations. For instance, the generative AI models that have been highlighted in popular media are able to swiftly produce persuasive essays across a diverse range of subjects, whereas some models exhibit the ability to create believable images with minimal input prompts (Office of Educational Technology, 2023).

On a global scale, there are over 60 commercial Intelligent tutoring systems currently accessible, including Alef, ALEKS, Byjus, Mathia, Qubena, Riiid, and Squirrel AI. A method dubbed Hi-Tech Hi-Touch, which seeks to amalgamate the finest qualities of intelligent tutoring systems and conventional teaching, is presently under evaluation by the Education Commission in Vietnamese educational institutions (UNESCO, 2021). Here are some categories:

- Squirrel AI is an online education technology platform from China that harnesses artificial intelligence to customize lesson plans for individual students. Collaborating with teachers, Squirrel AI identifies precise learning concepts ("knowledge points") to target specific gaps in understanding.
- eTeacher acts as an intelligent or pedagogical agent, analyzing student performance data to recommend personalized learning paths, aiding the learning process (Schiaffino et al., 2008).
- ZOSMAT serves as a human tutor, catering to the diverse needs of a classroom. By monitoring student progress and effort, this student-centric intelligent tutoring systems adjusts its program accordingly, guiding learners through various stages of learning (Keles et al., 2009).
- REALP, created to enhance reading comprehension, offers tailored lexical exercises and personalized training utilizing authentic reading materials sourced from online platforms (Maker et al., 2015).
- SmartTutor, developed by the University of Hong Kong, caters to the personalized learning requirements of adult learners and learns in continuation. By

amalgamating internet technology, educational research, and artificial intelligence, it delivers customized assistance to learners (Cheung et al., 2003)

- The Mathematics Tutor aids students in resolving word problems related to fractions, decimals, and percentages (Beal et al., 2002).
- ActiveMath is an adaptive online learning platform for mathematics (Melis et al., 2001).
- AdaptErrEx, an adaptive intelligent tutor, employs interactive erroneous examples to assist students in mastering decimal arithmetic (McLaren et al., 2015).
- Cognitive Algebra Tutor PAT, devised in Pittsburgh, immerses students in anchored learning scenarios, utilizing contemporary algebraic tools to nurture problem-solving skills (Institute of Education Sciences, U.S. Department of Education, 2016).
- Pearson's WriteToLearn software harnesses natural language processing technology to furnish students with personalized feedback, suggestions, and strategies for enhancing their writing aptitude (Pearson Education, 2019).

Special Education Teachers are tasked with modifying, adapting, and accommodating the general education curriculum to meet their students' diverse needs (Goldman et al., 2024). They also need to effectively communicate and collaborate with parents and general education teachers while monitoring progress on Individualized Education Program (IEP) goals, among other responsibilities. However, many Special Education Teachers, particularly those in more restrictive self-contained environments, report spending nearly half of their time on non-teaching duties (Goldman et al., 2024). An emerging and innovative solution to assist Special Education Teachers in managing these responsibilities is the use of AI. AI powers a variety of widely-used educational tools, including predictive text, adaptive learning platforms, and digital assistants. The introduction of generative pre-trained transformers (GPTs) like ChatGPT and Bard offers a promising opportunity to alleviate some of the administrative burdens faced by Special Education Teachers. These tools can generate human-like responses, aiding in tasks such as drafting essays, emails, and lists (Goldman et al., 2024).

Intelligent Textbooks and Techniques

The inception of intelligent textbooks was influenced by the notion of amalgamating adaptive hypermedia systems with intelligent tutoring systems (Weber & Brusilovsky, 2001). By utilizing advanced deep learning methodologies to absorb and evaluate prevailing educational materials like course resources, textbooks, and syllabi, the technology generates personalized learning tools, encompassing bespoke textbooks, succinct chapter summaries, and interactive quizzes.

Automated semantic connections are enabled by Interlingua, among different segments and subsections within textbooks, providing immediate access to pertinent reading materials in the learner's mother tongue (Chacon & Sosnovsky, 2019). Intelligent textbooks encompass a range of pedagogical methods, such as navigational tools, feedback sensitive to errors, tutorial dialogues, and personalized sequencing of content (Dresscher et al., 2021). These methods improve learning by offering multimedia resources, establishing semantic connections, creating concept maps, and engaging students with interactive simulations customized to their individual needs and preferences.

- Error-sensitive feedback constitutes an instructional methodology employed when learners provide erroneous responses, exhibit uncertainty regarding the accurate answer, or frequently solicit assistance. This pedagogical strategy transcends mere evaluation of answer precision; its principal objective is to rectify students' misconceptions. The Intextbooks application was developed with interactive assessment functionalities intended to reinforce students' comprehension of fundamental concepts (Dresscher, Chacon & Sosnovsky, 2021).
- Tutoring dialogues immerse students in natural language processing, exemplified by Inquiry's inquiry-based dialogue, MoFaCTS' rectification of conceptual inaccuracies (Pavlik et al., 2020), and LiveHint's provision of contextually pertinent hints (Fisher et al., 2020).
- Personalized content sequencing arranges educational trajectories predicated upon students' profiles and historical data, as observed in SmartBook's adaptive courseware (Koychev et al., 2009) and iRead's tailored activities (Deligiannis et al., 2019). A considerable amount of AI-enabled educational content is produced by an organization recognized as Content Technologies Inc. (Jiang et al., 2023).

Game-Based Learning

To make a game-like environment, in educational context, gamification applies such elements as competition, challenges and rewards. When it comes to making gamification better, AI technologies offer adaptive challenges, personalized feedback and dynamically generated content that is tailored to the progress of each student (Deterding et al., 2011). Teaching through games involves using interactive and engaging components similar to those seen in captivating games. Specifically employed for students with disabilities in special education, this technique allows for constant change and fun associated with learning situations which can be specialized for unique needs. Integrating both gamification and AI into education provides an interesting method of including students in the process of teaching while improving learning outcomes (Deterding et al., 2011). A special education adaption of Minecraft for Education Edition enables students to learn new things by exploring, building and solving problems virtually (Slattery et al., 2023). There are different games and activities incorporated into ABCmouse.com platform aimed at supporting basic knowledge acquisition in reading skills, mathematics among other subjects. The platform is especially useful for its target audience which is young learners as well as those having developmental delays (Age of Learning, Inc., 2016). OctoPlus from Zyrobotics is a math learning game that was developed for disabled children (MacCalla et al., 2015). Eye Gaze Games are built for people with severe physical disabilities who use eye-tracking systems to operate their computers. These games have been designed to enable students acquire eye tracking abilities and engage in academic content through simple means (Špakov et al., 2019). TeachTown, on the other hand, offers a software platform comprising of various games and activities aimed at training autistic learners how to be social, adaptive and academic minded (Whalen et al., 2010).

Predictive Analytics and Data-driven Insights

The future is foreseen by using past data through AI driven predictive analytics which involves the use of data, statistical algorithms and machine learning techniques. This helps teachers understand gaps in learning and make changes in order to improve student performance. Amazon Machine Learning, SageMaker, Microsoft Azure AI, Google Cloud AutoML, IBM Watson Studio and AIRWAT (Indian) are examples able to analyze students' information and predict what will happen next as well as identify possible barriers to learning (Alzahrani 2024; Liberty et al., 2020; Lai & Ma, 2023; Kanakanti & Sabitha, 2020; Hakkal, et al., 2017, Srinivasan et al., 2013). Incorporating AI algorithms enables precise assessment and diagnosis, personalized interventions, and data-driven decisions, thereby enhancing the evaluation process and improving outcomes for individuals with various disabilities and dysfunctioning (Medenica et al., 2023)

Communication

Communication is a fundamental human need, yet for many with speech or hearing impairments, it's a challenge fraught with frustration. The gap is being bridged by Artificial Intelligence through groundbreaking tools that transcribe verbal communication into text promptly, ensuring that individuals with hearing impairments or deafness can access conversations (Maples et al., 2023).

Intelligent Social Agents: Throughout history, interactions between humans and anthropomorphized machines were predominantly viewed as entertainment rather than emotionally significant for the majority of individuals.

However, XiaoIce developed by Microsoft for the Chinese market and Replika, created in the USA, both engage users in human-like conversations, positioning themselves as intelligent companions worthy of emotional trust. By gradually emulating the user's personality, these systems aim to provide users with a virtual best friend (Zubair & Rangreze, 2023).

Proloquo2Go is an innovative Alternative & Augmentative Communication tool designed to assist individuals with speech or language difficulties, including other Developmental disabilities. It offers a user-friendly, customizable interface that facilitates communication through text, images, and icons. Additionally, Proloquo2Go offers features like word prediction, message history, and voice output to enhance communication experiences for its users.

- ROYBI Robot is an AI robot specialized in aiding children with speech delays effectively.
- Google's Parrotron utilizes AI to interpret distorted speech patterns, transforming them into coherent conversations, providing invaluable support to those with speech impairments (Biadsy et al., 2019).
- Nuance, a speech recognition software used by students and faculty, boasts a transcription speed of up to 160 words per minute. Particularly beneficial for students facing writing challenges or needing accessibility accommodations (Poulter, 2020).
- KidSense offers AI educational solutions tailored for children, featuring a voice-to-text tool equipped with algorithms designed to understand the speech nuances of young learners.
- Language learning platforms like Duolingo, Babbel, Memrise, and Rosetta Stone employ gamified approaches to make language acquisition enjoyable, especially in the initial stages of learning (Kessler, Loewen, & Gonulal, 2023; Nuralisah & Kareviati, 2020; Şanverdi, 2021)
- Digital India Bhashini strives to create speech-to-speech machine translation systems for various Indian languages and dialects, enabling citizens to access digital services in their native languages to enhance digital inclusion and accessibility (Rabiyath & Kumar, 2024).

Enhancing Accessibility in Special Classrooms Through AI

Artificial Intelligence (AI) has shown immense potential in transforming the landscape for persons with disabilities (PwDs) by improving accessibility and fostering inclusivity. From education and healthcare to employment and daily living, AI-driven innovations are playing a critical role in addressing the barriers that PwDs face. The intersection of AI with assistive technologies offers personalized support, making environments more adaptable and accessible some of the ssuch AI driven technology apps are examples-

- Seeing AI is a free application that describes the user's surroundings. Developed in collaboration with and for the blind and visually impaired community, this ongoing research project leverages AI capabilities to reveal the visual surrounding (Granquist et al., 2021).
- SignReco, utilizes artificial intelligence to interpret sign language into spoken words instantly. Often described as the "Google translator for the deaf," this technology functions by positioning a smartphone in front of the user, employing neural networks and computer vision to comprehend the sign language speaker's gestures (Mendhe et al., 2022).
- Applications like Ava and RogerVoice offer transcription services through AI, swiftly transcribing group discussions for users. These telecommunications tools cater to individuals with hearing impairments, allowing them to initiate phone calls and receive immediate live transcriptions of the caller's speech (Zdravkova et al., 2022; Koshtura, Andrunyk, & Shestakevych et al., 2021).
- VoiceOver: Integrated directly into iPhones and TalkBack for Android smartphones, these screen readers utilize AI to describe icons, other updates and settings, and even interpret images to some extent (Diaz-Cintas & Orero, 2006; Mohammad & Nishida, 2007).
- Virtual assistants such as Siri, Google Assistant, and Google Voice Access empower individuals with limited mobility to control smartphones via voice prompts (Burbach et al., 2019). IFTTT, an app that connects other apps, helps users with poor dexterity to access all smartphone functionalities seamlessly. Even individuals with speech impediments, such as those with brain injuries or Parkinson's, can benefit from AI technology with apps like Voiceitt (Howarth et al., 2024). Google's Project Euphonia utilizes sound and gesture recognition to interact with the internet (MacDonald et al., 2021).
- *Accessible documents* with the help of Microsoft Accessibility Checker or Adobe Accessibility Checker, *Microsoft immersive Reader.*

Mobility and Navigation: Google Maps' wheelchair-accessible feature allows wheelchair users to locate ramps and elevators in the city (Mog, 2016). Similar to this, Wheelmap provides accessibility information (Mobasheri et al., 2017). Soundscape is an app that uses audio 3D technology to describe surroundings for blind individuals. Evelity, the pioneer indoor navigation app designed for individuals with disabilities, assists users in maneuvering through intricate indoor settings (Walle et al., 2022).

AI-Powered Assessment and Diagnosis

When examining the assessment and evaluation of the teaching-learning process, GradeGuardian utilizes predictive models and visualizations to track student performance. It features an interactive dashboard displaying the potential impact of policy changes and comprises three components: a Chatbot for student data input, an Advisor Console highlighting at-risk students, and a prediction module for policymakers.

In their chapter on "Analysis and Improvement of Classroom Teaching Based on Artificial Intelligence," Sun, Yu, and Xu explore how AI-based techniques can enrich our comprehension of classroom dynamics. They propose a blended analysis framework named TESTII, which integrates human and AI technologies to enhance traditional classroom teaching analysis, addressing issues of inefficiency and limited scalability (Sağdıç, et al., 2024). Some of the AI-driven technologies for assessment of disability in children with disability are discussed below.

- Canvas Dx by Cognoa: A digital assessment tool for children facing developmental concerns that bridges geographical gaps to access limited, overloaded specialty centers. Leveraging advanced AI technology, it consolidates data to generate insights aiding clinicians in either confirming or ruling out autism, facilitating personalized plans for both you and your child (Agency for Care Effectiveness, 2024).
- Eye tracking serves as a non-intrusive and effective technique for diagnosing autism in both children and adults. By assessing eye fixation points within specific regions of interest in images or videos, clinicians can determine the presence of ASD based on the duration of gaze fixation on non-biological, non-social movements (Chaddad et al., 2021).
- Neuroimaging studies have identified certain brain abnormalities associated with ASD, such as enlarged temporal and frontal lobes, excessive cerebrospinal fluid, and structural irregularities in white matter at distinct developmental stages (Sun et al., 2023).

- The Computerised Dynamic Assessment System focuses on evaluating cognitive abilities and learning potential in individuals with learning disabilities or developmental disorders (Sherkuziyeva, 2023).

When integrating AI into assessment practices, educators can use AI to enhance current strategies and develop innovative methods (Chassignol et al., 2018; Chen et al., 2020b, 2020c). Chatbots can serve as virtual assistants, guiding students through questions (Smutny & Schreiberova, 2020). AI-driven learning analytics help teachers understand learning behaviors and improve interventions by visualizing patterns like engagement and performance (Sedrakyan et al., 2020). AI tools, like writing assistants, can automatically evaluate student work, providing feedback on grammar and sentence structure (Ramesh & Sanampudi, 2021). Educators should harness AI to monitor progress and adapt teaching strategies.

AI-powered Assistive Robots for Educating Children with Special Needs

As AI technology progresses, machines now possess the ability to think, act, and mimic human behaviors. Notably, the concept of robots functioning as companions or educators has moved beyond the realm of science fiction and is now widely accepted in literature. Social robots are primarily engineered to enhance the speech and conversational abilities of children with ASD, while also instructing them in emotional intelligence. A British primary school has introduced NAO, a 2-foot-tall humanoid robot, to its students. NAO asks questions and responds to answers. Numerous studies confirm that individuals with autism exhibit increased interaction and prolonged eye contact with the robot Nao compared to interactions with humans. The efficacy of robotic interventions over traditional human-led approaches is well-established in the literature, with many suggesting a preference for robots among individuals with autism (Shamsuddin et al., 2011; Tapus et al., 2012; Mutawa et al., 2023). In addition, there is a robot called Romibo. This means that teachers and therapists who can monitor an individual student's progress in specific tasks can track them online and develop personalized lessons targeted at various focus areas. Some of these robots are iReCHeCk, an EPFL CHILI Lab groundbreaking project revolutionizing the way children learn to write (Tozadore et al., 2023).

Recent research has demonstrated the successful use of robots to teach autism patients a range of skills including eye contact, social interaction, emotion understanding, joint attention and imitation (Pennisi et al., 2016; Saleh et al., 2021). Moreover, some studies have examined the use of robots as AI technologies do for early detection of ASDs (Kumazaki et al., 2019).

AI-Powered Prosthetic, Health Monitoring and Assistance

The use of AI algorithms in prosthetic limbs has led to a new way of controlling and functioning for individuals who suffer from limb loss or disability. These algorithms are used to interpret muscle signals or neural data that can help the user have a more intuitive control of the prosthetic limb (Atzori et al., 2014). The development of AI-driven artificial body parts is a major step forward in assistive technology since they are able to mimic the movements and behaviours of their users' natural limbs. Robotic assistants powered by AI offer physical support, from enhancing mobility to assisting with household tasks, thereby enhancing the independence of individuals with physical disabilities. By using wearable devices powered by AI, healthcare providers can monitor vital health signs, predict possible health issues and provide timely feedbacks to users. Such prophylactic monitoring of one's health condition helps patients suffering from chronic ailments or requiring constant care outlive their diseases (Ogunbukola, 2024). The influence that AI has had on improving health care services for people with impairments cannot be underestimated (Bajwa et al., 2021).

POTENTIAL CHALLENGES OF AI IN SPECIAL EDUCATION

"Success in creating AI would be the biggest event in human history. Unfortunately, it might also be the last, unless we learn how to avoid the risks."

- Stephen Hawking, Famous Theoretical Physicist, Cosmologist, and Author

AI marks a landmark in human technological evolution, referring to a time when machines and algorithms are relied upon for decision-making at levels never seen before. Therefore, any efforts aimed at promoting AI ought to consider such issues as ethics, privacy and security concerns. This should be the heart of these strategies. Despite the significant impact of AI on students, educators, and parents, there is limited research on AI ethics in education, with a few exceptions (Adams et al., 2021; Holmes et al., 2021). AI highlights the dual nature, presenting significant benefits, such as personalized learning and automated assessments, as well as serious ethical concerns, including systemic bias and privacy issues (Akgun & Greenhow, 2022). Holmes and Tuomi (2022) indicate that AI in education systems can outperform human teachers in large classes but are slightly less effective than one-on-one human tutoring. This suggests that while AIED can enhance learning, it should not completely replace human interaction. Artificial Intelligence driven by data offers significant advantages in scalability, especially within today's interconnected ecosystems. This creates the potential for natural monopolies. Consequently, the future of AI in education is not just an educational matter but also an economic and geopolitical concern. Commercial AI in education companies are not only influencing individual learning experiences but are starting to shape governance and national policies as well. Their impact on society and culture may surpass immediate economic effects (Holmes & Tuomi, 2022). As Baker (2000) pointed out, these organizations may dictate what is considered knowledge in the first place (p. 127). In essence, the commercialization of education through AI in education introduces complex practical and ideological challenges.

Ethical Consideration Regarding AI

Integrating AI into the education system poses many ethical questions that need to be addressed (Floridi & Taddeo, 2016). Developers usually assume that comprehensive and diverse datasets provide accurate representations of reality leading them to the misconception that data-driven decision-making is objective. However, this view ignores the possibility of biases in data that may persist or get stronger over time affecting the fairness of decisions (Ferrara, 2024). Predictive analytics and algorithmic decision-making can jeopardize the autonomy of students and teachers, as these systems may dictate actions based on data-driven predictions rather than individual choices. Akgun and Greenhow (2022) state AI systems often reflect the biases of their creators, leading to discrimination based on gender, race, and socio-economic status. This bias can manifest in various educational applications, such as personalized learning and automated assessments, which may disadvantage certain groups of students. The use of AI in education can perpetuate existing inequalities, particularly for marginalized groups. Algorithms may reinforce systemic biases, leading to unfair treatment and outcomes for students from disadvantaged backgrounds (Akgun & Greenhow, 2022). In the study conducted by Holmes & Tuomi (2022), of an AI system used to support students with cognitive impairments, teachers expressed concern that the system was making educational decisions independently, leading to a diminished role for educators in the learning process.

Privacy and AI

AI systems that collect and analyze sensitive student data face an increased risk of privacy breach and unauthorized access (Floridi & Taddeo, 2016). To protect data privacy, strong encryption protocols should be used, storage must be safe and there is a need to have strict access controls put in place to curb probable risks (Floridi & Taddeo, 2016). AI technology, solutions, as well as their real-world applications are largely dependent on the generation, collection, and analysis of massive data sets reflecting individual behavior as well as at the organizational and community levels. There are issues with the unapproved collection of data, privacy vulnerabilities, biased selection of information sources for analysis purposes, and risks of profiling or discrimination. Secondly, AI solutions are not always transparent enough. Consequently, providing clear communication about how to handle information, get informed consent from people concerned and implementing strong security mechanisms is crucial for the maintenance of trust between educators and students so as to safeguard their privacy (Floridi & Taddeo, 2016). The collection of personal data by AI systems raises significant privacy issues. Students and teachers may unknowingly share sensitive information, undermining their autonomy and agency. Consent requests for data access often do not fully inform users about the extent of the data being shared (Akgun & Greenhow, 2022).

Security and AI

Failure prevention is often overlooked in AI discussions that tend to focus on attributing blame instead. The intricacy of AI systems and their absence of user-friendliness pose challenges for individuals with disabilities, impeding their effective utilization of and benefit from technology. Implementation obstacles, including high costs, limited technical support, and inadequate awareness and training among users and caregivers, negatively impact the overall accessibility and usability of AI systems (Lu et al., 2020; Cimolino et al., 2021; Theodorou et al., 2021; Chemnad & Othman, 2024). AI applications can involve monitoring students' activities, which may be perceived as invasive. This surveillance can limit students' willingness to express themselves freely, as they may feel their actions and thoughts are being policed (Akgun & Greenhow, 2022). UNESCO (2022) in the Recommendation on the Ethics of Artificial Intelligence guidelines states that unwanted harm (safety risk), as well as vulnerabilities to attack (security risk), should be avoided and should be addressed, prevented and eliminated throughout the life cycle of AI system to ensure human, environmental and ecosystem safety and security. Safe and secure ai will be enabled by development of sustainable privacy protected data access framework that foster better training and validation of AI model utilising quality data (UNESCO, 2022, p.7.).

Gender Inequality and AI

AI systems are developed utilizing historical datasets, and should these datasets embody biases, the algorithms possess the capacity to sustain and potentially exacerbate pre-existing inequalities (Floridi & Taddeo, 2016). A well-rounded strategy is proposed to confirm that the rewards of AI technologies are open to every person, while acknowledging the particular demands of varied age demographics, cultural settings, linguistic communities, individuals with disabilities, women and girls, as well as those who are underprivileged, marginalized, or in fragile situations (UNESCO, 2023). Gender bias has been manifested in various applications of AI, as exemplified by Amazon's 2018 decision to cease the employment of machine learning in recruitment processes due to discriminatory practices against female applicants (UNESCO, 2021). In the automation of selection processes, AI unavoidably magnifies and accentuates these initial biases. Recommendations have been articulated for Amazon to rectify the bias rather than entirely discontinuing the integration of AI in recruitment. Another pertinent example pertains to the creation of AI personalized assistants such as Apple's Siri, Amazon's Alexa, and Baidu's DuerOS (UNESCO, 2021).

The swift progression of technology has resulted in an increased reliance on digital devices for a multitude of applications, inclusive of the procurement of healthcare services. However, inequitable access to these digital utilities continues to be prevalent due to a variety of barriers, including physical, sensory, and cognitive impairments (Chemnad & Othman, 2024).

Other Challenges Are:

- **Lack of Public Trust:** AI is seen as a new technology, but there is little mention of public trust in current AI governance frameworks (Robles & Mallinson, 2023). This focus on public trust will help organizations integrate AI more responsibly and ethically, while also creating value for all stakeholders (Tambotoh et al., 2017). Public scepticism about the safety and reliability of AI technology impedes its acceptance and integration (Robles & Mallinson, 2023). A lack of public trust can cause dissatisfaction among the population, diminish respect for government authorities, and damage the image of official institutions (Littman et al., 2021). Müller and Bostrom (2016) highlights the significant ethical concerns related to data privacy when AI systems are used in special education. Students with disabilities often generate sensitive data (e.g., medical records, learning habits), and there are concerns about how this data is collected, stored, and shared by AI systems, designed to track the progress of students with physical disabilities. While the system provided valuable insights into student progress, it also collected detailed personal information, which was later accessed by third parties without the students' or parents' consent (Müller & Bostrom, 2016; Indrajith, 2024).
- **Limited Understanding of AI and its efficacy:** Many people don't have an overall understanding of the capabilities and applications of artificial intelligence. Research has largely focused on improving individual academic performance within narrow domains, often overlooking the broader impacts on

teachers, students, and classroom dynamics. As Nemorin et al. (2022) note, much of the current research examines AI's technical role in education without questioning its necessity (UNESCO, 2021a, p. 26). A key concern is AI in education's potential impact on cognition and brain development. While technology has long been known to influence cognition—Socrates even argued that writing diminished memory—its effects are complex. Some studies link GPS use to reduced spatial memory (Dahmani & Bohbot, 2020), while others suggest smartphone alerts free cognitive resources (Fröscher et al., 2022). This raises critical questions about how technology, particularly AI, might affect children's developing brains, including cognitive and behavioral outcomes, brain restructuring, and health risks (Gottschalk, 2019).

- **Absence of AI Standards and Fairness Assessment Tools:** The absence of standardized AI guidelines and fairness evaluation tools underscores the necessity for such resources to assess the ethical implications of AI systems. AI education tools can help bridge the gap in rural areas of developing countries where access to qualified teachers is limited (XPRIZE, 2015). However, challenges like inadequate infrastructure and lack of skilled support staff hinder their effectiveness. While AI tools may address immediate educational needs, they don't solve long-term issues like teacher shortages. The focus should be on using AI to support teacher development and foster networks of educators, ensuring technology enhances, rather than replaces, teachers. Broader socio-political changes and stakeholder involvement are also necessary for sustainable solutions (Krahulcova, 2021).
- **Accessibility:** Accessibility is paramount, necessitating the creation of AI tools that accommodate all students, including those with physical, sensory, or cognitive disabilities through functionalities like voice-activated interfaces, visual aids, and other assistive technologies (Alhosani & Alhashmi, 2024). Also, the infrastructure needed to support AI development and deployment is often inadequate or lacking. Scarcity of funding is noticeable, especially in early-stage AI research and the expansion of promising AI innovations.

While advanced tutorial systems endeavor to optimize educators' responsibilities for commercial benefits, the likelihood of machines supplanting human instructors appears unlikely in the imminent future. Nevertheless, a multitude of artificial intelligence developers seeks to alleviate educators from an array of tasks including progress assessment and assignment evaluation, thereby enabling them to focus on the interpersonal dimensions of pedagogy such as social engagement, compassion, and individualized mentorship (UNESCO, 2021). It is imperative to consider the societal ramifications associated with a potential cessation of conventional employment as a result of automation. Despite the unparalleled efficiency that artificial intelligence's automation capabilities can provide within educational frameworks, attaining an appropriate balance between mechanization and the essential human element constitutes a complex challenge (Floridi & Taddeo, 2016). Educators play a multifaceted role that extends beyond the mere transmission of knowledge, encompassing mentorship, emotional support, and the facilitation of socio-emotional development (Floridi & Taddeo, 2016). Robot Rights should be defined for ethical guidelines for the humane treatment of AI and robotic systems. If so, given robots' potential to develop into autonomous, thinking, moral agents, people may come to consider them comparably more entitled to rights like autonomy and social/civic participation than animals, which have a known ceiling in those capacities (Mays et al., 2024).

WAY FORWARD

Directions for Stakeholders

To address the gaps in privacy, ethics, and security in AI, a multifaceted approach is essential, incorporating stringent guidelines, robust safeguards, and continuous oversight (UNESCO, 2023). Curriculum developers should consider integrating culturally relevant and responsive pedagogies. This involves focusing on students' backgrounds and experiences while addressing ethical concerns like surveillance, privacy, and bias. It is important to provide more professional development opportunities for teachers, both pre-service and in-service. This could include sustained professional learning sessions about topics like understanding ai and its applications, culturally relevant pedagogy, reflective teaching practices, and ethical implications of AI, where teachers can engage with curriculum resources and share experiences. Further research on reflective teaching practices and students' sense-making processes about AI and ethics lessons is essential. This will aid in developing relevant curriculum materials and pedagogies for a diverse range of educators and students (Akgun & Greenhow, 2022).

Addressing Privacy and Security Concerns

Information stored through AI systems is usually large-scale, containing sensitive information. Consequently, this exposes the data to significant security and safety risks. Moreover, there is a great concern about data breaches given that cyber-attacks often target personal identifiable information (Schuster et al., 2021). Enact a legally backed system of data protection supported by industry-specific rules. It is advisable to compare domestic data protection and privacy regulations with global benchmarks such as the General Data Protection Regulation established by the European Union. These guidelines, which have been in effect since May 2018, promote the development of systems that intrude less on individual privacy (NITI Aayog, 2023). It is recommended to urge AI developers to conform to international norms. Authorities and experts from various regions have collaborated to establish standards that ensure the safety and privacy of AI systems. The Ethically Aligned Design of the IEEE's Global Initiative on Ethics of Autonomous and Intelligent Systems outlines fundamental principles of AI ethics, offers insights into handling personal data and implementing access control mechanisms, and addresses other crucial aspects to foster the ethical alignment of AI designs.

Holmes and Tuomi (2022) emphasize the importance of designing AI systems that empower teachers, providing them with tools that enhance their decision-making rather than replace it. Other resolutions are investing and collaboration in AI research, self-regulation, and spreading awareness (NITI Aayog, 2023). Differential Privacy a framework developed by Cynthia Dwork in 2006, that aims to safeguard individual user data, regardless of external information possessed by data aggregators. It guarantees that individuals' data inclusion in any analysis will not have either positive or negative effects, irrespective of other existing studies, datasets, or sources of information. This approach resolves the paradox of gaining valuable insights about a population without revealing anything specific about any individual (NITI Aayog, 2023). The 2022 Recommendation concerning the Ethics of Artificial Intelligence, published by UNESCO, articulates that "undesirable harms (pertaining to safety risks), alongside susceptibilities to aggression (relating to security risks), ought to be circumvented and must be systematically addressed, prevented, and eradicated throughout the entirety of the AI systems' lifecycle to ensure the safety and security of humans, the environment, and ecosystems. The establishment of safe and secure AI will be facilitated by the formulation of sustainable, privacy-preserving data access frameworks that promote enhanced training and validation of AI models through the utilization of high-quality data (UNESCO, 2022).

Transparency

Currently, many artificial intelligence solutions face challenges associated with the "Black Box Phenomenon", where understanding the processes between input and output is limited. This limitation arises from the focus on incremental performance enhancement within narrow parameters, rather than on understanding the algorithms' mechanisms for achieving success (NITI Aayog, 2023). Recent legislative frameworks, such as the General Data Protection Regulation, underscore the importance of protecting individuals' privacy rights in the digital age (Floridi & Taddeo, 2016). The development of comprehensive guidelines and policies that will prioritize data privacy and security while leveraging the benefits of artificial intelligence in the education sector is a must for researchers and policymakers (Floridi & Taddeo, 2016). The significance of protecting individuals' privacy rights in the digital era is emphasized by recent legal frameworks such as the General Data Protection Regulation (NITI Aayog, 2023).

AI Designed to Advance Gender Equality

If artificial intelligence is to provide real advantages to society, it is imperative to ensure that equity and fairness, including gender equality, are ingrained in its core principles. The mitigation of bias in AI algorithms demands continuous scrutiny of training data, ensuring diversity and inclusivity, and the adoption of techniques that promote fairness (Floridi & Taddeo, 2016). The achievement of goals for gender equality depends on sufficient number of women in the AI workforce, a matter that is currently problematic. Promoting gender diversity in the AI sphere is essential to upholding fundamental human rights and addressing the perpetuation and intensification of biases emanating from AI technologies (UNESCO, 2022).

Currently, equity as an idea has become a big discussion point in scholarly research and policy circles requiring a shared discussion and continuous search for solutions (NITI Aayog, 2023).

Creating resilient systems that can integrate AI sustainably and at scale, however, requires collective action among educators, technologists, and policy makers to establish robust frameworks for such integration (Jackson, 2015; Siemens & Long, 2011). Technology for people with disabilities may be severely complicated by complex system designs and lack of user-friendly interfaces. Additionally, challenges in adopting AI include high implementation costs, inadequate technical support, and lack of knowledge or training among users and caregivers which impair usability and accessibility of AI systems overall (Lu et al., 2020; Cimolino et al., 2021; Theodorou et al., 2021; Chemnad & Othman, 2024).

Direction for Teachers

Teachers should engage in professional development and training programs to enhance their AI knowledge, skills, and mindsets for effective teaching with AI tools. Schools need to upgrade their digital infrastructure and equipment to support teachers in developing their digital competencies and effectively using AI technologies. Educators should continuously update their knowledge about emerging technologies such as Metaverse, blockchain, and big data, and learn how to integrate these into their teaching practices. It is crucial to develop special educational programs that focus on enhancing digital literacy among pre-service special educators. This training should cover key content and activities that improve their digital knowledge and application skills, as current findings indicate a gap in these areas (Yao & Wang, 2024). Teachers must not only focus on technological skills but also develop life and career skills, multidisciplinary skills, and ethical mindsets to prepare students for the future (Ng et al., 2023). Ongoing professional development initiatives should be established to keep pre-service teachers updated on the latest AI in Education tools and practices, ensuring they remain competent and confident in their use of technology in education (Yao & Wang, 2024). Teachers should identify, select, and modify existing AI-driven learning resources to fit specific learning goals and pedagogical approaches. Educators need to learn about the positive and negative impacts of AI in education, including ethical considerations and how to use AI systems effectively in their instructional design. Teachers should leverage AI technologies to provide personalized learning experiences, addressing diverse learner needs and adapting their teaching strategies accordingly (Ng et al., 2023). Utilizing the Technology Acceptance Model framework in training can help educators understand the relationships between digital literacy, perceived ease of use, perceived usefulness, and behavioral intention. This understanding can guide the design of effective training programs (Yao & Wang, 2024).

Need of Further Research

The research is important in defining how artificial intelligence is used to address the unique requirements and challenges faced by students with disabilities or special learning needs. Researchers examining various methodologies, technologies and approaches can unearth new means through which artificial intelligence could potentially enhance the quality of educational experiences. Extensive research is focused on leveraging computers in education to develop learning environments that improve the learning experience across various contexts (Nanni & Lumini, 2009). Nations globally are recognizing the growing significance of harnessing and implementing artificial intelligence, understanding its capacity to yield both economic and societal advantages.

Figure 6. Citable documents in Artificial Education worldwide (1996-2023). Source: Scimago Journal and Country Rank (SJR)

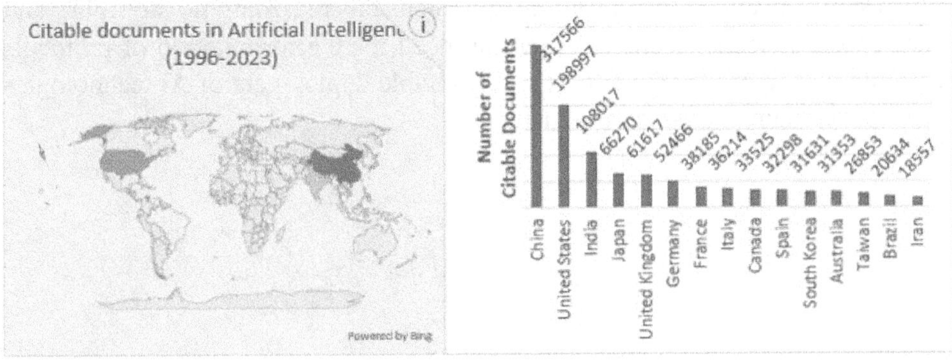

Between 1996 and 2023, research institutions from the United States, China, Japan, and more recently, India. primarily influenced the landscape of AI (Refer to Figure 6). The research ecosystem has shown promising growth in recent years. Notably, the number of published papers has increased more than tenfold. There has been a notable increase in academic research and technological advancements aimed at integrating AI into the realm of education and various other sectors. Nevertheless, there remains a significant requirement for further in-depth research in order to effectively tackle the ethical, privacy, and security issues associated with this integration. This is crucial to guarantee the optimal, transparent, explainable, and secure utilization of AI within the domain of special education. In order to surmount the potential obstacles linked to AI-driven special education, it is imperative that there be a concerted focus on intensive research and innovative solutions.

CONCLUSION

In nutshell, the incorporation of AI interventions in special education facilitates a harmonious blend of student autonomy and guidance, ultimately proving advantageous for children facing exceptional educational challenges. Our forthcoming endeavors will revolve around exploring the prospects of an AI-driven inclusive educational environment where every learner is anticipated to receive uniform learning opportunities and requisite support, while progressing alongside involved stakeholders. This ambitious goal cannot be realized without a substantial reservoir of data (Toyokawa et al., 2023). The urgency of promptly embracing AI solutions in the realm of special education, capable of furnishing a competitive edge and catering to the needs of struggling students, particularly those grappling with distinct learning requirements, cannot be overstated. Furthermore, there is a growing awareness regarding the ethical and societal consequences of employing AI in special education, encompassing apprehensions regarding privacy, bias, and fairness. Consequently, there is a pressing need for the formulation of protocols and regulations to ensure the ethical and equitable deployment of AI technologies within special educational environments.

REFERENCES

Abd El-Kader, S., & Mohammad El-Basioni, B. (2014). Independent Living for Persons with Disabilities and Elderly People using Smart Home Technology. *International Journal of Application or Innovation in Engineering & Management (IJAIEM)*, 3.

Abraham, T. H. (2002). (Physio)logical circuits: The intellectual origins of the McCulloch-Pitts neural networks. *Journal of the History of the Behavioral Sciences*, 38(1), 3–25. DOI: 10.1002/jhbs.1094 PMID: 11835218

Adams, C., Pente, P., Lemermeyer, G., & Rockwell, G. (2021). Artificial intelligence ethics guidelines for K-12 Education: A review of the global landscape. In Roll, I., McNamara, D., Sosnovsky, S., Luckin, R., & Dimitrova, V. (Eds.), *Artificial intelligence in education* (Vol. 12749, pp. 24–28). Springer International Publishing. DOI: 10.1007/978-3-030-78270-2_4

Age of Learning, Inc. (2016). *ABCmouse significantly improves student outcomes in pre-k and kindergarten*. Retrieved from https://www.ageoflearning.com/case_studies/ABCmouse_Research_Brief_Significantly_Improves_Student_Outcomes_in_Pre-K_and_Kindergarten.pdf

Agency for Care Effectiveness [ACE]. (2024). *ACE brief for new and emerging health technologies: canvas dx to aid the diagnosis of autism spectrum disorder.* https://www.ace-hta.gov.sg/docs/default-source/horizon-scanning/canvas-dx-to-aid-the-diagnosis-of-autism-spectrum-disorder.pdf?sfvrsn=a521d7c1_1

Akgun, S., & Greenhow, C. (2022). Artificial intelligence in education: Addressing ethical challenges in K-12 settings. *AI and Ethics*, 2(3), 431–440. DOI: 10.1007/s43681-021-00096-7 PMID: 34790956

Aldoseri, A., Al-Khalifa, K. N., & Hamouda, A. M. (2023). Re-thinking data strategy and integration for artificial intelligence: Concepts, opportunities, and challenges. *Applied Sciences (Basel, Switzerland)*, 13(12), 7082. DOI: 10.3390/app13127082

Algren, M., Fisher, W., & Landis, A. E. (2021). Machine learning in life cycle assessment. In Dunn, J., & Balaprakash, P. (Eds.), *Data science applied to sustainability analysis* (pp. 167–190). Elsevier., DOI: 10.1016/B978-0-12-817976-5.00009-7

Alhosani, K., & Alhashmi, S. M. (2024). Opportunities, challenges, and benefits of AI innovation in government services: A review. *Discover Artificial Intelligence*, 4(18), 1–19. DOI: 10.1007/s44163-024-00111-w

Alpizar-Chacon, I., & Sosnovsky, S. (2019). *Interlingua: Linking textbooks across different languages. In Proceedings of the 1st Workshop on Intelligent Textbooks, iText 2019* (pp. 104-117). https://ceur-ws.org/Vol-2384/paper11.pdf

Alzahrani, M. A. (2024). The user analysis of Amazon using artificial intelligence at customer churn. *Journal of Data Analysis and Information Processing*, 12(1), 40–48. DOI: 10.4236/jdaip.2024.121003

American Psychiatric Association. (2022). *Diagnostic and statistical manual of mental disorders* (5th ed., text rev.). American Psychiatric Association. https://doi/book/DOI: 10.1176/appi.books.9780890425787

Anderson, J. R., Corbett, A. T., Koedinger, K. R., & Pelletier, R. (1995). Cognitive tutors: Lessons learned. *Journal of the Learning Sciences*, 4(2), 167–207. DOI: 10.1207/s15327809jls0402_2

Atzori, M., Gijsberts, A., Castellini, C., Caputo, B., Mittaz Hager, A.-G., Elsig, S., Giatsidis, G., Bassetto, F., & Müller, H. (2014). Electromyography data for non-invasive naturally-controlled robotic hand prostheses. *Scientific Data*, 1(1), 140053. DOI: 10.1038/sdata.2014.53 PMID: 25977804

Awad, M., & Khanna, R. (2015). Machine learning. In *Efficient learning machines: Theories, concepts, and applications for engineers and system designers* (pp. 1–18). Apress., DOI: 10.1007/978-1-4302-5990-9_1

Bajwa, J., Munir, U., Nori, A., & Williams, B. (2021). Artificial intelligence in healthcare: Transforming the practice of medicine. *Future Healthcare Journal*, 8(2), e188–e194. DOI: 10.7861/fhj.2021-0095 PMID: 34286183

Baker, M. J. (2000). *The roles of models in artificial intelligence and education research: A prospective view*. Journal of Artificial Intelligence and Education, 11, 122–143. https://telearn.hal.science/hal-00190395/document

Beal, C. R., & Arroyo, I. (2002). The AnimalWatch project: Creating an intelligent computer mathematics tutor. In S. L. Calvert, A. B. Jordan, & R. R. Cocking (Eds.), *Children in the digital age: Influences of electronic media on development* (pp. 183–198). Praeger Publishers/Greenwood Publishing Group.

Biadsy, F., Weiss, R., Moreno, P., Kanevsky, D., & Jia, Y. (2019). Parrotron: An end-to-end speech-to-speech conversion model and its applications to hearing-impaired speech and speech separation. In *Proceedings of the Annual Conference of the International Speech Communication Association (Interspeech 2019)* (pp. 4115-4119). https://doi.org/DOI: 10.21437/Interspeech.2019-1789

Blikstein, P., & Worsley, M. (2016). Multimodal learning analytics and education data mining: Using Computational technologies to measure complex learning tasks. *Journal of Learning Analytics*, 3(2), 220–238. DOI: 10.18608/jla.2016.32.11

Brose, S. W., Weber, D. J., Salatin, B. A., Grindle, G. G., Wang, H., Vazquez, J. J., & Cooper, R. A. (2010). The role of assistive robotics in the lives of persons with disability. *American Journal of Physical Medicine & Rehabilitation*, 89(6), 509–521. DOI: 10.1097/PHM.0b013e3181cf569b PMID: 20134305

Burbach, L., Halbach, P., Plettenberg, N., Nakayama, J., Ziefle, M., & Calero Valdez, A. (2019). "Hey, Siri", "Ok, Google", "Alexa". Acceptance-Relevant Factors of Virtual Voice-Assistants. In *2019 IEEE International Professional Communication Conference (ProComm)* (pp. 101-111). IEEE. https://doi.org/DOI: 10.1109/ProComm.2019.00025

Canfield, W. (2001). ALEKS: A Web-based intelligent tutoring system. *Mathematics and Computer Education*, 35(2), 152–158. https://www.proquest.com/scholarly-journals/aleks-web-based-intelligent-tutoring-system/docview/235901507/se-2

Chaddad, A., Li, J., Lu, Q., Li, Y., Okuwobi, I. P., Tanougast, C., Desrosiers, C., & Niazi, T. (2021). Can autism be diagnosed with artificial intelligence? A narrative review. *Diagnostics (Basel)*, 11(11), 2032. DOI: 10.3390/diagnostics11112032 PMID: 34829379

Chassignol, M., Khoroshavin, A., Klimova, A., & Bilyatdinova, A. (2018). Artificial intelligence trends in education: A narrative overview. *Procedia Computer Science*, 136, 16–24. DOI: 10.1016/j.procs.2018.08.233

Chemnad, K., & Othman, A. (2024). Digital accessibility in the era of artificial intelligence: Bibliometric analysis and systematic review. *Frontiers in Artificial Intelligence*, 7, 1349668. Advance online publication. DOI: 10.3389/frai.2024.1349668 PMID: 38435800

Chen, H., Park, H. W., & Breazeal, C. (2020a). Teaching and learning with children: Impact of reciprocal peer learning with a social robot on children's learning and emotive engagement. *Computers & Education*, 150, 103836. DOI: 10.1016/j.compedu.2020.103836

Chen, L., Chen, P., & Lin, Z. (2020b). Artificial intelligence in education: A review. *IEEE Access : Practical Innovations, Open Solutions*, 8, 75264–75278. DOI: 10.1109/ACCESS.2020.2988510

Chen, P., & Lu, Y. (2023). An AI-powered teacher assistant for student problem behavior diagnosis. In Niemi, H., Pea, R. D., & Lu, Y. (Eds.), *AI in learning: Designing the future* (pp. 94–104). Springer., DOI: 10.1007/978-3-031-09687-7_6

Chen, X., Xie, H., Zou, D., & Hwang, G. J. (2020c). Application and theory gaps during the rise of artificial intelligence in education. *Computers and Education: Artificial Intelligence*, 1, 100002. DOI: 10.1016/j.caeai.2020.100002

Cheung, B., Hui, L., Zhang, J., & Yiu, S.-M. (2003). SmartTutor: An intelligent tutoring system in web-based adult education. *Journal of Systems and Software*, 68(1), 11–25. DOI: 10.1016/S0164-1212(02)00133-4

Chirvasiu, N. D. V., & Simion-Blândă, E. (2018). Alternative and augmentative communication in support of persons with language development retardation. *Revista Romaneasca Pentru Educatie Multidimensionala*, 10(2), 28–35. DOI: 10.18662/rrem/43

Cimolino, G., Askari, S., & Graham, T. C. N. (2021). The role of partial automation in increasing the accessibility of digital games. *Proceedings of the ACM on Human-Computer Interaction*, 5(CHI PLAY), 3474693. DOI: 10.1145/3474693

Collette, D., Brix, A., Brennan, P., DeRoma, N., & Muir, B. C. (2019). Proloquo-2Go enhances classroom performance in children with autism spectrum disorder. *Occupational Therapy Journal of Research: occupation, participation and health, 39*(3), 143–150. https://doi.org/DOI: 10.1177/1539449218799451

Contrino, M., Reyes-Millán, M., Vazquez-Villegas, P., & Membrillo-Hernández, J. (2024). Using an adaptive learning tool to improve student performance and satisfaction in online and face-to-face education for a more personalized approach. *Smart Learning Environments*, 11(1), 6. Advance online publication. DOI: 10.1186/s40561-024-00292-y

Crevier, D. (1993). *AI: The Tumultuous Search for Artificial Intelligence*. BasicBooks.

Cummings, M. L., Roff, H. M., Cukier, K., Parakilas, J., & Bryce, H. (2018). *Artificial intelligence and international affairs: Disruption anticipated*. Chatham House, International Security Department & US and the Americas Programme. Retrieved from https://www.chathamhouse.org/sites/default/files/publications/research/2018-06-14-artificial-intelligence-international-affairs-cummings-roff-cukier-parakilas-bryce.pdf

Dahmani, L., & Bohbot, V. D. (2020). Habitual use of GPS negatively impacts spatial memory during self-guided naviga-tion. *Scientific Reports*, 10(1), 6310. DOI: 10.1038/s41598-020-62877-0 PMID: 32286340

Dange, P., Mistry, T., & Mann, S. (2023). AI and assistive technologies for persons with disabilities: Worldwide trends in the scientific production using bibliometrix R tool. In *Communications in computer and information science* (pp. 24–43). https://doi.org/DOI: 10.1007/978-3-031-47997-7_3

Davids, J., Lidströmer, N., & Ashrafian, H. (2021). Artificial intelligence for physiotherapy and rehabilitation. In Lidströmer, N., & Ashrafian, H. (Eds.), *Artificial intelligence in medicine* (pp. 1–19). Springer., DOI: 10.1007/978-3-030-58080-3_339-1

Deligiannis, N., Panagiotopoulos, D., Patsilinakos, P., Raftopoulou, C., & Symvonis, A. (2019). Interactive and personalized activity eBooks for learning to read: The iRead case. In *Proceedings of the First Workshop on Intelligent Textbooks, International Conference on Artificial Intelligence in Education* (pp. 1-10). Chicago, IL, USA. https://ceur-ws.org/Vol-2384/paper06.pdf

Deterding, S., Dixon, D., Khaled, R., & Nacke, L. (2011, September). From Game Design Elements to Gamefulness: Creating Interactive Leisure with Gameful Design. In *Proceedings of the 15th International Academic MindTrek Conference: Envisioning Future Media Environments* (pp. 9-15). ACM. https://doi.org/DOI: 10.1145/2181037.2181040

Díaz-Cintas, J., & Orero, P. (2006). Voice-over. In Brown, K. (Ed.), *Encyclopedia of language & linguistics* (2nd ed., pp. 477–479). Elsevier., DOI: 10.1016/B0-08-044854-2/00473-9

Dresscher, L., Chacon, I. A., & Sosnovsky, S. A. (2021). *Generation of assessment questions from textbooks enriched with knowledge models* (Vol. 2895). [English], https://ceur-ws.org/Vol-2895/paper10.pdf

Drigas, A., Kouremenos, D., & Vrettaros, J. (2008). Teaching of English to hearing impaired individuals whose mother language is the sign language. In Lytras, M. D., Carroll, J. M., Damiani, E., & Tennyson, R. D. (Eds.), *Emerging technologies and information systems for the knowledge society. WSKS 2008 Lecture Notes in Computer Science* (Vol. 5288, pp. 263–270). Springer., DOI: 10.1007/978-3-540-87781-3_29

Duffy, E. I., Garry, J., Talbot, L., Pasternak, D., Flinn, A., Minardi, C., Dookram, M., Grant, K., Fitzgerald, D., Rubano, J., Vosswinkel, J., & Jawa, R. S. (2018). A pilot study assessing the spiritual, emotional, physical/environmental, and physiological needs of mechanically ventilated surgical intensive care unit patients via eye tracking devices, head nodding, and communication boards. *Trauma Surgery & Acute Care Open*, 3(1), e000180. DOI: 10.1136/tsaco-2018-000180 PMID: 30246152

Economic Commission for Latin America and the Caribbean. (2021). *Digital technologies for a new future: Production, productivity and management*. ECLAC Headquarters.

Ersozlu, Z., Ledger, S., Ersozlu, A., Mayne, F., & Wildy, H. (2021). Mixed-reality learning environments in teacher education: An analysis of TeachLivE™ research. *SAGE Open*, 11(3), 21582440211032155. Advance online publication. DOI: 10.1177/21582440211032155

Ferrara, E. (2024). Fairness and bias in artificial intelligence: A brief survey of sources, impacts, and mitigation strategies. *Science*, 6(1), 3. DOI: 10.3390/sci6010003

Ferrucci, D. A. (2012). Introduction to "This is Watson". *IBM Journal of Research and Development, 56*(3.4), 1:1-1:15. https://doi.org/DOI: 10.1147/JRD.2012.2184356

Fisher, J. D., Fancsali, S. E., Lewis, A. J., Fisher, V. A., Hausmann, R. G. M., Pavelko, M., Bartle Finocchi, S., & Ritter, S. (2020). *LiveHint: Intelligent digital support for analog learning experiences*. Carnegie Learning, Inc. Retrieved from http://CEUR-WS.org/Vol-2674/paper08.pdf

Floridi, L., & Taddeo, M. (2016). What is Data Ethics? *Philosophical Transactions. Series A, Mathematical, Physical, and Engineering Sciences*, 374(2083), 20160360. DOI: 10.1098/rsta.2016.0360 PMID: 28336805

Freund, Y., & Schapire, R. E. (1999). Large margin classification using the perceptron algorithm. *Machine Learning*, 37(3), 277–296. DOI: 10.1023/A:1007662407062

Fröscher, L., Friedrich, A.-K., Berentelg, M., Widmer, C., Gilbert, S. J., & Papenmeier, F. (2022). Framing cognitive off-loading in terms of gains or losses: Achieving a more optimal use of reminders. Cognitive Research: Principles andImplications, 7(1), 61. DOI: 10.1186/s41235-022-00416-3

Fulk, G. (2023). Artificial intelligence and neurologic physical therapy. *Journal of Neurologic Physical Therapy; JNPT*, 47(1), 1–2. DOI: 10.1097/NPT.0000000000000426 PMID: 36534016

Furlong, L., Morris, M., Serry, T., & Erickson, S. (2018). Mobile apps for treatment of speech disorders in children: An evidence-based analysis of quality and efficacy. *PLoS One*, 13(8), e0201513. DOI: 10.1371/journal.pone.0201513 PMID: 30092095

Garg, S., & Sharma, S. (2020). Impact of artificial intelligence in special need education to promote inclusive pedagogy. *International Journal of Information and Education Technology (IJIET)*, 10(7), 1418. Advance online publication. DOI: 10.18178/ijiet.2020.10.7.1418

Ghergulescu, I., Flynn, C., & O'Sullivan, C. (2015). Adaptemy Science: Adaptive learning for science for next generation classroom. In *E-Learn: World Conference on E-Learning in Corporate, Government, Healthcare, and Higher Education* (pp. 1477–1482). Association for the Advancement of Computing in Education (AACE). https://www.learntechlib.org/primary/p/152190/

Gliozzo, A., Ackerson, C., Bhattacharya, R., Goering, A., Jumba, A., Kim, S. Y., Krishnamurthy, L., Lam, T., Littera, A., McIntosh, I., Murthy, S., & Ribas, M. (2017). Building Cognitive Applications with IBM Watson Services: Volume 1 Getting Started. International Technical Support Organization, IBM RedBook. https://www.redbooks.ibm.com/redbooks/pdfs/sg248387.pdf

Goldman, S. R., Taylor, J., Carreon, A., & Smith, S. J. (2024). Using AI to support special education teacher workload. *Journal of Special Education Technology*, 39(3), 434–447. DOI: 10.1177/01626434241257240

Gottschalk, F. (2019). *Impacts of technology use on children: Exploring literature on the brain, cognition and well-being* (OECD Education Working Papers No. 195). OECD Publishing. https://doi.org/DOI: 10.1787/19939019

Granquist, C., Sun, S. Y., Montezuma, S. R., Tran, T. M., Gage, R., & Legge, G. E. (2021). Evaluation and Comparison of Artificial Intelligence Vision Aids: Orcam MyEye 1 and Seeing AI. *Journal of Visual Impairment & Blindness*, 115(4), 277–285. DOI: 10.1177/0145482X211027492

Gudlin, M., Ivanković, I., & Dadić, K. (2022). Robots used in therapy for children with autism spectrum disorder. *American Journal of Multidisciplinary Research & Development*, 4(3), 33–39. https://www.ajmrd.com/wp-content/uploads/2022/03/E433339.pdf

Guo, L., Wang, D., Gu, F., Zhang, Y., & Zhang, Y. (2021). Evolution and trends in intelligent tutoring systems research: A multidisciplinary and scientometric view. *Asia Pacific Education Review*, 22(3), 441–461. DOI: 10.1007/s12564-021-09697-7

Hakkal, S., & Ait Lahcen, A. (2021). An overview of adaptive learning fee-based platforms. In *Proceedings of the 2nd International Conference on Big Data, Modelling and Machine Learning (BML 2021)* (pp. 222-226). https://doi.org/DOI: 10.5220/0010731400003101

Hernandez, J., Mousalli, G., & Rivas, F. (2008). Expert system for the diagnosis of learning difficulties in children's basic education. In Proceedings of the 8th WSEAS International Conference on Applied Computer and Applied Computational Science: Italy. http://www.wseas.us/e-library/conferences/2009/hangzhou/ACACOS/ACACOS09.pdf

Holmes, W., Porayska-Pomsta, K., Holstein, K., Sutherland, E., Baker, T., Buckingham Shum, S., Santos, O. C., Rodrigo, M. M. T., Cukorova, M., Bittencourt, I. I., & Koedinger, K. (2021). Ethics of AI in education: Towards a community-wide

Holmes, W., Porayska-Pomsta, K., Holstein, K., Sutherland, E., Baker, T., Shum, S. B., Santos, O. C., Rodrigo, M. T., Cukurova, M., Bittencourt, I. I., & Koedinger, K. R. (2022, September). framework. *International Journal of Artificial Intelligence in Education*, 32(3), 504–526. DOI: 10.1007/s40593-021-00239-1

Holmes, W., & Tuomi, I. (2022). State of the art and practice in AI in education. *European Journal of Education*, 57(4), 542–570. DOI: 10.1111/ejed.12533

Holstein, K., McLaren, B. M., & Aleven, V. (2019). Co-designing a real-time classroom orchestration tool to support teacher–AI complementarity. *Journal of Learning Analytics*, 6(2). Advance online publication. DOI: 10.18608/jla.2019.62.3

Howarth, E., Vabulas, G., Connolly, S., Green, D., & Smolley, S. (2024). Developing accessible speech technology with users with dysarthric speech. *Assistive Technology*, •••, 1–8. DOI: 10.1080/10400435.2024.2328082 PMID: 38537126

Howlin, C., & Lynch, D. (2014). Learning and academic analytics in the RealizeIt system. https://doi.org/DOI: 10.13140/2.1.3811.1689

Hoy, M. B. (2018). Alexa, Siri, Cortana, and More: An Introduction to Voice Assistants. *Medical Reference Services Quarterly*, 37(1), 81–88. DOI: 10.1080/02763869.2018.1404391 PMID: 29327988

IBM. (n.d.). *What is artificial intelligence*? Retrieved June 30, 2024, from https://www.ibm.com/topics/artificial-intelligence

Indrajith, R. (2024). AI innovations for inclusive learning: Breaking down barriers. *International Journal of Research Publication and Reviews*, 5(4), 9742–9745. https://ijrpr.com/uploads/V5ISSUE4/IJRPR26119.pdf

Institute of Education Sciences, U.S. Department of Education. (2016). *Cognitive Tutor: WWC Intervention Report: A summary of findings from a systematic review of the evidence*. Retrieved from https://ies.ed.gov/ncee/wwc/Docs/InterventionReports/WWC_Cognitive_Tutor_061316.pdf

Jackson, E. A. (2015). Role of information science in sustainable development: Sierra Leone as a case study. *Management of Sustainable Development*, 7(2), 23–29. DOI: 10.1515/msd-2015-0026

Jain, M., Jain, S., Kesharwani, H., & Ahmed, A. E. (2023). Physiotherapeutic aid using ML and AI. *International Journal of Scientific Research in Computer Science Engineering and Information Technology*, 12(3), 245–251. DOI: 10.32628/CSEIT2390399C

Jiang, B., Gu, M., & Du, Y. (2023). Recent Advances in Intelligent Textbooks for Better Learning. In Niemi, H., Pea, R. D., & Lu, Y. (Eds.), *AI in Learning: Designing the Future*. Springer., DOI: 10.1007/978-3-031-09687-7_15

Johnson, C., Smart, K., & Mahar, P. (2023). Is there a place for generative artificial intelligence in special education? *National Social Science Technology Journal, 11*(2), 48-62. https://nssascholars.org/wp-content/uploads/2023/11/NSSA.Journal-11_2_v1.11.28.23.pdf

Kaelin, V. C., Valizadeh, M., Salgado, Z., Parde, N., & Khetani, M. A. (2021). Artificial Intelligence in Rehabilitation Targeting the Participation of Children and Youth with Disabilities: Scoping Review. *Journal of Medical Internet Research*, 23(11), e25745. DOI: 10.2196/25745 PMID: 34734833

Kahraman, H. T., Sağıroğlu, Ş., & Çolak, I. (2010). Development of adaptive and intelligent web-based educational systems. In *Proceedings of the 2010 4th International Conference on Application of Information and Communication Technologies* (pp. 1-5). IEEE. https://doi.org/DOI: 10.1109/ICAICT.2010.5612054

Kanakanti, C. R., & Sabitha, R. (2020). AI and ML based Google Assistant for an organization using Google Cloud Platform and Dialogflow. *International Journal of Recent Technology and Engineering*, 8(5), 2722–2727. DOI: 10.35940/ijrte.E6354.018520

Keles, A., Ocak, R., Keles, A., & Gülcü, A. (2009). ZOSMAT: Web-based intelligent tutoring system for teaching-learning process. *Expert Systems with Applications*, 36(2), 1229–1239. DOI: 10.1016/j.eswa.2007.11.064

Kessler, M., Loewen, S., & Gönülal, T. (2023). Mobile-assisted language learning with Babbel and Duolingo: Comparing L2 learning gains and user experience. *Computer Assisted Language Learning*, 1-25. Informa UK Limited. https://doi.org/DOI: 10.1080/09588221.2023.2215294

Khalid, U. B., Naeem, M., Stasolla, F., Syed, M. H., Abbas, M., & Coronato, A. (2024). Impact of AI-Powered Solutions in Rehabilitation Process: Recent Improvements and Future Trends. *International Journal of General Medicine*, 17, 943–969. DOI: 10.2147/IJGM.S453903 PMID: 38495919

King, P., & Martinez, E. G. (2020). Robotic Assistive Technologies: Principles and practice. *IEEE Pulse. IEEE Pulse*, 11(1), 27–28. DOI: 10.1109/MPULS.2020.2972726

Koshtura, D., Andrunyk, V., & Shestakevych, T. (2021). Development of a speech-to-text program for people with hearing impairments. *CEUR Workshop Proceedings*, 2917, Paper 38. Lviv Polytechnic National University. Retrieved from https://ceur-ws.org/Vol-2917/paper38.pdf

Kouroupa, A., Laws, K. R., Irvine, K., Mengoni, S. E., Baird, A., & Sharma, S. (2022). The use of social robots with children and young people on the autism spectrum: A systematic review and meta-analysis. *PLoS One*, 17(6), e0269800. DOI: 10.1371/journal.pone.0269800 PMID: 35731805

Koychev, I., Nikolov, R., & Dicheva, D. (2009, October 28-29). SmartBook: The new generation e-book meets University 2.0. In *Proceedings of the International Conference on Software, Services & Semantic Technologies* (pp. 60-67). Demetra EOOD. http://hdl.handle.net/10506/244

Krahulcova, L. (2021, March 24). Techno solutionism—Very few things actually need to be an app. Blogtext. Digital Rights Watch Website. https://digit alrightswatch .org.au/2021/03/25/technosolutionism/

Kumazaki, H., Muramatsu, T., Yoshikawa, Y., Matsumoto, Y., Ishiguro, H., Mimura, M., & Kikuchi, M. (2019). Role-play-based guidance for job interviews using an android robot for individuals with autism spectrum disorders. *Frontiers in Psychiatry*, 10, 239. Advance online publication. DOI: 10.3389/fpsyt.2019.00239 PMID: 31031664

Kurzweil, R. (1998). The age of spiritual machines: When computers exceed human intelligence. Viking Press. https://imrtc.org/RE/Books/Technology/THE_AGE_OF_SPIRITUAL_MACHINES_RAY_KURZWEIL.pdf

Labadze, L., Grigolia, M., & Machaidze, L. (2023). Role of AI chatbots in education: Systematic literature review. *International Journal of Educational Technology in Higher Education*, 20(1), 56. DOI: 10.1186/s41239-023-00426-1

Lai, K. H. A., & Ma, S. K. (2023). Sensitivity and specificity of artificial intelligence with Microsoft Azure in detecting pneumothorax in emergency department: A pilot study. *Hong Kong Journal of Emergency Medicine*, 30(1), 8–15. DOI: 10.1177/1024907920948994

Lee, Y., & Cho, J. (2021). Development of an artificial intelligence education model of classification techniques for non-computer majors. *JOIV: International Journal on Informatics Visualization*, 5(2), 113–119. DOI: 10.30630/joiv.5.2.552

Leka, H. B. (2016). *A spherical robot designed for children with special needs, seeks funding on Indiegogo*. TechCrunch. Retrieved from https://techcrunch.com/2016/05/03/lekaindiegogo/

Li, Y., Liao, I. Y., Zhong, N., Toshihiro, F., Wang, Y., & Wang, S. (2023, December). Generative AI Enables the Detection of Autism Using EEG Signals. In *Chinese Conference on Biometric Recognition*. 375-384. Springer Nature Singapore. https://doi.org/DOI: 10.1007/978-981-99-8565-4_35

Liberty, E., Karnin, Z., Xiang, B., Rouesnel, L., Coskun, B., Nallapati, R., Delgado, J., Sadoughi, A., Astashonok, Y., Das, P., Balioglu, C., Chakravarty, S., Jha, M., Gautier, P., Arpin, D., Januschowski, T., Flunkert, V., Wang, Y., Gasthaus, J., & Smola, A. (2020). Elastic machine learning algorithms in Amazon SageMaker. In *Proceedings of the 2020 ACM SIGMOD International Conference on Management of Data (SIGMOD '20)* (pp. 731–737). Association for Computing Machinery. https://doi.org/DOI: 10.1145/3318464.3386126

Lim, E. L., Murugesan, R. K., & Balakrishnan, S. (2024). Leveraging machine learning techniques for student's attention detection: A review. *IAES International Journal of Artificial Intelligence (IJ-AI), 13*(2), 1195-1205. https://doi.org/DOI: 10.11591/ijai.v13.i2.pp1195-1205

Lin, C., Huang, A. Y. Q., & Lu, O. H. T. (2023). Artificial intelligence in intelligent tutoring systems toward sustainable education: A systematic review. *Smart Learning Environments*, 10(1), 41. Advance online publication. DOI: 10.1186/s40561-023-00260-y

Littman, M. L., Ajunwa, I., Berger, G., Boutilier, C., Currie, M., Doshi-Velez, F., Hadfield, G., Horowitz, M. C., Isbell, C., Kitano, H., Levy, K., Lyons, T., Mitchell, M., Shah, J., Sloman, S., Vallor, S., & Walsh, T. (2021). *Gathering strength, gathering storms: The one hundred year study on artificial intelligence (AI100) 2021 study panel report*. Stanford University. https://ai100.stanford.edu/2021-report

Lu, W., Wei, Y., Yuan, J., Deng, Y., & Song, A. (2020). Tractor assistant driving control method based on EEG combined with RNN-TL deep learning algorithm. *IEEE Access : Practical Innovations, Open Solutions*, 8, 163269–163279. DOI: 10.1109/ACCESS.2020.3021051

MacCalla, J., Xu, J., & Howard, A. (2015). Integration of Common Core math standards into gaming apps for children with motor limitations. *Zyrobotics, LLC, Atlanta, GA*. Retrieved from https://www.resna.org/sites/default/files/conference/2015/parking_lot/pdfs/84.pdf

MacDonald, R. L., Jiang, P.-P., Cattiau, J., Heywood, R., Cave, R., Seaver, K., Ladewig, M. A., Tobin, J., Brenner, M. P., Nelson, P. C., Green, J. R., & Tomanek, K. (2021). Disordered speech data collection: Lessons learned at 1 million utterances from Project Euphonia. *Proceedings of Interspeech*, 2021, 4833–4837. DOI: 10.21437/Interspeech.2021-697

Maiseli, B., Abdalla, A. T., Massawe, L. V., Mbise, M., Mkocha, K., Nassor, N. A., Ismail, M., Michael, J., & Kimambo, S. (2023). Brain–computer interface: Trend, challenges, and threats. *Brain Informatics*, 10(1), 20. Advance online publication. DOI: 10.1186/s40708-023-00199-3 PMID: 37540385

Maker, J., Zimmerman, R., Alhusaini, A., & Pease, R. (2015). Real engagement in active problem solving (REAPS): An evidence-based model that meets content, process, product, and learning environment principles recommended for gifted students. *Apex*, 19(1), 1–24. DOI: 10.21307/apex-2015-006

Manyilizu, M. C. (2023). Effectiveness of virtual laboratory vs. paper-based experiences to the hands-on chemistry practical in Tanzanian secondary schools. *Education and Information Technologies*, 28(5), 4831–4848. DOI: 10.1007/s10639-022-11327-7 PMID: 36247025

Maples, B., Pea, R. D., & Markowitz, D. (2023). Learning from Intelligent Social Agents as Social and Intellectual Mirrors. In Niemi, H., Pea, R. D., & Lu, Y. (Eds.), *AI in Learning: Designing the Future*. Springer., DOI: 10.1007/978-3-031-09687-7_5

Mays, K. K., Cummings, J. J., & Katz, J. E. (2024). The Robot Rights and Responsibilities Scale: Development and Validation of a Metric for Understanding Perceptions of Robots' Rights and Responsibilities. *International Journal of Human-Computer Interaction*, •••, 1–18. DOI: 10.1080/10447318.2024.2338332

McCarthy, J. (2007). What is artificial intelligence. https://www-formal.stanford.edu/jmc/whatisai.pdf

McCulloch, W. S., & Pitts, W. (1943). A logical calculus of the ideas immanent in nervous activity. *The Bulletin of Mathematical Biophysics*, 5(4), 115–133. DOI: 10.1007/BF02478259

McLaren, B., Gog, T., Ganoe, C., Yaron, D., & Karabinos, M. (2015). RETRACTED ARTICLE: Worked examples are more efficient for learning than high-assistance instructional software. *International Journal of Artificial Intelligence in Education*, 26(4), 1117. Advance online publication. DOI: 10.1007/s40593-015-0046-z

Medenica, V., Ivanović, L., Ristic, I., & Čolić, G. (2023, September). *Artificial intelligence in occupational therapy and special education and rehabilitation*. In *Scientific conference SANUS2023, Prijedor, June 23 rd -24 th, 2023* (Conference presentation). Prijedor, BiH. https://doi.org/DOI: 10.7251/ZSAN2302033M

Melis, E., Andres, E., Budenbender, J., Frischauf, A., Goduadze, G., Libbrecht, P., Pollet, M., & Ullrich, C. (2001). ActiveMath: A generic and adaptive web-based learning environment. *International Journal of Artificial Intelligence in Education*, 12, 385–407. https://hal.archives-ouvertes.fr/ffhal-00197329

Mendhe, S., Bawankule, R., Udapurkar, A., Gogiya, R., Gaikwad, A., & Saggu, J. K. (2022). SignReco: Sign language translator. *International Research Journal of Engineering and Technology (IRJET), 9*(3). Retrieved from https://www.academia.edu/81754577/SignReco_Sign_Language_Translator

Microsoft. (n.d.). *Digital Learning Tools | Microsoft Education*. https://www.microsoft.com/en-us/education/products/learning-tools

Mobasheri, A., Deister, J., & Dieterich, H. (2017). Wheelmap: The wheelchair accessibility crowdsourcing platform. *Open Geospatial Data. Software and Standards*, 2(1), 27. Advance online publication. DOI: 10.1186/s40965-017-0040-5

Mog, L. K. (2016). Implementation of an electronic wheelchair with a Google Map and a smart phone's speaker-independent recognition engine. *Advanced Science Letters*, 22(11), 3333–3336. DOI: 10.1166/asl.2016.7900

Mohammad, Y., & Nishida, T. (2007). TalkBack: Feedback from a Miniature Robot. In T. Nishida & E. André (Eds.), *Toward Robotic Socially Believable Behaving Systems - Volume I: Modeling Emotions* (pp. 357-366). Springer. https://doi.org/DOI: 10.1007/978-3-540-76928-6_37

Mukherjee, P., S, G. R., Sadhukhan, S., Godse, M., & Chakraborty, B. (2023). Detection of Autism Spectrum Disorder (ASD) from Natural Language Text using BERT and ChatGPT Models. *International Journal of Advanced Computer Science and Applications*, 14(10). Advance online publication. DOI: 10.14569/IJACSA.2023.0141041

Müller, V. C., & Bostrom, N. (2016). Future Progress in Artificial Intelligence: A Survey of Expert Opinion. In Müller, V. C. (Ed.), *Fundamental Issues of Artificial Intelligence* (pp. 555–572). Springer., DOI: 10.1007/978-3-319-26485-1_33

Mutawa, A. M., Al Mudhahkah, H. M., Al-Huwais, A., Al-Khaldi, N., Al-Otaibi, R., & Al-Ansari, A. (2023). Augmenting mobile app with NAO robot for autism education. *Machines (Basel)*, 11(8), 833. DOI: 10.3390/machines11080833

Nanni, L., & Lumini, A. (2009). Ensemble generation and feature selection for the identification of students with learning disabilities. *Expert Systems with Applications*, 36(2), 3896–3900. DOI: 10.1016/j.eswa.2008.02.065

National Institute for Transforming India Aayog. (2023). National Strategy for Artificial Intelligence. Government of India. Retrieved [27th June 2024] from https://www.niti.gov.in/sites/default/files/2023-03/National-Strategy-for-Artificial-Intelligence.pdf

Nemorin, S., Vlachidis, A., Ayerakwa, H. M., & Andriotis, P. (2022). AI hyped? A horizon scan of discourse on artificialintelligence in education (AIED) and development. Online article. *Learning, Media and Technology*, •••, 1–14. DOI: 10.1080/17439884.2022.2095568

Ng, D. T. K., Leung, J. K. L., Su, J., Ng, R. C. W., & Chu, S. K. W. (2023). Teachers' AI digital competencies and twenty-first century skills in the post-pandemic world. *Educational technology research and development. Educational Technology Research and Development*, 71(1), 137–161. DOI: 10.1007/s11423-023-10203-6 PMID: 36844361

Nuralisah, A., & Kareviati, E. (2020). The effectiveness of using Memrise application in teaching vocabulary. [Professional Journal of English Education]. *PROJECT*, 3(4), 494–500. DOI: 10.22460/project.v3i4.p494-500

Office of Educational Technology. (2023, May). *Artificial intelligence and the future of teaching and learning: Insights and recommendations*. U.S. Department of Education. https://tech.ed.gov/files/2023/05/AI-Teaching-Learning-Insights-Recommendations.pdf

Ogunbukola, M. (2024). Empowering Abilities: How AI is Transforming Lives for People with Disabilities. https://www.researchgate.net/publication/378547809_Empowering_Abilities_How_AI_is_Transforming_Lives_for_People_with_Disabilities

Parekh, D., Poddar, N., Rajpurkar, A., Chahal, M., Kumar, N., Joshi, G. P., & Cho, W. (2022). A review on autonomous vehicles: Progress, methods and challenges. *Electronics (Basel)*, 11(14), 2162. DOI: 10.3390/electronics11142162

Patnaik, N., & Agrawal, K. (2022). Study on processor used in virtual assistants: Google Assistant, Alexa, Siri Alexa. *International Research Journal of Engineering and Technology (IRJET), 9*(3), 1874. Retrieved from https://www.irjet.net

Pattison, A. S., & Roopaei, M. (2023). An AI-based exergame to assist occupational and physical therapy. In *2023 IEEE World AI IoT Congress (AIIoT)* (pp. 0804-0807). IEEE. https://doi.org/DOI: 10.1109/AIIoT58121.2023.10174489

Pavlik, P. I., Jr., Olney, A. M., Banker, A., Eglington, L., & Yarbro, J. (2020). The mobile fact and concept textbook system (MoFaCTS). In S. Sosnovsky, P. Brusilovsky, R. Baraniuk, & A. Lan (Eds.), *Proceedings of the Second International Workshop on Intelligent Textbooks 2020 co-located with 21st International Conference on Artificial Intelligence in Education (AIED 2020)*. Institute for Intelligent Systems, University of Memphis. https://ceur-ws.org/Vol-2674/paper04.pdf

Pearson Education, Inc. (2019). *General overview of WriteToLearn and its components*. Retrieved from https://WriteToLearn.net

Pennisi, P., Tonacci, A., Tartarisco, G., Billeci, L., Ruta, L., Gangemi, S., & Pioggia, G. (2016). Autism and social robotics: A systematic review. *Autism research: official journal of the International Society for Autism Research, 9*(2), 165–183. https://doi.org/DOI: 10.1002/aur.1527

Peredo, R., Canales, A., Menchaca, A., & Peredo, I. (2011). Intelligent web-based education system for adaptive learning. *Expert Systems with Applications*, 38(12), 14690–14702. DOI: 10.1016/j.eswa.2011.05.013

Poulter, C. (2020). Voice recognition software—Nuance Dragon naturally speaking. *Occupational Medicine (Oxford, England)*, 70(1), 75–76. DOI: 10.1093/occmed/kqz128

Putra, A. (2023). The effect of EDAPP as LMS on students' English proficiency on junior high school student. *RETAIN: Journal of Research in English Language Teaching, 11*(03), 31-38. Retrieved from https://ejournal.unesa.ac.id/index.php/retain/article/view/56604

Rabiyath, S. S., & Kumar, M. N. (2024). Bashini Website and App – An Overview. *Journal of Emerging Technologies and Innovative Research*, 11(1). https://www.jetir.org/papers/JETIR2401141.pdf

Ramesh, D., & Sanampudi, S. K. (2022). An automated essay scoring system: A systematic literature review. *Artificial Intelligence Review*, 55(3), 2495–2527. DOI: 10.1007/s10462-021-10068-2 PMID: 34584325

Robert, A., Potter, K., & Frank, L. (2024). The impact of artificial intelligence on students' learning experience. *SSRN*. Advance online publication. DOI: 10.2139/ssrn.4716747

Robles, P., & Mallinson, D. J. (2023). Artificial intelligence technology, public trust, and effective governance. *The Review of Policy Research*, 00, 1–18. DOI: 10.1111/ropr.12555

Rumelhart, D. E., Hinton, G. E., & Williams, R. J. (1986). Learning representations by back-propagating errors. *Nature*, 323(6088), 533–536. DOI: 10.1038/323533a0

Russell, S., & Norvig, P. (2010). *Artificial intelligence: A modern approach* (3rd ed.). Prentice Hall, Pearson Education, Inc.

Russell, S., & Norvig, P. (2021). *Artificial Intelligence: A Modern Approach* (4th ed.). Prentice Hall, Pearson Education, Inc.

Sağdıç, A., Elumar-Efe, E., & Sani-Bozkurt, S. (2024). GenAI, robots, and inclusive special education: Autism spectrum disorder in the age of generative AI. In Sharma, R., & Bozkurt, A. (Eds.), *Transforming education with generative AI: Prompt engineering and synthetic content creation* (pp. 309–326). IGI Global., DOI: 10.4018/979-8-3693-1351-0.ch015

Salas-Pilco, S. Z., Xiao, K., & Hu, X. (2022). Artificial intelligence and learning analytics in teacher education: A systematic review. *Education Sciences*, 12(8), 569. DOI: 10.3390/educsci12080569

Saleh, M. A., Hanapiah, F. A., & Hashim, H. (2021). Robot applications for autism: A comprehensive review. *Disability and Rehabilitation. Assistive Technology*, 16(6), 580–602. DOI: 10.1080/17483107.2019.1685016 PMID: 32706602

Şanverdî, M. (2021). The use of Rosetta Stone application for vocabulary improvement in English: A review study. In *Proceedings of the International Conference on Language and Linguistics* (pp. 85–91). ISBN 978-605-196-721-9.

Sarker, I. H. (2021). Deep learning: A comprehensive overview on techniques, taxonomy, applications and research directions. *SN Computer Science*, 2(420), 420. Advance online publication. DOI: 10.1007/s42979-021-00815-1 PMID: 34426802

Schiaffino, S., Garcia, P., & Amandi, A. (2008). eTeacher: Providing personalized assistance to e-learning students. *Computers & Education*, 51(4), 1744–1754. DOI: 10.1016/j.compedu.2008.05.008

Schipor, O. A., Pentiuc, S. G., & Schipor, M. D. (2003). Improving computer-based speech therapy using a fuzzy expert system. *Computing and Informatics, 22*, 1001–1016. Retrieved from https://www.cai.sk/ojs/index.php/cai/article/view/193/130

Schuster, R., Song, C., & Tromer, E.. (2021). You autocomplete me: Poisoning vulnerabilities in neural code completion. In *Proceedings of the 30th USENIX Security Symposium* (pp. 1–18). USENIX Association., Retrieved from https://www.usenix.org/conference/usenixsecurity21/presentation/schuster

Sebesta, R. W. (2012). *Concepts of programming languages* (10th ed.). Pearson Education, Inc., https://www.ime.usp.br/~alvaroma/ucsp/proglang/book.pdf

Sedrakyan, G., Malmberg, J., Verbert, K., Järvelä, S., & Kirschner, P. A. (2020). Linking learning behavior analytics and learning science concepts: Designing a learning analytics dashboard for feedback to support learning regulation. *Computers in Human Behavior*, 107, 105512. Advance online publication. DOI: 10.1016/j.chb.2018.05.004

Shamsuddin, S., Yussof, H., Hanapiah, F. A., Mohamed, S., Ismail, L. I., & Pawi, S. (2011). Humanoid robot NAO: Review of control and motion exploration. In *2011 IEEE International Conference on Control System, Computing and Engineering* (pp. 511-516). Penang, Malaysia. https://doi.org/DOI: 10.1109/ICCSCE.2011.6190579

Shane, N. (2023). Artificial neural networks and the actiotope model of giftedness—Clever solutions from complex environments. *Journal of Intelligence*, 11(7), 128. DOI: 10.3390/jintelligence11070128 PMID: 37504771

Sharma, S., Tomar, V., Yadav, N., & Aggarwal, M. (2023). Impact of AI-based special education on educators and students. In *Advances in educational technologies and instructional design* (pp. 47–66). IGI Global. https://doi.org/DOI: 10.4018/979-8-3693-0378-8.ch003

Sherkuziyeva, N., Gabidullina, F. I., Ibrahim, K. A. A., & Bayat, S. (2023). The comparative effect of computerized dynamic assessment and rater mediated assessment on EFL learners' oral proficiency, writing performance, and test anxiety. *Language Testing in Asia*, 13(1), 15. Advance online publication. DOI: 10.1186/s40468-023-00227-3

Siemens, G. (2005). Connectivism: A learning theory for the digital age. *International Journal of Instructional Technology and Distance Learning, 2*. http://www.itdl.org/Journal/Jan_05/article01.htm

Siemens, G., & Long, P. (2011). Penetrating the fog: Analytics in learning and education. *EDUCAUSE Review*, 46(5), 30–32. DOI: 10.17471/2499-4324/195

Slattery, E. J., Butler, D., O'Leary, M., & Marshall, K. (2023). Primary school students' experiences using Minecraft Education during a national project-based initiative: An Irish study. *TechTrends: For leaders in education & training*, 1–13. Advance online publication. https://doi.org/DOI: 10.1007/s11528-023-00851-z

Smutny, P., & Schreiberova, P. (2020). Chatbots for learning: A review of educational chatbots for the Facebook Messenger. *Computers & Education*, 151, 103862. DOI: 10.1016/j.compedu.2020.103862

Špakov, O., Istance, H., Räihä, K.-J., Viitanen, T., & Siirtola, H. (2019). Eye gaze and head gaze in collaborative games. In *Proceedings of the 2019 CHI Conference on Human Factors in Computing Systems* (pp. 1-9). https://doi.org/DOI: 10.1145/3317959.3321489

Srinivasan, V., Vardhan, V., Kar, S., Asthana, S., Narayanan, R., Singh, P., Chakraborty, D., & Singh, A. (2013). Airavat: An automated system to increase transparency and accountability in social welfare schemes in India. In *ICTD '13: Proceedings of the Sixth International Conference on Information and Communications Technologies and Development: Notes*- Volume 2 (pp. 151–154). https://doi.org/DOI: 10.1145/2517899.2517937

Stoeger, H., Balestrini, D. P., & Ziegler, A. (2018). International perspectives and trends in research on giftedness and talent development. In Pfeiffer, S. I., Shaunessy-Dedrick, E., & Foley-Nicpon, M. (Eds.), *APA handbook of giftedness and talent* (pp. 25–37). American Psychological Association., DOI: 10.1037/0000038-002

Sun, Z., Yu, Z. C., & Xu, F. Y. (2023). Analysis and Improvement of Classroom Teaching Based on Artificial Intelligence. In Niemi, H., Pea, R. D., & Lu, Y. (Eds.), *AI in Learning: Designing the Future*. Springer., DOI: 10.1007/978-3-031-09687-7_7

Tambotoh, J., Kosala, R., Ranti, B., Prabowo, H., Supangkat, S., Isa, S. M., & Pudjianto, B. (2017, November). A conceptual model for creating effective public value through key practices in information technology governance mechanisms. In *2017 International Conference on Information Management and Technology (ICIMTech)* (pp. 128–132). IEEE. https://doi.org/DOI: 10.1109/ICIMTech.2017.8273524

Tapus, A., Peca, A., Amir, A., Pop, C., Jisa, L., Pintea, S., Rusu, A., & David, D. (2012). Children with autism social engagement in interaction with Nao, an imitative robot – A series of single case experiments. *Interaction Studies: Social Behaviour and Communication in Biological and Artificial Systems*, 13(3), 1–25. DOI: 10.1075/is.13.3.01tap

Theodorou, L., Massiceti, D., Zintgraf, L., Stumpf, S., Morrison, C., Cutrell, E., Harris, M. T., & Hofmann, K. (2021). Disability-first dataset creation: Lessons from constructing a dataset for teachable object recognition with blind and low vision data collectors. In *Proceedings of the 23rd International ACM SIGACCESS Conference on Computers and Accessibility*. ACM. https://doi.org/DOI: 10.1145/3441852.3471225

Toyokawa, Y., Horikoshi, I., Majumdar, R., & Ogata, H. (2023). Challenges and opportunities of AI in inclusive education: A case study of data-enhanced active reading in Japan. *Smart Learning Environments*, 10(67), 1–19. DOI: 10.1186/s40561-023-00286-2

Tozadore, D., Gauthier, S., Bruno, B., Wang, C., Zou, J., Aubin, L., Archambault, D., Chetouani, M., Dillenbourg, P., Cohen, D., & Anzalone, S. (2023). The iReCheck project: Using tablets and robots for personalized handwriting practice. *Proceedings of the 2023 ACM Conference on Human Factors in Computing Systems*, 297-301. https://doi.org/DOI: 10.1145/3610661.3616178

UNESCO. (2019). Leveraging AI towards improving learning and equity. In *Artificial intelligence in education: Challenges and opportunities for sustainable development* (pp. 12-16). UNESCO. https://unesdoc.unesco.org/ark:/48223/pf0000366994

UNESCO. (2021a). *AI and education: guidance for policy-makers* [English]. United Nations Educational, Scientific and Cultural Organization., DOI: 10.54675/PCSP7350

UNESCO. (2021 b). Reimagining Our Futures Together: A New Social Contract For Education [English]. International Commission on the Futures of Education. United Nations Educational, Scientific and Cultural Organization: France. https://doi.org/DOI: 10.54675/ASRB4722

UNESCO. (2022). Recommendation on the Ethics of Artificial Intelligence. United Nations Educational, Scientific and Cultural Organization: France. https://unesdoc.unesco.org/ark:/48223/pf0000381137

UNESCO. (2023). *Ethical impact assessment: A tool of the Recommendation on the Ethics of Artificial Intelligence*. United Nations Educational, Scientific and Cultural Organization., DOI: 10.54678/YTSA7796

UNESCO. (n.d.). Artificial intelligence in education. UNESCO. https://www.unesco.org/en/digital-education/artificial-intelligence#

Urrea, A. L., Fernández-Torres, V., Rodriguez-Ortiz, I. R., & Saldaña, D. (2024). The use of technology-assisted intervention in vocabulary learning for children with autism spectrum disorder: A systematic review. *Frontiers in Psychology*, 15, 1370965. Advance online publication. DOI: 10.3389/fpsyg.2024.1370965 PMID: 38817831

Velander, J., Taiye, M. A., Otero, N., & Milrad, M. (2024). Artificial intelligence in K-12 education: Eliciting and reflecting on Swedish teachers' understanding of AI and its implications for teaching & learning. *Education and Information Technologies*, 29(4), 4085–4105. DOI: 10.1007/s10639-023-11990-4

Vidhya, V., Ganesan, Lakshmanan, Arvind, T., Nithya, M., & Pranayini. (2009). T9++-Intelligent predictive text entry for mobile devices. *Journal of Theoretical and Applied Information Technology*, 52(1), 21–33.

Walle, H., De Runz, C., Serres, B., & Venturini, G. (2022). A survey on recent advances in AI and vision-based methods for helping and guiding visually impaired people. *Applied Sciences (Basel, Switzerland)*, 12(5), 2308. DOI: 10.3390/app12052308

Ward, N. (2006). SHRDLU. In Nadel, L. (Ed.), *Encyclopedia of cognitive science.*, DOI: 10.1002/0470018860.s00056

Weber, G., & Brusilovsky, P. (2001). *ELM-ART: An adaptive versatile system for web-based instruction. International Journal of Artificial Intelligence in Education (IJAIED)*, 12, 351–384. https://telearn.hal.science/hal-00197328

Weizenbaum, J. (1966). ELIZA: A computer program for the study of natural language communication between man and machine. *Communications of the ACM*, 9(1), 36–45. DOI: 10.1145/365153.365168

Whalen, C., Moss, D., Ilan, A., Vaupel, M., Fielding, P., Macdonald, K., Cernich, S., & Symon, J. (2010). Efficacy of TeachTown: Basics computer-assisted intervention for the Intensive Comprehensive Autism Program in Los Angeles Unified School District. *Autism*, 14(3), 179–197. DOI: 10.1177/1362361310363282 PMID: 20484002

World Health Organization. (n.d.). *International Classification of Functioning, Disability and Health (ICF)*. Retrieved June 29, 2024, from https://icd.who.int/dev11/l-icf/en

XPRIZE. (2015). XPRIZE. https://www.xprize.org/prizes/global-learning

Xu, Y., Liu, X., Cao, X., Huang, C., Liu, E., Qian, S., Liu, X., Wu, Y., Dong, F., Qiu, C.-W., Qiu, J., Hua, K., Su, W., Wu, J., Xu, H., Han, Y., Fu, C., Yin, Z., Liu, M., & Zhang, J. (2021). Artificial intelligence: A powerful paradigm for scientific research. *Innovation (Cambridge (Mass.))*, 2(4), 100179. DOI: 10.1016/j.xinn.2021.100179 PMID: 34877560

Xu, Z. (2024). AI in education: Enhancing learning experiences and student outcomes. *Applied and Computational Engineering*, 51(1), 104–111. DOI: 10.54254/2755-2721/51/20241187

Yao, N., & Wang, Q. (2024). Factors influencing pre-service special education teachers' intention toward AI in education: Digital literacy, teacher self-efficacy, perceived ease of use, and perceived usefulness. *Heliyon*, 10(14), e34894. DOI: 10.1016/j.heliyon.2024.e34894 PMID: 39149079

Zdravkova, K., Krasniqi, V., Dalipi, F., & Ferati, M. (2022). Cutting-edge communication and learning assistive technologies for disabled children: An artificial intelligence perspective. *Frontiers in Artificial Intelligence*, 5, 970430. DOI: 10.3389/frai.2022.970430 PMID: 36388402

Zubair, S., & Rangreze, I. (2023). AI-driven advancements in autism spectrum disorder: Early diagnosis, intervention, and genomic insights for enhanced social well-being. *European Chemical Bulletin*, 12, 6297–6313. DOI: 10.48047/ecb/2023.12.si8.533

Compilation of References

Abd El-Kader, S., & Mohammad El-Basioni, B. (2014). Independent Living for Persons with Disabilities and Elderly People using Smart Home Technology. *International Journal of Application or Innovation in Engineering & Management (IJAIEM)*, 3.

Abraham, T. H. (2002). (Physio)logical circuits: The intellectual origins of the McCulloch-Pitts neural networks. *Journal of the History of the Behavioral Sciences*, 38(1), 3–25. DOI: 10.1002/jhbs.1094 PMID: 11835218

Abramovich, S., Schunn, C., & Higashi, R. M. (2013). Are badges useful in education?: It depends upon the type of badge and expertise of learner. *Educational Technology Research and Development*, 61(2), 217–232. DOI: 10.1007/s11423-013-9289-2

Abuzakiyeh, K. (2018). Expert systems in artificial intelligence and their employment in education and education. *Journal of Faculties of Education, University of Al-Zawiya, 12*.

Adams, C., Pente, P., Lemermeyer, G., & Rockwell, G. (2021). Artificial intelligence ethics guidelines for K-12 Education: A review of the global landscape. In Roll, I., McNamara, D., Sosnovsky, S., Luckin, R., & Dimitrova, V. (Eds.), *Artificial intelligence in education* (Vol. 12749, pp. 24–28). Springer International Publishing. DOI: 10.1007/978-3-030-78270-2_4

Adiani, D., Itzkovitz, A., Bian, D., Katz, H., Breen, M., Hunt, S., Swanson, A., Vogus, T. J., Wade, J., & Sarkar, N. (2022). Career interview readiness in virtual reality (CIRVR): A platform for simulated interview training for autistic individuals and their employers. [TACCESS]. *ACM Transactions on Accessible Computing*, 15(1), 1–28. DOI: 10.1145/3505560

Afzal, S., Dempsey, B., D' Helon, C., Mukhi, N., Pribic, M., Sickler, A., Strong, P., Vanchiswar, M., & Wilde, L. (2019). The personality of AI systems in education: Experiences with the Watson Tutor, a one-on-one virtual tutoring system. *Childhood Education*, 95(1), 44–52. DOI: 10.1080/00094056.2019.1565809

Age of Learning, Inc. (2016). *ABCmouse significantly improves student outcomes in pre-k and kindergarten*. Retrieved from https://www.ageoflearning.com/case_studies/ABCmouse_Research_Brief_Significantly_Improves_Student_Outcomes_in_Pre-K_and_Kindergarten.pdf

Agency for Care Effectiveness [ACE]. (2024). *ACE brief for new and emerging health technologies: canvas dx to aid the diagnosis of autism spectrum disorder.* https://www.ace-hta.gov.sg/docs/default-source/horizon-scanning/canvas-dx-to-aid-the-diagnosis-of-autism-spectrum-disorder.pdf?sfvrsn=a521d7c1_1

Aggarwal, C. C. (2018). *Neural networks and deep learning*. Springer. DOI: 10.1007/978-3-319-94463-0

Aggarwal, D. (2023). Exploring the scope of artificial intelligence (AI) for lifelong education through personalised & adaptive learning. *Journal of Artificial Intelligence. Machine Learning and Neural Network*, 4(01), 21–26. DOI: 10.55529/jaimlnn.41.21.26

Aggarwal, D., Sharma, D., & Saxena, A. (2023). Adoption of artificial intelligence (AI) for development of smart education as the future of a sustainable education system. *Journal of Artificial Intelligence. Machine Learning and Neural Network*, 3(06), 23–28. DOI: 10.55529/jaimlnn.36.23.28

Agran, M., Jackson, L., Kurth, J. A., Ryndak, D., Burnette, K., Jameson, M., Zagona, A., Fitzpatrick, H., & Wehmeyer, M. (2020). Why aren't students with severe disabilities being placed in general education classrooms: Examining the relations among classroom placement, learner outcomes, and other factors. *Research and Practice for Persons with Severe Disabilities : the Journal of TASH*, 45(1), 4–13. DOI: 10.1177/1540796919878134

Ahmad, W., Parween, S., & Nazli. (2022). Concept of Normalization, Mainstreaming, Integration, and Inclusive Education: Implications in Educational Program. In Ahmad, W., Chavan, B.S., & Gupta, R.K. (Eds.), Comprehensive Textbook on Disability (pp. 8-12). New Delhi: Jaypee Brothers Medical Publishers.

Ahuja, N. J., Dutt, S., Choudhary, S., & Kumar, M. (2022). Intelligent tutoring system in education for disabled learners using human–computer interaction and augmented reality. *International Journal of Human-Computer Interaction*, 21(3), 1–13. DOI: 10.1080/10447318.2022.2124359

Akgun, S., & Greenhow, C. (2021). Artificial intelligence in education: Addressing ethical challenges in K-12 settings. *AI and Ethics*, 2(3), 431–440. DOI: 10.1007/s43681-021-00096-7 PMID: 34790956

Aksënova, A., van Esch, D., Flynn, J., & Golik, P. (2021). How might we create better benchmarks for speech recognition? In Church, K., Liberman, M., & Kordoni, V. (Eds.), *Proceedings of the 1st Workshop on Benchmarking: Past, present and future* (pp. 22–34)., https://aclanthology.org/2021.bppf-1.pdf DOI: 10.18653/v1/2021.bppf-1.4

Al Banna, M. H., Ghosh, T., Taher, K. A., Kaiser, M. S., & Mahmud, M. (2020, September). A monitoring system for patients of autism spectrum disorder using artificial intelligence. In *International conference on brain informatics* (pp. 251–262). Springer International Publishing. DOI: 10.1007/978-3-030-59277-6_23

Alam, A. (2021, November). Possibilities and apprehensions in the landscape of artificial intelligence in education. In *2021 International Conference on Computational Intelligence and Computing Applications (ICCICA)* (pp. 1-8). IEEE. DOI: 10.1109/ICCICA52458.2021.9697272

Albright, G., Bryan, C., Adam, C., McMillan, J., & Shockley, K. (2018). Using virtual patient simulations to prepare primary health care professionals to conduct substance use and mental health screening and brief intervention. *Journal of the American Psychiatric Nurses Association*, 24(3), 247–259. DOI: 10.1177/1078390317719321 PMID: 28754067

Aldoseri, A., Al-Khalifa, K. N., & Hamouda, A. M. (2023). Re-thinking data strategy and integration for artificial intelligence: Concepts, opportunities, and challenges. *Applied Sciences (Basel, Switzerland)*, 13(12), 7082. DOI: 10.3390/app13127082

Alghamdi, R., Alshehri, A., & Alqahtani, M. (2021). The impact of artificial intelligence on learning and teaching in higher education in Saudi Arabia. *Education and Information Technologies*, 26(3), 3547–3566.

Algren, M., Fisher, W., & Landis, A. E. (2021). Machine learning in life cycle assessment. In Dunn, J., & Balaprakash, P. (Eds.), *Data science applied to sustainability analysis* (pp. 167–190). Elsevier., DOI: 10.1016/B978-0-12-817976-5.00009-7

Alhashmi, M., Mubin, O., & Baroud, R. (2021). Examining the use of robots as teacher assistants in UAE classrooms: Teacher and student perspectives. *Journal of Information Technology Education*, 20, 245–261. DOI: 10.28945/4749

Alhosani, K., & Alhashmi, S. M. (2024). Opportunities, challenges, and benefits of AI innovation in government services: A review. *Discover Artificial Intelligence*, 4(18), 1–19. DOI: 10.1007/s44163-024-00111-w

Ali, B. M., Maheswari, M., Nagendrudu, P. V. V. S. D., Rani, D. L., & Hashmi, A. (2023). Application of Artificial intelligence Assisted Robots to Improve the Educational Outcome for Special Children in Disability Education. *Journal for ReAttach Therapy and Developmental Diversities*, 6(9s), 328–337.

Ali, Z., Ahmad, N., Rehman, H. U., Ullah, N., & Zahra, T. (2023). Investigating Teacher Educators' Perceptions on Technology Integration in Teacher Preparation Programs. *Journal of Social Sciences Review*, 3(2), 341–355. DOI: 10.54183/jssr.v3i2.272

Allebee, A. (2017). Equadex, Microsoft cognitive services. [Online]. Available: https://customers.microsoft.com/en-us/story/equadex-partner-professional-services-cognitive-services

Ally, L. (1948). About us. Retrieved from https://www.learningally.org/About-Us on 1 June 2024.

Ally, L. (2011). Learning Ally. https://learningally.org retrieved on 1 June 2024.

Almasri, F. (2022). Simulations to teach science subjects: Connections among students' engagement, self-confidence, satisfaction, and learning styles. *Education and Information Technologies*, 27(5), 7161–7181. DOI: 10.1007/s10639-022-10940-w PMID: 35153535

Almodaires, A. A., Almutairi, F. M., & Almsaud, T. E. A. (2021). Pre-Service Teachers' Perceptions of the Effectiveness of Microsoft. *International Education Studies*, 14(9), 108–121. DOI: 10.5539/ies.v14n9p108

Al-Obaydi, L. H., Pikhart, M., & Klimova, B. (2023). ChatGPT and the general concepts of Education: Can Artificial Intelligence-driven Chatbots Support the process of Language Learning? [IJET]. *International Journal of Emerging Technologies in Learning*, 18(21), 39–50. DOI: 10.3991/ijet.v18i21.42593

Alpizar-Chacon, I., & Sosnovsky, S. (2019). *Interlingua: Linking textbooks across different languages. In Proceedings of the 1st Workshop on Intelligent Textbooks, iText 2019* (pp. 104-117). https://ceur-ws.org/Vol-2384/paper11.pdf

Alraasibia, A. (2021). Mechanisms for developing teaching and learning in the Sultanate of Oman in accordance with the requirements of the Fourth Industrial Revolution. *Al-Andalus Journal for Humanities and Social Sciences, 45*(8). Retrieved from http://www.andalusuniv.net/AUSTNEW/ma gazine/sh/2021/8/45/7908bbd-5015f9b3e7b5 7ceefdd1580d1.pdf

Alsobeh, A., & Woodward, B. (2023). AI as a partner in learning: A novel student-in-the-Loop framework for enhanced student engagement and outcomes in higher education. *Proceedings of the 24th Annual Conference on Information Technology Education.* DOI: 10.1145/3585059.3611405

Alvarez-Alvarez, C., & Mischel, L. (2024). Edpuzzle for E-learning: A Study of Perceived Advantages and Limitations. *International Journal of Education and Development Using Information and Communication Technology*, 20(1), 134–145.

Alzahrani, M. A. (2024). The user analysis of Amazon using artificial intelligence at customer churn. *Journal of Data Analysis and Information Processing*, 12(1), 40–48. DOI: 10.4236/jdaip.2024.121003

Al-Zoubi, S. M., & Rahman, M. S. B. A. (2012). The Effect of Resource Room on improving Reading and Arithmetic Skills for Learners with Learning Disabilities. The. *International Journal of Scientific Research in Education*, 5(4), 269–277. Retrieved June 1, 2024, from http://www.ijsre.com

Al-Zyoud, H. M. M. (2020). The role of artificial intelligence in teacher professional development. *Universal Journal of Educational Research*, 8(11B), 6263–6272. DOI: 10.13189/ujer.2020.082265

Amaro, I., Della Greca, A., Francese, R., Tortora, G., & Tucci, C. (2023, July). AI unreliable answers: A case study on ChatGPT. In *International Conference on Human-Computer Interaction* (pp. 23–40). Springer Nature Switzerland. DOI: 10.1007/978-3-031-35894-4_2

Amazon (2021). What is artificial intelligence? Machine learning and deep learning. Retrieved from https://aws.amazon.com/machine-learning/what-is-ai/ on 11 October 2021.

Amazon. (2014). Amazon Alexa. Retrieved from https://www.amazon.com/alexa on 1 June 2024.

American Psychiatric Association. (2013). *Diagnostic and statistical manual of mental disorders* (5th ed.), American Psychiatric Association. https://dsm–psychiatry online–org.libproxy.library.unt.edu/doi/full/10.1176/appi.books.9780890425596 .dsm01

American Psychiatric Association. (2022). *Diagnostic and statistical manual of mental disorders* (5th ed., text rev.). American Psychiatric Association. https://doi/book/DOI: 10.1176/appi.books.9780890425787

Amiri, A. M., Peltier, N., Goldberg, C., Sun, Y., Nathan, A., Hiremath, S. V., & Mankodiya, K. (2017). WearSense: Detecting autism stereotypic behaviors through smartwatches. *Healthcare (Basel)*, 5(11), 2–9. DOI: 10.3390/healthcare5010011

Anagnostopoulou, P., Alexandropoulou, V., Lorentzou, G., Lykothanasi, A., Ntaountaki, P., & Drigas, A. (2020). Artificial intelligence in autism assessment. [iJET]. *International Journal of Emerging Technologies in Learning*, 15(6), 95–107. DOI: 10.3991/ijet.v15i06.11231

Anderson, J. R., Corbett, A. T., Koedinger, K. R., & Pelletier, R. (1997). K. R., & Pelletier, R. (1995). Cognitive tutors: Lessons learned. *Journal of the Learning Sciences*, 4(2), 167–207. DOI: 10.1207/s15327809jls0402_2

Anthony, L., Yang, J., & Koedinger, K. R. (2008). Toward Next-Generation Intelligent tutors: Adding natural Handwriting Input. *IEEE MultiMedia*, 15(3), 64–68. DOI: 10.1109/MMUL.2008.73

Anuradha, J., Ramachandran, V., Arulalan, K., & Tripathy, B. (2010). Diagnosis of adhd using svm algorithm. *Proceedings of the Third Annual ACM Bangalore Conference*, 1–4.

Archer, A. L., & Hughes, C. A. (2011). Explicit Instruction: Effective and efficient teaching (what works for special-needs learners). *The Journal of Special Education*, 36(4), 186–205.

Asfar, A. I. T., Asmawaty, A., Asfar, A. I. A., & Nursyam, A. (2019). Mathematical concept understanding: The impact of integrated learning model. *Al-Jabar: Jurnal Pendidikan Matematika*, 10(2), 211–222. DOI: 10.24042/ajpm.v10i2.3880

Ashraf, M. M., Ul-Haque, I., & Sangha, N. K. (2024). Navigating Autism Treatment: Unlocking New Frontiers with ChatGPT. *The International Journal of Neuroscience*, 1–3, 1–2. Advance online publication. DOI: 10.1080/00207454.2024.2341912

AssistiveWare. (2009). *Proloquo2Go*. AssistiveWare. https://www.assistiveware.com/products/proloquo2go

Atzori, M., Gijsberts, A., Castellini, C., Caputo, B., Mittaz Hager, A.-G., Elsig, S., Giatsidis, G., Bassetto, F., & Müller, H. (2014). Electromyography data for non-invasive naturally-controlled robotic hand prostheses. *Scientific Data*, 1(1), 140053. DOI: 10.1038/sdata.2014.53 PMID: 25977804

Aulisio, M. C., Han, D. Y., & Glueck, A. C. (2020). Virtual reality gaming as a neurorehabilitation tool for brain injuries in adults: A systematic review. *Brain Injury : [BI]*, 34(10), 1322–1330. DOI: 10.1080/02699052.2020.1802779

Awad, M., & Khanna, R. (2015). Machine learning. In *Efficient learning machines: Theories, concepts, and applications for engineers and system designers* (pp. 1–18). Apress., DOI: 10.1007/978-1-4302-5990-9_1

Ayuwanti, I., & Siswoyo, D. (2021). Teacher-student interaction in mathematics learning. *International Journal of Evaluation and Research in Education*, 10(2), 660–667.

Badawy, M. (2023). Integrating artificial intelligence and big data into smart health-care systems: A comprehensive review of current and future directions. *Artificial Intelligence Evolution. 4*(2),133-135. https://doi.org?DOI: 10.37256/aie/4220232980

Badmus, O. (2023). Application of AI technology in program management. *Journal of Engineering Research and Reports*, 25(8), 48–55. DOI: 10.9734/jerr/2023/v25i8958

Bailenson, J. (2020, September 18). Is VR the future of corporate training? *Harvard Business Review*.https://hbr.org/2020/09/is-vr-the-future-of-corporate-training

Bajwa, J., Munir, U., Nori, A., & Williams, B. (2021). Artificial intelligence in healthcare: Transforming the practice of medicine. *Future Healthcare Journal*, 8(2), e188–e194. DOI: 10.7861/fhj.2021-0095 PMID: 34286183

Baker, M. J. (2000). *The roles of models in artificial intelligence and education research: A prospective view*. Journal of Artificial Intelligence and Education, 11, 122–143. https://telearn.hal.science/hal-00190395/document

Baker, R. S. J. d., & Inventado, P. S. (2014). Educational data mining and learning analytics. In *Learning Analytics* (pp. 61–75). Springer. DOI: 10.1007/978-1-4614-3305-7_4

Baker, R. S., D'Mello, S. K., Rodrigo, M. M. T., & Graesser, A. C. (2010). Better to be frustrated than bored: The incidence, persistence, and impact of learners' cognitive–affective states during interactions with three different computer-based learning environments. *International Journal of Human-Computer Studies*, 68(4), 223–241. DOI: 10.1016/j.ijhcs.2009.12.003

Baldwin, L., Omdal, S. N., & Pereles, D. (2015). Beyond stereotypes: Understanding, recognizing, and working with twice-exceptional learners. *Teaching Exceptional Children*, 47(4), 216–225. DOI: 10.1177/0040059915569361

Ballesteros, S., Prieto, A., Mayas, J., Toril, P., Pita, C., Ponce de Leon, L., & Waterworth, J. (2014). Brain training with non-action video games enhances aspects of cognition in older adults: A randomized controlled trial. *Frontiers in Aging Neuroscience*, 6, 277. DOI: 10.3389/fnagi.2014.00277 PMID: 25352805

Bañeres, D., Rodríguez, M. E., Guerrero-Roldán, A. E., & Karadeniz, A. (2020). An Early Warning System to Detect at-risk Students in online Higher Education. *Applied Sciences (Basel, Switzerland)*, 10(13), 1–28. DOI: 10.3390/app10134427

Barkley, R. A. (2020). *Taking charge of ADHD: The complete, authoritative guide for parents*. Guilford Publications.

Barua, P. D., Vicnesh, J., Gururajan, R., Oh, S. L., Palmer, E., Azizan, M. M., & Acharya, U. R. (2022). Artificial intelligence enabled personalized assistive tools to enhance education of children with neurodevelopmental disorders: A review. *International Journal of Environmental Research and Public Health*, 19(3), 1–26. DOI: 10.3390/ijerph19031192

Baschera, G.-M., & Gross, M. (2010). Poisson-based inference for perturbation models in adaptive spelling training. *International Journal of Artificial Intelligence in Education*, 20, 333–360. DOI: 10.3233/JAI-2010-011

Baskara, R. (2023). Personalised learning with AI: Implications for Ignatian pedagogy. [International Journal of Educational Best Practices]. *IJEBP*, 7(1), 1–16. DOI: 10.31258/ijebp.v7n1.p1-16

Bateman, D., & Cline, J. (2019). *Special Education Leadership*. Routledge. DOI: 10.4324/9781351201353

Bausback, K. B., & Bunge, E. L. (2021). Meta-analysis of parent training programs utilizing behavior intervention technologies. *Social Sciences (Basel, Switzerland)*, 10(10), 367. DOI: 10.3390/socsci10100367

Beal, C. R., & Arroyo, I. (2002). The AnimalWatch project: Creating an intelligent computer mathematics tutor. In S. L. Calvert, A. B. Jordan, & R. R. Cocking (Eds.), *Children in the digital age: Influences of electronic media on development* (pp. 183–198). Praeger Publishers/Greenwood Publishing Group.

Beal, C. R., & Lee, H. (2019). Creating cognitive and metacognitive support for students in intelligent tutoring systems. *Journal of Educational Psychology*, 111(4), 666–677.

Beaulieu, L., & Jimenez-Gomez, C. (2022). Cultural responsiveness in applied behavior analysis: Self-assessment. *Journal of Applied Behavior Analysis*, 55(2), 337–356. DOI: 10.1002/jaba.907 PMID: 35266143

Behavior Analyst Certification Board. (2020). *Ethics code for behavior analysts.* https://bacb.com/wp-content/ethics-code-for-behavior-analysts/

Benfer, E. A., Mohapatra, S., Wiley, L. F., & Yearby, R. (2019). Health justice strategies to combat the pandemic: Eliminating discrimination, poverty, and health disparities during and after COVID-19. *SSRN*, 19(3), 122–171. DOI: 10.2139/ssrn.3636975

Bertacchini, F., Demarco, F., Scuro, C., Pantano, P., & Bilotta, E. (2023). A social robot connected with ChatGPT to improve cognitive functioning in autism subjects. *Frontiers in Psychology*, 14, 1232177. DOI: 10.3389/fpsyg.2023.1232177

Bérubé, M., Giannelia, T., & Vial, G. (2021). Barriers to the Implementation of AI in Organizations: Findings from a Delphi Study. *Proceedings of the 54th Hawaii International Conference on System Sciences*. 1-10. https://doi.org/DOI: 10.24251/HICSS.2021.805

Betsy, & Eubanck, G. (2012). *About ModMath*. Retrieved June 1, 2024, from https://www.modmath.com

Beukelman, D., & Light, J. (2020). Augmentative and alternative communication: Supporting children and adults with complex communication needs.

Bhatti, I., Mohi-U-din, S. F., Hayat, Y., & Tariq, M. (2024). Artificial Intelligence Applications for Students with Learning Disabilities: A Systematic Review. *European Journal of Science. Innovation and Technology*, 4(2), 40–56.

Biadsy, F., Weiss, R., Moreno, P., Kanevsky, D., & Jia, Y. (2019). Parrotron: An end-to-end speech-to-speech conversion model and its applications to hearing-impaired speech and speech separation. In *Proceedings of the Annual Conference of the International Speech Communication Association (Interspeech 2019)* (pp. 4115-4119). https://doi.org/DOI: 10.21437/Interspeech.2019-1789

Billingsley, B., & Bettini, E. (2019). *Special education teacher attrition and retention: A review of the literature*. AERA., DOI: 10.3102/0034654319862495

Birnbaum, B. W. (2006). *Foundations of special education leadership: Administration, assessment, placement and the law*. Edwin Mellen Press.

Blaas, S. (2014). The relationship between social-emotional difficulties and underachievement of gifted students. *Australian Journal of Guidance & Counselling*, 24(2), 243–255. DOI: 10.1017/jgc.2014.1

Black, P., & Wiliam, D. (2009). Developing the theory of formative assessment. *Educational Assessment, Evaluation and Accountability*, 21(1), 5–31. DOI: 10.1007/s11092-008-9068-5

Blair, C., & Ursache, A. (2021). A bidirectional model of executive functions and self-regulation. In Vohs, K. D., & Baumeister, R. F. (Eds.), *Handbook of Self-regulation: Research, Theory, and Applications* (pp. 300–320). Guilford Press.

Blasey, J., Wang, C., & Blasey, R. (2023). Accommodation use and academic outcomes for college students with disabilities. *Psychological Reports*, 126(4), 1891–1909. DOI: 10.1177/00332941221078011 PMID: 35303777

Blikstein, P., & Worsley, M. (2016). Multimodal learning analytics and education data mining: Using Computational technologies to measure complex learning tasks. *Journal of Learning Analytics*, 3(2), 220–238. DOI: 10.18608/jla.2016.32.11

Blömeke, S., Nilsen, T., & Scherer, R. (2021). School innovativeness is associated with enhanced teacher collaboration, innovative classroom practices, and job satisfaction. *Journal of Educational Psychology*, 113(8), 1645–1667. DOI: 10.1037/edu0000668

Bond, E. (2014). *Childhood, mobile technologies and everyday experiences: changing technologies changing childhoods?* Palgrave Macmillan. DOI: 10.1057/9781137292537

Borenstein, J., & Howard, A. (2020). The ethics of artificial intelligence in education: Emerging issues and the potential for lasting impact. *Educational Technology Research and Development*, 68(4), 1997–2011.

Borg, J., Larsson, S., Östergren, P. O., Rahman, A. A., Bari, N., & Khan, A. N. (2012). Assistive technology use and human rights enjoyment: A cross-sectional study in Bangladesh. *BMC International Health and Human Rights*, 12(1), 1–11. DOI: 10.1186/1472-698X-12-18 PMID: 22992413

Bouck, E. C. (2010), "Chapter 6 Technology and students with disabilities: Does it solve all the problems", Obiakor, F.E., Bakken, J.P. and Rotatori, n.F. (Ed.) *Current Issues and Trends in Special Education: Research, Technology, and Teacher Preparation (Advances in Special Education, Vol. 20)*, Emerald Group Publishing Limited, Leeds, pp. 91-104. https://doi-org.proxy1.library.jhu.edu/10.1108/S0270-4013(2010)0000020009

Bozkurt, A. (2020). Educational technology research patterns in the realm of the digital knowledge age. *Journal of Interactive Media in Education*, 2020(1), 1–17. DOI: 10.5334/jime.570

Bozkurt, A. (2023d). ChatGPT, generative artificial intelligence, and algorithmic paradigm shift. *CRES Journal Critical Reviews in Educational Sciences*, 4(1), 63–72. DOI: 10.59320/alanyazin.1283282

Bozkurt, A., & Sharma, R. C. (2023). Generative AI and prompt engineering: The art of whispering to let the genie out of the algorithmic world. *Asian Journal of Distance Education*, 18(2), i–vii. DOI: 10.5281/zenodo.8174941

Brahmi, Z., Mahyoob, M., Al-Sarem, M., Algaraady, J., Bousselmi, K., & Alblwi, A. (2024). Exploring the role of machine learning in diagnosing and treating speech disorders: A systematic literature review. *Psychology Research and Behavior Management*, 17(1), 2205–2232. DOI: 10.2147/PRBM.S460283 PMID: 38835654

Brand, D., Henley, A. J., DiGennaro Reed, F. D., Gray, E., & Crabbs, B. (2019). A review of published studies involving parametric manipulations of treatment integrity. *Journal of Behavioral Education*, 28(1), 1–26. DOI: 10.1007/s10864-018-09311-8

Brewer, J., Gerard, C., & Hakkinen, M. (2020). The Impact of AI on Accessibility. EDUCAUSE Review, November 4, 2020. https://er.educause.edu/articles/2022/6/3-ways-ai-can-help-students-with-disabilities

Breznitz, S., & Nachshon, I. (1999). Development of CogniFit. Retrieved from https://www.cognifit.com on 1 June 2024.

Brose, S. W., Weber, D. J., Salatin, B. A., Grindle, G. G., Wang, H., Vazquez, J. J., & Cooper, R. A. (2010). The role of assistive robotics in the lives of persons with disability. *American Journal of Physical Medicine & Rehabilitation*, 89(6), 509–521. DOI: 10.1097/PHM.0b013e3181cf569b PMID: 20134305

Brownell, M. T., Jones, N. D., Sohn, H., & Stark, K. (2020). Improving Teaching Quality for Students With Disabilities: Establishing a Warrant for Teacher Education Practice. *Teacher Education and Special Education*, 43(1), 28–44. DOI: 10.1177/0888406419880351

Brownell, M. T., & Leko, M. M. (2018). Advancing coherent theories of change in special education teacher education research: A response to the special issue on the science of teacher professional development. *Teacher Education and Special Education*, 41(2), 158–168. DOI: 10.1177/0888406417748430

Brownell, M. T., Ross, D. D., Colón, E. P., & McCallum, C. L. (2005). Critical features of special education teacher preparation: A comparison with general teacher education. *The Journal of Special Education*, 38(4), 242–252. DOI: 10.1177/00224669050380040601

Brownell, M. T., Sindelar, P. T., Kiely, M. T., & Danielson, L. C. (2010). Special education teacher quality and preparation: Exposing foundations, constructing a new model. *Exceptional Children*, 76(3), 357–377. DOI: 10.1177/001440291007600307

Brynjolfsson, E., & Mcafee, A. (2017). Artificial intelligence, for real. *Harvard Business Review*, 1(95), 1–31.

Bulman, G., & Fairlie, R. (2022). The impact of COVID-19 on community college enrollment and student success: Evidence from California administrative data. *Education Finance and Policy*, 17(4), 745–764. DOI: 10.1162/edfp_a_00384

Buolamwini, J., & Gebru, T. (2018, January). Gender shades: Intersectional accuracy disparities in commercial gender classification. In Conference on fairness, accountability and transparency (pp. 77-91). PMLR.Noble, S. U. (2018). Algorithms of oppression: How search engines reinforce racism. NYU Press.

Burbach, L., Halbach, P., Plettenberg, N., Nakayama, J., Ziefle, M., & Calero Valdez, A. (2019). "Hey, Siri", "Ok, Google", "Alexa". Acceptance-Relevant Factors of Virtual Voice-Assistants. In *2019 IEEE International Professional Communication Conference (ProComm)* (pp. 101-111). IEEE. https://doi.org/DOI: 10.1109/ProComm.2019.00025

Burke, S. L., Bresnahan, T., Li, T., Epnere, K., Rizzo, A., Partin, M., Ahlness, R. M., & Trimmer, M. (2018). Using virtual interactive training agents (ViTA) with adults with autism and other developmental disabilities. *Journal of Autism and Developmental Disorders*, 48(3), 905–912. DOI: 10.1007/s10803-017-3374-z PMID: 29168090

Burm, E., Chun, Y. E., & Han, J. Y. (2023). Validation of the effectiveness of AI-Based Personalized Adaptive Learning: Focusing on basic math class cases. *Journal of Internet of Things and Convergence*, 9(3), 35–43.

Byrd, D. R., & Alexander, M. (2020). Investigating special education teachers knowledge and skills: Preparing general teacher preparation for professional development. *Journal of Pedagogical Research*, 4(2), 72–82. DOI: 10.33902/JPR.2020059790

Callender, A., King, S. A., & Howard, M. (2020). Social validity assessment: Examples from a functional skills training intervention. In Jaworski, J. A. (Ed.), *Advances in Sociology Research* (Vol. 31). Nova Science Publishers.

Calloway-Appleton, T. April 15, 2023, "Mom couldn't find a show tailored to her son's special needs—so she made her own!" Inspiremore.com https://www.inspiremore.com/ms-rachel-developmental-programming-for-kids/

Canfield, W. (2001). ALEKS: A Web-based intelligent tutoring system. *Mathematics and Computer Education*, 35(2), 152–158. https://www.proquest.com/scholarly-journals/aleks-web-based-intelligent-tutoring-system/docview/235901507/se-2

Carales, V. D. (2020). Examining educational attainment outcomes: A focus on Latina/o community college students. *Community College Review*, 48(2), 195–219. DOI: 10.1177/0091552120903087

Caramancion, K. M. (2024). Large Language Models vs. Search Engines: Evaluating User Preferences Across Varied Information Retrieval Scenarios. *arXiv preprint arXiv:2401.05761*.

Cardona, M. A., Rodríguez, R. J., & Ishmael, K. (2023). Artificial Intelligence and the Future of Teaching and Learning. Office of Educational Technology, U.S. Department of Education, 1-67. Retrieved from https://tech.ed.gov

Carnegie Learning, Inc. (n.d.). *Carnegie Learning*. Retrieved from https://www.carnegielearning.com on 27 June 2024.

Caro, M. F., Quitian, L., Giraldo, J. C., & Lengua-Cantero, C. (2023, November). A Formal Model for Personalized Learning Path using Artificial Intelligence for Instructional Planning with a Focus on 21st-Century Skills and Environmental Awareness. In *2023 IEEE Colombian Caribbean Conference (C3)* (pp. 1-6). IEEE. DOI: 10.1109/C358072.2023.10436195

Carroll, R. A., Owsiany, J., & Cheatham, J. M. (2018). Using an abbreviated assessment to identify effective error-correction procedures for individual learners during discrete-trial instruction. *Journal of Applied Behavior Analysis*, 51(3), 482–501. DOI: 10.1002/jaba.460 PMID: 29675825

CAST. (2011). *UDL guidelines* [Web tool]. Retrieved from https://udlguidelines.cast.org on 1 June 2024.

Cefai, J., Smith, D., & Pushak, R. E. (2010). Parenting wisely: Parent training via CD-ROM with an Australian sample. *Child & Family Behavior Therapy*, 32(1), 17–33. DOI: 10.1080/07317100903539709

Centers for Disease Control and Prevention. (2022). *Prevalence and characteristics of autism spectrum disorder*. Retrieved at https://www.cdc.gov/mmwr/volumes/72/ss/ss7202a1.htm?s_cid=ss7202a1_w

Chaddad, A., Li, J., Lu, Q., Li, Y., Okuwobi, I. P., Tanougast, C., Desrosiers, C., & Niazi, T. (2021). Can autism be diagnosed with artificial intelligence? A narrative review. *Diagnostics (Basel)*, 11(11), 2032. DOI: 10.3390/diagnostics11112032 PMID: 34829379

Chai, C. S., Lin, P. Y., Jong, M. S. Y., Dai, Y., Chiu, T. K., & Qin, J. (2021). Perceptions of and behavioral intentions towards learning artificial intelligence in primary school students. *Journal of Educational Technology & Society*, 24(3), 89–101.

Chang, A. A., Kazemi, E., Esmaeili, V., & Davies, M. S. (2023). The effectiveness of virtual reality training: A systematic review. *Journal of Organizational Behavior Management*, 44(3), 214–232. DOI: 10.1080/01608061.2023.2240767

Charlton, J. I. (1998). *Nothing about us without us: Disability oppression and empowerment*. University of California Press.

Chassignol, M., Khoroshavin, A., Klimova, A., & Bilyatdinova, A. (2018). Artificial intelligence trends in education: A narrative overview. *Procedia Computer Science*, 136, 16–24. DOI: 10.1016/j.procs.2018.08.233

ChatGPT. (2024, January 19). How do you cite an answer in ChatGPT. Retrieved from [https://chat.openai.com/]

Chazin, K. T., Barton, E. E., Ledford, J. R., & Pokorski, E. A. (2018). Implementation and intervention practices to facilitate communication skills for a child with complex communication needs. *Journal of Early Intervention*, 40(2), 138–157. DOI: 10.1177/1053815118771397

Chemnad, K., & Othman, A. (2024). Digital accessibility in the era of artificial intelligence: Bibliometric analysis and systematic review. *Frontiers in Artificial Intelligence*, 7, 1349668. Advance online publication. DOI: 10.3389/frai.2024.1349668 PMID: 38435800

Chen, G., Davis, D., Hauff, C., & Houben, G. J. (2016, April). Learning transfer: Does it take place in MOOCs? An investigation into the uptake of functional programming in practice. In *Proceedings of the Third(2016) ACM Conference on Learning@ Scale* (pp. 409-418).

Chen, C.-M. (2009). Personalized E-learning system with self-regulated learning assisted mechanisms for promoting learning performance. *Expert Systems with Applications*, 36(5), 8816–8829. DOI: 10.1016/j.eswa.2008.11.026

Cheng, K. H., & Tsai, C. C. (2020). The interactions between self-regulation of learning and the use of AI-based applications in learning. *Journal of Educational Computing Research*, 57(6), 1585–1602.

Chen, H., Park, H. W., & Breazeal, C. (2020a). Teaching and learning with children: Impact of reciprocal peer learning with a social robot on children's learning and emotive engagement. *Computers & Education*, 150, 103836. DOI: 10.1016/j.compedu.2020.103836

Chen, J., & Miao, W. (2021). Application and inspiration of virtual reality technology in vocational education in the United States. *Adult Education*, 41(06), 90–93.

Chen, L., Chen, P., & Lin, Z. (2020). Artificial intelligence in education: A review. *IEEE Access : Practical Innovations, Open Solutions*, 8, 75264–75278. DOI: 10.1109/ACCESS.2020.2988510

Chen, P., & Lu, Y. (2023). An AI-powered teacher assistant for student problem behavior diagnosis. In Niemi, H., Pea, R. D., & Lu, Y. (Eds.), *AI in learning: Designing the future* (pp. 94–104). Springer., DOI: 10.1007/978-3-031-09687-7_6

Chen, X., Xie, H., Zou, D., & Hwang, G. J. (2020c). Application and theory gaps during the rise of artificial intelligence in education. *Computers and Education: Artificial Intelligence*, 1, 100002. DOI: 10.1016/j.caeai.2020.100002

Chen, X., Zou, D., Xie, H., Cheng, G., & Liu, C. (2022). Two decades of artificial intelligence in education. *Journal of Educational Technology & Society*, 25(1), 28–47.

Chermesh, O. (2009). *Ghotit Real Writer and Reader*. Retrieved from https://www.ghotit.com on 20 June 2024.

Cheung, B., Hui, L., Zhang, J., & Yiu, S.-M. (2003). SmartTutor: An intelligent tutoring system in web-based adult education. *Journal of Systems and Software*, 68(1), 11–25. DOI: 10.1016/S0164-1212(02)00133-4

Chiam, B. S. W., Leung, I. M. W., Devilly, O. Z., Da Ow, C. Y., Guan, F. Y., & Tan, B. L. (2021, October). Novel augmented reality enhanced solution towards vocational training for people with mental disabilities. In *2021 IEEE International Symposium on Mixed and Augmented Reality Adjunct (ISMAR-Adjunct)* (pp. 195–200). IEEE. DOI: 10.1109/ISMAR-Adjunct54149.2021.00047

Chirvasiu, N. D. V., & Simion-Blândă, E. (2018). Alternative and augmentative communication in support of persons with language development retardation. *Revista Romaneasca Pentru Educatie Multidimensionala*, 10(2), 28–35. DOI: 10.18662/rrem/43

Chiu, T. K. (2021b). Applying the self-determination theory (SDT) to explain student engagement in online learning during the COVID-19 pandemic. *Journal of Research on Technology in Education, 54*(sup1), S14-S30.

Chiu, T. K. F. (2020). Six key principles in designing AI curriculum for middle schools. Association for Educational Communications and Technology (AECT) International Convention, November 3–7, Jacksonville, Florida. Retrieved from https://members.aect.org/pdf/Proceedings/proceedings20/2020i/20_03.pdf

Chiu, T. K. (2021a). A holistic approach to the design of artificial intelligence (AI) education for K-12 schools. *TechTrends*, 65(5), 796–807. DOI: 10.1007/s11528-021-00637-1

Chiu, T. K. (2021c). Digital support for student engagement in blended learning based on self-determination theory. *Computers in Human Behavior*, 124, 106909. DOI: 10.1016/j.chb.2021.106909

Chiu, T. K. (2021d). Student engagement in K-12 online learning amid COVID-19: A qualitative approach from a self-determination theory perspective. *Interactive Learning Environments*, 31(6), 3326–3339. DOI: 10.1080/10494820.2021.1926289

Chiu, T. K., & Chai, C. S. (2020). Sustainable curriculum planning for artificial intelligence education: A self-determination theory perspective. *Sustainability (Basel)*, 12(14), 5568. DOI: 10.3390/su12145568

Chiu, T. K., Chai, C. S., Williams, P. J., & Lin, T. J. (2021). Teacher professional development on self-determination theory–based design thinking in STEM education. *Journal of Educational Technology & Society*, 24(4), 153–165.

Chiu, T. K., & Churchill, D. (2016). Adoption of mobile devices in teaching: Changes in teacher beliefs, attitudes and anxiety. *Interactive Learning Environments*, 24(2), 317–327. DOI: 10.1080/10494820.2015.1113709

Chiu, T. K., Jong, M. S. Y., & Mok, I. A. (2020). Does learner expertise matter when designing emotional multimedia for learners of primary school mathematics? *Educational Technology Research and Development*, 68(5), 2305–2320. DOI: 10.1007/s11423-020-09775-4

Chiu, T. K., & Lim, C. P. (2020). Strategic use of technology for inclusive education in Hong Kong: A content-level perspective. *ECNU Review of Education*, 3(4), 715–734. DOI: 10.1177/2096531120930861

Chiu, T. K., Meng, H., Chai, C. S., King, I., Wong, S., & Yam, Y. (2021). Creation and evaluation of a pretertiary artificial intelligence (AI) curriculum. *IEEE Transactions on Education*, 65(1), 30–39. DOI: 10.1109/TE.2021.3085878

Chiu, T. K., & Mok, I. A. (2017). Learner expertise and mathematics different order thinking skills in multimedia learning. *Computers & Education*, 107, 147–164. DOI: 10.1016/j.compedu.2017.01.008

Chiu, T. K., Xia, Q., Zhou, X., Chai, C. S., & Cheng, M. (2023). Systematic literature review on opportunities, challenges, and future research recommendations of artificial intelligence in education. *Computers and Education: Artificial Intelligence*, 4, 100118. DOI: 10.1016/j.caeai.2022.100118

Choi, D., Lee, S., Kim, S. I., Lee, K., Yoo, H. J., Lee, S., & Hong, H. (2024, May). Unlock Life with a Chat (GPT): Integrating Conversational AI with Large Language Models into Everyday Lives of Autistic Individuals. In *Proceedings of the CHI Conference on Human Factors in Computing Systems* (pp. 1–17). DOI: 10.1145/3613904.3641989

Christensen, H., Cunningham, S. P., Fox, C., Green, P. D., & Hain, T. (2012, September). A comparative study of adaptive, automatic recognition of disordered speech. In *Interspeech* (pp. 1776-1779). DOI: 10.21437/Interspeech.2012-484

Christian, B. (2020). *The Alignment Problem: Machine Learning and Human Values*. W.W. Norton & Company.

Chua, N. A., Soon, G. Y., Mansor, N. R. B. M., Rashid, R. A., Ahmad, M., Musa, A., Rahman, N. A. A., Noh, C. H. C., Ibrahim, M. Y., & Dollah@Abdullah, A. B. (2021). 'CLASSKICK' an interactive online app to support students' learning: A case study on Mandarin as a foreign learning. *Journal of Physics: Conference Series,* 1874(1), 012084. IOP Publishing. https://doi.org/DOI: 10.1088/1742-6596/1874/1/012084

Chun, D., Kaplan-Rakowski, R., Ovsiannikova, U., Thrasher, T., & Yuan, Y. (2024). AI-mediated high-immersion virtual reality for language learning. In Lan, Y. J., Qi, G., & Chun, D. (Eds.), *AI-mediated language education in the metaverse era*. Springer.

Cibrian, F. L., Lakes, K. D., Schuck, S. E. B., & Hayes, G. R. (2022). The potential for emerging technologies to support self-regulation in children with ADHD: A literature review. *International Journal of Child-Computer Interaction*, 31, 100421. Advance online publication. DOI: 10.1016/j.ijcci.2021.100421

Cimolino, G., Askari, S., & Graham, T. C. N. (2021). The role of partial automation in increasing the accessibility of digital games. *Proceedings of the ACM on Human-Computer Interaction*, 5(CHI PLAY), 3474693. DOI: 10.1145/3474693

CityTeachingAlliance. (n.d.). The program. https://cityteachingalliance.org/the-program/

Clark, A., & Chalmers, D. (1998). The extended mind. *Analysis*, 58(1), 7–19. DOI: 10.1093/analys/58.1.7

Clay, C. J., Schmitz, B. A., Balakrishnan, B., Hopfenblatt, J. P., Evans, A., & Kahng, S. (2021). Feasibility of virtual reality behavior skills training for preservice clinicians. *Journal of Applied Behavior Analysis*, 54(2), 547–565. DOI: 10.1002/jaba.809 PMID: 33482023

Cochran-Smith, M., Keefe, E. S., Carney, M. C., Sánchez, J. G., Olivo, M., & Smith, R. J. (2020). Teacher preparation at new graduate schools of education. *Teacher Education Quarterly*, 47(2), 8–37.

Cole, S. M., Murphy, H. R., Frisby, M. B., & Robinson, J. (2023). The relationship between special education placement and high school outcomes. *The Journal of Special Education*, 57(1), 13–23. DOI: 10.1177/00224669221097945

Collette, D., Brix, A., Brennan, P., DeRoma, N., & Muir, B. C. (2019). Proloquo-2Go enhances classroom performance in children with autism spectrum disorder. *Occupational Therapy Journal of Research: occupation, participation and health, 39*(3), 143–150. https://doi.org/DOI: 10.1177/1539449218799451

Collier, M., Keefe, E., & Hirrel, L. (2015). Preparing special education teachers to collaborate with families. *School Community Journal*, 25, 117–136.

Confer, C. A. (2023). The Use of Artificial Intelligence to Create Inclusivity in Special Education Classrooms. *Journal of Applied Professional Studies*, 4(9).

Connor, F. P. (1976). The past is prologue: Teacher preparation in special education. *Exceptional Children*, 42(7), 366–378. DOI: 10.1177/001440297604200702

Contrino, M., Reyes-Millán, M., Vazquez-Villegas, P., & Membrillo-Hernández, J. (2024). Using an adaptive learning tool to improve student performance and satisfaction in online and face-to-face education for a more personalized approach. *Smart Learning Environments*, 11(1), 6. Advance online publication. DOI: 10.1186/s40561-024-00292-y

Cooc, N. (2023). National trends in special education and academic outcomes for English learners with disabilities. *The Journal of Special Education*, 57(2), 106–117. DOI: 10.1177/00224669221147272

Cook, B. G., & Odom, S. L. (2013). Evidence-based practices and implementation science in special education. *Exceptional Children*, 79(2), 135–144. DOI: 10.1177/0014402913079002021

Cooper, B. R., Parker, L. A., & Diaz Martinez, A. (2019). *Balancing fidelity and adaptation: A guide for evidence-based program implementation*. Washington State University Extension. http://hdl.handle.net/2376/16873

Cooper, J. O., Heron, T. E., & Heward, W. L. (2020). *Applied behavior analysis* (3rd ed.). Pearson.

Cornelius, K. E., Rosenberg, M. S., & Sandmel, K. N. (2020). Examining the impact of professional development and coaching on mentoring of novice special educators. *Action in Teacher Education*, 42(3), 253–270. DOI: 10.1080/01626620.2019.1638847

Corralejo, S. M., & Rodríguez, D. M. M. (2018). Technology in parenting programs: A systematic review of existing interventions. *Journal of Child and Family Studies*, 27(9), 1–15. DOI: 10.1007/s10826-018-1117-1

Council for Exceptional Children. (2014). *Standards for evidence-based practices in special education.* CEC. https://exceptionalchildren.org/sites/default/files/2021-04/EBP_FINAL.pdf

Council for Exceptional Children. (2015). *What every special educator must know: Professional ethics and standards* (7th ed.). Council for Exceptional Children. https://www.archive.org/details/isbn_9780865865044

Council for Exceptional Children. (2022). *Practice-based standards for the preparation of special educators.* Council for Exceptional Children.

Council for Exceptional Children. (n.d.). *Special Education Technology.* Retrieved March 22, 2024, from https://exceptionalchildren.org/

Cox, D. J., & Jennings, A. M. (2024). The promises and possibilities of artificial intelligence in the delivery of behavior analytic services. *Behavior Analysis in Practice*, 17(1), 123–136. DOI: 10.1007/s40617-023-00864-3 PMID: 38405282

Crevier, D. (1993). *AI: The Tumultuous Search for Artificial Intelligence.* BasicBooks.

Cross, J. R., & Cross, T. L. (2015). Clinical and mental health issues in counseling the gifted individual. *Journal of Counseling and Development*, 93(2), 163–172. DOI: 10.1002/j.1556-6676.2015.00192.x

Cummings, M. L., Roff, H. M., Cukier, K., Parakilas, J., & Bryce, H. (2018). *Artificial intelligence and international affairs: Disruption anticipated.* Chatham House, International Security Department & US and the Americas Programme. Retrieved from https://www.chathamhouse.org/sites/default/files/publications/research/2018-06-14-artificial-intelligence-international-affairs-cummings-roff-cukier-parakilas-bryce.pdf

Cummings, L. (2014). *The communication disorders workbook.* Cambridge University Press. DOI: 10.1017/CBO9781107295117

Curtin, D. (2023). *Evidence-based practices in education.*https://plt4m.com/blog/evidence-based-practices-in-education/

Dafoe, A., Hughes, E., Bachrach, Y., Collins, T., McKee, K., Leibo, J., Larson, K., & Graepel, T. (2020). Open Problems in Cooperative AI. *ArXiv*, abs/2012.08630.

Dahmani, L., & Bohbot, V. D. (2020). Habitual use of GPS negatively impacts spatial memory during self-guided naviga-tion. *Scientific Reports*, 10(1), 6310. DOI: 10.1038/s41598-020-62877-0 PMID: 32286340

Dange, P., Mistry, T., & Mann, S. (2023). AI and assistive technologies for persons with disabilities: Worldwide trends in the scientific production using bibliometrix R tool. In *Communications in computer and information science* (pp. 24–43). https://doi.org/DOI: 10.1007/978-3-031-47997-7_3

Darling-Hammond, L., DiNapoli, M.Jr, & Kini, T. (2023). *The Federal Role in Ending Teacher Shortages*. Learning Policy Institute. DOI: 10.54300/649.892

Darvishi, A., Khosravi, H., Sadiq, S., Gašević, D., & Siemens, G. (2024). Impact of AI assistance on student agency. *Computers & Education*, 210, 104967. DOI: 10.1016/j.compedu.2023.104967

Das, A. J., & Shah, R. (2014). *Special Education Today in India [PDF]*. ResearchGate. Retrieved from https://www.researchgate.net/publica

Davids, J., Lidströmer, N., & Ashrafian, H. (2021). Artificial intelligence for physiotherapy and rehabilitation. In Lidströmer, N., & Ashrafian, H. (Eds.), *Artificial intelligence in medicine* (pp. 1–19). Springer., DOI: 10.1007/978-3-030-58080-3_339-1

Davidson Academy. (2021). *Underachievement in gifted students*. https://www.davidsonacademy.unr.edu/blog/underachievement-in-gifted-students/

Davidson Institute. (2024). *Roles in gifted education: A parent's guide*.https://www.davidsongifted.org/gifted-blog/roles-in-gifted-education-a-parents-guide/#:~:text=CLASSROOM%20TEACHER&text=In%20fact%2C%20most%20teacher%20preparation,professional%20development%20on%20gifted%20education

Davis, J., Smith, L., & Anderson, A. (2021). Artificial Intelligence-Powered Social Skills Training for Students with Autism Spectrum Disorder. *Journal of Educational Technology & Society*, 24(2), 145–158.

de Boer, A., Pijl, S. J., Post, W., & Minnaert, A. (2013). Peer acceptance and friendships of students with disabilities in general education: The role of child, peer, and classroom variables. *Social Development*, 22(4), 831–844. DOI: 10.1111/j.1467-9507.2012.00670.x de Freitas, M. P., Piai, V. A., Farias, R. H., Fernandes, A. M. R., de Moraes, R. A. G., & Leithardt, V. R. Q. (2022). Artificial Intelligence of Things Applied to Assistive Technology: A Systematic Literature Review. *Sensors (Basel)*, 22(21), 8531. DOI: 10.3390/s22218531

Delaine, D. A., Williams, D. N., Sigamoney, R., & Tull, R. G. (2016). Global Diversity and Inclusion in Engineering Education: Developing Platforms toward Global Alignment. *International Journal of Engineering Pedagogy*, 6(1), 56. DOI: 10.3991/ijep.v6i1.5372

Deligiannis, N., Panagiotopoulos, D., Patsilinakos, P., Raftopoulou, C., & Symvonis, A. (2019). Interactive and personalized activity eBooks for learning to read: The iRead case. In *Proceedings of the First Workshop on Intelligent Textbooks, International Conference on Artificial Intelligence in Education* (pp. 1-10). Chicago, IL, USA. https://ceur-ws.org/Vol-2384/paper06.pdf

Dempsey, N., Brown, C., & Bramley, G. (2012). The key to sustainable urban development in UK cities? The influence of density on social sustainability. *Progress in Planning*, 77(3), 89–141. DOI: 10.1016/j.progress.2012.01.001

Deshpande, S. (April, 2023). Supporting K-12 Learners: The Importance of Executive Functioning Development.State of Neurodiversity 2023 Report. Learnfully blog. https://learnfully.com/state-of-neurodiversity-2023-report/

Deterding, S., Dixon, D., Khaled, R., & Nacke, L. (2011, September). From Game Design Elements to Gamefulness: Creating Interactive Leisure with Gameful Design. In *Proceedings of the 15th International Academic MindTrek Conference: Envisioning Future Media Environments* (pp. 9-15). ACM. https://doi.org/DOI: 10.1145/2181037.2181040

Dhimolea, T. K., Kaplan-Rakowski, R., & Lin, L. (2022). Supporting social and emotional well-being with artificial intelligence. In Albert, V. M., Lin, L., & Spector, J. M. (Eds.), *Bridging Human and Artificial Intelligence* (pp. 125–138). Springer., DOI: 10.1007/978-3-030-84729-6_8

Diamond, A. (2013). Executive functions. *Annual Review of Psychology*, 64(1), 135–168. DOI: 10.1146/annurev-psych-113011-143750 PMID: 23020641

Diana, V. (1970). State Board of Education. Civil Action No. C-70-37 (N. D. Cal. 1970)

Díaz-Cintas, J., & Orero, P. (2006). Voice-over. In Brown, K. (Ed.), *Encyclopedia of language & linguistics* (2nd ed., pp. 477–479). Elsevier., DOI: 10.1016/B0-08-044854-2/00473-9

Dieker, L. A., Hynes, M. C., Hughes, C. E., Hardin, S., & Becht, K. (2015). TLE TeachLive (TM): Using technology to provide quality professional development in rural schools. *Rural Special Education Quarterly*, 34(3), 11–16. DOI: 10.1177/875687051503400303

Diffit. (2024). *Learning resources for all.* https://web.diffit.me/

Dillenbourg, P., & Fischer, F. (2007). Basics of computer-supported collaborative learning. Zeitschrift für Berufs- und Wirtschaftspädagogik, 21, 111-130.

Dimian, A. F., & Symons, F. J. (2022). A systematic review of risk for the development and persistence of self-injurious behavior in intellectual and developmental disabilities. *Clinical Psychology Review*, 94, 102158. Advance online publication. DOI: 10.1016/j.cpr.2022.102158 PMID: 35580423

Disability. (2023, March 7). World Health Organization (WHO). https://www.who.int/news-room/fact-sheets/detail/disability-and-health

Doidge, N. (2007). *The Brain That Changes Itself: Stories of Personal Triumph from the Frontiers of Brain Science*. Viking Penguin.

Don Johnston Incorporated. (2006). *Coby*. Don Johnston Incorporated.

Donath, J. L., Lüke, T., Graf, E., Tran, U. S., & Götz, T. (2023). Does professional development effectively support the implementation of inclusive education? A meta-analysis. *Educational Psychology Review*, 35(30), 30. Advance online publication. DOI: 10.1007/s10648-023-09752-2

Dreaver, J., Thompson, C., Girdler, S., Adolfsson, M., Black, M. H., & Falkmer, M. (2019). Success factors enabling employment for adults on the autism spectrum from employers' perspective. *Journal of Autism and Developmental Disorders*, 50(5), 1657–1667. DOI: 10.1007/s10803-019-03923-3

Desscher, L., Chacon, I. A., & Sosnovsky, S. A. (2021). *Generation of assessment questions from textbooks enriched with knowledge models* (Vol. 2895). [English], https://ceur-ws.org/Vol-2895/paper10.pdf

Drigas, A. S. (2012, June). Artificial Intelligence in Special Education: A Decade Review. *British Journal of Educational Technology*, 43(3), 498–513.

Drigas, A. S., & Ioannidou, R. E. (2013). A Review on Artificial Intelligence in Special Education. *InInternational Conference on Knowledge Systems and Web Engineering*. Springer, Berlin, Heidelberg.385-391. DOI: 10.1007/978-3-642-35879-1_46

Drigas, A., & Ioannidou, R.-E. (2012). Artificial intelligence in special education: A decade review. *International Journal of Engineering Education*, 28(1), 135–146.

Drigas, A., Kouremenos, D., & Vrettaros, J. (2008). Teaching of English to hearing impaired individuals whose mother language is the sign language. *Emerging Technologies and Information Systems for the Knowledge Society: First World Summit on the Knowledge Society,* WSKS 2008, Athens, Greece, September 24-26, 2008 *Proceedings, 1*, 263–270.

Drigas, A., Kouremenos, D., & Vrettaros, J. (2008). Teaching of English to hearing impaired individuals whose mother language is the sign language. In Lytras, M. D., Carroll, J. M., Damiani, E., & Tennyson, R. D. (Eds.), *Emerging technologies and information systems for the knowledge society. WSKS 2008 Lecture Notes in Computer Science* (Vol. 5288, pp. 263–270). Springer., DOI: 10.1007/978-3-540-87781-3_29

Drigas, A., Papanastasiou, G., & Skianis, S. (2023). The role of digital technologies, metacognition and emotional intelligence. *International Journal of Emerging Technologies.*, 18(9), 65–85. DOI: 10.3991/ijet.v18i09.38133

Drigas, S., & Ioannidou, R.-E. (2012). Artificial intelligence in special education: A decade review. *International Journal of Engineering Education*, 28(6), 1366–1372.

Duchemin, T., & Doevendans, P. (2014). AVA. Retrieved from https://www.ava .me/blog on 20 June 2024.

Duffy, E. I., Garry, J., Talbot, L., Pasternak, D., Flinn, A., Minardi, C., Dookram, M., Grant, K., Fitzgerald, D., Rubano, J., Vosswinkel, J., & Jawa, R. S. (2018). A pilot study assessing the spiritual, emotional, physical/environmental, and physiological needs of mechanically ventilated surgical intensive care unit patients via eye tracking devices, head nodding, and communication boards. *Trauma Surgery & Acute Care Open*, 3(1), e000180. DOI: 10.1136/tsaco-2018-000180

Ebo, B. A. (2018). Constructivism or Behaviorism: What is the Best Method to Teach Special Needs Students? *Journal of Healthcare, Science and the Humanities*, 8(2), 45–56.

Economic Commission for Latin America and the Caribbean. (2021). *Digital technologies for a new future: Production, productivity and management*. ECLAC Headquarters.

Eden, C. A., Nneamaka, O. N., & Adeniyi, I. S.Chima Abimbola EdenOnyebuchi Nneamaka ChisomIdowu Sulaimon Adeniyi. (2024). Parent and community involvement in education: Strengthening partnerships for social improvement. *International Journal of Applied Research in Social Sciences*, 6(3), 372–382. DOI: 10.51594/ijarss.v6i3.894

Edpuzzle, Inc. (n.d). Edpuzzle. Retrieved [27th June 2024], from https://edpuzzle.com on 20 June 2024.

Edutopia. (2023). *Using ChatGPT to support student-led inquiry.*https://www.edutopia.org/article/using-chatgpt-support-student-led-inquiry/?gad_source=1&gclid=CjwKCAjwrIixBhBbEiwACEqDJYrYiCqWwl0YSCWwSupsfjRx0s_VWTDIQg1anQ2hBIFQUn8NMNJhlRoCDoIQAvD_BwE

Edwards, E., & Vlachokyriakos, V. (2017). Artificial intelligence in the home: How to help humans think. In *Proceedings of the 2017 ACM Conference on Computer Supported Cooperative Work and Social Computing*, 363-375

Edyburn, D. L. (2023). Reimagining the Future of Special Education Technology. In *Reimagining Education: Studies and Stories for Effective Learning in an Evolving Digital Environment* (pp. 281–292). Springer International Publishing. DOI: 10.1007/978-3-031-25102-3_23

Elasri, M., Elharrouss, O., Al-Maadeed, S., & Tairi, H. (2022). Image generation: A review. *Neural Processing Letters*, 54(5), 4609–4646. DOI: 10.1007/s11063-022-10777-x

Elevenlabs. (2023). *Generative voice AI.* https://elevenlabs.io/

Ellis, V., Steadman, S., & Mao, Q. (2020). 'Come to a screeching halt': Can change in teacher education during the COVID-19 pandemic be seen as innovation? *European Journal of Teacher Education*, 43(4), 559–572. DOI: 10.1080/02619768.2020.1821186

Elsahar, Y., Hu, S., Bouazza-Marouf, K., Kerr, D., & Mansor, A. (2019). Augmentative and Alternative Communication (AAC) Advances: A Review of Configurations for Speech Disabled Individuals.

Emerging Technologies and Trends. (June 3, 2022). *3 Ways AI Can Help Students with Disabilities.*" *The Voice of the Higher Education Technology Community: EDUCAUSE Review.* https://er.educause.edu/articles/2022/6/3-ways-ai-can-help-students-with-disabilities

Emotiplay. (n.d). Emotiplay. Retrieved from https://www.emotiplay.com/blog/ on 1 June 2024.

Entenberg, G. A., Areas, M., Roussos, A. J., Maglio, A. L., Thrall, J., Escoredo, M., & Bunge, E. L. (2021). Using an artificial intelligence-based chatbot to provide parent training: Results from a feasibility study. *Social Sciences (Basel, Switzerland)*, 10(11), 426. DOI: 10.3390/socsci10110426

Er, M., Andres, E., Budenbender, J., Frischauf, A., Goguadze, G., Libbrecht, P., Pollet, M., & Ullrich, C. (2001). ActiveMath: A generic and adaptive web-based learning environment. *Artificial Intelligence in Education, 12*.

Er, M., & Siekmann, J. (2004). ActiveMath: An intelligent tutoring system for mathematics. In Rutkowski, L., Siekmann, J., Tadeusiewicz, R., & Zadeh, L. A. *(Eds.),Seventh International Conference on Artificial Intelligence and Soft Computing (ICAISC)* (pp. 91–101). Springer-Verlag. https://doi.org/DOI: 10.1007/978-3-540-24844-6_12

Ersozlu, Z., Ledger, S., Ersozlu, A., Mayne, F., & Wildy, H. (2021). Mixed-reality learning environments in teacher education: An analysis of TeachLivE™ research. *SAGE Open*, 11(3), 21582440211032155. Advance online publication. DOI: 10.1177/21582440211032155

Ertmer, P. A., Paul, A., Molly, L., Eva, R., & Denise, W. (2012). Examining teachers' beliefs about the role of technology in the classroom. *Journal of Research on Technology in Education*, 45(2), 101–125.

Espinoza, D., Saunders, R., Kini, T., & Darling-Hammond, L. (2018). Taking the long view: state efforts to solve teacher shortages by strengthening the profession. *Learning Policy Institute*. https://learningpolicyinstitute.org/product/long-view-report

Esposito, M. C., Hamdan, K., & Benitez, X. (2014), "Providing Effective Special Education Teachers in Low-Income Urban Settings: Implications for Educational Leadership", *Pathways to Excellence: Developing and Cultivating Leaders for the Classroom and Beyond* (*Advances in Educational Administration, Vol. 21*), Emerald Group Publishing Limited, Leeds, pp. 205-219.

Exploring the Role of AI in Special Education. (2024, February 29). 21K Schools. https://www.21kschool.com/us/blog/ai-in-special-education/#:~:text=The%20Potential%20of%20AI%20in%20Special%20Education,-AI%20holds%20immense&text=This%20personalization%20can%20maximize%20learning,with%20speech%20impairments%20communicate%20effectively

Eynon-Lynch, R., & Eynon-Lynch, M. (2015). *Pear Deck*. Pear Deck, Inc.

Falcomata, T. S., Roane, H. S., Muething, C. S., Stephenson, K. M., & Ing, A. D. (2012). Functional communication training and chained schedules of reinforcement to treat challenging behavior maintained by terminations of activity interruptions. *Behavior Modification*, 36(5), 630–649. DOI: 10.1177/0145445511433821 PMID: 22327267

Family Educational Rights and Privacy Act (FERPA), 20 U.S.C. § 1232g; 34 CFR Part 99 (1974).

Faris, D. (2024). Why are professors trying to escape their jobs? *The Week*. https://theweek.com/education/professors-leaving-academia

Federal Trade Commission. (2024). Children's Online Privacy Protection Rule. Retrieved from https://www.ftc.gov/legal-library/browse/rules/childrens-online-privacy-protection-rule-coppa

Ferguson, J., Craig, E. A., & Dounavi, K. (2019). Telehealth as a model for providing behavior analytic interventions to individuals with autism spectrum disorder: A systematic review. *Journal of Autism and Developmental Disorders*, 49(2), 582–616. DOI: 10.1007/s10803-018-3724-5 PMID: 30155578

Fernandez, N., & Hynes, J. W. (2016). The Efficacy of Pullout Programs in Elementary Schools: Making it work. *The Journal of Multidisciplinary Graduate Research*, 2 (3),32-47. Retrieved from https://www.shsu.edu/academics/education/journal-of-multidisciplinary-graduate-research/documents/2016/Article%203%20-%202016%20-%20Fernandez%20and%20Hynes.pdf on 1 June 2024.

Fernandez, M., Hernandez, A., & Garcia, R. (2022). Predicting Learning Disabilities using Machine Learning Algorithms. *Computers & Education*, 178, 104388.

Ferrara, E. (2024). Fairness and bias in artificial intelligence: A brief survey of sources, impacts, and mitigation strategies. *Science*, 6(1), 3. DOI: 10.3390/sci6010003

Ferrer, X., Van Nuenen, T., Such, J. M., Coté, M., & Criado, N. (2021). Bias and discrimination in AI: A cross-disciplinary perspective. *IEEE Technology and Society Magazine*, 40(2), 72–80. DOI: 10.1109/MTS.2021.3056293

Ferrucci, D. A. (2012). Introduction to "This is Watson". *IBM Journal of Research and Development, 56*(3.4), 1:1-1:15. https://doi.org/DOI: 10.1147/JRD.2012.2184356

Filatov, V., Zolotukhin, O., Yerokhin, A., & Kudryavtseva, M. (2019, September). Personalized adaptation of learning environments. In *2019 IEEE 8th International Conference on Advanced Optoelectronics and Lasers (CAOL)* (pp. 584-587). IEEE. DOI: 10.1109/CAOL46282.2019.9019525

Fisher, J. D., Fancsali, S. E., Lewis, A. J., Fisher, V. A., Hausmann, R. G. M., Pavelko, M., Bartle Finocchi, S., & Ritter, S. (2020). *LiveHint: Intelligent digital support for analog learning experiences*. Carnegie Learning, Inc. Retrieved from http://CEUR-WS.org/Vol-2674/paper08.pdf

Fisher, W. W., Greer, B. D., Querim, A. C., & DeRosa, N. (2014). Decreasing excessive functional communication responses while treating destructive behavior using response restriction. *Research in Developmental Disabilities*, 35(11), 2614–2623. DOI: 10.1016/j.ridd.2014.06.024 PMID: 25036315

Fitch, F. (2003). Inclusion, exclusion, and ideology: Special education students' changing sense of self. *The Urban Review*, 35(3), 233–252. DOI: 10.1023/A:1025733719935

Fitria, T. N. (2021, December). Artificial Intelligence in Education: Using AI tools for Teaching and Learning Process [Conference paper]. *ResearchGate*. https://www.researchgate.net/publication/357447234

Flores, M. A., & Craig, C. J. (2023). Reimagining teacher education in light of the teacher shortage and the aftershock of COVID-19: Adjusting to a rapidly shifting world. *European Journal of Teacher Education*, 46(5), 772–788. DOI: 10.1080/02619768.2023.2294697

Floridi, L., & Taddeo, M. (2016). What is Data Ethics? *Philosophical Transactions. Series A, Mathematical, Physical, and Engineering Sciences*, 374(2083), 20160360. DOI: 10.1098/rsta.2016.0360 PMID: 28336805

Floyd, D. L., & Walker, D. A. (2003). Community college teacher education: A typology, challenging issues, and state views. *Community College Journal of Research and Practice*, 27(8), 643–663. DOI: 10.1080/713838241

Ford, D. Y., Hines, E. M., Middleton, T. J., & Moore, J. L.III. (2024). Brown vs. Board of Education: Implications for Gifted and Talented Education. *Gifted Child Today*, 47(3), 216–220. DOI: 10.1177/10762175241242493

Forgatch, M. S., & Gewirtz, A. H. (2018). The evolution of the Oregon Model of Parent Management Training: An Intervention for Antisocial Behavior in Children and Adolescents. In Weisz, J. R., & Kazdin, A. E. (Eds.), *Evidence-based psychotherapies for children and adolescents* (pp. 85–102). The Guilford Press.

Francois, J. (2020) "Teaching Beliefs and Their Relationship to Professional Development in Special Education Teachers," Educational Considerations: Vol. 45: No. 3. DOI: 10.4148/0146-9282.2195

Francom, G. M., Lee, S. J., & Pinkney, H. (2021). Technologies, Challenges and Needs of K-12 Teachers in the Transition to Distance Learning during the COVID-19 Pandemic. *TechTrends*, 65(4), 589–601. DOI: 10.1007/s11528-021-00625-5 PMID: 34223560

Frederick, D. E. (2024). Prompt engineering–a disruption in information seeking? *Library Hi Tech News*, 41(3), 1–5. DOI: 10.1108/LHTN-03-2024-0037

Freund, Y., & Schapire, R. E. (1999). Large margin classification using the perceptron algorithm. *Machine Learning*, 37(3), 277–296. DOI: 10.1023/A:1007662407062

Fridenson-Hayo, S., Berggren, S., Lassalle, A., Tal, S., Pigat, D., Meir-Goren, N., O'Reilly, H., Ben-Zur, S., Bölte, S., Baron-Cohen, S., & Golan, O. (2017). 'Emotiplay': A serious game for learning about emotions in children with autism: Results of a cross-cultural evaluation. *European Child & Adolescent Psychiatry*, 26(8), 979–992. DOI: 10.1007/s00787-017-0968-0

Frolli, A., Ricci, M. C., Di Carmine, F., Lombardi, A., Bosco, A., Saviano, E., & Franzese, L. (2021). The Impact of COVID-19 on Cognitive Development and Executive Functioning in Adolescents: A First Exploratory Investigation. *Brain Sciences*, 11(9), 1222. Advance online publication. DOI: 10.3390/brainsci11091222 PMID: 34573241

Frontline Education. (1998). Special Ed & Interventions [Educational software]. Retrieved from https://www.frontlineeducation.com/products/special-education-interventions/ on 1 June 2024.

Frontline Education. (2021). *Teacher shortages: The new normal.*https://www.frontlineeducation.com/solutions/recruiting-hiring/insights/teacher-shortages-new-normal/

Fröscher, L., Friedrich, A.-K., Berentelg, M., Widmer, C., Gilbert, S. J., & Papenmeier, F. (2022). Framing cognitive off-loading in terms of gains or losses: Achieving a more optimal use of reminders. Cognitive Research: Principles andImplications, 7(1), 61. DOI: 10.1186/s41235-022-00416-3

Fryling, M. J., Wallace, M. D., & Yassine, J. N. (2012). Impact of treatment integrity on intervention effectiveness. *Journal of Applied Behavior Analysis*, 45(2), 449–453. DOI: 10.1901/jaba.2012.45-449 PMID: 22844155

Fuches, W. (2009). Examining teachers perceived barriers associated with inclusion. *SRATE Journal*, 19(1), 30–35.

Fuchs, L. S., Fuchs, D., Hamlett, C. L., & Stecker, P. M. (2021). Bringing data-based individualization to scale: A call for the next-generation technology of teacher supports. *Journal of Learning Disabilities*, 54(5), 319–333. DOI: 10.1177/0022219420950654 PMID: 33813936

Fulk, G. (2023). Artificial intelligence and neurologic physical therapy. *Journal of Neurologic Physical Therapy; JNPT*, 47(1), 1–2. DOI: 10.1097/NPT.0000000000000426 PMID: 36534016

Fullan, M. (2007). Change theory as a force for school improvement. In *Intelligent leadership: Constructs for thinking education leaders* (pp. 27–39). Springer Netherlands. DOI: 10.1007/978-1-4020-6022-9_3

Furlong, L., Morris, M., Serry, T., & Erickson, S. (2018). Mobile apps for treatment of speech disorders in children: An evidence-based analysis of quality and efficacy. *PLoS One*, 13(8), e0201513. DOI: 10.1371/journal.pone.0201513 PMID: 30092095

Gal, N., Andrei, D., Nemeş, D. I., Nădăşan, E., & Stoicu-Tivadar, V. (2015). A Kinect based intelligent e-rehabilitation system in physical therapy. *Studies in Health Technology and Informatics*, 210, 489–493.

Gander, T., & Shaw, B. (2024). AI in education 2023: Understanding the impact on effective pedagogy, inclusive learning and equitable outcomes. *He Rourou*, 1(1), 15. DOI: 10.54474/herourou.v1i1.9137

García-Martínez, I. (2023). Analyzing the Impact of Artificial Intelligence and Computational Sciences on Student Performance: Systematic Review and Meta-Analysis. *Journal of Educational Technology*, 45(2), 123–145.

Garg, S., & Sharma, S. (2020). Impact of Artificial Intelligence in Special Need Education to Promote Inclusive Pedagogy. *International Journal of Information and Education Technology (IJIET)*, 10(7), 514–519. DOI: 10.18178/ijiet.2020.10.7.1418

Garrad, T.-A., Vlcek, S., & Page, A. (2022). The importance of the promotion of evidence-based practice as a reasonable adjustment in mainstream education settings for students with Autism Spectrum Disorder. *Australasian Journal of Special and Inclusive Education*, 46(1), 101–112. DOI: 10.1017/jsi.2022.5

Garrett, B., Taverner, T., Gromala, D., Tao, G., Cordingley, E., & Sun, C. (2018). Virtual reality clinical research: Promises and challenges. *JMIR Serious Games*, 6(4), e10839. Advance online publication. DOI: 10.2196/10839 PMID: 30333096

Garza-Mitchell. Geier, & Singleton. (2019). Community college teacher education: Fulfilling the workforce development mission for diverse geographies. In C. Lewis & M. D'Amico (Eds.), Community college teacher preparation for diverse geographies (pp. 15-32). Information Age Publishing, Inc.

Gelbar, N. W., Smith, I., & Reichow, B. (2014). Systematic review of articles describing experience and supports of individuals with autism enrolled in college and university programs. *Journal of Autism and Developmental Disorders*, 44(10), 2593–2601. DOI: 10.1007/s10803-014-2135-5

Georgopoulos, V. C., Malandraki, G. A., & Stylios, C. D. (2003). A fuzzy cognitive map approach to differential diagnosis of specific language impairment. *Artificial Intelligence in Medicine*, 29(3), 261–278. DOI: 10.1016/S0933-3657(02)00076-3

Ge, S., Zhu, Z., Wu, B., & McConnell, E. S. (2018). Technology-based cognitive training and rehabilitation interventions for individuals with mild cognitive impairment: A systematic review. *BMC Geriatrics*, 18(1), 213. DOI: 10.1186/s12877-018-0893-1 PMID: 30219036

Getting Smart. (2016). *Bridging the Knowledge Gap on Special Needs Learner Support.* Retrieved March 22, 2024, from https://www.gettingsmart.com/2016/07/11/bridging-the-knowledge-gap-of-special-education-students/

Ghaemmaghami, M., Hanley, G. P., & Jessel, J. (2021). Functional communication training: From efficacy to effectiveness. *Journal of Applied Behavior Analysis*, 54(1), 122–143. DOI: 10.1002/jaba.762 PMID: 32929757

Ghafghazi, S., Carnett, A., Neely, L., Das, A., & Rad, P. (2021). AI-augmented Behavior Analysis for Children with Developmental Disabilities: Building towards Precision Treatment. Child and Adolescent Policy and Research Institute (CAPRI); *Secure AI Laboratory for Autonomy* (AILA). 1-6.

Ghanouni, P., Jarus, T., Zwicker, J. G., & Lucyshyn, J. (2020). The use of technologies among individuals with autism spectrum disorders: Barriers and challenges. *Journal of Special Education Technology*, 35(4), 286–294. DOI: 10.1177/0162643419888765

Ghergulescu, I., Flynn, C., & O'Sullivan, C. (2015). Adaptemy Science: Adaptive learning for science for next generation classroom. In *E-Learn: World Conference on E-Learning in Corporate, Government, Healthcare, and Higher Education* (pp. 1477–1482). Association for the Advancement of Computing in Education (AACE). https://www.learntechlib.org/primary/p/152190/

Ghosh, S., & Sankar, C. S. (2024). Competency-Based Teacher Education in Gender and Inclusive Practices. *Social Science Journal for Advanced Research*, 4(5), 18–25.

Giani, M. S., Krawietz, C. E., & Whittaker, T. A. (2023). The Role of Student Beliefs in Dual-Enrollment Courses. *Research in Higher Education*, 64(8), 1113–1142. DOI: 10.1007/s11162-023-09740-z PMID: 37359447

Gierdowski, D. C., & Galanek, J. D. (2020). *ECAR Study of the Technology Needs of Students with Disabilities, 2020. Research report.* ECAR.

Gillett-Swan, J., & Grant-Smith, D. (2018). A framework for managing the impacts of work-integrated learning on student quality of life. *International Journal of Work-Integrated Learning*, 19(2), 129–140. https://eprints.qut.edu.au/223863/

Gliozzo, A., Ackerson, C., Bhattacharya, R., Goering, A., Jumba, A., Kim, S. Y., Krishnamurthy, L., Lam, T., Littera, A., McIntosh, I., Murthy, S., & Ribas, M. (2017). Building Cognitive Applications with IBM Watson Services: Volume 1 Getting Started. International Technical Support Organization, IBM RedBook. https://www.redbooks.ibm.com/redbooks/pdfs/sg248387.pdf

Goeke, J. L., Kossar, K. R., & Mitchem, K. J. (Eds.). (2018). *Redesigning special education teacher preparation : challenges and solutions / edited by Jennifer L. Goeke, Katherine J. Mitchem, and Kalie R. Kossar* (1st ed.). Routledge.

Goe, L. (2006). *The teacher preparation teacher practices student outcomes relationship in special education: Missing links and next steps. A research synthesis.* National Comprehensive Center for Teacher Quality.

Goldman, S. R., Taylor, J., Carreon, A., & Smith, S. J. (2024). Using AI to support special education teacher workload. *Journal of Special Education Technology*, 39(3), 434–447. DOI: 10.1177/01626434241257240

Gonzalez-Calatayud, V., Prendes-Espinosa, P., & Roig-Vila, R. (2021). Artificial intelligence for student assessment: A systematic review. *Applied Sciences (Basel, Switzerland)*, 11(12), 5467. Advance online publication. DOI: 10.3390/app11125467

Google, A. I. (2024). *Gemini* [Large language model]. https://gemini.google.com/app/d0458de8087b1246

Google. (2016). Google Assistant. Retrieved from https://assistant.google.com on 1 June 2024.

Google. (n.d.). *AI data analytics*. https://cloud.google.com/use-cases/ai-data-analytics

Gormley, L., Healy, O., O'Sullivan, B., O'Regan, D., Grey, I., & Bracken, M. (2019). The impact of behavioural skills training on the knowledge, skills and well-being of front line staff in the intellectual disability sector: A clustered randomised control trial. *Journal of Intellectual Disability Research*, 63(11), 1291–1304. DOI: 10.1111/jir.12630 PMID: 31106922

Goswami, U. (2004). Neuroscience, education and special education. *British Journal of Special Education*, 31(4), 175–183. DOI: 10.1111/j.0952-3383.2004.00352.x

Goswami, U. (2008). Principles of learning, implications for teaching: A cognitive neuroscience perspective. *Journal of Philosophy of Education*, 42(3/4), 381–399. DOI: 10.1111/j.1467-9752.2008.00639.x

Grabowski, C. (2023). *A review of the use of artificial intelligence to enhance the practice of speech-language pathology*. Abe Books.

Graesser, A. C. (2013). Evolution of advanced learning technologies in the 21st century. *Theory into Practice*, 52(1), 93–101. DOI: 10.1080/00405841.2013.795446

Graham, S., & Harris, K. R. (2003). *Writing Better: Teaching Writing Process and Self-Regulation to Students with Learning Problems*. Brookes Publishing.

Granquist, C., Sun, S. Y., Montezuma, S. R., Tran, T. M., Gage, R., & Legge, G. E. (2021). Evaluation and Comparison of Artificial Intelligence Vision Aids: Orcam MyEye 1 and Seeing AI. *Journal of Visual Impairment & Blindness*, 115(4), 277–285. DOI: 10.1177/0145482X211027492

Gravel, J., D'Amours-Gravel, M., & Osmanlliu, E. (2023). Learning to fake it: Limited responses and fabricated references provided by ChatGPT for medical questions. *Mayo Clinic Proceedings. Digital Health*, 1(3), 226–234. DOI: 10.1016/j.mcpdig.2023.05.004

Grawemeyer, B., Holmes, W., Mavrikis, M., Hansen, A., Loibl, K., & Gutiérrez-Santos, S. (2017). Affective versus cognitive behavior modeling for better educational outcomes. In Leonidis, A., & Bouras, C. (Eds.), *UMAP 2017: Proceedings of the 25th Conference on User Modeling, Adaptation, and Personalization* (pp. 268-279). Springer. DOI: 10.1007/978-3-319-93843-1_19

Grewal, S. (2014). A critical conceptual analysis of definitions of AI as applicable to computer. *IOSR Journal of Computer Engineering*, 16(2), 9–13. DOI: 10.9790/0661-16210913

Griffiths, A. J., Giannantonio, C. M., Hurley-Hanson, A. E., & Cardinal, D. N. (2016). Autism in the workplace: Assessing the transition needs of young adults with autism spectrum disorder. *Journal of Business and Management*, 22(1), 5–22. DOI: 10.1504/JBM.2016.141233

Gruber, A., & Kaplan-Rakowski, R. (2020). User experience of public speaking practice in virtual reality. In Zheng, R. Z. (Ed.), *Cognitive and affective perspectives on immersive technology in education* (pp. 235–249). IGI Global. DOI: 10.4018/978-1-7998-3250-8.ch012

Gudlin, M., Ivanković, I., & Dadić, K. (2022). Robots used in therapy for children with autism spectrum disorder. *American Journal of Multidisciplinary Research & Development*, 4(3), 33–39. https://www.ajmrd.com/wp-content/uploads/2022/03/E433339.pdf

Guerriero, S. (Ed.). (2017). *Educational research and innovation pedagogical knowledge and the changing nature of the teaching profession*. OECD Publishing., DOI: 10.1787/9789264270695-

Guilherme, A. (2019). AI and education: The importance of teacher and student relations. *AI & Society*, 34(1), 47–54. DOI: 10.1007/s00146-017-0693-8

Gunnar, F. (2024). A Systematic Review of Special Educational Interventions for Student Attention: Executive Function and Digital Technology in Primary School. *Journal of Special Education Technology*, 39(2), 264–276. DOI: 10.1177/01626434231198226

Guo, L., Wang, D., Gu, F., Zhang, Y., & Zhang, Y. (2021). Evolution and trends in intelligent tutoring systems research: A multidisciplinary and scientometric view. *Asia Pacific Education Review*, 22(3), 441–461. DOI: 10.1007/s12564-021-09697-7

Guo, Y., Liu, Y., Oerlemans, A., Lao, S., Wu, S., & Lew, M. S. (2016). Deep learning for visual understanding: A review. *Neurocomputing*, 187, 27–48. DOI: 10.1016/j.neucom.2015.09.116

Gupta, R. K., & Ahmad, W. (2022). Universal Design for Learning. In Ahmad, W., Chavan, B. S., & Gupta, R. K. (Eds.), *Comprehensive Textbook on Disability* (pp. 558–563). Jaypee Brothers Medical Publishers.

Hakkal, S., & Ait Lahcen, A. (2021). An overview of adaptive learning fee-based platforms. In *Proceedings of the 2nd International Conference on Big Data, Modelling and Machine Learning (BML 2021)* (pp. 222-226). https://doi.org/DOI: 10.5220/0010731400003101

Hallahan, D. P., & Kauffman, J. M. (1977). Labels, categories, behaviors: ED, LD, and EMR reconsidered. *The Journal of Special Education*, 11(2), 139–149. DOI: 10.1177/002246697701100202

Han, X., Hu, L., Han, D., Peng, Y., Wang, Y., Yan, C., & Wang, Z. (2022). International Conference on Social Science, Education and Management (ICSSEM 2022). CSP.

Han, X., Hu, L., Han, D., Peng, Y., Wang, Y., Yan, C., & Wang, Z. (2022). Research on the Application of Artificial Intelligence in Special Education. In *International Conference on Social Science, Education and Management*. Harvard University's Graduate School of Education.(nd). https://www.gse.harvard.edu/ideas/usable-knowledge/24/09/students-are-using-ai-already-heres-what-they-think-adults-should-know#:~:text=Many%20participants%20reported%20using%20AI,use%20it%20to%20write%20code

Haneya, H., AlKaf, D., Bajammal, F., & Brahimi, T. (2021). A meta-analysis of artificial intelligence applications for tracking COVID-19: The case of the UAE. *Procedia Computer Science*, 194, 180–189. DOI: 10.1016/j.procs.2021.10.072 PMID: 34876933

Hanley, G. P., Iwata, B. A., & Thompson, R. H. (2001). Reinforcement schedule thinning following treatment with functional communication training. *Journal of Applied Behavior Analysis*, 34(1), 17–38. DOI: 10.1901/jaba.2001.34-17 PMID: 11317985

Haoues, M., & Mokni, R. (2023). Toward an autism-friendly environment based on mobile apps user feedback analysis using deep learning and machine learning models. *PeerJ. Computer Science*, 9, e1442. DOI: 10.7717/peerj-cs.1442

Hardy, J. L., Drescher, D., Sarkar, K., Kellett, G., & Scanlon, M. (2011). Enhancing visual attention and working memory with a web-based cognitive training program. *Mensa Research Journal*, 42(2), 13–20.

Harfouche, A., Quinio, B., & Bugiotti, F. (2023). Human-Centric AI to Mitigate AI Biases. *Journal of Global Information Management*, 31(5), 1–23. Advance online publication. DOI: 10.4018/JGIM.331755

Harry, A., & Sayudin, S. (2023). Role of AI in education. [INJURITY]. *Interdisciplinary Journal and Humanity*, 2(3), 260–268. DOI: 10.58631/injurity.v2i3.52

Ha, S. H., & Park, C. G. (2017). The use of artificial intelligence in educational systems: Benefits and challenges. *Journal of Educational Technology Development and Exchange*, 10(1), 55–66.

Hasanov, A., Laine, T. H., & Chung, T. S. (2019). A survey of adaptive context-aware learning environments. *Journal of Ambient Intelligence and Smart Environments*, 11(5), 403–428. DOI: 10.3233/AIS-190534

Hatch, D. K., & Garcia, C. E. (2017). Academic advising and the persistence intentions of community college students in their first weeks in college. *Review of Higher Education*, 40(3), 353–390. DOI: 10.1353/rhe.2017.0012

Hedges, S. H., Odom, S. L., Hume, K., & Sam, A. (2018). Technology use as a support tool by secondary students with autism. *Autism*, 22(1), 70–79. DOI: 10.1177/1362361317717976

Heffernan, N. T., & Heffernan, C. L. (2014). The ASSISTments ecosystem: Building a platform that brings scientists and teachers together for minimally invasive research on human learning and teaching. *International Journal of Artificial Intelligence in Education*, 24(4), 470–497. DOI: 10.1007/s40593-014-0024-x

Hegde, M. N., & Freed, D. (2020). *Assessment of communication disorders in adults: Resources and protocols*. Plural Publishing.

Heng, L. E., Voon, W. P., Jalil, N. A., Kwun, C. L., Chieh, T. C., & Subri, N. F. (2021). Personalization of learning content in learning management system. *Proceedings of the 2021 10th International Conference on Software and Computer Applications*. DOI: 10.1145/3457784.3457819

Heppen, J. B., & Therriault, S. B. (2008). Developing Early Warning Systems to Identify Potential High School Dropouts. Issue Brief. *National High School Center*.

Hernandez, J., Mousalli, G., & Rivas, F. (2008). Expert system for the diagnosis of learning difficulties in children's basic education. In Proceedings of the 8th WSEAS International Conference on Applied Computer and Applied Computational Science: Italy. http://www.wseas.us/e-library/conferences/2009/hangzhou/ACACOS/ACACOS09.pdf

Herrero, S., & Sabrià, Q. (2013). *Edpuzzle*. Edpuzzle, Inc.

Hessen, S. H., Abdul-Kader, H. M., Khedr, A. E., & Salem, R. K. (2022). Developing Multiagent E-Learning System-Based Machine Learning and Feature Selection Techniques. *Computational Intelligence and Neuroscience*, 2022(1), 2941840. DOI: 10.1155/2022/2941840 PMID: 35140765

Hester, O. R., Bridges, S. A., & Rollins, L. H. (2020). 'Overworked and underappreciated': Special education teachers describe stress and attrition. *Teacher Development*, 24(3), 348–365. DOI: 10.1080/13664530.2020.1767189

Hiebert, J., & Grouws, D. A. (2007). The effects of classroom mathematics teaching on students' learning. *Second handbook of research on mathematics teaching and learning*, 1(1), 371-404.

Hill-Jackson, V., & Lewis, C. W. (Eds.). (2023). *Transforming teacher education: What went wrong with teacher training, and how we can fix it*. Taylor & Francis.

Hind, M., Mehta, S., Mojsilovic, A., Nair, R., Ramamurthy, K., Olteanu, A., & Varshney, K. R. (2018). Increasing trust in AI services through supplier's declarations of conformity. *arXiv*. https://arxiv.org/abs/1808.07261

Hirsch, S. E., Kennedy, M. J., Haines, S. J., Thomas, C. N., & Alves, K. D. (2015). Improving preservice teachers' knowledge and application of functional behavioral assessments using multimedia. *Behavioral Disorders*, 41(1), 38–50. DOI: 10.17988/0198-7429-41.1.38

Hmelo-Silver, C. E. (2004). Problem-based learning: What and how do students learn? *Educational Psychology Review*, 16(3), 235–266. DOI: 10.1023/B:EDPR.0000034022.16470.f3

Hobson v. Hansen (1967) 269 F.Supp. 401; (1971) 327 F.Supp 844.

Holmes, W., Porayska-Pomsta, K., Holstein, K., Sutherland, E., Baker, T., Buckingham Shum, S., Santos, O. C., Rodrigo, M. M. T., Cukorova, M., Bittencourt, I. I., & Koedinger, K. (2021). Ethics of AI in education: Towards a community-wide

Holmes, W. (2020). Artificial intelligence in education. In Tatnall, A. (Ed.), *Encyclopedia of education and information technologies* (pp. 88–103). Springer., DOI: 10.1007/978-3-030-10576-1_107

Holmes, W., Bialik, M., & Fadel, C. (2019). *Artificial Intelligence in Education: Promises and Implications for Teaching and Learning*. Center for Curriculum Redesign.

Holmes, W., Porayska-Pomsta, K., Holstein, K., Sutherland, E., Baker, T., Shum, S. B., Santos, O. C., Rodrigo, M. T., Cukurova, M., Bittencourt, I. I., & Koedinger, K. R. (2022, September). framework. *International Journal of Artificial Intelligence in Education*, 32(3), 504–526. DOI: 10.1007/s40593-021-00239-1

Holmes, W., & Tuomi, I. (2022). State of the art and practice in AI in education. *European Journal of Education*, 57(4), 542–570. DOI: 10.1111/ejed.12533

Holstein, K., McLaren, B. M., & Aleven, V. (2019). Co-designing a real-time classroom orchestration tool to support teacher–AI complementarity. *Journal of Learning Analytics*, 6(2). Advance online publication. DOI: 10.18608/jla.2019.62.3

Homer, B. D., Plass, J. L., Raffaele, C., Ober, T. M., & Ali, A. (2018). Improving High School Students' Executive Functions through Digital Game Play. *Computers & Education*, 117, 50–58. DOI: 10.1016/j.compedu.2017.09.011

Hopcan, S., Polat, E., Ozturk, M. E., & Ozturk, L. (2023). Artificial intelligence in special education: A systematic review. *Interactive Learning Environments*, 31(10), 7335–7353. DOI: 10.1080/10494820.2022.2067186

Horváth, I. (2020). Personalized learning opportunity in 3D VR. In 2020 11th IEEE International Conference on Cognitive Infocommunications (CogInfoCom) (pp. 425-430). Mariehamn, Finland. DOI: 10.1109/CogInfoCom50765.2020.9237895

Hough, L. (2018, May 22). Tool in school: Quizlet. ED. Magazine, Harvard Graduate School of Education. https://www.gse.harvard.edu/news/ed/18/05/tool-school-quizlet

Howarth, E., Vabulas, G., Connolly, S., Green, D., & Smolley, S. (2024). Developing accessible speech technology with users with dysarthric speech. *Assistive Technology*, •••, 1–8. DOI: 10.1080/10400435.2024.2328082 PMID: 38537126

Howlin, C., & Lynch, D. (2014). Learning and academic analytics in the RealizeIt system. https://doi.org/DOI: 10.13140/2.1.3811.1689

Hoy, M. B. (2018). Alexa, Siri, Cortana, and More: An Introduction to Voice Assistants. *Medical Reference Services Quarterly*, 37(1), 81–88. DOI: 10.1080/02763869.2018.1404391 PMID: 29327988

Hu, C., Li, W., Ruan, M., Yu, X., Paul, L. K., Wang, S., & Li, X. (2024). Exploiting ChatGPT for Diagnosing Autism-Associated Language Disorders and Identifying Distinct Features. *arXiv preprint arXiv:2405.01799.*

Huang, L. (2023). *Ethics of artificial intelligence in education: Student privacy and data protection*. Science Insights Education Frontiers., DOI: 10.15254.sief.23.re202

Huang, W., Billinghurst, M., Alem, L., Xiao, C., & Rasmussen, T. (2024). *Computer-Supported Collaboration: Theory and Practice*. John Wiley & Sons. DOI: 10.1002/9781119719830

Huera, E. N. M., Novay, E. G. Z., Meneses, A. L. T., & Villacrés, R. C. I. (2024). Curricular adaptations based on Information and Communication Technologies for students with special educational needs. *Sinergias Educativas, 9*(1).

Hughes, C., Dieker, L., Glavey, E., Hines, R., Wilkins, I., Ingraham, K., Bukaty, C., Ali, K., Shah, S., Murphy, J., & Taylor, M. (2022). RAISE: Robotics & AI to improve STEM and social skills for elementary school students. *Frontiers in Virtual Reality*, 3, 968312. Advance online publication. DOI: 10.3389/frvir.2022.968312

Hume, K., Steinbrenner, J. R., Odom, S. L., Morin, K. L., Nowell, S. W., Tomaszewski, B., Szendrey, S., McIntyre, N. S., Yücesoy-Özkan, S., & Savage, M. N. (2021). Evidence-based practices for children, youth, and young adults with autism: Third generation review. *Journal of Autism and Developmental Disorders*, 51(11), 4013–4032. DOI: 10.1007/s10803-020-04844-2

Hunt, X., Saran, A., White, H., & Kuper, H. (2021). PROTOCOL: Effectiveness of Interventions for Improving Educational Outcomes for People With Disabilities in Low- and Middle-income Countries: A Systematic Review. *Campbell Systematic Reviews*, 17(4), e1197. DOI: 10.1002/cl2.1197

Huron & Ohio., (2024, June 6). n2y wins "Special Education Solution of the Year" designation in 6th annual EdTech Breakthrough Awards program: Prestigious international awards program recognizes outstanding educational technology products and companies [Press release]. PR Newswire.

Hussain, Z., Binz, M., Mata, R., & Wulff, D. U. (2024). A tutorial on open-source large language models for behavioral science. *Behavior Research Methods*. Advance online publication. DOI: 10.3758/s13428-024-02455-8 PMID: 39147947

Iannone, A., & Giansanti, D. (2023). Breaking Barriers-The Intersection of AI and Assistive Technology in Autism Care: A Narrative Review. *Journal of Personalized Medicine*, 14(1), 41. DOI: 10.3390/jpm14010041

Ibe, N. A., Howsmon, R., Penney, L., Granor, N., DeLyser, L. A., & Wang, K. (2018, February). Reflections of a diversity, equity, and inclusion working group based on data from a national CS education program. In *Proceedings of the 49th ACM Technical Symposium on Computer Science Education* (pp. 711-716). DOI: 10.1145/3159450.3159594

IBM. (n.d.). *What is artificial intelligence*? Retrieved June 30, 2024, from https://www.ibm.com/topics/artificial-intelligence

Ibrahim, Z., Mohamed, J., Kassim, N., & Bahrudin, I. A. (2023). The Assistive Technology for Teaching and Learning of Social Skills for Autism Spectrum Disorder Children: Multimedia Interactive Social Skills Module Application. *European Journal of Educational Research*, 12(3), 1465–1477. DOI: 10.12973/eu-jer.12.3.1465

Ifenthaler, D., & Schumacher, C. (2023). Reciprocal issues of artificial and human intelligence in education. *Journal of Research on Technology in Education*, 55(1), 1–6. DOI: 10.1080/15391523.2022.2154511

Imam, A. A. (2021). Historically recontextualizing Sidman's Tactics: How behavior analysis avoided psychology's methodological Ouroboros. *Journal of the Experimental Analysis of Behavior*, 115(1), 115–128. DOI: 10.1002/jeab.661 PMID: 33336404

Indrajith, R. (2024). AI innovations for inclusive learning: Breaking down barriers. *International Journal of Research Publication and Reviews*, 5(4), 9742–9745. https://ijrpr.com/uploads/V5ISSUE4/IJRPR26119.pdf

Ingersoll, R. M., & Tran, H. (2023). Teacher shortages and turnover in rural schools in the US: An organizational analysis. *Educational Administration Quarterly*, 59(2), 396–431. DOI: 10.1177/0013161X231159922

Inoferio, H. V., Espartero, M., Asiri, M., Damin, M., & Chavez, J. V. (2024). Coping with math anxiety and lack of confidence through AI-assisted Learning. *Environment and Social Psychology, 9*(5).

Institute for Educational Advancement. (2022). *Defining gifted.* https://educationaladvancement.org/what-is-gifted/?gad_source=1&gclid=CjwKCAjwz42xBhB9EiwA48pT75g3YhNOgcSkc9VYLksuh9Ow8PfrUyaOgFAAROCHL-Krlfpa1nIBXhoCvqEQAvD_BwE

Institute of Education Sciences, U.S. Department of Education. (2016). *Cognitive Tutor: WWC Intervention Report: A summary of findings from a systematic review of the evidence.* Retrieved from https://ies.ed.gov/ncee/wwc/Docs/InterventionReports/WWC_Cognitive_Tutor_061316.pdf

Institute of Education Sciences. (n.d.). *What works clearinghouse.* https://ies.ed.gov/ncee/wwc

Interaction Design Foundation. (2016, June 1). What is accessibility? Interaction Design Foundation - IxDF. https://www.interaction-design.org/literature/topics/accessibility

International Dyslexia Association. (n.d). IDA and Learning Ally to get struggling readers much-needed help. https://dyslexiaida.org/ida-and-learning-ally-to-get-struggling-readers-much-needed-help/

International Gifted Consortium. (2020). *High, exceptional, and profound giftedness.* https://giftedconsortium.com/high-exceptional-profound-giftedness/

International Society for Technology in Education (ISTE). (2023, July). *Bringing AI to school: Tips for School Leaders.* https://cms-live-media.iste.org/Bringing_AI_to_School-2023_07.pdf?_ga=2.148286964.278272055.1709340314-1629594781.1707762420

Islam, S. N. (2013, November). ShellAg: Expert system shell for agricultural crops. In *2013 International Conference on Cloud & Ubiquitous Computing & Emerging Technologies* (pp. 83-86). IEEE DOI: 10.1109/CUBE.2013.24

Israni, B. (2019). *Combining artificial intelligence with special education.*

Itsquiz. (2016). AI in special education. [Online]. Available: https://medium.com/@itsquiz15/artificial-intelligence-in-special-educ ation-dab27649b9b6

Iuculano, T., Rosenberg-Lee, M., Richardson, J., Tenison, C., Fuchs, L., Supekar, K., & Menon, V. (2015). Cognitive tutoring induces widespread neuroplasticity and remediates brain function in children with mathematical learning disabilities. *Nature Communications*, 6(1), 8453. DOI: 10.1038/ncomms9453 PMID: 26419418

Jackson, E. A. (2015). Role of information science in sustainable development: Sierra Leone as a case study. *Management of Sustainable Development*, 7(2), 23–29. DOI: 10.1515/msd-2015-0026

Jadán-Guerrero, J., Tamayo-Narvaez, K., Méndez, E., & Valenzuela, M. (2024, June). Adaptive Learning Environments: Integrating Artificial Intelligence for Special Education Advances. In *International Conference on Human-Computer Interaction* (pp. 86-94). Cham: Springer Nature Switzerland. DOI: 10.1007/978-3-031-61953-3_10

Jain, K., Manghirmalani, P., Dongardive, J., & Abraham, S. (2009). Computational diagnosis of learning disability. *International Journal of Recent Trends in Engineering*, 2(3), 64–69.

Jain, M., Jain, S., Kesharwani, H., & Ahmed, A. E. (2023). Physiotherapeutic aid using ML and AI. *International Journal of Scientific Research in Computer Science Engineering and Information Technology*, 12(3), 245–251. DOI: 10.32628/CSEIT2390399C

Jaliaawala, M. S., & Khan, R. A. (2020). Can autism be catered with artificial intelligence-assisted intervention technology? A comprehensive survey. *Artificial Intelligence Review*, 53(2), 1039–1069. DOI: 10.1007/s10462-019-09686-8

Jameel, T., & Arsalan, H. (2024). *Adapting education for the AI era: Strategies for generative AI integration*. https://doi.org/DOI: 10.13140/RG.2.2.10251.50723

Jämsä, T., Kangas, M., Vikman, I., Nyberg, L., & Korpelainen, R. (2014). Fall detection in older people: From laboratory to real-life. *Proceedings of the Estonian Academy of Sciences*, 63(3), 341–345. DOI: 10.3176/proc.2014.3.08

Jeannel, O. (2012). Roger Voice. Retrieved from https://rogervoice.com/solutions/the-rogervoice-app/ on 1 June 2024.

Jensen, L., & Konradsen, F. (2018). A review of the use of virtual reality head-mounted displays in education and training. *Education and Information Technologies*, 23(4), 1515–1529. DOI: 10.1007/s10639-017-9676-0

Jha, M. M. (2002). *School Without Walls: Inclusive Education for All*. Heinemann.

Jiang, B., Gu, M., & Du, Y. (2023). Recent Advances in Intelligent Textbooks for Better Learning. In Niemi, H., Pea, R. D., & Lu, Y. (Eds.), *AI in Learning: Designing the Future*. Springer., DOI: 10.1007/978-3-031-09687-7_15

Jian, M. (2023). Personalized learning through AI. *Advances in Engineering Innovation*, 5(1), 16–19. Advance online publication. DOI: 10.54254/2977-3903/5/2023039

Johnson, C., Smart, K., & Mahar, P. (2023). Is there a place for generative artificial intelligence in special education? *National Social Science Technology Journal, 11*(2), 48-62. https://nssascholars.org/wp-content/uploads/2023/11/NSSA.Journal-11_2_v1.11.28.23.pdf

Johnson, D., & Johnson, R. T. (2015). Cooperation and competition. In *International encyclopedia of the social & behavioral sciences: Second edition* (pp. 856–861). https://doi.org/DOI: 10.1016/B978-0-08-097086-8.24051-8

Johnson, D. W., & Johnson, R. (1989). *Cooperation and competition: Theory and research*. Interaction Book Company.

Johnson, D., Alsharid, M., El-Bouri, R., Mehdi, N., Shamout, F., Szenicer, A., Toman, D., & Binghalib, S. (2022, June). An experience report of executive-level artificial intelligence education in the united arab emirates. *Proceedings of the AAAI Conference on Artificial Intelligence*, 36(11), 12766–12773. DOI: 10.1609/aaai.v36i11.21555

Johnson, J. M., Paris, J. H., Curci, J. D., & Horchos, S. (2024). Beyond college access: An exploration of the short-term impact of a dual enrollment program. *Journal of College Student Retention*, 26(1), 41–63. DOI: 10.1177/15210251211056319

Johnson, K. R. (2022). Using a Strengths–Based Approach to Improve Employment Opportunities for Individuals with Autism Spectrum Disorder. *New Horizons in Adult Education and Human Resource Development*, 34(1), 16–25. DOI: 10.1002/nha3.20321

Johnson, K. R., Ennis–Cole, D., & Bonhamgregory, M. (2020). Workplace success strategies for employees with autism spectrum disorder: A new frontier for human resource development. *Human Resource Development Review*, 19(2), 122–151. DOI: 10.1177/1534484320905910

Johnson, K. R., & Williams, K. (2022). Workplace Training for Employees with Autism Spectrum Disorder. In *Generation A* (pp. 7–18). Emerald Publishing Limited. DOI: 10.1108/978-1-80071-256-020211001

Jones, S., Wilson, K., & Green, L. (2022). Assistive Technologies for Students with Disabilities: A Systematic Review. *Disability and Rehabilitation. Assistive Technology*, 17(5), 663–677.

Joseph, R. (2020). The theory of empowerment: A critical analysis with the theory evaluation scale. *Journal of Human Behavior in the Social Environment*, 30(2), 138–157. DOI: 10.1080/10911359.2019.1660294

Juanis, A. A., Anak Mundu, J., & Tati, J. S. (2023). Student's engagement with interactive online learning by Pear Deck. *Jurnal Pengajian Umum / Journal of General Studies, 1*. https://myjms.mohe.gov.my/index.php/jpu/article/view/22743

K-12 Education : Education Should Assess Its Efforts to Address Teacher Shortages : Report to Congressional Committees / United States Government Accountability. Office. (2022). United States Government Accountability Office. Print

Kadaruddin, K. (2023). *Empowering education through generative AI: Innovative instructional strategies for tomorrow's learners*. International Journal of Business, Law, and Education., DOI: 10.56442/ijble.v4i2.215

Kaelin, V. C., Valizadeh, M., Salgado, Z., Parde, N., & Khetani, M. A. (2021). Artificial Intelligence in Rehabilitation Targeting the Participation of Children and Youth with Disabilities: Scoping Review. *Journal of Medical Internet Research*, 23(11), e25745. DOI: 10.2196/25745 PMID: 34734833

Kahraman, H. T., Sağıroğlu, Ş., & Çolak, I. (2010). Development of adaptive and intelligent web-based educational systems. In *Proceedings of the 2010 4th International Conference on Application of Information and Communication Technologies* (pp. 1-5). IEEE. https://doi.org/DOI: 10.1109/ICAICT.2010.5612054

Kalil, T. (2017). Policy entrepreneurship at the White House. *Innovations: Technology, Governance, Globalization*, 11(3/4), 4–21. DOI: 10.1162/inov_a_00253

Kalonde, G., Boateng, S., Sanni, L., Chotwe, S., & Ododo, F. (2024, March). Artificial Intelligence and Special Education: The use and the integration. In *Society for Information Technology & Teacher Education International Conference* (pp. 1926-1932). Association for the Advancement of Computing in Education (AACE).

Kambalimath, S., & Deka, P. C. (2020). A basic review of fuzzy logic applications in hydrology and water resources. *Applied Water Science*, 10(8), 1–14. DOI: 10.1007/s13201-020-01276-2

Kanakanti, C. R., & Sabitha, R. (2020). AI and ML based Google Assistant for an organization using Google Cloud Platform and Dialogflow. *International Journal of Recent Technology and Engineering*, 8(5), 2722–2727. DOI: 10.35940/ijrte.E6354.018520

Kaplan-Rakowski, R., Grotewold, K., Hartwick, P., & Papin, K. (2023). Generative AI and teachers' perspectives on its implementation in education. *Journal of Interactive Learning Research*, 34(2), 313–338. https://www.learntechlib.org/primary/p/222363/

Kaplan-Rakowski, R., & Gruber, A. (2023). The impact of high-immersion virtual reality on foreign language anxiety when speaking in public. *Smart Learning Environments*, 10(46), 46. Advance online publication. DOI: 10.1186/s40561-023-00263-9

Kapoor, R., Sharma, A., & Gupta, V. (2023). AI-driven Social Skills Training for Students With Autism Spectrum Disorder in India. *Journal of Autism and Developmental Disorders*, 53(6), 2345–2359.

Karnes, F. A., & Stephens, K. R. (2008). *Achieving excellence: Educating the gifted and talented*. Pearson Education, Inc.

Kast, M., Baschera, G.-M., Gross, M., Jäncke, L., & Meyer, M. (2011). Computer-based Learning of Spelling Skills in Children with and without Dyslexia. *Annals of Dyslexia*, 61(2), 177–200. DOI: 10.1007/s11881-011-0052-2

Katoch, S., Chauhan, S. S., & Kumar, V. (2021). A review on genetic algorithm: Past, present, and future. *Multimedia Tools and Applications*, 80(5), 8091–8126. DOI: 10.1007/s11042-020-10139-6 PMID: 33162782

Kaur, J., Khan, M. A., Iftikhar, M., Imran, M., & Haq, Q. E. U. (2021). Machine learning techniques for 5G and beyond. *IEEE Access : Practical Innovations, Open Solutions*, 9, 23472–23488. DOI: 10.1109/ACCESS.2021.3051557

Ke, F., & Im, T. (2013). Virtual-reality-based social interaction training for children with high-functioning autism. *The Journal of Educational Research*, 106(6), 441–461. DOI: 10.1080/00220671.2013.832999

Ke, F., Moon, J., & Sokolikj, Z. (2022). Virtual reality–based social skills training for children with autism spectrum disorder. *Journal of Special Education Technology*, 37(1), 49–62. DOI: 10.1177/0162643420945603

Keles, A., Ocak, R., Keles, A., & Gülcü, A. (2009). ZOSMAT: Web-based intelligent tutoring system for teaching-learning process. *Expert Systems with Applications*, 36(2), 1229–1239. DOI: 10.1016/j.eswa.2007.11.064

Kempt, H., Heilinger, J. C., & Nagel, S. K. (2022). Relative explainability and double standards in medical decision-making: Should medical AI be subjected to higher standards in medical decision-making than doctors? *Ethics and Information Technology*, 24(2), 20. Advance online publication. DOI: 10.1007/s10676-022-09646-x

Kennett, D. W., Gardner, A., Scott, L., Patterson, M. S., Zhang, L., & Carter, R. A. (2022). Choice and voice: Emerging questions of personalised professional learning. *Practice*, 4(2), 103–109. DOI: 10.1080/25783858.2022.2086061

Ke, Q., & Wang, P. (2019). Research progress of educational applications of brain-computer interface technology. *China Electro-Chemical Education*, (10), 14–22.

Kessler, M., Loewen, S., & Gönülal, T. (2023). Mobile-assisted language learning with Babbel and Duolingo: Comparing L2 learning gains and user experience. *Computer Assisted Language Learning*, 1-25. Informa UK Limited. https://doi.org/DOI: 10.1080/09588221.2023.2215294

Khairi, F., & Yhya Alhafidh, F. (2024). *Navigating the five stages of AI adoption in higher education: A simplified guide*. https://doi.org/DOI: 10.13140/RG.2.2.15679.52641

Khalid, U. B., Naeem, M., Stasolla, F., Syed, M. H., Abbas, M., & Coronato, A. (2024). Impact of AI-Powered Solutions in Rehabilitation Process: Recent Improvements and Future Trends. *International Journal of General Medicine*, 17, 943–969. DOI: 10.2147/IJGM.S453903 PMID: 38495919

Khanzanchi, R., & Khanzanchi, P. (2024). Generative AI to improve special education teacher preparation for inclusive classrooms. In Searson, M., Langran, E., & Trumble, J. (Eds.), *Exploring new horizons: Generative artificial intelligence and teacher education* (pp. 159–177). Association for the Advancement of Computing in Education., https://www.learntechlib.org/primary/p/223928/

Kharbat, F. F., Alshawabkeh, A., & Woolsey, M. L. (2021). Identifying gaps in using artificial intelligence to support students with intellectual disabilities from education and health perspectives. *Aslib Journal of Information Management*, 73(1), 101–128. DOI: 10.1108/AJIM-02-2020-0054

Khosravi, H., Denny, P., Moore, S., & Stamper, J. (2023). Learnersourcing in the age of AI: Student, educator, and machine partnerships for content creation. *Computers and Education: Artificial Intelligence*, 5, 100151. DOI: 10.1016/j.caeai.2023.100151

Kim, J., Merrill, K., Xu, K., & Sellnow, D. D. (2020). My teacher is a machine: Understanding students' perceptions of AI teaching assistants in online education. *International Journal of Human-Computer Interaction*, 36(20), 1902–1911. DOI: 10.1080/10447318.2020.1801227

Kim, S. I., Jang, S. Y., Kim, T., Kim, B., Jeong, D., Noh, T., Jeong, M., Hall, K., Kim, M., Yoo, H. J., Han, K., Hong, H., & Kim, J. G. (2024). Promoting Self-Efficacy of Individuals With Autism in Practicing Social Skills in the Workplace Using Virtual Reality and Physiological Sensors: Mixed Methods Study. *JMIR Formative Research*, 8, e52157. DOI: 10.2196/52157

Kim, Y. D., Hong, J. W., Kang, W. S., Baek, S. S., Lee, H. S., & An, J. (2010). Design of robot-assisted observation system for therapy and education of children with autism. In Ge, S. S., Li, H., Cabibihan, J. J., & Tan, Y. K. (Eds.), *Social robotics* (Vol. 6414, pp. 218–227). Springer., DOI: 10.1007/978-3-642-17248-9_23

King, M. R., & Chat, G. P. T. (2023). A conversation on artificial intelligence, chatbots, and plagiarism in higher education. *Cellular and Molecular Bioengineering*, 16(1), 1–2. DOI: 10.1007/s12195-022-00754-8 PMID: 36660590

King, P., & Martinez, E. G. (2020). Robotic Assistive Technologies: Principles and practice. *IEEE Pulse. IEEE Pulse*, 11(1), 27–28. DOI: 10.1109/MPULS.2020.2972726

King, S. A. (2022). The education context for twice-exceptional students: An overview of issues in special and gifted education. *Neurobiology of Learning and Memory*, 193, 107659. Advance online publication. DOI: 10.1016/j.nlm.2022.107659 PMID: 35835373

King, S. A., Boyer, J., Bell, T., & Estapa, A. (2022). An automated virtual reality training system for teacher-student interaction: A randomized controlled trial. *JMIR Serious Games*, 10(4), e41097. Advance online publication. DOI: 10.2196/41097 PMID: 36480248

King, S. A., Dzenga, C., Burch, T., & Kennedy, K. (2021). Teaching partial-interval recording of problem behavior with virtual reality. *Journal of Behavioral Education*, 30(2), 202–225. DOI: 10.1007/s10864-019-09363-4

King, S. A., Estapa, A., Bell, T., & Boyer, J. (2024). Behavioral skills training through smart virtual reality: Demonstration of feasibility for a verbal mathematical questioning strategy. *Journal of Behavioral Education*, 33(2), 396–420. DOI: 10.1007/s10864-022-09492-3

King, S. A., Feng, L., Glazek, C., Ross, K. M., Green, M., Lele, H., & Bell, T. (2024, October 11). (in press). Developing smart virtual reality to teach functional communication training. *Journal of Behavioral Education*. Advance online publication. DOI: 10.1007/s10864-024-09569-1

King, S. A., Nylen, B., Enders, O., Wang, L., & Opeoluwa, O. (2024). Examining the impact of design-comparable effect size on the analysis of single-case design in special education. *School Psychology*. Advance online publication. DOI: 10.1037/spq0000628 PMID: 38753395

King, S. A., Ross, K. M., Glazek, C., Feng, L., Green, M., Bell, T., & Lele, H. (2024). Integrating artificial intelligence and virtual reality to train educators in functional communication training—Results from exploratory studies. In Eom, M., Kim, Y., Lee, K., Lee, S., & Oh, H. (Eds.), *Proceedings of the 24th International Conference on Educational Research: Reimaging Teaching and Teachers in a Changing World* (pp. 1–5)., https://icer.snu.ac.kr/sub_proceeding/icer_add.php?mode=view&year=2024&number=31

King, S. A., Wang, L., Nylen, B., & Enders, O. (2023). Prevalence of research design in special education: A survey of peer-reviewed journals. *Remedial and Special Education*, 44(6), 480–494. DOI: 10.1177/07419325231152453

Kinteract. (n.d). Kinteract. Retrieved June 27, 2024, from https://www.kinteract.co.uk/ on 1 June 2024.

Kirkpatrick, M., Akers, J., & Rivera, G. (2019). Use of behavioral skills training with teachers: A systematic review. *Journal of Behavioral Education*, 28(3), 344–361. DOI: 10.1007/s10864-019-09322-z

Kirongo, A., Bundi, D., Kitaria, D., Huka, G., & Muketha, G. (2022). *Implementation of AI-based assistive technologies for learners with physical disabilities in Kenya: a practical design thinking approach.* African Journal of Science, Technology and Social Sciences., DOI: 10.58506/ajstss.v1i1.71

Kisker, C. B., Cohen, A. M., & Brawer, F. B. (2023). *The American community college*. John Wiley & Sons.

Kizilcec, R. F. (2023). To Advance AI Use in Education, Focus on Understanding Educators. *International Journal of Artificial Intelligence in Education*, 34(1), 12–19. DOI: 10.1007/s40593-023-00351-4 PMID: 37359103

Klarin, J., Hoff, E., Larsson, A., & Daukantaite, D. (2024). Adolescents' use and perceived usefulness of generative AI for schoolwork: Exploring their relationships with executive functioning and academic achievement. *Frontiers in Artificial Intelligence*, 7, 1415782. https://www.frontiersin.org/journals/artificial-intelligence/articles/10.3389/frai.2024.1415782 doi.org/10.3389/frai.2024.1415782. DOI: 10.3389/frai.2024.1415782 PMID: 39263526

Klimova, B., Pikhart, M., & Kacetl, J. (2023). Ethical issues of the use of AI-driven mobile apps for education. *Frontiers in Public Health*, 10, 1118116. DOI: 10.3389/fpubh.2022.1118116

Kloos, E., Nacik, E., & Ward, C. (2023). Developing implementation capacity of a state education agency to improve outcomes for students with disabilities. *Journal of Disability Policy Studies*, 34(2), 127–136. DOI: 10.1177/10442073221096393

KnowledgeWorks. (2020). *State policy framework for personalized learning*. KnowledgeWorks. https://knowledgeworks.org/resources/state-policy-framework-personalized-learning/

Kofler, M. J., Irwin, L. N., Soto, E. F., Groves, N. B., Harmon, S. L., & Sarver, D. E. (2019). Executive Functioning Heterogeneity in Pediatric ADHD. *Journal of Abnormal Child Psychology*, 47(2), 273–286. DOI: 10.1007/s10802-018-0438-2 PMID: 29705926

Kohli, R., Phutela, S., Garg, A., & Viner, M. (2021).Review on Artificial Intelligent in Special Education.*TLDR*,385-391.

Kohli, M., & Prasad, T. (2010). Identifying dyslexic students by using artificial neural networks. *Lecture Notes in Engineering and Computer Science*, 2183, 118.

Konrad, A. (2022, July 21). ClassDojo won Over Classrooms. Now it's on a $125 million mission to bring kids to the metaverse. *Forbes*.

Kopf, B., & Kopf, D. (2011). Remind [Mobile app]. Remind. https://www.remind.comNisbet, Kelsey and Opp, Allison. (2017). Effects of the Remind App on Parent-Teacher Communication at a Mixed-Income Middle School. Retrieved from Sophia, the St. Catherine University repository website: (https://sophia.stkate.edu/maed/227) on 1 June 2024.

Kornack, J., Persicke, A., Cervantes, P., Jang, J., & Dixon, D. (2014). Economics of autism spectrum disorders: An overview of treatment and research funding. In Tarbox, D. J., Dixon, D. R., Sturmey, P., & Matson, J. L. (Eds.), *Handbook of early intervention for autism spectrum disorders: Research, policy, and practice* (pp. 165–178). Springer. DOI: 10.1007/978-1-4939-0401-3_9

Kornbluh, M. (2020). Untold student stories: Examining educational budget cuts within urban school settings. *Journal of Urban Affairs*, 42(5), 731–749. DOI: 10.1080/07352166.2019.1607748

Koshtura, D., Andrunyk, V., & Shestakevych, T. (2021). Development of a speech-to-text program for people with hearing impairments. *CEUR Workshop Proceedings*, 2917, Paper 38. Lviv Polytechnic National University. Retrieved from https://ceur-ws.org/Vol-2917/paper38.pdf

Kotter, J. P. (2012). *Leading change*. Harvard business press.

Koubaa, A., Boulila, W., Ghouti, L., Alzahem, A., & Latif, S. (2023). Exploring ChatGPT Capabilities and Limitations: A Survey. *IEEE Access : Practical Innovations, Open Solutions*, 11, 118698–118721. DOI: 10.1109/ACCESS.2023.3326474

Kouroupa, A., Laws, K. R., Irvine, K., Mengoni, S. E., Baird, A., & Sharma, S. (2022). The use of social robots with children and young people on the autism spectrum: A systematic review and meta-analysis. *PLoS One*, 17(6), e0269800. DOI: 10.1371/journal.pone.0269800 PMID: 35731805

Koychev, I., Nikolov, R., & Dicheva, D. (2009, October 28-29). SmartBook: The new generation e-book meets University 2.0. In *Proceedings of the International Conference on Software, Services & Semantic Technologies* (pp. 60-67). Demetra EOOD. http://hdl.handle.net/10506/244

Krahulcova, L. (2021, March 24). Techno solutionism—Very few things actually need to be an app. Blogtext. Digital Rights Watch Website. https://digit alrightswatch .org.au/2021/03/25/technosolutionism/

Krezmien, M. P., Travers, J. C., & Camacho, K. (2017). Suspension rates of students with autism or intellectual disabilities in Maryland from 2004 to 2015. *Journal of Intellectual Disability Research*, 61(11), 1011–1020. DOI: 10.1111/jir.12406 PMID: 28836311

Krijan, I. P., Jurčec, L., & Borić, E. (2015). Primary school teachers' attitudes toward gifted students. *Croatian Journal Educational.*, 17, 681–707. DOI: 10.15516/cje. v17i3.1199

Kruk, M. (2020). Fluctuations in self-perceived foreign language anxiety during visits to Second Life: A case study. *Innovation in Language Learning and Teaching*. Advance online publication. DOI: 10.1080/17501229.2020.1813737

Kruse, C. S., Karem, P., Shifflett, K., Vegi, L., Ravi, K., & Brooks, M. (2018). Evaluating barriers to adopting telemedicine worldwide: A systematic review. *Journal of Telemedicine and Telecare*, 24(1), 4–12. DOI: 10.1177/1357633X16674087 PMID: 29320966

Kuleto, V., Ilić, M., Dumangiu, M., Ranković, M., Martins, O. M., Păun, D., & Mihoreanu, L. (2021). Exploring opportunities and challenges of artificial intelligence and machine learning in higher education institutions. *Sustainability (Basel)*, 13(18), 10424. DOI: 10.3390/su131810424

Kulik, J. A., & Fletcher, J. D. (2016). Effectiveness of intelligent tutoring systems: A meta-analytic review. *Review of Educational Research*, 86(1), 42–78. DOI: 10.3102/0034654315581420

Kumagai, H., & Nagai, N. (2022). Challenges and Opportunities of AI in Inclusive Education: A Case Study of Data-Enhanced Active Reading In Japan. *Smart Learning Environments*, 1(1), 1–13.

Kumar, A., Raghunathan, A., Jones, R., Ma, T., & Liang, P. (2022). Fine-tuning can distort pretrained features and underperform out-of-distribution. *arXiv preprint arXiv:2202.10054*.

Kumar, A., Nayyar, A., Sachan, R. K., & Jain, R. (Eds.). (2023). *AI-assisted Special Education for Students with Exceptional Needs*. IGI Global. DOI: 10.4018/979-8-3693-0378-8

Kumar, K., & Thakur, G. S. M. (2012). Advanced applications of neural networks and artificial intelligence: A review. *International Journal of Information Technology and Computer Science*, 6(6), 57–68. https://doi-org.proxy1.library.jhu.edu/10.5815/ijitcs.2012.06.08. DOI: 10.5815/ijitcs.2012.06.08

Kumazaki, H., Muramatsu, T., Yoshikawa, Y., Matsumoto, Y., Ishiguro, H., Mimura, M., & Kikuchi, M. (2019). Role-play-based guidance for job interviews using an android robot for individuals with autism spectrum disorders. *Frontiers in Psychiatry*, 10, 239. Advance online publication. DOI: 10.3389/fpsyt.2019.00239 PMID: 31031664

Kuprenko, V. (2020). Artificial Intelligence in education: benefits, challenges, and use cases. Retrieved from https://pub.towardsai.net/artificial-intelligence-in-education-benefits-challenges-and-use-cases-db52d8921f7a

Kurth, J. A., Turner, E. L., Gerasimova, D., Hicks, T. A., Zagona, A., Lansey, K., Mansouri, M. C., Lyon, K. J., Jameson, M., Loyless, R., & Pace, J. R. (2022). An investigation of IEP quality associated with Special Education Placement for Students with Complex Support Needs. *Research and Practice for Persons with Severe Disabilities : the Journal of TASH*, 47(4), 244–260. DOI: 10.1177/15407969221134923

Kurzweil Education. (1996). Kurzweil 3000 [Computer software]. Retrieved from https://www.kurzweiledu.com, on 1 June 2024.

Kurzweil, R. (1998). The age of spiritual machines: When computers exceed human intelligence. Viking Press. https://imrtc.org/RE/Books/Technology/THE_AGE_OF_SPIRITUAL_MACHINES_RAY_KURZWEIL.pdf

Laabidi, M. (2013). *Jemni, L. J. B. Ayed, H. B. Brahim, and A. B. Jemaa, "Learning technologies for people with disabilities," Research Laboratory of Technologies of Information and Communication & Electrical Engineering LaTICE*. National Higher School of Engineering of Tunis.

Laal, M., & Ghodsi, S. M. (2012). Benefits of collaborative learning. *Procedia: Social and Behavioral Sciences*, 31, 486–490. DOI: 10.1016/j.sbspro.2011.12.091

Laal, M., Khattami-Kermanshahi, Z., & Laal, M. (2014). Teaching and education: Collaborative style. *Procedia: Social and Behavioral Sciences*, 116, 4057–4061. DOI: 10.1016/j.sbspro.2014.01.890

Labadze, L., Grigolia, M., & Machaidze, L. (2023). Role of AI chatbots in education: Systematic literature review. *International Journal of Educational Technology in Higher Education*, 20(1), 56. DOI: 10.1186/s41239-023-00426-1

Labs, E. (2014). Elevate - Brain Training [Mobile application software]. App Store. https://www.elevateapp.com

Labs, W. (2017). Woebot. Retrieved from https://woebothealth.com on 2 June 2024.

Ladson-Billings, G. (2006). From the Achievement Gap to the Education Debt: Understanding Achievement in U.S. Schools. *Educational Researcher*, 35(7), 3–12. DOI: 10.3102/0013189X035007003

Lai, K. H. A., & Ma, S. K. (2023). Sensitivity and specificity of artificial intelligence with Microsoft Azure in detecting pneumothorax in emergency department: A pilot study. *Hong Kong Journal of Emergency Medicine*, 30(1), 8–15. DOI: 10.1177/1024907920948994

Lakes, K. D., Cibrian, F. L., Schuck, S. E. B., Nelson, M., & Hayes, G. R. (2022). Digital health interventions for youth with ADHD: A mapping review. *Computers in Human Behavior Reports*, 6, 100174. Advance online publication. DOI: 10.1016/j.chbr.2022.100174

Lambora, A., Gupta, K., & Chopra, K. (2019, February). Genetic algorithm-A literature review. In 2019 international conference on machine learning, big data, cloud and parallel computing (COMITCon) (pp. 380-384). IEEE.

Lamb, R., Choi, I., & Owens, T. (2023). Artificial intelligence and sensor technologies: The future of special education for students with intellectual and developmental disabilities. *Global Journal of Intellectual & Developmental Disabilities*, 11(3), 555814. Advance online publication. DOI: 10.19080/GJIDD.2023.11.555814

Lameras, P., & Arnab, S. (2021). Power to the teachers: An exploratory review on artificial intelligence in education. *Information (Basel)*, 13(1), 14–20. DOI: 10.3390/info13010014

Lampropoulos, G., Ferdig, R. E., & Kaplan-Rakowski, R. (2024). A social media data analysis of general and educational use of ChatGPT: Understanding emotional educators. *Journal of Educational Technology & Society.*

Larry P. v. Riles is 495 F. Supp. 926 (N.D. Cal. 1979).

Lasrado, F. (2019). *Sustaining Innovation and Future Research Implications.* Fostering Creativity and Innovation., DOI: 10.1007/978-3-319-99121-4_6

Leaf, J. B., Cihon, J. H., Javed, A., Klick, S., Ferguson, J. L., Milne, C., Creem, A., Arthur, S., Saunders, M., Olive, M. L., Ross, R. K., Leaf, R., & McEachin, J. (2022). A call for discussion on stereotypic behavior. *European Journal of Behavior Analysis*, 23(2), 156–180. DOI: 10.1080/15021149.2022.2112810

Learning Ally. (n.d). Learning Ally: Audiobooks for students with dyslexia & learning disabilities. https://learningally.org/

Lebovitz, S., Lifshitz-Assaf, H., & Levina, N. (2022). To engage or not to engage with AI for critical judgments: How professionals deal with opacity when using AI for medical diagnosis. *Organization Science*, 33(1), 126–148. DOI: 10.1287/orsc.2021.1549

Lee, J., & Obinata, G. (2013, March). Developing therapeutic robot for children with autism: A study on exploring colour feedback. In *Human-Robot Interaction (HRI), 8th Association for Computing Machinery/Institute of Electrical and Electronics Engineers (ACM/IEEE)* (pp. 10–15). IEEE. https://doi.org/DOI: 10.1109/HRI.2013.6483557

Lee, J., Takehashi, H., Nagai, C., & Obinata, G. (2012). Design of a therapeutic robot for interacting with autistic children through interpersonal touch. In *IEEE RO-MAN: The 21st IEEE International Symposium on Robot and Human Interactive Communication* (pp. 712–717). IEEE. https://doi.org/DOI: 10.1109/ROMAN.2012.6343835

Lee, S. (2024). *3 types of learning environments.* https://www.wgu.edu/blog/3-types-learning-environments2111.html#:~:text=Studies%20have%20shown%20that%20positive,they%20learn%20evolve%20as%20well

Lee, J., Solomon, M., Stead, T., Kwon, B., & Ganti, L. (2021). Impact of COVID-19 on the mental health of US college students. *BMC Psychology*, 9(1), 95–102. DOI: 10.1186/s40359-021-00598-3 PMID: 34103081

Lee, Y., & Cho, J. (2021). Development of an artificial intelligence education model of classification techniques for non-computer majors. *JOIV: International Journal on Informatics Visualization*, 5(2), 113–119. DOI: 10.30630/joiv.5.2.552

Leka, H. B. (2016). *A spherical robot designed for children with special needs, seeks funding on Indiegogo*. TechCrunch. Retrieved from https://techcrunch.com/2016/05/03/lekaindiegogo/

Li, Y., & Chiu, C. Y. (2024, June). Redefining Truth in the Context of AI-Truth Era: A Practice-Led Research of "From Post-Truth to AI-Truth". In *International Conference on Human-Computer Interaction* (pp. 245-257). Cham: Springer Nature Switzerland. DOI: 10.1007/978-3-031-60913-8_17

Li, Y., Liao, I. Y., Zhong, N., Toshihiro, F., Wang, Y., & Wang, S. (2023, December). Generative AI Enables the Detection of Autism Using EEG Signals. In *Chinese Conference on Biometric Recognition*. 375-384. Springer Nature Singapore. https://doi.org/DOI: 10.1007/978-981-99-8565-4_35

Liang, M. (2020). Research on the application of brain-computer interface technology in the education of special children attending classes. *Computer Knowledge and Technology*, 16(18), 200–201.

Libbrecht, P., & Melis, E. (2006). Methods to access and retrieve mathematical content in ActiveMath. In A. Iglesias & N. Takayama (Eds.), *Mathematical software - ICMS 2006* (Vol. 4151, pp. 331–342). Springer. https://doi.org/DOI: 10.1007/11832225_33

Liberty, E., Karnin, Z., Xiang, B., Rouesnel, L., Coskun, B., Nallapati, R., Delgado, J., Sadoughi, A., Astashonok, Y., Das, P., Balioglu, C., Chakravarty, S., Jha, M., Gautier, P., Arpin, D., Januschowski, T., Flunkert, V., Wang, Y., Gasthaus, J., & Smola, A. (2020). Elastic machine learning algorithms in Amazon SageMaker. In *Proceedings of the 2020 ACM SIGMOD International Conference on Management of Data (SIGMOD '20)* (pp. 731–737). Association for Computing Machinery. https://doi.org/DOI: 10.1145/3318464.3386126

Lift lab. (2012). Liftware. Retrieved from https://www.liftware.com, on 1 June 2024.

Lim, E. L., Murugesan, R. K., & Balakrishnan, S. (2024). Leveraging machine learning techniques for student's attention detection: A review. *IAES International Journal of Artificial Intelligence (IJ-AI), 13*(2), 1195-1205. https://doi.org/DOI: 10.11591/ijai.v13.i2.pp1195-1205

Lin, C., Huang, A. Y. Q., & Lu, O. H. T. (2023). Artificial intelligence in intelligent tutoring systems toward sustainable education: A systematic review. *Smart Learning Environments*, 10(1), 41. Advance online publication. DOI: 10.1186/s40561-023-00260-y

Linstrom, K. R., & Boye, A. J.Neural Network Prediction Model for a Psychiatric Application, Proceedings of the Sixth International Conference on Computational Intelligence and Multimedia Applications (2005).

Littman, M. L., Ajunwa, I., Berger, G., Boutilier, C., Currie, M., Doshi-Velez, F., Hadfield, G., Horowitz, M. C., Isbell, C., Kitano, H., Levy, K., Lyons, T., Mitchell, M., Shah, J., Sloman, S., Vallor, S., & Walsh, T. (2021). *Gathering strength, gathering storms: The one hundred year study on artificial intelligence (AI100) 2021 study panel report*. Stanford University. https://ai100.stanford.edu/2021-report

Liu, H., Wang, Y., Fan, W., Liu, X., Li, Y., Jain, S., Liu, Y., Jain, A., & Tang, J. (2021). Trustworthy AI: A Computational Perspective. *ACM Transactions on Intelligent Systems and Technology*, 14(1), 1–59. DOI: 10.1145/3546872

Liu, V., & Chilton, L. B. (2022, April). Design guidelines for prompt engineering text-to-image generative models. In *Proceedings of the 2022 CHI Conference on Human Factors in Computing Systems* (pp. 1–23). DOI: 10.1145/3491102.3501825

Lizotte, M. (2018). I Am a College Graduate: Postsecondary Experiences as Described by Adults with Autism Spectrum Disorders. *International Journal of Education and Practice, 6*(4), 179-191.Limna, P., & Kraiwanit, T. (2023). The role of chatgpt on customer service in the hospitality industry: An exploratory study of hospitality workers' experiences and perceptions. *Tourism and Hospitality Management*, 29(4), 583–592.

Long, D., & Magerko, B. (2020, April). What is AI literacy? Competencies and design considerations. In *Proceedings of the 2020 CHI Conference on Human Factors in Computing Systems* (pp. 1-16). DOI: 10.1145/3313831.3376727

López Jiménez, E. A., & Ouariachi, T. (2021). An exploration of the impact of artificial intelligence (AI) and automation for communication professionals. *Journal of Information. Communication and Ethics in Society*, 19(2), 249–267. DOI: 10.1108/JICES-03-2020-0034

Lorenzo, G., Lorenzo-Lledó, A., Lledó Carreres, A., & Pérez-Vázquez, E. (2020). Approach from a bibliometric perspective of the educational application of virtual reality in people with autism spectrum disorder. *Education in the Knowledge Society*, 21(4), 1–14. DOI: 10.14201/eks.19522

Losavio, M. (2023). Forensic proof and criminal liability for development, distribution and use of artificial intelligence. In Wang, C., Iyengar, S. S., & Sun, K. (Eds.), *AI Embedded Assurance for Cyber Systems* (pp. 37–48). Springer., DOI: 10.1007/978-3-031-42637-7_3

Luckin, R. (2017). Towards Artificial Intelligence-based Assessment Systems. *Nature Human Behaviour, 1*, 0028. https://doi.org/DOI: 10.1038/s41562-016-0028

Lugrin, J. L., Latoschik, M. E., Habel, M., Roth, D., Seufert, C., & Grafe, S. (2016). Breaking bad behaviors: A new tool for learning classroom management using virtual reality. *Frontiers in ICT (Lausanne, Switzerland)*, 3(26), 1–21. DOI: 10.3389/fict.2016.00026

Luka.inc (2017). Replika. Retrieved from https://replika.ai on 1 June 2024.

Lukins, J. M., Able, H., & Hume, K. (2023). Novice teachers' implementation of evidence-based practices in autism education: Examining the roles of preparation and perception. *Focus on Autism and Other Developmental Disabilities*, 38(1), 5–16. DOI: 10.1177/10883576221144734

Lund, B. D., Wang, T., Mannuru, N. R., Nie, B., Shimray, S., & Wang, Z. (2023). ChatGPT and a new academic reality: Artificial Intelligence-written research papers and the ethics of the large language models in scholarly publishing. *Journal of the Association for Information Science and Technology*, 74(5), 570–581. DOI: 10.1002/asi.24750

Lu, O. H. T., Huang, A. Y. Q., & Azar, P. (2018). AI-based assessment and feedback in education: Enhancing student learning outcomes. *Journal of Learning Analytics*, 5(2), 91–104.

Lu, W., Wei, Y., Yuan, J., Deng, Y., & Song, A. (2020). Tractor assistant driving control method based on EEG combined with RNN-TL deep learning algorithm. *IEEE Access : Practical Innovations, Open Solutions*, 8, 163269–163279. DOI: 10.1109/ACCESS.2020.3021051

Luzmo. (2023). *Using AI for data analysis: The ultimate guide (2024)*.https://www.luzmo.com/blog/ai-data-analysis

Lytras, M., Drigas, A., & Ioannidou, R. (2020). Artificial Intelligence in Special Education: A Systematic Review. *International Journal of Disability and Development*, 16(2), 232–241.

MacCalla, J., Xu, J., & Howard, A. (2015). Integration of Common Core math standards into gaming apps for children with motor limitations. *Zyrobotics, LLC, Atlanta, GA*. Retrieved from https://www.resna.org/sites/default/files/conference/2015/parking_lot/pdfs/84.pdf

MacDonald, R. L., Jiang, P.-P., Cattiau, J., Heywood, R., Cave, R., Seaver, K., Ladewig, M. A., Tobin, J., Brenner, M. P., Nelson, P. C., Green, J. R., & Tomanek, K. (2021). Disordered speech data collection: Lessons learned at 1 million utterances from Project Euphonia. *Proceedings of Interspeech*, 2021, 4833–4837. DOI: 10.21437/Interspeech.2021-697

Mackie, R., & Dunn, L. (1954). *College and university programs for the preparation of teachers of exceptional children*. U.S. Department of Health, Education, and Welfare, Office of Education.

Maddox, R. P.II, Rujimora, J., Nichols, L. M., Williams, M. K., Hunt, T., & Carter, R. A.Jr. (2022). Trauma-informed schools: Implications for special education and school counseling. *Teaching Exceptional Children*, 56(6), 510–520. DOI: 10.1177/00400599221107142

Maghsudi, S., Lan, A., Xu, J., & van Der Schaar, M. (2021). Personalized education in the artificial intelligence era: What to expect next. *IEEE Signal Processing Magazine*, 38(3), 37–50. DOI: 10.1109/MSP.2021.3055032

Magic School. (2024a). *Mission*. https://www.magicschool.ai/mission

Magic School. (2024b). *Tools*. https://app.magicschool.ai/tools

Mahini, S. (2024). Virtual reality as a tool for children with autism spectrum disorder. *Digital Technologies Research and Applications*, 3(1), 16–23. DOI: 10.54963/dtra.v3i1.211

Maiseli, B., Abdalla, A. T., Massawe, L. V., Mbise, M., Mkocha, K., Nassor, N. A., Ismail, M., Michael, J., & Kimambo, S. (2023). Brain–computer interface: Trend, challenges, and threats. *Brain Informatics*, 10(1), 20. Advance online publication. DOI: 10.1186/s40708-023-00199-3 PMID: 37540385

Maker, J., Zimmerman, R., Alhusaini, A., & Pease, R. (2015). Real engagement in active problem solving (REAPS): An evidence-based model that meets content, process, product, and learning environment principles recommended for gifted students. *Apex*, 19(1), 1–24. DOI: 10.21307/apex-2015-006

Makhlouf, M. K. I. (2021). Effect of artificial intelligence-based application on Saudi preparatory-year students' EFL speaking skills at Albaha university. *International Journal of English Language Education*, 9(2), 36–56. DOI: 10.5296/ijele.v9i2.18782

Malach, J., & Javorcik, T. (n.d.). Conditions and bases of incorporation of artificial intelligence into Czech school environment. *European Conference on Learning and Instruction (EClAIR)*. https://doi.org/DOI: 10.34190/EClAIR.19.077

Manyilizu, M. C. (2023). Effectiveness of virtual laboratory vs. paper-based experiences to the hands-on chemistry practical in Tanzanian secondary schools. *Education and Information Technologies*, 28(5), 4831–4848. DOI: 10.1007/s10639-022-11327-7 PMID: 36247025

Marin, I., & Popovici, D. (2022). Teachers-students-parents digital portal need analysis designed for abroad studies. In *Proceedings of the 14th International Conference on Education and New Learning Technologies (EDULEARN)* (pp. 3373–3382). https://doi.org/DOI: 10.21125/edulearn.2022.0826

Marino, M. T., Basham, J. D., Courtade, G., Hott, B. L., Howorth, S. K., Goldman, S. R., & Vasquez, E. (2024). Inclusive intelligence: The impact of AI on education for all learners. Center for Innovation, Design, and Digital Learning (CIDDL). https://ciddl.org/inclusive-intelligence-the-impact-of-ai-on-education-for-all-learners/

Marino, M. T., Vasquez, E., Dieker, L., Basham, J., & Blackorby, J. (2023). The future of artificial intelligence in special education technology. *Journal of Special Education Technology*, 38(3), 404–416. DOI: 10.1177/01626434231165977

Mason-Williams, L., Bettini, E., Peyton, D., Harvey, A., Rosenberg, M., & Sindelar, P. T. (2020). Rethinking shortages in special education: Making good on the promise of an equal opportunity for students with disabilities. *Teacher Education and Special Education*, 43(1), 45–62. DOI: 10.1177/0888406419880352

Massoumeh, Z., & Jamshidi, L. (2012). An investigation of medical model and special education methods. *Procedia: Social and Behavioral Sciences*, 46, 5802–5804. DOI: 10.1016/j.sbspro.2012.06.518

Matsuda, K., Garcia, Y., Catagnus, R., & Brandt, J. A. (2020). Can behavior analysis help us understand and reduce racism? A review of the current literature. *Behavior Analysis in Practice*, 13(2), 336–347. DOI: 10.1007/s40617-020-00411-4 PMID: 32642393

Ma, W., Adesope, O. O., Nesbit, J. C., & Liu, Q. (2014). Intelligent tutoring systems and learning outcomes: A meta-analysis. *Journal of Educational Psychology*, 106(4), 901–918. DOI: 10.1037/a0037123

Mayer-Schönberger, V., & Cukier, K. (2013). *Big data: A revolution that will transform how we live, work, and think*. Houghton Mifflin Harcourt.

Mays, K. K., Cummings, J. J., & Katz, J. E. (2024). The Robot Rights and Responsibilities Scale: Development and Validation of a Metric for Understanding Perceptions of Robots' Rights and Responsibilities. *International Journal of Human-Computer Interaction*, •••, 1–18. DOI: 10.1080/10447318.2024.2338332

McArdle, L. (2022). Artificial Intelligence and Inclusive Education: Speculative Futures and Emerging Practices. *Journal of Interdisciplinary Studies in Education*, 11(2), 210–211.

McArthur, D., Lewis, M., & Bishay, M. (1993). The roles of artificial intelligence in education: Current progress and future prospects. *Journal of Educational Computing Research*, 9(2), 165–189.

McCall, M. P., Anton, M. T., Highlander, A., Loiselle, R., Forehand, R., Khavjou, O., & Jones, D. J. (2023). Technology-enhanced behavioral parent training: The relationship between technology use and efficiency of service delivery. *Behavior Modification*, 47(5), 1094–14. DOI: 10.1177/01454455231165937

McCarthy, J. (2007). What is artificial intelligence. https://www-formal.stanford.edu/jmc/whatisai.pdf

McCoach, D. B., Siegle, D., & Rubenstein, L. D. (2020). Pay attention to the inattention: Exploring ADHD symptoms in a sample of underachieving gifted students. *Gifted Child Quarterly*, 64(2), 100–116. DOI: 10.1177/0016986219901320

McCray, E. D. (2023). *Handbook of research on special education teacher preparation*. E. Bettini, M. T. Brownell, J. McLeskey, & P. T. Sindelar (Eds.). Taylor & Francis Group. DOI: 10.4324/9781003297093

McCulloch, W. S., & Pitts, W. (1943). A logical calculus of the ideas immanent in nervous activity. *The Bulletin of Mathematical Biophysics*, 5(4), 115–133. DOI: 10.1007/BF02478259

McFayden, T. C., Bristol, S., Putnam, O., & Harrop, C. (2024). ChatGPT: Artificial Intelligence as a Potential Tool for Parents Seeking Information About Autism. *Cyberpsychology, Behavior, and Social Networking*, 27(2), 135–148. Advance online publication. DOI: 10.1089/cyber.2023.0202

McGrath, D. (2023, July 12). Using AI to write IEPs: A tool to help educators reduce workload. *Edutopia*. https://www.edutopia.org/article/using-ai-write-ieps-help-educators-reduce-workload/

McGraw-Hill. (n.d). ALEKS. Retrieved, from https://www.aleks.com on 27 June 2024.

McKenney, S. (2018). How can the learning sciences (better) impact policy and practice? *Journal of the Learning Sciences*, 27(1), 1–7. DOI: 10.1080/10508406.2017.1404404

McLaren, B., Gog, T., Ganoe, C., Yaron, D., & Karabinos, M. (2015). RETRACTED ARTICLE: Worked examples are more efficient for learning than high-assistance instructional software. *International Journal of Artificial Intelligence in Education*, 26(4), 1117. Advance online publication. DOI: 10.1007/s40593-015-0046-z

McNamara, K. (2023). "The Magic of Numbers is Strong": Hobson v Hansen and Contested Social Science in Judicial Decision Making. *Social Science History*, 47(4), 641–664. DOI: 10.1017/ssh.2023.16

Medenica, V., Ivanović, L., Ristic, I., & Čolić, G. (2023). *Artificial intelligence in occupational therapy and special education and rehabilitation*. https://doi.org/DOI: 10.7251/ZSAN2302033M

Mehrotra, S., Degachi, C., Vereschak, O., Jonker, C., & Tielman, M. (2023). A systematic review on fostering appropriate trust in human-AI interaction. *ARXiv*, abs/2311.06305. https://doi.org//arXiv.2311.06305DOI: 10.48550

Mehta, P., Chillarge, G. R., Sapkal, S. D., Shinde, G. R., & Kshirsagar, P. S. (2023). Inclusion of Children With Special Needs in the Educational System, Artificial Intelligence (AI). In *AI-Assisted Special Education for Students With Exceptional Needs* (pp. 156-185). IGI Global.

Melis, E., Andres, E., Budenbender, J., Frischauf, A., Goduadze, G., Libbrecht, P., Pollet, M., & Ullrich, C. (2001). ActiveMath: A generic and adaptive web-based learning environment. *International Journal of Artificial Intelligence in Education*, 12, 385–407. https://hal.archives-ouvertes.fr/ffhal-00197329

Mendhe, S., Bawankule, R., Udapurkar, A., Gogiya, R., Gaikwad, A., & Saggu, J. K. (2022). SignReco: Sign language translator. *International Research Journal of Engineering and Technology (IRJET), 9*(3). Retrieved from https://www.academia.edu/81754577/SignReco_Sign_Language_Translator

Menezes, D. (2024). Student fights AI cheating allegations for using Grammarly. NewsNation. https://www.newsnationnow.com/business/tech/ai/student-fights-academic-probation-ai-tool/

Mentegram. (n.d). Mentegram. Retrieved from https://mentegram.com.au/how-it-works/ on 1 June 2024.

Meskó, B. (2023). Prompt engineering as an important emerging skill for medical professionals: Tutorial. *Journal of Medical Internet Research*, 25, e50638. DOI: 10.2196/50638

Meulen, R., Bruggen, C., Spilt, J., Verouden, J., Berkhout, M., & Bögels, S. (2014). The pull-out program day a week school for gifted children: Effects on social- emotional and academic functioning. *Child and Youth Care Forum*, 43(3), 287–314. DOI: 10.1007/s10566-013-9239-5

Miao, F., & Holmes, W. (2021). *Artificial intelligence and education. Guidance for policy-makers*. United Nations Educational, Scientific and Cultural Organization (UNESCO).

Michelson, D., Davenport, C., Dretzke, J., Barlow, J., & Day, C. (2013). Do Evidence-based Interventions work when Tested in the "real world?" A Systematic Review and Meta-analysis of Parent Management Training for the Treatment of Child Disruptive Behavior. *Clinical Child and Family Psychology Review*, 16(1), 18–34. DOI: 10.1007/s10567-013-0128-0

Microsoft. (1975). Accessibility Tools for Learning. Retrieved June 28, 2024, from https://www.microsoft.com/en-in/education/learning-tools/accessibility-tools

Microsoft. (2017). Seeing AI. Retrieved from https://www.microsoft.com/seeing-ai on 1 June 2024.

Microsoft. (2023). Seeing AI. Retrieved from https://www.seeingai.com/

Microsoft. (n.d.). *Digital Learning Tools | Microsoft Education*. https://www.microsoft.com/en-us/education/products/learning-tools

Middeke, A., Anders, S., Schuelper, M., Raupach, T., & Schuelper, N. (2018). Training of clinical reasoning with a Serious Game versus small-group problem-based learning: A prospective study. *PLoS One*, 13(9), e0203851. Advance online publication. DOI: 10.1371/journal.pone.0203851 PMID: 30204773

Miesenberger, K., & Kouroupetroglou, G. (Eds.). (2018). Computers Helping People with Special Needs*:16th International Conference, ICCHP 2018,* Linz, Austria, July 11-13, 2018*, Proceedings, Part I* (Vol. 10896). Springer.

Milat, A., King, L., Bauman, A., & Redman, S. (2013). The concept of scalability: Increasing the scale and potential adoption of health promotion interventions into policy and practice. *Health Promotion International*, 3(28), 285–298. DOI: 10.1093/heapro/dar097 PMID: 22241853

Mills v. Board of Education of District of Columbia: 348 F. Supp. 866 (D.D.C. 1972)

Ministry of Education, Government of India. (2023). *Strategic Framework for the Integration of AI in Special Education.*

Ministry of Education, Government of India. (n.d.). *Samagra Shiksha*. Retrieved from https://samagra.education.gov.i NCERT (National Council of Educational Research and Training). (2024). *AI-powered Assessment and Monitoring Systems for Learning Disabilities in India*. New Delhi, India.

Mitchell, M. (2019). *Artificial Intelligence: A Guide for Thinking Humans*. Farrar, Straus and Giroux.

Mobasheri, A., Deister, J., & Dieterich, H. (2017). Wheelmap: The wheelchair accessibility crowdsourcing platform. *Open Geospatial Data. Software and Standards*, 2(1), 27. Advance online publication. DOI: 10.1186/s40965-017-0040-5

ModMath. (2023). ModMath. Retrieved from https://www.modmath.com/

Mog, L. K. (2016). Implementation of an electronic wheelchair with a Google Map and a smart phone's speaker-independent recognition engine. *Advanced Science Letters*, 22(11), 3333–3336. DOI: 10.1166/asl.2016.7900

Mohammad, Y., & Nishida, T. (2007). TalkBack: Feedback from a Miniature Robot. In T. Nishida & E. André (Eds.), *Toward Robotic Socially Believable Behaving Systems - Volume I: Modeling Emotions* (pp. 357-366). Springer. https://doi.org/ DOI: 10.1007/978-3-540-76928-6_37

Mohammed, P. S., & 'Nell'Watson, E. (2019). Towards inclusive education in the age of artificial intelligence: Perspectives, challenges, and opportunities. *Artificial Intelligence and Inclusive Education: Speculative futures and emerging practices*, 17-37.

Mokhlis, S., & Abdullah, A. H. (2024). Does teacher empowerment contribute to innovative work behaviour? *International Journal of Management Education*, 18(2), 147–172.

Molenaar, I., de Mooij, S., Azevedo, R., Bannert, M., Järvelä, S., & Gašević, D. (2022). Measuring self-regulated learning and the role of AI: Five years of research using multichannel data. *Computers in Human Behavior*, 139, 1–9. DOI: 10.1016/j.chb.2022.107540

Montesinos López, O. A., Montesinos López, A., & Crossa, J. (2022). Fundamentals of artificial neural networks and deep learning. In *Multivariate statistical machine learning methods for genomic prediction* (pp. 379–425). Springer International Publishing. DOI: 10.1007/978-3-030-89010-0_10

Moon, M. (2023). Searching for inclusive artificial intelligence for social good: Participatory governance and policy recommendations for making AI more inclusive and benign for society. *Public Administration Review*, 83(6), 1496–1505. DOI: 10.1111/puar.13648

Morales, M. (2021). Enhancing student engagement in math education through the use of gamified AI virtual assistants. *Frontiers in ICT (Lausanne, Switzerland)*, 8, 614019.

Morawska, A., Tometzki, H., & Sanders, M. R. (2014). An Evaluation of the Efficacy of a Triple P-Positive Parenting Program podcast series. *Journal of Developmental and Behavioral Pediatrics*, 35(2), 128–137. DOI: 10.1097/DBP.0000000000000020

Moriña, A., Carballo, R., & Castellano-Beltran, A. (2023). A systematic review of the benefits and challenges of technologies for the learning of university students with disabilities. *Journal of Special Education Technology*, 39(1), 41–50. DOI: 10.1177/01626434231175357

Morrison, E. C., & Dhareshwar, A. "Imagining AI applications with people with visual disabilities using tactile ideation," in *Proc. ASSETS '17*, 2017. DOI: 10.1145/3132525.3132530

Mosito, C. P., Warnick, A. M., & Esambe, E. E. (2017). Enhancing Reading Abilities of Learners with Intellectual Impairments through Computer Technology. *African Journal of Disability*, 6, 206. DOI: 10.4102/ajod.v6i0.206

Mountjoy, J. (2022). Community colleges and upward mobility. *The American Economic Review*, 112(8), 2580–2630. DOI: 10.1257/aer.20181756

Mühlhoff, R. (2021). Predictive privacy: Towards an applied ethics of data analytics. *Ethics and Information Technology*, 23(4), 675–690. DOI: 10.1007/s10676-021-09606-x

Mukherjee, P., S, G. R., Sadhukhan, S., Godse, M., & Chakraborty, B. (2023). Detection of Autism Spectrum Disorder (ASD) from Natural Language Text using BERT and ChatGPT Models. *International Journal of Advanced Computer Science and Applications*, 14(10). Advance online publication. DOI: 10.14569/IJACSA.2023.0141041

Mukhtarkyzy, K., Abildinova, G., & Sayakov, O. (2022). The use of augmented reality for teaching Kazakhstani students physics lessons. *International Journal of Emerging Technologies in Learning*, 17(12), 215–235. DOI: 10.3991/ijet.v17i12.29501

Mulfari, D., Carnevale, L., & Villari, M. (2023). Toward a lightweight ASR solution for atypical speech on the edge. *Future Generation Computer Systems*, 149(1), 455–463. DOI: 10.1016/j.future.2023.08.002

Muller, E. (2011, July). *Nasdse.* inForum. https://nasdse.org/docs/72_f2f7f9b7-ff92-4cda-a843-c817497e81e4.pdf

Müller, V. C., & Bostrom, N. (2016). Future Progress in Artificial Intelligence: A Survey of Expert Opinion. In Müller, V. C. (Ed.), *Fundamental Issues of Artificial Intelligence* (pp. 555–572). Springer., DOI: 10.1007/978-3-319-26485-1_33

Munro, E. (2019). *Predictive analytics in child protection* (CHESS Working Paper No. 2019-03). Durham University. https://www.dur.ac.uk/resources/chess/CHESSWorkingPaper2019-03.pdf

Mursion. (n.d.). *Mursion* [software]. https://www.mursion.com/

Mutawa, A. M., Al Mudhahkah, H. M., Al-Huwais, A., Al-Khaldi, N., Al-Otaibi, R., & Al-Ansari, A. (2023). Augmenting mobile app with NAO robot for autism education. *Machines (Basel)*, 11(8), 833. DOI: 10.3390/machines11080833

n2y. (2004). Unique Learning System [Educational software]. Retrieved from https://www.n2y.com/unique-learning-system/ on 1 June 2024.

N2Y. 2021, October 21). *N2Y wins Special Education Solution of the Year designation in 6th annual EdTech Breakthrough Awards program.* PR Newswire. https://www.prnewswire.com/news-releases/n2y-wins-special-education-solution-of-the-year-designation-in-6th-annual-edtech-breakthrough-awards-program-302166212.html

Namachivayam, A. (2021). An Appraisal of Microsoft Teams and Its Features. 462-478.

Nanni, L., & Lumini, A. (2009). Ensemble generation and feature selection for the identification of students with learning disabilities. *Expert Systems with Applications*, 36(2), 3896–3900. DOI: 10.1016/j.eswa.2008.02.065

Nathan, M. J., & Sawyer, R. K. (2014). Foundations of the learning sciences. In Sawyer, R. K. (Ed.), *The Cambridge Handbook of the Learning Sciences* (2nd ed., pp. 21–43). Cambridge University Press. DOI: 10.1017/CBO9781139519526.004

National Association for Gifted Children. (n.d.). *What is giftedness.*https://nagc.org/page/what-is-giftedness

National Association of School Psychologists. (2020). *The professional standards of the National Association of School Psychologists.* https://www.nasponline.org/standards-and-certification/professional-ethics

National Center for Special Education Research. (2023). *Special education research grants program.* US Department of Education. Institute of Education Sciences. https://ies.ed.gov/funding/pdf/2024_84324A.pdf

National Forum on Education Statistics. (2019). Forum Guide to Personalized Learning Data (NFES2019160). U.S. Department of Education. Washington, DC: National Center for Education Statistics.

National Informatics Centre. (n.d.). KVS Shala Darpan. Retrieved on june 1, 2024, from https://information.nic.in/kvs-shala-darpan

National Institute for Transforming India Aayog. (2023). National Strategy for Artificial Intelligence. Government of India. Retrieved [27th June 2024] from https://www.niti.gov.in/sites/default/files/2023-03/National-Strategy-for-Artificial-Intelligence.pdf

National Institute for Transforming India Aayog. (2023). National Strategy for Artificial Intelligence. Government of India. Retrieved from https://www.niti.gov.in/sites/default/files/2023-03/National-Strategy-for-Artificial-Intelligence.pdf) on 27th June 2024.

Nayak, J., Bhat, P. S., Acharya, R. U. V., & Aithal, U. V. (2005). Classification and analysis of speech abnormalities. *ITBM-RBM*, 26(5–6), 319–327. DOI: 10.1016/j.rbmret.2005.05.002

Nayak, S., & Das, R. K. (2020). Application of artificial intelligence (AI) in prosthetic and orthotic rehabilitation. In *Service Robotics*. IntechOpen. DOI: 10.5772/intechopen.93903

Nazaretsky, T., Cukurova, M., & Alexandron, G. (2022, March). An instrument for measuring teachers' trust in AI-based educational technology. In *LAK22: 12th international learning analytics and knowledge conference* (pp. 56-66).

Neal, T. (2016). *Teacher, parent, and student perceptions of adolescent giftedness and self- concept in rural northeast Louisiana schools* (10148471) [Doctoral dissertation, University of Louisiana at Monroe]. ProQuest Dissertations and Theses database.

Neamtu, R., Camara, A., Pereira, C., & Ferreira, R. (2019). Using artificial intelligence for augmentative alternative communication for children with disabilities. In Lamas, D., Loizides, F., Nacke, L., Petrie, H., Winckler, M., & Zaphiris, P. (Eds.), Lecture Notes in Computer Science: Vol. 11746. *Human-Computer Interaction – INTERACT 2019*. Springer., DOI: 10.1007/978-3-030-29381-9_15

Neeharika, C., & Riyazuddin, Y. (2023). Artificial Intelligence in Children with Special Need Education. *2023 International Conference on Intelligent Data Communication Technologies and Internet of Things*, 519-523. DOI: 10.1109/IDCIoT56793.2023.10053420

Neely, L., MacNaul, H., Gregori, E., & Cantrell, K. (2021). Effects of telehealth-mediated behavioral assessments and interventions on client outcomes: A quality review. *Journal of Applied Behavior Analysis*, 54(2), 484–510. DOI: 10.1002/jaba.818 PMID: 33621358

Neihart, M., Reis, S. M., Robinson, N. M., & Moon, S. M. (Eds.). (2002). *The social and emotional development of gifted children: What do we know?* Prufrock Press, Inc.

Nelson, E. L., & Bui, T. (2010). Rural telepsychology services for children and adolescents. *Journal of Clinical Psychology*, 66(5), 490–501. DOI: 10.1002/jclp.20682 PMID: 20306524

Nemorin, S., Vlachidis, A., Ayerakwa, H. M., & Andriotis, P. (2022). AI hyped? A horizon scan of discourse on artificialintelligence in education (AIED) and development. Online article. *Learning, Media and Technology*, •••, 1–14. DOI: 10.1080/17439884.2022.2095568

Nesbitt, S. (2000). Why and why not? Factors impacting employment for individuals with Asperger syndrome. *Autism*, 4(4), 357–369. DOI: 10.1177/1362361300004004002

Newhall, P. W. (2012). *Language-based learning disabilities*. Landmark School Outreach Program.

Newsroom (2019, July 21). How Education Software Company Kami entered America's Classrooms. University of Auckland Centre for Innovation and Entrepreneurship. https://www.example.com/kami-article retrieved on 20 June 2024.

Ng, D. T. K., Leung, J. K. L., Chu, S. K. W., & Qiao, M. S. (2021). Conceptualizing AI literacy: An exploratory review. *Computers and Education: Artificial Intelligence, 2*, article 100041.

Ng, D. T. K., Lee, M., Tan, R. J. Y., Hu, X., Downie, J. S., & Chu, S. K. W. (2023). A review of AI teaching and learning from 2000 to 2020. *Education and Information Technologies*, 28(7), 8445–8501. DOI: 10.1007/s10639-022-11491-w

Ng, D. T. K., Leung, J. K. L., Chu, K. W. S., & Qiao, M. S. (2021). AI literacy: Definition, teaching, evaluation and ethical issues. *Proceedings of the Association for Information Science and Technology*, 58(1), 504–509. DOI: 10.1002/pra2.487

Ng, D. T. K., Leung, J. K. L., Su, J., Ng, R. C. W., & Chu, S. K. W. (2023). Teachers' AI digital competencies and twenty-first century skills in the post-pandemic world. *Educational technology research and development. Educational Technology Research and Development*, 71(1), 137–161. DOI: 10.1007/s11423-023-10203-6 PMID: 36844361

Nguyen, T., Lee, J., & Chen, H. (2022). AI-powered Language Processing Tools for Supporting Students with Speech and Language Impairments. *Assistive Technology*, 34(3), 145–158.

Nicholas, D. B., Zwaigenbaum, L., Zwicker, J., Clarke, M. E., Lamsal, R., Stoddart, K., Carroll, C., Muskat, B., Spoelstra, M., & Lowe, K. (2018). Evaluation of employment support services for adults with autism spectrum disorder. *Autism*, 22(6), 693–702. DOI: 10.1177/1362361317702507

Nicholas, D., Mitchell, W., Zulla, R., & Dudley, C. (2019). Perspectives of employers about hiring individuals with autism spectrum disorder: Evaluating a cohort of employers engaged in a job–readiness initiative. *Journal of Vocational Rehabilitation*, 50(3), 353–364. DOI: 10.3233/JVR-191018

Ntoutsi, E., Fafalios, P., Gadiraju, U., Iosifidis, V., Nejdl, W., Vidal, M., Ruggieri, S., Turini, F., Papadopoulos, S., Krasanakis, E., Kompatsiaris, I., Kinder-Kurlanda, K., Wagner, C., Karimi, F., Fernández, M., Alani, H., Berendt, B., Kruegel, T., Heinze, C., & Staab, S. (2020). Bias in data-driven artificial intelligence systems—An introductory survey. *Wiley Interdisciplinary Reviews. Data Mining and Knowledge Discovery*, 10(3), e1356. DOI: 10.1002/widm.1356

Nuralisah, A., & Kareviati, E. (2020). The effectiveness of using Memrise application in teaching vocabulary. [Professional Journal of English Education]. *PROJECT*, 3(4), 494–500. DOI: 10.22460/project.v3i4.p494-500

Nylen, B., & King, S. A. (2023). Training practitioners to conduct a functional behavior assessment via telehealth-delivered behavioral skills training: A systematic literature review. *Journal of Behavioral Education*. Advance online publication. DOI: 10.1007/s10864-023-09514-8

O'Brien, K. M., Nagro, S. A., Binkert, G. D., Szocik, K., & Gerry, M. (2024). Field experiences in special education teacher preparation: A review of the literature. *Teacher Education and Special Education*, 47(1), 5–25. DOI: 10.1177/08884064231177662

O'Brien, M. J., Pelzel, K. E., Hendrix, N. M., Schieltz, K. M., Miller, K., Call, N. A., Tsami, L., Lerman, D. C., Berg, W. K., Kopelman, T. G., Wacker, D. P., & Lindgren, S. D. (2022). Parent ratings of generalized and indirect effects of functional communication training for children with autism spectrum disorder. *Behavior Modification*, 46(5), 971–1001. DOI: 10.1177/01454455211018815 PMID: 34041956

O'Connor, S., & Liu, H. (2024). Gender bias perpetuation and mitigation in AI technologies: Challenges and opportunities. *AI & Society*, 39(4), 2045–2057. DOI: 10.1007/s00146-023-01675-4

Obiakor, F. E., Bakken, J. P., & Rotatori, A. F. (2010). *Current issues and trends in special education.Research, technology, and teacher preparation / edited by Festus E. Obiakor, Jeffrey P. Bakken, Anthony F. Rotatori.* (1st ed.). Emerald.

Ochoa, S. H., Rivera, B., & Ford, L. (1997). An investigation of school psychology training pertaining to bilingual psycho-educational assessment of primarily Hispanic students: Twenty-five years after Diana v. California. *Journal of School Psychology*, 35(4), 329–349. DOI: 10.1016/S0022-4405(97)00009-5

Office of Educational Technology. (2023). *Artificial intelligence and the future of teaching and learning: Insights and recommendations*. U.S. Department of Education. https://tech.ed.gov/ai-report-2023

Office of Educational Technology. (2023, May). *Artificial intelligence and the future of teaching and learning: Insights and recommendations*. U.S. Department of Education. https://tech.ed.gov/files/2023/05/AI-Teaching-Learning-Insights-Recommendations.pdf

Office of Special Education and Rehabilitative Services. (2024). *Applications for new awards; Educational technology, media, and material for individuals with disabilities program-stepping-up technology implementation*. US Department of Education. https://www.federalregister.gov/documents/2024/03/01/2024-04316/applications-for-new-awards-educational-technology-media-and-materials-for-individuals-with

Office of the High Commissioner for Human Rights (OHCHR). (2022, May 9.). Humanity should get the best from AI, not the worst - UN disability. https://www.ohchr.org/

Ogunbukola, M. (2024). Empowering Abilities: How AI is Transforming Lives for People with Disabilities. https://www.researchgate.net/publication/378547809_Empowering_Abilities_How_AI_is_Transforming_Lives_for_People_with_Disabilities

Ojha, S. T. (2022). Artificial Intelligence In Special Education, Id& Cp. *Journal of Positive School Psychology*, 6(6), 8341–8345. https://journalppw.com/index.php/jpsp/article/view/9109/5928

Okamura, K., & Yamada, S. (2020). Adaptive trust calibration for human-AI collaboration. *PLoS One*, 15(2), e0229132. Advance online publication. DOI: 10.1371/journal.pone.0229132 PMID: 32084201

Olasik, M. (2023). "Good morning, ChatGPT, Can We Become Friends?" An Interdisciplinary Scholar's Experience of 'Getting Acquainted'with the OpenAI's Chat GPT: An Auto Ethnographical Report. *European Research Studies*, 26(2), 269–284. DOI: 10.35808/ersj/3168

Olton-Weber, S., Hess, R., & Ritchotte, J. A. (2020). Reducing levels of perfectionism in gifted and talented youth through a mindfulness intervention. *Gifted Child Quarterly*, 60(4), 319–330. DOI: 10.1177/0016986220953392

Open, A. I. (2022). *Introducing Whisper*. https://openai.com/research/whisper

Open, A. I. (2023). ChatGPT (June 2023 version) [Large language model]. https://www.openai.com/

Open, A. I. (2024). *ChatGPT* [Large language model]. https://chat.openai.com/

OpenLearning. (2024, March 7). AI in education: Benefits, challenges, and best practices. Learning Design Theories, Micro-credentials and Online Education - OpenLearning Blog. https://blog.openlearning.com/ai-in-education

Ouyang, F., & Jiao, P. (2021). Artificial intelligence in education: The three paradigms. *Computers and Education: Artificial Intelligence*, 2, 100020. DOI: 10.1016/j.caeai.2021.100020

Ouyang, F., Zheng, L., & Jiao, P. (2022). Artificial intelligence in online higher education: A systematic review of empirical research from 2011 to 2020. *Education and Information Technologies*, 27(6), 7893–7925. DOI: 10.1007/s10639-022-10925-9

Özdemir, O., & Kalınkara, Y. (2020). Bulanık Mantık: 2000-2020 Yılları Arası Tez ve Makale Çalışmalarına Yönelik Bir İçerik Analizi. *Acta Infologica*, 4(2), 155–174. DOI: 10.26650/acin.762872

Palacios, A. M., Sánchez, L., & Couso, I. (2010). Diagnosis of dyslexia with low quality data with geneticfuzzy systems. *International Journal of Approximate Reasoning*, 51(8), 993–1009. DOI: 10.1016/j.ijar.2010.07.008

Panitz, T. (1999). Benefits of cooperative learning in relation to student motivation. In Theall, M. (Ed.), *Motivation from within: Approaches for encouraging faculty and students to excel* (pp. 59–68). Josey-Bass Publishing.

Panjwani-Charani, S., & Zhai, X. (2023). AI for Students with Learning Disabilities: A Systematic Review. In *X. Zhai & J. Krajcik (2023), Uses of Artificial Intelligence in STEM Education* (pp. 1–28). Oxford University Press.

Pantziaras, I., Fors, U., & Ekblad, S. (2015). Training with virtual patients in transcultural psychiatry: Do the learners actually learn? *Journal of Medical Internet Research*, 17(2), e46. Advance online publication. DOI: 10.2196/jmir.3497 PMID: 25689716

Parekh, D., Poddar, N., Rajpurkar, A., Chahal, M., Kumar, N., Joshi, G. P., & Cho, W. (2022). A review on autonomous vehicles: Progress, methods and challenges. *Electronics (Basel)*, 11(14), 2162. DOI: 10.3390/electronics11142162

Park, T. J., Tandberg, D. A., Shim, H. K., Hu, S., & Herrington, C. D. (2018). Community college teacher education baccalaureate programs: Early evidence yields mixed results. *Educational Policy*, 32(7), 1018–1040. DOI: 10.1177/0895904816682317

Parmaxi, A., Athanasiou, A., & A Demetriou, A. (2021). Introducing a Student-led Application of Google Expeditions: An exploratory study. *Educational Media International*, 58(3), 1–23. DOI: 10.1080/09523987.2021.1908497

Parre, M. D.; Sujatha, B. (2021): Novel human-centered robotics: towards an automated process for neurorehabilitation. Neurology Research International, 2021 (1). https://doi.org/DOI: 10.1155/2021/6690715

Parsons, J. A. (2021). The telemedical imperative. *Bioethics*, 35(4), 298–306. DOI: 10.1111/bioe.12847 PMID: 33586790

Parsons, S., & Mitchell, P. (2002). The potential of virtual reality in social skills training for people with autistic spectrum disorders. *Journal of Intellectual Disability Research*, 46(5), 430–443. DOI: 10.1046/j.1365-2788.2002.00425.x PMID: 12031025

Patil, S., Gupta, N., & Rao, J. (2022). Implementing AI-powered Assistive Robotics in Special EducationAI-power in Rural India: A Case Study. *Assistive Technology*, 34(4), 211–223.

Patnaik, N., & Agrawal, K. (2022). Study on processor used in virtual assistants: Google Assistant, Alexa, Siri Alexa. *International Research Journal of Engineering and Technology (IRJET), 9*(3), 1874. Retrieved from https://www.irjet.net

Pattison, A. S., & Roopaei, M. (2023). An AI-based exergame to assist occupational and physical therapy. In *2023 IEEE World AI IoT Congress (AIIoT)* (pp. 0804-0807). IEEE. https://doi.org/DOI: 10.1109/AIIoT58121.2023.10174489

Pavlik, P. I., Jr., Olney, A. M., Banker, A., Eglington, L., & Yarbro, J. (2020). The mobile fact and concept textbook system (MoFaCTS). In S. Sosnovsky, P. Brusilovsky, R. Baraniuk, & A. Lan (Eds.), *Proceedings of the Second International Workshop on Intelligent Textbooks 2020 co-located with 21st International Conference on Artificial Intelligence in Education (AIED 2020)*. Institute for Intelligent Systems, University of Memphis. https://ceur-ws.org/Vol-2674/paper04.pdf

Pavlik, J. V. (2023). Collaborating with ChatGPT: Considering the implications of generative artificial intelligence for journalism and media education. *Journalism & Mass Communication Educator*, 78(1), 84–93. DOI: 10.1177/10776958221149577

Pavlopoulos, J., Vrettaros, J., Vouros, G., & Drigas, A. S. (2008). The development of a self-assessment system for the learners' answers with the use of GPNN. In Lytras, M. D., Carroll, J. M., Damiani, E., & Tennyson, R. D. (Eds.), *Emerging technologies and information systems for the knowledge society: WSKS 2008* (Vol. 5288, pp. 332–340). Springer., DOI: 10.1007/978-3-540-87781-3_37

Pearson Education, Inc. (2019). *General overview of WriteToLearn and its components*. Retrieved from https://WriteToLearn.net

Pearson, E., Gkatzidou, V., & Green, S. (2010). From a personal Learning environment to an adaptable personal learning environment: Meeting the needs and preferences of disabled learners. 2010 10th IEEE International Conference on Advanced Learning Technologies, 333–335. DOI: 10.1109/ICALT.2010.94

Pennington, B. F., McGrath, L. M., Peterson, R., & Peterson, R. L. (2019). *Diagnosing learning disorders: From science to practice*. Guilford Publications.

Pennisi, P., Tonacci, A., Tartarisco, G., Billeci, L., Ruta, L., Gangemi, S., & Pioggia, G. (2016). Autism and Social Robotics: A Systematic Review. *Autism Research: official journal of the International Society for Autism Research,* 9(2), 165–83. https://doi.org/DOI: 10.1002/aur.1527

Pennsylvania Association for Retarded Citizens (PARC) v. Commonwealth of Pennsylvania (1972, 334 F. Supp. 1257 Rajesh, R., & Joseph, Z. C. (2023). Competency-based teacher education (CBTE): A training module to improve knowledge, attitude, and practices (KAP) of school teachers on learning disabilities in children. *Journal of Family Medicine and Primary Care, 12*(5), 874-880.

Peredo, R., Canales, A., Menchaca, A., & Peredo, I. (2011). Intelligent web-based education system for adaptive learning. *Expert Systems with Applications*, 38(12), 14690–14702. DOI: 10.1016/j.eswa.2011.05.013

Peterson, A. K., Fox, C. B., & Israelsen, M. (2020). A systematic review of academic discourse interventions for school-aged children with language-related learning disabilities. *Language, Speech, and Hearing Services in Schools*, 51(3), 866–881. DOI: 10.1044/2020_LSHSS-19-00039 PMID: 32525756

Peterson-Karlan, G. R. (2015). Assistive technology instruction within a continuously evolving technology environment. *Quarterly Review of Distance Education*, 16(2), 61.

Petroni, F., Rocktäschel, T., Lewis, P., Bakhtin, A., Wu, Y., Miller, A. H., & Riedel, S. (2019). Language models as knowledge bases? *arXiv preprint arXiv:1909.01066*. DOI: 10.18653/v1/D19-1250

Peyton, D. J., Acosta, K., Harvey, A., Pua, D. J., Sindelar, P. T., Mason-Williams, L., Dewey, J., Fisher, T. L., & Crews, E. (2021). Special education teacher shortage: Differences between high and low shortage states. *Teacher Education and Special Education*, 44(1), 5–23. https://doi-org.ezproxy.ecu.edu.au/10.1177/0888406420906618. DOI: 10.1177/0888406420906618

Picard, R. W. (2000). *Affective computing*. MIT press. DOI: 10.7551/mitpress/1140.003.0008

Pidano, A. E., & Allen, A. R. (2015). The Incredible Years series: A Review of the Independent Research base. *Journal of Child and Family Studies*, 24(7), 1898–1916. DOI: 10.1007/s10826-014-9991-7

Pierres, O., Darvishy, A., & Christen, M. (2023). AI in Higher Education: Ethical Concerns for Students with Disabilities. In Alvarez, J.M., Fabris, A., Heitz, C., Hertweck, C., Loi, M., Zehlike, M. Proceedings of the European Workshop on Algorithmic Fairness (EWAF'23). Winterthur: CEUR-WS, 7-9.

Pilling, K. (2015). Special Needs for Special Kids [Mobile app]. Special Needs for Special Kids. https://www.specialneedsforspecialkids.org

Pintrich, P. R. (2000). The role of goal orientation in self-regulated learning. In *Handbook of Self-Regulation* (pp. 451–502). Academic Press. DOI: 10.1016/B978-012109890-2/50043-3

Podoletz, L. (2023). We have to talk about emotional AI and crime. *AI & Society*, 38(3), 1067–1082. DOI: 10.1007/s00146-022-01435-w

Porayska-Pomsta, K., Alcorn, A. M., Avramides, K., Beale, S., Bernardini, S., Foster, M. E., Frauenberger, C., Good, J., Guldberg, K., Keay-Bright, W., Kossyvaki, L., Lemon, O., Mademtzi, M., Menzies, R., Pain, H., Rajendran, G., Waller, A., Wass, S., & Smith, T. J. (2018). Blending human and artificial intelligence to support autistic children's social communication skills. [TOCHI]. *ACM Transactions on Computer-Human Interaction*, 25(6), 1–35. DOI: 10.1145/3271484

Poulter, C. (2020). Voice recognition software—Nuance Dragon naturally speaking. *Occupational Medicine (Oxford, England)*, 70(1), 75–76. DOI: 10.1093/occmed/kqz128

Praglin, L. J. (2007). Ida Cannon, Ethel Cohen, and early medical social work in Boston: The foundations of a model of culturally competent social service. *The Social Service Review*, 81(1), 27–45. DOI: 10.1086/511013

Prain, V., Cox, P., Deed, C., Dorman, J., Edwards, D., Farrelly, C., Keeffe, M., Lovejoy, V., Mow, L., Sellings, P., Waldrip, B., & Yager, Z. (2013). Personalised learning. *Journal of Educational Psychology*, 38(1), 54–68. DOI: 10.1080/01443410.2013.857010

Prenner. (2015, August 5). *Ghotit Real Writer*. Dyslexia Help at the University of Michigan. https://dyslexiahelp.umich.edu/home/ghotit-real-writer

Prykanowski, D. A., Conroy, M. A., & Reichow, B. (2021). Schedule thinning during functional communication training in the home for young children with autism. *Journal of Positive Behavior Interventions*, 23(4), 257–271. DOI: 10.1177/1098300721994204

Puglisi, A., Caprì, T., Pignolo, L., Gismondo, S., Chilà, P., Minutoli, R., Marino, F., Failla, C., Arnao, A. A., Tartarisco, G., Cerasa, A., & Pioggia, G. (2022). Social Humanoid Robots for Children with Autism Spectrum Disorders: A Review of Modalities, Indications, and Pitfalls. *Children (Basel, Switzerland)*, 9(7), 953. DOI: 10.3390/children9070953

Pullen, P. C., & Kennedy, M. J. (Eds.). (2019). *Handbook of response to intervention and multi-tiered systems of support*. Routledge.

Putra, A. (2023). The effect of EDAPP as LMS on students' English proficiency on junior high school student. *RETAIN: Journal of Research in English Language Teaching, 11*(03), 31-38. Retrieved from https://ejournal.unesa.ac.id/index.php/retain/article/view/56604

Rabiyath, S. S., & Kumar, M. N. (2024). Bashini Website and App – An Overview. *Journal of Emerging Technologies and Innovative Research*, 11(1). https://www.jetir.org/papers/JETIR2401141.pdf

Radianti, J., Majchrzak, T. A., Fromm, J., & Wohlgenannt, I. (2020). A systematic review of immersive virtual reality applications for higher education: Design elements, lessons learned, and research agenda. *Computers & Education*, 147, 103778. Advance online publication. DOI: 10.1016/j.compedu.2019.103778

Rajaraman, A., Austin, J. L., Gover, H. C., Cammilleri, A. P., Donnelly, D. R., & Hanley, G. P. (2022). Toward trauma-informed applications of behavior analysis. *Journal of Applied Behavior Analysis*, 55(1), 40–61. DOI: 10.1002/jaba.881 PMID: 34525220

Rakap, S. (2024). Chatting with GPT: Enhancing Individualized Education Program Goal Development for Novice Special Education Teachers. *Journal of Special Education Technology*, 39(3), 339–348. DOI: 10.1177/01626434231211295

Ramesh, D., & Sanampudi, S. K. (2022). An automated essay scoring system: A systematic literature review. *Artificial Intelligence Review*, 55(3), 2495–2527. DOI: 10.1007/s10462-021-10068-2 PMID: 34584325

Ratican, J., & Hutson, J. (2023). The Six Emotional Dimension (6DE) Model: A Multidimensional Approach to Analyzing Human Emotions and Unlocking the Potential of Emotionally Intelligent Artificial Intelligence (AI) via Large Language Models (LLM). *Journal of Artificial Intelligence and Robotics*, 1(1), 481.

Reid, D. H., O'Kane, N. P., & Macurik, K. M. (2011). Staff training and management. In Fisher, W. W., Piazza, C. C., & Roane, H. S. (Eds.), *Handbook of applied behavior analysis* (pp. 281–296). The Guilford Press.

Reinholz, D. L., & Andrews, T. C. (2020). Change theory and theory of change: What's the difference anyway? *International Journal of STEM Education*, 7(1), 1–12. DOI: 10.1186/s40594-020-0202-3

Reis, S. (2023). *Reconsidering regular curriculum for high achieving students, gifted underachievers, and relationship between gifted and regular education*. https://gifted.uconn.edu/schoolwide-enrichment-model/reconsidering_regular_curriculum/#:~:text=Sixty%2Done%20percent%20of%20public%20school%20teachers%20and,to%20meet%20the%20needs%20of%20gifted%20students

Reis, S., & Renzulli, J. (2004). Current research on the social and emotional development of gifted and talented students: Good news and future possibilities. *Psychology in the Schools*, 41(1), 119–130. DOI: 10.1002/pits.10144

Rejmaniak, R. (2021). Bias in Artificial Intelligence Systems. *Białostockie Studia Prawnicze*, 26(3), 25–42. DOI: 10.15290/bsp.2021.26.03.02

Rello, L., & Ballesteros, M. (2015, May). Detecting readers with dyslexia using machine learning with eye tracking measures. In *Proceedings of the 12th international web for all conference* (pp. 1-8). DOI: 10.1145/2745555.2746644

Rende, F. Ş., Bütün, G., & Karahan, Ş. (2016). Derin Öğrenme Algoritmalarında Model Testleri: Derin Testler. 10. Ulusal yazılım Mühendisliği Sempozyumu,24-26 Ekim, pp:54-59, Çanakkale. Russell, S. J., & Norvig, P. (2020). Artificial intelligence: a modern approach (Fourth edition), Pearson Education.

Renz, A., & Hilbig, R. (2020). Prerequisites for artificial intelligence in further education: Identification of drivers, barriers, and business models of educational technology companies. *International Journal of Educational Technology in Higher Education*, 17(1), 1–21. DOI: 10.1186/s41239-020-00193-3

Rhodes, B. J., & Maes, P. (2000). Just-in-time information retrieval agents. *IBM Systems Journal, 39*(3.4), 685–704.

Rice, M. F., & Dunn, S. (2023). The use of artificial intelligence with students with identified disabilities: A systematic review with critique. *Computers in the Schools*, 40(4), 370–390. Advance online publication. DOI: 10.1080/07380569.2023.2244935

Riedl, M., Arriaga, R., Boujarwah, F., Hong, H., Isbell, J., & Heflin, J. (2009). Graphical social scenarios: Toward intervention and authoring for adolescents with high functioning autism. In 2009 AAAI Fall Symposium Series. AAAI. https://cdn.aaai.org/ocs/945/945-4144-1-PB.pdf

Riedl, M., Arriaga, R., Boujarwah, F., Hong, H., Isbell, J., & Heflin, L. J. (2007). *Graphical social scenarios: Toward intervention and authoring for adolescents with high functioning autism.* Virtual Healthcare Interaction. Papers from the AAAI Fall Symposium, 64-73. https://aaai.org/papers/00945-945-graphical-social-scenarios-toward-intervention-and-authoring-for-adolescents-with-high-functioning-autism/

Rimm, S. B., Siegle, D., & Davis, G. A. (2018). *Education of the gifted and talented* (7th ed.). Pearson Education, Inc.

Ritonga, M., Zulmuqim, Z., Bambang, B., Kurniawan, R., & Pahri, P. (2022). SIAKAD Machine Learning for Correcting Errors in Speaking Arabic. *World Journal on Educational Technology: Current Issues*, 14(3), 768–780. DOI: 10.18844/wjet.v14i3.7214

Rittle-Johnson, B., Siegler, R. S., & Alibali, M. W. (2001). Developing conceptual understanding and procedural skill in mathematics: An iterative process. *Journal of Educational Psychology*, 93(2), 346–362. DOI: 10.1037/0022-0663.93.2.346

Rizky, R., & Hakim, Z. (2020). *International Conference on Science, Health, Economics, Education and Technology (ICoSHEET 2019)*. Atlantis Press.

Rizvi, M. (2023). Investigating AI-Powered Tutoring Systems that Adapt to Individual Student Needs, Providing Personalized Guidance and Assessments. *The Eurasia Proceedings of Educational and Social Sciences*, 31, 67–73. DOI: 10.55549/epess.1381518

Roach, J. (2018). AI technology helps students who are deaf learn. *Microsoft*. https://blogs.microsoft.com/ai/ai-powered-captioning/

Robert, A., Potter, K., & Frank, L. (2024). The impact of artificial intelligence on students' learning experience. *SSRN*. Advance online publication. DOI: 10.2139/ssrn.4716747

Robledo-Castro, C., Catillo-Ossa, L. F., & Corchado, J. M. (2023). Artificial Cognitive Systems Applied in Executive Function Stimulation and Rehabilitation Programs: A Systematic Review. *Arabian Journal for Science and Engineering*, 48(2), 2399–2427. DOI: 10.1007/s13369-022-07292-5 PMID: 36185593

Robles, P., & Mallinson, D. J. (2023). Artificial intelligence technology, public trust, and effective governance. *The Review of Policy Research*, 00, 1–18. DOI: 10.1111/ropr.12555

Robokind. (n.d). Milo Robot. Retrieved from https://www.robokind.com/advanced-social-robots on 1 June 2024.

Robson, D. A., Allen, M. S., & Howard, S. J. (2020). Self-regulation in childhood as a predictor of future outcomes: A meta-analytic review. *Psychological Bulletin*, 146(4), 324–354. DOI: 10.1037/bul0000227 PMID: 31904248

Rogoshui, A. Z. (2023) The effect of digital educational game on the visual perception of dyslexic first grade students [thesis]. Tehran, Iran: Allameh Tabataba'i University

Roll, I., & Wylie, R. (2016). Evolution and revolution in artificial intelligence in education. *International Journal of Artificial Intelligence in Education*, 26(2), 582–608. DOI: 10.1007/s40593-016-0110-3

Ronksley-Pavia, M. (2024). Curriculum in special school contexts: A collaged framework for personalised, individual student learning. *Curriculum Journal*, 35(1), 56–72. DOI: 10.1002/curj.235

Rose, D. H., & Meyer, A. (2002). Teaching every student in the digital age: Universal design for learning. Association for Supervision and Curriculum Development, 1703 N. Beauregard St., Alexandria, VA 22311-1714 (Product no. 101042: $22.95 ASCD members; $26.95 nonmembers).

Rose, D. (2018). *Universal Design for Learning Environments*. Harvard Education Press.

Rosen, R., Weiss, P. L., Zancanaro, M., & Gal, E. (2017). Usability of a video modeling computer application for the vocational training of adolescents with autism spectrum disorder. *British Journal of Occupational Therapy*, 80(4), 208–215. DOI: 10.1177/0308022616680367

Roth, R. A. (1977). How effective are CBTE programs? *Phi Delta Kappan*, 58(10), 757–760.

Rowland, A., Do, P., & Aylward, J. (2014). Classkick. https://www.classkick.com

Ruan, M., Peng, X., & Zhang, Y. (2022). Modeling self-regulated learning with AI: A case study using multimodal data. In Aleven, V., Roll, I., & Koedinger, K. R. (Eds.), Lecture Notes in Computer Science: Vol. 13291. *Artificial Intelligence in Education* (pp. 90–101). Springer., DOI: 10.1007/978-3-031-06017-9_7

Rude, H., & Miller, K. J. (2018). Policy challenges and opportunities for rural special education. *Rural Special Education Quarterly*, 37(1), 21–29. DOI: 10.1177/8756870517748662

Rufo, J. M., & Causton, J. (2022). *Reimagining special education: Using inclusion as a framework to build equity and support all students*. Brookes Publishing.

Rumelhart, D. E., Hinton, G. E., & Williams, R. J. (1986). Learning representations by back-propagating errors. *Nature*, 323(6088), 533–536. DOI: 10.1038/323533a0

Ruppar, A., Kurth, J., Bubash, S., & Lockman Turner, E. (2023). A framework for preparing to teach students with extensive support needs in the 21st century. *Teacher Education and Special Education*, 46(1), 26–43. DOI: 10.1177/08884064211059853

Russell, S., & Norvig, P. (2010). *Artificial intelligence: A modern approach* (3rd ed.). Prentice Hall, Pearson Education, Inc.

Russell, S., & Norvig, P. (2021). *Artificial Intelligence: A Modern Approach* (4th ed.). Prentice Hall, Pearson Education, Inc.

Sadhana, & Yadav, D. S. (2024). Ethical Considerations in AI-Driven Education: Balancing Innovation and Responsibility. International Journal Of Innovative Research In Technology, 10(10), 49-53. https://ijirt.org/master/publishedpaper/IJIRT162392_PAPER.pdf

Sağdıç, A., Canpolat Çığ, N., Çelenk, U., Takı, Z., Çetin, İ., Feyzullahoğlu, P., Altuğ Ateş, M., & Doğan, O. (2023). Teaching following instructions and responding skills to children with autism with an AI-supported mobile application. In *ICERI2023 Proceedings* (pp. 7658-7664). IATED. https://doi.org/DOI: 10.21125/iceri.2023.1920

Sağdıç, A., Elumar-Efe, E., & Sani-Bozkurt, S. (2024). GenAI, robots, and inclusive special education: Autism spectrum disorder in the age of generative AI. In Sharma, R., & Bozkurt, A. (Eds.), *Transforming education with generative AI: Prompt engineering and synthetic content creation* (pp. 309–326). IGI Global., DOI: 10.4018/979-8-3693-1351-0.ch015

Salas-Pilco, S. Z., Xiao, K., & Hu, X. (2022). Artificial intelligence and learning analytics in teacher education: A systematic review. *Education Sciences*, 12(8), 569. DOI: 10.3390/educsci12080569

Saleh, M. A., Hanapiah, F. A., & Hashim, H. (2021). Robot applications for autism: A comprehensive review. *Disability and Rehabilitation. Assistive Technology*, 16(6), 580–602. DOI: 10.1080/17483107.2019.1685016 PMID: 32706602

Saleh, M. A., Hashim, H., Mohamed, N. N., & Almisreb, A. A. (2020). Robots and autistic children: A review. *Periodicals of Engineering and Natural Sciences*, 8(3), 1247–1262. DOI: 10.21533/pen.v8i3.790

Salkever, D. S. (2000). Activity status, life satisfaction and perceived productivity for young adults with developmental disabilities. *Journal of Rehabilitation*, 66(3), 4.

Samara, M., George, T., & Ali, M. (2021). AI-based adaptive intelligent systems: A comprehensive review. *iJAI, 4*(3), 319-330. https://doi.org/DOI: 10.1016/j.jai.2021.11.005

Sancenon, V., Wijaya, K., Wen, X. Y., Utama, D. A., Ashworth, M., Ng, K. H., Cheong, A., & Neo, Z. (2022). A new web-based personalized learning system improves student learning outcomes. *International Journal of Virtual and Personal Learning Environments*, 12(1), 1–21. DOI: 10.4018/IJVPLE.295306

Santos, L., Annunziata, S., Geminiani, A., Ivani, A., Giubergia, A., Garofalo, D., Caglio, A., Brazzoli, E., Lipari, R., Carrozza, M. C., Ambrosini, E., Olivieri, I., & Pedrocchi, A. (2023). Applications of robotics for autism spectrum disorder: A scoping review. *Review Journal of Autism and Developmental Disorders*. Advance online publication. DOI: 10.1007/s40489-023-00402-5

Şanverdi, M. (2021). The use of Rosetta Stone application for vocabulary improvement in English: A review study. In *Proceedings of the International Conference on Language and Linguistics* (pp. 85–91). ISBN 978-605-196-721-9.

Sarker, I. H. (2021). Deep learning: A comprehensive overview on techniques, taxonomy, applications and research directions. *SN Computer Science*, 2(420), 420. Advance online publication. DOI: 10.1007/s42979-021-00815-1 PMID: 34426802

Sato, M., Ishikawa, S., & Tanaka, H. (2023). Virtual Assistants for Students with Intellectual Disabilities: Enhancing Independence and Confidence. *Journal of Special Education Technology*, 38(1), 23–37.

Saxena, N. B. (2020). AI as awakened intelligence: Buddha, Kurzweil and the film Her. *Theology and Science*, 18(1), 74–85. DOI: 10.1080/14746700.2019.1710351

Sayed, W. S., Noeman, A. M., Abdellatif, A., Abdelrazek, M., Badawy, M. G., Hamed, A., & El-Tantawy, S. (2023). AI-based adaptive personalized content presentation and exercises navigation for an effective and engaging E-learning platform. *Multimedia Tools and Applications*, 82(3), 3303–3333. DOI: 10.1007/s11042-022-13076-8 PMID: 35789938

Scassellati, B., Admoni, H., & Matarić, M. (2012). Robots for use in autism research. *Annual Review of Biomedical Engineering*, 14(1), 275–294. DOI: 10.1146/annurev-bioeng-071811-150036 PMID: 22577778

Schiaffino, S., Garcia, P., & Amandi, A. (2008). eTeacher: Providing personalized assistance to e-learning students. *Computers & Education*, 51(4), 1744–1754. DOI: 10.1016/j.compedu.2008.05.008

Schiff, D. (2021). Out of the lab and into the classroom: The future of artificial intelligence in education. *AERA Open*. Advance online publication. DOI: 10.1177/23328584211037513

Schiff, D. (2021). Out of the laboratory and into the classroom: The future of artificial intelligence in education. *AI & Society*, 36(1), 331–348. DOI: 10.1007/s00146-020-01033-8 PMID: 32836908

Schipor, O. A., Pentiuc, S. G., & Schipor, M. D. (2003). Improving computer-based speech therapy using a fuzzy expert system. *Computing and Informatics, 22*, 1001–1016. Retrieved from https://www.cai.sk/ojs/index.php/cai/article/view/193/130

Schipor, O., Pentiuc, S., & Schipor, M.-D. (2010). Improving computer-based speech therapy using a fuzzy expert system. *Computer Information*, 29(1), 303–318.

Schmidt, P., Biessmann, F., & Teubner, T. (2020). Transparency and trust in artificial intelligence systems. *Journal of Decision Systems*, 29(2), 260–278. DOI: 10.1080/12460125.2020.1819094

Schradie, J. (2020). The great equalizer reproduces inequality: How the digital divide is a class power divide. In *Rethinking class and social difference* (Vol. 37, pp. 81–101). Emerald Publishing Limited. DOI: 10.1108/S0198-871920200000037005

Schrauben, K., Owen-DeSchryver, J., & Cale, S. (2019). STRIVE to improve educational outcomes: Supporting students with disabilities in the general education classroom. *Educational Psychology*, 58(16), 171–185. Advance online publication. DOI: 10.5604/01.3001.0013.6372

Schreuter, D., van der Putten, P., & Lamers, M. H. (2021). Trust me on this one: Conforming to conversational assistants. *Minds and Machines*, 31(4), 535–562. DOI: 10.1007/s11023-021-09581-8

Schunk, D., & Ertmer, P. (2000). Self-Regulation and academic learning. Handbook of Self-Regulation, 631–649. DOI: 10.1016/B978-012109890-2/50048-2

Schuster, R., Song, C., & Tromer, E.. (2021). You autocomplete me: Poisoning vulnerabilities in neural code completion. In *Proceedings of the 30th USENIX Security Symposium* (pp. 1–18). USENIX Association., Retrieved from https://www.usenix.org/conference/usenixsecurity21/presentation/schuster

Schworm, R. (1979). Task Analysis in Special Education: Definition and Clarification. *Journal of Special Education Technology*, 2(3), 37–44. DOI: 10.1177/016264347900200305

ScootPad Corporation. (n.d). ScootPad. Retrieved from https://www.scootpad.com 27th June 2024.

Scott, M., Milbourn, B., Falkmer, M., Black, M., Bölte, S., Alycia, H., Lerner, M., Taylor, J. L., & Sonya, G. (2019). Factors impacting employment for people with autism spectrum disorder: A scoping review. *Autism*, 23(4), 869–901. DOI: 10.1177/1362361318787789

Sebe, N., Cohen, I., Gevers, T., & Huang, T. S. (2006). Emotion recognition based on joint visual and audio cues. In *Proceedings of the 18th International Conference on Pattern Recognition (ICPR'06)* (pp. 1136–1139). IEEE. https://doi.org/DOI: 10.1109/ICPR.2006.489

Sebesta, R. W. (2012). *Concepts of programming languages* (10th ed.). Pearson Education, Inc., https://www.ime.usp.br/~alvaroma/ucsp/proglang/book.pdf

Sedrakyan, G., Malmberg, J., Verbert, K., Järvelä, S., & Kirschner, P. A. (2020). Linking learning behavior analytics and learning science concepts: Designing a learning analytics dashboard for feedback to support learning regulation. *Computers in Human Behavior*, 107, 105512. Advance online publication. DOI: 10.1016/j.chb.2018.05.004

Semmel, M. I., & Semmel, D. S. (1976). Competency-based teacher education: An overview. *Behavioral Disorders*, 1(2), 69–82. DOI: 10.1177/019874297600100205

Şen, N., & Akbay, T. (2023). Artificial intelligence and innovative applications in special education. Öğretim Teknolojisi ve Hayat Boyu Öğrenme Dergisi - Instructional Technology and Lifelong Learning. https://doi.org/DOI: 10.52911/itall.1297978

Şen, N., & Akbay, T. (2023). Artificial intelligence and innovative applications in special education. *Instructional Technology and Lifelong Learning*, 4(2), 176–199.

Setiawan, M. R., & Wiedarti, P. (2020). The effectiveness of Quizlet application towards students' motivation in learning vocabulary. *Studies in English Language and Education*, 7(1), 83–95. DOI: 10.24815/siele.v7i1.15359

Settembre, J. (2024). College student put on academic probation for using Grammarly: "AI violation. https://nypost.com/2024/02/21/tech/student-put-on-probation-for-using-grammarly-ai-violation/

Shadiev, R., Wu, T. T., Sun, A., & Huang, Y. M. (2018). Applications of speech-to-text recognition and computer-aided translation for facilitating cross-cultural learning through a learning activity: Issues and their solutions. *Educational Technology Research and Development*, 66(1), 191–214. DOI: 10.1007/s11423-017-9556-8

Shahamiri, S. R., & Thabtah, F. (2020). Autism AI: A new autism screening system based on artificial intelligence. *Cognitive Computation*, 12(4), 766–777. DOI: 10.1007/s12559-020-09743-3

Shakhnoza, M. (2023). The role of AI in teaching: Advantages, disadvantages, and future implications. *Genius Repository, 24*, 8–12. Retrieved from https://www.geniusrepo.net/index.php/1/article/view/43

Shamim, M., Ademola, A. H., & Uz, Z. T. (2022). Special education: Learning theories and educational models. In B. S. Chavan, W. Ahmad, R. K. Gupta, M. Shamim, A. H. Ademola, & Z. T. Uz (Eds.), *Comprehensive textbook on disability*. Jaypee Brothers Medical Publishers (P) Ltd. https://doi.org/DOI: 10.5005/jp/books/18613_5

Shams, L., & Seitz, A. R. (2008). Benefits of multisensory learning. *Trends in Cognitive Sciences*, 12(11), 411–417. DOI: 10.1016/j.tics.2008.07.006 PMID: 18805039

Shamsuddin, S., Yussof, H., Hanapiah, F. A., Mohamed, S., Ismail, L. I., & Pawi, S. (2011). Humanoid robot NAO: Review of control and motion exploration. In *2011 IEEE International Conference on Control System, Computing and Engineering* (pp. 511-516). Penang, Malaysia. https://doi.org/DOI: 10.1109/ICCSCE.2011.6190579

Shane, N. (2023). Artificial neural networks and the actiotope model of giftedness—Clever solutions from complex environments. *Journal of Intelligence*, 11(7), 128. DOI: 10.3390/jintelligence11070128 PMID: 37504771

Shapiro, M., & Kazemi, E. (2017). A review of training strategies to teach individuals implementation of behavioral interventions. *Journal of Organizational Behavior Management*, 37(1), 32–62. DOI: 10.1080/01608061.2016.1267066

Sharma, A., Kapoor, R., & Gupta, V. (2023). Assistive Technologies Powered by AI in Special Education Schools in India. *International Journal of Special Education*, 38(1), 45–61.

Sharma, N., Kaur, A., & Aggarwal, N. (2020). Impact of Artificial Intelligence in Special Need Education to Promote Inclusive Pedagogy. In *International Conference on Artificial Intelligence and Sustainable Computing*. Springer, Singapore. 1047-1054.

Sharma, S., Tomar, V., Yadav, N., & Aggarwal, M. (2023). Impact of AI-based special education on educators and students. In *Advances in educational technologies and instructional design book series* (pp. 47–66). IGI Global., DOI: 10.4018/979-8-3693-0378-8.ch003

Shashua, A., & Aviram, Z. (2010). OrCam MyEye. Retrieved from https://www.orcam.com, 1 June 2023.

Shepherd, K. G., Fowler, S., McCormick, J., Wilson, C. L., & Morgan, D. (2016). The search for role clarity: Challenges and implications for special education teacher preparation. *Teacher Education and Special Education*, 39(2), 83–97. DOI: 10.1177/0888406416637904

Shepley, C., Lane, J. D., & Ault, M. J. (2019). A review and critical examination of the system of least prompts. *Remedial and Special Education*, 40(5), 313–327. DOI: 10.1177/0741932517751213

Sherkuziyeva, N., Gabidullina, F. I., Ibrahim, K. A. A., & Bayat, S. (2023). The comparative effect of computerized dynamic assessment and rater mediated assessment on EFL learners' oral proficiency, writing performance, and test anxiety. *Language Testing in Asia*, 13(1), 15. Advance online publication. DOI: 10.1186/s40468-023-00227-3

Shia College. (n.d.). *Special Education Legislation in India*.

Shivers, C. M., Sonnier-Netto, L., & Lee, G. K. (2019). Needs and experiences of family caregivers of individuals with autism spectrum disorders across the lifespan. *Journal of Policy and Practice in Intellectual Disabilities*, 16(1), 21–29. DOI: 10.1111/jppi.12272

Shores, R. E., Cegelka, P. T., & Michael Nelson, C. (1973). Competency Based Special Education Teacher Training. [Web]. *Exceptional Children*, 40(3), 192–197. DOI: 10.1177/001440297304000305

Shortliffe, E. H., & Buchanan, B. G. (1975). A model of inexact reasoning in medicine. *Mathematical Biosciences*, 23(3-4), 351–379. DOI: 10.1016/0025-5564(75)90047-4

Siemens, G. (2005). Connectivism: A learning theory for the digital age. *International Journal of Instructional Technology and Distance Learning, 2*. http://www.itdl.org/Journal/Jan_05/article01.htm

Siemens, G., & Long, P. (2011). Penetrating the fog: Analytics in learning and education. *EDUCAUSE Review*, 46(5), 30–32. DOI: 10.17471/2499-4324/195

Sindelar, P. T., Brownell, M. T., & Billingsley, B. (2010). Special education teacher education research: Current status and future directions. *Teacher Education and Special Education*, 33(1), 8–24. DOI: 10.1177/0888406409358593

Skansi, S. (2018). *Introduction to Deep Learning: from logical calculus to artificial intelligence*. Springer. DOI: 10.1007/978-3-319-73004-2

Skiba, R. J., Simmons, A. B., Ritter, S., Gibb, A. C., Rausch, M. K., Cuadrado, J., & Chung, C. G. (2008). Achieving equity in special education: History, status, and current challenges. *Exceptional Children*, 74(3), 264–288. DOI: 10.1177/001440290807400301

Slattery, E. J., Butler, D., O'Leary, M., & Marshall, K. (2023). Primary school students' experiences using Minecraft Education during a national project-based initiative: An Irish study. *TechTrends: For leaders in education & training*, 1–13. Advance online publication. https://doi.org/DOI: 10.1007/s11528-023-00851-z

SmartClick. (2022). Machine Learning Solutions & Artificial Intelligence https://www.smartclick.ai/

Smiderle, R., Rigo, S. J., Marques, L. B., Peçanha de Miranda Coelho, J. A., & Jaques, P. A. (2020). The impact of gamification on students' learning, engagement, and behavior based on their personality traits. *Smart Learning Environments*, 7(1), 3. DOI: 10.1186/s40561-019-0098-x

Smith, M. J., Ginger, E. J., Wright, K., Wright, M. A., Taylor, J. L., Humm, L. B., Olsen, D. E., Bell, M. D., & Fleming, M. F. (2014). Virtual reality job interview training in adults with autism spectrum disorder. *Journal of Autism and Developmental Disorders*, 44(10), 2450–2463. DOI: 10.1007/s10803-014-2113-y

Smith, P. S. (2024). (Re) presenting race: An analysis of special education textbooks for engagement with race and ethnicity. *Race, Ethnicity and Education*, •••, 1–22. DOI: 10.1080/13613324.2024.2306409

Smith, T., Johnson, M., & Diaz, N. (2021). Personalized Learning with AI-powered Platforms: Improving Academic Outcomes for Students with Learning Disabilities. *International Journal of Artificial Intelligence in Education*, 31(2), 321–345.

Smutny, P., & Schreiberova, P. (2020). Chatbots for learning: A review of educational chatbots for the Facebook Messenger. *Computers & Education*, 151, 103862. DOI: 10.1016/j.compedu.2020.103862

SoftBank Robotics. (n.d). NAO Robot. Retrieved from https://emea.softbankrobotics.com/industries/higher-education on 1 june 2024.

Soleimani, M., Intezari, A., Taskin, N., & Pauleen, D. (2021). Cognitive biases in developing biased artificial intelligence recruitment systems. In *Proceedings of the 54th Hawaii International Conference on System Sciences* (pp. 1-9). DOI: 10.24251/HICSS.2021.620

Sonuga-Barke, E., Brandeis, D., Holtmann, M., & Cortese, S. (2014). Computer-based cognitive training for ADHD: A review of current evidence. *Child and Adolescent Psychiatric Clinics of North America*, 23(4), 807–824. DOI: 10.1016/j.chc.2014.05.009 PMID: 25220088

Soria, K. M., Horgos, B., & Shenouda, J. D. (2023). Disparities in college students' financial hardships during the COVID-19 pandemic. *Journal of Student Affairs Research and Practice*, 60(1), 31–48. DOI: 10.1080/19496591.2022.2046597

Sourander, A., McGrath, P. J., Ristkari, T., Cunningham, C., Huttunen, J., Lingley-Pottie, P., Hinkka-Yli-Salomäki, S., Kinnunen, M., Vuorio, J., Sinokki, A., Fossum, S., & Unruh, A. (2016). Internet-Assisted Parent Training Intervention for Disruptive Behavior in 4-Year-Old Children: A Randomized Clinical Trial. *JAMA Psychiatry*, 73(4), 378–387. DOI: 10.1001/jamapsychiatry.2015.3411

Špakov, O., Istance, H., Räihä, K.-J., Viitanen, T., & Siirtola, H. (2019). Eye gaze and head gaze in collaborative games. In *Proceedings of the 2019 CHI Conference on Human Factors in Computing Systems* (pp. 1-9). https://doi.org/DOI: 10.1145/3317959.3321489

Sperling, K., Stenberg, C. J., McGrath, C., Åkerfeldt, A., Heintz, F., & Stenliden, L. (2024). In search of artificial intelligence (AI) literacy in teacher education: A scoping review. *Computers and Education Open*, 6, 100169. DOI: 10.1016/j.caeo.2024.100169

Srihari, S., Collins, J., Srihari, R., Srinivasan, H., Shetty, S., & Brutt-Griffler, J. (2008). Automated Scoring of Handwritten essays in Reading Comprehension tests. *Artificial Intelligence*, 172(3), 300–324. DOI: 10.1016/j.artint.2007.06.005

Srinivasan, B., & Parthasarathi, R. (2013). An intelligent task analysis approach for special education based on MIRA. *Journal of Applied Logic*, 11(1), 137–145. DOI: 10.1016/j.jal.2012.12.001

Srinivasan, R., & Chander, A. (2021). Biases in AI Systems. *ACM Queue; Tomorrow's Computing Today*, 19(2), 45–64. DOI: 10.1145/3466132.3466134

Srinivasan, V., Vardhan, V., Kar, S., Asthana, S., Narayanan, R., Singh, P., Chakraborty, D., & Singh, A. (2013). Airavat: An automated system to increase transparency and accountability in social welfare schemes in India. In *ICTD '13: Proceedings of the Sixth International Conference on Information and Communications Technologies and Development: Notes*- Volume 2 (pp. 151–154). https://doi.org/DOI: 10.1145/2517899.2517937

Sripan, R., & Suksawat, B. (2010, January). Proposal of Fuzzy Logic-based Students´ Learning Assessment Model. ResearchGate. https://www.researchgate.net/publication/238519325_Propose_of_fuzzy_logic-based_students'_learning_assessment

Stabback, P. (2016). What Makes a Quality Curriculum? In-Progress Reflection No. 2 on" Current and Critical Issues in Curriculum and Learning". *UNESCO International Bureau of Education.* Retrieved from https://unesdoc.unesco.org/ark:/48223/pf0000243975

Stoeger, H., Balestrini, D. P., & Ziegler, A. (2018). International perspectives and trends in research on giftedness and talent development. In Pfeiffer, S. I., Shaunessy-Dedrick, E., & Foley-Nicpon, M. (Eds.), *APA handbook of giftedness and talent* (pp. 25–37). American Psychological Association., DOI: 10.1037/0000038-002

Strickland, D. C., Coles, C. D., & Southern, L. B. (2013). JobTIPS: A transition to employment program for individuals with autism spectrum disorders. *Journal of Autism and Developmental Disorders*, 43(10), 2472–2483. DOI: 10.1007/s10803-013-1800-4

Stupar-Rutenfrans, S., Ketelaars, L. E. H., & Van Gisbergen, M. S. (2017). Beat the fear of public speaking: Does the 360° video virtual reality exposure training in home environment reduces speech anxiety? *Cyberpsychology, Behavior, and Social Networking*, 20, 624–633. DOI: 10.1089/cyber.2017.0174

Suh, A., & Prophet, J. (2018). The state of immersive technology research: A literature analysis. *Computers in Human Behavior*, 86, 77–90. DOI: 10.1016/j.chb.2018.04.019

Sun, X., Ma, R., Zhao, X., Li, Z., Lindqvist, J., Ali, A. E., & Bosch, J. A. (2024). Trusting the Search: Unraveling Human Trust in Health Information from Google and ChatGPT. *arXiv preprint arXiv:2403.09987*.

Sun, S., Else-Quest, N., Hodges, L., French, A., & Dowling, R. (2021). The effects of ALEKS on mathematics learning in K-12 and higher education: A meta-analysis. *Investigations in Mathematics Learning*, 13(3), 1–15. DOI: 10.1080/19477503.2021.1926194

Suppan, P. (2006). Differentiated instruction: A research base. *International Education Journal*, 7(7), 935–947.

Sutherland, A. (2005). Quizlet. https://www.quizlet.com

Swan, C. (2017). Personalized learning: Understandings and effectiveness in practice. *Journal of Initial Teacher Inquiry*, 3, 3–6. DOI: 10.26021/834

Tahiru, F. (2021). AI in education: A systematic literature review. *Journal of Cases on Information Technology*, 23(1), 1–20. DOI: 10.4018/JCIT.2021010101

Tambotoh, J., Kosala, R., Ranti, B., Prabowo, H., Supangkat, S., Isa, S. M., & Pudjianto, B. (2017, November). A conceptual model for creating effective public value through key practices in information technology governance mechanisms. In *2017 International Conference on Information Management and Technology (ICIMTech)* (pp. 128–132). IEEE. https://doi.org/DOI: 10.1109/ICIMTech.2017.8273524

Tan, B. L., Guan, F. Y., Leung, I. M. W., Kee, S. Y. M., Devilly, O. Z., & Medalia, A. (2022). A gamified augmented reality vocational training program for adults with intellectual and developmental disabilities: A pilot study on acceptability and effectiveness. *Frontiers in Psychiatry*, 13, 966080. DOI: 10.3389/fpsyt.2022.966080

Tan, H. C., Hughes, M. R., & Toogood, S. (2016). Using task analysis to promote engagement in special educational settings. *European Journal of Behavior Analysis*, 17(2), 116–130. DOI: 10.1080/15021149.2016.1247575

Tan, S. C., Lee, A. V. Y., & Lee, M. (2022). A systematic review of artificial intelligence techniques for collaborative learning over the past two decades. *Computers and Education: Artificial Intelligence*, 3, 100097. DOI: 10.1016/j.caeai.2022.100097

Tanveer, M., Hassan, S., & Bhaumik, A. (2020). Academic Policy Regarding Sustainability and Artificial Intelligence (AI). *Sustainability (Basel)*, 12(22), 9435. DOI: 10.3390/su12229435

Tapalova, O., & Zhiyenbayeva, N. (2022). Artificial intelligence in education: AIEd for personalised learning pathways. *Electronic Journal of e-Learning*, 20(5), 639–653. https://files.eric.ed.gov/fulltext/EJ1373006.pdf. DOI: 10.34190/ejel.20.5.2597

Tapscott, D., & Tapscott, A. (2016). *Blockchain revolution: how the technology behind bitcoin is changing money, business, and the world*. Penguin.

Tapus, A., Peca, A., Aly, A., Pop, C., & Jisa, L.. (2012). Children with autism social engagement in interaction with Nao, an imitative robot: A series of single case experiments. *Interaction Studies: Social Behaviour and Communication in Biological and Artificial Systems*, 13(3), 315–347. DOI: 10.1075/is.13.3.01tap

Teach, A. I. (2023). AI guidance for schools toolkit - AI Education in School Presentation. https://www.teachai.org/toolkit

Terra, M., Baklola, M., Ali, S., & El-Bastawisy, K. (2023). Opportunities, applications, challenges and ethical implications of artificial intelligence in psychiatry: A narrative review. *The Egyptian Journal of Neurology, Psychiatry and Neurosurgery*, 59(1), 80. DOI: 10.1186/s41983-023-00681-z

Texthelp. (2023). Equatio. Retrieved from https://www.texthelp.com/

The Aditya Birla Integrated School. (2023). *History of Special Education*.https://www.adityabirlaintegratedschool.com/blog/history-of-special-education

The Pecan Team. (2023, December 15). 3 Ways to Build Your Own AI Model. Blog post. https://www.pecan.ai/blog/3-ways-build-your-own-ai-model/#:~:text=Building%20an%20AI%20model%20requires,customization%20needs%2C%20and%20time%20availability

Theodorou, L., Massiceti, D., Zintgraf, L., Stumpf, S., Morrison, C., Cutrell, E., Harris, M. T., & Hofmann, K. (2021). Disability-first dataset creation: Lessons from constructing a dataset for teachable object recognition with blind and low vision data collectors. In *Proceedings of the 23rd International ACM SIGACCESS Conference on Computers and Accessibility*. ACM. https://doi.org/DOI: 10.1145/3441852.3471225

Therapy Box Ltd. Predictable, [Mobile application software]. Retrieved on 1 June 2024.

Tholfsen, M. (2020, January 13). Pear Deck integrates with Microsoft Immersive Reader to make Learning more Accessible for all. Microsoft Tech Community. https://techcommunity.microsoft.com/t5/education-blog/pear-deck-integrates-with-microsoft-immersive-reader-to-make/ba-p/1101740

Thompson, J. R., Walker, V. L., Felce, D., Jenkins, R., Kerr, M., Lowe, K., & Linehan, C. (2020). Planning supports for students with intellectual disability in general education classrooms. *Inclusion (Washington, D.C.)*, 8(1), 27–42. DOI: 10.1352/2326-6988-8.1.27

Thrasher, T., Kaplan-Rakowski, R., Ovsiannikova, U., Meyr, J., & Yuan, Y. (2023). *"I can talk to Spanish speakers in Illinois!": Student perspectives on AI-avatar role plays in virtual reality*. WorldCALL2023: Conference Proceedings. DOI: 10.22492/issn.2759-1182.2023.18

Tobii Dynavox. (2023). *Tobii Dynavox I-Series*. Retrieved from Tobii Dynavox.

Tokuhama-Espinosa, T. (2019). The learning sciences framework in educational leadership. *Frontiers in Education*, 4(136), 1–20. DOI: 10.3389/feduc.2019.00136

Tomczak, M. T. (2021). Employees with autism spectrum disorders in the digitized work environment: Perspectives for the future. *Journal of Disability Policy Studies*, 31(4), 195–205. DOI: 10.1177/1044207320919945

Touretzky, D., Gardner-McCune, C., Breazeal, C., Martin, F., & Seehorn, D. (2019). A year in K–12 AI education. *AI Magazine*, 40(4), 88–90. DOI: 10.1609/aimag.v40i4.5289

Toyokawa, Y., Horikoshi, I., Majumdar, R., & Ogata, H. (2023). Challenges and Opportunities of AI in Inclusive Education: A case Study of Data-enhanced Active Reading in Japan. *Smart Learning Environments*, 10(67), 1–19. DOI: 10.1186/s40561-023-00286-2

Tozadore, D., Gauthier, S., Bruno, B., Wang, C., Zou, J., Aubin, L., Archambault, D., Chetouani, M., Dillenbourg, P., Cohen, D., & Anzalone, S. (2023). The iReCheck project: Using tablets and robots for personalized handwriting practice. *Proceedings of the 2023 ACM Conference on Human Factors in Computing Systems*, 297-301. https://doi.org/DOI: 10.1145/3610661.3616178

Trewin, S., Basson, S., Muller, M., Branham, S., Treviranus, J., Gruen, D., Herbert, D., Lyckowski, N., & Manser, E. (2019). Considerations for AI Fairness for People with Disabilities. *AI Matters*, 5(3), 40–63. DOI: 10.1145/3362077.3362086

Tripp, B., & Shortlidge, E. (2019). A Framework to guide undergraduate education in interdisciplinary science. *CBE Life Sciences Education*, 18(2), es3. Advance online publication. DOI: 10.1187/cbe.18-11-0226 PMID: 31120394

Trust, T., Whalen, J., & Mouza, C. (2023). Editorial: ChatGPT: Challenges, Opportunities, and Implications for Teacher Education. *Contemporary Issues in Technology and Teacher Education, 23*(1), 1-23. Waynesville, NC USA: Society for Information Technology & Teacher Education. Retrieved September 27, 2024 from https://www.learntechlib.org/primary/p/222408/

Trust, T., Whalen, J., & Mouza, C. (2023). Editorial: ChatGPT: Challenges, opportunities, and implications for teacher education. *Contemporary Issues in Technology & Teacher Education*, 23(1).

Turi, L. F., Cavalini, A., Comarela, G., Oliveira-Santos, T., Badue, C., & De Souza, A. F. (2024). Analysis of Bias in GPT Language Models through Fine-tuning Containing Divergent Data. In *2024 International Joint Conference on Neural Networks (IJCNN)* (pp. 1-8). IEEE. DOI: 10.1109/IJCNN60899.2024.10650574

U. S. Department of Education. (2004). Individuals with Disabilities Education Act (IDEA). https://sites.ed.gov/idea/about-idea/

U.S. Department of Army–Medical Research Acquisition Activity. (2024). *Autism research program idea development award.* U.S. Department of Defense. https://cdmrp.health.mil/funding/arp

U.S. Department of Education. Office of Educational Technology, Artificial Intelligence and Future of Teaching and Learning: Insights and Recommendations, Washington, DC, 2023. https://tech.ed.gov

U.S. Equal Employment Opportunity Commission. (2022). *Elementary-secondary staff information report (EEO-5) data collection*. https://www.eeoc.gov/employers/eeo-5-elementary-secondary-staff-information-report-data-collection

UNESCO. (2019). Leveraging AI towards improving learning and equity. In *Artificial intelligence in education: Challenges and opportunities for sustainable development* (pp. 12-16). UNESCO. https://unesdoc.unesco.org/ark:/48223/pf0000366994

UNESCO. (2021 b). Reimagining Our Futures Together: A New Social Contract For Education [English]. International Commission on the Futures of Education. United Nations Educational, Scientific and Cultural Organization: France. https://doi.org/DOI: 10.54675/ASRB4722

UNESCO. (2021a). *AI and education: guidance for policy-makers* [English]. United Nations Educational, Scientific and Cultural Organization., DOI: 10.54675/PCSP7350

UNESCO. (2022). Recommendation on the Ethics of Artificial Intelligence. United Nations Educational, Scientific and Cultural Organization: France. https://unesdoc.unesco.org/ark:/48223/pf0000381137

UNESCO. (2023). *Ethical impact assessment: A tool of the Recommendation on the Ethics of Artificial Intelligence*. United Nations Educational, Scientific and Cultural Organization., DOI: 10.54678/YTSA7796

UNESCO. (n.d.). Artificial intelligence in education. UNESCO. https://www.unesco.org/en/digital-education/artificial-intelligence#

United Nations Educational, Scientific and Cultural Organization (UNESCO). (2023). Guidance for generative AI in education and research. https://unesdoc.unesco.org/ark:/48223/pf0000386693

University of Amsterdam. (2022). *How to develop learner autonomy*. https://www.itta.uva.nl/learnerautonomy/how-to-develop-learner-autonomy-59

University of Pennsylvania. (2023). *Confronting perfectionism, inspiring excellence*. https://almanac.upenn.edu/articles/confronting-perfectionism-inspiring-excellence

Urrea, A. L., Fernández-Torres, V., Rodriguez-Ortiz, I. R., & Saldaña, D. (2024). The use of technology-assisted intervention in vocabulary learning for children with autism spectrum disorder: A systematic review. *Frontiers in Psychology*, 15, 1370965. Advance online publication. DOI: 10.3389/fpsyg.2024.1370965 PMID: 38817831

US Bureau of Labor Statistics. (2023). *People with a disability: Labor Force Characteristics*. Retrieved at https://www.bls.gov/news.release/disabl.a.htm

Van der Vorst, T., & Jelicic, N. (2019). *Artificial intelligence in education: Can AI bring the full potential of personalized learning to education? 30th European Conference of the International Telecommunications Society (ITS): "Towards a Connected and Automated Society", Helsinki, Finland, 16th-19th June, 2019, International Telecommunications Society*. ITS., https://hdl.handle.net/10419/205222

Vanderbilt University. (2023). *Evidence-based resources for EBP.*https://my.vanderbilt.edu/spedteacherresources/evidence-based-resources-for-ebp/

Vanderbilt University. (2024). *Bloom's taxonomy*. https://cft.vanderbilt.edu/guides-sub-pages/blooms-taxonomy/

VanLehn, K. (2011). The relative effectiveness of human tutoring, intelligent tutoring systems, and other tutoring systems. *Educational Psychologist*, 46(4), 197–221. DOI: 10.1080/00461520.2011.611369

VanLehn, K., Lynch, C., Schulze, K., Shapiro, J. A., Shelby, R., Taylor, L., & Wintersgill, M. (2005). The Andes physics tutoring system: Lessons learned. *International Journal of Artificial Intelligence in Education*, 15(3), 147–204.

Varona, D., & Suárez, J. (2022). Discrimination, Bias, Fairness, and Trustworthy AI. *Applied Sciences (Basel, Switzerland)*, 12(12), 5826. Advance online publication. DOI: 10.3390/app12125826

Velander, J., Taiye, M. A., Otero, N., & Milrad, M. (2024). Artificial intelligence in K-12 education: Eliciting and reflecting on Swedish teachers' understanding of AI and its implications for teaching & learning. *Education and Information Technologies*, 29(4), 4085–4105. DOI: 10.1007/s10639-023-11990-4

Vembi Technologies. (2024). Hexis-Antara: Braille reader for visually impaired children. Retrieved from https://vembi.in/wp/hexis/

Vidhya, V., Ganesan, Lakshmanan, Arvind, T., Nithya, M., & Pranayini. (2009). T9++-Intelligent predictive text entry for mobile devices. *Journal of Theoretical and Applied Information Technology*, 52(1), 21–33.

Vince-Garland, K. M., Holden, K., & Garland, D. P. (2016). Individualized clinical coaching in the TLE TeachLivE lab: Enhancing fidelity of implementation of system of least prompts among novice teachers of students with autism. *Teacher Education and Special Education*, 39(1), 47–59. DOI: 10.1177/0888406415600769

Vincent-Lancrin, S., & van der Vlies, R. (2020). Trustworthy artificial intelligence (AI) in education: Promises and challenges. *OECD Education Working Papers*, No. 218, OECD Publishing, Paris. DOI: 10.1787/19939019

Vincent-Lancrin, S., & Van der Vlies, R. (2020). Trustworthy artificial intelligence (AI) in education: Promises and challenges. In *OECD education working papers* (Vol. 218). OECD Publishing.

Vivanti, G., & Stahmer, A. (2018). Early intervention for autism: Are we prioritizing feasibility at the expense of effectiveness? A cautionary note. *Autism*, 22(7), 770–773. DOI: 10.1177/1362361318803043 PMID: 30235939

Voiceitt Ltd. (2012). Voiceitt. Retrieved from https://www.voiceitt.com on 2 June 2024.

Vygotsky, L. S. (1978). *Mind in society: The development of higher psychological processes*. Harvard University Press.

Wainer, J., Ferrari, E., Dautenhahn, K., & Robins, B. (2010). The effectiveness of using a robotics class to foster collaboration among groups of children with autism in an exploratory study. *Personal and Ubiquitous Computing*, 14(5), 445–455. DOI: 10.1007/s00779-009-0266-z

Wald, M. (2021). AI data-driven personalization and disability inclusion. Secondary Machine Learning and Artificial Intelligence. *Frontier Artificial Intelligences*, 3, 1–14. DOI: 10.3389/frai.2020.571955 PMID: 33733215

Waldron, N., & McLeskey, J. (2010). Establishing a Collaborative School Culture Through Comprehensive School Reform. *Journal of Educational & Psychological Consultation*, 20(1), 58–74. DOI: 10.1080/10474410903535364

Wali, A., Mahamad, S., & Sulaiman, S. (2023). Task automation intelligent agents: A review. *Future Internet*, 15(6), 196. Advance online publication. DOI: 10.3390/fi15060196

Walker, V. L., Carpenter, M. E., Clausen, A., Ealer, K., & Lyon, K. J. (2021). Special educators as coaches to support paraprofessional implementation of functional communication training. *Journal of Positive Behavior Interventions*, 23(3), 174–184. DOI: 10.1177/1098300720957995

Walker, V., Carpenter, M., Kittelman, A., & Rowe, D. (2023). Supports planning to improve access and participation in general education classrooms for students with disabilities. *Teaching Exceptional Children*, 55(4), 232–235. DOI: 10.1177/00400599231167479

Wallace, B. C., & Abel, Y. (2021). Utilizing specially designed, instructional evidence-based practices and family engagement: Increasing African American student achievement in digital literacies. In *Connecting Disciplinary Literacy and Digital Storytelling in K-12 Education* (pp. 24–37). IGI Global. DOI: 10.4018/978-1-7998-5770-9.ch002

Walle, H., De Runz, C., Serres, B., & Venturini, G. (2022). A survey on recent advances in AI and vision-based methods for helping and guiding visually impaired people. *Applied Sciences (Basel, Switzerland)*, 12(5), 2308. DOI: 10.3390/app12052308

Wang, H., & Woodworth, K. (2011). *Evaluation of Rocketship Education's use of DreamBox Learning's online mathematics program.* Center for Education Policy, SRI International. https://www.sri.com/publication/evaluation-rocketship-educations-use-dreambox-learnings-online-mathematics-program/

Wang, Y., Skerry-Ryan, R. J., Stanton, D., Wu, Y., Weiss, R. J., Jaitly, N., . . . Saurous, R. A. (2017). Tacotron: Towards end-to-end speech synthesis. *arXiv preprint arXiv:1703.10135*. DOI: 10.21437/Interspeech.2017-1452

Wang'ang'a, A. W. (2024). Consequences of Artificial Intelligence on Teaching and Learning in Higher Education in Kenya. *Literature Review East African Journal of Education Studies*, 7(1), 202–215. DOI: 10.37284/eajes.7.1.1718

Wang, H. (2013). Instruction in American academic libraries. In Wang, H., & Latham, B. (Eds.), *Academic libraries in the US and China* (pp. 3–49). Chandos Publishing., DOI: 10.1016/B978-1-84334-691-3.50001-9

Wang, M., Wang, M., Xu, X., Yang, L., Cai, D., & Yin, M. (2023). Unleashing ChatGPT's Power: A Case Study on Optimizing Information Retrieval in Flipped Classrooms via Prompt Engineering. *IEEE Transactions on Learning Technologies*, 17, 629–641. DOI: 10.1109/TLT.2023.3324714

Wang, Y. (2021). When artificial intelligence meets educational leaders' data-informed decision-making: A cautionary tale. *Studies in Educational Evaluation*, 69, 100872. DOI: 10.1016/j.stueduc.2020.100872

Ward, N. (2006). SHRDLU. In Nadel, L. (Ed.), *Encyclopedia of cognitive science.*, DOI: 10.1002/0470018860.s00056

Ward, S. J., & King, L. A. (2017). Work and the good life: How work contributes to meaning in life. *Research in Organizational Behavior*, 37, 59–82. DOI: 10.1016/j.riob.2017.10.001

Waterfield, D. A., Watson, L., & Day, J. (2024). Applying Artificial Intelligence in Special Education: Exploring Availability and Functionality of AI Platforms for Special Educators. *Journal of Special Education Technology*, 39(3), 448–454. DOI: 10.1177/01626434241257237

Waymo. (2023). Waymo Self-Driving Cars. Retrieved from Waymo

Webb, J. J., Cook, M. A., Grant, A. A., & Ross, S. M. (2023). *A study of educator attitudes and beliefs and Goalbook Toolkit usage* (Doctoral dissertation). Johns Hopkins University. Available from Johns Hopkins University Repository. https://jscholarship.library.jhu.edu/server/api/core/bitstreams/a052eaae-7035-4200-b8a1-e9260ffa92b0/content

Weber, G., & Brusilovsky, P. (2001). *ELM-ART: An adaptive versatile system for web-based instruction. International Journal of Artificial Intelligence in Education (IJAIED)*, 12, 351–384. https://telearn.hal.science/hal-00197328

Wehman, P., Schall, C. M., McDonough, J., Graham, C., Brooke, V., Riehle, J. E., Brooke, A., Ham, W., Lau, S., Allen, J., & Avellone, L. (2017). Effects of an employer–based intervention on employment outcomes for youth with significant support needs due to autism. *Autism*, 21(3), 276–290. DOI: 10.1177/1362361316635826

Weiler, S. C., & Bauries, S. R. (2021). Special Education's Lessons for School Funding Litigation. *Education Law & Policy Review, 6*, 126. Westerns Governors University. Nd. *Special education: History, resources, and advice.*https://www.wgu.edu/blog/special-education-history-resources-advice2001.html

Weiser, B. (2023). Here's what happens when your lawyer uses ChatGPT. *The New York Times*. https://www.nytimes.com/2023/05/27/nyregion/avianca-airline-lawsuit-chatgpt.html

Weitzman, T. (2023, June 16). Empowering individuals with disabilities through AI technology. *Forbes Business Council*. https://www.forbes.com/sites/forbesbusinesscouncil/2023/06/16/empowering-individuals-with-disabilities-through-ai-technology/

Weizenbaum, J. (1966). ELIZA: A computer program for the study of natural language communication between man and machine. *Communications of the ACM*, 9(1), 36–45. DOI: 10.1145/365153.365168

Welker, Y. (2023). Algorithmic Diversity: Mitigating AI Bias and Disability Exclusion. Forbes Technology Council. https://www.forbes.com/sites/forbestechcouncil/2023/05/09/algorithmic-diversity-mitigating-ai-bias-and-disability-exclusion/

Weng, Y., Chen, H., & Lee, J. (2021). Ethical Considerations in the Development and Deployment of AI-powered Technologies in Special Education. *Journal of Special Education Technology*, 36(4), 247–260.

West, D. M. (2012). Big data for education: Data mining, data analytics, and web dashboards. *Governance studies at Brookings, 4*(1), 1-10.

West, S. M., Kraut, R. E., & Chew, H. E. (2019). I'd blush if I could: Closing gender divides in digital skills through education. *AI & Society*, 34(1), 31–46.

Whalen, C., Moss, D., Ilan, A., Vaupel, M., Fielding, P., Macdonald, K., Cernich, S., & Symon, J. (2010). Efficacy of TeachTown: Basics computer-assisted intervention for the Intensive Comprehensive Autism Program in Los Angeles Unified School District. *Autism*, 14(3), 179–197. DOI: 10.1177/1362361310363282 PMID: 20484002

What Works Clearinghouse. (2010, August 31). *Carnegie Learning curricula and Cognitive Tutor software*. U.S. Department of Education, Institute of Education Sciences. https://ies.ed.gov/ncee/wwc/InterventionReport/Index/408

What Works Clearinghouse. (2013). Elementary School Mathematics December 2013: DreamBox Learning. U.S. Department of Education, Institute of Education Sciences. https://ies.ed.gov/ncee/wwc/Docs/InterventionReports/wwc_dreambox_123013.pdf

Whill. (n.d). Whill Autonomous Drive System. Retrieved from https://www.whill.us on 2 June 2024.

White paper on rights of persons with disabilities. (2015). [Online]. Available: https://www.ru.ac.za/media/rhodesuniversity/content/equityinstitution alculture/documents/White%20Paper%20on%20the%20Rights%20of %20Persons%20with%20Disabilities.pdf

Wiberg, H. H. (2012). Be My Eyes. Retrieved from https://www.bemyeyes.com on 2 June 2024.

Williams, M. K., Christensen, R., McElroy, D., & Rutledge, D. (2023). Teacher self-efficacy in technology integration as a critical component in designing technology-infused teacher preparation programs. *Contemporary Issues in Technology & Teacher Education*, 23(1), 228–259.

Wilson, K., Davis, J., & Anderson, A. (2022). Assistive Robotics in Special Education: A Systematic Review. *International Journal of Social Robotics*, 14(4), 321–338.

Wilson, T. D. (1981). On user studies and information needs. *The Journal of Documentation*, 37(1), 3–15. DOI: 10.1108/eb026702

Wong, P. C. M., Vuong, L. C., & Liu, K. (2017). Personalized learning: From neurogenetics of behaviors to designing optimal language training. *Neuropsychologia*, 98, 192–200. DOI: 10.1016/j.neuropsychologia.2016.10.002 PMID: 27720749

Woolf, B. P. (2010). *Building Intelligent Interactive Tutors: Student-Centered Strategies for Revolutionizing E-learning*. Morgan Kaufmann.

World Health Organization. (n.d.). *International Classification of Functioning, Disability and Health (ICF)*. Retrieved June 29, 2024, from https://icd.who.int/dev11/l-icf/en

Wozniak, M., Krishnaswamy, D., Callegari, C., Takagi, H., Prasad, N. R., Que, X., & Sandhu, R. (2015). *Advances in Computing, Communications and Informatics*. ICACCI.

Wu, T. K., Meng, Y. R., & Huang, S. C. (2006). Application of artificial neural networks to the identification of students with learning disabilities. *International Conference on Artificial Intelligence*, 162–168. https://www.semanticscholar.org/paper/Application-of-Artificial-Neural-Network-to-the-of-Wu-Meng/7826dcbacc ba15159a69c16750ced68b5f818132

Wu, T., He, S., Liu, J., Sun, S., Liu, K., Han, Q. L., & Tang, Y. (2023). A brief overview of ChatGPT: The history, status quo and potential future development. *IEEE/CAA Journal of Automatica Sinica, 10*(5), 1122–1136.

Wu, P. (2024). The Influence of Holistic Leadership of Administrators on Teachers Empowerment Program. *Journal of Education and Educational Research*, 7(2), 71–78. DOI: 10.54097/qcdv1t54

Xia, Q., Chiu, T. K., Lee, M., Sanusi, I. T., Dai, Y., & Chai, C. S. (2022). A self-determination theory (SDT) design approach for inclusive and diverse artificial intelligence (AI) education. *Computers & Education*, 189, 104582. DOI: 10.1016/j.compedu.2022.104582

Xie, L., Smith, T., & Diaz, N. (2023). Adaptive Learning Systems for Students with ADHD: Improving Focus, Task Completion, and Academic Performance. *Computers & Education*, 182, 104023.

XPRIZE. (2015). XPRIZE. https://www.xprize.org/prizes/global-learning

Xu, Y., Liu, X., Cao, X., Huang, C., Liu, E., Qian, S., Liu, X., Wu, Y., Dong, F., Qiu, C.-W., Qiu, J., Hua, K., Su, W., Wu, J., Xu, H., Han, Y., Fu, C., Yin, Z., Liu, M., & Zhang, J. (2021). Artificial intelligence: A powerful paradigm for scientific research. *Innovation (Cambridge (Mass.))*, 2(4), 100179. DOI: 10.1016/j.xinn.2021.100179 PMID: 34877560

Xu, Z. (2024). AI in education: Enhancing learning experiences and student outcomes. *Applied and Computational Engineering*, 51(1), 104–111. DOI: 10.54254/2755-2721/51/20241187

Yale University. (2021). *Formative and summative assessments*. https://poorvucenter.yale.edu/Formative-Summative-Assessments

Yang, C., Rho, E., Lin, X., & Stomski, M. (2024). Empowerment and Silence: A Grounded Theory Exploration Among New Teachers. *School Psychology*, 39(3), 291–301. DOI: 10.1037/spq0000612 PMID: 38095960

Yang, H. S., & Wu, J. P. (2017). Exploration on cultivation of application-oriented and innovative talents in the information field under "Internet +" environment. *Eurasia Journal of Mathematics, Science and Technology Education*, 13(8), 5607–5614. DOI: 10.12973/eurasia.2017.01014a

Yang, S. J. H., & Wang, Y. (2019). The impact of AI on learning: Future perspectives. *Interactive Learning Environments*, 27(7), 1020–1033.

Yao, N., & Wang, Q. (2024). Factors influencing pre-service special education teachers' intention toward AI in education: Digital literacy, teacher self-efficacy, perceived ease of use, and perceived usefulness. *Heliyon*, 10(14), e34894. DOI: 10.1016/j.heliyon.2024.e34894 PMID: 39149079

Yi, H., Liu, T., & Lan, G. (2024). The key artificial intelligence technologies in early childhood education: A review. *Artificial Intelligence Review*, 57(1), 12. DOI: 10.1007/s10462-023-10637-7

Yilin, T., & Wang, C. (2020). Research on the application of artificial intelligence in individualized education for special children. *Journal of Suihua College*, 40(07), 126–129.

Yoo, J. D. (2011). Goalbook Toolkit. https://goalbookapp.com/ retrieved on 2 June 2024

Yu, S., & Lu, Y. (2021). *An introduction to artificial intelligence in education*. Springer. DOI: 10.1007/978-981-16-2770-5

Yu, Z., & Xu, W. (2022). A meta-analysis and systematic review of the effect of virtual reality technology on users' learning outcomes. *Computer Applications in Engineering Education*, 30(5), 1470–1484. DOI: 10.1002/cae.22532

Zablotsky, B., Ng, A. E., Black, L. I., & Blumberg, S. J. (2023). Diagnosed developmental disabilities in children aged 3–17 years: United States, 2019–2021. *NCHS Data Brief*, 473, 1–8. DOI: 10.15620/cdc:129520 PMID: 37440277

Zammarchi, G., & Conversano, C. (2021). Application of eye tracking technology in medicine: A bibliometric analysis. *Vision (Basel)*, 5(4), 56. DOI: 10.3390/vision5040056

Zavaraki, E. Z. (2023). Artificial Intelligence for Quality Education [Working Title]. DOI: 10.5772/intechopen.1004158

Zdravkova, K. (2022). The potential of artificial intelligence for assistive technology in education. In *Handbook on Intelligent Techniques in the Educational Process: Vol 1 Recent Advances and Case Studies* (pp. 61-85). Cham: Springer International Publishing. DOI: 10.1007/978-3-031-04662-9_4

Zdravkova, K., Krasniqi, V., Dalipi, F., & Ferati, M. (2022). Cutting-edge communication and learning assistive technologies for disabled children: An artificial intelligence perspective. *Frontiers in Artificial Intelligence*, 5, 970430. DOI: 10.3389/frai.2022.970430 PMID: 36388402

Zhang, Y., Li, Y., Cui, L., Cai, D., Liu, L., Fu, T., . . . Shi, S. (2023). Siren's song in the AI ocean: a survey on hallucination in large language models. *arXiv preprint arXiv:2309.01219.*

Zhang, F., Yu, H.-L., Wang, L.-L., Meng, Q., Li, S.-J., & Ni, W. (2017). Exploring the classification of rehabilitation robots. *Chinese Journal of Physical Medicine and Rehabilitation*, 39(08), 633–636.

Zhao, M., Hernandez, A., & Garcia, R. (2023). Early Warning Systems for Learning Difficulties: A Machine Learning Approach. *Educational Assessment, Evaluation and Accountability*, 35(2), 189–208.

Zigmond, N. P., & Kloo, A. (2017). General and special education are (and should be) different. In *Handbook of special education* (pp. 249–261). Routledge. DOI: 10.4324/9781315517698-21

Zimmerman, B. J. (2000). Attaining self-regulation. *Handbook of self-regulation*, 13–39. DOI: 10.1016/B978-012109890-2/50031-7

Zimmerman, B. J. (2008). Investigating self-regulation and motivation: Historical background, methodological developments, and future prospects. *American Educational Research Journal*, 45(1), 166–183. DOI: 10.3102/0002831207312909

Zisser-Nathenson, A. R., Herschell, A. D., & Eyberg, S. M. (2018). Parent-child interaction therapy and the treatment of disruptive behavior disorders. In Weisz, J. R., & Kazdin, A. E. (Eds.), *Evidence-Based Psychotherapies for Children and Adolescents* (pp. 103–121). The Guilford Press.

Zubair, S., & Rangreze, I. (2023). AI-driven advancements in autism spectrum disorder: Early diagnosis, intervention, and genomic insights for enhanced social well-being. *European Chemical Bulletin*, 12, 6297–6313. DOI: 10.48047/ecb/2023.12.si8.533

About the Contributors

Annette Walters has been in the field of K-12 education for over 20 years. She has presented on educational topics that include Diversity and Equity, Using Data to Guide Practices, Special Education, Staff Development, and Restorative Practices. She is passionate about classroom management, teacher retention, coaching, and staffing strategies that are aligned to student achievement and success. Dr. Walters' experience has led her to work and research in various aspects of education from Pre-K through college. She shares her knowledge and expertise with others in the educational field, to improve a quality learning experience for all. Dr. Walters has also worked as an adjunct professor for over fifteen years in both the traditional and online platform. She has earned an earned doctorate in Education and three graduate degrees in the areas of Educational Leadership, Management and Policy; Education; and Special Education with a minor in Developmental Disabilities.

* * *

Yolanda Abel is an Associate Professor and immediate past chair of the Department of Advanced Studies in Education at Johns Hopkins University School of Education. She is also a faculty affiliate with Center for Social Organization of Schools, the Center for Safe and Healthy Schools and the Center for Africana Studies. Her publications appear in American Educational Research Journal, Journal of Negro Education, Education and Urban Society, and School Science and Mathematics Journal. Abel has held several leadership roles within the American Educational Research Association specifically in the Family School Community Partnership Special Interest Group where she is past chair. Her dissertation, African-American Father Involvement in Their Children's School-Based Lives, earned the 2008 Judith Ruchkin Research Award from the Maryland Association for Supervision and Curriculum Development. In 2017 she was awarded the inaugural Excellence in Mentorship Award for providing a quality mentoring experience for a junior faculty at the School of Education. In 2019 she was named Honorable Mention for the 2019 Provost's Prize for Faculty Excellence in Diversity.

Wasim Ahmad was born on 2-11-1986. Dr Ahmad holds M. Ed. M. Phil and PhD in Special Education (Intellectual Disability) beside M. Sc. Applied Psychology and MA Sociology. Dr Ahmad is a determined academician and dedicated researcher in the field of Special Education. He is currently working as Faculty in Special Education (Intellectual Disability) at National Institute for the empowerment of Persons with Intellectual Disabilities NIEPID, Regional Centre, Navi Mumbai, India. For his exemplary work, academics and outstanding professional services in the rehabilitation of persons with disabilities he has been honoured with Late Shri N.D. Diwan Memorial Award-2016, Dr Reeta Peshawaria Award-2017, Dr JK Trivedi Award-2017, Kalyanam Karoti Award-2017, Sarovar Award-2017, Chandigarh State Award for his Meritorious Services 2018, Prof. Puran Singh Award 2018 and Academic Brilliance Award 2019. Dr Ahmad has more than 50 publications to his credit which appeared in the International and National journals of repute. He has also authored several chapters in the edited books.

Oindrila Chakraborty is a gold medalist in her MBA programme from University of Calcutta. She has 15 years of teaching experience in management education. She has completed her PhD from University of Calcutta and has several publications to furnish in National and International Journals of high repute.

Srimani Chakravarthi is a professor at the College of Education, University of St. Francis, at Joliet, IL. She has over 20 years of experience in teaching children with LD, ADHD and other mild disabilities at the school level and as a teacher educator for undergraduate and graduate aspiring teachers. She teaches special education, assistive technology and culturally relevant practices to future teachers. Her own experiences as an immigrant, coupled with diverse school teaching experiences in low-performing schools have helped shape her teaching beliefs and practices to ensure cultural relevancy.

Jennifer Gallup researches and publishes in the area of special education with an emphasis in secondary transitions related to autism spectrum disorders and innovative technology. Additionally, she does work in the area of depression and autism and the effects of depression on post-secondary outcomes. Dr. Gallup conducts research on a national and international level and is an expert in preparing individuals to work with those who have autism or developmental disabilities.

Karen R. Johnson is an associate professor in the department of Learning Technologies at the University of North Texas. Her research focuses on factors that influence the learning process and the outcomes of learning on employee performance. In her research, she also investigates organization development interventions that can aid the transition, retention, and work outcomes of young adults with autism to the workplace. She also serves as associate editor for the Advances in Developing Human Resources journal.

Regina Kaplan-Rakowski is an Assistant Professor of Learning Technologies at the University of North Texas. She is also Vice President of the Computer-Assisted Language Instruction Consortium (CALICO). Her research interests include immersive learning technologies (e.g., virtual reality, augmented reality, mixed reality), emotional responses to learning technologies, and computer-assisted language learning. She serves on the Editorial Board of Educational Technology & Society (ET&S) and the Journal of Technology and Teacher Education (JTATE).

Brady Lund is an assistant professor of information science at the University of North Texas, Denton, Texas, USA. He received his Ph.D. in information management from Emporia State University. His research aims to understand and address important issues at the intersection of information, data, and people, and to promote ethical and responsible practices in these fields, with a particular emphasis on international development.

Mohsen Mahmoudi-Dehaki is an Assistant Professor of TEFL at the Islamic Azad University of Najafabad, Iran. With over a decade of experience teaching undergraduate and postgraduate students, he has established himself as a respected educator and scholar. His research has been widely published in national and international journals, solidifying his reputation as a prominent voice in the field. Dr. Mahmoudi-Dehaki serves as a peer reviewer for several esteemed scientific journals, including RELP, ensuring the highest standards of academic rigor and integrity. His academic achievements include winning the prestigious first place in the English Writing Award in Iran, a distinction earned among all university students from state universities and institutes of higher education. His paper "COVID-19 Lingo or Covidipedia" has garnered significant attention, with over 70,000 visits, making it the most visited paper in Iranian scientific journals. This remarkable achievement underscores his significant impact on the academic community. Dr. Mahmoudi-Dehaki's research and teaching interests span a diverse range of novel branches in applied linguistics, including psycho/cognitive/neurocognitive/forensic/jury/sociocultural/ecological, and clinical linguistics. He is also well-versed in educational technology, educational psychology, and psychometrics, demonstrating his versatility and breadth of expertise in the interdisciplinary fields of education and linguistics.

Nasim Nasr-Esfahani, PhD, is an Assistant Professor of TEFL at the Islamic Azad University of Isfahan (Khorasgan), Iran. She earned her PhD in TEFL at the Islamic Azad University of Isfahan, Khorasgan. She has over two decades of experience teaching undergraduate and postgraduate students in Iran. Her publications have appeared in leading international journals, such as the Australian Journal of Teacher Education. She serves as a reviewer and article editor of RELP Journal. Her areas of research and teaching interests are dynamic and evolving and span language education, generative artificial intelligence (GenAI) in education, critical thinking skills, oral and written communication skills, student engagement, advancing equity in education, brain-based teaching and learning, neurolinguistics, psycholinguistics as well as teaching and research methodologies.

Tia Neal's educational journey reflects a deep commitment to academic excellence and ongoing learning. With a BA in pre-law, a Master of Arts in Teaching, and a Doctorate in Curriculum and Instruction, alongside certifications in gifted education and educational diagnostics, Dr. Neal's expertise spans diverse educational domains. Now in her 22nd year in education, she has transitioned from teaching to roles such as lead researcher for the Associated Professional Educators of Louisiana and adjunct professor at ULM. Beyond academia, she finds joy in family life with her husband, two children, and two pets. Actively engaged in professional organizations, Dr. Neal's multifaceted career epitomizes dedication to student success and ongoing professional growth.

Krishna Kumari R. is working as an Assistant Professor in the Department of Career Development Centre in SRM Institute of Science and Technology has about 8 years of teaching experience. Her areas of research include Formal Languages and Automata Theory, Theory of Computation. She holds a diverse array of qualifications including M.Sc., M.Phil., M.Ed., TNSET, and a Ph.D. She has authored a total of 25 publications, all indexed in SCOPUS, with 17 being published post-Ph.D. Additionally, she has authored 3 books/book chapters and holds 1 patent published and 1 granted. She serves as a reviewer in 4 SCOPUS indexed journals and 2 SCOPUS and ESCI indexed journals. Dr. Krishna Kumari has been a resource person for 3 Faculty Development Programs (FDPs), presented at 2 conferences/symposiums, and chaired 2 conferences. She has also attended 3 workshops and participated in 10 FDPs. Furthermore, Dr. Krishna Kumari is an active member of 10 professional memberships, showcasing her commitment to professional development and academic excellence.

Rishu Raj, born on the 26th of September 1998, armed with distinction in B.Ed Special Education Delhi University; top second institute in NIRF ranking 2024 and

M.A in English honours. She has now embarked Master's degree in Education at NIEPID; an apex institute of India recognised by RCI. She exemplifies an unwavering testament to diligence and commitment.

Rajesh Kanna Rajendran is an accomplished academic with over 16 years of experience in the field of computer science and information technology. He holds a Ph.D. from Bharathiar University, Coimbatore, and an M.Phil from Vinayaka Missions University, Salem. Dr. Rajeshkanna has made significant academic contributions through his research and scholarly activities. He has published 35 papers in reputed international journals with high impact factors and has contributed 16 book chapters through IGI Global Publications. His active participation in the academic community is demonstrated by presenting 47 papers at various national and international conferences and participating in 27 workshops. Additionally, he has published seven books with ISBN numbers and completed over 25 MooC courses on platforms such as NPTEL, Coursera, Infosys Springboard, and Udemy. Dr. Rajeshkanna's dedication to academia, coupled with his extensive research and teaching experience, continues to contribute significantly to the advancement of computer science and information technology education. He is a recognized reviewer and editorial board member for various UGC-approved, Web of Science, SCI, and Scopus-indexed journals. Dr. Rajeshkanna has also served as a resource person for numerous national seminars and guest lecture programs and has organized various faculty development programs, workshops, seminars, and conferences.

Tamar F. Riley, PhD, holds a master's and Doctor of Philosophy degrees in special education from the University of Florida (UF). Dr. Riley was a faculty member at The University of Alabama (UA) for four years, Florida Memorial University (FMU) for nineteen years, and is in her second year with Alabama A&M University, teaching in both the undergraduate and graduate programs in Special Education. She has a strong commitment to prepare teachers of color who are highly effective special education teachers and leaders as demonstrated by more than two decades of work at HBCUs, both private and public institutions. Dr. Riley has extensive experience in working with the Florida Department of Education (FDOE) in program improvement and evaluation and held a multi-year appointment by the Florida Commissioner of Education to serve on the State Advisory Committee for Special Education as the Institutions for Higher Education representative. She has secured, directed, and managed almost $10M in external funds, both federal and foundation, to help support the recruitment and retention of minority teachers in Evidence-Based Practices (EBPs) for special education. Dr. Riley almost two decades (2005-present) of experience in the role of Project Director and Co-Director for seven federally-funded projects and mentors novice grant writers and directors in her department as evidenced by three separate OSEP grant awards. She has extensive experience in working with teachers on research-based instructional strategies to improve the academic success of students with disabilities, with particular focus on intensive interventions for students with persistent and severe learning and behavioral issues. Her research interests include minority teacher recruitment and retention, teacher wellness, implementation of EBPs, trauma informed practices for the classroom, and intensive interventions. Dr. Riley is a national instructor for Youth Mental Health First Aid, a Board-Certified Advocate in Special Education (B-CASE) and trained in Trauma Informed Care. Dr. Riley has more than two decades of experience in providing professional development to pre-service and in-service teachers in virtual and physical settings.

Annette Romualdo, Ph.D., is an Assistant Professor of Special Education at University of Minnesota Duluth. Annette's passion is to increase the inclusion of individuals with disabilities into the general education classroom, with an emphasis on post-secondary inclusion and transition. Annette has worked in both medical- and school-based settings promoting self-advocacy and empowerment. Annette regularly collaborates with disability advocacy organizations to amplify self-advocate and family voices within special education. Annette is also the parent of a child with an intellectual disability.

Nobhonil Roy Choudhury is an Assistant Professor with 9 years of experience in Computer Science and BCA curriculum development, known for fostering student engagement and supporting learning objectives. With expertise in PC programming and subjects like C, Java, and Cyber Security, they have a proven track record in academic advisement and technology integration in education. Career Highlights: Current role at Brainware University, focusing on up-to-date technology curriculum and NAAC work. Previous position at GitaRam Institute of Management, where they enhanced computer literacy and monitored industry trends. Started as a Teaching Assistant at Narula Institute of Technology, providing personalized student support. This educator is dedicated to technological proficiency and academic excellence, continually advancing student success.

Saptarshi Kumar Sarkar is an Assistant Professor at Brainware University. With a dedication to academic excellence, he brings a wealth of knowledge and experience to his students. His research interests include AI, ML and Social Networking, contributing significantly to advancements in his field.

Lynn Scott, Ph.D., serves as an Assistant Professor of Special Education at Indiana State University, drawing from her extensive experience in teaching and educational leadership to support students with exceptionalities at all stages of life.

With a strong commitment to promoting inclusivity and equity in education, her goal is to enhance the training of pre-service and in-service teachers and administrators by utilizing simulation and multimodal data collection techniques. By doing so, she aims to improve outcomes for diverse populations and advance the adoption of more inclusive educational practices.

Shiwangi Sharma is Assistant Professor School of Leadership and Management-PG Manav Rachna International Institute of Research and Studies, Faridabad. She has more than 7 years of total experience with 5 years of experience as an academician in the field of management education and 2 years in corporate as HR Executive with a digital marketing company. She has a flair for academic as well as web content writing as a freelancer. Currently, she is working in the area of talent management and employee development. She has been in organizing committee of various Conferences and MDPs.

Ruchika Shokeen, born on January 31, 1998, is a dedicated and accomplished educator in the field of Special Education, with a focus on Intellectual Disabilities. She is currently pursuing a Master of Arts in Psychology, adding to her extensive academic background and deep commitment to supporting individuals with special needs. Ruchika is pursuing Master of Education in Special Education (Intellectual Disability) from the National Institute for the Empowerment of Persons with Intellectual Disabilities (NIEPID), the apex institute of the Government of India dedicated to empowering persons with intellectual disabilities. Her journey in special education began with a Bachelor of Education in Special Education (Intellectual Disability) from Delhi University, recognized as one of the top institutes in India. Ruchika's academic prowess is further highlighted by her Bachelor of Science in Chemistry from the esteemed Delhi University, followed by a Master of Science in Chemistry. This diverse academic foundation has equipped her with a unique perspective and a multifaceted approach to education. She is dedicated to advancing research and practice in the academic field of special education, striving to make significant contributions to better serve this sector.

Mohana Priya T. is Assistant Professor at CHRIST(Deemed to be University), Bangalore, India. She Holds a PhD degree in Computer Science in Machine learning at Bharathiar University, Coimbatore, India. Her research areas are Machine Learing and medical image analysis. She is acted as Coordinator for curriculum development cell and Software development cell.She published 10 Journal articles in various international peer reviewed journals, 2 Book publications and 15 presentations in various international level conference held in India and abroad.

Brandon C. S. Wallace is a full professor at Montgomery College, and a faculty associate at Johns Hopkins University. Dr. Wallace has received many awards for his work in education, most notably the Diane Tobin Award for Excellence in Teaching from the Johns Hopkins University's School of Education, the Bowie Black Male Educators and Leaders Alliance's Outstanding Professor Award in 2020, from Bowie State University, the Outstanding Faculty Member (2023) and Team Effort Award (2023) from Montgomery College, as well as the nationally recognized 2024 NISOD Excellence Award. Dr. Wallace's research interests include English language and literature, qualitative methodology, multiculturalism, assessment theory, Universal Design for Learning, specialized education, behaviorism, and restorative justice. Brandon lives in Prince George's County, Maryland and enjoys leisurely reading the works of Toni Morrison, John Milton, Jane Elliott, James Baldwin, and Damon Young.

Tahnee L. Wilder, Ph.D., CCC-SLP, is a speech-language pathologist and researcher, who has dedicated her life to transforming the educational landscape. With a Ph.D. in Education (Exceptional Education Track) and a cognate in Cognitive Neuroscience from the University of Central Florida, she has gained profound insights into the intricate workings of the human brain and its impact on learning. Driven by a deep commitment to uplifting historically marginalized communities, Dr. Wilder's research interests span educational neuroscience, educational technology, speech and communication disorders, and special education. Prior to her doctoral studies, Dr. Wilder earned a Master of Science in Speech and Language Pathology from Nova Southeastern University, where she honed her skills in addressing communication disorders. She has practiced as a Speech-Language Pathologist in an array of education and medical settings over the past 15 years. With her extensive educational background, professional experience as a speech-language pathologist, and fervent dedication to marginalized communities, Dr. Tahnee Wilder is uniquely positioned to make transformative contributions that bridge the gap between neuroscience, common communication disorders, and equitable educational practices.

Tiffanie Zaugg is an influential figure in the field of exceptional education, particularly known for her contributions to improving accessibility in learning environments for students with disabilities. She is a Ph.D. candidate in Exceptional Education, which equips her with a profound understanding of the needs of students who require special educational adjustments. Throughout her career, Mrs. Zaugg has been actively involved in research and development of assistive technologies that enhance educational opportunities for these students. Her work often involves collaborating with educational institutions, technology developers, and policy-makers to create inclusive educational practices and tools. Mrs. Zaugg is also a respected educator and mentor, sharing her expertise through teaching at the university level and conducting workshops and seminars across the country. Her publications and presentations at academic conferences contribute significantly to ongoing discussions and advancements in her field. As an advocate for the integration of technology in education for students with disabilities, Mrs. Zaugg continues to push the boundaries of what is possible in special education, ensuring that learning is accessible to all students, regardless of their individual challenges.

Index

A

B

C

D

E

P

S

T

U

V

W

www.ingramcontent.com/pod-product-compliance
Lightning Source LLC
LaVergne TN
LVHW080616300926
849162LV00005B/1175
* 9 7 9 8 3 6 9 3 5 5 3 8 1 *